# India's National Security Annual Review 2003

# India's National Security Annual Review 2003

*Editor-in-Chief*
**Satish Kumar**
Former Professor of Diplomacy
Jawaharlal Nehru University
New Delhi

India Research Press
New Delhi

**India Research Press**
B-4/22, Safdarjung Enclave,
New Delhi – 110 029.
Ph.: 24694610; Fax : 24618637
bahrisons@vsnl.com
contact@indiaresearchpress.com
**www.indiaresearchpress.com**



**ISBN : 81-87943-56-4**


**India's National Security 2003**
**by Satish Kumar**

*Cataloguing in Publication Data*
Includes bibliographical references and index.
1. National Security 2. India 3. South Aisa Security
I. Title II. Author

*Printed in India at Focus Impressions, New Delhi – 110 003.*

# Editor's Note

*India's National Security Annual Review* was launched in September 2000 as an independent project to make a holistic assessment of India's national security every year. India's experience after the nuclear tests of 1998 made it obvious that the national security of India was threatened as much in the fields of technology and economy, as in the fields of military capability, political relationships, and internal security. Non-traditional security issues like food, energy, climate change, demography, and terrorism, and new concerns like higher defence management and national security decision-making also needed to be factored in while evaluating national security. The initiative to examine all these aspects in one volume every year was welcomed by the National Security Council Secretariat which decided to support this project.

The present volume is the third in the series. The volume covers the developments in the year 2002, although in many cases the analysis of the issues concerned covers a much larger span. The earlier two volumes were vindicated by the enthusiastic response of the national security and strategic studies community within and outside the country. This volume also draws on the expertise of scholars, administrators, foreign policy experts, technocrats, military officers, economists and trade and industry specialists who have first hand experience of handling national security issues in their respective fields.

The overall security environment of the country has been dealt with under the heads: Global Security Trends, External Security Environment, and Internal Security Threats. Articles on Global Military Environment and India's Military Modernisation scrutinise the military challenges that India faces. The need for further globalisation of the Indian economy and the relationship of economic security with national security has been stressed in the two articles on External Economic

Environment and India's Economic Security. The article, Some Concerns about Internal Security, makes a thorough investigation of the dynamics of internal security. The role of technology in security and the degree of self-reliance in defence technologies have been examined in Technology and Security and Self-Reliance in Defence Technologies. Regarding non-traditional security issues, there are articles on Health Hazards and National Security, Security Implications of Climate Change, and Urban India's Security Concerns.

**The volume also carries a National Security Index which compares India's national power with fifty top countries of the world. This volume has a new feature on Acquisition of Arms and Military Technology by India and Its Neighbours during the year. There are regular sections on Chronology of Major Events, Select Documents, and Basic Statistics.**

We are happy to say that the Confederation of Indian Industry (CII) also agreed to support this annual publication from the third volume onwards. We are grateful to the CII for agreeing to support this venture. We also highly appreciate the continuing support of the National Security Council Secretariat. We must state, however, that the views expressed in this volume are not necessarily those of the NSC Secretariat, or any of the government agencies, or of the Confederation of Indian Industry.

Ambassador M. Rasgotra, Chairman, and other members of the Editorial Board provided indispensable direction and guidance in the preparation of the volume. Sanghita Bhattacharya, a PhD scholar in the Centre for Study of Regional Development, School of Social Sciences, Jawaharlal Nehru University, assisted the editor in the preparation of the National Security Index. Manoranjan Pattanayak, a PhD scholar in the Centre for Diplomacy, International Law and Economics, School of International Studies, JNU, worked on the Basic Statistics. Pooja Rishi, Samuel Rajiv, and Joseph Kuba, PhD scholars in the Centre for International Politics, Organisation and

Disarmament, School of International Studies, JNU, in their capacity as Research Assistants for *INSAR*, put in sustained and meticulous hard work to see this volume through. Mukesh Pokhriyal, the Computer-cum-Office Assistant, provided long hours of infrastructural support. I would like to record my grateful acknowledgement of the extremely valuable and commendable work done by all my colleagues mentioned above.

November 2003 Prof. Satish Kumar

## About the Contributors

1. **Tarun Das** is Director-General, Confederation of Indian Industry (CII), New Delhi. He started with the predecessor body of CII in November 1963 and has been the Chief Executive of its permanent secretariat since April 1974 when CII (formerly AIEI) was formed. He is an Honours Graduate in Economics and Commerce. He was educated at Calcutta University, India, and Manchester University, UK, and has been awarded an Honorary Degree of Doctorate in Science by the University of Warwick, UK. Tarun Das is also the non-executive Chairman of The Associated Cement Companies Ltd., India.

2. **Dr. Shubhashis Gangopadhyay** did his PhD in Economics from Cornell University, Ithaca, New York, USA. He joined the Delhi Centre of the Indian Statistical Institute as a Lecturer in 1983. He became a full Professor in 1991. He took over as Founder-Director of India Development Foundation in July 2002. He has published widely in journals on development economics, international trade, industrial organisation, regulatory economics and finance. He has also co-authored and co-edited a number of books in economics and finance.

3. **Air Marshal B. D. Jayal** (Retd.) has a service career which involved extensive fighter and test flying operations. He is an alumnus of the National Defence College. His staff appointments in Air HQ have included the operational and planning posts of ACAS (Operations), ACAS (Plans) and Deputy Chief of the Air Staff. He was AOC-in-C Eastern Air Command and later AOC-in-C South Western Air Command from which appointment he retired in 1993.

4. **Dr. Amitav Mallik** has over 35 years of experience in post-graduate teaching, Defence R&D and technology analysis

& planning. As India's first Adviser, Defence Technology, at Washington DC between 1988-1994, he played a pivotal role in building Indo-US technology cooperation. On his return to India, he served as Secretary, Self-Reliance Implementation Council of MOD. He has made a significant contribution to the development of high power lasers in the country for which he was awarded a Padma Shri' in 2002. He is presently a Member of the National Security Advisory Board.

5. **Admiral Raja Menon** retired from the Navy as the Assistant Chief of Naval Staff (Operations) in 1994. He was a Senior Research Fellow at the Institute for Defence Studies and Analyses for two years where he did some pioneering work on the economic factors in war. He has published three books: *Maritime Strategy and Continental Wars (1998)*, *A Nuclear Strategy for India (2000)*, and *The Indian Navy: A Photo Essay*.

6. **Dr. Saumitra Mukherjee**, Associate Professor at the School of Environmental Sciences, Jawaharlal Nehru University, is an MSc and PhD (Geology) and PG Diploma in Environment, Ecology, Hydrogeology, Remote Sensing and GIS from reputed Institutes. He has published more than 60 national and international papers in reputed journals and is the author of three books. Dr. Mukherjee is collaborating with NASA, USA in various projects related to "Sun-Earth Environment". He is Convenor of the Third World Water Forum, 2003 (Japan).

7. **Lt. Gen. Vijay Oberoi**, PVSM, AVSM, VSM was commissioned in the Maratha Light Infantry in June 1961 and retired on 1 October 2001. Despite losing his right leg during the Indo-Pak War of 1965, he soldiered on till he retired as the Vice Chief of the Army Staff. He was an International Fellow at the US Army War College, and had commanded an armoured division, a strike corps, and

the Training and Western Commands. His other important appointments were Military Advisor in Malaysia and the DGMO.

8. **Lt. Gen. D. Raghunath** (Retd.) is the Principal Executive of Sir Dorabji Tata Centre for Research in Tropical Diseases, Bangalore. He received his MBBS (1959), DCP (1964) and MD Pathology/Bacteriology (1975) from Poona University. He was a Fellow of Royal College of Pathologists and Fellow of National Academy of Medical Sciences. As for professional experience, he was Medical Officer in Armed Forces Medical Services, Pathologist, Army Medical Corps, Professor and Head of the Dept. of Microbiology of Armed Forces Medical College, Dean and Commandant, AFMC, Pune, Director-General of Medical Services, Army and DG Armed Forces Medical Services. He was decorated with Param Vishist Seva Medal (PVSM) and Ati Vishist Seva Medal (AVSM).

9. **K. C. Sivaramakrishnan** joined the Indian Administrative Service (IAS) in 1958 and after holding various assignments in West Bengal, he moved to Delhi in 1985 as Additional Secretary in the Ministry of Environment. In 1988, he became Secretary in the Ministry of Urban Development. Mr. Sivaramakrishnan retired from the IAS in 1992. Thereafter, he became Sr. Adviser, Urban Management, in the World Bank. In 1996 he joined the Centre for Policy Research as Professor. Mr. Sivaramakrishnan was a Parvin Fellow at Woodrow Wilson School, Princeton University in 1965, Visiting Professor and Homi Bhabha Fellow at the Indian Institute of Management, Calcutta in 1977, and Senior Lecturer at the Economic Development Institute of the World Bank from 1978 to 1982.

10. **N. N. Vohra** was educated at the Punjab and Oxford Universities. He was a member of the Indian Administrative Service (1959-1994). He served in the Special Services

Bureau in the Western Indo-Tibetan theatre (1962-64) and as Home Secretary Punjab (1984-85). With the Government of India, he served as Secretary Defence Production, Defence Secretary and Home Secretary (1985-94). He was recalled from retirement to serve as Principal Secretary to the Prime Minister (1997-98). His other appointments were Member, National Security Advisory Board (1998-01), Chairman, IDSA Review Committee (1999-01), Chairman, Task Force on Internal Security (2000), Chairman, Military History Review Committee (2001-02), Representative of Union Government for J&K Dialogue (2003- ), Director, India International Centre (1995-97; 1998-2003).

## Contents

## III. Select Documents

# I

# Review and Analysis

# Global Security Trends

*Satish Kumar*

## Introduction

Global security remained a victim of terrorism and proliferation of weapons of mass destruction. The United States and its allies had succeeded in eliminating the Taliban from their control over Afghanistan, which had become the home of Al-Qaeda. Most countries of the world had extended their sympathy and support to the United States in this venture. But terrorism spearheaded by extremist Islamic groups showed its deadly face in various parts of the world. The anxiety that terrorist groups might get hold of weapons of mass destruction reinforced the efforts of the Bush administration to stop or counter WMD proliferation but without much success. While major powers of the world shared the anxieties of the Bush administration on account of terrorism and WMD proliferation, they were jolted out of their wits by President Bush's withdrawal from the ABM treaty, initiation of a missile defence programme, release of a new nuclear policy which would legitimise the use of nuclear weapons against certain states and in certain situations, and the identification by Bush of North Korea, Iran, and Iraq as the "axis of evil", which could be the targets of American wrath.

These unilateralist pronouncements of the United States became a major source of concern to the rest of the world, which gradually learnt to live with them because of the overwhelming power of the United States and the highly indispensable economic and strategic interdependencies that all major powers have with the United States. The Bush administration announced its national security strategy whose most striking feature was the doctrine of "pre-emptive strikes" against state or non-state actors suspected of planning hostile attacks against US interests. In a sense, this was a precursor to the March 2003 US attack on Iraq, a case for which was gradually built throughout 2002. The security environment of the world was thus surcharged with tension, fear and instability. This led major powers like China and Japan and regional powers all over the world to revise their security doctrines and to upgrade their capabilities in conventional and nuclear fields.

**US Defines the Global Security Agenda**

The global security agenda tended to be defined in terms of US interests and perceptions. The entire security discourse was dominated by issues which were of importance to the United States. The decisions taken by the United States, despite reservations of other major powers, were pushed to their bitter end. Other powers protested, not too loudly but insistently, and then fell in line or kept quiet.

A case in point was the US decision to withdraw from the ABM Treaty. President George W. Bush announced on 13 December 2001 that the United States would withdraw from the Treaty in six months. The justification given was that the Treaty is outdated. Today's threats differ drastically from when the two super powers signed the Treaty in 1972. Then, the two super powers posed the greatest threat to each other's security. Now, terrorism and rogue states pose the greatest danger.

The Russian Federation disagreed. President Putin in an interview to *The Financial Times* on 13 December said that neither terrorists nor rogue states "have or are likely to ever have" strategic ballistic missiles. Putin also said that Russia had been ready to modify the Treaty but the United States chose to limit discussions "to jointly leave this Treaty." Earlier in 2001, Putin and other top Russian officials had warned that a unilateral US withdrawal from the ABM Treaty could lead to the demise of more than 30 other security and disarmament agreements.[1]

China, which had been consistently opposed to US missile defences, commented after the Bush announcement that Beijing hopes Washington "will seriously consider the opinions of the majority of nations on the ABM Treaty." The Chinese spokesperson was referring to a resolution supporting preservation of the ABM Treaty passed by the UN General Assembly by a vote of 82 to 5 with 62 abstentions on 29 November. France spoke in favour of "binding international rules and instruments" to help guarantee strategic stability.

However, President Bush announced the US withdrawal from the ABM Treaty on 13 June 2002, six months after the expiry of the notice period. Most countries of the world, including United States until Bush took over, had referred to this Treaty as a "cornerstone of strategic stability" because it had made possible for the US and Russia to reach agreements limiting and reducing their deployed strategic nuclear arsenals. A day after the ABM Treaty was dead, on 14 June, Russia announced that it would no longer be bound by the START II offensive arms reduction treaty. The move, of course, was symbolic because the START II had never entered into force and had been superceded by the Strategic Offensive Reductions Treaty of 24 May 2002.

Consistent with the strategic thinking inherent in it's decision to withdraw from the ABM Treaty, the Bush administration announced its Nuclear Posture Review in a briefing to the Congress on 8 January and to the press on 9 January 2002. The review of United States' nuclear policy, a secret exercise undertaken for the first time since 1994, was based on two assumptions. One, that the relationship with Russia was no longer based on "mutual assured destruction", and two, that the threats to the United States were "uncertain" and emanated from "multiple" sources. Accordingly, the Bush administration wanted to shift from a "threat-based" approach to a "capability-based" approach, from greater emphasis on offensive nuclear forces to greater emphasis on enhanced conventional capabilities and missile defences.[2]

Fuller details of the Nuclear Posture Review were, however,

obtained and published by *The Los Angeles Times* on 9 March, and subsequently by *The New York Times* and the website www.globalsecurity.org. This leaked version gave an alarming list of seven countries that could be involved in "immediate", "potential", or "unexpected" contingencies necessitating the use of nuclear weapons against them by the United States. These countries were Iran, Iraq, Libya, North Korea, Syria, China and Russia.[3] The Review pointed out that nuclear weapons "provide credible military options to deter a wide range of threats, including WMD and large-scale conventional military force." The Review also said, "nuclear weapons could be employed against targets able to withstand non-nuclear attack (for example, deep underground bunkers or bio-weapon facilities)." Three specific "nuclear strike" contingencies the Review discussed were "an Iraqi attack on Israel or its neighbours, a North Korean attack on South Korea, or a military confrontation [with China] over the status of Taiwan."[4]

The Nuclear Posture Review raised hackles in various parts of the world as also within the United States. A Chinese Foreign Ministry spokesman said that "the Chinese government is deeply shocked over news that the US Defence Department has outlined the possible use of nuclear weapons against countries including China." Mr. Sun Yuxi added, "the US side bears the responsibility to make an explanation on this matter."[5] Within the United States, the Review came in for severe criticism from responsible and well-informed quarters. Daryl G. Kimball, the Executive Director of Arms Control Association, pointed out:

> If the Bush administration fails to follow through on US NPT disarmament commitments, and if it renounces its long-standing pledge not to use nuclear weapons against non-nuclear weapon states in good standing with the NPT, some states may see that the rule of law is breaking down and conclude that they too need nuclear, chemical, or biological weapons to ward off attack. And if the United States asserts that pre-emptive use of nuclear weapons

against terrorist-related WMD threats is justified, a state such as India might assert the same right and consider launching its own pre-emptive strike against Pakistan.[6]

The general sentiment across the United States was perhaps summed up by a US analyst, Jill Nelson: "I can't be the only one struck by the irony that as people across the United States peacefully observe the passage of six months since the terrorist attacks on America, the Pentagon is considering a fundamental change in established policy on nuclear weapons, lowering the threshold from their use as tools of deterrence to active instruments of conventional warfare."[7]

The third major pronouncement which set the tone for global security agenda was the declaration that North Korea, Iran and Iraq constituted an "axis of evil" getting armed to threaten world peace. The declaration was made by President Bush in his State of the Union address on 29 January. Bush observed that North Korea, Iran and Iraq "pose a grave and growing danger" and could provide WMD and missiles to "terrorists, giving them the means to match their hatred". He affirmed that the United States "will not wait on events" and warned that his administration "will not permit the world's most dangerous regimes to threaten us with the world's most destructive weapons."[8]

George Bush's use of the appellation "axis of evil" to characterise the three states caused quite a consternation across the world. China mildly said, "we disapprove of the use of such words in international relations". The French President Jacques Chirac's Assistant pointed out that Chirac "does not subscribe to the 'Axis of Evil' theory" and that "the good-and-evil view does not conform to the actual conditions in the present day world." Former US Secretary of State Madeleine Albright described Bush's "Axis of Evil" remark as "a gross mistake."[9]

As for North Korea, Iran, and Iraq themselves, they all reacted angrily. North Korea called Bush a "nuclear maniac" and characterised his remarks as "reckless" and "tantamount to a declaration of war." Iran said Bush's rhetoric was "intervening, war-mongering, [and] insulting". Iraq described Bush's charges as "stupid" and "inappropriate."[10]

The abrogation of the ABM Treaty by the Bush administration, its new policy with regard to the use of nuclear weapons, called the Nuclear Posture Review, and its virtual declaration of war against the so-called rogue states of North Korea, Iran, and Iraq were to cast their shadow on the entire global security discourse of the next two years and determine the policies and attitudes of all major powers. Most of the ideas inherent in these three strategic policy statements were later consolidated in the National Security Strategy of the United States announced by President Bush on 20 September 2002.

**Terrorism Remains a Global Threat**

Terrorism continued to be a major security threat throughout the world. Despite the overthrow of the Taliban in Afghanistan, neither the Taliban, nor Al-Qaeda, nor terrorism in the rest of the world was anywhere near eradication. According to the US State Department's report on "Patterns of Global Terrorism 2002", the total number of international terrorist attacks in 2002 was 199, as against 355 such attacks in 2001.[11] This reduction is attributed by the report to a number of steps taken by the international community through means of diplomacy, intelligence, law enforcement, financial controls, and military. And yet the report admits, terrorism plagued the world, "from Bali to Grozny to Mombasa". Out of 199 terrorist attacks, 99 took place in Asia, 50 in Latin America, 29 in the Middle East, 9 in Western Europe, 7 in Eurasia, and 5 in Africa. The report concludes by saying, "Al-Qaeda is still planning attacks. Every Al-Qaeda operations officer captured so far was involved in some stage of preparation for a terrorist attack at the time of capture. Recent audiotapes by Al-Qaeda leaders contain exhortations to further violence and threaten the United States and our coalition allies."[12]

Al-Qaeda as a non-state actor seems to have emerged as the most powerful threat to the security of the international system, feared as much by the major powers as by the middle and small powers. Al-Qaeda has become synonymous with terrorism. And counter-terrorism has come to imply the campaign against Al-Qaeda. A survey carried out by *Jane's Intelligence Review* in July and August 2002 came to the following conclusions: i) Al-Qaeda has active cells around the world including in the USA, Europe and Asia, and it retains an ability to carry out attacks; ii) Over the next two years, attacks using conventional explosives will continue to be the most likely form of terrorist activity, while the use of chemical, biological, radiological and nuclear weapons (CBRN) was a threat in the ten-year time horizon; iii) There will be an increase in Islamist-related terrorism and instability in almost all parts of the globe, although the dynamics behind the increase are complex. South and Southeast Asia, for instance, will witness an increasing growth in the power of dissenting Islamist groups. The Middle East may also experience a hardening of the Islamist stance.[13]

The JIR survey also points out that the most serious threat from extremist religious groups, mainly Islamist, derives from the fact that "the root causes motivating these groups are unlikely to disappear", giving rise to "copycat" attacks encouraged by the success of the previous attacks such as 11 September 2001.[14] Unfortunately, scant attention is being paid either to the root causes motivating the religious extremist groups or to the specificities of terrorism in different parts of the world, whether it is South Asia, Southeast Asia, Central Asia or the West. A careful look at incidence of terrorism around the world will reveal that a broad-brush approach centred around Western concerns alone will not help eliminate the threat of global terrorism.

### WMD Non-Proliferation: An Elusive Goal

Non-proliferation of weapons of mass destruction (WMD) remained a major concern of the international community. Several major powers as well as lesser powers were allegedly involved in transfer of nuclear weapons and missile-related equipment and technology. Sanctions were imposed by the United States on some of these powers. But neither the exporters nor recipients of equipment and technology demonstrated any change in their policies.

China was accused by the United States of violating a November 2000 agreement by which Beijing had committed not to help other states in developing ballistic missiles to deliver nuclear weapons and to enact a comprehensive export control system. In January 2002, the CIA accused China of breaching its commitments and pointed out that during the first half of 2001, China had provided Pakistan with "missile-related technical assistance" and Chinese firms had transferred "dual-use missile related items" to Iran, North Korea and Libya.[15] President George W. Bush during his official visit to Beijing on 21-22 February 2002 failed to resolve the differences on this question.

Sanctions were imposed against China by the US administration on 16 January 2002 for transferring to Iran sensitive equipment and technology to manufacture chemical and biological weapons. Again, sanctions were imposed against China by the Bush administration on 9 July for contributing to the efforts of Iran and possibly Iraq to acquire weapons of mass destruction or advanced conventional weapons.

Similarly, the alleged Russian assistance to Iran's nuclear and ballistic missile programmes remained a matter of deep concern to the United States. The question was discussed at two high-level meetings in Moscow, by the US Assistant Secretary of State John Wolf in January and the US Under Secretary of State for Arms Control in February, with the Russian Deputy Minister of Foreign Affairs, Georgy Mamedov.[16] The two sides could not resolve their differences on this question even when President Bush and President Putin met in Moscow on 24 May to sign a new nuclear arms reduction treaty and a joint declaration.[17]

Despite US objections, Russia went ahead and signed another draft document with Iran on 26 July that included plans to build five nuclear reactors in Iran in addition to the reactor currently under construction near Bushehr.[18] While the Bush administration refrained from imposing sanctions against the Russian government, it did impose sanctions against 12 Chinese, Moldavian, and Armenian firms and individuals on 9 May for transferring items to Iran that could be used for missile development or the production of chemical or biological weapons.[19]

Attempts by North Korea to develop its nuclear weapons programme also dominated the non-proliferation discourse. On 20 March, the White House declared that it would not certify to the Congress that Pyongyang was adhering to the 1994 Framework Agreement under which North Korea agreed to freeze its nuclear programme and ultimately dismantle it in exchange for two civilian nuclear power reactors. The White House did so on the basis of the report of the State Department that North Korea was resisting comprehensive international inspections of its nuclear programme.[20]

It was during the talks held by the US Assistant Secretary of State for East Asian and Pacific Affairs, James Kelly, in Pyongyang on 3-5 October that North Korea admitted that it was attempting to obtain enriched uranium and also claimed that it had some "powerful things". This revelation was made by the United States much after the talks, on 17 October. A statement by the North Korean Foreign Ministry on 25 October asserted the country's entitlement to nuclear weapons and demanded a non-aggression pact with the USA that guaranteed North Korea's sovereignty.[21]

On 15 November, US, South Korea, Japan and the EU – members of the Korean Peninsula Energy Development

Organisation (KEDO) – decided to suspend the monthly shipments of heavy fuel oil to North Korea until the North Korean government took "concrete and credible actions" to dismantle its nuclear weapons programme.[22] North Korea escalated its confrontation with the US on the nuclear question by announcing on 12 December that it was going to restart a nuclear power plant capable of producing weapons grade plutonium at the Yongbyon complex, 90 kms north of Pyongyang. This reactor complex was at the heart of the 1994 Agreed Framework concluded between North Korea and the US under President Clinton.[23] North Korea, apart from being engaged in producing nuclear weapons, was also found to be openly engaged in exporting missile technology to Pakistan in exchange for nuclear expertise.[24]

The Bush administration released its strategy of combating weapons of mass destruction – biological, chemical and nuclear – on 11 December. Divided into sections on counter-proliferation, non-proliferation, and consequence management, it was essentially a part of the National Security Strategy released in September. The most striking part of the strategy was the administration's readiness to act pre-emptively against potential adversaries and to consider using nuclear weapons in retaliation for any attack on the United States using weapons of mass destruction.[25]

## NATO Expands its Membership and Role

After the end of the Cold War and the dissolution of the Warsaw Pact, questions had arisen about the relevance of NATO, its relationship with erstwhile members of the Soviet bloc, and its new role, if any. Although since its creation in 1949, NATO had expanded its membership four times, the last expansion in 1999 which led to the addition of the Czech Republic, Hungary and Poland indicated the desire of the Western leadership to expand eastwards and occupy the strategic space vacated by the former Soviet Union.

The events of 11 September 2001 had provided a reason to the Russian Federation to come closer to the West to fight the common threat of terrorism jointly, despite its discomfort about NATO's eastward expansion. At a meeting on 25 February 2002, NATO's 19 ambassadors reached an agreement on proposals to offer Russia a new relationship with NATO. Under this relationship, Russia would have a seat in NATO's political body, the North Atlantic Council (NAC), but without a veto on military decisions.[26]

The new relationship took shape on 28 May at Pratica di Mare air force base near Rome. The Heads of State of the 19-member NATO and Russia signed the Rome Declaration creating a NATO-Russia Council (NRC). This would be a mechanism whereby Russia would be included in discussions with NATO members on areas such as terrorism, crisis management, peacekeeping, and preventing the spread of weapons of mass destruction. For the first time, Russia would have a permanent office in NATO's headquarters in Brussels. It was agreed, however, that Russia's membership of NRC would give it no veto over the proposed further expansion of NATO.[27]

US Defence Secretary Donald Rumsfeld tried to "educate" the fellow Defence Ministers of NATO at a meeting in Brussels on 6-7 June on the danger of biological and chemical weapons being obtained by terrorists, such as Al-Qaeda, and "terror-states", such as Iraq, Iran and North Korea. He also warned the member states that they should be prepared for worse attacks than those of 11 September 2001 and that the organisation "should countenance the idea of pre-emptive strikes against terrorists". The counterview expressed by the NATO Secretary General, Lord Robertson, was that NATO was a "defensive alliance and will remain a defensive alliance."[28] And yet, Donald Rumsfeld reiterated at an informal meeting of Defence Ministers in Warsaw on 24-25 September that NATO "must transform itself from a collective defence organisation into one that was ready to fight terrorists and rogue states." He also pointed out that if NATO could not deploy a mobile strike force able to operate worldwide, it "would not have much to offer the world."[29]

It was in the context of such strategic thinking that the NATO members held their summit meeting in Prague on 21-22 November. The highlight of the summit, of course, was the decision to invite 7 new countries to join the organisation. But the decision that imperceptibly changed the character and role of the organisation was the one to create a NATO Response Force (NRF) capable of fighting around the globe to defend its members' interests.

The NATO Summit invited Bulgaria, Estonia, Latvia, Lithuania, Romania, Slovakia, and Slovenia to begin accession talks immediately with the goal of becoming full members by May 2004. The invitation was notable because three of the invitees, i.e. Estonia, Latvia and Lithuania were parts of the former Soviet Union, and one, i.e. Slovenia, a part of former Yugoslavia. All the seven new invitees had a total military strength of 227,000 personnel and military budgets which totalled $ 2.8 billion, as against the US active duty strength of 1.4 million and the 2003 military budget of $ 355 billion.[30] Security analysts, however, believed that "their usefulness to US and NATO planning was largely in terms of political and geographical enlargement, providing fixed bases and communication facilities as well as specialist units and capabilities."[31]

Another significant decision of this summit, as mentioned earlier, was to support a US initiative to create a roughly 21,000 troop NATO Response Force (NRF) "capable of fighting around the globe on as little as seven days' notice". Use of the force would require consensus by NATO's decision-making body, the North Atlantic Council. Expected to be ready initially by October 2004, and fully operational by October 2006, the force could comprise sea, air, and ground assets and be able to operate independently for up to a month. Establishment of the NRF was thus evidence of the fact that NATO under US exhortation did shift its focus "of defending against a massive conventional attack from the east to the more disparate and asymmetrical threats posed by rogue states and terrorism."[32]

### Bush Proclaims a Doctrine of Pre-Emptive Strikes

President George W. Bush released his National Security Strategy (NSS) on 20 September bringing together all strands of his strategic thinking since he assumed office in January 2001. This was the most comprehensive statement of US strategy in recent years, analysing the whole range of threats that the US faced and laying down the kind of responses that America was determined to offer. The strategy was carved in the backdrop of the terrorist attack of 11 September 2001.

The most salient features of the strategy were: first, the US will disrupt and destroy terrorist organisations of global reach and attack their leadership, command, control and communications; material support; and finances. The immediate focus will be those terrorist organisations and State sponsors of terrorism, which attempt to gain or use weapons of mass destruction. Even if the support of the international community is not available in this respect, the US "will not hesitate to act alone, if necessary, to exercise our right of self-defence by acting pre-emptively against such terrorists, ..."[33]

Second, the national security strategy unfolded a comprehensive approach to combat the threat of weapons of mass destruction. States like Iraq, North Korea, and other "rogue regimes" were acquiring nuclear, biological and chemical weapons. To meet this threat, a three-part strategy would be: i) Proactive counter-proliferation efforts; ii) Strengthened non-proliferation efforts; and iii) Effective consequence management. Given the goals of rogue states and terrorists, the US "can no longer solely rely on a reactive posture." The US "will, if necessary, act preemptively."[34] (Emphasis added)

Third, the NSS Document described Russia, India and China as "potential great powers" and emphasised the importance of developing strong relations with them. The central reality of the 21st country is that "the United States and Russia are no longer strategic adversaries." The US policy seeks to "refocus our relationship on emerging and potential common interests and challenges." The US and India are two largest democracies. They have a common interest in the free flow of commerce, including through the vital sea-lanes of the Indian Ocean. They share an interest in fighting terrorism and in creating a strategically stable Asia. The United States seeks a "constructive relationship with a changing China." The two countries already cooperate in the field of terrorism. They have an annual two-way trade of $ 100 billion, China being America's fourth largest trading partner. The two countries have profound disagreements over Taiwan, human rights, and non-proliferation issues. The United States "will work to narrow differences where they exist, but not allow them to preclude cooperation where we agree."[35] The NSS document had also sections on defusing regional conflicts, promoting economic growth through free markets and free trade, building open societies, and transforming America's national security institutions.

The national security strategy of President Bush attracted considerable international attention for enunciation of the doctrine of pre-emptive action against threats of terrorism as well as weapons of mass destruction. Within the United States too, the Bush strategy was subjected to severe scrutiny. Writing under the title "National Insecurity Strategy", Daryl Kimball said, "In the long run, this approach is unsustainable and self-defeating. The strategy minimises the role of diplomacy and arms control and seeks to maintain and even expand US nuclear capabilities. This combination threatens to erode the credibility of the laws and norms against WMD upon which our security and the security of our allies depend."[36] John Steinbrunner, Director of the Center for International and Security Studies at

Maryland, commented thus: "The Bush doctrine of pre-emption apparently proposes to rely primarily on coercive power, that is, to initiate violence in order to prevent it, and it appears to neglect and indeed to disdain international legal restraint. In the judgement of much of the world, that formula is more likely to generate violence than to contain it."[37]

## China's Growing Military Power and Security Strategy

The US Department of Defence submitted its annual report on China's military power to the US Congress on 12 July. The report carried a wide-ranging analysis of China's military capability, security strategy, threat perceptions and military modernisation. Some of the highlights of this report were:[38]

### 1. Military Capability

(i) Chinese doctrine is moving towards the goal of surprise, deception, and shock effect in the opening phase of a campaign. China is exploring coercive strategies designed to bring Taipei to terms quickly.

(ii) In March 2002, China announced a 17.6 per cent or $ 3 billion increase in defence spending, bringing the public reported total to $ 20 billion. Total spending is closer to $ 65 billion, and annual spending could increase in real terms over three-to-four-fold by 2020.

(iii) Beijing's military training exercises increasingly focus on the United States as an adversary.

(iv) China has approximately 350 short-range ballistic missiles (SRBMs) already in its deployed inventory, increasing at about 50 missiles per year. The accuracy and lethality of this force are also increasing. The PLA is developing variants of the CSS-6 that enable attacks against Okinawa when forward-deployed or against Taiwan when deployed further inland.

(v) All of China's known SRBM assets are believed to be based in the Nanjing Military Region (MR). The number of conventional ballistic missiles deployed opposite Taiwan is expected to increase substantially over the next several years.

## 2. Grand Strategy

(i) China's grand strategy attempts to balance two often competing objectives: a) developing the nation's "comprehensive national power" (CNP); and b) exploiting to maximum advantage the existing "strategic configuration of war", or "shi".

(ii) Three essential "conditions" – national unity, stability, and sovereignty – must exist if China is to survive and develop as a nation.

## 3. Security Strategy

(i) Beijing believes that the United States poses a significant long-term challenge. The United States, according to the Chinese leaders, seeks to maintain a dominant geo-strategic position by containing the growth of Chinese power and preventing a resurgence of Russian power. Beijing has interpreted the strengthened US-Japan security alliance, increased US presence in the Asia Pacific region, and efforts to expand NATO as manifestations of US strategy.

(ii) Chinese analyses indicate a concern that Beijing would have difficulty in managing potential US military intervention in crises in the Taiwan Strait or the South China Sea. There are even indications of a concern that the United States might intervene in China's internal disputes with ethnic Tibetans or Muslim minorities.

(iii) A key variable in China's security strategy is Taiwan. A priority security concern of Beijing is to prevent further steps by Taiwan towards independence and to secure resolution of the Taiwan issue on China's terms.

(iv) Beijing also seeks to counter Japan's growing military cooperation with the United States and to prevent a re-birth of Japanese militarism. At the same time, it will continue to value the access to Japanese technology, trade, and foreign investment.

(v) Beijing's other security goals in East Asia include preventing the development of a regional theatre missile defence system, particularly one involving Taiwan, coping with challenges to its claims in East and South China Seas, and furthering its economic interests through ASEAN, APEC and ARF.

The Chinese government released its new Defence Policy Paper on 9 December 2002. The last such paper called "China's National Defence in 2000" had been released on 17 October 2000. The US Defence Department's report on China's Military Power discussed earlier had based some of its observations on China's Defence Paper of 17 October 2000. The new Defence Policy Paper of China does not make any significant departures from the previous paper. However, some important observations with regard to the security situation in this paper[39] are:

(i) World multi-polarisation and economic globalisation are developing amid twists and turns.

(ii) Since the terrorist attacks of 11 September 2001, major countries of the world have stepped up their coordination and cooperation against terrorism, even though they are competitive in other fields.

(iii) The developing countries are actively pushing forward the establishment of a fair and rational new international order.

(iv) A new world war is unlikely in the foreseeable future.

(v) In the Asia-Pacific region, APEC, ASEAN, and Shanghai

Cooperation Organisation are mentioned as playing a positive role.

(vi) However, the world is far from being tranquil. The old international political and economic order, which is unfair and irrational, has yet to be changed fundamentally. Economic development of the world is materially unbalanced, and the North-South gap is further widening. Democracy in international relations remains elusive and there are new manifestations of hegemonism and power politics.

(vii) Rapid and drastic changes are taking place in the military field around the world, and a new serious disequilibrium has occurred in the balance of military power. The extensive applications of high technologies led by IT have stretched the battlefield into a multi-dimensional space. In military technology, the gap between the developed and developing countries is wider than ever before. The developing countries are facing a serious challenge in their efforts to safeguard sovereignty and security.

(viii) Factors of instability still exist in the Asia-Pacific region. Besides traditional security issues left over from history, non-traditional security issues are looming large. Tensions in South Asia have remained fundamentally unchanged. Afghanistan has not regained full stability. Reconciliation in the Korean peninsula is moving haltingly. The basic pattern of development of relationship in the cross-Taiwan Straits has remained unchanged.

## Japan Rethinks its Nuclear and Security Policy

There were some indications that Japan might rethink its longstanding policy of forswearing nuclear weapons. On 31 May, Japan's Chief Cabinet Secretary Yasuo Fukuda said that "in the face of calls to amend the [no-war provisions of the Japanese] constitution, the amendment of the principles is also possible."[40]

Fukuda was referring to Japan's three non-nuclear principles, which state that Tokyo will never produce, possess, or allow nuclear weapons on its territory. These principles were set out in the late 1960s by the then Prime Minister Eisaku Sato and have been subsequently endorsed by successive Japanese governments. When subjected to harsh domestic criticism, the Japanese government subsequently somewhat retracted from the remarks. During a parliamentary session on 10 June, Fukuda noted that his "remarks did not indicate the government's future policy." At the same session, Prime Minister Junichiro Koizumi also made clear that his government did not support revising the non-nuclear principles.[41]

Fukuda's remarks had also upset Japan's neighbours. On 4 June, Chinese Foreign Ministry spokesman called the remarks "really shocking" and observed that "they obviously run counter" to Japanese policy. Two days later, North Korea's state-run news agency criticised the comments as an "ill-boding act" warning that "Japanese militarists are well-advised to behave with discretion, mindful of what disaster their reckless moves for nuclear armament will bring."[42] South Korean officials also expressed concern.

Japan's rethinking of its security strategy was also reflected in the three War Contingency Bills submitted to the Diet (Japanese Parliament) in April 2002, and the Defence White Paper 2002 presented at a cabinet meeting on 1August.

The first War Contingency Bill (WCB) titled "Emergency Legislation to Deal with Military Attacks from Abroad" provides for the Self-Defence Force (SDF) of Japan to be deployed in the event of "an attack from any country, the fear that such an attack may occur, or a situation in which an attack is likely to occur." The second WCB titled "The Security Council Revision Law" authorises the Prime Minister to convene a special panel to deal with any military situation. This panel would allow for special attendance of cabinet officials in addition to elected Diet members.

The third WCB titled the "Self-Defence Revision Law" would allow the SDF to take possession of privately-held properties, re-locate structures on them, take strict action against those found to be illegally storing fuel or provisions, ask medical and other professionals to render compulsory service, and so on.[43]

The Defence Ministry's White Paper 2002 points out that North Korea, in addition to developing and deploying weapons of mass destruction and guided missiles, maintains a 100,000 strong special forces contingent active in all forms of activity from espionage and sabotage to guerilla warfare. Therefore, "DPRK action raises the level of military tension on the peninsula and is also the main agent of instability in the entire East Asian region." The White Paper says that the DPRK continues R & D on long-range missiles, and the Nodong, with a range of 1300 kms capable of reaching Japanese territory has already been perfected. There are also orders to deploy Taepodong 2 with a range of 3,500-6,000 kms, greater than the 1500 km Taepodong 1, which overflew northern Japan three years ago. A two-stage Taepodong 2 could reach Alaska and an improved three-stage version could also possibly reach the US mainland, the White Paper states.

On Russia, the White Paper says that since its peak period, the number of Russian forces has been reduced substantially, with a scaling back of funding, training exercises, and the number of ground troops "limited to a special-response unit." The White Paper attributes these changes to the disarray and contraction of the Russian economy, a relaxation of military tension with the US, the reduced necessity of showing military strength in the Far East, and an easing of tensions with China. The White Paper concludes, "In the foreseeable future there is little possibility of the Russian army returning to the posture of the Cold War Soviet era", but contends, "there is still reason for caution."

On China, the White Paper says that its defence spending has increased 10 per cent a year in the 14 years since 1989 and this fiscal year shows a large 17.6 per cent jump. But the budget figures made public by Beijing are only a small part of total expenditures for the armed forces. Additionally, the fiscal review reported in the National People's Congress notes increased expenditures for "modern technology, especially to strengthen high-tech defence capability." Regarding China's nuclear capability, the White Paper states that in addition to the estimated 20 ICBMs concerning which the last year's White Paper said "the whole of Asia including Japan falls within their range", are the medium range missiles. Last year's figure of 100 has been updated to 130-150, plus an entry for the first time of 335 short-range missiles, suggesting a build-up in the Taiwan Straits. Summarising the situation about China, the White Paper says, "Modernisation of China's armed forces extends beyond defence. It portends a wider scale of action and bears close watch in the future."

The White Paper makes the following prescription for Japan: "To self-reliantly maintain our country's peace and independence in the present international milieu necessitates a defensive posture that assures response to all varieties of military action from nuclear devices to threats of invasion."[44]

Hisao Maeda, a former Defence Ministry analyst of Japan, criticised the White Paper for evoking images of "survival of the fittest", and asserting that given the opportunity, "evil doers" are "prepared to pounce at any time." If this is the worldview of the defence establishment, Maeda says, "Japan would necessarily have to become a heavily armed and fortified country." Reviewing the War Contingency Bills and the White Paper, Maeda warned of "the emergence of a national warfare state and the further decimation of the provisions of Japan's peace constitution."[45]

❖❖❖❖❖

**NOTES**

1. See *Arms Control Today,* January/February 2002, p. 27.
2. Ibid., pp. 28-29.
3. *See Arms Control Today*, April 2002, pp. 20-21.
4. Ibid.
5. http://english.peopledaily.com.cn/200203/12/ eng200203'2_91927.st...n
6. Daryl G. Kimball, "Do As I Say, Not As I Do", *Arms Control Today*, July/August 2002, p. 2
7. http://english.peopledaily.com.cn/200203/12/ eng20020312_91983.st...n
8. *Arms Control Today*, March 2002, p. 25.
9. http://english.peopledaily.com.cn/20020204/ print20020204_89898.html
10. *Arms Control Today*, March 2002, p. 25.
11. http://www.state.gov/s/ct/rls/pgtrpt/2002/html/19980.htm
12. http://www.state.gov/s/ct/rl/pgtrpt/2002/html/19977.htm
13. For more details, see Christopher Aaron, "Terrorism Threat Survey 2002", *Jane's Intelligence Review*, October 2002, pp. 8-13.
14. Ibid., p. 11.
15. *Arms Control Today*, March 2002, p. 27.
16. Ibid., p. 32.
17. *Arms Control Today*, June 2002, p. 27.
18. *Arms Control Today*, September 2002, p. 14.
19. *Arms Control Today*, June 2002, p. 31.
20. *Arms Control Today*, April 2002, p. 26.
21. *Keesing's Record of World Events,* October 2002, p. 45039.
22. Ibid., November 2002, p. 45088.
23. Ibid., December 2002, p. 45138.
24. See Ibid., October 2002, p. 45039 and November 2002, p. 45089.
25. *Arms Control Today*, January/ February 2003, pp. 22 and 34.

26. *Keesing's Record of World Events,* February 2002, pp. 44651-52.

27. Ibid., May 2002, pp. 44818 and 44820.

28. Ibid., June 2002, p. 44877.

29. Ibid., September 2002, p. 45019.

30. *Arms Control Today*, December 2002, p. 24.

31. *Keesing's Record of World Events*, November 2002, p. 45122.

32. *Arms Control Today*, December 2002, p. 27.

33. The National Security Strategy of the United States of America, September 2002; see http://www.whitehouse.gov/nsc/nss.pdf.

34. Ibid.

35. Ibid.

36. Daryl G. Kimball, "National Insecurity Strategy", *Arms Control Today*, December 2002, p. 2.

37. John Steinbruner, "Confusing Ends and Means: The Doctrine of Coercive Pre-emption", *Arms Control Today,* January/February 2003, p. 3.

38. See Annual Report on the Military Power of the People's Republic of China, July 2002, at www.defenselink.mil/news/Jul2002/d20020712China.pdf.

39. See China's Defence Policy Paper for 2002, at http://www.China.org.cn/e-white/20021209 /index.htm

40. *Arms Control Today*, July/August 2002, p.26

41. Ibid.

42. Ibid.

43. See Hisao Maeda, "Full Speed Ahead to the National Warfare State", 13 February 2003, at http://www.japanfocus.org/018.html

44. For a summary and review of the White Paper, see http://www.japanfocus.org/018.html

45. Hisao Maeda, n. 43

# Global and Regional Military Environment

*Vijay Oberoi*

## Introduction

Globalisation has had a profound effect in making the world smaller and more accessible, but it has also had a major effect on the military environment. Military force factors continue to retain their significance in international relations, but increasingly economic, political, technological, ecological, information and energy factors also play a dominant role in the shaping of the security environment.

The global military environment is influenced by the unilateralism of the sole super power, USA; war on terrorism; the vast potential of the information revolution; the growing potential of regional powers, particularly China; the spread of fundamentalism; and the social upheaval in many developing countries due to the rising expectations of their people. The scenario is further complicated by a rise in trans-border terrorism, sponsored ethnic strife, and low intensity conflicts.

Asia's power structure continues to be polycentric, with the power centres being China, India, Japan, and to an extent, Russia. Regional groupings are exerting their influence on strategic issues, particularly economic. East, South and West Asia, have ongoing bilateral and multilateral conflicts, which impact on the overall military environment.

## Global Military Environment

### An Overview

The 21st century had opened with the global environment focused more on economic issues and multilateral and bilateral cooperation amongst nations. However, after the events of 11 September 2001 (9/11), security issues have re-emerged and taken centre-stage. The global security environment has become increasingly unpredictable. Individual nations, notably India and Israel, but also many others, have been coping with terrorist threats for decades, but after the events of 9/11, terrorism has taken on a global dimension. In addition to terrorism, the world continues to be plagued with conventional military threats, as well as non-military threats. The Revolution in Military Affairs (RMA) has also impacted heavily on the global security environment. Militaries are now focusing on rapidly imbibing the latest technological tools, so that they are not left behind and are able to field modern military forces.

Besides, nuclear and missile proliferations are on the increase. The recent revelations relating to North Korea are pointers in this respect. Conventional conflicts are gradually giving way to trans-border terrorism, engineered ethnic strife and sponsored insurgency.

## Influencing Factors

The global military environment is influenced by many factors, which include regional conflicts, proliferation and transfer of weapons, advancements in military technology, the changing nature of war, and a recent addition, terrorism.

### *Regional Conflicts*

Conflicts have continued, in varying intensities, in many regions of the world. Most have a historical past, with solutions so intractable that they linger despite many changes in the security environment. Like volcanoes, they erupt once in a while and then lie dormant, but festering within, till another catalyst causes yet another eruption.

In South Asia, the notable conflicts are the India-Pakistan adversarial relationship, the India-China border stand-off, and internal conflicts like the LTTE problem in Sri Lanka, the Maoist insurgency in Nepal and the plethora of insurgencies in India. In East Asia, the dispute between the two Koreas and the problem of sovereignty between China and Taiwan are notable conflicts. In West Asia, the ongoing confrontation between Israel and Palestine on the one hand, and the simmering dispute between the Arabs and Israel on the other, have in recent months been eclipsed by the war in Iraq.

The Chechnya problem for Russia, the Tibetan and Xinjiang ethnicity-related problems for China, the continuing ethnic divide in Afghanistan, the simmering discontent in erstwhile Yugoslavia and in the Balkans in general; all affect the global military situation, directly or indirectly. The disputed Paracel and Spratly islands in the South China Sea are a potential flashpoint, but a recent political understanding amongst the concerned nations has shelved the problem temporarily.

***Proliferation and Transfer of Weapons***

The proliferation of weapons of mass destruction (WMD), especially in the hands of non-state actors, is of grave concern, particularly when the countries involved are those which are prone to be influenced by terrorist activities or have a history of promoting terrorism, either as state policy, or by ignoring its rise.

In recent years, China's export of high-grade steel, navigational guidance systems, and missile technologies to Pakistan has enabled it to arm itself with nuclear weapons, with matching delivery capabilities. China is also believed to have provided technologies for manufacturing WMD and missiles to North Korea, Iran and Iraq. China has also provided conventional weaponry to many countries of our region, particularly to Bangladesh and Myanmar. Such actions can threaten the regional military balance. The recent revelations of proliferation of nuclear technology and missiles by Pakistan and

North Korea, in a barter arrangement, have highlighted the perils of proliferation of weapons.

### *Military Technology*

Rapid advancements in technology, in the fields of information, nuclear energy, biotechnology, aviation and underwater operations, are changing the concept of warfare.[1] In the field of information technology (IT), digitisation, networked communications, electronic warfare, as well as information warfare (IW), have highlighted the importance of systems integration and the concept of 'system of systems'.

The proliferation of all types of missiles, the versatility of modern aviation platforms, the precision guided and terminally guided munitions (PGMs and TGMs); and multi-dimensional manoeuvre vehicles, are some of the breakthrough technologies which have changed the nature of warfare. Technology is now evolving exponentially, which means the rate of change, is accelerating.[2]

Missile Defence (MD), whether at the national or theatre levels, is another technological advancement which will have a major effect on warfare in future. MD is a strategic shift from a doctrine of deterrence to that of interdictory interception, and is the new face of the Strategic Defence Initiative (SDI) which could not achieve technological maturity in the 1980s.

### *Changing Nature of War*

Concepts and methodologies of waging war are also changing. Asymmetric Warfare, for example, focuses on fighting a stronger enemy and still winning. In the same context, non-nuclear deterrence is aimed at deterring regional conflicts with only conventional weapons. President Bush has recently added 'regime change' and 'pre-emption' to the lexicon of politico-military terminology. The world is also greatly concerned with 'non-state actors', who could cause havoc at a scale quite disproportionate to their size or strength.

It is now difficult to divide operations into conventional and low intensity conflicts. The modern battlefield demands that wars be fought in all six dimensions — space, cyber, air, land, sea and sub-surface. Increased use of various types of sensors has brought total transparency to the battlefield, affecting the achievement of surprise.

Today, joint and combined operations are the norm. IT, in all its manifestations, affects decision-making. At the same time, IW, including the creation of a favourable public opinion, is a necessary adjunct to the higher direction of war. The fast pace of operations and high attrition rates result in greater physical and psychological strain on all combatants.

***Terrorism***

Terrorism has been part of the security scene for decades. However, after the terrorist attacks of 9/11, it has assumed global dimensions. It has had a profound effect on international security, and strategic planning of many countries has been affected. The overall effect is that terrorism has created a sense of worry in the international community.

Military planners too have to now give considerable thought to the likelihood of terrorist threats, while formulating plans for military operations. Resultantly, greater number of troops and equipment would be required to cope with such threats.

**Major Players**

Nations which play a major role in shaping the military environment at the global level are the United States, Russia, and China. Japan is currently in the shadows and is deliberately maintaining a low profile, but it has great potential. The military developments in these countries are discussed in the following paragraphs.

*United States*

The stated goal of US global strategy is to ensure its national security and economic interests, while promoting democracy and peace around the world. The unstated goal is to take all actions to ensure that its pre-eminent position as the sole super power of the world is fully safeguarded. By implication, it would prevent the rise of any other power or power group from challenging its dominance in any of the parameters of national power. For at least the next 50 years, the US is not likely to be challenged as the sole super power.[3]

In the Report of the Quadrennial Defence Review, released in September 2001, the US Department of Defence (DoD) drew a new blueprint for the national defence strategy, stressing homeland security as the top priority, and emphasising capabilities in response to surprise attacks and terrorist activities. The defence budget in fiscal year (FY) 2003 was $ 364.6 billion and the projection for FY 2004 is $ 379.9 billion, which is an increase of $ 15.3 billion.[4]

During 2002, the US attack in Afghanistan was only partially successful. While a new government was installed, the Al-Qaida and Taliban leadership escaped. US troops continue to be present in Afghanistan and Pakistan, and operations to hunt down the terrorists are continuing.

A significant reorganisation of the worldwide command structure, known as the Unified Command Plan, was approved. This includes the new US Northern Command responsible for USA, Canada and Mexico. It will be the lead instrument to tackle terrorist attacks, civil disturbances and natural disasters. The Joint Forces Command (JFCOM) took on a new focus as the lead command for the transformation of the military forces. The Space Command (SPACECOM) was merged with the Strategic Command (STRATCOM), to eliminate redundancies and streamline decision-making. The regional combatant commands' boundaries were also realigned, to reflect the new changes in the geo-political environment.[5]

In 2002, the DoD reorganised and revitalised the missile defence research and testing programme, free of constraints of the ABM Treaty. The new Missile Defence Agency established a programme to develop an integrated missile defence system. On the other hand, the Navy Area-Wide Theatre Missile Defence Programme was eliminated and a second programme, the Space Based Infra-Red (Low) programme, was restructured. The outmoded Crusader artillery system was eliminated and the funds saved were diverted to develop and field precision munitions and non-line-of-sight artillery systems. The development and deployment of UAV's was accelerated significantly.[6]

The transformation of the Navy's ballistic missile submarine fleet continued in 2002. Four of the older Ohio-class ballistic missile submarines (SSBN's) are being converted to guided missile submarine (SSGN) systems. The Navy also decided to cancel production of the DD-21 destroyer and shift resources to the DD-X family of ships. This move is likely to produce a family of surface combatants that uses advanced technology on a wide range of ships.[7]

In the field of R&D, a new process called spiral development, or evolutionary acquisition, allows the Department of Defence to put systems in the field without going to 100 per cent capability, but with the potential to develop further. Spiral development shortens the time to field systems. The Training Transformation Strategic Plan, which aims to provide dynamic, capability-based training, as the key enabler to achieve objectives, was also approved.[8]

National Missile Defence (NMD) continued to get priority. On 17 December 2002, President Bush stated that the US would field a limited missile defence shield by 2004. The blueprint called for 10 ground-based interceptor missiles at Fort Greeley in Alaska by 2004, and another 10 interceptors by 2005 or 2006.

Many US academics feel that the proposed missile system, which suffered its third failure in eight tests in mid-December 2002, was unworkable and a waste of money. The DoD has spent $ 8 billion per year in the last two years, on this project, and it is likely to spend more than $ 17.5 billion in the next two years.[9]

The US still maintains approximately 1,00,000 troops in the Asia-Pacific region. Through combined military exercises with Japan and South Korea, it retains its influence in the region.[10] US military deployment in the Asia-Pacific region focuses on building a multilateral security network, reinforcing forward deployment and power projection capability, enhancing military alliances with Japan, South Korea and Australia, and maintaining US interests. In addition, the US is building intelligence exchange and military consultation mechanisms through bilateral or multilateral military exercises and strengthening military alliances. The US is reinforcing its ability to tackle contingencies in the West Pacific and East Asia. It is planning to add a few emergency bases in the Pacific and Indian Oceans. The US is promoting military cooperation with some countries of South and Southeast Asia.

***Russia***

Soon after Putin assumed office as President of Russia, he made China a strategic partner of Russia. Moscow has stepped up military cooperation with China, including the acceleration of China's military modernisation. President Jiang visited Russia in July 2001 and signed the PRC-Russia Good-Neighbourly Treaty of Friendship and Cooperation. With NATO's active eastward expansion, Russia is making use of the treaty with China and other mechanisms to reaffirm its interest in the Asia-Pacific region and to indicate that its strategic significance had not declined with the collapse of the Soviet Union.

After the 9/11 incident, Russia rendered strong support for the global war on terrorism. In May 2002, USA and Russia signed the Moscow Treaty, which is expected to slash each side's

6000 active strategic nuclear warhead stocks to a number between 1700 and 2200. However, no definite timeframe for phasing out the stocks was mentioned.[11]

Russia is aggressively selling military hardware to China and Third World countries. Besides improving the economy, developing and maintaining defence industries, and replenishing stocks of military equipment, these arms deals also serve the strategic purpose of maintaining Russia's influence and involvement in regional affairs.

The size of Russia's military is currently in the region of 12,22,000, comprising 1,50,000 in the Strategic Deterrent Force; 4,40,000 in the Army; 2,00,000 in the Navy; 2,10,000 in the Air Force; and 2,00,000 command and logistical personnel. The major weapon systems are 21,970 tanks, 67 submarines, one aircraft carrier, 34 main surface combatants, and 2,733 combat aircraft.[12]

Russia continues to follow an aggressive policy in Chechnya against terrorism and insurgency.

*China*

Although the modernisation of the People's Liberation Army (PLA) is placed last amongst the 'four modernisations', yet the reality is that China's military spending is the third or fourth largest in the world. The focus of military development is on enhancing the capabilities of the Navy and the Air Force, strengthening the Second Artillery, and creating a Rapid Response Force. China is improving the precision and lethality of ballistic missiles, while developing cruise missiles and submarine-launched missiles. China has also launched several satellites, aimed at enhancing the PLA's 'Command, Control, Communications, Intelligence, Surveillance and Reconnaissance' (C3ISR) capability. The PLA has 500 DF-series short, medium, long-range, and inter-continental missiles in its inventory. In recent years, the PLA's efforts in IW have been focused on electronic warfare, command and control (C2) warfare, cyber warfare, and psychological warfare.

China's publicly acknowledged defence budget was RMB$160 billion in 2002. This was an increase of 17.6 per cent from the previous year. However, US sources estimate China's actual budget for 2002 in the region of RMB$498 billion, i.e. three to four times higher than the official figures.[13] Russia has become China's chief supplier of modern weapons and military technology. About 70 per cent of Russia's foreign arms sales went to China in 2000.[14] Recent Russian weapon and equipment sales have included 72 Su-27 fighter-ground aircraft, 100 S-30 surface to air missiles, 10 Il-76 transport aircraft, four kilo-class submarines, and two Sovremenny-class destroyers.[15] China is expected to have 300 Su-27s in operation by 2003. In addition, Russia and China have finalised a deal to co-produce 200 Su 27s in China by 2012. Using in-flight air refuelling kits obtained from Russia, five B-6 bombers have been converted into aerial refuelling tankers.[16]

The ground troops have started to convert to newly developed armour, extended range artillery, rockets, armed helicopters, air defence missiles, tactical ballistic missiles, and so on. The amount of equipment purchased from Russia confirms the selective modernisation of a few units throughout the Chinese military. Only enough equipment has been purchased to develop 'pockets of excellence' among the PLA forces.[17]

The PLA Navy is carrying out research and development (R&D) on advanced submarines, large combat ships, and an aircraft carrier. US sources have, however, assessed that China appears to have set aside indefinitely plans to acquire an aircraft carrier. The PLA Navy's next objective is to become a 'green water' navy. China's 'green water' extends eastward in the Pacific Ocean, out to the first island chain. Further eastward is what the Navy calls 'blue water'. China hopes to have a 'green water' navy early in this century and a 'blue water' navy by 2050.[18]

The PLA Air Force has already introduced Sukhoi fighters, airborne early warning (AEW) aircraft, heavy transport aircraft, and air-refuelling planes. Other weapon systems, such as multi-function fighters, electronic counter-measure aircraft, area air defence missiles, unmanned reconnaissance aerial vehicles, medium range air to air missiles, anti radiation missiles and air launched cruise missiles are expected to complete the R&D phase and enter into service in the near future.

The Second Artillery is phasing out old fixed-site missiles, with vehicle mounted mobile launchers, so as to increase survivability and rapid response.

*Japan*

Japan has a security alliance with USA and is under its nuclear umbrella. Japan's major concern is the security of its sea routes for trade. Earlier, according to the US-Japan Security Treaty, the Japanese Self-Defence Force (SDF) was only responsible for the defence of Japanese territory. However, under the New Guidelines for US-Japan Defence Cooperation, the SDF may operate outside Japanese territory. The question whether the increased scope of Japanese defence responsibility includes the Taiwan Straits, has been deliberately left vague, to avoid friction with China. The Guidelines had evoked a strong reaction from China.

In December 2000, Japan had launched the Fourth Defence Build-up Plan, which stressed sufficiency in responding to various situations, improving defence capabilities, creating a more stable security environment, and building an appropriate self-defence force that is efficient, small, powerful and sophisticated. Besides deciding to purchase advanced equipment, such as shipboard helicopter destroyers, Kongo-class destroyers, and refuelling planes, the plan emphasised the SDF making contributions at the international level, such as in disaster relief operations.[19]

The Japanese SDF has approximately 2,43,000 servicemen,

with the most sophisticated array of weaponry in Asia, and an annual defence budget that ranks third behind USA and Russia.[20] The ground elements number about 1,50,000, the maritime component about 43,000, and the air force comprises about 45,000 personnel. The major weapon systems include 1,070 main battle tanks, 16 submarines, 55 main surface combatants, and 331 combat aircraft.[21]

In October 2001, as a sequel to 9/11, Japan passed the Anti Terrorism Special Measures Law, which further broadened the legal basis for Japan's participation in overseas military missions.

## Regional Military Environment

*Pakistan*

Pakistan's intransigence has now become a permanent feature of the security environment of South Asia. Its Kashmir policy has fostered militancy and terrorism in all parts of J&K. Pakistan's 6,10,000 member armed forces, the world's eighth largest, are well trained. However, their involvement in various aspects of governance has diluted their combat potential. Fiscal and other constraints have affected the government's efforts to modernise the armed forces.

Pakistan's ballistic missile programme continues to progress with the assistance of China and North Korea. Pakistan has been test firing its Shaheen and Ghauri missiles, to demonstrate its capability, and deter India. Pakistan inducted the Ghauri missile in the Army in January 2003. After the purchase of 320 T- 80 UD main battle tanks from Ukraine in 1999, no other tanks have been acquired. However, technology transfer for the assembly of 30 M-113A2 APC's from USA has been arranged and 500 AT-11 Sniper/9M 119 anti-tank missiles have been acquired from Belarus.[22]

Technology transfer for the construction of two Jalalatclass FAC's and four Jiangwei frigates from China and 40 SM-39 Exocet anti-ship missiles for submarines from France, have been obtained. The first indigenously built submarine, an Agosta 90-B, was received by the Navy for sea trials on 20 January 2003. With the assistance from China, the Ormara naval base, on the Makran coast, has been commissioned. Pakistan and China are also jointly building a multi-purpose deep-water port at Gwadar in Balochistan, for which China announced a preferential loan, for US $ 58.21 million, in December 2002.

Approximately 75 to100 K-8 fighter/trainer aircraft are being procured from China during the period 2000-08. Pakistan is planning to buy F-7 fighter aircraft from China and six C-130 Hercules transport aircraft from USA.[23] A media report stated that Pakistan was planning to acquire an anti-ballistic missile system from USA, at an estimated cost of over US $1.5 billion.

Pakistan has been sharing sophisticated technology, warhead design information, prototypes of high-speed centrifuge machines and weapon testing data, with North Korea, probably since 1997. In return, North Korea gave surface-to-surface missiles to Pakistan.

Pakistan has claimed that it has developed complete UAV's, and is now engaged in the production of advanced UAV systems, anti-armour bombs, cluster bomb units, starfish naval mines and other defence systems. Pakistan has also claimed that it has developed a turbojet target variant, as a small step towards indigenous cruise missile capability.

*India*

India has major concerns about the Sino-Pak and Pak-North Korea defence cooperation. It also sees serious security implications in China's strategic partnership with Pakistan, and China's efforts to build strategic relations with India's neighbours, by providing military aid and weapons at 'friendship' prices.[24]

The Indian Army has been fighting terrorism in J&K and in the northeastern States, for many years. Terrorism and insurgency in J&K are Pakistan-sponsored, but on account of their own interests, USA and other Western countries are hesitating to confront Pakistan on this issue. In India's view, as also of many countries, Pakistan is now the epicentre of terrorism.

For nearly ten months in 2002, the armed forces of India were deployed in their operational locations on the western borders. Tension between India and Pakistan was very high during the deployment and at least on two occasions the two nations came very close to waging a war.

Modernisation of India's armed forces has been a slow process. The bottlenecks are paucity of funds, and antiquated procurement and decision-making procedures. Nevertheless, some acquisitions have been made and others are on the anvil. India's defence budget for the year 2002-03 was Rs 65, 000 crores, an increase of 14 per cent over last year's revised estimates. As a proportion of GDP, it was only about 2.5 per cent. The defence budget for the year 2003-04 is only marginally higher at Rs 65,300 crores.[25]

The Army has accorded priority to the modernisation of the infantry and the special forces.[26] There hundred and ten T-90 tanks, contracted in 2001, are being introduced in service. Future inductions include eight AN/TPQ 37 weapon-locating radars and ground sensors from USA; UAVs and surveillance equipment from Israel; the Smerch 300 mm multiple launch rocket system from Russia; and the next generation 155 mm towed and self-propelled artillery guns.[27]

The Navy is hopeful of clinching a deal with Russia, involving the purchase of the refitted Kiev-class aircraft carrier, Admiral Gorshokev; six MiG-29K aircraft, which it will carry; leasing of two Akula-class nuclear submarines, and Tu-22 M3 strategic bombers. In addition, the three Krivak-III class stealth frigates, already on order, were planned to be inducted by April 2003, but this has been delayed. The Navy is also planning to acquire two sets of Deep Submergence Rescue Vessels (DSRV) and technology transfer for the French Scorpene submarines.[28]

By end-2003, the Indian Air Force (IAF) would have inducted most of its SU-30MK I aircraft, with another 140 to be license-produced in India, from 2004 onwards. MiG-27s are in the process of being upgraded to fire PGMs. 40 additional Mi-17 IV helicopters were added to the fleet in 2001.[29] India and Russia have also decided to jointly work on the 5th generation fighter, which will be the frontline fighter aircraft in the next decade.[30] Launching the IRS-TES satellite has enhanced surveillance capabilities.

Acquisition of mid-air refuelling aircraft in 2003 and AWAC's a little later, will give the IAF significant force-multipliers.[31]

India has also purchased hi-tech defence equipment from Israel in recent years. India's other plans to acquire arms include the purchase of 66 Hawk advanced jet trainers from UK, 10 Mirage 2000H from France and the upgrading of 130 mm M-46 guns.[32]

In the nuclear arena, a tri-service Strategic Forces Command has come into existence, in January 2003. India has also announced its command and control structure for handling all aspects of nuclear weapons. The ballistic missile Agni-I and the supersonic cruise missile 'BrahMos' may be inducted by end-2003. The short range 'Prithvi' missile has been in service for a number of years now.[33]

### *The Indian Ocean*

The northern Indian Ocean region is an important area in the security calculus of India. India's overseas trade is considerable and is poised for more growth. Almost all of India's oil imports come from the Gulf, and if they are cut off or otherwise hindered, the country's interests will be very seriously affected. Major sea-lanes of the world pass through this area and India uses them extensively. The exploitation of resources, both within the respective Exclusive Economic Zones (EEZs) of littoral countries, and beyond, is also steadily increasing.

The United States has a major base in the Indian Ocean at Diego Garcia, which is always operationally active. US forces are also well established in the Gulf Region, and now in Afghanistan and Pakistan too. Their presence is likely to increase manifold, following the successful completion of the war in Iraq. The United States would like to see the Indian Navy safeguarding the sea-lanes of the Indian Ocean, so that its own commitments in this regard, are reduced.

***Other Countries***

Practically all other countries of South Asia are faced with internal threats, which require to be tackled by their armed forces. The danger of their spilling over into India is a major concern.

The Nepalese Army is fighting the Maoist rebels. The Bhutan Army is trying to ensure that the insurgents from India are persuaded to leave their sanctuaries in Bhutan. The Myanmar Army continues to operate against insurgent groups along their western borders. Bangladesh has to deal with small insurgent groups operating in the Chittagong Hill Tracts. Bangladesh also provides shelter to insurgents from India, and reportedly permits Pakistani Intelligence to operate against India, by assisting these insurgents. In Sri Lanka, after years of internal strife, the government and the Liberation Tigers of Tamil Eelam (LTTE) are having a dialogue and a temporary ceasefire prevails.

India has land or sea frontiers with all its neighbours, who themselves, in most cases, have such borders only with India. This has an 'in built' scope for irritation and exploitation by vested interests.

## Other Regions

### Central Asia

Although a transitional government has been established in Kabul, Afghanistan continues to be mired in uncertainties. Ethnic groups and warlords are still active. The reconstruction process is continuing, although USA and other Western nations have now shifted focus to Iraq. Coalition forces continue to be deployed in Kabul and some other areas.

The Central Asian Republics (CARs) continue to face the menace of Islamic fundamentalism and terrorism.[34] The armed forces of most CARs are still in a nascent stage and are dependent on Russia. Central Asia had anticipated an oil boom after the Soviet Union disintegrated, but the situation in Afghanistan has denied them a safe export route and also discouraged foreign-investment.[35]

Central Asia has served as a back door for China. The promotion of the 'Shanghai Five' dialogue mechanism and the establishment of the Shanghai Cooperation Organisation[36], are good indicators of the importance China attaches to the region.

### West Asia

The security environment in West Asia revolves around the Arab-Israeli dispute over Palestine. The United States is providing arms to most West Asian states, to have a degree of control over this oil-rich region. The security situation in the region has exacerbated by the acquisition of missiles by some countries like Iran and Saudi Arabia.[37]

US-Iran relations remain frozen, despite the moderate policies of Iran now, under the leadership of President Khatami.[38] Iran is steadily building up its military strength. The Iranian Navy is the strongest in the region, and Iran has a relatively large ballistic missile force. With help from China, it is believed to have developed a potent anti-ship cruise missile. It has test-fired a medium range missile, Shahab-3, with a range of 1300 kms. Another missile Shahab-4, meant for launching satellites into space, is under development.[39]

Following the attack on Iraq by the Coalition Forces, led by USA, Iraq is in a state of flux. The Americans are likely to ensure their permanent presence in this strategically important area. The war is a precursor to strategic changes of great import in the entire West Asian region. This war may create an upsurge in anti-American feelings, throughout the Muslim world and particularly amongst the Arabs.

Israel has adopted a hard-line for handling the Palestinian question. Israel's defence industry has made rapid strides. Israel is a major exporter of high technology equipment to India and China. Israel has successfully tested the Arrow anti-missile missile and also a cruise missile. Israel is widely believed to be a nuclear weapons state, with an arsenal of around 100 nuclear warheads.[40]

**Korean Peninsula**

In recent years, South Korea has promoted the 'Sunshine Policy', for accelerating the process of unification with North Korea. However, major uncertainties persist. South Korea is engaged in major modernisation of its troops. It is planning to acquire new-generation fighters, warships, air defence missiles and early warning aircraft. It is also increasing its C3I capabilities. South Korea wants to establish a 21st century military, which can work with US troops in maintaining regional stability.[41]

North Korea continues to stress its 'military first' policy. It is producing long-range missiles and submersibles, producing and deploying Chonma tanks, and seeking to introduce major conventional forces, including armoured personnel carriers, combat vessels, and fighter aircraft.[42]

North Korea recently startled the world by announcing that it had reactivated its plutonium-producing reactors. It also threw out international inspectors of nuclear facilities and withdrew from the Non-Proliferation Treaty. The defence budget of North Korea in 2001 was US$1.42 billion, which amounted to 14.5 per cent of its national budget.[43]

**Conclusion**

In the global military environment, the immediate and overriding priority at the beginning of 2002 was terrorism. However, in the last few months of the year, the focus shifted, as two issues upstaged it. The first was the build-up to the Iraq war, and the second was the sudden upping of the nuclear ante by North Korea. As events have developed, the Iraq war is now a reality, but the North Korean crisis is hopefully being resolved diplomatically.

The United States, as the sole super power of the world, is readjusting its security and military relations with selected countries, especially those that are likely to be regional powers of the future. In the near-term, it is forging ties with countries that can assist in its war on global terrorism. It is also continuing to sustain its balancing role in high threat areas. It is in the process of developing a long-term strategic relationship with India. At the same time, Pakistan continues to be of importance to USA, at least in the short term.

Russia will continue to be a major exporter of military hardware, particularly to the two regional powers, India and China. The overriding priority of China continues to be economic development. However, missile defence, selective modernisation of the PLA, Islamic terrorism in its periphery, and export of military hardware and technology to selected countries, remain as principal blips on its security radar screen.

India's military environment continues to be in a state of flux. There is no let up in the proxy war in J&K. Modernisation of the armed forces is proceeding slowly. The dangers of increasing Chinese influence in the affairs of Myanmar; the illegal migrations and tacit support to Indian insurgent groups in Bangladesh; and keeping the Indian Ocean a conflict free area are major challenges, which directly affect the security environment of India.

❖❖❖❖❖

## NOTES

1. *Defence Report Republic of China,* Ministry of National Defence, ROC, internet, http://www.mnd. gov.tw/report/revised/bb/NDI.htm.
2. Kip P. Nugren, "Emerging Technologies and Exponential Change: Implications for Army Transformation", *Parameters,* Vol. XXXII, No. 2, Summer 2002, pp. 86-89.
3. K Subrahmanayiam, "US Super League", *The Times of India*, 17 March 2003.
4. US Department of Defence (DoD), *Budget Release for Fiscal 2004*, internet,http://www.defencelink.mil/news/Feb2003/b02032003bt044-03.html.
5. US Department of Defence (DoD), *2002 Year in Review*, 31 December 2002.
6. Ibid.
7. Ibid.
8. Ibid.
9. *The Tribune*, Chandigarh, 19 December 2002.
10. *Defence Report Republic of China*, Chapter 3.
11. Ibid.
12. Ibid.
13. *Defence Report Republic of China*, Chapter 4.
14. Catherine Bilton and Stan Crock, "Washington and Moscow : Back to the Cold War", *Business Week*, 5 March 2001, p. 61.
15. Frances Omori and Mary A. Sommerville, eds, *Strength Through Cooperation: Military Forces in the Asia Pacific Region* (Washington: National University Press, 1999), p. 181.

16. Bill Gertz, Office of Naval Intelligence (ONI) Report, quoted in 'Betrayal' (Washington: Regency Press, 1999), p. 104.

17. Andrew Scobell, *Chinese Army Building in the Era of Ziang Zemin* (Carlisle, Pa.: US Army War College, Strategic Studies Institute, 2000), p. 6.

18. *Jane's Sentinel Security Assessment – China and Northeast Asia* (Coulsdon, Eng.: Jane's Information Group, 1999), p. 96.

19. *Defence Re ort Republic of China*, Chapter 3.

20. Jayant Baranwal, ed. *SP's Military Year Book 2001* (Guide Publications, New Delhi, India), pp. 258-259.

21. *Defence Report Republic of China*, Chapter 3.

22. Shalini Chawla, "Pakistan's Arms Procurement: Shifting Balance with India," *Indian Defence Review*, Vol. 17 (3), July – September 2002, pp. 135-136.

23. Ibid., p. 136.

24. Baranwal, p. 239.

25. Lt Gen Vijay Oberoi, "Fund Surrender Despite Crunch," *The Tribune*, Chandigarh, 28 March 2003.

26. *The Times of India*, 15 January 2003.

27. *The Times of India*, 1 January 2003.

28. *The Tribune*, 26 December 2002.

29. Air Marshal R. S. Bedi, "Pak Must Reconcile to India's Potential," *Hindustan Times*, Chandigarh Live, 30 December 2002, p. 2.

30. *The Times of India*, 19 January 2003.

31. Bedi, p. 2.

32. Baranwal, p. 239.

33. *The Times of India*, 2 January 2003.

34. Kanwal Sibal, "Challenges Ahead - India's Views on Regional Development," speech at the French Institute for International Relations, Paris, on 17 December 2002, excerpted in *The Indian Express*, Chandigarh, January 3, 2003.

35. Baranwal, p. 227.

36. In 1996, heads of states from China, Russia, Kazakhstan, Kyrgyzstan, and Tajikistan had gathered at Shanghai and established the organisation called 'Shanghai Five', with the aim of strengthening economic cooperation and jointly fighting terrorism. On 14 June 2001, another meeting was held in Shanghai, where Uzbekistan was formally admitted as a member. On 5 July 2001, heads of state of the six member countries had issued the 'Dushanbe Statement' in the Tajik capital; renaming 'Shanghai Five' as 'Shanghai Cooperation Organisation', to further enhance cooperation.

37. Baranwal, pp. 277-278.

38. Ibid.

39. Ibid., p. 287.

40. Ibid., p. 291.

41. *Defence Report Republic of China*, Chapter 3.

42. *Global and Northeast Asian Environment*, Republic of Korea (ROK), Ministry of Defence (MND), December 2001, p. 2-1 (internet, http: // www.mnd.go.kr/mndn/sub_menu/w_book/2001/1-2-3.htm).

43. Ibid., p.2-3.

# External Economic Environment: A Globalised India?

*Shubhashis Gangopadhyay*

## Introduction

Citizens in civilised countries should be able to live out their aspirations for a reasonable quality of life. This encompasses more than being able to earn sufficient income, or purchasing power, by being engaged in productive economic activity. It also means being empowered to lead a life free from the basic insecurities of daily existence. Good health, basic education, safeguards from unforeseen shocks, freedom from harassment by state authority, gender equality, etc. are some of the things that guarantee this security. The market economy, private enterprise, democracy, rule of law and other appropriate institutions can go a long way in making these things possible. The basic philosophy of strong societies is one where all citizens are equal regardless of race, religion, creed and gender. It is this goal that India must reach, and quickly.

India's human development rank is 124 among 173 countries. This is not acceptable for two reasons. First, this actually shows a slippage in our relative position since the time of Independence. Though such rankings are not available for the early 1950s, when we look at the 1950 values of some of the variables that go into these rankings, India was well ahead of most of its Asian neighbours of that time. India, at the time of Independence, had almost similar levels of per-capita income as that of China or Korea, but since then both these economies have out-performed us in terms of per-capita income or even in terms of share in the global economy, whether in manufacturing output or in global trade. Second, India is a large country with a one-sixth share of the global population. Thus, if India does not perform well, a large part of humanity is in distress.

Some of the problems facing us are poverty, lack of education and good health among a significant proportion of its people, gender inequality, high infant mortality rates, undernourishment especially among young girls, a rapid degradation of the environment and the lack of social security. However, two major achievements are a thriving democracy and an income distribution that is less equal than only nine other countries in the world.

**Where Do We Stand?**

Table 1 gives our relative position in terms of other comparable countries. We had referred to China and Korea as having started off, during our Independence, at positions similar to us in terms of GDP per capita. In 2000, Korea had a per capita GDP of USD 17,380 while China had a figure of USD 3,976. India, on the other hand, had only USD 2,358. What is probably worse is that India was below the average for all the four regions given at the end of the Table. Indeed, both in terms of life expectancy and adult literacy, India's position is bad.

Table 2 is even more illuminating in terms of how poorly we fare with respect to some of the assets we are proud of. We often boast of our higher education system and the number of skilled personnel we produce in the country. Unfortunately, Korea has 14 times the number of scientists and engineers involved in R&D compared to us. Even China has three times the number we have, while Philippines and Malaysia have numbers comparable to us.

China faces many of the same problems we do. It is a big country, with diverse topographical features and difficult geographical terrain. And yet, it has four times the telephone density that we have.

## Strategic Error

Our major problem is the low productivity of our workers. This is a result of many factors, but particularly those of poor technology, low amounts of physical capital (one has to see the highways being built with bare hands to understand the magnitude of this problem), inadequate training of labour and the lack of economies of scale and scope. How did these come about?

A strategic error was the attempt at being self-sufficient without comprehending the role of international trade in development. This prevented us from accessing bigger markets for our products or from using quality inputs. We wanted to produce everything in the production chain, regardless of whether we had the expertise, technology or market. Consequently, whenever a process was less efficient than what was available internationally, the entire production chain was affected adversely. For instance, by forcing the Indian fertiliser industry to use only Indian designed catalysts, the entire fertiliser industry's productivity suffered. The same was true of the electronics sector where our software industry took time to take off because of the insistence on the use of domestic computer hardware.

Thankfully, there has been a major departure from the original Indian model since 1991. The country has opened up to trade and to foreign investment. Custom duties have been reduced, quantitative restrictions on imports have gone and foreign investment can now come in more freely in most sectors. We still have a long way to go but have certainly embarked on the road to globalisation.

## Opening up the Economy

Before the reform process that started in 1991, India was a country largely protected from imports by high tariffs. High custom duties also implied that the domestic market faced minimal competition from foreign producers, making it more lucrative for domestic producers who, therefore, were not interested in the export market. This also meant that India was a high cost country, with little or no technological improvements. The country has been systematically opened up to the outside world since then. Custom duties have been reduced and foreign investors have been allowed to come in and invest, through both the direct investment and the portfolio investment routes. Many markets where foreign presence was unthinkable have now been thrown open. It is interesting to see how this has affected the Indian economy.

In 1993, India's export was 0.6 per cent of world trade having fallen from 2.2 per cent in 1948. By 2001, this had marginally increased to 0.7 per cent. This is low when compared to other countries like China (4.3 per cent), Korea (2.4 per cent), Malaysia (1.4 per cent), Thailand (1.1 per cent) and Indonesia (0.9 per cent). The world economy has been sluggish since the 11 September terrorist attack on USA and this had affected our export growth in 2002. However, this year exports are faring much better. In terms of foreign investment, in 1991-92, foreign direct investment was at 129 million US dollars while foreign portfolio investment was at a miniscule 4 million US dollars. In 2001-02, the corresponding figures were 3904 million US dollars and 2021 million US dollars. This meant an increase in foreign direct investment of about 2926 per cent and an increase in foreign portfolio investment of a whopping 73050 per cent. Of the total foreign investment, portfolio investment constitutes 34 per cent.

While these are impressive figures, given our past performance in world trade and investment, it is important to put them in perspective. Over the last decade, world imports increased from 20 per cent of world GDP to 22 per cent while exports moved from 20 to 23 per cent. India's globalisation of trade showed much higher growth during the same decade. India's import trade increased from 10 to 17 per cent of GDP, while export doubled from 7 to 14 per cent. Indeed, India increased its trade openness more than any country in the subcontinent (barring Bangladesh in terms of export), or by comparison to any comparable country or region. However, even though the growth in trade has been impressive, India still remains around the bottom of the Table (topping only Japan) when it comes to trade as a percentage of GDP (Table 3).

In the decade of the 1990s, India experienced the second largest increase, after Korea, in net foreign direct investment as a percentage of GDP. This ratio increased from a paltry 0.1 to 0.5. However, this increase disguises the fact that India, along with Pakistan, has the lowest ratio of net foreign direct investment to GDP among a set of comparable countries (Table 4). This is a problem when we are looking for an overhaul of our old and inefficient technologies that we have been able to maintain through years of protection from foreign competition. Most East Asian economies have a direct investment to GDP ratio more than five times that of India's while China has a ratio of 3.6. Even strife-torn Sri Lanka at 1.1 is more than double that of India.

**Are We Globalised Enough?**

Using data from 2001, 62 countries were ranked according to the Globalisation Index. India's rank was a lowly 56, with Saudi Arabia, Venezuela, Peru, Indonesia and Brazil being the countries less globalised than India. These rankings were part of a joint project of *Foreign Policy*, a publication of the Carnegie Endowment for International Peace and A. T. Kearney, an international business-consulting firm. It consists of the combined score of a dozen weighted variables and concluded that global economic integration actually declined during 2001 owing to the sharp slowdown in the world economy in the aftermath of the 11 September terrorist attacks on the United States. There was a 1.5 per cent decline in trade levels during the year, while global FDI dropped by more than 50 per cent, from 1.5 trillion dollars in 2000 to 735 billion dollars in 2001.

The report also compared the Globalisation Index with different indicators of development worked out by other reporting agencies. More globalised countries enjoyed more political freedom, have less corruption and have a more equal income distribution. The Yale Centre for Environmental Law and Policy has ranked 23 countries based on their commitment to a sound environment. Greater globalisation was positively correlated to greater environmental protection. The report also used the results of a survey undertaken by the World Bank that investigated the wages paid to workers in the manufacturing sector of various countries. The greater the globalisation index, the higher was the wage in the manufacturing sector. Not surprisingly, the report concluded that greater globalisation is associated with a higher level of development.

The rankings were based on a number of economic variables including the percentage of trade as a share of the country's gross domestic product (GDP); inward and outward foreign direct investment (FDI) and other portfolio investment; and, international income payments and receipts as shares of GDP. In addition to economic variables, the index included personal, technological and political variables. An interesting finding of the study was that even though globalisation declined according to the economic variables, there was an overall increase in economic integration in the world. This was because the political, social and technological connections among nations continued to grow at a rate that offset the fall in economic integration. For instance, indicators of personal connections across borders, such as international telephone traffic, saw steady growth during the year, while political engagement deepened as a result of factors like the 'war on terrorism' and China's membership in the World Trade Organisation (WTO).

Globalisation does not work simply through greater efficiency and better technology leading to higher growth and hence, more resources for the eradication of poverty and an improvement in the quality of life. It will help India to play a positive role in maintaining stability, not only in its immediate region but also in the global arena. However, this cannot come about simply through the opening up of the economy to trade and investment. India must not only benefit from global technology, it must also contribute to the global pool of knowledge and innovation. Here, our performance is woefully short. One way of measuring contribution to innovation or growth of knowledge is by counting the number of patents a country obtains. In 1999, India obtained 114 patents in the US; for Taiwan and Korea this figure was as high as 4000. Even in terms of domestic patents, India (1660 patents) was far behind China (12,000) or Japan (300,000).

The point I wish to make here is that the world integration is more than the trade and investment on which we tend to concentrate. At one level, the forces of world integration are much stronger and more varied than the simple economic variables on which we focus attention. At another level, and more importantly, the forces of globalisation make economic isolation irrelevant, or contrived. It is impossible to keep oneself insulated from global events even if one tries to follow a policy of relatively closed economic borders. Consequently, one needs to accept globalisation as given and try to make the best of it, rather than wishing it away.

India can have a strong global presence by integrating its economy with other countries. Interdependence among economies adds to the strength of each one of them; the collective strength often being more than the sum of each of their military might. China's importance in today's world is largely because it is seen as a business destination by the rest of the world. It has a huge domestic market and cheap labour where foreigners flock to do business. India can easily be in a similar situation if it can make the world perceive it the same way they perceive China.

**Can Globalisation Go Wrong?**

While globalisation can open up new opportunities for

development, it will be a mistake to think that globalisation is a panacea for all that plagues India. Indeed, if one is not careful, globalisation can actually backfire. When a country opens up to the world, its economy is no longer completely controlled by the domestic authorities. In other words, the collapse of a market, or currency, or the stock index in some distant country, or region, can adversely affect the Indian economy.

This will be a new phenomenon, something that we have never seen before during our long experience with a closed economy. For instance, many argue that India survived the Asian crisis of the late 1990s simply because we had more controls on the movement of capital than these countries. This should not, however, encourage us to keep our economy closed and hence, insulated from the external world. The lesson learnt from the Asian crisis is that there are certain important things that one needs to do before completely opening up the market to the world market uncertainties. The power of the market lies in its ability to be a self-correcting mechanism. Anything that prevents the market from playing its disciplining role is dangerous. There is enough evidence to suggest that the Asian crisis was triggered by government guaranteed foreign loans in some of the countries and, by foreign currency denominated loans in other countries that maintained fixed exchange rates. Our experience with government guaranteed price for electricity from the Dabhol power plant should be a pointer in this regard-government intervention in economic activity was bad during the planning period and it continues to be bad in today's world of globalisation.

In addition to market uncertainties, one other thing to worry about is labour that is currently employed in industry. Globalisation will put pressure on our companies to become more efficient. Some will be able to re-organise and re-structure themselves to take on this challenge, while others will be forced to shut shop. This disciplining role played by the global market will enable the re-deployment of resources from the inefficient to the efficient companies. Such a re-deployment, however, can become very costly for India.

One of the most important resources that will need to be re-deployed is labour. The new and more competitive industry will need to economise on labour costs. They will demand higher productivity levels from their employees, who will need to be trained and will work with more capital and new technologies. The currently employed labour may find this a difficult process and lose out to new and fresh entrants into the labour force. The redundant older labour may have to be retrenched before they can be rehabilitated.

Most market-based economies also have very strong unemployment insurance schemes. It is unfortunate that India, whose Constitution describes it as a socialist economy, has absolutely no such scheme. What is even more astonishing is that our intelligentsia, which is so vociferous about changing the labour laws that make it difficult to fire employees, provides no meaningful suggestions to develop a programme that insures labour against sudden job-loss. If we do not take this seriously, our experience with globalisation will be mired in social unrest and political instability.

The other important area of discontent could be agriculture and rural India. The WTO agreements will push the services and industrial sectors towards greater integration with world markets. This push will come mostly from developed countries. However, these very same countries will resist tooth and nail, any opening up of their own agricultural sector. Thus, while we will face global competition in services and industry, our agriculture will not be able to reap the benefits of a global market.

Too often, globalisation seems to benefit the urban elite in developing countries. This raises discontent among the large chunk of the population that gets left behind and is outside the process of integration with the world economy. The majority of our population stays in rural India and are employed mostly in agriculture. However, globalisation seems to have passed them by. This is because of the developed countries that prevent imports of agricultural produce from less developed countries. While most emerging market countries are pressured in world forums to open up their industry and services, the developed countries resent similar moves in agriculture. It is in agriculture that developing countries have their comparative advantage. Trade in agriculture will not only bring incomes to those who are most poor, but will also help in rural industrialisation through the development of food-processing industries. The latter will release the burden on agriculture to provide employment in rural India and help increase the productivity of those remaining in the agriculture sector.

A large part of the globalisation battle is politics and not economics. India, as the largest developing economy after China, has to play an important role in winning concessions that will help not only its own rural poor, but also those in other developing countries. The developed countries have been able to keep the agenda of WTO negotiations focussed on matters other than agriculture by constantly introducing newer and newer items. None of the committed deadlines of the Doha Development Agenda has been met by them and, by all indications the upcoming discussions in Cancun will stay away, or provide lip service to the developmental issues. The gains that world trade can bring about to developing countries will be lost if the world fails to open up the sector in which developing countries have comparative advantage.

India has to bargain hard in WTO. It is the largest developing economy and can offer market opportunities to a number of foreign players. This will also improve the incomes and productivity of a large group of its own citizens. However, it may also improve the gap between those who participate in the globalisation process and those who do not. The non-participants will be mostly in rural India, if the developed world continues to protect its agriculture from the cheaper imports from developing countries. Agriculture and food processing can be a boon to most emerging countries — helping in increased agricultural productivity as well as rural industrialisation. This is the challenge the Indian negotiators must take up in Cancun. And, in this regard, China is more of an ally than a competitor.

❖❖❖❖❖

Table 1: Human Development

| HDI Rank | Country | GDP per capita (PPP USD) | Adult Literacy Rate (% 15 & above) | Life Expectancy at birth (years) |
|---|---|---|---|---|
| 9 | Japan | 26,755 | | 81.0 |
| 23 | Hong Kong, China (SAR) | 25,153 | 93.5 | 79.5 |
| 25 | Singapore | 23,356 | 92.3 | 77.6 |
| 27 | Korea, Rep. of | 17,380 | 97.8 | 74.9 |
| 59 | Malaysia | 9,068 | 87.5 | 72.5 |
| 70 | Thailand | 6,402 | 95.5 | 70.2 |
| 77 | Philippines | 3,971 | 95.3 | 69.3 |
| 89 | Sri Lanka | 3,530 | 91.6 | 72.1 |
| 96 | China | 3,976 | 84.1 | 70.5 |
| 110 | Indonesia | 3,043 | 86.9 | 66.2 |
| **124** | **India** | **2,358** | **57.2** | **63.3** |
| 138 | Pakistan | 1,928 | 43.2 | 60.0 |
| 145 | Bangladesh | 1,602 | 41.3 | 59.4 |
| | South Asia | 2,404 | 55.6 | 62.9 |
| | East Asia and the Pacific | 4,290 | 85.9 | 69.5 |
| | Developing Countries | 3,783 | 73.7 | 64.7 |
| | WORLD | 7,446 | | 66.9 |

Source: UNDP, *Human Development Report 2002*, New Delhi, Oxford University Press, 2002.

## Table 2: Science and Technology

| HDI Rank | Country | Telephone Mainlines (per 1000) 2000 | Scientists & Engineers in R&D (per million) 2000 |
|---|---|---|---|
| 9 | Japan | 586 | 4,960 |
| 23 | Hong Kong, China (SAR) | 583 | 93 |
| 25 | Singapore | 484 | 2,182 |
| 27 | Korea, Rep. of | | 464 2,139 |
| 59 | Malaysia | 199 | 154 |
| 70 | Thailand | 92 | 102 |
| 77 | Philippines | 40 | 156 |
| 89 | Sri Lanka | 40 | 188 |
| 96 | China | 112 | 459 |
| 110 | Indonesia | 31 | |
| **124** | **India** | **32** | **158** |
| 138 | Pakistan | 22 | 78 |
| 145 | Bangladesh | 4 | 51 |
| | South Asia 33 | 158 | |
| | East Asia and the Pacific | 104 | 496 |
| | Developing Countries | 78 | |
| | WORLD 163 | | |

Source: UNDP, *Human Development Report 2002*, New Delhi, Oxford University Press, 2002.

### Table 3: Trade Figures

| HDI Rank | Country | Imports of Goods and Services (as percentage of GDP) 1990 | 2000 | %change | Exports of Goods and Services (as percentage of GDP) 1990 | 2000 | %change |
|---|---|---|---|---|---|---|---|
| 9 | Japan | 9 | 8 | -11.11 | 10 | 10 | 0.00 |
| 23 | Hong Kong, China (SAR) | 126 | 145 | 15.08 | 134 | 150 | 11.94 |
| 25 | Singapore | 195 | 161 | -17.44 | 202 | 180 | -10.89 |
| 27 | Korea, Rep. of | 30 | 42 | 40.00 | 29 | 45 | 55.17 |
| 59 | Malaysia | 72 | 104 | 44.44 | 75 | 125 | 66.67 |
| 70 | Thailand | 42 | 59 | 40.48 | 34 | 67 | 97.06 |
| 77 | Philippines | 33 | 50 | 51.52 | 28 | 56 | 100.00 |
| 89 | Sri Lanka | 38 | 51 | 34.21 | 29 | 40 | 37.93 |
| 96 | China | 14 | 23 | 64.29 | 18 | 26 | 44.44 |
| 110 | Indonesia | 24 | 31 | 29.17 | 25 | 39 | 56.00 |
| **124** | **India** | **10** | **17** | **70.00** | **7** | **14** | **100.00** |
| 138 | Pakistan | 23 | 19 | -17.39 | 16 | 16 | 0.00 |
| 145 | Bangladesh | 14 | 19 | 35.71 | 6 | 14 | 133.33 |
| | South Asia | 15 | 19 | 26.67 | 11 | 18 | 63.64 |
| | East Asia and the Pacific | 40 | 51 | 27.50 | 41 | 56 | 36.59 |
| | Developing Countries | 26 | 32 | 23.08 | 26 | 34 | 30.77 |
| | WORLD | 20 | 22 | 10.00 | 20 | 23 | 15.00 |

Source: UNDP, *Human Development Report 2002*, New Delhi, Oxford University Press, 2002.

### Table 4: FDI Figures

| HDI Rank | Country | Net Foreign Direct Investment (as percentage of GDP) | | | Other Private Flows (as percentage of GDP) | | |
|---|---|---|---|---|---|---|---|
| | | 1990 | 2000 | %change | 1990 | 2000 | %change |
| 9 | Japan | | | | | | |
| 23 | Hong Kong, China (SAR) | | | | | | |
| 25 | Singapore | 15.2 | 6.9 | -54.61 | | | |
| 27 | Korea, Rep. of | 0.3 | 2.0 | 566.67 | 0.1 | 0.9 | 800 |
| 59 | Malaysia | 5.3 | 1.9 | -64.15 | -3.6 | 1.7 | 147 |
| 70 | Thailand | 2.9 | 2.8 | -3.45 | 2.3 | -3.9 | -270 |
| 77 | Philippines | 1.2 | 2.7 | 125.00 | 0.2 | 0.6 | 200 |
| 89 | Sri Lanka | 0.5 | 1.1 | 120.00 | 0.1 | 0.5 | 400 |
| 96 | China | 1.0 | 3.6 | 260.00 | 1.3 | 1.8 | 38 |
| 110 | Indonesia | 1.0 | -3.0 | -400.00 | 1.9 | -4.3 | -326 |
| **124** | **India** | **0.1** | **0.5** | **400.00** | **0.5** | **1.4** | **180** |
| 138 | Pakistan | 0.6 | 0.5 | -16.67 | -0.2 | -0.6 | 200 |
| 145 | Bangladesh | | 0.6 | | 0.2 | | |
| | South Asia | | 0.5 | | 0.3 | 0.8 | 166.67 |
| | East Asia and the Pacific | 1.7 | 2.8 | 64.71 | 0.8 | 0.7 | -12.50 |
| | Developing Countries | 0.9 | 2.5 | 177.78 | 0.5 | 1.0 | 100.00 |
| | WORLD | 1.0 | 3.8 | 280.00 | | | |

Source: UNDP, *Human Development Report 2002*, New Delhi, Oxford University Press, 2002.

# External Security Environment

*Satish Kumar*

## Introduction

The security environment of India in the year 2002 was dominated by the possibility of war with Pakistan in the midst of incessant terrorist attacks by Pakistan-sponsored militants on high value targets in India. Considerable diplomatic effort was invested by India in persuading major powers of the world, particularly the United States, to pressurise Pakistan to stop abetting cross-border terrorism. While counsels of restraint from external powers came in plenty, none of them had any effect on Pakistan. India resorted to near full-scale mobilisation of its troops and their deployment on the international border with Pakistan. The deployment continued from December 2001 to October 2002 costing India a huge sum of money.

India remained engaged in countering Pakistan-sponsored infiltration across the Line of Control and incidents of terrorist violence in Jammu and Kashmir and other parts of India. Apprehending a long-term terrorist threat from across the borders, India beefed up its security infrastructure. A process of consultation and cooperation was kept up with the United States and Russia. Other major powers like Britain, France, and China were also kept informed. Relations with China marked an upward trend.

The security environment in the South Asian region was not ideal. Nepal was beset with Maoist violence which had potentially disturbing implications for Indian security. Bangladesh showed signs of yielding to pressures of extremist Islamic elements with adverse repercussions on India. Sri Lanka, while entering into a phase of negotiated settlement of its ethnic conflict, was nowhere near an early end to it. The situation in

Afghanistan remained turbulent with the Hamid Karzai government facing the double challenge of residual resistance of the Al-Qaeda and Taliban as well as assertions of authority by provincial warlords. Pakistan's interference in Afghanistan increased. Myanmar's nexus with China remained a cause of concern although India in the last few years has tried to create a strategic space for itself in that country. Overall, there was a sense of challenge.

**United States**

The role of the United States was extremely significant in the external security environment of India. In the backdrop of the 13 December attack on Parliament House and the subsequent massive troop mobilisation by India and Pakistan, the United States sought to defuse the situation by pressurising Pakistan to desist from involvement in terrorist activities directed against India and to dismantle the infrastructure of terror. Despite Pakistani assurances that it would do the needful, cross-border terrorism against India continued.

There were a number of high-profile visits to the region by American officials. These included the visits of the US Secretary of State Colin Powell, Deputy Secretary of State Richard Armitage, Defence Secretary Donald Rumsfeld, Under-Secretary of State for South Asia, Christina Rocca, FBI Director Robert Mueller, the Chief of the Defence Intelligence Agency, Admiral Thomas Wilson, the Counter-terrorist Head of the State Department Francis Taylor, the Chairman of the Joint Chiefs of Staff Richard B. Myers, among others.

The war on terror should have made the United States more sensitive to the travails of India vis-à-vis Pakistan-sponsored terrorism in Jammu and Kashmir. But, the post-9/11 importance of Pakistan and the belief that Pervez Musharraf was its best bet explain perhaps the fact that the US did not move more forcefully to influence Pakistan to curb its involvement with cross-border terrorism. The United States has military personnel stationed at Jacobabad, Pasni and Dalbandin, who are operating in conjunction with Pakistani forces in mopping up the remnants of the Al-Qaeda and the Taliban. By the middle of 2003, Pakistani authorities were said to have handed over more than 500 Al-Qaeda men to the United States. At the same time it is also clear that Pakistan not only provides shelter to some Al-Qaeda and Taliban elements but it is also supporting them materially in their efforts to find a niche for themselves in Afghanistan.

The war on terror reinvigorated the US-Pakistan relationship. After Musharraf's visit to Washington in February, Pakistan was given a 'soft' International Monetary Fund (IMF) loan and donor assistance for economic restructuring and poverty alleviation at the rate of $ 1 billion a year, $ 150 million for military education and training, among other things including $ 300 million for its help in 'Operation Enduring Freedom'.[1] The US also promised that $ 1 billion of Pakistan's nearly $ 3 billion debt to the United States would be written off.

The US reluctance to censure Pakistan led to a sense of anguish in India that the United States was adopting double standards and distinguishing between terrorist violence against America and the violence that India was being subjected to. Prime Minster Vajpayee told reporters in London that "the West finds its terrorism more serious, not ours. It has a double-standard to measure terrorism."[2] India spent considerable diplomatic energy to convince Washington of the common origins of terrorism in the *madrasas* of Pakistan, and the organic link between the Taliban, the Al-Qaeda, the terrorist groups operating in Jammu and Kashmir, and the Pakistani establishment, especially the ISI.

The fall of the Taliban and the Al-Qaeda in Afghanistan was a major gain for India as it denied Pakistan the strategic depth that it so desperately craves. But it but it came at the price of bringing the US strategic presence much closer to the Indian soil. The United States became India's new neighbour. The

United States' military presence in Afghanistan, Pakistan, and Central Asia added a new strategic dimension to the security situation in the region.

India-US defence interaction increased during the year. It began with the meeting of the Defence Policy Group (DPG) and the subsequent signing of the General Security of Military Information Agreement (GSO-MIA) in Washington by the Defence Minister George Fernandes in January. The agreement provides for sharing information relating to security, terrorism, military intelligence, guaranteed protection of technology secrets involving weapons sales, among others. India also clinched a $ 146 million deal to buy 8 Raytheon AN|TPQ-37 Firefinder Weapons Locating Radars (WLR's) which enable detection of enemy artillery, missile and mortar positions, in April. The need for these radars was acutely felt during the Kargil war. The Bush administration during the year also approved the sale of 40 GE F404-GE-F2J3 engines and advanced avionics for India's Light Combat Aircraft (LCA), submarine rescue facilities, satellite-backed ground sensors and electronic fencing for the Line of Control, in collaboration with the Sandia Laboratories Cooperative Monitoring Centre. Besides, the United States cleared the sale of the Israeli Airborne Early Warning And Control (AWAC) Phalcon system as well as the sale of multi-mission maritime reconnaissance aircraft and Harpoon anti-ship missiles.[3] The Chairman of the US Joint Chiefs, Gen. Richard Myers, remarked that the US sees its relations with India as central to maintaining long-term stability in Asia and in fighting terrorism.[4] India and the United States also conducted joint exercises in Agra (army), Alaska (air force) and both Navies patrolled the maritime trade routes between the Suez Canal and the Malacca Straits. The year also saw the aircraft carrier USS Carl Vinson touching port in Mumbai.

The increased level of cooperation and interaction prompted the view that the United States would be a new strategic partner of India, be it in the war against terrorism, containment of China, or promotion of liberal democracy. This assumption, however, was not fully borne out by the ground realities. The United States seemed more interested in the short-term goal of neutralising Al-Qaeda and took the view that Pakistan held the key to achieving this objective. This prevented the United States from pressurising Pakistan to stop cross-border terrorism against India. The United States also turned a blind eye to Pakistan's proliferation activities and to General Musharraf's strangling of democracy in the country.

**Europe**

Europe witnessed momentous changes during the year. Domestically, there was considerable churning on the political spectrum. Centre-left governments lost power in Italy, Norway, Denmark, Portugal and right-wing parties did consistently well. The most prominent right-wing performer was Jean Marie Le Pen of the extreme-right Front National (FN) in France, who was a close second to the eventual winner Jacques Chirac. Mr. Le Pen succeeded in eliminating the socialist Prime Minister Lionel Jospin, securing 19.2 per cent of the vote. He campaigned on a platform of racist xenophobia and ultra nationalism, themes which were very popular with the extreme right throughout Europe. Other prominent rightists who did well in elections or cornered attention included Joerg Haider in Austria, who became part of the coalition government there, and Pim Fortuyn in the Netherlands. The rightists' campaign thrived on the discontent in European society and the perceived injustices meted out to Europeans on account of forces as varied as Islamic fundamentalism and the militancy that it spawned, and illegal immigration, among others. France with a population of 4 million Muslims and Spain with around 500,000 out of a population of 40 million were two of the countries that had to deal with these problems. In fact, Mohammed Atta, the coordinator of the 11 September attacks in New York, visited Spain twice before the attacks and the Spanish police carried out arrests of members belonging to the sleeper cells of the Al-Qaeda network.[5] In order to deal with these problems more effectively, European governments proposed to enact tougher new laws. UK Defence White Paper identified international terrorism as the country's primary enemy.[6] The EU Heads of Government meeting in Seville, Spain on 21-22 June reached an agreement to tackle illegal immigration.[7] On a suggestion from the US, NATO also decided to establish a "find and strike" rapid response force of about 20,000 troops, capable of being deployed within 5-15 days, backed by air and naval support, at the Prague summit in November.[8]

Europe's response to the war plans against Iraq was also varied. While Britain supported the idea wholeheartedly, along with Italy and Spain, France and Germany opposed US plans to invade Iraq. Chancellor Schroeder maintained that Germany would not be party to an attack against Iraq and that he would withdraw German forces in Kuwait. President Chirac was of the opinion that US unilateralism was contrary to France's vision of collective security, based on cooperation between states, respect for law and authority of the UN Security Council.[9] Even in Britain, where Prime Minister Blair was willing to pay the "blood price" for the war on Iraq, he had to face consistent domestic opposition, even from members of his cabinet like the International Development Secretary, Clare Short.[10] French Foreign Minister Dominique de Villepin wrote in *Le Monde* that France does not want to give a blank cheque to military action, as it would like to shoulder the responsibility to the end.[11] The stand taken by France and Germany hurt their bilateral relations with the US. US Defence Secretary Donald Rumsfeld took the position that Chancellor Schroeder's stand on Iraq, in the run-up to the general election, had "poisoned" German-US relations.[12] European leaders were wary of the foreign policy being followed by the Bush administration, which they variously termed as "unilateralist" and "simplistic".[13]

Ten new nations joined the EU at the Copenhagen Summit held on 12-13 December. These included Latvia, Lithuania,

Estonia, Poland, Hungary, Czech Republic, Slovakia, Slovenia, Malta, and Cyprus. Bulgaria and Romania will become full members in 2007.[14] Efforts to create a European constitution received a boost when Valery Giscard d'Estaing, the chairman of the 105-member convention tasked with the job under the Laeken Declaration of December 2001, published a draft of the EU constitution. Article 1 of the 46-article document defines the EU as "a union of European states", retaining their national identities, but cooperating and sharing power, sometimes on a federal basis.[15]

The India-Pakistan standoff cornered the diplomatic attention of European states during the first half of the year. European governments were sympathetic to the position of India and urged Pakistan to stop cross-border terrorism. This was conveyed during the series of high-level contacts European leaders had with their counterparts from the subcontinent.[16] India had a fruitful interaction with Europe in the form of the India-EU bi-annual summit in the first week of May. The Gujarat incidents had an echo at the summit when the EU expressed concern "regarding violence, loss of life and property" in these incidents. In fact, the EU issued a *demarche* to India on 23 April when Dilip Lahiri, India's ambassador to Spain, the current chair of the Union, was summoned by the EU. The incident threatened to become a major diplomatic row when conflicting reports did the rounds as to the exact nature of the said interaction, with the MEA spokesperson in Delhi denying that the EU had issued the *demarche*.

Prime Minister Vajpayee went on a tour to Europe from 7-13 October when he visited Cyprus, Copenhagen and London. The third Indo-European Business Summit was held in Copenhagen during his stay there. There was a public falling out with EU at Copenhagen as the EU refused to include a reference to Pakistan in the context of cross-border terrorism.

India-EU strategic interaction also increased during the year.

The British government tried hard to finalise the nearly $1 billion deal to sell 66 advanced jet trainers (AJTs) manufactured by BAE Systems to India. Indo-French strategic dialogue took place in January. Joint Indo-French air exercises were also decided to be held in 2003 in Gwalior, home of India's Mirage squadron. France also offered to sell its Rafale fighter jets for the aircraft carrier Admiral Gorshkov, which India plans to induct into its fleet. France also agreed to transfer technology for the Mirage 2000 V aircraft.[17]

**Russia**

Russia had to contend with the growing presence of the United States in the Central Asian region following the war in Afghanistan and the possibility of expansion of NATO near its borders. Russia was earlier against the scrapping of the ABM treaty but later backed down in its criticism. Russia had the visit of President Bush to Moscow in the last week of May and to St. Petersburg in November. During the Moscow summit, the Treaty of Moscow was signed by the US and Russia, which commits both sides to reduce their nuclear arsenals to 1700-2200 warheads by 2012. The 22 November summit between President Putin and President Bush followed the 21 November Prague meeting of NATO, during which the membership claims to NATO of Latvia, Lithuania, Estonia, Romania, Bulgaria, Slovenia and Slovakia were considered. Russia was naturally alarmed over the NATO encroachment of its traditional spheres of influence. Bush tried to soothe Russian feelings by saying that Russia does not need a buffer zone for protection. He added that what it needed were "peaceful and prosperous neighbours who are also friends."[18] Moscow became a junior partner in NATO formally on 28 May, when the 19 members of NATO and Moscow formed the NATO-Russia Council at the Pratica-di-Mare air base in Italy. The agreement gave Moscow equal footing with NATO on issues ranging from terrorism to arms control, missile defence, among other things. The agreement, however, gave Moscow no power of veto.

The US presence in the region saw a closer level of interaction among Moscow, Beijing, and New Delhi. Russian Foreign Minister, Igov Ivanov, who was in Delhi in the first week of February, reiterated the need for it.[19] Closer Sino-Russian ties culminated in the Sino-Russian Joint Communiqué of 22 August in Shanghai, which aimed to build "a just and rational international order on the basis of mutual trust, equality and cooperation". The communiqué appealed to the international community to safeguard the outer space from the weaponisation moves of any country, particularly the US, and called for a greater role for the United Nations and its Security Council in "international anti-terror operations."[20]

President Putin paid a high profile visit to China in December which gave content to the July 2001 Treaty of Good Neighbourliness, Friendship and Cooperation. The two countries stepped up their cooperation to combat terrorism, particularly in the framework of the Shanghai Cooperation Organisation. They also enhanced their cooperation in the military and energy sectors. Russia continues to remain the main supplier of military technology to China. China is also viewing Russia as a major supplier of hydrocarbons in future. An agreement was reached to build a Russia-China oil pipeline.

To the increasing US military presence in Central Asia, Russia responded by stepping up its military ties with the CARs in the framework of the Collective Security Treaty. Russia secured a military base at Kant in Kyrgyzstan. In order to assert its interests in the region, Russia held naval exercises in the Caspian Sea.

Indo-Russian ties continued on the upswing. President Putin visited India in the first week of December and signed the Delhi Declaration for enhanced strategic cooperation. The two countries agreed to begin "tactical cooperation against terrorism on an unprecedented scale, involving cooperation at operational and diplomatic levels.[21] Eight other documents were signed including one on strengthening economic, scientific and cultural cooperation. President Putin publicly expressed apprehension about the continued presence of terrorists in Pakistan and the danger of WMDs falling in their hands. Greater impetus was given to improving bilateral economic trade. ONGC (Videsh) in a joint venture with Exxon-Mobil is already operating an offshore project in Sakhalin. It has a share of 20 per cent in the project Sakhalin-I. Russian companies are also in the fray to bring Iranian gas to India.

Indo-Russian military-technical cooperation also showed progress. A bright example of joint efforts to develop high-technology military hardware was the successful flight test of the supersonic cruise missile, Brahmos. Russia's annual weapons sales to India were in the range of $ 1.0 to $ 1.2 billion, and improving.[22]

The year saw the reaffirming of the traditionally close ties between India and Russia, grudging acknowledgement of US supremacy in world affairs by Russia, and a closer interaction and cooperation among Russia, China and India to offset the US presence in the region.

## Japan

The year 2002 saw the 50th anniversary of the establishment of diplomatic relations between India and Japan. Contacts at the highest level were maintained, when Prime Minister A. B. Vajpayee met his Japanese counterpart Junichiro Koizumi in New York on the sidelines of the UN General Assembly meetings in September. Both leaders discussed projects in which Japan was collaborating, like the Metro rail project in Delhi and the Ganga water pollution project. Prime Minister Koizumi also praised India's hosting of the Conference of Parties to the Kyoto Protocol.[23]

Former Prime Minister Yoshiro Mori also visited India as a special envoy of Prime Minister Koizumi on 20 October, at the beginning of the Japan Week celebrations commemorating the

50th anniversary of the establishment of diplomatic relations between the two countries. Japan's leader of the opposition Hatoyama Yukio, leader of the Japan Democratic Party, visited India during January on an invitation from the Bharatiya Janata Party, to develop closer inter-party links.

Both the countries also lobbied for a seat at the UN Security Council. Japanese Ambassador to India, Hiroshi Hirabayashi, said that Japan perceived India as "a power that could play a role in securing the sea lanes."[24]

The North Korean stalemate saw Japan play a leading role to bring about a rapprochement. There was a historic summit in Pyongyang on 17 September between Japan and the Democratic People's Republic of Korea. In the resulting Pyongyang Declaration, North Korea expressed its intention "to further maintain moratorium on missile launches in and after 2003."[25]

Japan also took a consistent view on Indo-Pak relations when it urged both countries to resume dialogue at the earliest and noted with satisfaction the withdrawal of troops from the border, the conduct of the elections in Jammu and Kashmir and the general elections in Pakistan.[26]

**China**

There was a marked improvement in India-China relations during the year, relations that had taken a downturn after the 1998 Pokhran nuclear tests and the subsequent characterisation of China as India's enemy. This was all the more significant given Indian concerns about the deep Sino-Pak linkages and Chinese apprehensions about the possibility of the US building India as a counter to it. The positives included the visit of the Chinese Prime Minister Zhu Rongji to India during the second week of January and the visit of the External Affairs Minister Jaswant Singh to China in March. During Mr. Rongji's visit, business contracts worth over $100 million were signed.[27] Addressing a meeting jointly organised by the Federation of Indian Chambers of Commerce and Industry (FICCI) and the Confederation of Indian Industry (CII) in Mumbai, Prime Minister Rongji hoped that the volume of trade between the two countries, currently valued at around $3 billion, would grow to around $10 billion in the near future.[28]

There was some positive movement forward to resolve the contentious border dispute between the two countries. India and China share a disputed border area of nearly 125,000 sq.kms, spread over three sectors. During Rongji's visit, the Chinese side reiterated that the dispute could be settled through "mutual understanding, mutual accommodation and mutual adjustment."[29] Maps were exchanged on the middle sector during Mr. Rongji's visit in January. This was done to facilitate better understanding of each other's position vis-à-vis the disputed areas.

The US war on terror in Afghanistan and its military presence in the Central Asian region with which China shares its borders added to Beijing's disquiet during the year. It was also a year that saw greater levels of cooperation and interaction between New Delhi and Washington, which Beijing believes is part of Washington's game plan to build India as a counter to it. This is a position further buttressed by statements made by the US Ambassador to India, Robert Blackwill, who is reported to have said that India and the US should together prepare to face the enemy "beyond the third mountain range."[30]

China and Russia, sharing similar concerns over Washington's moves in the region, came together in Shanghai to sign the Sino-Russian Joint Communique on 22 August. The communiqué states that it would be the Sino-Russian joint effort to build a "just and rational international order" based on "mutual trust, equality, and cooperation", and on the principle of "multi-polarisation process in global politics".[31] Both the countries have used the renewed sense of urgency post-11 September 2001 terror attacks to crack down on their respective separatist/terrorist movements in Xinjiang and Chechnya.

China's all-weather friendship with Pakistan continued to trouble India. Some of the missiles in Pakistan's inventory like Hatf I (range of 300 kms), and Hatf III (range of 600 kms), are in fact the Chinese M-11 and M-9 missiles. US had imposed Category-II sanctions against China and Pakistan (China's Metallurgical Export Corporation and Pakistan's National Development Council), which would continue till 31 August 2003, for failing to live up to the MTCR specifications regarding missile transfers.[32] China of course denies having supplied Pakistan with the relevant technology.

China's leadership changed hands at the 16th Congress of the Chinese Communist Party that concluded on 18 November. Hu Jintao took over as the new General Secretary while President Jiang Zemin continued in his post as the Chairman of the powerful Central Military Commission. It was also a year that saw the Chinese economy perform admirably, registering a growth of nearly 7.5 per cent, with the foreign direct investment touching US $ 50 billion, the largest ever annual inflow. The year also saw the hosting of the Boao Forum by China, billed as an Asian equivalent of the annual Davos economic summit of government and business leaders.

**Pakistan**

The 13 December attack on Parliament House set the tone for the India-Pakistan relations. The subsequent troop mobilisation by India on its borders with Pakistan and the reciprocal actions by Pakistan brought the two South Asian neighbours to the brink of war. Nearly 3/4th of India's million-strong army was massed along the border. India terminated the 25-year-old Samjhauta Express, the two-year-old Lahore-Delhi bus service, recalled its High Commissioner and banned Pakistani flights to India. These steps were an indication of India's extreme displeasure at Pakistani abetment of cross-border terrorism in Jammu and Kashmir and elsewhere in India, with the attack on Parliament testing India's patience to the limit. Even during the

1971 Bangladesh war of liberation, India had not taken the step of recalling its High Commissioner.

The increased levels of tension between the two South Asian neighbours saw a greater degree of diplomatic engagement by the United States especially and the world community in general. Gen. Pervez Musharraf's 12 January speech was an indication of the pressure that was being applied on the Pakistani president as a result of the Indian actions. In his speech, which even Union Home Minister L.K. Advani appreciated, Gen. Musharraf promised to end cross-border terrorism against India.

The United States designated the Lashkar-e-Taiba (LeT) and the Jaish-e-Mohammed (JeM), two Pakistan-based terrorist organisations, as foreign terrorist organisations under US laws in the aftermath of the parliament attack. President Bush expressed satisfaction at the efforts of the Pakistani leader when he observed that President Musharraf was responding to the Indian request. The US urged India to give the Pakistani ruler breathing space and resume dialogue. New Delhi insisted that cross-border terrorism and Pakistan's sponsorship and abetment of it should end conclusively before they could think of resuming dialogue. This was a position the US also acknowledged when Secretary of State Colin Powell told reporters in New Delhi that it was up to India to decide whether the steps undertaken by Gen. Musharraf constituted the basis for the resumption of a bilateral dialogue.[33]

Aware of India's sensitivities vis-à-vis Jammu and Kashmir, the US sought to characterise its enhanced role as that of a 'facilitator' and not that of a 'mediator', in spite of Pakistan's efforts to involve the US in a more substantial role.[34] There was even a proposal for joint US-British patrolling of the 776-km-long LoC, which India rejected. New Delhi instead proposed joint patrolling by both the countries, which Pakistan was unwilling to accept.

Internally, Pakistan was in a state of flux. The overt support being given to the US in its war on terror and the presence of US troops on the ground in Jacobabad, Pasni, and Dalbandin inflamed the fundamentalist crowd. The US support to Gen. Musharraf stemmed from the belief that it was the Pakistani President who could help them in ensuring that the war on terror reaches its logical conclusion. Events on the ground, however, testified to the fact that the military regime of Gen. Musharraf did not live up to its promise. The killing of church-goers in Islamabad on 17 March, the 8 May attack at Hotel Sheraton in Karachi killing 11 French Navy personnel, and the 14 June bombing of the US Consulate in Karachi were all pointers to the freedom with which terrorists could strike as also the deep antagonisms nurtured by these groups against the West, and the United States particularly. The US declared Pakistan "a non family station" after the 17 March attack.[35]

In order to further consolidate his position, Gen. Musharraf conducted a doctored referendum on 30 April, which he "won" with a handsome majority of 98 per cent. He also proposed setting up a National Security Council (NSC), which would have powers to decide on all matters related to "security and national interest". He would also have supreme powers to dismiss and appoint prime ministers at will and even declare a state of emergency.[36]

The 14 May Kaluchak massacre in which 34 innocent civilians were killed pointed to the fact that India was unable to pressure Pakistan into to reducing either the infiltration across the LoC or the levels of violence executed by terrorist groups based there. The Kaluchak massacre proved that terrorist groups could operate with impunity in the face of India's threat of a full-scale military response. It was evident that General Musharraf was only making a pretence of fighting terrorism. In fact, the ISI's interactions with terrorist groups involved in cross-border terrorism continued unabated as did Pakistan's support to them.[37]

India officially ended its massive troop mobilisation,

codenamed 'Operation Parakram' on 16 October. The decision led to a huge sense of relief in India and the international community but left several questions unanswered as to the costs and benefits of the nearly 10-month-long troop deployment.

Landmark elections were held in Jammu and Kashmir in October and a new government assumed office on 2 November under the Chief Ministership of Mufti Mohammad Sayeed. General elections were held in Pakistan in October which saw the ascendance of fundamentalist religious parties, especially the Muttahida-Majlis-e-Amal (MMA), a combine of six Islamist parties. A government under the Prime Ministership of Mir Zafarullah Khan Jamali took over on 23 November.

No progress was made on forging closer economic ties between the two countries. The SAARC summit which Pakistan was to hold in January 2003 was postponed indefinitely. India blames Pakistan for not being serious about regional economic integration.[38]

The year 2002 saw a new low in India-Pakistan relations which threatened to spill over into a major war that, the world feared, might escalate to a full scale nuclear conflagration. De-escalation finally took place. India still seems to be groping to find the right strategy to deal with Pakistan.

**Nepal**

As Nepal entered the terrorism map of the world, it was witness to continually deteriorating internal security owing to the Maoist rebellion. The rebellion, serious as it was, assumed even more dangerous proportions in the context of the constitutional crisis in the country which arose from the Monarchy's desire to garner an enhanced role for itself. The fast unfolding Maoist insurgency had obviously detrimental cross-border implications.

The constitutional crisis continued due to divergent

approaches of the three key players of the Nepali polity. The Maoists demanded a republican form of government either without monarchy or with a king being a ceremonial figure; the political parties desired a constitutional monarchy; and the king desired to have more powers than envisaged in either of these two alternatives. The continued political stalemate accompanied by political agitation by the main political parties and the upgradation of fighting capability by the Maoists created a vacuum that attracted foreign powers to this country.

The "People's War" was launched in Rolpa by the Communist Party of Nepal (Maoists) in February 1996 to establish a democratic republic in Nepal. The Maoists established a People's government in about 22 districts of Nepal's total of 75 districts while threatening to engulf the whole of Nepal into chaos and instability. The Maoists have a two-fold strategy ¾ on the one hand, they execute armed attacks in militant style while on the other hand, they announce democratic forms of protests such as bandhs. Due to the deteriorating law and order situation, the Sher Bahadur Deuba government announced a state of emergency in Nepal in November 2001. Though the emergency was widely criticised within Nepal and raised concerns of human rights violations by the army, the Nepal government maintained that imposing an emergency was the only recourse left for the government to deal with the difficult situation.

Indian security was intertwined with the fast unfolding situation in Nepal in two ways. The first was the cross-border implication of the Maoist rebellion in terms of the activities of ultra-Left groups like the People's War Group in India. The second was the ever-increasing role of the US in Nepal's efforts to counter the threat.

The cross-border implication of Nepal's Maoist rebellion cannot go unnoticed. Many political analysts are of the opinion that a coordinated scheme could be seen in the actions of the ultra-Left groups, which could be detrimental for Indian and

Nepali internal security. At the ground level, within India the activities of ultra-Left groups like the Maoist Communist Centre (MMC) in Bihar and the People's War Group (PWG) in Andhra Pradesh were proscribed. More substantially, the Indian government assured King Gyanendra of Nepal during his visit to India in the last week of June that India was willing to assist Nepal in all possible ways to bring peace to the troubled state.[39] To prevent any unwarranted spill over of the Maoist rebellion into India, vigilance was intensified on the 1800-km border between India and Nepal. Although within Nepal there was considerable suspicion that India might provide refuge to the Maoist leaders, it is important to remember that within India a number of ultra-Left groups operate. To encourage links between groups such as the PWG and the Nepali Maoists whether by design or inadvertently due to a lax security system would be detrimental not only to Indian security, but also to the whole region.[40] India had a huge stake in Nepal's success against the Maoist insurgency.

The Maoist rebellion pushed Nepal into the terrorism map of the world and consequently into the American spotlight on terrorism. Despite the deteriorating law and order situation within Nepal, the ruling establishment was bolstered by unflinching support from the US and India. The American Secretary of State, Colin Powell, in an unprecedented move visited Nepal in January 2002 and expressed the US support for Nepal's fight against terrorism.[41] The Bush administration also requested a congressional sanction of $ 20 million in April as military and economic assistance to Nepal to fight the Maoist insurgency.[42] A dozen US military experts had visited the Maoist infested areas in Rolpa district and elsewhere on 21 April to assess Nepal's military and development needs.[43] Apart from the role of the US in countering insurgency in Nepal, it may be recalled that Nepal already has a large USAID programme and an active Peace Corps programme.

It should be remembered that the issue of external aid in

fighting internal security problems is a sensitive one in any nation and Nepal is no exception. The ruling establishment in Nepal, therefore, had to tread a delicate line in accepting external aid to fight the domestic menace. India dispatched two MI-17 transport helicopters to Nepal, apart from giving training to 100 Royal Nepal Army personnel at the Counter Insurgency and Jungle Warfare School in Mizoram.[44] Though the Nepali Prime Minister had dismissed the need for foreign troops to quash the insurgency, there were reports that Nepal was seeking to import logistical support from the US, UK and India. From the Indian perspective, however, the role of external powers would remain a cause of concern.

**Bangladesh**

Bangladesh was rocked by a crisis of ungovernability. The growing nexus between crime and politics, the uninhibited violation of human rights, extra-judicial killings, and the repression and torture of political opponents, all mounted concerns about the inability of the government to provide a secure and transparent governance. Indian security was adversely affected because of three reasons. First, the growth of religious fundamentalism and its corollary of high political rhetoric affected any progress in trade and border management between the two countries. Second, the fact that Bangladesh was increasingly described at least in the Western media as the latest stop of militant Islamic fundamentalism did not augur well for Indian security. And third, India had to deal with a large number of illegal Bangladeshi migrants, which threatened to affect the demography of the border states.[45]

The government in Bangladesh was a four party alliance led by the Bangladesh Nationalist Party (BNP). It included most of Bangladesh's fundamentalist religious organisations that had a Talibanesque quality to them. Mostly it was an alliance of religious nationalists and militant fundamentalists. The presence of such elements inadvertently affected the bilateral equation between Bangladesh and India. Though the Khaleda Zia government had by and large distanced itself from the anti-India rhetoric, it had to tread carefully lest it be accused of caving in to Indian demands by its allies and the opposition. Therefore, progress in relations in spheres such as trade, especially export of natural gas, travel and border management was excruciatingly slow and politically volatile in Bangladesh.

From the long-term perspective and perhaps having a greater impact on Indian security was Bangladesh's association, at least in the Western media, with fundamentalist and jehadi Islamic forces. An article in the October 2002 issue of *Time* magazine alleged that in December 2001 as the war on terrorism in Afghanistan was intensified a ship m.v. Mecca transported about 150 Al-Qaeda fighters from Pakistan to Chittagong. It further unravelled the nexus between Bangladeshi intelligence agencies and their Pakistani counterparts, the Inter-Services Intelligence (ISI).[46] Apparently they have had a long history of providing refuge to secessionist forces within India such as the United Liberation Front of Assam (ULFA). Even more inimical to Bangladesh's own social fabric and to Indian security was the Jamaat-i-Islami's patronage to about 15,000-20,000 (Qaumi) madrasas. Apparently about 30-40 of these were run by Mujahideen veterans and they sheltered militants and also recruited fresh fighters.

The Bangladesh government, however, denied these allegations. Moreover, the Bush administration stood firmly behind the Bangladeshi official establishment and its efforts to curb terrorism. President Bush in a letter to Bangladesh President Prof. Tajuddin Ahmed lauded the country's commitment to combating terrorism.

The developments in Bangladesh during the last year did not augur well for Indian security. Issues such as trade, especially the export of natural gas to India and border management became mired in high political rhetoric on both sides of the border.[47]

Indian security interests would be served well if the Bangladeshi establishment is able to control the spread of fundamentalism at the grass roots level, and also if the government is able to build a consensus within Bangladesh with respect to the export of natural gas to India. Increased trade and inter dependence will also bode well for the security of the two countries.

**Sri Lanka**

The year 2002 saw considerable progress towards resolution of the 20-year-old ethnic conflict in Sri Lanka. The ethnic conflict saw a flicker of hope as talks began between the Liberation Tigers of Tamil Eelam (LTTE) under the auspices of Norwegian mediation. For India it was a delicate balancing act between keeping abreast of all the developments in the peace talks while at the same time resisting the active role that was expected of it. For Sri Lanka itself continuing the dialogue with the LTTE was the only ray of hope in crafting a solution to the bitter ethnic conflict. Though the LTTE suspended talks with the Sri Lankan government in April 2003, it ostensibly remained committed to seek a negotiated political solution to the ethnic conflict.

The post-11 September discourse on terrorism had left the LTTE with few options with respect to its political agenda. The fact that the US along with Canada and Britain had categorised LTTE as a terrorist organisation led the Eelam to rethink its strategy. A formally agreed ceasefire with rules of conduct came into being in February 2002 between the LTTE and Sri Lankan government.[48] The balancing act for Sri Lanka while the talks were on was to build a consensus within the establishment while the President Chandrika Kumaratunga had differences with the Ranil Wickremasinghe led United National Front (UNF) government. The President was of the view that the LTTE was being given undue concessions.[49] As a symbolic gesture the Prime Minister, Ranil Wickremasinghe, visited Jaffna and also met the US Assistant Secretary of State for South Asia, Christina Rocca, there.[50] The fact that the Sri Lankan government had eased the economic embargo on the northern areas held by LTTE as a confidence building measure for the peace initiative helped in the rousing welcome that the Prime Minister got. Between September and December 2002, three rounds of talks were held between the LTTE and the Sri Lankan government with Norwegian mediation. Of significance were the pronouncements made by LTTE's chief negotiator and political adviser, Anton Balasingham, on the issue of the LTTE's political aspirations. Balasingham announced during the first round that the LTTE would settle for regional autonomy with self-governance; secession was only the last option. During the second round of talks too he repeated that self-governance and autonomy could be the basis for a solution.[51] Other agreements negotiated related to demilitarisation and rehabilitation of displaced people. The LTTE plunged the talks into a phase of uncertainty by pulling out of them in April 2003. For many Eelam watchers the fact that secession was not even put forward by the Tigers raised concerns about the seriousness with which the LTTE was negotiating. Within Sri Lanka itself the issue of how much trust to place on the fickle organisation is a much-debated one. The only ray of hope in this scenario was the fact that at least in public the LTTE remained committed to a negotiated political settlement.

The Indian position on the ethnic conflict in Sri Lanka was that the sovereignty and territorial integrity of the island be maintained and that the solution to the ethnic conflict should accommodate the aspirations of all the ethnic groups. In the South Asian subcontinent where ethnicity transcends borders it is imperative to maintain the status quo of borders if peace in the region is to be maintained. India has a huge stake in the peaceful resolution of the ethnic conflict. Since 1983 when the conflict boiled over, about 63,000 Sri Lankan Tamil refugees are accommodated in about 110 government run camps in Tamil Nadu. While not seeking an active role in conflict resolution, India has keenly followed all the developments in the peace talks.

President Chandrika Kumuarantunga was in constant touch with the Indian establishment on all developments relating to the peace talks. The Sri Lankan Prime Minister, Ranil Wickremashinghe, visited New Delhi twice within a period of six months in 2002 to brief the Indian leadership on the initiatives of his UNF government to resolve the government. He apparently assured India that its political and strategic interests would not be compromised. The LTTE has constantly appealed to India to play a proactive role in the talks. In fact, when the modalities of the peace talks were being structured the LTTE had requested India not only to host the talks but also to relocate its political adviser, Anton Balasingham, in Chennai.[52] The reaction within India to even the hint of such a suggestion was very hostile. The hostility was especially evident in Southern India where the Tamil Nadu State Assembly in April 2002 passed a special resolution demanding the extradition of LTTE chief Prabhakaran to New Delhi to stand trial in the Rajiv Gandhi assassination case.[53] Besides, even from a long-term perspective India would prefer that the status quo be maintained in South Asia as far as boundaries are concerned.

The fact that the LTTE is a banned terrorist organisation does not help in its efforts to refashion its profile and agenda. India has therefore resisted all invitations to play a more active role in the conflict resolution keeping in mind the adverse effects that an association with the LTTE can have for the fissiparous tendencies within the country. Though it has remained a stated aim with India to get extradition of Prabhakaran, the demand, however, was put on the back burner. The fact that both Sri Lanka and India agree that a permanent negotiated solution has to be structured within the territorial boundaries of Sri Lanka has helped to strengthen the Sri Lankan government's hands while negotiating with the LTTE.[54]

The real challenge in the solution of the ethnic conflict in Sri Lanka is whether the LTTE can transform from a banned terrorist organisation into a political party. That notwithstanding,

Indian interests are best served by at least a continuation of the peace talks and ultimately a negotiated solution emerging.

## South-East Asia

### *Myanmar*

Indo-Myanmar relations were conducted in the backdrop of India's renewed emphasis to build better economic and strategic ties with South-East Asia. Myanmar occupies an important place in India's security framework. India shares a 1640-km-long border with Myanmar and four of India's north-eastern states ¾ Arunachal Pradesh, Nagaland, Manipur, and Mizoram ¾ share their borders with Myanmar. Militants from the four states are known to have training camps across the border. In fact, Myanmar released 192 Manipur rebels apprehended in November 2001 in Sagaing division of Myanmar, purportedly under pressure from China. India wanted the militants to be released to it but the military junta ruling Myanmar refused to do so saying that they were in fact Burmese.[55]

Apart from the role of Myanmar in providing safe haven to militants operating in India's North-East, the Myanmar-China relationship has also cast a shadow on Indo-Myanmar relations. China and Myanmar share a close defence relationship with China supplying arms to Myanmar. China also has plans to build the Irawaddy corridor, giving China direct access to the Indian Ocean. There are also reports of China building new radar facilities at Cocos Island in the Bay of Bengal.

One of the high points of Myanmar's domestic political scene was the release of the independence leader Aung San Suu Kyi on 6 May. This was a few months after the ruling military junta, the State Peace and Development Council (SPDC) arrested a son-in-law and three grandsons of the former General Ne Win on charges of plotting a coup. Observers believe this was an indication of the power struggle in the ruling junta. UN special envoy Razali Ismail had to postpone his visit to the country owing to this development.

In order to carry forward the process and continue maintaining contacts at the highest level, Vice President B. S. Shekhawat is scheduled to go to Myanmar early 2003. This would be the highest-ranking visit to Yangon since Prime Minister Rajiv Gandhi's visit in December 1987.[56]

### *Others*

India's renewed emphasis in improving economic ties with South-East Asia resulted in the Indo-ASEAN Summit in Phnom Penh in November and the visit of Prime Minister Vajpayee to Laos and Cambodia during the year. The trilateral initiative linking India and Thailand through Myanmar to build an East-West transport corridor was also part of the effort. Foreign Minister Jaswant Singh travelled to Yangon on 5 April along with his Thai counterpart Surakiart Sathirathai to meet the Myanmarese leadership in order to carry forward this process.[57] A dominant view gaining ground in the foreign policy establishment is to use Myanmar as a land-bridge to South-East Asia and help transform the North-East into a zone of economic opportunity.[58]

## Central Asia-Caspian Sea

The US war on terror in Afghanistan brought into sharp focus the strategic importance of the Central Asian region. The region is not only home to great reserves of oil and natural gas but is also strategically placed as it abuts South West Asia, South Asia and Russia to the north. The Central Asian region played a very important role for the US in the war against the Taliban and Al-Qaeda in Afghanistan. The US established military bases in Uzbekistan, Kyrgyzstan, Tajikistan and facilities in Kazakhstan. It provided economic and humanitarian aid worth $ 600 million to Central Asian countries, and also gave them military equipment and military training. The US was involved in training Georgia's elite forces to take on the militants in its troubled Pankisi gorge area. The increased US involvement in the region raised the anxiety levels in Moscow and Beijing, which consider the region to be under their traditional spheres of influence.

The oil wealth of the Central Asian region, especially the Caspian Sea region, was also the subject of international attention and speculation. Countries like the US want to have their share of the pie in the oil wealth. During the visit of Kazakh President Nursultan Nazarbayev to New Delhi in February, ONGC (Videsh) decided to invest in four identified Caspian Sea oil fields in Kazakhstan.[59] Agro and food processing industries were also identified as potential sectors for immediate investment. Kazakhstan also urged India to join the Shanghai Cooperation Organisation (SCO), the Central Asian grouping of four Central Asian states (Kazakhstan, Kyrgyzstan, Uzbekistan, and Turkmenistan) and China and Russia. Pakistan also expressed its desire to join the organisation.[60] The charter of the SCO was signed on 7 June in St. Petersburg making it a full-fledged international body. The charter listed three priority tasks ¾ regional security, economic and humanitarian cooperation, and the fight against terrorism and separatism.

The Conference on Interaction and Confidence-Building Measures in Asia was held in Almaty, which adopted the Almaty Declaration on 4 June. The Declaration identified terrorism as "a trans-national threat". The Declaration on Eliminating Terrorism and Promoting Dialogue among Civilisations was signed by 16 countries. These included Afghanistan, Azerbaijan, China, Egypt, India, Iran, Israel, Kazakhstan, Kyrgyzstan, Mongolia, Pakistan, Palestine, Russia, Tajikistan, Turkey, and Uzbekistan.[61]

India's plans for Central Asia during the year included a software facility in Kyrgyzstan and the building of a fast-track communication network, the North-South corridor, linking Russia, Belarus, Iran and India.[62]

## South-West Asia

### *Afghanistan*

The year 2002 was witness to the deep difficulties involved

in rebuilding Afghanistan, after the fall of the Taliban regime. After taking over the reins of the country on 22 December 2001, along with a 30-member Executive Council, Hamid Karzai had an unenviable task at hand. He had to restore a sense of normalcy and order in the war-torn country, mop up the remnants of the Taliban and the Al-Qaeda, and do a balancing act to keep in good humour the provincial warlords so that they do not derail the peace efforts. In addition, he had to contend with the Pashtun-Tajik divide in the echelons of the government. At the end of the year, though Kabul saw a semblance of order and normalcy, and his individual position was strengthened, President Karzai was still grappling with Afghanistan's myriad problems. The most serious of these was how to prevent external interference into Afghanistan's internal affairs.

The US bombing campaign was a bone of contention at the beginning of the year between the Afghan interim administration and the US military. The civilian deaths that resulted due to the bombing were further alienating the US among ordinary Afghanis. US Defence Secretary Donald Rumsfeld dismissed the talk of massive civilian casualties owing to US bombing as "enemy propaganda".[63]

In order to mop up the remaining elements of the Al-Qaeda and the Taliban, the US launched '*Operation Anaconda*' in March, which lasted 12 days. At the end of the campaign, the US claimed that it killed over 700 fighters, and destroyed their command and control system in the Shah-E-Kot Mountains. Given the fact that the US failed to capture Mullah Omar and Osama bin Laden and reports that fighters had escaped from Tora Bora Mountains into Pakistan, scepticism greeted US claims.

Added to this was the open rivalry among the warlords controlling the provinces of Afghanistan, and the differences rampant among warlords belonging to different ethnic groups. The interim administration had its hands full dealing with the competing pulls and pressures from Gen. Rashid Dostum (an ethnic Uzbek from Mazar-e-Sharif), Gen. Mohammad Fahim (an ethnic Tajik from Panjshir valley), Padshah Khan Zadran in Paktia province, and Ismail Khan in Herat, among others.

The Loya Jirga was convened in the middle of June at which Hamid Karzai was reappointed the President. Over 1,656 delegates attended the meeting. President Karzai was promised aid worth $ 4.5 billion in the donor conferences at Berlin and Tokyo, aid which would not be distributed properly unless there was a semblance of normalcy in the country. The International Security Assistance Force (ISAF) was doing a commendable job in Kabul, but the situation overall was not very encouraging. Even in Kabul, the assassination of Civil Aviation Minister Abdul Rehman in February and of Vice-President Abdul Qadir in July were signs of growing anarchy in the troubled capital.

Pakistan took advantage of the uncertainties in the country and once again became active in cultivating and encouraging the disgruntled Pushtun elements in the South and South Eastern parts of the country. Hekmatyar's JEI, supported by the ISI, declared a jehad against the western supported Karzai government. Towards the end of the year, there were signs that Taliban and Al-Qaeda elements were regrouping. The Western forces came under sporadic attack from disgruntled Taliban/ Al-Qaeda cadres.

Hamid Karzai was active on the diplomatic front. He visited Pakistan, India, Iran, Russia, China, US, Japan and a number of Western countries. In his visits he candidly admitted that the prevailing security situation was a matter of concern. He pleaded for non-interference in Afghanistan's internal affairs and asked for speedy international assistance as committed by various countries at the Donor's Conference in Tokyo in January.

It was in this backdrop that India moved to reestablish its ties with the Afghan government and the Afghan people. A substantial, wide-ranging assistance and rehabilitation programme worth about $ 100 million was announced by India.

A large portion of the programme was implemented. India also reopened its Mission in Kabul and Consulates in Jalalabad, Kandahar and Herat. It announced its willingness to build a road between Iranian port of Chabahar and Western Afghanistan. The Pakistanis took exception to Indian activism in Afghanistan and sought to pressurise Hamid Karzai to deny permission to Indians to open Consulates in Jalalabad and other towns. The Afghan government ignored Pakistani pressures but privately cautioned Indian diplomats that Afghanistan should not become an arena of Indo-Pak rivalry.

The fall of the Taliban brought about an improvement in the socio-cultural environment of the country. The position of women improved. Under the Taliban, life was very difficult for them as they were banned from even attending colleges and working in a professional environment. Most importantly, the fall of the Taliban denied Pakistan the strategic depth. Pakistan was unable to reconcile with this. The coming to power of Karzai and of elements of the Northern Alliance, with which India had traditionally good relations, augured well for India strategically, but unnerved Pakistan. Whether the positive changes in Afghanistan could be sustained was still a question mark at the end of 2002.

### *Iran*

Iran occupies an important place in India's strategic calculus. It is not only the repository of one of the world's largest reserves of gas but plays a major role on issues of India's immediate concern, namely, Afghanistan and terrorism.

The fall of the Taliban in Afghanistan was a positive development for both India and Iran as it removed a destabilising force in the regional security situation. It also brought into the neighbourhood the world's only superpower which viewed the theocracy in Iran in an unfriendly manner. In fact, Iran was one of the three countries, apart from Iraq and North Korea, that

President Bush had included in his 29 January State of the Union address as states constituting an "axis of evil". The Iranian leadership reacted strongly against this characterisation. President Mohammed Khatami described President Bush's speech as "bellicose and insulting".[64]

Iran, apprehensive of US designs once the war on Iraq would be over, climbed down from its rhetoric and even requested the help of US in manning the 560-mile-long porous border with Afghanistan. Iran did help the US in its anti-Taliban campaign, promising to rescue grounded pilots and even providing an air cover for US fighter planes.[65]

Indo-Iranian relations during the year were dominated by the possibility of bringing gas to India. Considerable progress was made with the Gas Authority of India Limited (GAIL) being made a co-client with the National Iranian Oil Company (NIOC) in carrying out pre-feasibility studies for the project. Italy's Snamprogeti was given the task of conducting the undersea pre-feasibility study while Australia's BHP was given the task of doing it for the overland route. The Iranian Foreign Minister Kamal Kharazzi in New Delhi on 21 May called the pipeline project a "peace pipeline" and added that the project would promote peace and security in the region by itself. Pakistan was keen on this project as it would get transit fees from India and royalties from Iran for the passage of gas through its territory. But whether Pakistan would be able to provide security for this pipeline remained one of India's dominant concerns.

Foreign Ministers Kamal Kharazzi and Jaswant Singh reviewed the entire gamut of Indo-Iranian economic issues during the meeting of the Indo-Iranian Joint Commission in New Delhi in May. Strategic dialogue between the two countries was also held when the chief of the Supreme National Security Council of Iran, Hassan Rouhani, visited New Delhi in the last week of June, and held wide-ranging talks with his Indian counterpart, Brajesh Mishra. Both sides agreed on the need to cooperate in dealing with Al-Qaeda.[66] Foreign Secretary Kanwal Sibal also visited Tehran in October to carry forward the dialogue with Iran.

Iran's nuclear programme and the Russian help to it was also the subject of international attention. Iran has maintained that the reactors that Russia is building at Bushehr and plans to build in Akhraz and Bushehr are strictly for commercial purposes. The US is not willing to take at face value the Russian assertion that its assistance will not help Iran in acquiring a nuclear weapon capability. Russia is involved in the 1,000 MW Bushehr project, worth nearly $ 800 million. The US believes Iran is pursuing a nuclear weapons development programme at the Natanz Plant in Isfahan province of Central Iran.[67]

The year saw deeper interaction between India and Iran on issues ranging from economic cooperation to strategic partnership, in the backdrop of the US war on terror, and increased pressure on Iran on account of its nuclear programme.

❖❖❖❖❖

## NOTES

1. B. Muralidhar Reddy, "Musharraf's New High," *Frontline*, Vol. 19, No.5, 2-15 March 2002, pp. 113-115; Sridhar Krishnaswami, "Romancing the US," Ibid., pp. 115-116.
2. Praveen Swami, "Beating the Retreat", *Frontline*, Vol. 19, No. 22, 26 October – 8 November 2002, p. 15.
3. Rahul Bedi, "The Disarming Pitch", *Frontline*, Vol. 19, No. 12, 8-21 June 2002, pp. 22-23; and Rahul Bedi, "A Spreading Menace", *Frontline,* Vol. 19, No. 15, 20 July – 2 August 2002, pp. 51-60.
4. Ibid.
5. Vaiju Naravane, "Islamic Militancy, a Cause for Concern", *The Hindu,* 15 March 2002.
6. *Keesings Record of World Events*, Vol.48, No. 7, July 2002, p. 44911.
7. *Keesings Record of World Events*, Vol.48, No. 6, June 2002, p. 44859.

8. "NATO'S Anti-Terror Force may Strike without Permission", *Hindustan Times*, 17 November 2002.

9. Vaiju Naravane, "Europe's Dilemmas", *Frontline*, Vol. 19, No. 19, 14-27 September 2002, pp. 54-56.

10. Hasan Suroor, "Unease in Europe", *Frontline*, Vol. 19, No. 20, 28 September - 11 October 2002, pp. 14-15.

11. Sukumar Muralidharan, "The Prey and the Predator", *Frontline*, Vol. 19, No. 21, 12-25 October 2002, pp. 22.

12. John Cherian, "German Assertion", ibid., pp. 56-58.

13. "France hits out at US Foreign Policy", *The Times of India*, 7 February 2002.

14. Batuk Gathani, "Ten Nations Join EU", *The Hindu*, 15 December 2002.

15. *Keesings Record of World Events*, Vol. 48, No. 10, October 2002, p. 45063.

16. "Blair Pledges Total Solidarity with India in Fight against Terrorism", *The Hindu*, 15 January 2002.

17. "France Offers Technology for Advanced Jets", *The Times of India*, 1 October 2002.

18. Charu Singh, "Russia's Worries", *Frontline*, Vol. 19, No. 25, 7-20 December 2002, pp. 54-56.

19. "India Yields to Russia on Tripartite Ties with China", *The Times of India*, 5 February 2002.

20. P. S. Suryanarayana, "A Strategic Entente", *Frontline*, Vol. 19 Issue 19, 14-27 September 2002, pp. 51-52.

21. "Russia, India Bolster Ties to Tackle Terror", *Hindustan Times*, 5 December 2002.

22. John Cherian, "Re-Affirming Traditional Ties", *Frontline*, Vol. 19, No. 26, 2002, 21 December 2002 – 3 January 2003, pp. 49-51.

23. Sridhar Krishnaswami, "India, Japan to Broaden Areas of Cooperation", *The Hindu*, 14 September 2002.

24. Aunohita Mojumdar, "India, Japan Unite for Security Council Seat", *The Times of India*, 26 April 2002.

25. P. S. Suryanarayana, "The Signal from Pyongyang", *Frontline*, Vol. 19, No. 20, 28 September – 11 October 2002, pp. 46-47.

26. P. S. Suryanarayana, "Japan for Resumption of Indo-Pak Talks", *The Hindu*, 13 October 2002.

27. John Cherian, "Some Positive Movement", *Frontline*, Vol. 19, No. 8, 13-26 April 2002, pp. 48-49.

28. John Cherian, "Zhu Rongji in India", *Frontline*, Vol. 19, No. 3, 2-15 February 2002, pp. 122-123.

29. Cherian, "Some Positive Movement", *Frontline*, Vol. 19, No. 8, 13-26 April 2002, p. 48.

30. Cherian, ibid., p. 49.

31. P. S. Suryanaraya, "A Strategic Entente", *Frontline*, Vol. 19, No. 19, 14-27 September 2002, pp. 51-52.

32. P. Ramachandran, "Missile Match", *Frontline*, Vol.19, No. 12, 8-21 June 2002, pp.18-21.

33. John Cherian, "Visitors and Messages", *Frontline,* Vol. 19, No. 3, 2-15 February 2002, pp. 21-22.

34. Praful Bidwai, "Nuclear Ostriches All," *Frontline,* Vol. 19, No. 13, 22 June – 5 July 2002, pp. 30-31.

35. Rahul Bedi, "Infiltration Worries", *Frontline,* Vol. 19, No. 13, 22 June – 5 July 2002, pp. 25-28.

36. B. Muralidhar Reddy, "Assuming Supreme Powers", *Frontline,* Vol. 19, No. 14, 9-16 July 2002, pp. 114-115.

37. Sukumar Muralidharan, "Lacking in Strategy", *Frontline,* Vol. 19, No. 11, 25 May – 7 June 2002, pp. 10-12.

38. B. Muralidhar Reddy, "The Growing Chill", *Frontline,* Vol. 19, No. 25, 7-20 December 2002, pp. 126-127.

39. "Military Help to Nepal will Continue", *The Hindu*, 26 June 2002.

40. Keshav Pradhan, "Nepal Sees PWG Hand in Maoist Attacks", *Hindustan Times*, 24 February 2002; Keshav Pradhan, "India: PWG Training in Nepal", *Hindustan Times*, 21 December 2002.

41. "Nepal gets $ 200 Million American Aid to Combat Maoists", *The Times of India*, 1 March 2002.

42. Suman Pradhan, "140 Maoists Shot Dead, Nepal Says No to Peace Talks", *The Times of India*, 4 May 2002.

43. "US Military Experts in Nepal to Advise Government", *The Times of India*, 22 April 2002.

44. Gaurav C. Sawant, "India to Supply Nepal Arms, Military Tactics", *The Indian Express*, 26 June 2002.

45. Swati Chaturvedi, "Militants Got Dhaka Address", *Hindustan Times*, 17 February 2002; Chandan Nandy, "Bangla Outfit Gives Security Agencies Sleepless Nights", *Hindustan Times*, 10 June 2002; C. Raja Mohan, "Indo-Bangla Ties Turning Sour", *The Hindu*, 30 November 2002.

46. "*Time*: Dhaka Hub of Anti-India Activities", *Hindustan Times*, 14 October 2002; "Bangladesh, A Hotbed of Anti-India Terror", *The Hindu*, 14 October 2002. Also see, "Dhaka is Nerve Centre of ISI: Yashwant Sinha", *The Times of India*, 28 November 2002.

47. Sanjay Datta, "Bangla May Not Agree on Gas Flow to India", *The Times of India*, 29 July 2002.

48. "Lanka, Tigers Sign Pact on Truce", *The Times of India*, 23 February 2002; Nirupama Subramanian, "Sri Lanka Government, LTTE Sign Ceasefire Accord", *The Hindu*, 23 February 2002.

49. "Chandrika Denies Scuttling Peace Bid", *The Times of India*, 20 March 2002.

50. Nirupama Subramanian, "Christina Rocca Visits Jaffna", *The Hindu*, 16 March 2002.

51. V. S. Sambandan, "Separation Only if Autonomy Denied: LTTE", *The Hindu*, 19 September 2002.

52. D. B. S. Jeyaraj, "LTTE Seeks India's Help for Talks with Colombo", *The Hindu*, 8 January 2002; Nirupama Subramanian, "Lets Bury the Past: LTTE Tells India", *The Hindu*, 3 February 2002.

53. Farah Mihlar Ahamad, "Ranil to Brief Vajpayee on Peace Process", *The Times of India*, 22 April 2002.

54. V. S. Sambandan, "India Adds Clause for the Resolution of Sri Lankan Conflict", *The Hindu*, 10 December 2002.

55. Rahul Karmakar, "Myanmar Snubs India, Frees Rebels", *Hindustan Times*, 18 March 2002.

56. Amit Baruah, "Vice-President to Visit Myanmar", *The Hindu*, 14 December 2002.

57. C. Raja Mohan, "Trilateral Move for Transport Corridor", *The Hindu*, 6 April 2002.

58. C. Raja Mohan, "Looking East: Phase Two, *The Hindu*, 11 April 2002.

59. Rajesh Ramachandra, "India to Tap Caspian Sea Oil", *The Times of India*, 4 June 2002.

60. Atul Aneja, "India urged to Join Central Asian Grouping", *The Hindu*, 13 February 2002.

61. "Almaty Declaration vows to Eliminate Terrorism", *The Hindu*, 5 June 2002.

62. Atul Aneja, "India, Iran Wooing Central Asia", *The Hindu*, 21 October 2002.

63. John Cherian, "War and Resistance", *Frontline*, Vol. 19, No. 7, 30 March – 12 April 2002, pp. 46-47.

64. Kesava Menon, "Bush Speech Bellicose, Insulting: Iran", *The Hindu*, 1 February 2002.

65. Kesava Menon, "Iran None Too Happy About US Warning", *The Hindu*, 13 January 2002.

66. C. Raja Mohan, "India, Iran to Combat Terrorism, *The Hindu*, 28 June 2002.

67. "Iran Pursuing Nuclear Programme", *The Hindu*, 15 December 2002.

# India's Military Modernisation

*B. D. Jayal*

## Background

Over the years, modernisation of the armed forces has continued to suffer. Reasons have varied from resource constraints on one hand to paralysis, within the procurement system as a result of real or perceived scandals, on the other. It was therefore no surprise that in the midst of the Kargil conflict the Army Chief while addressing a Press conference admitted rather helplessly that if war were thrust on the army, it would do its best with what it had!

It was anticipated that with the Kargil Review Committee and the follow- on GOM recommendations in February 2001, things would eventually improve. Even as these were being processed for implementation, the 9/11 attacks in the US brought terrorism onto international centre stage. Closer home, the subsequent terrorist attack on the J&K Assembly followed by one on the Parliament in December 2001 brought home vividly the changing security dynamics and the need to evolve appropriate responses. Commencement of Operation 'Parakram', the large-scale Indian troop deployments on the Indo-Pak border, brought to fore additional weaknesses.

The aim of this paper is to review modernisation of the military machine during the year 2002 when fortuitously due to the factors mentioned, the political climate and national mood were fully supportive of making good, past lapses in modernising the military machine.

## Factors Inhibiting Modernisation in the Past

Weaknesses in defence management and procurement that have in the past (before the GOM recommendations) resulted in successive years of neglected modernisation of the military machine can broadly be summarised as follows:

- Authority for equipment procurement rested with MOD. The latter was neither equipped professionally for this responsibility nor accountable for operational consequences of this authority.
- The Services HQ who are accountable for operational performance had no control apart from laying down initial staff requirements and priorities, as the HQ were outside the governmental structure.
- Integrated military planning was absent. The apex joint institution of COSC was found wanting by the GOM in its ability to provide single point advice to the government, and resolve inter-Service doctrinal, planning, policy and operational issues adequately.
- In essence each service planned for and budgeted for its modernisation in isolation. Share of the defence budget of each service generally followed historical percentages and was not driven by integrated security priorities.
- The procurement system had become immobilised for fear of being drawn into controversies and scandals.
- In the name of self-reliance Defence PSUs had been given preference to respond to Services Staff requirements, sometimes against Service advice. Cost, and time over runs and performance shortfalls have been endemic.
- Licence production has been seen as self-reliance. Yet import dependence on sub assemblies/detailed parts/spares remains, thereby affecting availability of systems in service.

**Reorganisation of Defence Management**

It may appear irrelevant to discuss reorganisation when in effect the topic is about modernisation of the military machine in terms of weapon systems. As the following discussion indicates, however, there are close linkages in the entire military management system.

The GOM did not recommend integrating the Services HQ into the MOD although it had recognised that there was a marked difference in the perception of civil and military officials regarding their respective roles and functions with lack of synchronisation among and between the departments in the MOD. The reorganisation that occurred in the year has left the Services HQ still outside the apex government structure and the Chiefs of Staff continue as Operational Commanders rather than COS to PM & RM. The weaknesses highlighted by the KRC in this model, namely that of service long-term planning and higher operational decisions being command-oriented rather than collegiate have therefore remained. Two negative fallouts which have been inhibitors to modernisation in the past need highlighting since they have continued to come in its way even this year, in spite of an otherwise favourable climate. Firstly hierarchies in the Service HQ rotate frequently while staff requirements and procurements have longer gestation time frames. Command oriented decision-making results in frequent changes of requirements and priorities depending on individual perceptions rather than institutional long-term interests. Secondly, the old system of Service HQ putting up cases to MOD, which still has the authority, remains with detrimental consequences.

**Chief of Defence Staff**

The GOM brought out serious weaknesses in the institution of the Chiefs of Staff Committee and recommended the institution of CDS (along with an integrated staff). The CDS was to be the principal military adviser to the RM, provide single point military advice to the government, promote efficiency in planning, budget and equipment prioritisation within the services, be responsible to promote jointness in training and operations and to administer the Strategic Forces. This charter makes it clear that such an appointment is an essential prerequisite for integrated and meaningful military equipment planning and modernisation. It is possible that had the CDS been appointed, to some extent the drawbacks mentioned in the previous paragraphs could have been neutralised and some success achieved this year.

For reasons not dictated by compulsions of national security, the appointment of a CDS was held in abeyance while the Chief of Integrated Staff to COSC (CISC) along with a HQ was established. The CISC reports to the COSC, the efficacy of which institution has been found wanting. Amongst the many weaknesses of this half-hearted reorganisation, two merit mention. Firstly, no amount of integrated staff work will produce integrated and prioritised modernisation if at the COSC level, issues will still be subject to inter service pulls and pressures. This in turn will undermine the very concept of the institution of an integrated defence staff and nullify efforts at jointness, inter service equipment and budget prioritisation. This is precisely why the erstwhile Defence Planning Staff did not achieve much.

While procrastination on the appointment of CDS seriously undermines the very modernisation of integrated military management including equipment, the CCS approved model has another drawback. Responsibility for planning and conduct of operations is not vested with the CDS although he is tasked to prioritise equipment, force levels and budget within the services and to promote jointness in training and operations. Clearly such authority without consequential operational accountability then becomes misplaced and to the CsOS who remain responsible for conduct of operations of their respective services, as before, this will be viewed as one more layer of bureaucracy, albeit in uniform.

**Joint Services Commands**

Andaman and Nicobar Command was the first integrated

theatre command to be formed this year with the Strategic Forces Command following soon after the year ended. Operationally this is a welcome step towards developing an integrated war fighting capability. Since the joint Commands have only recently been set up and are still in the process of establishing themselves, the issues discussed below with respect to modernisation did not come into play this year. They need mention, as they could seriously undermine these commands achieving operational status.

These integrated commands will evolve their operational plans based on their integrated fighting capability. From these will emerge their concepts and plans for modernisation of weapons and systems. Once these reach the HQ CISC and are processed and prioritised, they will be put up to the COSC. The COSC will face the dilemma of prioritising between the perceptions of their own HQ and the needs of these integrated commands!

By far the most fundamental modernisation has been the announcement of India's nuclear doctrine followed by the setting up of a Strategic Force Command. Much work needs to be done before this command can become operational backed by necessary hardened infrastructure, manning, C4I2, weapon systems, training, operational and emergency procedures and synergy with different agencies. The existing system of equipment and infrastructure modernisation single service- wise will not permit the desired operational capability to be harnessed and harmonised in the absence of a CDS. Operationally also what is needed is single point military advice to the Defence Minister, Prime Minister and the NCA. Even in peacetime, the CDS with his stature and experience would need to be vested with the authority to evolve operational doctrines and ensure synergy between the many different agencies that would be involved apart from the armed forces.

## Changing Nature of Threat – Modernising For What?

If beyond operationalising the nuclear doctrine, there was one priority that should have featured high enough on the national security agenda during the year, the place must go to counter- terrorism, as urban warfare is now a reality. An important lesson of the year was India's inability to use military force, having come to a stone's throw from it. The reasons are beyond the scope of this paper, but it is important to determine the type of threat and responses that the military must plan and prepare for into the future. These are issues for the NSAB and NSC, but only from these directives can emerge meaningful future force and equipment modernisation plans and inter- service priorities. As far as the year under discussion goes, almost all the major modernisation plans under consideration were ones that have been under consideration for some time.

## Roles and Missions

With the current RMA and evolution of information and military technologies, traditional roles and missions of the respective services have blurred and in many areas are overlapping. The need is for the services to jointly face these challenges by innovating, adapting/discarding old doctrines, reorganising, redefining and integrating roles and missions for optimum effectiveness through scientific systems analysis and cost-effectiveness criteria and not resorting to ad hocism and traditional turf wars. Such an exercise may well reveal that many service staff requirements or force plans need change. Absence of a CDS is preventing such an approach.

## Military Equipment Modernisation

Over the years equipment modernisation of the services has continued to suffer with the result that the backlog is now huge. While the genuine needs and the wish lists of the three services are thus substantial, this was one more year of missed opportunities. Defence procurement has been one of the many weak links in the Indian security chain and recognising this, the Defence Procurement Board and associated institutions were set up in the year 2001 itself. There was great hope that unnecessary delays in military procurement would now be a thing of the past and this year would usher in change. Revised Estimates for the FY 2002-03 indicate a shortfall in defence expenditure of Rs. 9000 crores in spite of the added burden of Op Parakram. It is probable that more than Rs. 9000 of capital expenditure and modernisation plans did not progress to anticipated fruition. Indifferent progress on this front in spite of the most adverse security conditions prevailing indicates that problems are deeper than mere organisational.

A review of the year reveals that major modernisation programmes which have featured in the press for some time and are under discussion, did not reach fruition.

Having earlier finalised the contract for the T90 tanks, perhaps the biggest achievement for the Army in the year was placement of orders for 8 US Weapon Locating Radars after many years. Procurement of Smerch multiple rocket launchers from Russia is also awaited. There were reports of delay in upgrading of T72 tank weapon systems owing to shortage of resources. Reports that upwards of 80 casualties during mine laying operations were due to old mines and fuses with later reports that demining operations had to be held up for want of safety clothing, reveal weaknesses in basic areas.

Aircraft Carrier Gorshkov along with its complement of Mig 29s and Kamov helicopters, lease of two Akula class Nuclear submarines and four TU 22 M3 aircraft, and contract for production of French Scorpene submarines and deep submergence rescue vessels, though under discussion for long, still did not materialise. Delivery of the first of the three Krivak III multi-purpose stealth frigates from Russia also was delayed due to technical problems. It is reported that the TU 22 M3 aircraft is intended to carry nuclear weapons. Should this be so then their ownership should vest with the IAF whose designated role is long-range strategic strike by shore-based aircraft. What is of greater concern is the operational, technical and financial non-viability of a force of a mere four combat aircraft. This highlights the importance of rationalising roles and missions earlier discussed, in the absence of which valuable resources are put to infructuous use.

While the IAF has inducted the Mig 21-93 after prolonged delays, the controversy about the safety and reliability of spares for the Mig 21 fleet continued to dog the IAF. Accusations by the Mig Corporation of unreliable spares procurements by IAF and HAL do not bode well for Indo-Russian partnership. Considering that this still remains the largest fighter in the IAF inventory, there is need to put this bogey behind. The AJT still eluded the air force. The complement of Su 30 MKI continues to build up and plans for licence production at HAL till 2017 continue. At 2000 levels, some estimates indicate that this single weapon system will on an average continue to consume 50 per cent of the IAF's capital budget. Mid air refuellers were expected to join the IAF although the AWACS still seemed some distance away. While the LCA continues its flight-testing and is more than a decade away from operational service, there are reports of licence producing the Mirage 2000H. Quite apart from these high profile items there is need for precision-guided weapons, modern radar systems, surface to air missile systems, communications and electronic warfare equipment.

Such prolonged induction time frames when not only technology, but also threats are rapidly changing, spell danger that some of the plans may well be overtaken by events. For example when the IAF inducts the LCA around 2010, it will be faced with threats and challenges that were unknown when the air staff requirements were spelt out in the early 1980s.

The services have inducted the Prithvi and Agni missiles and RPVs. In the context of RPVs and Cruise Missiles two areas need mentioning. First is the need for uninterrupted availability of space based GPS and terrain/target mapping data towards mission accomplishment. The second issue relates to avoiding turf wars and streamlining roles and missions for efficient exploitation, of which more below.

While the Army was fortunate in placing orders for the US weapon locating radars, the issue of procurements from the USA leaves unresolved the possibility of future US congressional embargoes. There were conflicting signals from the services on the approach to weapon procurements from the US. The Indian Navy Sea Kings and Sea Harriers suffered as a result of post-Pokhran embargoes on US made spares. For its AJT programme the IAF initially deleted all US equipment, but was later reported to be considering one option with US equipment. Clearly there is need for a centralised policy directive on this issue, embarked as India and US are on a strategic partnership.

In essence space technologies have brought in a military revolution in the command, control, communication, computerisation, intelligence, information, surveillance and reconnaissance (C4I2SR) functions of warfare. Not much is known of the military establishment's plans in this regard. Those aspects of GPS, high-resolution imagery, communications, EW, command and control that are force- multipliers need be developed indigenously to guard against denial, interference and sanction regimes. There is need to clearly articulate these within a joint and coordinated strategy not only amongst the military, but all national security agencies.

While major service procurements always steal the limelight, it is the relatively low profile items like small arms, night vision equipment, precision guided weapons, EW equipment, secure communications, safety equipment, arctic clothing, etc. that never reach our fighting forces in time. Ordnance is stored in vintage depots where major fires have cost the nation dear in wasted weapons. During mining operations for Op Parakram over 80 soldiers lost their lives because of vintage mines and fuses and during demining the army was compelled to halt operations owing to non-availability of safety clothing. Major areas of modernisation are not always the high profile weapon systems much publicised, but these low-ticket items, infrastructure and living conditions of our forces. So unresponsive has our procurement system become that even these essentials need wars or disasters for us to send emergency procurement teams scurrying abroad. These then become the subject of audit scrutiny and comment further paralysing normal peacetime procurement progress.

In spite of a positive national mood, this year was generally one of failed equipment modernisation as surrender of funds later has revealed. One silver lining this year was reported ambitious plans for large-scale enhancement of service-married accommodation, an aspect always ignored. This welcome move deserved greater publicity, if for nothing else then at least for the sake of the morale of our forces.

**Information Age Warfare**

Traditionally in the military domain, information-based warfare is not new although evolution of IT has made it far more potent and complex. The greatest threat, however, is that it can be waged in political, economic and social fields both in peace and war and can be mounted by non- state actors manipulating information databases, such that one may not even know whether one is under attack and if so from whom.

Information revolution is being driven by the ongoing evolution of microprocessors and related technologies and rapid changes make it difficult for security planners to contemplate their precise impact on current and future threats. Reducing cost factor makes these available even to would- be hackers and terrorist organisations. By the very nature of the subject, little is known about what was planned for and achieved during the year. Being an important aspect of security planning not just for the military but in the civil domain as well, it merits mention in this analysis.

### Defence/Private Partnership in Defence Production

For decades, under the slogan of self-reliance, ordnance factories and Defence PSUs have held the armed forces as captive customers. All have stagnated and suffered. For survival in the defence equipment market, strong investment in R&D, exports and economies of scale are prerequisites. During the year initiatives like amendment to the Industrial Policy Resolution, allowing private sector participation in defence production, limited foreign participation and joint development projects with some countries have been initiated and are positive landmarks. In the information age when computer, telecom and other IT technologies are being driven more by the civil sector than the defence, it becomes vital that a close public and private sector partnership is nurtured. If success is to be achieved, much more than policy announcements are needed and the government must consider playing the role of active catalyst till these initiatives gain self-sustaining momentum and beyond.*

---

* Editor's Note: India's Ministry of Defence (MoD) recently awarded licenses to two Indian private companies to design and manufacture a range of military equipment as part of its long-standing bid to privatise its defence industry. These two companies, Larsen and Toubro (L&T) and Mahindra and Mahindra (M&M) were amongst 10 manufacturers to apply for licenses to the MoD after defence production was thrown open to the private sector two years ago with a foreign direct investment (FDI) limit of 26 per cent. Five licenses have been given to L&T to build warships, submarines, weapon platforms (offshore, floating and submerged), high speed boats, radar, sonar, electronic warfare equipment and armoured and combat vehicles including associated systems and sub-systems such as turrets and bridge layers. India's leading jeep maker Mahindra and Mahindra (M&M) is the other company to be awarded a licence to supply the army vehicles developed with foreign assistance, possibly from an Israeli company. M&M too have had a long association with the military. (*Jane's Defence Weekly,* 26 March 2003).

## Joint Programmes

One of the positive outcomes of the Military Cooperation Agreement with Russia has been joint development of the supersonic 290 Km BrahMos anti-ship cruise missile, which underwent tests in the year. Other items under discussion have been fifth generation fighter, advanced electronic warfare equipment, aircraft engines and marine propulsion systems. It is significant that after nearly four decades of a pure buyer-seller or licenser-licensee relationship, practical considerations from both sides have enabled graduation to a mature and equal relationship. However welcome this change, there is need for caution. Projects conceived for joint development must clearly have a service application in mind, be based on Staff Requirements, be funded equally and jointly by both parties and the products must find markets in both countries and beyond to derive benefits of scale. One wonders if plans to develop a fifth generation fighter measure up to such criteria, when LCA is still under development and the Su 30 MKI will continue in production till 2017!

In the larger interest of expanding India's technological base and widening technological and marketing options, joint programmes in specific areas also need to be explored with armament industries of the US and Europe.

## Educating Security Leaders

This topic again may appear incongruous to the subject under discussion, but it is only enlightened security leadership that will ultimately put in place institutions and organisations that will enable meaningful long-term equipment planning and modernisation of the security machine The GOM had accepted the need for a National Defence University and a broad based committee set up to make detailed proposals submitted its report to the Defence Minister by mid year with a clearly defined road map. The proposed National Defence University aims to educate national security leaders on all aspects of national security strategy, military strategy, resource strategy, information strategy and technology strategy through teaching and research. It also aims to promote policy-oriented research and provide a war gaming and simulation center for policy makers at the strategic level. Unless NDU graduates start to occupy higher-level leadership positions in the civil and military areas, the central place of resource management in promoting national security will not be recognised.

**Conclusion**

Coming as it did on the heels of the post-Kargil GOM recommendations and terrorist attacks on Parliament, the year 2002 was poised to usher in a new era in modernisation of the military. With Op Parakram and the nation poised at the brink of war, national polity and mood were fully supportive of any moves that would have been initiated towards this.

As one reviews the year, it emerges as one of failed opportunities much like periods preceding it. Major modernisation programmes on the anvil for many years continued to be on hold while the services continued to fall short of even basic war fighting and living needs. The one silver lining was major plans to increase the level of married accommodation for the armed forces. While the GOM did not approve of integrating the service HQ within the MOD, the appointment of a CDS was held up for want of political will. Without such organisational backing, identifying the nature of threat and response, rationalising service roles and missions and modernising the equipment of the forces become unfocused exercises leading to duplication, stagnation and wastage; luxuries that benefit the nation's enemies.

One could argue that this has been the situation in the past. The reality is that today the nation faces security challenges as never before with the added responsibility of being a nuclear weapons power. Past performance is thus no guarantor of security into the future. The best that one can hope for is for objective case studies to be conducted to identify reasons why modernisation of the armed forces continues to stagnate and why at every security crisis our armed forces are found wanting in material and infrastructure essentials.

❖❖❖❖❖

# Internal Security Threats

*Satish Kumar*

## Introduction

Governance in India has never been easy, given the enormous linguistic, religious, ethnic, and cultural diversities, the history of communal violence on the eve of Independence, and a socio-political dynamic in which caste still occupies an important place. Although much progress has been made since independence towards national integration, there has, particularly over the last decade, been an unfortunate move towards polarisation both in communal and caste terms.

The year under review witnessed serious violence in Jammu and Kashmir, North-East, and by Left Wing extremist groups. Besides, there were unfortunate communal incidents. While there were reports of corruption in high places, attacks on Dalits, suicide by farmers, and problems related to water sharing between states, the major issues of concern pertained to terrorism, communalism, and illegal migration from Bangladesh.

There were some positive aspects to the security situation as well. The government's persistent engagement and ceasefire agreements with insurgent groups, particularly the two factions of the NSCN in Nagaland and two smaller groups in Assam, contributed to a decline in violence in the troubled north-east. State Assembly elections in Manipur in early 2002 were followed by similar elections in Nagaland, Tripura, and Meghalaya in early 2003. In these elections, violence levels were contained although insurgent groups continued to engage in extortions and support to individual candidates and parties. The successful conduct of polls in Jammu and Kashmir in 2002 despite determined efforts by Pakistan-sponsored terrorist groups to disrupt the process marked a significant step forward on the path to restoration of normalcy. The political initiatives aimed at settling the problem were supplemented with announcements by the Prime Minister of large economic assistance packages to generate socio-economic development of the regions both in the north-east and Jammu and Kashmir. While Gujarat witnessed serious and disquieting communal violence, the worst in several years, it was by and large confined to the state.

## Terrorism

Terrorism as a method to achieve political objectives, whether in national politics or international politics, has acquired greater salience in the last few decades. To the extent terrorism is a manifestation of unfulfilled sub-national aspirations, it can be controlled through a mix of dialogue and coercion. But, when terrorism becomes the official instrument of policy of an adversary state, which has the capacity and unflinching intent to resort to this instrument, the response is not easy. Pakistani sponsored terrorism continued to play a major role in disrupting internal security of the country. Despite a massive deployment of troops in response to Pakistan-sponsored terrorism, India refrained from carrying its actions to a logical conclusion because of its endeavour to avoid escalation of conflict, and assurances from the international community that Musharraf would put an end to cross border terrorism.

Terrorism in India manifested itself in various forms. These included attacks on high value political targets; inciting election related violence in Jammu and Kashmir; and engineering attacks elsewhere in the country with the objective of igniting communal conflagrations.

### *Political Targets*

Among the high value political targets, the most important was the attack on Parliament House on 13 December 2001. This was followed by the attack on American Information Resource Centre (AIRC) in Kolkata on 22 January 2002. Earlier, the

Jammu and Kashmir Assembly premises had been attacked on 1 October 2001. All these attacks brought home the vulnerability of India to Pakistan-sponsored terrorism, made more poignant by the fact that these incidents occurred soon after the 9/11 terrorist attacks in New York and Washington. The Parliament House attack brought Pakistan and India once again into a diplomatic standoff and a near military confrontation when India responded to the attack by deploying on a massive scale its troops on the international border leading to counter deployment by Pakistan.

### *Jammu and Kashmir*

Jammu and Kashmir remained the most serious cause for concern with regard to terrorist activities sponsored from across the border. The overall security situation remained grim with reports of terrorist killings, ambushes and massacres coming in at regular intervals. Despite President Musharraf's announcement on two occasions (12 January and 27 May) that Pakistan will not allow its territory to be used for terrorist strikes against other countries, there was no let up in infiltration and support for terrorist activities in Jammu and Kashmir. Media reports pointed out that in mid-June 2002 there were over 30,000 Islamic mercenaries trained in guerilla warfare in Pakistan waiting to be transported to the next jehad. Significantly, there was increased dependence on foreign mercenaries to sustain the movement in Jammu and Kashmir.

The civilian population, particularly Hindus, came under heavy terrorist attacks aimed at fomenting communal disturbances. Attacks on Hindus were reported between January and June 2002 in Doda, Rajouri and Udhampur districts taking a heavy toll of lives. On 13 July, terrorists suspected to belong to Lashkar-e-Taiba (LET) killed 28 persons including 13 women and a child and injured several others in Jammu. The outfit also targeted Amarnth yatris and on 6 August killed 9 and injured 30 in an attack on a yatri camp in Pahalgam (Anantnag). On 24

November, the LET targeted for the second time the Raghunath Temple complex in Jammu by launching a suicide attack, killing 12 persons and injuring 53 others. Earlier on 14 May in a major strike, terrorists suspected to belong to LET/ Jamait-ul-Mujahideen targeted civilians travelling in a bus and family members of army personnel residing in army quarters at Kaluchak, Jammu, resulting in the death of 31 persons and injuries to 49 others. These attacks were meant to provoke a communal backlash, but achieved little success in this respect.

Attempts at initiating a political dialogue in Kashmir during the period also proved futile. In a bid to smother the voice of moderation and conciliation, terrorists short dead on 21 May in Srinagar Abdul Gani Lone, a veteran politician of All Party Hurriyat Conference (AHPC) who had questioned the wisdom of pursuing a violent 'jehadi' agenda and had earned the odium of the militant elements. Abdul Majid Dar of the Hizbul Mujahideen was expelled from the organisation on 3 May for taking a pro-dialogue position with the Government of India, bypassing Pakistan.

In the run up to the elections in Jammu and Kashmir, Pakistan sponsored terrorists made determined attempts to disrupt the process launching more than 200 violent incidents from the day of notification of elections on 22 August. In these incidents 112 persons including 42 political activists and 38 personnel were killed. The successful conduct of polls in the state in September-October 2002, with encouraging response from the people, marked a significant step towards restoration of normalcy.

### *North-East*

In the north-east too, despite a statistical decline in violence in relation to the previous year, the situation remained disturbed. While Assam and Tripura witnessed a declining trend in violence, the two states nevertheless remained the worst affected, followed by Manipur and Nagaland. The overall decrease in incidents of violence was attributable to continuing talks with the National

Socialist Council of Nagaland [NSCN (IM)], and cease-fire agreement with the NSCN (K) in Nagaland, and Bodo Liberation Tigers (BLT), DHD and a faction of the UPDS in Assam.

In Assam while the violence profile of United Liberation Front of Assam (ULFA) showed a decline, the organisation maintained its fighting potential. The mortar attacks by it on Dispur and Guawahati in the latter half of 2002 signalled its ability to strike at will and create terror. No talks could be initiated with the outfit in view of the serious division on this issue between the civilian and military wings within the organisation, with the latter obdurately opposed to the talks under strong influence of the ISI. The suspension of operations by the BLT for the past few years and its talks with the Government of India on the Bodoland Territorial Council (BTC) resulted in a progressive decline in its violent activities. However, the National Democratic Front of Bodoland (NDFB), which is opposed to the BTC and BLT, continued to create terror in the state especially by targeting non-Bodos, particularly the Bengalis and Biharis. NDFB was responsible for over 40 per cent incidents of violence in the state.

In Nagaland the security situation was vitiated largely by the feud between the two NSCN factions, which impacted adversely on the situation in Dimapur, Kohima, Zunheboto, Wokha, Mokokchung, Tuensang and Mon. efforts aimed at bringing peace and unity amongst the Naga tribes continued under the aegis of Naga Hoho; the NSCN (IM) also held two consultation meetings in Bangkok to generate a consensus on the issue of the talks with the Government of India. The NSCN (IM), however, continued its efforts at spreading its influence in some districts of Arunachal Pradesh and to extend support to allied insurgent groups in other states. Elections were held in the state in early 2003. Although no serious incidents of killing occurred, clashes between political opponents and intimidation of workers and voters were reported. S. C. Jamir, former Chief

Minister, and leader of the Congress blamed the NSCN (IM) for the Congress defeat.

In Manipur, violence by Meitei, Kuki and Naga groups continued, with the Meitei being responsible for the preponderant share, followed by the Kukis. Security forces remained the prime target. The Naga peace process accentuated apprehension among Meitei groups over the territorial integrity of Manipur, which was countered through Meitei revivalism. The NSCN (IM) sought to isolate Meitei groups by shoring its influence in the hill district of the state. There was no major violence involving the NSCN (IM). The demand by the NSCN (IM) leaders for the inclusion of the Naga hill districts of Manipur into any settlement of the Naga issue has not only accentuated ethnic polarities but could prove an intractable issue. State Assembly elections were held in early 2002 when several Meitei groups were reported to have indulged in extortions from candidates.

In Tripura, the activities of the National Liberation Front of Tripura (NLFT) were a major cause of concern with the group being responsible for around 60 per cent of violence and deaths in the state. Regular attacks on non-tribals (Bengalis) were reported. While the violence profile of the ATTF sowed some decline, the group exhibited considerable growth both in manpower and firepower, thus maintaining a strong potential for mischief.

***Left Wing Groups***

The violent activities of Naxalite groups witnessed a rise in scale, intensity and spatial spread with the CPML-PW and Maoist Communist Centre (MCC) responsible for the preponderant portion of the violence, i.e. 88 per cent of the violent incidents and over 55 per cent deaths. The worst affected state was Jharkhand followed by Andhra Pradesh, Chattisgarh, Bihar, Maharashtra and Orissa, in terms of violent incidents perpetrated by Naxalite groups.

In a carefully conceived move, the CPML (PW) proposed a unilateral ceasefire in Andhra Pradesh in the first half of 2002, to inveigle the state government to suspend operations. The ensuing temporary calm and a decline in violence in Andhra was, however, tactfully exploited by the outfit to consolidate within the state, intensify its militarization drive and expand its activities in other states notably Jharkhand, Chattisgarh, Eastern Maharashtra, Orissa and Bihar. In July the outfit reneged on its cease-fire and reverted to its violent ways following the killing of some of its activists by the police in Karimnagar district. On 18 November, landmine blast by the PW on a state-owned bus killed 14 people in Warangal district of Andhra Pradesh. Peace with the group remained a far cry.

Both the CPML (PW) and MCC, which were declared terrorist organisations under Prevention of Terrorism Act (POTA), continued to build on their strategic ties with the Communist Party of Nepal (Maoist) in pursuit of their common objective to develop a Compact Revolutionary Zone stretching southwards from the borders of Nepal through contiguous Indian states down to Andhra Pradesh. Both the organisations were also engaged in efforts to evolve an entente and its fructification would lend an ominous impetus to the movement.

**Communalism**

The 27 February 2002 burning of a coach of a Sabarmati Express in Godhra killing 58 Kar Sevaks and the communal mayhem that followed in which over 950 people were killed and roughly 1.5 lakh people rendered homeless was one of the worst communal conflagrations in the recent history of India. The violence remained confined to the state and had little repercussions in other parts of the country. However, Indians as a whole, whether within India or abroad, felt acutely embarrassed and ashamed of these incidents.

The Gujarat government was widely accused of being complacent and even inciting the riots. The preliminary comments and recommendations submitted by National Human Rights Commission (NHRC) on 1 April challenged the state government's claim that it was able to bring the situation under control within 72 hours and noted that the government of Gujarat had 'comprehensively' failed to protect the people of Gujarat. In other reports by independent civil society groups such as Sabarmati, the People's Union of Civil Liberties and Citizen's Initiative (Ahmedabad), the Modi government was found guilty of negligence. Several political leaders including the members of the Legislative Assembly have been named in the 3800 FIRs filed since the riots broke out in Gujarat. On 16 August the Election Commission ordered the postponement of elections to the Gujarat Assembly on the plea that conditions were not favourable for the elections to be held.

Following the riots, Pakistan sponsored terrorist organisations and crime syndicates are reported to have hatched plans to attack targets to create a communal backlash and engender destabilisation. Attacks on Akshardham and Raghunath temples (suspected to be LET actions) were part of such machinations although they failed to achieve the desired objective.

While on the surface quiet, communal tensions in Gujarat continue to simmer. These tensions are further fuelled by the non-resolution of sensitive issues such as Babri Masjid/Ram Janmabhoomi, and the efforts of Pakistan to fish in troubled waters. The democratic and secular character of India's constitution and the credibility of its institutions like the judiciary and the National Human Rights Commission can, however, be relied on to contain the damage.

**Illegal Migration**

The uninterrupted flow of the illegal migrants from Bangladesh remained a serious security threat. Their cumulative numbers, pegged at 15 - 18 million, and their vast spread from the states bordering Bangladesh to interior areas including Delhi and Mumbai is becoming increasingly ominous. Apart from generating socio-economic and communal tensions, the incremental change in demography in several bordering areas and the simultaneous growth in fundamentalist and ISI activities and terrorist and insurgent groups is a significant factor impacting adversely on India's internal security. The consistent refusal of Bangladesh to even acknowledge the existence of the problem underlines the need for unilateral, strong and concerted physical measures to stem the flow of illegal migrants. These include the accelerated construction of good quality fencing along the entire border, strengthening of the BSF through augmentation of manpower and high-tech equipment, detection and deportation of illegal migrants, and the early implementation of the scheme for issue of multi-purpose national identity cards to Indian citizens.

## Problems of Governance

### *Corruption*

Corruption at high places continued to pose a problem of governance. In August 2002, five retired judges who were Chairmen of the Dealer Selection Boards for the allotment of petrol pumps, LPG, and kerosene at various times, broke their silence on how they were pressurised to favour certain quarters. These revelations came after the uncovering of a nationwide scam by *The Indian Express*. To redress the situation, the Prime Minister cancelled all petrol pumps, cooking gas and kerosene dealerships awarded since January 2000. In another incident involving the government, the parent body of Xerox Corporation disclosed that Xerox ModiCorp Ltd., its Indian subsidiary, had paid bribes to government officials with regard to sales of Xerox equipment to government agencies. There were also reports of alleged scams in the purchase of arms and equipment pertaining to defence of the country, one of which was by Tehelka.com. The government was worried about the veracity of these reports on the one hand, and how to prevent corrupt practices on the other.

### *Attacks on Tribals and Dalits*

Attacks on Tribals and Dalits by the majority community and sometimes by the police to displace them and grab their lands and forests were reported from time to time. On 3 January, eight members of a tribal family were arrested and harassed in Dharmapuri district of Tamil Nadu. It was reported that female members of the family were sexually assaulted. On 5 September, in Kaundampatti, Dindigul district of Tamil Nadu, Dalit members were attacked and two individuals were made to consume human waste. In Haryana, five Dalits were killed in a mob frenzy in front of the police station allegedly for killing and skinning a cow on 15 October. Post-mortem reports, however, indicated that the cow had died the previous night. These incidents were of course a matter of grave concern for the government.

### *Distress of Farmers*

Suicides by farmers for such reasons as crop failure, high sales tax, lack of marketing opportunities, debts from moneylenders and no debt relief from cooperative banks have been a cause of serious concern. During the year reports of suicides by farmers came in from some parts of country. Cases from Karnataka and Andhra Pradesh were the most serious. On 23 February, the Human Rights Council, Visakapatnam, sought the intervention of the NHRC to direct an enquiry. The Council said that of the 490 suicides reported in the country during 2001-2002, 385 were from Andhra Pradesh.

❖❖❖❖❖

# Some Concerns about Internal Security

*N. N. Vohra*

## Introduction

National security encompasses any threat to the Indian state, from any possible source within the country, from across the air space or the land and sea borders. Thus, in a broad sense, national security concerns can be viewed as falling under two major heads: internal and external security. In the management context, national security would include every aspect of security—territorial security, internal security, food security, energy security, science and technology security, environmental security, fiscal security, et al. In the paper I shall comment briefly on certain aspects of internal security management.

In any discussion on security it would be useful to keep in mind the physical parameters of our concerns. In this context, the following facts may be recounted:

India is the seventh largest country in the world. It has an area of about 33,00,000 sq. kms, land boundaries of 15,200 kms, a coastline of over 7500 kms, over 600 island territories, and an EEZ of 25,00,000 sq. kms. We have land frontiers with seven countries and maritime borders with five countries. Our island territories in the east, 1300 kms away from the mainland, are far closer to our ASEAN neighbours. Except a few hinterland areas, like Haryana and Madhya Pradesh, all other States and some of the Union Territories have land or maritime borders which require to be safeguarded. Our borders with Pakistan and China are militarised; those with Pakistan have been generating a variety of threats to our country.

It is also necessary to keep in mind that our country represents an immense cultural and geographical diversity and socio-religious traditions, which go back to 5000 years of recorded history. The well over a billion people of India constitutes a multi-racial, multi-religious, multi-lingual and multi-cultural society. Every major religion in the world is practised in India; our Muslim population is the second largest in the world, significantly larger than that of Pakistan. The roots of India's secular and pluralistic traditions are imbedded deep in our ancient history.

India's internal security problems, arising from varied sources, are influenced by a host of factors among which are its past history, geography, colonial legacy, a very large number of political parties at the regional and sub-regional levels and a polity which is still in the process of stabilising, an inadequate electoral system which has still to prevent persons with known criminal backgrounds getting into the legislature, a burgeoning population, economic disparities and complex socio-cultural and ethno-religious traditions which interplay freely in our secular democracy. As developments in the past five decades have shown, regional and global developments also impact significantly on our security interests.

India is a Union of States. Our Constitution demarcates the executive and legislative powers of the Union and the States. The States have the responsibility of maintaining law and order within their jurisdictions. Consequently, "Public Order" and "Police" are included in the State List (List II, Seventh Schedule of the Constitution). Thus, the States have the exclusive powers [Article 246(3)] to make laws in respect of the aforesaid matters and, in the normal circumstances, the maintenance of public order is the sole responsibility of the States. In this context, it would be useful to recall the Sarkaria Commission's view that the States should themselves handle the problems of law and order and the Centre should provide aid to a State only when a specific request to that effect is received. In such situations the Centre may deploy one or more of its Police forces and/or the

Army in aid of the civil authority (Item 2A, List I, Seventh Schedule).

In so far as the Centre's responsibility is concerned the Constitution lays down that it shall be the duty of the Union to protect the States against external aggression and internal disturbances and to ensure that the governance of every State is carried on in accordance with the constitutional provisions (Article 355), failing which Presidential Rule may be imposed (Article 366) till constitutional functioning is restored. The Constitution also provides for the enforcement of Emergency if a situation exists or there is an imminent danger of the security of India being threatened by war or an armed rebellion (Article 352).

Five years ago, the Ministry of Home Affairs had reported to the Parliamentary Standing Committee (43rd Report, 1998) that 210 out of the 535 districts in the country were affected by grave public disorders of militancy, insurgency or ethnic violence. The security environment in the country has since become more complex and cause for even greater concern. The Home Ministry has reported to the aforesaid Committee (98th Report, 2003) that there "would be no immediate respite from cross-border terrorism primarily in J&K but aided and abetted elsewhere also in the country". In this background it may not be purposeful to draw up a chronological list of the serious internal security problems which have been faced by the country in the years past. However, it would be relevant to recognise that while it is the constitutional responsibility of the States to maintain peace and public order, the ground realities have changed most significantly in the past years. Unlike in the initial period after the country attained freedom, the State Police forces have, for well over two decades now, been called upon to deal with serious disturbances created by highly trained and motivated insurgent and terrorist groups which possess unlimited resources, sophisticated weaponry and communication systems and enormous mobility. While this factor would require to be kept in view while making any assessment of the manner in which the States have been discharging their constitutional responsibility to maintain law and order, it may be said that almost all the States have defaulted their crucial obligation to progressively expand and maintain fully trained and equipped Police forces in adequate strength and commensurate intelligence organisations to meet the arising challenges to the maintenance of internal security.

**The Pakistan Factor**

Taking an across the board view it may be said that a large majority of the serious threats to the country's internal security have emanated from Pakistan's unceasing attempts to seize J&K, which commenced within weeks of the partition of the country, and continued with sustained strategy to launch varied subversive activities to create chaos and disorder to destabilise the country.

Commencing from the early 1980s, Pakistan's ISI succeeded in inducting terrorism in Punjab which suffered enormous human and economic losses till the situation was normalised in the mid-1990s. Benefiting from the experience gained from its foray into Punjab, Pakistan launched a proxy-war in J&K from around the end of 1989. The continuing wave of terrorism and ethnic cleansing has resulted in the loss of thousands of lives, rendered lakhs into refugees, ruined the economy and shattered the secular fabric of J&K. In the north-east region several States have been facing varied insurgencies on a continuing basis. While the level of violence in the region has shown a relative decline the internal security situation requires to be handled with sensitivity and urgency, particularly in Nagaland, Manipur, Tripura and Assam. An aspect of the militancy in the north-east region which is a cause for growing concern are the trans-national linkages of some of the militant groups with the Pakistan ISI and other inter-group relations within the region. Of equal concern is the unabated illegal immigration from Bangladesh which has resulted in a demographic upheaval and generated serious communal, political, social and economic tensions in several areas of this region.

There has been a growing increase in the emergence of pan-Islamic militant outfits which have been establishing madrasas, spreading hatred and violence in several parts of the country. The systematic indoctrination of Muslims in fundamentalist ideology has resulted in creating communal unrest, specially in the border areas. Abetted and supported by the ISI the so-called 'Mujahideen' and 'Jehadi' elements, operating from bases along the LoC, have been supporting and controlling the activities of the various fundamentalist and terrorist groups operating in J&K. The fundamentalist elements have also been active in the North-East region and West Bengal and have been able to extend their reach as far south as Tamil Nadu. To carry out its subversive activities in India the ISI has established its networks all along our borders, particularly in Nepal and Bangladesh.

**Left-Wing Extremism**

There has been an upswing in the scale and intensity of Left-wing extremist violence which has spread to 53 districts in 9 States. Advancing from its traditional strongholds the movement has since spread its influence in Chattisgarh, western districts of West Bengal, parts of North Bihar, eastern UP and eastern and southern parts of Jharkhand and the CPML-PW has extended its activities to Tamil Nadu, Karnataka and Kerala. The CPML-PW, MCC and CPN (Maoist) are collaborating to establish a Compact Revolutionary Zone by linking up their respective strongholds, spreading from Telengana to Nepal. There has also been a rapid increase in the visible militarisation of the formations of these groups. Caste-based senas, supported and exploited by local political groups, are continuing with their atrocities in Bihar.

Several underworld crime and mafia groups, the leading among which originated in Mumbai and still flourish there, have linked up with adversary external agencies and progressively extended their criminal and subversive activities in the country. There has been expansion in the activities of the narcotics and drug mafia outfits which have a close nexus with the organised smuggling of arms, explosives and varied gadgetry for causing death and destruction. The operations of the narcotics and weapon smuggling networks are also linked to large-scale hawala and money laundering activities. The enormous funds generated by these criminal groups are laundered and utilised for carrying out varied serious crimes; the growing nexus between the mafia and the ISI-supported subversive and terrorist networks is cause for most serious concern.

The aforesaid are among the more significant factors which have generated serious internal security concerns and, for over two decades now, kept the Centre constantly engaged in dealing with the arising situations, some of which have posed grave threats to the very unity and integrity of the nation. Keeping in view the experience gained in the past years, it would be useful to comment, even though briefly, on certain aspects of internal security management which call for high priority attention.

**Internal Security Management**

It would not be feasible to embark upon an exhaustive delineation of the varied and continuing failures of the States in not taking timely action to adequately handle emerging security situations and allowing serious disorders to get built up. However, a commonly shared failure, which has a serious adverse impact on internal security management, arises from the fact that despite the passage of over five and a half decades since we gained Independence, the State Police organisations continue to function under a colonial statute, the Police Act of 1861. Enacted by our imperial masters nearly a century and a half ago this legislation is altogether incompatible with the requirements of policing within a democratic framework. This serious constraint is compounded by the severe inadequacies suffered by the State Police forces on account of continued neglect and, worse still, the systematic erosion of discipline and professionalism which has arisen from the day-to-day interference in their functioning and the sustained politicisation to which the forces have been subjected in the past years. While the States would need to take various necessary measures to improve the functioning of their security administrative apparatus, their very first task should be to ensure that the Police forces are urgently rid of the indiscipline, corruption and unaccountability with which they are plagued. The Police cannot, however, be restored to effective functioning unless the States are seriously committed to ensuring against any interference, whatsoever, in their working and, besides, provide the required resources for the modernisation of the existing organisations which would also need to be progressively expanded to maintain fully trained and equipped forces in the required strength.

For the past over two decades, ever since Pakistan's initial adventure in fomenting militancy in Punjab, the Union Ministry of Home Affairs (MHA) has, for reasons which are not far to seek, been essentially engaged in tackling arising disorders by deploying the armed forces of the Union, i.e. the Central Police Forces and, as required, the Army in the affected areas. Needless to say, the restoration of normalcy in any disturbed area inescapably involves the application of the State's coercive power which, in other words, means deploying the required quantum of Central forces to bring the disturbed area under control. However, it is a matter for concern that, faced with problems on various fronts and the unceasing demands for the deployment of Central forces, even in situations which could have been handled by the States, the MHA has been kept perpetually engaged in making available the required assistance even if this has involved pulling away the border guarding forces, which were specially established to keep a vigil on our frontiers, to perform internal security duties in various parts of the country.

Having been continuously occupied with the deployment

and re-deployment of its forces to deal with serious existing and arising situations, the MHA has not had the time, and perhaps also not the administrative and other required resources, to devote due attention to the factors which have contributed to the emergence of internal disorders in various parts of the country, notwithstanding the essential assumption that the ISI would not have lost any opportunity of exploiting any arising situation which has the potential of being converted into a serious disorder. In this context MHA would need to enlarge and strengthen its resources to constantly monitor emerge situations and ensuring that the concerned States take the required steps to see that all aspects of an arising disorder are dealt with effectively.

From the experience gained in combating insurgencies in the past years, specially in the north-east region, it would be altogether unsound to assume that the ultimate resolution of serious breakdowns of the public order would relate merely to the speed and efficiency with which MHA deploys Central armed forces to contain and control a given disorder. In this regard it is essential to remember that, contrary to the mistaken belief in certain quarters, the ultimate responsibility for dealing with an internal disorder cannot be "handed over" to any of the armed forces of the Union, under any circumstances. The constitutional responsibility to run the administration in accordance with the terms of the Constitution cannot be abdicated by the States.

It requires to be kept in mind that the prolonged deployment of Central Police Forces, and even the Army, to carry out counter insurgency operations may not invariably result in restoring normalcy unless the State Chief Ministers, their Cabinets and the entire administrative apparatus which functions under their control devotes prompt and simultaneous attention to providing effective governance and pays particular heed to resolving the day-to-day difficulties faced by the common man on account of the disruption of normal functioning caused by an ongoing insurgent situation. It is, therefore, of vital importance that the Chief Ministers and the entire governmental machinery which runs under their direction devotes special attention to ensure the time-bound implementation of all schemes and programmes which promote the welfare of the people at large, specially those who have been seriously affected and disadvantaged by the disorder being tackled by the Security Forces. In the past years State-level bodies, called by various names, e.g. Unified or Combined Command Hqrs, have been set up to coordinate the counter insurgency/terrorism operations being carried out by the security forces. It is extremely necessary that the functioning of such apex bodies is chaired by the Chief Ministers to ensure that normal administration is not suspended merely because the security forces are engaged in carrying out operations in the State. If normalcy is to be restored it is of the highest importance to ensure that the Security Forces and the Civil Administration discharge their respective roles in complete unison under the overall direction of the State Chief Minister. As, in the ultimate analysis, the Centre remains responsible for protecting the States against internal disorders, the MHA will need to exert its influence, and even compulsion if persuasion fails, to secure the required performance by the States. As past experience has shown any dithering on this score leads to grave consequences and much larger responsibility having to be borne by the Centre for want of adequate and timely responses by the States in meeting their constitutional duties to maintain public order.

Considering the irreparable damage caused by the disruption of the established order and the severe human and economic losses which are suffered when a serious internal disorder takes place it would be stating the obvious to stress that the States require to deliver good governance and display much greater concern and urgency to ensure against any significant security problem arising in their jurisdictions. Towards this end the States have to be constantly vigilant and altogether sensitive in timely understanding and critically assessing the likely consequences of an arising situation and, based on a careful analysis, promptly implementing the required remedial measures. This would, inter alia, involve the political leadership of the States and the senior bureaucracy undertaking timely and meaningful interaction with the leaders or representatives of any segment of society which is agitating its demands. The Centre must exercise its constitutional powers to ensure that the States do not default on this account, under any circumstances.

Experience has shown that the lack of timely concern or failure to deal understandingly with the demands of the aggrieved elements invariably leads to enhanced estrangements and, subsequently, resort to violence. When such situations get out of hand the traditional approach is to deal with them merely as law and order problems. In many such cases the disgruntled elements, abetted and supported by adversary foreign agencies, are easily persuaded to adopt the gun culture. And when such developments take place, we see the beginning of militancies and insurgencies. In this context it is necessary to ensure that the coercive powers of the State are applied after due deliberation and, while dealing with an arising disorder, the States must remain equally responsible for taking timely and effective measures to identify and deal with the root causes of any situation which is likely to evolve into an internal security problem. The achievement of such an objective would call for prompt and systematic attention being given for dealing with the socio-economic problems of the masses and showing sensitive concern for understanding their political demands and aspirations. The aforesaid approach can materialise only if MHA constantly monitors developments all over the country and ensures that the required steps are timely taken by the concerned States. For this purpose the MHA has to adequately enlarge its resources and specially ensure that the Intelligence Bureau maintains constant connectivity with the intelligence wings in the States.

The despair and consequent alienation of the disadvantaged communities is heightened by the social and economic exploitation to which they are subjected. Feudal systems are still in existence in several parts of the country where the much needed land, agrarian and other reforms have still to be implemented. It is indeed most unfortunate that besides the economic disparities and severe disadvantages from which they suffer the neglected segments of society are also subjected to continual harassments which arise from the various political parties exploiting religious, ethnic and caste factors for electoral gains.

## Socio-Religious Organisations Create Conflictual Environment

Another factor which is cause for serious concern is the growing trend of certain socio-religious organisations, which are supported by interested political parties, resurrecting centuries old issues which generate a conflictual environment. As events in the past decade and more have shown the agitation of religious claims of one or another kind, apparently with no other objective than to garner electoral advantages, have generated serious communal dissensions and led to disorders involving enormous human and economic losses and, besides, contributed to destroying the harmony of inter-community relations. If internal security is to be maintained the States have to take prompt and stringent steps to ensure against any disruption of the secular environment. Such an objective cannot be achieved unless the most stringent action is taken to ensure against politicising religious issues and leaving the the police and civil administration altogether unfettered in enforcing the Rule of Law. Political interference in the functioning of the law enforcement agencies shall lead to disastrous consequences, as seen in the Babri Masjid episode and the more recent communal carnage in Gujarat.

Besides the failures of governance to pursue the avowed welfare state goals and deliver social and economic justice to the masses, the States have also failed to timely and sensitively respond to the felt needs and aspirations of ethnic and tribal groups and communities, most of whom live in remote, difficult and under developed areas. It has been seen that the demands of such neglected communities are ignored for prolonged periods and, if and when considered, being viewed essentially in terms of the likely electoral gains to the political parties in power. Such attitudes have contributed to promoting distrust and alienation among the affected communities which have lost faith and trust in their elected representatives and the State Governments, which are expected to attend to their problems.

Another factor which contributes to causing despair and anger among the under-privileged and economically disadvantaged segments of the population arises from the failures of the States to efficiently execute even the poverty alleviation schemes and programmes. The large financial outlays and outright grants provided to the States by the Centre for such programmes are not timely utilised. These are illegitimately diverted to ease the ways and means position of the State exchequers and, in many cases, the grants are even embezzled. Needless to say, such gross failures result only in creating hopelessness, cynicism and consequential alienation among the poorest segments of society.

Failures of the aforesaid kind are due to maladministration, unaccountability and corruption. Notwithstanding the endless public criticism over the past many years effective steps have still to be taken to deal with corruption at the highest levels and enforcing efficiency, honesty and accountability in the functioning of the public services. The Lok Pal Bill has been awaiting enactment for the past nearly four decades and the functioning of the Lok Ayukts, established in many States, has still to result in bringing the dishonest to book. Corruption weakens the very foundations of the administrative and legal frame work and disrupts the Rule of Law. Thus, eradicating corruption from the functioning of the governmental apparatus is a sine qua non of internal security.

**Criminal-Politician Nexus**

The brazen lack of accountability which has permeated governmental functioning has, interalia, contributed to the growth of threatening linkages between unprincipled politicians, dishonest public servants and the criminal and mafia elements. Consequent to the serial bomb blasts in Mumbai in March 1993, which were carried out by the Dawood Ibrahim gang in concert with the ISI, a committee appointed by the Centre under the chairmanship of the Union Home Secretary had submitted its report, in September 1993, which concluded that crime syndicates and mafia organisations had established themselves in various parts of the country and developed significant' muscle and money power to carry out their activities with impunity. It was brought out that such syndicates thrived on the strength of their linkages with political leaders, governmental functionaries and other influential elements. The action taken on the aforesaid report, commonly referred to as the Vohra Committee Report, is not publicly known.

While there are various factors which contribute to the lack of good governance in the States, a major reason is that the political parties in power remain perennially preoccupied with retaining their positions, by whatever means, instead of being engaged in resolving problems which promote the welfare of their people. This unfortunate situation is further vitiated by the rampant corruption and lack of accountability in the public services at all levels of functioning. Efforts to contain and reduce corruption do not yield the desired outcome as the tainted elements in the administrative system enjoy the patronage and protection of their political masters who have placed them in key positions. An extremely worrying aspect of this situation is that functionaries of highly questionable integrity, some of whom maintain close linkages with criminal and anti-national elements, continue to hold responsible positions in the administrative apparatus. The potential of such elements subverting governmental functioning from within poses a grave threat to the security of the State.

The problems arising from the failures of governance have been compounded by the continuing determined efforts of adversary foreign agencies to destabilise the country by investing enormous resources for spreading religious fundamentalism, generating conflicts and perpetrating violence and subversion. The result is that, today, we face an extremely worrying situation in which our internal and external security concerns have got inextricably interwoven.

The internal security problems of the country cannot be effectively managed if the States fail to discharge their constitutional duty of maintaining peace and public order in their realms and, instead, cast this crucial responsibility on the Centre, as has been the continuing trend in the past years. It must be recognised that, notwithstanding the strong financial, technical and material support which is provided by the Centre to enable the States to enlarge and strengthen their Police forces, the Centre would be unable to discharge its constitutional responsibility of protecting the States against internal disturbances unless the States wholeheartedly support the Centre's initiatives to secure effective internal security management of the country. In this context it must be noted that MHA's responsibility cannot remain limited to providing adequate financial and other required support to the States to upgrade and improve the functioning of their Police forces. MHA would need to undertake a sustained campaign to educate and sensitise the States to display a far more responsible attitude with regard to their role in maintaining internal security.

**Political Interference in Law Enforcement**

It is also relevant to emphasise that a stable security environment cannot be engendered merely by promulgating new laws on the specious ground that an existing law has been misapplied and misused, as happened in the case of TADA. The application of any law is likely to be abused if the very functioning of the law enforcement agencies is politicised and subjected to extra-constitutional influences. It is, therefore, of crucial importance that the working of the law enforcement agencies is urgently liberated from day-to-day political interference. It is also necessary to recognise that, in the ultimate analysis, every citizen must discharge his duty to uphold and protect the sovereignty, unity and integrity of the country. It is indeed unfortunate that while the vast majority of our people are concerned only about their Fundamental Rights there are not very many, even among the educated classes, who are even aware of their Fundamental Duties, laid down in Article 51A of the Constitution. Even if action were to be taken to enforce the Fundamental Duties of our citizens which, most regrettably, has not so far been done, it would be unsound to assume that the citizenry of India shall be overnight imbued with patriotic feelings to protect national interests if the environment in which they live and work continues to be vitiated by discrimination, corruption and injustice. The requisite environment can be engendered only if the States perpetually demonstrate and ensure that the laws of the land apply equally to the rich and influential and the highest placed public servants. Side by side, it must be ensured that no injustice is done to the poor and the disadvantaged segments of society as this would result only in promoting distrust and despair among the masses and further eroding their loyalties.

In the aforesaid context it has also to be noted that lawlessness cannot be controlled and internal security maintained unless the entire framework of the criminal justice system functions with speed, fairness and transparent honesty. From the statistics collected and annually published by MHA it would be observed that while, on an average, over 5 million criminal cases are registered every year, well over 20 million cases continue to await trials in Courts and the number of pending cases is progressively increasing. Besides the gargantuan logistical inadequacies in the justice delivery system the integrity of the magistracy and the subordinate judiciary is seriously tainted. In the recent past serious allegations of financial and moral corruption have been raised even against Judges in the High Courts. Needless to say, the most urgent measures need to be taken to clean up the justice administration apparatus and enlarge and strengthen it to ensure speedy trials. Internal security cannot be maintained if rampant lawlessness pervades the realm and lawlessness cannot be eradicated unless the necessary measures are taken on a time limited basis to make the criminal justice system work with speed, fairness and honesty.

Another cause for serious concern is that while we continue to have hundreds of altogether obsolete and irrelevant laws, most of which were enacted during the colonial period, we do not have an adequately stringent law, applicable all over the country, which can meet the requirements of effectively dealing with terrorist offences, cyber crimes and the fast growing areas of organised criminality which pose a grave threat to the nation's unity and integrity. We also do not have a Federal Crime Agency which can deal with the serious offences committed by criminal networks whose activities spread across several States or even the entire country. It is indeed most unfortunate that MHA's initiative to establish such an Agency has been thwarted by the irresponsible postures taken by several States which have argued that the proposal militates against their constitutional jurisdictions. MHA must continue with its efforts to educate the recalcitrant States to better understand the grave consequences of playing politics with serious issues relating to the effective management of internal security.

**Economic Offences**

The country also does not have a comprehensive law for dealing with serious economic offences which, if not timely checked, have the potential of disrupting the national economy. Today, terrorist and criminal networks operate in a borderless world and, needless to say, the grave challenges posed by their activities cannot be tackled if the various concerned law-enforcing agencies continue to operate within their respective limited jurisdictions. What is urgently required is an appropriate legal framework and a well planned strategy which is executed in the most effective coordination between the Centre and the States to deal with each and every aspect of internal security management. The MHA must pursue unceasing efforts to achieve this objective.

Many of the fundamental factors which generate grievances among the people at large, and some of which may cause serious internal disorders, would start getting resolved when the people are empowered and the communities are enabled to manage most of their affairs. Such a goal was sought to be achieved through the crucial 73rd and 74th Amendments to the Constitution. The States would need to pursue this objective with far greater commitment and faster pace than has been evidenced in the past two decades.

The Centre would require to allocate progressively increasing resources to MHA for better internal security management and taking all necessary measures to effectively enforcing a constant vigil across the length and breadth of the country. Side by side, the States, which are receiving significant assistance from the Centre to modernise and upgrade their Police forces, shall have to improve the functioning of their security administrative apparatus without any further loss of time. As earlier noted, among the most urgent steps required to be taken by the States is to depoliticise the functioning of the State Police organisations and to specially strengthen their Intelligence wings which should operate in close and effective collaboration with the Central intelligence agencies.

In the aforesaid background it would not be out of place to reiterate that in the security scenario which has been evolving over the past more than two decades issues pertaining to internal security management have got inextricably interwoven with those relating to safeguarding external security. In this context it is no longer feasible to deal separately with internal and external security concerns. It is, therefore, extremely necessary that a holistic view is taken of all our security concerns, both internal and external, and a comprehensive strategy is planned and executed, in the fullest coordination between the Centre and the States, to effectively safeguard national security.

I would conclude by stressing, once again, that internal security cannot be preserved and maintained without enforcing the Rule of Law. And there cannot be any Rule of Law except the constitutional Rule of Law. Thus, it is of the highest importance that the command of the Constitution is scrupulously obeyed by the Executive, Legislature and the Judiciary. Any threat to the constitutional values would pose a threat to the very foundations of the polity and society and, as a consequence, to national security.

❖❖❖❖❖

# India's Economic Security*

*Tarun Das*

## Introduction

This is clearly a world of increasing interdependence. Technology has made it so, and borders between countries and continents are being bridged by the power of information and financial flows. In this framework, is there a place for national economic security? If the answer is in the positive, then how does a nation consider itself economically secure? And, is India's economic security in good shape?

To develop this thought process further, it is necessary to first get a basic sense of what one means by "economic security". It means that, in an interdependent world, the country concerned has sufficient resources and reserves at its command to minimize its vulnerability to different kinds of threats, volatility and fluctuations, which might occur in this uncertain and complex world, and impact on the stability of the country. By that basic yardstick, USA is seemingly most economically secure. So, also seems to be China. A few other countries, such as France, Germany, Singapore and Malaysia have the economic power, depth and strength, but whether that constitutes "economic security" in the face of severe and sustained global shocks may be debatable.

Once upon a time, the Soviet Union was surely one such secure nation; and hopefully, the Russia of tomorrow will rank in this number in future.

There are different views and perceptions regarding the economic security of India. As far as military and defence security

* The views expressed inthis paper are personal to the author and do not necessarily represent the views of the Confederation of Indian Industry.

goes, few will doubt that the answer is yes. Economic security was a question mark earlier. It is less so now. The international environment, India's foreign exchange reserves, her technology revolution, her food safety net, her human resource strength and the steady, ongoing economic reform process — all of these have helped to make India stronger, more economically secure.

The question is: What are the factors which give a nation that strength and security? There are clearly quite a few: size and scale of the country and its domestic economy; food availability; quality and adequacy of infrastructure; size and depth of manufacturing; the services sector; human resources; energy resources; financial resources; the financial services sector; technology, and more. It is now possible to have a checklist of "National Security" factors and create a matrix that gives ratings to different factors in different countries.

Since India has achieved food self-sufficiency, this paper focuses on other issues. It is my view that the first need for a country has to be technology, after food. This is an area of strength in many countries. However, it seems clear that on the technology front USA leads all others.

**Technology**

Technology does not necessarily mean pure research though that is part of it. It also means applied research. It includes commercialisation of technology. The founding fathers who led India post-independence understood the need for national capability to be developed in technology, and therefore created an infrastructure of R&D institutes and labs across disciplines, across India. But, the infrastructure was not fully utilised because the missing link of competition was largely absent till 1991. The impetus to build new technology and to focus on technology development really came after 1991.

However, where international technology denial took place such as in the areas of space, nuclear, missiles and defence, India adopted a mission approach. The country allocated national resources and achieved self-reliance. These were also the areas where, for national security and strategic reasons, India had to develop these technologies and could not afford to be out in the cold.

A nation gains from the development of strategic technologies through their use and application in the civilian and commercial sector. This did not happen adequately in India. However, a new trend has begun. Recently, the private sector is being allowed and encouraged to enter these areas such as defence production. The scenario will be transformed over the next seven to ten years.

Technology, then, is an important key not only to military but also to economic security. And, India is finding it increasingly difficult to import technology, to access technology. As a result, there is greater pressure on domestic effort — also, a greater need and challenge.

The US sanctions on India in 1998, and their restrictions on export of dual-use technology to India have impacted the civilian sector and, necessarily, got reflected in flat US exports to India.

Today, not only is Indian industry paying far greater attention to technology development, but, the S&T people available in the country are bringing major MNCs to establish technology development centres in India. This is an amazing turnaround the impact of which will be felt in India by 2010 in terms of technology capability.

**Manufacturing**

The second area of priority in terms of economic security is the area of manufacturing. India will necessarily import all kinds of products and services including, of course, manufactured products. As India's growth increases, these imports will also rise — and must do so. But, at the same time, India's manufacturing development has to be given enormous priority.

Manufacturing provides products, employment, technology, ancillarisation, a market for the services sector and more. It has a huge importance in the economy of the country and the emphasis that was placed on building manufacturing capabilities in the 1950s and 60s needs to be revived again. In those days, the priority was to build manufacturing in the public sector and to allocate government resources for this purpose. In today's context, and tomorrow's, the manufacturing capacity will by and large be in the private sector with only select, strategic sectors falling under the government ambit. And, internationally, even key defence production has come into the private sector, which has been at least as competent and trustworthy as the public sector.

So, a key agenda in the maintenance of national security is the manufacturing industries of India — their growth, their strength and their development. Happily, with the euphoria of the 1990s in regard to IT and software having passed, manufacturing industry and manufacturing technology are again moving back to centre stage. And, equally important, individual public and private sector companies are achieving global standards, global competitiveness and, not only excelling internationally, but also, withstanding pressures of competition within India.

The unique strength of India, so far not fully utilised, is the SME sector which is rich in entrepreneurship. The policy of reservation of 800 plus products for SSI units has inhibited growth, efficiency, management and competitiveness. Otherwise, the low technology, labour intensive production of India, manufactured to large scale, would have rivaled China in the markets of the world.

Again, the Indian elephant is making a slow U-turn. In a

variety of products made by Indian companies, the world has become the marketplace and zero defect supplies, over the years, is happening. Indian companies are winning the most prestigious global awards in manufacturing quality products and this is a growing phenomenon. India must now have a very different "Manufacturing Policy", adopt a "Manufacturing Mission" and work to be the second "factory to the world".

**Services**

In addition to manufacturing, the new environment has made the services sector assume critical importance. Fortunately, the 1990s saw the emergence of India as a strong player in the IT software industry. In more recent times, business process outsourcing and IT enabled services have come to play a major role in India's IT sector. The challenge now is to go up the value chain, to take on higher value added work.

In addition, India has to focus on some niche products in IT hardware. This has been a weak area for India, which has galloped ahead on software and services but done very poorly in hardware for the IT industry. This must be an area of focus over the next five to ten years in order that India is not completely dependent on imports of IT hardware. The learning is not from the giants of USA but from the midsize companies of smaller, highly successful economies of East Asia and the Middle East.

But, reverting to services, the focus must not be only on IT-related services. India can be the global hub and resource for the entire services sector which includes training, recruitment, healthcare, education, engineering, maintenance, R&D, and so on. Gradually, these services are evolving and making a mark in the global arena. A consistent plan to build India's services sector will aid the national security process enormously.

With the kind of human resource skills in India, and the large numbers, India is likely to emerge as the global hub and resource for services. "Served from India" can become an internationally recognised and respected brand as the country explodes with an abundance of talented, young people. As against this, many countries, including Europe and Japan, will have ageing populations, higher costs and outsourcing dependency. One important facet is that these services can be provided out of India to other countries. Technology makes this possible. Therefore, large-scale migration will be unnecessary and the services sector which is now being led by the southern states of India, will find emerging competition from the east, north and west, which is all to the good.

**Infrastructure**

Infrastructure is another key area of focus — railways, ports, roads, airports, power, and telecom. These are crucial areas of the economy, and can be strengths or weaknesses. For many years, these were neglected. But, in the last few years, there has been steady progress, thanks to clearer focus. The national highway construction programme is an outstanding example.

Unfortunately, the railways and power sectors continue to cause huge concern. If the same Mission approach is applied there, as was done for highways, the problems could be resolved in three to five years. Essentially, these are man-made problems based on inadequate leadership within these sectors and the reluctance to embrace new ways of working. For example, the power strategy of the country needs to go beyond large projects to small local power generating capacities serving local needs. Such power will be low cost, owned by local communities, based on local resources and serving a cluster of villages. No one will mind paying for power at one rupee per unit. Everyone objects to paying five rupees per unit and everyone cannot afford it.

For the railways, a road map for reform exists but, sadly, neglected.

Telecom, in spite of tensions and controversy, is moving ahead rapidly and transforming the nation in many many ways beneficially.

Ports, too, are developing except the three old, major ports.

Airports still suffer from backlog, which can be resolved quickly, given the will.

A specific aspect of national security is civil aviation. The country has a huge network of small airports and airfields all over the country. To build economic strength and national integration, India needs to use small aircraft to link states, districts and clusters of villages, transporting people and goods at low cost. This could be a daylight operation so as to avoid the need for expensive night-landing facilities at these airfields. National efficiency would be enhanced enormously, the productivity of the agricultural sector, in particular, will be augmented, wastage will be drastically cut and the standard of life of farmers improved. A related effect — higher purchasing power, new levels of demand, rising investments and higher growth.

The 'usual' focus in any national economic security issue or debate is energy, especially oil and gas. Clearly, these are strategic sectors. Indigenous production, import dependency, consumption levels, the conservation agenda — all these offer challenges and concerns.

To add to these are issues of inter-state policy differences, time and cost overruns on projects, lack of autonomy for the public sector, lack of adequate and timely investments, etc. The supply and availability of energy has to be given maximum attention to minimise exposure to geopolitical uncertainties. So much has been written and spoken on energy security that there is little new to add except one word — implementation. Stop the debate. Do the things which have to be done for India.

**Banking and Financial Services**

In this era of globalisation, another aspect determines economic security — the banking and financial services sectors.

The South-east Asian financial crisis highlighted this fully. India's conservative policies paid good dividends. However, the current, unprecedented foreign exchange reserves — $ 75.5 billion and rising — should not lead to complacency. The composition of India's foreign exchange reserves could be a cause for alertness, constant vigilance and an approach of carefully calibrated capital account liberalisation. Financial stability is crucial and caution is essential to ensure and insure economic security. In every aspect — capital account convertibility, exchange controls and exchange rate policy — a step-by-step approach is essential.

Side by side, there must be concern about the size of the fiscal deficit and the extent to which the country is living beyond its means. This is clearly an area of anxiety, an area of concern, an area for action. Good fiscal health is an imperative for economic security.

The country needs to debate and decide whether it can afford the huge establishment of people on the rolls of governments. A simple action could be to ask 33 per cent of government employees to stay home on full pay for three years and give them freedom to earn additional income through self-employment or additional employment. In these times, when new opportunities are opening up daily, many might prefer to opt out of government employment after some time based on the safety net of continued government pay.

**Human Resource**

India's most abundant resource is human resources. The much-criticised Indian educational system has produced human resources of global standards. In fact, there is no country in the world today which has the quality and quantity of human resource strength as India. This has fuelled India's services sector explosion. It should also enable India to become the second "factory to the world" in manufacturing, after China, and also be the S&T hub for many corporates around the world.

What is now needed is to focus on spreading primary education like wildfire throughout the country. Happily, a public private partnership approach is working and the spread of the midday meal scheme is bringing, and keeping, children in school.

In addition, there is a need to incentivise students to pursue science, technology and engineering studies, to take an M.Tech and Ph.D so that India is truly a technology resource to the world. It can and must be done. India must not have all its technical people drifting into general management and becoming investment bankers!

**Other Concerns**

With all these resources at India's command, what else is needed?

Of course, there are several issues, but, four, in particular, need highlighting.

First, competition, especially domestic competition in this time of low world growth, increased focus on India as a market, increased pressure on India to open up to imports, etc. In international trade, India will need to negotiate hard for mutuality. Opening of markets must be a two-way traffic, not one-way. Today, the developed nations are adopting numerous protectionist measures to save jobs, save votes, serve political needs. These are understandable in democracies.

The same issues apply to India — equally, actually, more so, with huge unemployment and underemployment to deal with.

But, concurrently, the policy of giving the consumer a choice and fostering fierce domestic competition is essential to fulfil the tremendous potential of India's industries. National economic security is served by domestic competition and not by monopolies. The lessons of the period from 1956 (the Second Plan) to 1991 are to be remembered forever. The comfort level of all suppliers has to be kept low so that there is a constant incentive to innovate, to improve, to perform. Gone are the days when anyone could sell anything at any price.

The second issue relates to ownership. Who owns the nation's economy has an impact on security. Who owns the key sectors of the economy has an implication for national security. This is why even the most developed nations control ownership in key sectors, e.g. USA and telecom; USA and media.

Foreign investment is important. FDI is essential and must be welcome. Clarity on FDI issues, learning from international experience and policy is crucial. There is need for balance in strategy and policy so as to access FDI and yet assure that national interest is served in terms of economic security.

Third, the public sector. It is much criticised and maligned. But I believe wrongly so. Public sector workers, managers, executives and Chief Executives are of high quality competence and integrity. They are wrongly criticised because they are given an impossible framework to work in. They are given the worst possible batting wicket where performance is impossible.

That results in the constant cry for privatisation. Of course, privatisation should happen. It is the natural order of things. But, every PSU cannot be privatised or disinvested for many years. The process will take time. Meanwhile, providing the public sector with a deregulated environment will enable them to be more efficient, competitive and profit making. And, hence more valuable.

The new aspect is that, in the interest of economic security, there are public sector companies which need to remain in the public sector. These are companies of strategic importance. And, providing their boards with freedom to take decisions will make a considerable difference to India's security interests.

The final point relates to management of the economy. In

a complex world, competent professional management is imperative to understand issues and take the right decisions at the right time. Does India today have people of this quality available? Yes. But, they are all outside government and it is important to consider new strategy to serve national security needs. A strategy of inducting people into the economic management structure and system is required so as to strength the nation's economic management team. This has been done in the S&T, R&D policy making area.

There are also strong intangibles which must be taken into account. Culture and values are crucial to national security as positive factors; corruption, on the other hand, is a negative factor which undermines a nation.

Similarly, unemployment is a great threat to national security because of the negative forces which are released by people out of jobs, families living in poverty and despair, without confidence about their future.

Another factor which causes concern is the lack of development in the East and North-East. This has a huge bearing on a very large part of India and, strategically, a crucial region. There is hardly any economic activity in the North-East, greater Eastern India including Eastern UP. In fact, all of UP is getting out of the economic map.

**Conclusion**

In conclusion, it must be said that India lacks a vibrant economic security debate. It is not only food or energy. There are many other issues. In this paper, some have been highlighted. Separately, water and rivers need to be fully debated. But, competition, manufacturing, banking services, infrastructure, human resources, technology management, culture, unemployment, value systems, etc. need to be highlighted because these are almost taken for granted and, yet, these have a sizeable impact on a nation's economic security.

In this framework, the National Economic Security of India in 2003 needs higher priority attention and strategic planning. There is not sufficient initiative to build advanced technology or to support national ownership of strategic industries, technologies and sectors as, for example, USA does. National Economic Security is not only about growth or liberalisation or disinvestments — in fact, these sometimes weaken economic security if not consciously addressed. The 2002 scenario, therefore, gives cause for concern and these anxieties need to be addressed, not through ad hoc decisions but through a structured approach and strategy.

It is a complex matrix but one which can be framed and managed. India has the leadership and the management capability to make the nation truly economically secure. If the objective is an economically secure country, every piece of the puzzle needs to fall into place. An Economic Security Council needs to be constituted as a broad-based body but not too large. This structure could monitor all aspects of economic security and influence — strategy, policy and action — and all parts of Government — Central and States — as well as other "players", e.g. industry, academia, research, media, etc. need to be involved and engaged so that 2003 and beyond will see an India which is more economically secure for the one billion plus people of the nation.

❖❖❖❖❖

# Technology and Security

*Raja Menon*

## Introduction

Most scholars agree that there has been considerable overlap between the nature of society and the manner in which that society makes war. Before the Industrial Revolution, people depended largely on agriculture for their incomes and that era has sometimes been dubbed, rightly or wrongly, the agricultural era. The doubt arises because of the geographical areas that achieved high levels of prosperity through trade, even in the agricultural era, like Venice, Lebanon, Saurashtra, Malabar, Chettinad, etc.[1] The importance of agriculture and the imperatives of sowing and harvesting inhibited the campaign season frequently to two months in fertile lands, and often explains the conquest of agricultural lands by pastoral people. The next economic revolution, we see, also automatically revolutionised warfare, as the factories set in motion by the steam engine produced a vast tax paying middle class, increased revenues, paid armies and mass produced weapons. The inventor of the cotton gin, Eli Whitney, offered to make in 1797 for the US army, fifteen thousand stand of arms 'including a musket, bayonet, ramrod, wiper and screw driver by using forging, rolling, floating, boreing, grinding and polishing.'[2] Lest this era be considered passé, it is interesting to note that up to the 1970s, it was a widely held belief in both India and Pakistan that wars could only be fought in September or October between the monsoon harvest and winter sowing in the Punjab.

The industrial era has admittedly given way to the information or technological, best understood by the radical change in the constituent costs of a product. While Marx held that it was labour during the industrial age, with materials making up the rest of the costs, today the quotient for technological amortisation and advertising costs of a product often dwarfs the material and labour costs. Not surprisingly, technology has become the foundation for economic prosperity. It would be missing the point therefore if the implications of high or low technologies was seen to affect only military security, when it may well initially decide the economic security of a people. Paul Kennedy's study of the continued economic growth of Japan for four decades, and the move of Japanese companies up the manufacturing ladder of value-added items is illustrative.[3]

### Security of Indian Society

Nearer home, our President, Dr. Abdul Kalam has addressed the issue of the role of technology in improving the life of a people rather more directly. His case is strongly, if inconsistently argued. There are many indications of what a nation's position in the world is and some conventional indices include the GDP, balance of payments, rate of economic growth, per capita income and all the social indicators like infant mortality, etc. However, these indices will not really give any indication of the quality of a people's lives, as per capita income, for instance, does not indicate income distribution. Kalam feels that a country's weight in international trade today is dependent on its technological levels, which grows out of the opportunities given to the people to better themselves. He goes on to classify the areas where the country needs to concentrate on in the growth of 'core competence'. These are self-reliance in critical technologies and strategic industrial infrastructure.[4] While there is no doubt that Kalam's arguments in support of a central strategy for technology development are well taken, less certain is that this is the sole answer to India's problems. The only Indian economics Nobel Prize winner has often emphasised in his speeches that India's primary requirement is to 'expand social opportunities'.[5] That there is a conflict between the two is evident in the case of agriculture in India. Even without the benefits of biotechnology, Indian agricultural output has grown embarrassingly large. So large has it become that the state continues to subsidise the support price of wheat and rice to the farmer, incurring huge losses in the budget, which makes it difficult to balance the current account, thereby denying funds for development. The large number of people dependent on agriculture, and who generate large numbers of votes may prevent a democracy like India from accepting that migration from villages to cities is inevitable and should be encouraged. Biotechnology may then become the answer in increasing agricultural incomes, but only if the government stops bankrupting the treasury buying whatever the farmer produces.[6] Biotechnology could initially make the food grain surplus even larger.

To take the idea mooted by Kalam further; that countries need independent organisations to forecast and choose appropriate technologies, the USA has the well known Office of Technology Management (OTA) which works for the US Congress. The Chairman and Vice Chairman are leading figures from the House of Representatives and there are four members each from the two Houses. Below them is the Advisory Council consisting of 16 CEO/CTOS and academics from companies like General Motors and from Universities and faculties.[7] The UK has a Technology Foresight Programme which is funded by the government. Germany has more or less copied the Japanese method of periodically writing a 25-year Technology Vision Statement. Against what these countries have done, the Indian effort to centrally project the country's technological requirements have been timely, relevant, and probably more comprehensive than the European documents. First set up in 1988, the Technology Information Forecasting and Assessment Council (TIFAC) under the Department of Science and Technology, brought together government, industry, scientific and technological institutions and intellectuals. TIFAC has produced a number of reports, but its greatest achievement was probably to inspire some of the technology-related 'missions' as for example for drinking water and telephones. The people in TIFAC were only too aware that they had had only limited successes when the entire body met in 1993 to review the situation.[8] At the 1993 meeting the sector-wise initiatives to make India a developed country was discussed as a result of which seventeen panels were set up. To enable Industry to have a full voice in what needs to be researched, ten of these panels were headed by experts from industry. These seventeen panels produced twenty-five technology vision statements, and most of the important areas were addressed including food, healthcare, engineering, life sciences, electronics and communication, defence, chemical, industries, materials and strategic industries.

Perhaps the best of the technology vision statements pertain, not surprisingly, to agriculture since the country has a history of applying science effectively to agriculture. Eventually, what assessment can one make about the efforts of TIFAC? For no fault of this organisation, the actual work in the field of technology has continued to be done autonomously by the existing bureaucratic structures, in cases where the R&D money came from the government. For instance, the TIFAC report on defence, space and atomic energy read more or less like autonomous documents put together by the Defence Research Organisation, and the Departments of Space and Atomic Energy. TIFAC may have been able to influence the autonomous organisations only in two ways. Either through funding against specific projects, or by bringing to bear an overwhelming weight of intellectual brilliance. Looking carefully through the defence portion of TIFAC's report it is clear that TIFAC has had virtually no effect on what DRDO had decided to do in its many laboratories, in any case.[9] The difficulty in influencing the practical world has obviously been realised by TIFAC since pressure has been brought to bear on the working ministries through the Planning Commission, particularly in the case of the Ninth Plan 1997-2002.

In the case of private industry it doesn't need emphasis that in India the financial allocation for R&D is negligible. Could government laboratories spin-off the dual use technologies to the civilian sector? A good example of this is the NASA which produces an excellent document every year.[10] A glance at the report for 2000 shows that the report includes two separate sets of products ¾ one at the strategic level and the other at the commercial. The strategic spin-offs include objects like a space re-entry 'lifeboat' like the Mach 10 speed X-42, a fuel cell powered UAV and an Ion engine with 10 times the thrust of a solid fuel rocket. Commercial products include human hand-like robots, bioscans to detect breast cancer by a blood test, mechanically advantaged aged person lifters, complicated geometry CAD/CAM, direct osmosis water purifiers and many others. The DRDO has done something similar by putting into the market almost 25 products for civilian use which are defence research spin-offs.[11] Some queries with Indian industry representatives showed that all of them are unaware of the US spin-offs while many of them are also unaware of the Indian DRDO's spin-offs. Might it make some sense if the Indian scientific organisations were to simplify the NASA spin-offs and put them out in the Indian market as an Indian publication?

### Cyber and Information Security

Seminars and conferences on information security have often elicited the view that prime societal targets in attacking the information system of a country would be the financial system for money and cheque transfers, the national civil aviation flight control system, military command and control systems, immigration and customs software and the software systems of large companies like Reliance and Tata's ( in case of India). The threat from non-state actors with no assets to punish requires that strategy be primarily defensive. The largest two private software systems in the USA are apparently the Walmart management system and the New York stock exchange. It's likely that the Bombay stock exchange will soon be one of India's biggest systems. In the United States, a white paper has been published which contains the proposed regulations to strictly monitor money laundering and prevent large benami transactions. The

US example would be useful for India to follow in protecting our financial systems.[12] Similar attempts have recently begun with the US government having appointed a commission to go into promulgating a national strategy to secure cyber space.[13] In India, writers on info-security have made a number of suggestions on what should be done, but as in the US case a comprehensive set of recommendations have not yet been promulgated. In the meanwhile, new software tools are being developed that will prevent attacks rather than merely warn of an attack in progress or record an attack that has occurred.[14]

**Technology Export and Denial**

India has had one of the longest experiences of being on the wrong side of technology denial regimes. Fortunately the regimes have never been watertight. Of the five multilateral regimes — the Zangger Committee, the Nuclear Suppliers Group, the Australia Group, the MTCR and the Wassenaar Arrangement, the first two were probably put in place to specifically target India after Pokhran 1. The coordination committee on Multilateral Exports (COCOM) was the one really intended to prevent the export of dual use technologies, after a visiting Western delegation saw virtual copies of three- axes milling machines in the Warsaw Pact countries used to produce submarine propellers. The dichotomy between technology export and denial will become clear from what has been written earlier. If labour costs are high in the developed countries, and export targets can only be met by exporting technologically advanced items, how can a technology denial regime be put in place? This riddle is at the heart of the differences between the US and Europe where the former feels that 'Europe leaks', whereas the American system is stringent. According to US sources, Israel received reactor and reprocessing technology from France, and uranium from Belgium and Germany. Pakistan acquired enrichment technology from Holland and many manufactured items from Germany.[15]

Perhaps the reason why the USA is able to export larger

numbers of its hi-tech equipment, like radars and EW systems is that their equipment is sold to a large US armed force, apart from sales to client states of the USA like Japan whose military equipment is solely American. Some of the European nations also buy American Elint systems, leaving only a small export window to the European hi-tech exporters who must sell or perish. Opposition is now building up inside the USA also, that technology denial regimes would cripple many industries in the USA. Bitter complaints have been made by the satellite industry association in California.[16] Certainly the experience of the Indian armed forces have been that European manufacturers have never hesitated to tender for the supply of hi-tech systems like radars and ESM despite the Wassenaar Agreement, but American companies have far more advanced systems which they are not prepared to sell. The Europeans generally compete with the Israelis. Today the thaw in Indo-US relations and the beginning of military equipment transfers will still not mean that India will be offered what the US armed forces themselves use, although the equipment offered will satisfy Indian needs. Hence a balance may be found by the USA between exporting technology and denying anything from the top shelf. The conflict between US export interests, particularly to a large buyer like China, and national security interests has been well summed up in a CSIS study.[17] In the meanwhile, where the buyer has plenty of money to offer and the off-take is quite large, hi-tech manufacturers often circumvent export controls.[18] One example is the Chinese attempt to beat the restriction on the manufacture of next generation microchips, when equipment to manufacture circuitry to 0.13 microns was obtained from Europe despite US bans.[19]

The Indian attempt to be independent of foreign technology has met with mixed successes. Induction of hi-tech equipment like radars and ESM has followed two routes. The first involved the production of a prototype by DRDO and technology was then transferred to a defence PSU like Bharat Dynamics. In the second case a Defence PSU or a service like the Air Force went into direct collaboration with a foreign manufacturer. The largest number of inductions and successes fall into the latter category, but the former produces higher indigenous technology. The scientists prefer the former, while the services rely more on the latter method, which has produced the Jaguar, the Mig series, the Leander frigates, search radars, the Bofors gun and the T-72 tank. Major successes in pure indigenous technology are mainly with the Navy in the form of the APSOH and Panchendriya sonars and the Air Force's Indra radar. Producing a world-class piece of equipment in India required the maintenance of 'islands of excellence' amidst a generally low-tech ambience. The pay scales of those in the island were never conducive to retaining them in that island. On the other hand, it is reported that the CEO of Northrop Grumman when told of India's stuttering LCA project, said that the Indians in his company could have produced an aircraft ahead of the LCA all on their own.[20] It is clear that what India defends itself with is far below the standard of what Indians in the world can produce. The reasons for not being able to tap NRI talents are fairly well known, and are symptomatic of a backward and jealous bureaucracy.

The island of excellence story is not relevant any more, of course. Both in the USA and India the technology in the civil sector has rapidly sped past the defence requirements with microprocessors and the telecommunication revolution. In fact the revolution in military affairs (RMA) was largely enabled by advances in civilian technology. As we shall see later, many in the armed forces who still believe in the Island theory are responsible for keeping the services from progressing into the stage of developing modern warfare techniques.

## Space

There is little doubt that space has now become what the oceans were in the 16th and 17th centuries. Then, a well found three masted sailing ship capable of circumnavigating the world and fighting in any part of it became the symbol of colonial power, vast riches and a regenerating economy. Today space may become the theatre which is sought to be dominated as a prelude to regional or world domination. The capture and holding of high ground has always been critical in war. Technology has gradually pushed high ground into space, which today is already militarised.[21] International efforts to prevent it from being weaponised are blocked at the CD in Geneva. In the meanwhile, dependence on space grows exponentially for communication, television, surveillance, cartography and national security. Admissions have already been made by American commanders that the victory in Afghanistan could not have been achieved without extensive use of space assets.[22] The possibility of weaponisation comes from the NMD concepts of a boost phase intercept, which today is aircraft borne, but which eventually may go into orbit. At present, the Outer Space Treaty bans strike weapons in space, but the treaty dated 1967 was agreed to when the possibilities of weaponising space did not exist.[23] The ability to execute boost phase interception will not be scenario specific, since some claims have already been made that if India and Pakistan were to get into a state of creeping escalation, they could be cooled down with a threat of a laser blast from outer space.[24]

### Technology in Defence

Victory, which is the objective of all armed forces is thought to be ensured by a combination of leadership, morale, logistics, numbers, training, tradition and finally, the correct technology. It is not always that the technology relevant to the war being fought is present. Numbers are always thought to be inadequate. Recently commissioned unclassified studies on the Navy and the Air Force complain that neither service is big enough.[25] On the contrary most literature from the West emphasises that the revolution in military affairs (RMA) is not being instituted fast enough, and that if it was, superiority in numbers would be a marginal factor. The USA in its effort to mould the information systems of the Army, Navy and the Air Force into one system, called the Cooperative Engagement Capability is about to announce the parameters of the new system.[26] In the meanwhile, none of the Indian armed forces has a common information system even within the service, despite all the three services having acknowledged that an RMA exists. The passion for acquiring more hardware without putting much money into increasing the speed of battle continues eleven years after the RMA was demonstrated. Similarly, thirteen years after the country began its war on terrorism, it still does not possess a night flying helicopter over land, resulting in thousands of commandos being un-useable offensively. There are many more anecdotes which are disturbing, like the digital mapping system being incomplete after eight years of trying.

Stepping backward to get a fuller picture, it becomes clear that technological reform of the armed forces will not occur without organisational reform. This is not a new discovery but something that has been established to be the root cause of technical obsolescence over two centuries. The higher command organisations of the three armed forces fiercely reflect the 1947 culture that they were handed over, with no regard for the organisational changes that have swept the military staffs of advanced countries. Activities like space, wide band connectivity, satellite surveillance, UAV's and air borne sensors are reflected poorly in the command structure, leading to inadequate funding, and poor management efforts in these areas. In many cases the scientists who received no direction from the service staffs, took their own initiative to produce the nuclear weapon, the Prithvi and Agni and the nuclear submarine. A committee constituted to set up a National Defence University (NDU) saw the problem in the officer corps and has recommended the setting up of an Information and Technology Management College in Bangalore to train service officers to interact better with scientists. The NDU report is still circulating after one year.

A country as poor as India is unlikely to be an independent player in producing the top end of weaponry like combat aircraft, stealth frigates, submarines and main battle tanks. Countries with the GDP of India, like France are getting into multi-national Consortia to produce expensive weaponry. India needs to look at cost sharing with Asian partners such as Iran, Malaysia, Thailand and even Australia and New Zealand. The problem of organisational obsolescence of the armed forces without curing which technological resurgence will not occur can only be attacked with outside consultancy services, since the senior officer corps are the problem and cannot be the solution. The Defence Research Organisation can only produce what Indians can produce and a little more. Their claims to be able to indigenise anything cannot and must not be taken seriously. Service staffs will continue to make their choices, but the staffs cannot claim more resources to overcome the consequences of bad choices. What can be done in the country will improve dramatically in any case as the civil sector catches up with the microchip and telecommunications revolution. Spin offs will inevitably flow through the DRDO into the services. Organisational change in the services is a more serious matter and something only the MOD can tackle, albeit with a little ruthlessness. However nothing substantial can be achieved if the problem of technological change is approached as a purely technical problem without recourse to changing the structure of the service hierarchies. The CDS and the Integrated Defence Staff is only a small beginning to bringing about jointness. Cleaning up the single service hierarchies is still a long way from being approached.

**The Russia Factor**

The Indian armed forces today virtually run on Russian hardware. Acquired when the Soviet Union could invest billions in weapons research, today the successor state Russia, has a GDP barely larger than Belgium, lower than Italy's and even the state of Texas. The implication for India could be hugely beneficial or hugely catastrophic. These factors need study. Firstly, the giant military complexes like Mikoyan, Sukhoi and Nikolayev haven't got the money to put into R & D to produce world class weapon systems. In fact, today, Sukhoi is kept going by China and India. Secondly, even if the money was found to be put into R &D, it can be recovered only if sales are amortised over the armed forces of Russia, China and India. The largest purchaser may be China and that may produce its own complications. Thirdly, the Russians have offered India joint production instead of the old sales programmes. It is unlikely that a similar offer has been made to China. Now comes the rub. Getting into a joint venture for top of the line equipment with another country requires a level of managerial expertise not available in the MOD or the existing armed forces structures. The European experience with consortia will bear this out. High-level groups like the Inter Governmental Commission on Military Cooperation composed of ministers, bureaucrats and senior service officers cannot put a giant joint venture together without literally hundreds of middle seniority management groups. The Russians are probably even more deficient in this respect than we are. The danger is that if we bumble along without progress in joint ventures with Russia, two things could happen – either the Russians will go to the Chinese or, the large production centres in Russia will collapse.

❖❖❖❖❖

**NOTES**

1. The main part of the revenue of the Mughal empire reached its peak during the end of Shahjahan's reign and was purely of agricultural origin and stood at 60,000 lakh dams @ 40 dams to a silver rupee, or Rs. 2025 crores (current value). W. H. Morland, *From Akbar to Aurangzeb: A Study in Indian Economic History,* Delhi, Low Price Publications, 1994, p. 32.
2. Quoted by Alvin and Heidi Toffler in War and Anti-War, taking the quote from Jeanette Mirsky and Alan Nevins, *The World of Eli Whitney,* New York, Macmillan, 1952, pp. 136-138.
3. Paul Kennedy, *Preparing for the Twenty-First Century,* New Delhi, Harper

Collins, 1993, p. 148; see Table 4.

4. A. P. J. Abdul Kalam, *India 2020: A Vision for the New Millennium*, New Delhi, Viking, 1998, pp. 9-20.

5. For example, see Amartya Sen's *First Lakdavala Memorial Lecture* given at the Indian Institute of Social Sciences, New Delhi, 29 June 1994, available at www.economics.pomona.edu/Andrabi/Sen_Beyond%20Liberalization.pdf.

6. Amartya Sen, *Development as Freedom*, New Delhi, OUP, 1999, pp. 206-209. Between 1950 and 1997 wheat prices have fallen 62.71, rice by 64.2, sorghum by 66.2 and maize by 68 per cent in constant dollar terms, because during this period world food production went up by 94 per cent per hectare. These increases are only marginal compared to what biotech could achieve.

7. The Office of Technology Assessment was set up for the Congressional Office in 1972 and closed on 19 September 1995. The composition of the members of the Board of the OTA is taken from an old PR pamphlet issued while the office was extant.

8. Kalam, n. 4, p. 48.

9. DRDO, *Status of Science & Technology in India: Defence R & D* (TIFAC Study), New Delhi, Department of Science and Technology, 1996.

10. See for example *Spinoff 2000*, Center for Aerospace Information, NASA, USA.

11. TIFAC Study, n. 9, pp. 24-27, which includes 4 food technologies, 30 chemical, 8 electronic and 16 transport industry spinoffs.

12. The Federal Government of the USA publishes a white paper on New Stringent Regulations of the Financial System. See also Ephrain Schutz, Loretta Principe and Brian Fonseca, Regulation of Financial Institutions, *Infoworld*, Vol. 24, 9 September 2002, p. 2.

13. Dennis Fisher, "National Security to Secure Cyberspace," *E-week*, 23 September 2002, p. 1.

14. Dennis Fisher, 'New Tools to Prevent Attacks', *E-week,* 16 September 2002, p. 12.

15. Ernst Piffl, Managing Director of a German firm in Stuttgant received a 3½-year sentence for exporting thousands of scoops for uranium gas centrifuges to Pakistan. See www.http.Pakistan. facts.com appearing in

the website of the *Bulletin of Atomic Scientists.* See also the trial of Ortmayer who helped Pakistan with boosted fission technology in David Albright and Mark Hibbs, "Pakistan's bomb of the Closet", *Nuclear Fuels and Nucleonics Week*, 6 February 1989.

16. Satellite Industries Association, *A Report on the Impact of the Federal Export Control Law on the California Space Industry,* 13 December 2000, available at http: //www.sia.org/papers/satexport01.pdf.

17 See John Hamre, Jay Farrar and James Lewis, *Technology and Security in the 21st Century,* Washington, CSIS, 2002.

18. Zoli Simon, "Hi Tech Transfers to China Continues," *Insight on the News*, Vol. 18, 29 July 2002, p. 22.

19. See *New York Times*, 6 May 2002, p. 4.

20. In a conversation with a US Embassy official.

21. Dawn Stover, "The New War in Space", *Popular Science*, Vol. 261, September 2002, p. 40.

22. Peter Grier, "Afghanistan", *Air Force Magazine*, Vol. 85, April 2002, p. 30, quoting General Tommy Franks and USAF Lt. Gen. Ralph Eberhart.

23. George Baran and John Rhinelander, "Outer Space Treaty Bans Strike Weapons", *Arms Control Today Vol.* 32, January 2002, p. 24.

24. John Miller, "May Sound like 21st Century Imperialism", *National Review*, Vol. 54, 15 July 2002, p. 35.

25. R. Adm. R. B. Suri (retired), "The Shape and Size of the Navy in the 21st Century", *USI Paper*, May 98; and Air Marshal Bharat Kumar, "The Impact of Emerging Technologies on Air Power", *USI Paper* 1/98.

26. Sandra Erwin, "Cooperative Engagement Capability", *National Defence*, Vol. 87, September 2002, p. 17.

# Self-Reliance in Defence Technologies

*Amitav Mallik*

## Introduction

Technologically the past decade has been very eventful in the world in general and India in particular. Following the collapse of the Soviet Union, the sole superpower USA demonstrated its unique skills in preventive nuclear disarmament by successfully containing the potential nuclear proliferation in the former Soviet states. At the same time, while most others were looking for peace dividend, the USA wasted no time in further improving its lead in conventional weapon technologies, as demonstrated in the recent Iraq operations. This was a high-tech military operation with full use of information networking as well as the full range of advanced sensors and weapons in an integrated joint operation with unprecedented real time flexibility. Importance of technology in matters of military superiority, national security and international affairs has never before been demonstrated so vividly on millions of TV sets worldwide.

Back home, the past decade has been witness to the superior calibre of Indian software engineers, earning for the first time a good measure of technological recognition in the world. The decade also saw the historic unveiling of project 'Shakti' on 11 May 1998 at Pokhran which caused sharp international rebuke at first but has also obtained some grudging acquiescence and even some respect over time. The successful launch of 'GLSV', maiden flights of LCA and successful tests of a range of missiles also added to the recognition of India as a potential technological power of the future. And yet, the post-Kargil analysis exposed the weakness of indigenous R&D and production capabilities that are not yet mature enough to meet routine expectations of our armed services, which continue to rely heavily on imports for most of their modernisation requirements. Fifty-five years after gaining independence, India continues to struggle with a rather paradoxical situation, where a few pockets of excellence create cheer in the midst of overall hollowness owing to inherent unattended weaknesses and unprofessionalism of its so-called professional people, who do exceedingly well once outside India. There must be something wrong in the way we address very important issues like technology and security here in the country.

In the emerging new world order dictated by core techno-economic strengths, India is still hesitating or unable to take bold strides to prove itself fully competitive with the best in the world. While the Western advanced nations are forging cooperative security and risk reduction programmes, India continues to be perceived as a 'Country of Concern' that is unable to resolve its regional disputes as well as the internal disorder. One could blame it on governance or political will, but in actual tangible terms, it is the lack of indigenous techno-economic capabilities that is holding us down. This paper attempts a re-visit of the core issues of technology in terms of why we lag behind as we do, what are the critical areas of technology for defence and security and what we should be doing for reaching where we ought to be particularly in the context of 'Self-Reliance' in defence technologies. The subject has often been examined by many experts in the past and we seem to know most of the answers to our problems. But somehow, we appear incapable of implementing our own recommendations and plans, to succeed within the cost-time boundaries of national requirements as well as global competition.

**Self-Reliance**

An important key to India's defence technology problems is obviously achieving 'Self-Reliance' (SR) in defence systems and critical technologies. This in fact is the well established 'Techno-Military' strategy to ensure that the national security interests of the country are not compromised due to any technological shortcomings. In the long term, 'SR' must mean that the country should not have to import 'Defence Systems and Equipment' for want of indigenous technology capability. As things stand today, India may continue to remain among the targets for export controls and technology denial regimes until it is proven that these controls are counter-productive in terms of international commercial or political interests. It is becoming increasingly important for a country like India to be able to exercise its own independent foreign policy in the interest of its own national security. This can be achieved only through a sustained effort at technological Self-Reliance that would not only enable the country to have an independent techno-military strategy for defence but also provide the nation with the vital techno-economic strength to leverage its political standing in the world.

Self-Reliance in defence systems and technology may be perceived in two different ways. One-way is to define an 'SR Index' in terms of modernisation expenditure by the armed forces. It would then be the ratio of the expenditure on the indigenous part of the defence procurement to the total expenditure on all defence procurement in a given financial year. Thus defined, the SR Index certainly indicates the extent to which our fighting forces depend on indigenous equipment. However, as is well-known, such an index can be influenced by many factors that are not necessarily technology dependent. In areas where the world market does not offer the desired systems for reasons of export controls and other political priorities, the Indian defence forces have to depend on the indigenous technology and the necessary fine tuning between indigenous R&D and defence procurement happens more naturally, thus boosting the SR index. But in other areas as soon as indigenous technology is established in important dual-use technologies, often the import options open up because denials then would only hurt the supplier states. Indigenous R&D and production agencies then have to compete with the defence industrial giants among the foreign exporters and the race becomes uneven because indigenous industries neither have the depth or the width to compete nor can they match the attractive package deals associated with overseas procurement. For most conventional weapon systems and support equipment the import option thus becomes the preferred choice, bringing the SR index tumbling down, despite the availability of indigenous technology in the country.

The real measure of Self-Reliance should thus be the indigenous technology maturity and timely availability of indigenous systems. The self-reliance could be assessed by an 'Index of Indigenisation' that would be a more appropriate representation of the technological capability to meet the nation's requirement of defence systems and equipment. Another dimension of the problem is the fact that modern defence systems need substantial development time but the rate of obsolescence in defence technology is very fast. Hence, while indigenous R&D and production may strive to provide the latest possible technology particularly in critical or strategically important areas, the defence forces on their part must have a well-planned procurement policy to allow adequate time for development, trials and production cycle. This kind of matching between the needs of the defence forces and the R&D programmes leading to production and availability of suitable equipment is very important. All this is well recognised in theory and such mutual tuning has actually succeeded in the specific areas of strategic technologies such as electronic warfare systems, radar and sonar systems, certain missile systems and nuclear weapon technology where even older generation technologies are carefully protected through export control regimes of the advanced states.

For a country like India the main thrust of an 'SR Plan' should inlclude: (i) Support existing systems through indigenising critical spares, (ii) Upgrade existing systems by stretching life and capability; and (iii) Introduce indigenous systems progressively, minimising import of major systems. 'Self-Reliance in Defence Systems' should be a national objective that requires full commitment of all concerned Government departments as well as the user service wings. With the indigenous

R&D and Production capabilities rapidly maturing, it could be expected that our armed forces would break away from the old practice of first shopping abroad for their immediate requirements of weapons and equipment and then settling for in-country Licence-Production for the long term, under the so-called 'Transfer of Technology' (TOT) agreements. For any SR plan to succeed adequate planning and forecasting must be incorporated to allow indigenous equipment to be ready on time. The 'Make or Buy' decision-making should be participatory with all involved agencies and "Make" option ought to be the first choice. Of course, operational urgencies and non-availability of indigenous options could always be valid reasons for choosing "Import" options. But by and large, once a 'Make' decision is made and funding provided for the indigenous effort, all parties including the user service would need to remain fully committed to the ultimate success of the indigenous project leading to timely induction of the desired equipment.

Every procurement of imported equipment actually pays for foreign R&D expenditure that is amortised over the life cycle of the equipment which is often over 10 to 15 years. This obviously undercuts the indigenous R&D efforts over significantly long periods, pushing the indigenous technology further back in competition. Hence with a view to enhancing Self-Reliance in these competitive areas, the emphasis of Indian Defence R&D has rightly been on force multiplier technologies and systems such as advanced armaments, infantry fighting vehicles, combat aircraft, un-manned aerial vehicles (UAV), modernisation of naval platforms, underwater systems, radar systems, electronic warfare systems, electro-optical systems and battlefield missiles systems. The SR plan must have special emphasis to make the nation less vulnerable to technology denial regimes or the single vendor situations, where in the event of conflict indigenous capabilities could be checked through politicaliy motivated limits on supply and even sanctions. The quantum of effort and need for matching resources for this mission was recognised by the 'Parliamentary Committee on Defence' which has always recommended progressively increasing allocation for indigenous R&D and production. In all fairness it must be acknowledged that availability of funds has never been a major problem in the areas of Defence R&D.

In the complex matrix of achieving Self-Reliance, the role of Defence R&D is clearly to provide the 'Critical Technologies' for Defence needs and to build the 'Core Competence' for enriching the technology base in the country. Criteria for critical technologies are primarily based on their importance to military capabilities and industrial development, both being vital components of national security. Other factors such as enabling or pervasive nature of technology, concerns of vulnerability owing to non-availability, capacity to improve performance, quality and productivity, leverage on other technologies, etc. also matter in the assessment of criticality. 'Breakthrough Technologies' like the Nuclear Submarine, Stealth Aircraft, High Precision Satellite Surveillance and Guidance or the futuristic Directed Energy Weapons that can provide a technology 'Trump Card' to sustain long-term advantage, are also critical to technology superiority in the future. An effective long-term 'SR Implementation Plan' therefore must advocate selective investments in 'Critical Technologies' that would help realise the SR objectives specific to a nation's needs, both in the short-term as well as in the long-term.

**Defence Systems and Technologies**

A possible future war situation in the region of the Indian subcontinent perhaps can be comprehensively addressed by some or all of the following defence systems and technology components:

- Small Arms and Artillery Weapon Systems
- Mountain Warfare Technology
- Missile warfare and Missile Defence Systems

- Under Water Systems and Anti-submarine Warfare Systems
- Secure Communication and $C^4$ $I^2$ Systems
- Intelligent Electronic Warfare and Information Warfare Systems
- Air Defence System against High Density Air Attack or Missile Attack
- Satellite-based Surveillance, Intelligence and Communication Systems
- Electronic / Electro Optical Counter Measure Systems (EOCM))

Hence the likely future technology requirements may be summarised as:*

- Advanced Air-defence Technologies
- Air and Space-based Sensors and Radars
- Airborne EW Technology including ECM, ECCM and EOCM
- Advanced Battle Field Radars, Weapon Locating Radars
- Long Range Radars and Synthetic Aperture Technology
- Underwater Sensors and Weapons
- Flexible Launch, Medium and Long Range Guided Missiles
- Unmanned Air Vehicles and Cruise Missiles
- New Generation Combat Aircraft, Helicopters and Transporters
- New Generation Battle Tanks and ICVs
- MBRL Systems, Futuristic Field Guns, AD Guns and Rocket Artillery
- Smart Weapons and High Precision Terminal Guidance.
- Futuristic Ammunition such as Sub-munitions, Smart Mines, etc.

While the above short-listing is representative of a wish list of any modern fighting force, the changes in threat perceptions, strategic considerations, economic compulsions and available indigenous expertise and infrastructure would finally determine the operational priorities and time scheduling of the specific systems and technology requirements.

### Critical Technologies

Several technologies are needed for the development and production of the various systems listed above. In addition, the basic design know-how and the knowledge of integration, testing of the many subsystems and technologies, is another dimension of the expertise that is critical to being self-reliant in fielding these weapon systems. Technologies that are critical to some of the existing requirements may include:

- Microwave and mm Wave Integrated Circuits
- Fly-By-Wire Digital Flight Control Technology
- Advanced Gas Turbine Engines
- Ram Rocket Propulsion and Hyper Velocity Missiles
- Atmospheric Re-entry Technology
- Infra-Red Search and Track Technology
- Advanced Inertial Navigation Systems and Technology
- Smart Materials and Structures
- Advanced Simulation Techniques

Technologies that would be vital for new generation weapon systems may include:

- Sensors and Active Arrays
- Smart Weapon Sub-systems
- Intelligent Terminal Guidance
- Supersonic and Hypersonic Propulsion

- Satellite-based Communication and Intelligence
- Advanced Radars and Stealth Detection
- Ceramics and Metal Matrix Materials
- Advanced VLSI Devices and ASICs
- Photonics and Integrated Optics
- High Power Lasers and Microwaves
- Software and Information System Technologies

Self-reliance in these technologies can be achieved only when indigenous know-how and competence is backed with in-country availability of all critical materials and components as well as the necessary integration and test facilities for some of these highly complex advanced systems. These being very advanced technologies at the cutting-edge, expecting foreign help in these areas would be futile unless we have some demonstrated in-house capabilities. Once basic competence is established through convincing technology demonstrator programmes, often forging cooperation or joint development programmes with other countries or multinational industries becomes viable and even mutually profitable.

A new dimension to the international security perceptions is emerging due to abolition of the ABM Treaty and the US resolve to deploy NMD. Weaponisation of outer space will certainly create new security concerns for all sovereign nations with space assets. Today safety and reliability of satellite systems is vital not only for surveillance and guidance applications for defence but more so for several essential civilian applications such as communication, information transfer, financial transactions, etc. Definition of critical technology will then have to include most of the space technologies as well as directed energy weapon technologies for anti-satellite capabilities for the defence of one's own satellites. Advanced research in mini-nukes may also open up issues such as nuclear powering of satellites with associated increasing concerns about misuse of outer space. For a nation with 'No First Use' doctrine, survivability of its nuclear and missile assets also becomes very critical and technologies for protection from EMP effects can assume major significance. The nature or level of criticality of technology therefore is a time and environment variable phenomena and a progressive country must be sensitive to creating technological core competence to take up fresh challenges of new technologies.

**Core Competence**

While indigenous strengths in enabling technologies may be built-up progressively as part of indigenous system development programmes built into the national five year plans, a well conceived 'Self-Reliance Plan' must envisage acceleration of the processes through 'Critical Technology Development' programmes, to be undertaken at appropriate work-centres where core competence already exists or can be created. The long-term SR Plan for Defence Systems would thus require that while the relative benchmarking for technology maturity gets enhanced at the various R&D labs and Production centres as an evolutionary process, there should be a renewed focus on creating 'Core Competence' in new and revolutionary technology areas as well.

The Defence R&D is normally required to initiate fast track projects to meet immediate requirements but the real challenge is to succeed in projects with emphasis on development of critical enabling technologies. Such technologies need to be developed indigenously in order to ensure independence from foreign control, as also to provide the basic technological backbone for development of the defence systems. In the area of Critical Technology development, some notable achievements in the country would include the Gallium Arsenide and Silicon Foundries, Application Specific ICs (ASIC), Phase Shifters for Phased Array Radars, Parallel Processing and Super Computers, Titanium Sponge and Aerospace Materials, Composites and Special Alloys, Advanced Avionics, Electro-Optical Counter Measures and High Power Lasers-Microwaves, etc.

With reference to the Kargil experience a review was undertaken to identify specific technology and equipment that could be offered to the user services within a short time from the existing indigenous technology capabilities. These could well include Satellite and UAV-based Surveillance, Battle Field Surveillance Radars (BFSR), Weapon Locating Radars, Night Vision devices, Secure communication systems, Electro-Optic Counter Measures (EOCM) and other technologies for support to soldiers for better mobility, firepower and survivability. Steps should also include quick conversion of existing technology capability to usable equipment for 'Low Intensity Conflict' to fight insurgency and terrorism, which has become a very complicated problem eating into our defence efforts as well as economic development. But all this is very easily said than done because the process of converting a laboratory success into a successful, reliable and cost-effective product is very complex, involving many players. All these agencies and key players need to be equally capable, have adequate infrastructure and resource support and also have professional approach with full commitment for the whole team effort to succeed.

**Issues of Concern**

As already pointed out, mere technology development will be insufficient. Translating R&D success to actual equipment in the hands of the defence forces involves several steps and many agencies, all of which may not share the same motivation to fielding indigenous equipment as the first choice. For a variety of reasons, the anticipated induction of indigenous equipment into the inventory of the three Services does not happen easily. User services have a natural preference acquisition of imported equipment and often, major Defence contracts get finalised based on perceived urgent operational requirements irrespective of prior plans of procurement or induction. The second preference of the user services is invariably the 'TOT' route for licence production. Funds committed for such major contracts have a significant spillover to following financial years. As a result, the funds available for induction of indigenous equipment is always in short supply and often, indigenous R&D success does not even get a fair chance for efficient production and induction.

The "Make or Buy" decision-making process continues to be somewhat ad hoc. Even for proven indigenously developed systems, there is often a procedural/bureaucratic delay in terms of placing production orders for indigenously developed systems. This leads to a situation where the specifications (Qualitative Requirements) defined some years ago tend to get outdated and operational requirements become predominant factors in decision-making in favour of either 'Imports or License Production'. There appears to be a misplaced perception that the TOT for License Production (LP) is equivalent to technology acquisition. In reality, the latest technology is very rarely transferred to the recipient country. It is only the assembly and integration process instructions that are given under license production and a tight control is maintained on critical sub-systems or technologies. Heavy dependence on import or LP, particularly in the area of critical systems is highly undesirable, as the country can be choked by external forces at most inconvenient times.

Given certain limitations of the Government funded R&D and production centres, the policy for Self-Reliance should certainly encourage R&D and production at suitable private sector industries. However, because of the uncertainty of orders as well as inadequate numbers, very often the private sector in the country finds it difficult to enter into Defence R&D and production. A possible solution could be to form consortiums of Government R&D and private production partners in select technology areas to address specific needs of the services. Another aspect of cooperation outside the Government system is the all important involvement of the academic institutions that can provide valuable scientific and technological support to the national R&D efforts.

An important point to note is that every programme must have a prime motivator who should be in final control. For defence procurement the prime motivator is the user. Unless the user preference changes to indigenous systems over imported options, mere policy changes in favour of indigenous R&D and private industry participation is unlikely to make much difference. There is therefore a need to evolve a mechanism to ensure actual implementation of the ideals of SR doctrine through participatory enforcement of certain basic guidelines for long-term Self-Reliance with user interest in focus.

Another point of caution is the fact that even the few success stories that we feel good about, like missiles or radars or underwater systems, rarely match the latest advances in technology. Often these use technologies proven in advanced countries some 10-15 years ago, but still very relevant in our context because of the similar level of technology available to our adversaries. However, this could change significantly if an advanced country were to take extraordinary interest in our region and introduce the latest technologies in our neighbourhood. The recent Iraq operation has demonstrated how a single superpower can marginalise even the established UN structure and enforce its will and policy on other sovereign states. In this age of rapid changes in strategies by powerful nations, a country like India that is not a party to any alliance group, needs to be mindful of the level of indigenous technology capabilities compared to the latest in the world. Real 'Self-Reliance' in defence technologies is thus now more critical than ever before.

**Some Prescriptions**

What India really needs is a full scope 're-engineering' of the defence technology efforts in the country according to the collective wisdom that has emerged in the GOM (Group Of Ministers) recommendations based on the various 'Post-Kargil' soul searching reviews. Defence R&D in future perhaps should therefore concentrate only on futuristic enabling technologies, much along the successful DARPA model of USA and leave jobs such as performance upgradation and import substitution to the base workshops of the individual user services. Defence scientists of course could give valuable assistance and training for the purpose of transforming these units into modern workshops. At the other end of the spectrum, the major platform and systems projects should be handled by the defence industry with the Defence R&D assisting in the capacity of a design consultant. This would allow Defence R&D to give better attention to the challenges of modern high technology areas including system design, system simulation and system integration of complex military systems as well as concentrate on emerging critical technologies of the future to create the necessary core competence for the next generation systems. Such a re-orientation would require strong policy level decisions and political will to enforce implementation, like what China has been able to do in the past decade. Done properly, this may even regenerate interest among the future generation to face the challenging opportunities in science and technology.

Another dimension of the problem is the inadequate defence industrial infrastructure in the country to undertake real major challenges. A 'back-of-the-envelope' calculation will indicate that, if one were to apportion about 30 per cent of our total defence allocation for modernisation, the scope of defence procurement expenditure on capital equipment would be of the order of Rs. 20,000 crores in a year. At present all our defence PSUs and the ordnance factories together are not equipped to handle such a large turnover of high-tech production, even if indigenous technology were to be available. While this capacity gap is easily appreciated in terms of the volume of work, the real issue is the intangible gap in technology maturity that is essential for ensuring world-class quality and the gap in management skills needed to make things happen within the 'cost-time' boundaries of the market forces. The remedy here again would be a major overhaul to convert the defence PSUs into unprotected competitive entities to succeed in the new environment of economic reforms and open market competition. And of course, with the laws for development and export of high tech equipment being progressively liberalised, the Indian industry must also now pitch-in in a big way to energise the industrial environment in the country. No defence industry can ever succeed merely on domestic demands and hence it is imperative that we get competitive enough to export at least in our own region. These are tall challenges but there can be no shortcuts to 'Self-Reliance'.

The third important consideration is the user. Our defence forces have to be weaned away from looking at the glossy product catalogues to identify the modernisation requirements. Integrated defence planning must be a serious ongoing exercise that is forward looking as well as pragmatic. Knowing how a poor country like India must optimise its resources, the defence requirements should be fine-tuned to specific perceptions of our national security threats. Defence technology is always changing at a very rapid rate, whereas the R&D and production lead time needed for modern high-tech products is quite considerable. In order to cut this time gap, it is essential that the requirements get projected well in advance through a long-term perspective planning process. The defence forces must learn to avoid the perpetual traps of buying yesterday's products at tomorrow's prices, never getting the technology know-how in the hitherto practice of licence-production. Arms exporters get rich and support their R&D at our country's expense while we continue to pay heavily throughout the life cycle of the equipment, well beyond the warranty periods. An honest survey of the existing inventory of imported equipment with our armed forces today may probably show that perhaps a substantial percentage of the inventory is either unserviceable or beyond economic repairs. This indeed would be a case of avoidable waste of precious resources and of the lost opportunities for the indigenous industry.

Today India enjoys a relatively high degree of appreciation of its security concerns by the international community and yet we ourselves continue to be a 'country of concern' owing to lack of proper articulation of our legitimate national priorities and security compulsions. The environment of dual use technology controls is currently undergoing a major change with the forces of globalisation and rapid technology diffusion gaining momentum since the IT revolution. Large industrial houses have become transnational with flexibility to operate at the 'speed of business' and national boundaries are getting less relevant to technology operators. The bureaucratic government agencies are thus getting less forceful with their cold-war mindsets and export control agenda. With our exceptionally good record at unilateral control over sensitive technologies, India has a unique opportunity to break into the international system of high technology cooperation and ending the history of isolation as a target country. Diplomatic engagement on all issues of proliferation and arms control with other established nations will be vital for opening up areas of international cooperation in technologies that are important for India. That in turn could spur the techno-economic development in the country and help us bridge the technology gaps and be counted among the developed nations of the world within a decade from now.

Last but not the least, it is the quality of people that makes or breaks a nation. If one looks at the formative years soon after independence, the leaders of that era were an inspired lot with selfless visions for the country. The phenomenal success of our nuclear and space programmes can be attributed to visionaries such as Bhabha, Sethna, Sarabhai and the likes. Even at the political level, leaders then showed an intense awareness of the importance of science and technology. Over the years we have got so bogged down with the issues of political survival and individual pursuit of prosperity and personal well-being that everyone is tending to become self-serving. We only pay lip service to the virtues of science and technology, with almost every parent totally absorbed in how to make the child earn maximum money in his or her lifetime. For every difficult challenge, there is always a need for a champion, someone with conviction and missionary zeal to make the impossible happen. India probably has no dearth of such people as can be seen by Indians performing so well the world over. But at home there is a distinct lack of professionalism at every stage that throttles even the few that are exceptionally endowed, leading to frustration and mediocrity. It is extremely important for the social reformists, educationists and political leaders to appreciate that if we can convert a sizeable majority of our one billion population into a creative and productive force, we could well outshine many of today's leading nations. These are those philosophical observations that no one may ever dispute and yet no one will do anything about it either. The devil is always in the details and it is these details of how, when and by whom that will have to be addressed by the thinkers and planners of our generation.

**Conclusion**

Self-Reliance in Defence should be a 'National Mission' with wholehearted commitment from the Defence R&D, the three armed services, the defence production agencies and of course the Department of Defence. The nation's Industry and Academic Institutions must also play a very significant role. For effective long-term Self-Reliance, incremental increase or improvement in indigenous R&D alone will not be sufficient. An integrated approach to defence planning, defence technology development, defence system productionisation and a policy of 'Preferential, Planned Indigenous Procurement' of Defence equipment and systems is absolutely essential. This will be the essence of a step-by-step long-term road map for Self-Reliance in Defence. This should not be left to any ad hoc methods of implementation. This must be carefully structured and effectively institutionalised on highest priority. The step-by-step action plan for future sustained Self-Reliance depends on such a coordinated effort at the MOD level in particular and at the national level in general. Undoubtedly, this cannot happen without a robust political resolve and sustained professional will. The 'Self-Reliance' plans for defence must become a part of the larger 'National Plan' for economic and industrial development so that together they drive the nation to the status of a 'developed nation'.

❖❖❖❖❖

# Health Hazards and National Security

*D. Raghunath*

## Introduction

National Security defined as the ability of a state to maintain its integrity and assure the welfare of its peoples has various contributing factors built in. The physical development of the population of a country is an important component. The mental attitude in terms of willingness to undertake strenuous activities, ability to exert over long periods and withstand stressful situations is determined to a large extent by the overall health of the individual and collectively the nation. There is evidence accumulating that even the intrauterine environment has an influence on the health of an individual after birth. A society burdened by a large proportion of malnourished, sick or handicapped individuals in its population would certainly not be secure. The health of the people determines their level of economic activity since debilitated individuals not only have a low efficiency but also drain the resources of the state. India has a long way to go before it can attain optimum levels of health. Though the country has managed to control some diseases and improve its life expectancy, it still has high levels of infectious and communicable diseases, nutritional maladies, maternal mortality and childhood mortality. This has affected the performance of the nation. These are inherent problems that are being tackled by the development process and, hopefully, will improve in the long run. Such issues are not being addressed in this paper, which would dwell on the hazards that are posed by diseases that could cause major perturbations in the normal health state. Infectious diseases have the greatest potential to cause this.

A constant burden of infection is borne by every community, the spectrum dependent on the level of infrastructural development. However, this can be altered by epidemics that could be caused by a change in the population-pathogen dynamics, or the emergence of new strains of endemic infectious agents with enhanced disease causing potential. The outbreaks of malaria following changed weather patterns or regional ecology owing to man-made projects are examples where a stable state has been altered by human activity. The outbreaks of infection following natural calamities would also fall in this category. The widespread epidemics of influenza A are due to the virus changing its properties. Similarly, human activity can expose susceptible persons to viruses restricted to special ecologic niches, e.g. the outbreaks of Ebola and Marburg virus infection due to human invasion of their environment. Such outbreaks impinge directly on nations' security by imposing a burden of infections that immobilise increasing numbers of the population and affect the social services. The dislocation of national activity that followed the Surat plague epidemic in 1993 illustrates the potential of such epidemics.

### Infections in Military Operations

The association of disease with war has been a part of the folklore of all the ancient civilisations. The outbreak of infectious diseases has modified the outcome of a number of wars. The role bubonic plague played during the Crusades and its subsequent spread to Europe (as Black Death) in the 14th century and the decimation of the native tribes by smallpox and measles (immigrant introduced) in the Indian Wars of North America are two historical examples. Even in the wars fought in the 20th century 'medical' casualties have been many fold more than the 'surgical' (battle) casualties. The realisation of the importance of this stimulated medical research. The side that managed to contain the health hazards better had a tactical advantage. World War (WW) I research by Germany developed synthetic antimalarials and WWII was the stimulus that kick-started the antibiotic era. In fact, in military circles penicillin, mepacrine and dimethylphthalate (DMP) have been accorded the status of munitions for their role in salvaging soldiers infected by pyogenic bacteria, malaria and preventing scrub typhus respectively in the South East Asia theatre. The Allied army possessed these 'weapons' not available to the Axis forces. Military medical research has traditionally been directed towards the control of 'battlefield' diseases. Thus, some of the most spectacular research efforts have emerged from studies on diseases that had military importance. The pioneering works of Walter Reed in Panama (on yellow fever), Ronald Ross in India (on malaria) and Leonard Rogers (on cholera) are examples that readily come to mind.

Thus, it is evident that the health status of a nation and naturally occurring infections have an important bearing on the ability of a nation to maintain its integrity. These factors are normally taken into consideration in planning and even naturally occurring exotic infections are not surprising. However, the rise of biotechnology in the 20th century has enabled ambitious countries, groups or individuals to use microorganisms and their products as weapons. This artificially created health hazard has developed into a major Weapon of Mass Destruction (WMD). This Biological Warfare is now a serious health hazard that has to be factored into the security planning

## Biological Warfare

The association of death caused by disease with war has been known from the dawn of history. It was also realised that outbreaks of infectious diseases could determine the outcome of a campaign and upset well laid out plans. The contagious nature of the diseases was surmised. Many a commander prayed for a pestilence to affect his enemies while sparing his own force. The inability to control the spread of the infections prevented them from using the infectious materials as an adjunct to their munitions except when the enemy was in a confined space and methods of delivery were available. Thus, practice of catapulting dead bodies into besieged forts evolved with the hope that the contagion would start epidemics that would further debilitate the inmates. Indeed, there is historic evidence that the manoeuvre did start an outbreak of plague during the siege of Caffa in Crimea in the 14th century. In fact, the outbreak probably developed into the infamous Black Death that ultimately accounted for a third of the population of Europe. The colonial expansions of the 16th and 17th centuries brought sequestered indigenous populations who were ignorant of infections like measles, smallpox, tuberculosis etc. into contact with the 'Old World' invaders with disastrous consequences. Of course the New World people too gave their diseases (like syphilis) to their conquerors.

However, the net effect has been a devastation of the indigenous peoples. This contact afforded an opportunity to try out introduction of lethal infections to which own troops were immune. The first documented instance of a biological attack took place in such an environment when General Amherst distributed smallpox infected blankets to unvaccinated Amerindians loyal to the French. Developments in vaccinology and the advent of antibiotics gave a further fillip to the expansion of the activity. The former Soviet Union initiated its Biological Warfare programme in the late 1920s and a number of other countries followed suit. During WW II both sides started work to produce usable biological weapons (BW). To date as many as 17 countries are suspected to have developed (BW).

The burgeoning stockpiles of BW alarmed the world community and a Biological and Toxin Weapons Convention (BWC) was proposed by the United Kingdom in1968 to examine and improve upon the earlier Geneva Protocol of 1925. The resultant document was first signed by the Soviet Union, USA and the UK on 10 April 1972. It is a landmark document that outlaws an entire weapon category. BWC was then presented to the nations of the world. The convention came into force in March 1975 and has 143 state parties and 18 signatories. BWC is a strongly worded document, but has not achieved its purpose. The convention was violated by its originators and a number of other countries. The United States continued to develop BW till 1969 when under the Nixon administration the programme was discontinued. The Soviet Union, however, continued to produce BW till its disintegration. Another significant weapons programme has been that of Iraq, which had produced 380,000 litres of Botulinum toxin, more than 80,000 litres of anthrax spores, a considerable amount of Clostridium perfringes spores and over 2000 litres of aflatoxin. Iraq also produced ricin toxin, crop pathogens and worked on camel pox (as a model for smallpox). In 1991 the third review meeting of BWC decided to draft a verification protocol for consideration of the signatories. It was fondly hoped by the world community that the world would be rid of BW and any infringement would be detected and eliminated. This was not to be as both the developed and developing nations felt threatened by the clauses that permitted intrusions. It has now become clear that without a certain degree of acquiescence on the issue of sovereignty no progress is possible.

It is evident that many countries actively pursued the issue of BW and serious efforts were made to develop effective weapons. Nevertheless, despite many allegations of use there have been no proven instances of the deployment of BW. Innate abhorrence as well as a fear of retaliation has probably been the deterrent to major attacks. However, this has largely been superseded by the rise of bioterrorism, which has been used by diverse political, religious and criminal groups. Bioterrorism is unpredictable, more clandestine and less easily defensible. It is, thus, a greater threat to security than a Biological War.

Biological Warfare has been defined by Nobel Laureate Joshua Lederberg as "... use of agents of disease for hostile purposes." This is a broad definition that covers medical veterinary and agricultural pathogens. That is the larger scope of Biological Warfare. In this paper only medical aspects are covered.

Any human pathogen can be used as a BW provided it is introduced in a suitable form under appropriate conditions. Thus, introduction of pathogens that are transmitted by contaminated water would not be successful in an environment that has protected water supply but would be effective in areas without the infrastructure. Cholera, typhoid or water borne Hepatitis E can be introduced in areas of India but cannot take root in the USA. The list of potential BW agents would be large and include bacteria, viruses, fungi and parasites. While it is relatively easy to cultivate most of the pathogens in the average microbiology laboratory, converting them to weapons requires processing technology that is not easily available. It is this that requires a specialised facility. However, the machinery that is required is available today in most countries and has other legitimate uses, e.g. fermenters used in preparation of biological products. BW production, if decided upon is within the reach of most reasonably developed countries, groups and even individuals. This has been the theme of a number of works of fiction. In Richard Preston's book *The Cobra Event*, an individual prepares smallpox for bioterrorist attacks. Likewise, a number of toxic derivatives can be used to cause harm but only a few lend themselves to being used as BW. Bearing these factors in mind the agents that have the potential for use as BW agents are enumerated in Table I.

While BW is recognised as a weapon of mass destruction along with nuclear and chemical weapons, grouped together under the acronym NBC, it differs from the other two in some basic characteristics. These are:

(a) BW cause diseases that are replicas of naturally occurring infections except when unusual routes are employed, e.g. Staphylococcal enterotoxin causes a pneumonia when it is spread by aerosols, while naturally it causes gastroenteritis.

(b) As in the case of natural infections there is an incubation period, when no symptoms are evident. In contrast, the effects of nuclear and chemical attacks are evident immediately.

(c) Due to a variation in the parameters of infection, like

individual susceptibility, infecting dose, mode of infection, etc. all the cases do not appear simultaneously. In the Sverdlovsk (Siberia) episode of 1979, persistently denied by Soviet authorities but admitted by Boris Yeltsin in 1991, the earliest cases appeared within the accepted incubation period of 1-6 days but the last few cases appeared as late as 43 days after the accident.

(d) The moment of attack may not be appreciated by the community particularly in bioterrorist attacks. The perpetrator as well as the first victims (in the incubation period) may travel away from the incident site and mingle with the community. This has a disastrous consequence in the case of BW like smallpox, that cause secondary infections.

(e) The infected cases turn up at the normal medical treatment centres and the first cases are likely to be missed because of the low level of suspicion or delay in the development of the characteristic clinical features, e.g. smallpox cases in the prodromal phase. Even when fully developed the diagnosis may not be made unless appropriate laboratory tests are ordered.

(f) Unlike the case of nuclear and chemical attacks the victims of biological attacks are seen by the first contact medical attendant, doctor, nurse or medical technician. The speed of arriving at the correct diagnosis depends largely on the level of training of these personnel. Presently, the average medical care person is not aware of the properties of the agents that are used in biological warfare. This is largely due to the extreme reticence in medical circles to talk about the subject. Fortunately, recent events have brought the issue into the open.

India has had a taste of the effects biological warfare would have on the civilian population during the Surat plague epidemic of 1994. The epidemic was caused by a natural infection but the panic response it generated was similar to the projected scenarios in cases of biological attacks. The national and international ramifications of the outbreak resulted in a political and economic setback. Assessments have been made on the economic impact of biological attacks on the United States. It has been estimated that an attack using an organism with moderate infectivity and low mortality like Brucella melitensis would have an economic impact of about $(US) 477.7 million per 100,000 exposed persons, whereas the damage in the case of a highly infective agent with a high mortality could go up to $(US) 26.2 billion for the same number exposed. There would be similar impacts in the case of attacks on livestock and crops. Thus, biological weapons are effective agents that are relatively cheap. They have been estimated to be 1/25th as costly as the other two WMD.

We have so far been considering the impact of deliberate introduction of pathogenic organisms. Natural infections too can spread across the country and cause serious economic damage. Historically, the two major epidemics of the 20th century that overshadowed the periodic outbreaks (of cholera, smallpox, measles, dysentery etc.) were the influenza epidemic of 1917-18 and the long drawn out plague epidemic of 1896-1945. Both of them were parts of global pandemics and caused high mortality in India. The influenza epidemic impacted on the rural economy and the about 17 million deaths that occurred within the span of a few months caused a decline in the population numbers. The plague epidemic did not have a serious demographic impact but it did dislocate people. Natural hazards that have made an impact in the last half-century are Japanese encephalitis, drug resistant malaria, multidrug resistant Salmonellae of the enteric and nonenteric types.

## Protecting National Security from Health Hazards

At the outset it is necessary to assess whether there is a threat. It has already been pointed out that the health status of the nation is not sound. While we are not the sickliest country, we are ranked amongst the lowest 1/3rd of the nations of the world. Countries with modest per capita incomes are better off than us. Even within the country the health status varies significantly. At one end of the spectrum we have a state that can match some of the developed countries while at the other end we have states that are not better than the poor nations of Central Africa. There is a difference in the productivity of the populations. Not only does this poor level of health of the people make the country vulnerable to exploitation but it also creates tensions within the country. As regards the threat perception regarding biological attacks, it is evident in the present post—11 September 2001 security scenario that moral and ethical inhibitions against the use of biological weapons have largely disappeared. When the first use of the nuclear option can be openly discussed it would not be surprising if the far more cost effective WMD (BW) were chosen. Likewise at the terrorist level BW offer a viable option with the added advantage of difficult detection. Therefore, it is high time we take note of the challenge. The national initiatives needed to counter the challenge of health hazards are dealt with below.

It is worthwhile noting that Sri Lanka (which has better health statistics than India) spent more than twice the amount per capita on health even during the civil war. Expenditure in health in India has only lately started showing an upward trend. This requires to be maintained. It is only then that there would be some hope of achieving good primary health care for the majority of the population in rural areas. Good quality primary health care is the key to the improvement of maternal and child well-being.

The allocation of funds would by itself not be sufficient until effective leadership is in place. Motivated medical staff is essential. The medical education initiatives in the past few years have been largely elitist. This trend needs to be changed. Balanced nutrition, protected water supply, employment and adequate purchasing power would automatically have salutary effects on general health. These are 'more easily said than done' and we will probably have to wait for adequate economic growth unless we can generate the necessary political will.

The steps necessary to be taken for protecting the country against biological attacks are, however, very much more specific and within the capabilities of the health services. Broadly, the actions necessary are:

(a) Have in place an efficient disease surveillance system that can quickly pick up even minor perturbations in the disease pattern across the country.

(b) Strengthen the public health system, particularly epidemiology. This would need training field epidemiologists – a rare commodity in this country! This activity would include having mobile investigation teams.

(c) Build up the laboratory infrastructure in the country. It is a sad commentary on the state of affairs when it is realized that this country of sub-continental proportions has no Level 4 facility for investigation of highly virulent pathogens. The country requires at least four such facilities across its territory. In addition every medical college and district hospital should have a Level 3 facility. These facilities are labour-intensive and require specially trained personnel where there are none available. A special cadre has to be developed.

(d) Official guidelines need to be drawn up to lay down the ground rules for combating the important agents like anthrax, smallpox, botulism, etc. The diagnostic methods need to be specified and an adequate number of quality-controlled kits require to be centrally stocked at all times.

(e) Antibiotics, sera and vaccines should be stocked in an adequate amount for counteracting the important BW agents, e.g. ciprofloxacin for anthrax, tetracyclines for

Brucella, smallpox vaccine, etc. It is a paradox that India was self-sufficient in freeze-dried smallpox vaccine after 1974. It not only had enough to execute the Smallpox Eradication Programme in the subcontinent but also managed to help the process elsewhere.

(f) An important task would be to train the primary health care providers in the prompt recognition of infections caused by BW agents. This would be a major task that would require a degree of coercion.

(g) Last but certainly not the least is the requirement of enlightening the general public and decision-makers. An enlightened public is less likely to panic. A proper handling of the Surat plague outbreak would have minimised the individual dislocation and national chaos.

It is worthwhile following the steps taken by US governmental authorities to tackle the hazard of smallpox in the country. A policy that follows the detection and containment strategy, which succeeded in eliminating the scourge, has been formulated. Stocks of smallpox vaccine have been augmented to 100 per cent vaccination capability. Detailed research into the molecular biology of smallpox stocks held in the US has been undertaken with a view to identify drug development prospects. A public debate has been initiated on the issue of voluntary vaccination after the hazards inherent in the procedure have been adequately publicised.

A healthy, strong nation will certainly be secure. The country requires to be protected against efforts to upset this balance. This is a major issue that needs to be addressed urgently.

❖❖❖❖❖

**Table 1***
**Critical Biological Weapon Agents**

| Biological Agent(s) | Disease |
|---|---|
| **Category A** | |
| *Variola major* | Smallpox |
| *Bacillus anthracis* | Anthrax |
| *Yersinia pestis* | Plague |
| *Clostridium botulinum* (botulinum toxins) | Botulism |
| *Francisella tularensis* | Tularemia |
| *Filoviruses and Arenaviruses (e.g. Ebola virus, Lassa virus)* | Viral haemorrhagic fevers |
| **Category B** | |
| *Coxiella burnetii* | Q fever |
| *Brucella spp.* | Brucellosis |
| *Burkholderia mallei* | Glanders |
| *Burkholderia pseudomallei* | Melioidosis |
| Alphaviruses (VEE, EEE, WEE)** | Encephalitis |
| *Rickettsia prowazekii* | Typhus fever |
| Toxins (e.g. Ricin, Staphylococcal enterotoxin B) | Psittacosis |
| *Chlamydia psittaci* | |
| Food safety threats (e.g. *Salmonella spp., Escherichia coli* O157:H7) | |
| Water safety threats (e.g. Vibrio cholerae, Cryptosporidium parvum) | |
| **Category C** | |
| *Emerging threat agents (e.g. Nipah virus, hantavirus)* | |

* Modified from Lisa D. Rotz, Ali S. Khan, Scott R. Lillibridge et al., Public Health Assessment of Potential Biological Terrorism Agents, Emerging Infectius Diseases, 2002, 8 (2) : 225-230.

** Venezuelan equine (VEE), estern equine (EEE), and western equine encephalomyelitis (WEE) viruses.

# Security Implications of Climate Change

*Saumitra Mukherjee*

## Introduction

There is no doubt about the changing climate and its influence on various sectors of earth. This has been established by the research carried out by various agencies across earth. Extensive work has been carried out to understand the influence of climate changes on the security of earth and its various environmental components. It has been a matter of great concern to understand and analyse seismic security, food security (related to agriculture and rainfall), water security and other associated phenomena. Lately it has been felt that climate change and security from earthquakes, cyclones, global warming, sea level rise, erratic rainfall, variations in temperature on earth and other related phenomena are in coherence with each other. Scientists have been anxious to understand the possibilities of interrelationship of various phenomena and the impact of climate change on them.

Natural processes involving changes in the sun could have at least as powerful an effect on global temperature as increased emissions of carbon dioxide (CO2). These two factors are related to the hydrological cycle of nature. Climate scientists have already looked at changes related to sun spot activity – a cycle of approximately 11 years – and long-term changes in the sun's brightness, which has a cycle that lasts for centuries. Scientists have discounted the effect of both the factors on the temperature increase over the last century because they either happen over too short a timescale, or they are too weak.

## The Many Causes of Climatic Change

Between 1850 and 1990 the global-mean temperature at

the surface of the earth was warmed by approximately 0.5° C (about 1° F). During the same period, the amount of carbon dioxide measured in the earth's atmosphere increased by about 25 per çent, as a consequence of our ever- increasing use of fossil fuels. This raises the possibility that the two trends are directly connected, and that the century-long warming is a long-anticipated sign of the climate system's response to human activities.

Still, more factors were obviously perturbing the climate system than the lone hand of greenhouse gases. The global-mean temperature did not rise steadily: statistical analyses of the temperature record since 1850 reveal significant year-to-year and decade-to-decade variability. Moreover, what is known of the longer climatic record suggests that surface temperatures may have been systematically increasing since the late 17th century well before the onset of the Industrial Revolution, when greenhouse gas concentrations first began their upward climb. Other natural perturbations, which have also varied during the past few centuries, might help explain the difference between the change expected from a simple increase in greenhouse gases and what has been observed.

Like the concentrations of greenhouse gases, solar activity has risen systematically through the past 100 years, as recorded in the number of sunspots. An upward trend is found in the number of solid particles, or aerosols, in the lower atmosphere. The burning of fossil fuels that has led to an increase in greenhouse gases has introduced an ever-increasing load of sulfur-bearing or sulfate aerosols, which affect the temperature on the surface of earth. In contrast, the aerosols ejected into the atmosphere by volcanic eruptions decreased markedly during most of the 20th century, compared to conditions in the century preceding, as a result of a presumably random drop in the long-term average of volcanic activity. Other potential causes of climate change include the depletion of stratospheric ozone in recent decades, again through human activities, and global changes in the surface reflectivity – or albedo – of the planet, as we modify the patterns of vegetation that cover the land. In conjunction with possible internal system changes such as variations in ocean circulation, these influences define the most likely causes of climatic change in the recent era.

Different influences on climate affect the system in ways that in principle can be distinguished on the basis of geography, altitude, and time history. More often, however, the impacts of multiple influences are mixed together, and further confused by imperfect knowledge of how each of them has changed, and uncertainties in how climate itself has varied.

In global average, increases in greenhouse gas concentrations or in solar radiation bring warmer surface temperatures since they add energy to the climate system. In contrast, increased industrial and volcanic aerosols restrict the penetration of solar radiation to earth's surface and lead to surface cooling. A drop in the concentration of ozone in the lower stratosphere should also produce a net cooling at the surface. Changes in albedo that increase the planet's reflectivity will lead to cooling, and those that make it less reflective and more absorbing, to a temperature rise.

**Climate Change: Fifty Years Past and Possible Futures**

A new NASA-funded study used a computer climate model to simulate the last 50 years of climate changes, project warming over the next 50 years regardless of whether or not nations curb their greenhouse gas (GHG) emissions soon. If no emission reductions are made and they continue to increase at the current rate, global temperatures may increase by 1-2° Celsius (1.8°-3.6° Fahrenheit). But if the growth rate of carbon dioxide does not exceed its current rate and if the growth of true air pollutants (things that are harmful to human health) is reversed, temperatures may rise by only 0.75C (1.35F).

"Some continued global warming will occur, probably

about 0.5C (0.9F) even if the greenhouse gases in the air do not increase further, but the warming could be much less than the worst case scenarios," observed Jim Hansen, lead researcher on the study from NASA's Goddard Institute for Space Studies (GISS), NY. This research was a collaborative effort of 19 institutions, including 7 universities, federal agencies, private industry and other NASA centres.

The GISS "SI2000" climate model provided a convincing demonstration that global temperature change of the past half-century is mainly a response to climate forcing agents, or imposed perturbations of earth's energy balance. This is especially true of human-made forcings, such as carbon dioxide and methane, which trap earth's heat radiation as a blanket traps body heat; thus they cause warming.

The computer model's ability to simulate the past 50 years of global temperature change provided confidence in understanding the causes behind climate changes that have occurred over that time period. The sensitivity of the "SI2000" model to a climate forcing is comparable to that of other climate computer models. Model results from 1951-2000 are in close agreement with observed changes; the surface has warmed by about .5°C (0.9°F) while the upper atmosphere (10-15 mile altitudes) has cooled by about 1°C (1.8°F).

The climate model was then used to simulate global temperature change during the next 50 years, under two contrasting assumptions for future growth of human-made forcings. The first assumption for the emissions of GHGs is the "business-as-usual" scenario where GHGs continue to increase rapidly. This scenario leads to an accelerating rate of global warming, raising global temperature to levels that have not existed during the past several hundred thousand years. In the 'alternative' scenario, in which air pollution is decreased and fossil fuel CO2 emissions are stabilised, further global warming is limited to 0.75°C (1.35°F) in the next 50 years. Hansen cautioned that the 'alternative' scenario will not be easy to achieve. It requires that the world begin to reverse the growth of true air pollution (especially 'soot' and the gases that control surface ozone, including methane) and also that we flatten out and eventually begin to decrease CO2 emissions.

The climate forcing agents that Hansen and his co-authors include in their climate simulations are:

(1) Long-lived greenhouse gases such as carbon dioxide, methane and the chlorofluorocarbons;

(2) Stratospheric aerosols (fine particles) from volcanic eruptions;

(3) Variations in the sun's energy indicated by sunspots;

(4) Ozone changes - both at the surface (a pollutant) and upper atmosphere (protects from the sun's ultraviolet rays);

(5) Stratospheric water vapor; and

(6) Tropospheric air pollution aerosols, including black and organic carbon (soot) and sulfates.

For achievement of stable CO2 emissions, as required in the alternative scenario that yields minimal climate change, it is likely to require some combination of increased energy efficiencies, a growing role for renewable energies, capture and sequestration of CO2 emissions, and/or increased use of nuclear power. All these possibilities are being addressed by the National Climate Change Technology Initiative.

"Decision-makers, including the public, may need to consider all of these options as climate change becomes more apparent and as our understanding of the climate forcing agents improves," Hansen said. "Halting and reversing the growth of air pollution is possible with existing and developing technologies. It would have other benefits, especially for human health and agricultural productivity."

## India Specific Impacts of Climate Change

A study conducted by the Tata Energy Research Institute in 2003 states that in developing countries like India, climate change could represent an additional stress on ecological and socio-economic systems that are already facing tremendous pressures due to rapid urbanisation, industrialisation and economic development. With its huge and growing population, a 7500-km long densely populated[1] and low-lying coastline, and an economy that is closely tied to its natural resource base, India is considerably vulnerable to the impacts of climate change.

Lonergan estimates that India's climate could become warmer under conditions of increased atmospheric carbon dioxide. The average temperature change is predicted to be in the range of 2.33° C to 4.78° C with a doubling in CO2 concentrations[2]. It is also likely that there will be an increase in the frequency of heavy rainfall in South and Southeast Asia.[3] A study by Lal, Cubasch, Voss and Waszkewitz presents a climate change scenario for the Indian subcontinent, taking projected emissions of greenhouse gases and sulphate aerosols into account. It predicts an increase in annual mean maximum and minimum surface air temperatures of 0.7° C and 1.0° C over land in the 2040s with respect to the 1980s.[4] Since the warming over land is projected to be lower in magnitude than that over the adjoining ocean, the land-sea thermal contrast that drives the monsoon mechanism could possibly decline. However, there continues to be considerable uncertainty about the impacts of aerosols on the monsoon.

## Agriculture

Agriculture and allied activities constitute the single largest component of India's economy, contributing nearly 27 per cent of the Gross Domestic Product (GDP) in the year 1999-2000.[5] Agricultural exports account for 13 to 18 per cent of total annual exports of the country.[6] However, given that 62 per cent of the cropped area is still dependent on rainfall[7], Indian agriculture continues to be fundamentally dependent on weather.

A few studies on the impact of climate change on agriculture have been reported for India in the IPCC Third Assessment Report.[8] While Saseendran et al., have reported decrease in rice yields by 3 to 15 per cent under a scenario of 1.50C rise in temperature and a 2 mm day -1 increase in precipitation, Lal et al., have reported that yields of soyabean in India would vary between 22 to 18 per cent under different climate scenarios considering +2 and +40C change in temperature; ± 20 and ± 40 per cent change in precipitation.

In an ongoing study supported by CIDA and the Government of Norway, TERI along with CICERO and IISD is working on a project, "Vulnerability of Indian Agriculture to Climate Change and Globalisation". The macro level vulnerability is assessed at a district level using GIS-based techniques. This involves the development of a climate change vulnerability map and a globalisation vulnerability map. Based on an overlay of these two maps, regions across India that are doubly exposed to both climate change and globalisation are identified.

To study the micro-level implications of vulnerability, detailed case studies are being conducted. The case studies aim to see how economic factors within the context of domestic policies have either enhanced or reduced the capacity of farmers to cope with climate change. The pilot case study was undertaken in district Jhalawar of Rajasthan. Three other case studies are to be conducted over 2003-2004. This is done using a detailed questionnaire survey, through group discussions and interviews with villagers and meetings with village heads and district officials.

**Forestry**

In addition to their crucial ecological role, forests make a considerable contribution to the Indian economy. Forests contribute 1.7 per cent to the GDP of the country.[9] Moreover, non-timber forest products provide about 40 per cent of total official forest revenues and 55 per cent of forest-based employment. Nearly 55 million people living in and around forests in India depend upon non-timber forest products as a critical component for their sustenance.[10]

Climate is an important determinant of the geographical distribution, composition and productivity of forests. Therefore, changes in climate could alter the configuration and productivity of forest ecosystems. These changes in turn could have profound implications for traditional livelihood, industry, biodiversity, soil and water resources, and hence, agricultural productivity. Moreover, these climate change induced effects would aggravate the existing stresses due to non-climate factors, such as land use changes and the unsustainable exploitation of natural resources.

Ravindranath and Sukumar discuss the impacts of two climate change scenarios on tropical forests in India — one involving greenhouse gas forcing and the other incorporating the effects of sulphate aerosols.[11] The first scenario, associated with increased temperature and rainfall, could result in increased productivity, migration of forest types to higher elevations, and transformation of drier forest types to moister types. The second scenario, involving a more modest increase in temperature and a decrease in precipitation in central and northern India, could have adverse effects on forests.

In a case study of the southern Indian state of Kerala, Achanta and Kanetkar link the precipitation effectiveness index to net primary productivity of teak plantation.[12] Results indicate that under the climate scenarios generated by the ECHAM3 climate model, the soil moisture is likely to decline and, in turn reduce teak productivity from 5.40 m3/ha to 5.07 m3/ha. The study also shows that the productivity of moist deciduous forests could decline from 1.8 m3/ha to 1.5 m3/ha.

In a study conducted by the Stockholm Environment Institute in collaboration with TERI, Deshingkar, Bradley,

Chadwick and Leach apply the BIOME model to project future climate-induced shifts in geographical location and changes in area under different forest types in the north Indian state of Himachal Pradesh.[13] The social and economic impacts of changes in forest structure on rural communities and the local economy are examined through a case study of the Mandi district in Himachal Pradesh.

**Coastal Zones**

India has a low-lying densely populated coastline extending for about 7500 kms. UNEP (1989) identifies India among the 27 countries that are most vulnerable to sea level rise. Most of the coastal regions are agriculturally fertile, with paddy fields that are highly vulnerable to inundation and salinisation. Coastal infrastructure, tourist actitivites, and onshore oil exploration are also at risk. The impacts of any increase in the frequency and intensity of extreme events, such as storm surges, could be disproportionately large, not just in heavily developed coastal areas, but also in terms of the paralysing devastation in low-income rural areas. The 1999 tropical cyclone that hit Orissa resulted in a death toll of about 10,000, and demonstrates the extreme significance of impacts related to climate variability.

A case study of Orissa and West Bengal estimates that in the absence of protection, a one-meter sea level rise would inundate 1700 km2 of predominantly prime agricultural land.[14] A JNU study shows that in the absence of protection, a one-meter sea level rise on the Indian coastline is likely to affect a total area of 5763 km2, and put 7.1 million people at risk.[15] TERI has done a district level ranking of vulnerability to one-metre sea level rise by constructing a weighted index.[16] The study also assesses the economic implications of such a rise on the most and least vulnerable districts in order to provide the range of projected economic impacts on the Indian coast. In present value terms, the results range from Rs 2287 billion in the case of Mumbai, to Rs 3.6 billion in the case of Balasore.

**Water Resources**

India is considered rich in terms of annual rainfall and total water resources available at the national level. However, these resources are unevenly distributed and result in spatial and temporal shortages, hence limiting availability across regions.

Increased demand has further increased the pressure on the resource. The demand for water has increased tremendously over the years due to an increasing population, expanding agriculture, and rapid industrialisation. However, the amount of water available on earth that can actually be beneficially utilised, is limited. Fulfilling demands has led to considerable imbalances in the quantity and quality of water resources.

Climate change and variabilty are likely to worsen the existing situation by further limiting water availability. Under a changed climatic regime for any given region, the combined effect of lower rainfall and more evaporation would have dire consequences. Both these would lead to less runoff, substantially changing the availability of freshwater in the watersheds. Also, potential changes in temperature and precipitation might have a dramatic impact on the soil moisture and aridity level of hydrological zones. With changes in the flows, annual runoff, and ground water recharge, water available for usage will further be decreased.

An assessment of the implications of climate change for hydrological regimes and water resources using scenarios developed from Hadley Centre Model Simulations indicates that by the year 2050, the average annual runoff in the river Brahmaputra will decline by 14 per cent. Studies have indicated that the impact of snow melting in the high Himalayas will lead to flood disasters in Himalayan catchments. Impacts will be observed more in the western Himalayas as the contribution of snow to the runoff of major rivers on the western side is about 60 per cent compared to 10 per cent on the eastern side.[17] Singh suggests that an increase in surface temperatures will lead to a rise in the snowline, increasing the risk of floods in North India during the wet season.[18]

## Earthquakes

Besides agriculture, forestry, costal zones and water resources being affected by climatic factors, the possibility of increase in earthquakes also exists. The associate factors of climate changes are directly related with the changes within Sun. The Solar Maximum repeats its peak within the 11-year cycle which leads to the changes in thermosphere, ionosphere, atmosphere as well as geosphere. This fact was revealed in TIGER project. It is possible to forecast the possibility of triggering of earthquake by looking into the location of active sunspots before it harbours energy towards earth. It has been observed that when Coronal Mass Ejections (CME) are not earth directed but pass/sweep away from earth from a very short distance, it may produce sudden changes in atmosphere. Whatever be the manifestations in the environment of the atmosphere or geosphere there is a positive correlation of CME with change in magnetic field followed by aurora borealis or a sudden spark of light from sky before an earthquake. It is possible to correlate the occurrence of global earthquake and earth directed coronal mass ejections and change in magnetic field (Kp indices) and electron flux of earth-sun environment. On 24 January 2001, an Earth directed coronal mass was ejected which took two days to reach earth's surface and a major earthquake of magnitude 7.9 occurred in Gujarat, west coast of India. This area was reportedly seismically active. In the entire world, a total of 65 earthquakes were reported on the same day. Earth directed coronal mass ejection produced a suspected invisible tail of electrified gas. IMAGE spacecraft spotted the tail that stream from earth towards the sun.

❖❖❖❖❖

## NOTES


1. DOD, *Annual Report 2001/02,* New Delhi, Department of Ocean Development, 2002.
2. S. Lonergan, "Climate Warming and India", in *Measuring the Impact of Climate Change on Indian Agriculture*, edited by A. Dinar, et al. Washington DC: World Bank, 1998. [World Bank Technical Paper No. 402].
3. Inter-Governmental Panel on Climate Change (IPCC), *The Regional Impacts of Climate Change: An Assessment of Vulnerability*, Cambridge: Cambridge University Press, 1998.
4. M. Lal,, U. Cubasch, R. Voss and J. Waszkewitz., "Effect of Transient Increase in Greenhouse Gases and Sulphate Aerosols on Monsoon Climate", *Current Science*, 69(9): 752-763, 1995.
5. TERI, *Energy Data Directory and Yearbook 2001/2002*, New Delhi, Tata Energy Research Institute, 2002.
6. *Economic Survey 2001-2002*, New Delhi, Ministry of Finance, Economic Division, Government of India, 2002.
7. *Agenda 21: An Assessment*, New Delhi, Ministry of Environment and Forests, Government of India, 2002.
8. IPCC, Climate Change 2001: *Impacts, Vulnerability and Adaptation* (Contribution of Working Group II to the Third Assessment Report of the Intergovernmental Panel on Climate Change), Cambridge: Cambridge University Press, 2001.
9. *National Forestry Action Plan*, New Delhi, Ministry of Environment and Forests, Government of India, 1999.
10. TERI, *Energy Data Directory and Yearbook 1999/2000,* New Delhi, Tata Energy Research Institute, 2000.
11. N. H. Ravindranath and R. Sukumar, "Climate Change and Tropical Forests in India", *Climatic Change*, 39(2-3): 563-581, 1998.
12. A. Achanta and R. Kanetkar, "Impact of Climate Change on Forest Productivity: A Case Study of Kerala, India", in Paper Presented at the Asian and Pacific Workshop on Climate Change Vulnerability and Adaptation Assessment [Manila, Philippines, 15-19 January 1996].
13. P. Deshingkar, P. N. Bradley, M. J. Chadwick and G. Leach, *Adapting*

*to Climate Change in a Forest-Based Land Use System: A Case Study of Himachal Pradesh*, India, Stockholm, Stockholm Environment Institute, 1996.

14. IPCC, *Global Climate Change and the Rising Challenge of the Sea: Supporting Document for the Intergovernmental Panel on Climate Change*, World Meteorological Organization, and United Nations Environment Programme, Geneva, 1992.

15. JNU, *Impacts of Greenhouse Inducted Sea-Level Rise on the Islands and Coasts of India*, New Delhi, School of Environmental Sciences, Jawaharlal Nehru University, 1993.

16. TERI, *The Economic Impact of a One Metre Sea Level Rise on the Indian Coastline: Method and Case Studies,* Report submitted to the Ford Foundation, 1996.

17. See n. 8.

18. Singh, "Effect of Global Warming on the Streamflow of High Altitude Spiti River", in *Enhydrology of High Mountain Areas*, pp. 103-114, edited by S. R. Chalise, A. Hermann, N. R. Khanal, H. Lang, L. Molnar and A. P. Pokhrel, Kathmandu, International Centre for Integrated Mountain Development, 1998.

# The Shape of Urban India and Some Security Concerns

*K. C. Sivaramakrishnan*

## Introduction

Urbanisation in India is neither unique nor exclusive but is part of a worldwide phenomenon. It is a manifestation of economic change and growth in agriculture, industry and services. According to the 2001 Census, the urban population of India is 285.35 million. The percentage is 27.78 per cent in 2001 as against 25.72 per cent in 1991, 23.73 per cent in 1981 and 20.22 per cent in 1971. But these figures alone do not portray the urban picture. The state-wise variations are significant. The pace and spread of urbanisation are not uniform. Among major states, Tamil Nadu's level of urbanisation is 43.86 per cent (27 million) followed by Maharashtra with 42.40 per cent (41 million), Gujarat with 37.35 per cent (19 million), and Karnataka with 33.98 per cent (18 million). The least urbanised states are Bihar with 10.47 per cent (8 million), followed by Assam with 14.9 per cent (3 million), Orissa with 14.9 per cent (5 million) and Himachal Pradesh with 9.79 per cent (0.6 million). Smaller states like Goa (49.77 per cent), Pondicherry (66.57 per cent) and the city-states of Delhi (93.01 per cent) and Chandigarh (89.78 per cent) are also highly urbanised.

Absolute numbers and physical patterns of urban growth are more important than arithmetical averages. There are 5161 urban centres in the country, a thousand more than the number in 1981. In 1991, about 71 million (33 per cent of the urban population) resided in 23 metropolitan cities each with a population of a million or more; another 68 million (32 per cent) were in the remaining 277 Class I cities. In comparison about 108 million (37.81 per cent) are now in 35 metropolitan cities, 88 million (31 per cent) in 358 other Class I Cities and the rest about 90 million in the remaining towns. According to a recent estimate, the number of these million plus cities will increase to 51 by 2011 and 75 by 2021. Thus the bulk of urban population will be living in metropolitan regions and other urban agglomerations, covering several municipal jurisdictions. These will emerge as a distinct feature of India's urbanisation. Most of these agglomerations will grow along transport corridors. Growth will be unrestrained by municipal jurisdictions; the distinction between urban and rural will get blurred.

### Urban Corridors

The emergence of transport corridors with a substantial increase in industrial investment, services, flow of goods and people along them has been a significant feature of spatial change in many countries in recent years. The north-eastern corridor in the US labelled as Megalopolis by the geographer, Jean Gottman some thirty years ago is a well-documented region but similar corridors have been emerging elsewhere. The phenomenon is not new but the spatial pattern emerging along such transport corridors needs careful attention. If the 'towns and cities' are merely urbanised stretches along the corridors, they will only be a shapeless mass and a creeping sprawl. Many of the transport-cum-urban corridors in India are of this nature. In some cases, trading centres and agricultural mandi towns, new industrial and service centres, may be distinct and even spectacular such as in Gurgaon or Panipat or Kota but do not necessarily reflect any harmonised pattern. The Prime Minister's national highways development project establishing a network called the 'golden quadrilateral' linking Delhi, Mumbai, Chennai and Kolkata as well as north south and east-west corridors, will reinforce this corridor type growth. This 5,851-kilometre project is heading for completion in December 2003. Transport and urbanisation will thus mutually reinforce each other.

Last time we took a serious look at the shape of India's

urbanisation was when the National Commission on Urbanisation (NCU) was set up in 1988. The NCU had identified 329 urban centres all over the country as generators of economic momentum (GEMs) where development activities should converge. The Commission also identified 49 Spatial Priority Urban Regions (SPURs). A subsequent study titled 'India-Urban Corridors' based on the 1991 Census by the National Atlas and Thematic Mapping Organisation (NATMO) identified 25 urban corridors at the country level. This was a diagnostic and descriptive delineation and was, therefore, different from the SPURs. The Centre for Policy Research (CPR) in a recent study (2001) looked at the evidence available in the past decade in the states of Maharashtra, Gujarat, Tamil Nadu, Karnataka and Andhra Pradesh. Investment data on industry and infrastructure obtained from government or CMIE data and the spatial changes as indicated by satellite imageries were used to discuss the spatial manifestation of urban growth. The findings of the study have reconfirmed the emergence of the earlier corridors as well as a few new corridors.

The prominent urban corridors of growth in the five states (Maharashtra, Gujarat. Tamil Nadu, Karnataka and Andhra Pradesh) covered in the CPR study are given in Table 1. The percentages of the state's urban population, which are located in these corridors is also indicated. It is important to note that about 80 per cent of the urban population in these states are to be found in these corridors. Tamil Nadu is an exception where the corridors account for about 60 per cent of the state's total urban population. While the CPR study is limited to five states, similar corridors have also emerged in the North, East and North-East of the country such as Ambala-Delhi, Amritsar-Mohali, Ratlam-Bhopal, Kolkata-Asansol or Shillong-Dispur. Here again the bulk of the urban population of the concerned states are located in the corridors. The maps in Annexures 1 and 2 will convey some idea about these corridors in the southern states and elsewhere.

## Metropolitanisation

In keeping with the global trends some major changes have taken place in the country. The liberalisation of economy has enabled a wider choice for investors in locating industrial and other economic activities. Agricultural development and productivity enhancement with increased incomes have given a spurt to off farm and non-farm jobs. This is in contrast to past history where urban growth has been mainly due to distress-induced migration. However, in the past two decades, we have seen districts like Ludhiana. Jullundhur, Karnal, Kurukshetra, Bardhamen, Krishna or Chenglepattu which are in the frontline of wheat and rice production in the country showing rates of urban growth higher than their respective states. This is the type of prosperity induced migration and urbanisation witnessed in other developed economies.

Industrialisation has continued to influence urban growth and a high level of urbanisation is associated with industrial development. Urban corridors have been attracting a substantial volume of economic activities as per CMIE's database providing details of investments in industrial and infrastructure projects. An analysis of total industrial and infrastructure investments based on this database containing information up to March 1999 has been shown in Table 3 in respect of five states included in the CPR study. Coastal corridors have emerged as the most preferred destinations for new investments in industry and infrastructure. These coastal corridors in Andhra Pradesh, Gujarat, Karnataka, Maharashtra and Tamil Nadu have attracted a high proportion of investment ranging from 40 to 76 per cent of the state's total industrial investment respectively. Other corridors like Mahesana-Ahmedabad-Surat-Valsad (29.29 per cent), Mumbai-Thane (23.73 per cent), Bangalore-Belgaum (38.66 per cent) and Chennai-Krishnagiri-Hosur (32.99 per cent) have also attracted significant industrial investments. Much of these new investments have been located in areas adjoining a large city rather than within the city itself. Such investments further increase the agglomeration aspect of the economy and consequent metropolitanisation

**Concentration of Investments**

It is useful to have an idea of the magnitude of such investments. In the coastal corridors of Saurashtra, i.e. Bhavnagar-Porbandar-Okha-Morvi-Bhuj investment in industry and infrastructure exceed 120,000 crores. This includes the vast petro-chemical complex of Reliance at Jamnagar. Investments made and proposed in Saurashtra exceed the figures of Maharashtra. Of course, Maharashtra had received equally large investments in earlier periods. Coastal corridors in Andhra, Karnataka and Tamil Nadu have also received massive investments.

Such scales of investments and their comparative concentration in urban corridors make them highly important parts of the country's economic assets. The safe upkeep of these assets and their competent performance are crucial to the country's economy. Such performance is needed both in times of peace and conflict. It can be argued that concentration increases the vulnerability of these assets in times of conflicts. But concentration is prompted by agglomeration economies and locational advantages. It is wishful thinking to seek dispersal of industries for security considerations. What is important is to ensure efficient performance of these concentrations, in terms of infrastructure, services, trade and industry, on a regular basis, rather than during times of crisis only.

**Infrastructure Deficiencies**

Regrettably, the infrastructure facilities required to support such large concentration of population has been lagging far behind the pace of urbanisation. Some industrial and residential enclaves may be the exception but most agglomerations and cities have severe shortages of water supply, sewerage, developed land, housing, transportation and other facilities. The level, quality and distribution of services have been very poor. Large segments of urban population do not have access to drinking water, sanitation, basic health services and education. These deficiencies have serious health impacts particularly affecting the urban poor. Deteriorating infrastructure, weak municipal institutions and poor delivery systems have constrained the urban economy and its ability to generate employment, incomes and services for the poor.

The periodic scarcity of water and the frequent conflicts over water between rural, urban and industrial users in Gujarat is an apt illustration of the problem of basic infrastructure. Gujarat as a whole is a water scarce area and past history shows that the State is affected by drought once or twice every five years. Rainfall varies from 1800 mm in Dangs to 300 mm in Kutch. Rajkot, Jamnagar, Junagadh, Amreli, Bhavnagar and Kutch have always been critical districts. Yet, Saurashtra has undergone one of the most spectacular transformations owing to industry and port development, but infrastructure problems persist. Ground water has been particularly scarce and extraction has been at unsustainable rates exceeding 60 per cent of the recharge. In other parts of Gujarat particularly along the Vadodara, Ahmedabad and Gandhinagar corridors ground water is increasingly saline due to over extraction. All large cities and industries have been looking towards Narmada Dam but in the absence of water management and conservation, the urban and industrial consumers in Gujarat may be very simply drinking tomorrow's water, today. Alternate sources have been developed in some cases such as desalination of seawater as in the Reliance Petro Chemical complex but frequently they have to make available some of this water to neighbouring municipalities because of their absolute scarcity. Conflicts over water between riparian parties have also turned violent in the past.

Turning our attention to another part of the country the situation is not very different in the Delhi-Agra or Delhi-Ambala corridors. For most of its length from Yamunanagar downwards, the river Yamuna is a veritable ditch heavily polluted. Delhi itself has an insatiable demand requiring that Haryana, Himachal and Uttaranchal should meet its needs by providing water from the upper Ganga and upper Yamuna canals as well as far removed sources like Renuka and Kishau Dams in Himachal. Delhi being a rich city may be able to buy its way out temporarily but it also discharges 70 per cent of the water consumed as untreated waste downstream which has rendered surface and ground water in Mathura and Agra highly polluted. Besides, Delhi cannot withstand even brief periods of water scarcity being a highly vocal capital city. If this be the peacetime attitude its vulnerability in times of conflict and the inadequacy to cope with it, can be well imagined.

**Poor Connectivity within Corridors**

While connectivity itself has been a major reason for transport corridors to come into existence in the first place, the paradox is that subsequent growth has in fact reduced this connectivity. This is mainly because the movement of people and goods increase at a rate faster than what the infrastructure can accommodate. It is widely known that rise in incomes usually generate more travel trips. This in turn results in the increase of transport fleet as such. Where there is priority for public transport some balance is maintained between public transport and private transport vehicles. However, in India over the past decade the tilt has been heavily in favour of private transport considering the investment in vehicle manufacture as well as in the infrastructure being provided in many of our cities. Public policy pronouncements however, may be, contrary to this, but the scale of investment hardly match these promises. According to the data compiled by the Ministry of Transport, the total number of motor vehicles registered in the country rose from 337 lakhs in 1996 to 484 lakhs in 2000. Out of this, two wheelers alone increased from 232 lakhs to 239 lakhs, while cars, jeeps and taxis increased from 42 lakhs to 60 lakhs. The increase in buses, on the other hand, was much less in comparison from about 4.5 lakhs to 5.6 lakhs

Metropolitan cities and regions which have multiple nodes of residence and work have high demands of commuting traffic. Only in Chennai, Mumbai and Kolkata, there are at least suburban railway and rapid transit service in existence which account for a significant share of the transit volume. Most other urban agglomerations such as Bangalore, Hyderabad, Pune-Pimpri-Chinchwad or Gandhinagar-Ahmedabad-Vadodara corridors have very limited public transport facilities. The Delhi Union Territory as well as the larger national region which includes various centres like Gurgaon, Faridabad, Noida, Ghaziabad, Panipat, Rewari etc are heavily dependent on private transport. The motor vehicles break-up in some metropolitan cities given in Table 5 amply illustrates this. Within the Union Territory of Delhi itself there is a total of 33.34 lakhs vehicles as of 2000 out of which two wheelers are nearly 22 lakhs, cars about 9 lakhs, and buses about 38,000 only. In fact the total number of vehicles in Delhi exceed the totals of Chennai, Kolkata and Mumbai put together. The enormous increase in private vehicles makes significant demand on road space. Almost all the investments made in constructing flyovers and expressways are mainly for the benefit of these private vehicles. In contrast, the MRTS system has made only a belated start with a very limited line and as of now funding is limited to only the first line from Shahdara to Tees Hazari.

Public transport continues to suffer more because of distortions in taxation and charges for use of road space, which clearly benefit private vehicles. In many states motor vehicle taxes on cars still vary from Rs 200 to Rs 600 per year, while in some, one-time taxes are charged as in Haryana (Rs 1500), UP (Rs 5000), Delhi (Rs 3850 to Rs 7050), etc. These levels of taxation bear no relation to capital cost of the car or the extent of road space usage. Yet, in contrast, public transport vehicles including taxis and buses are charged on the basis of passengers on an annual basis. The incidence of taxation invariably falls more heavily on people using public transport rather than users of private cars.

This is yet another way by which public transport and its growth suffers which in turn adversely affects the performance of urban places and thereby increases their vulnerability in situations of conflict.

**Moving about in the Region**

What happens within the metropolitan city itself can be easily amplified to the region. Apart from infrastructure investment decisions, there are also serious distortions in taxation and pricing for road space use which clearly benefit private vehicles. With continued growth in and alongside the corridors per capita trip rates and trip lengths will steadily increase, often at a higher rate than population growth. Connectivity within the corridor will therefore have to be addressed with foresight and imagination. Transportation needs have to be examined carefully and new strategies formulated including demand management and multi nodal balance with the objective of providing maximum access at a minimum cost.

Connectivity in the urban corridors in terms of transportation network through secondary arterial roads is crucial. This will indeed help in redistribution of population as well as efficient patterns of urban development. In the absence of such a network, the urban corridor will experience an unprecedented volume of traffic, both freight as well as passenger. In case of congestion and bottleneck near the metro cities, the likelihood of accidents, violence due to strikes, delays and unrest apart from undesired increase in fuel consumption as well as environmental hazards cannot be avoided. This will have a far-reaching impact not only on the quality of life but also in terms of economic development at the regional and national levels. In densely populated areas, the transport corridor will have environmental as well as rehabilitation and livelihood related impacts. The obstruction in traffic flow in the corridor can only be avoided through the development of secondary and tertiary road networks as well as linking all the settlements falling within the corridor.

The programme of 'golden quadrangle' now underway aims to bring the inter-city road traffic upto international standards. However, in the overall interest of the planned development of the areas along the corridor, it is essential to develop a sub-arterial system of road network simultaneously according to area-wise strategic plans.

### Violence and Social Vulnerability

Urban India has seen during the recent decades a significant increase in crime and incidents of communal conflicts. Metropolitan cities are increasingly becoming a melting pot for different strata of society. In some cases, there have been amalgamation and fusion. But in the majority of situations, separation of different groups and social strata is observed. Globalisation so far has aggravated rather than moderated inequalities. The rise in incomes and wealth has not been equitable and the differences have become sharper. If housing and access to service is considered more than a third of the urban residents are marginalised. The larger the city the greater and faster the slum growth in the city's core and the periphery. As the disparities widen unrest accumulates. Given the comparative ease of communication in metropolitan cities it becomes easier for dissent and dissatisfaction to spread.

These are not musings but facts borne out by the National Crime Record Bureau. In 1998 cognisable crime reported in Delhi was the highest (59,011) followed by Mumbai (30,017) and Bangalore (29,265). Crimes against women have also been high in the cities. Here again, Delhi takes the lead. Incidents of social unrest are prompted by circumstances as varied as hike in transport fares, water shortages, religious sentiments, political differences or even screening of a film or a play not liked by some.

These again are not extraordinary or unusual phenomena. Across the world whether in Rio de Janeiro or Caracas, Seattle or San Francisco, Lagos or Nairobi, Karachi, Mumbai or

Bangkok, unrest has become a recurring feature of urban life. To the extent the cities and the larger society are in a comparatively stable economic situation, they are able to recover: but retrieval is that much harder if the cities are beset by faltering economies and fractured institutions of governance.

As India's urbanisation grows, large cities become larger and more metropolitan corridors take shape, their future cannot be secured by a conventional approach to town planning and city management. In fact, security hardly features as a concern in urban planning, whether at the neighbourhood or the city level. It matters little whether such concern is focused on the internal or the external. Without addressing the first, the second is unlikely to be answered.

❖❖❖❖❖

**Table 1: Population of Urban Corridors in Major States-2001**

| S. No | Urban Corridor | Population 2001 | % urban population |
|---|---|---|---|
| **Gujarat** | | | |
| 1 | Mahesana- Ahmedabad- Surat-Valsad | 12,065,680 | 66.20 |
| 2 | Coastal Corridor-I (Bhavnagar-Porbandar-Okha) | 1,371,416 | 7.52 |
| 3 | Coastal Corridor-II (Okha- Morvi- Bhuj) | 782,042 | 4.29 |
| 4 | Ahmedabad-Rajkot-Junagadh | 2,137,490 | 11.73 |
| | **Total** | **16,356,628** | **89.74** |
| **Maharashtra** | | | |
| 1 | Mumbai-Thane | 17,781,449 | 43.35 |
| 2 | Mumbai-Nashik -Nagpur | 8,056,082 | 19.64 |
| 3 | Mumbai-Pune | 4,081,851 | 9.95 |
| 4 | Pune-Solapur | 1,476,352 | 3.60 |
| 5 | Pune-Kolhapur | 1,748,949 | 4.26 |
| 6 | Coastal Corridor (Mumbai-Raigad-Ratnagiri) | 139,419 | 0.34 |
| 7 | Pune- Aurangabad-Jalgoan | 1,370,438 | 3.34 |
| 8 | Aurangabad-Parbhani-Nanded | 1,193,922 | 2.91 |
| 9 | Solapur-Parbhani | 526,519 | 1.28 |
| | **Total** | **36,374,981** | **88.68** |
| **Andhra Pradesh** | | | |
| 1 | Hyderabad-Ananthpur-Hindupur | 7,182,888 | 35.03 |
| 2 | Hyderabad-Vijaywada | 2,321,250 | 11.32 |
| 3 | Hyderabad-Nizamabad-Adilabad | 854,931 | 4.17 |
| 4 | Coastal Corridor (Srikakulam-Vishakhapattam-Guntur-Nellore) | 5,353,828 | 26.11 |
| | **Total** | **15,712,897** | **76.63** |

| Karnataka | | |
|---|---|---|
| 1 Bangalore-Belgaum | 11,183,091 | 62.41 |
| 2 Mysore-Bangalore-Kolar | 2,871,165 | 16.02 |
| 3 Coastal Corridor (Mangalore-Udupi-Karwar) | 1,055,127 | 5.89 |
| **Total** | **15,109,383** | **84.32** |
| **Tamil Nadu** | | |
| 1 Chennai-Krishnagiri-Hosur | 7,495,922 | 27.52 |
| 2 Coimbatore -Salem-Krishnagiri | 3,577,975 | 13.13 |
| 3 Coastal Corridor-I (Chennai- Tanjavur-Karaikudi) | 3,535,535 | 12.98 |
| 4 Coastal Corridor-II (Tuticorin-Nagarcoil) | 1,383,098 | 5.08 |
| **Total** | **15,992,530** | **58.71** |

**Table 2: Population of Urban Corridors (Contd.)**

| S.No | Urban Corridor | Population 2001 (In Million) | % Urban Population to State's Urban Population |
|---|---|---|---|
| 1 | Amritsar-Jullundur-Ludhiana-Mohali | 3.90 | 47.29 |
| 2 | Ambala-Karnal-Panipat-Sonipat-Delhi | 1.45 | 23.65 |
| 3 | Delhi-Jaipur-Ajmer | 3.49 | 26.46 |
| 4 | Kolkata-Barddhaman-Durgapur-Asansol | 15.37 | 68.37 |
| 5 | Ranchi-Bokaro-Dhanbad-Kolkata | 2.92 | 48.77 |
| 6 | Brahmapur-Bhubaneshwar-Cuttack-Baleshwar | 2.17 | 39.55 |
| 7 | Shillong-Nongpoh-Dispur | 0.28 | 62.09 |
| 8 | Guwahati-Dispur | 1.13 | 33.19 |
| 9 | Ratlam-Indore-Bhopal | 6.53 | 40.56 |

## Table 3: Investments along Urban Corridors - 1999

*(Rs. in crore)*

| S.No | Urban Corridor | Total (Ind.+Inf.) | | Industry | | Infrastructure | |
|---|---|---|---|---|---|---|---|
| | | Invest-ment | % age | Invest ment | % age | Inves ment | % age |
| ***Gujarat*** | | | | | | | |
| 1 | Mahesana-Ahmedabad-Surat-Valsad | 89,448 | 40.60 | 22,585 | 29.29 | 66,863 | 30.35 |
| 2 | Coastal Corridor-I (Bhavnagar-Porbandar-Okha) | 113,660 | 51.59 | 53,687 | 69.62 | 59,973 | 27.22 |
| 3 | Coastal Corridor-II (Okha- Morvi- Bhuj) | 17,195 | 7.80 | 825 | 1.07 | 16,370 | 7.43 |
| 4 | Ahmedabad-Rajkot-Junagadh | 29 | 0.01 | 18 | 0.02 | 11 | 0.00 |
| | **Total** | **220,332** | **100.00** | **77,115** | **100.00** | **143,217** | **100.00** |
| ***Maharashtra*** | | | | | | | |
| 1 | Mumbai-Thane | 32,943 | 27.60 | 16,233 | 23.73 | 16,710 | 14.00 |
| 2 | Mumbai-Nashik-Nagpur | 15,306 | 12.82 | 10,446 | 15.27 | 4,860 | 4.07 |
| 3 | Mumbai-Pune | 15,46 | 2 12.95 | 12,703 | 18.57 | 2,759 | 2.31 |
| 4 | Pune-Solapur | 524 | 0.44 | 174 | 0.25 | 350 | 0.29 |
| 5 | Pune-Kolhapur | 4,158 | 3.48 | 441 | 0.64 | 3,717 | 3.11 |
| 6 | Coastal Corridor (Mumbai-Raigad-Ratnagiri) | 43,97 | 9 36.84 | 25,001 | 36.55 | 18,978 | 15.90 |
| 7 | Pune- Aurangabad-Jalgoan | 3,816 | 3.20 | 3,364 | 4.92 | 452 | 0.38 |
| 8 | Aurangabad-Parbhani-Nanded | 50 | 0.0 4 | 46 | 0.07 | 4 | 0.00 |
| 9 | Solapur-Parbhani | 3,140 | 2.63 | 0 | 0.00 | 3,140 | 2.63 |
| | **Total** | **119,378** | **100.00** | **68,408** | **100.00** | **50,970** | **100.00** |

| *Andhra Pradesh* | | | | | | | |
|---|---|---|---|---|---|---|---|
| 1 | Hyderabad-Ananthpur-Hindupur | 12,291 | 19.06 | 6,823 | 20.69 | 5,468 | 17.36 |
| 2 | Hyderabad-Vijaywada | 2,013 | 3.12 | 820 | 2.49 | 1,193 | 3.79 |
| 3 | Hyderabad-Nizamabad -Adilabad | 273 | 0.42 | 173 | 0.52 | 100 | 0.32 |
| 4 | Coastal Corridor (Srikakulam-Vishakhapattam- Guntur-Nellore) | 49,893 | 77.39 | 25,165 | 76.30 | 24,728 | 78.53 |
| | **Total** | **64,470** | **100.00** | **32,981** | **100.00** | **31,489** | **100.00** |
| *Karnataka* | | | | | | | |
| 1 | Bangalore-Belgaum | 17,711 | 34.55 | 7,212 | 38.66 | 10,499 | 25.56 |
| 2 | Mysore-Bangalore-Kolar | 5,683 | 15.04 | 171 | 0.92 | 5,512 | 38.98 |
| 3 | Coastal Corridor (Mangalore-Udupi-Karwar) | 25,840 | 50.41 | 11,273 | 60.43 | 14,567 | 35.46 |
| | **Total** | **49,234** | **100.00** | **18,656** | **100.00** | **30,578** | **100.00** |
| *Tamil Nadu* | | | | | | | |
| 1 | Chennai-Krishnagiri-Hosur | 37,391 | 39.82 | 20,730 | 32.99 | 16,661 | 53.66 |
| 2 | Coimbatore- Salem-Krishnagiri | 4,577 | 4.87 | 4,143 | 6.59 | 434 | 1.40 |
| 3 | Coastal Corridor-I (Chennai- Tanjavur-Karaikudi) | 45,439 | 48.40 | 34,835 | 55.43 | 10,604 | 34.15 |
| 4 | Coastal Corridor-II (Tuticorin-Nagarcoil) | 6,482 | 6.90 | 3,132 | 4.98 | 3,350 | 10.79 |
| | **Total** | **93,889** | **100.00** | **62,840** | **100.00** | **31,049** | **100.00** |

## Table 4: Total Registered Motor Vehicles in India

| Year | All Vehicles | Two Wheelers | Cars, Jeeps, and Taxis | Buses | Goods Vehicles | Others |
|---|---|---|---|---|---|---|
| 1996 | 3,37,83,000 | 2,32,52,000 | 42,04,000 | 4,49,000 | 20,31,000 | 38,47,000 |
| 1997 | 3,72,31,000 | 2,56,93,000 | 46,62,000 | 4,88,000 | 22,60,000 | 41,28,000 |
| 1998 | 4,09,39,000 | 2,83,42,000 | 50,56,000 | 5,35,000 | 25,29,000 | 44,77,000 |
| 1999 | 4,48,75,000 | 3,13,28,000 | 55,56,000 | 5,40,000 | 25,54,000 | 48,97,000 |
| 2000 | 4,83,93,000 | 3,39,13,000 | 60,42,000 | 5,59,000 | 26,81,000 | 51,98,000 |

Source: Motor Transport Statistics of India, 1999-2000

## Table 5: Registered Motor Vehicles in Major Metropolitan Cities - 2000

| Type of Vehicle | Bangalore | Chennai | Delhi | Kolkata | Mumbai |
|---|---|---|---|---|---|
| ***Transport Vehicles*** | | | | | |
| (A) Goods Vehicles | 32,190 | 32,411 | 212,705 | 59,576 | 53,980 |
| (B) Passenger | 83,755 | 49,425 | 142,480 | 50,532 | 171,675 |
| - Buses | 6,380 | 4,409 | 37,733 | 8,586 | 15,414 |
| - Taxis | 8,638 | 9,596 | 17,762 | 32,199 | 58,696 |
| - Others | 68,737 | 35,420 | 86,985 | 9,747 | 97,565 |
| **Sub-total (A+B)** | **1,15,945** | **81,836** | **3,55,185** | **1,10,108** | **2,25,655** |
| ***Non-Transport Vehicles*** | | | | | |
| Two wheelers | 11,64,204 | 8,48,118 | 21,84,581 | 2,98,959 | 4,07,306 |
| Cars | 2,30,388 | 1,99,848 | 8,69,820 | 2,38,560 | 3,03,108 |
| Others | 39,158 | 19,824 | 13,888 | 16,419 | 33,611 |
| Sub-total | 14,33,750 | 10,67,790 | 30,68,289 | 5,53,938 | 7,44,025 |
| **Total** | **15,49,695** | **11,49,626** | **34,23,474** | **6,64,046** | **9,69,680** |

Source: Motor Transport Statistics of India, 1999-2000

**Table 6: Share of Public Transport in Four Metropolitan Cities**

| City | Share of Public Transport (%) | Share of Suburban Railway (%) |
|---|---|---|
| Mumbai | 88.0 | 44.0 |
| Kolkata | 79.0 | 14.0 |
| Chennai | 67.0 | 16.0 |
| Delhi | 62.0 | 1.0 |

*India's Urban Sector Profile, Research Study Series - 61, NIUA, 1998.*

## Annexure - 1

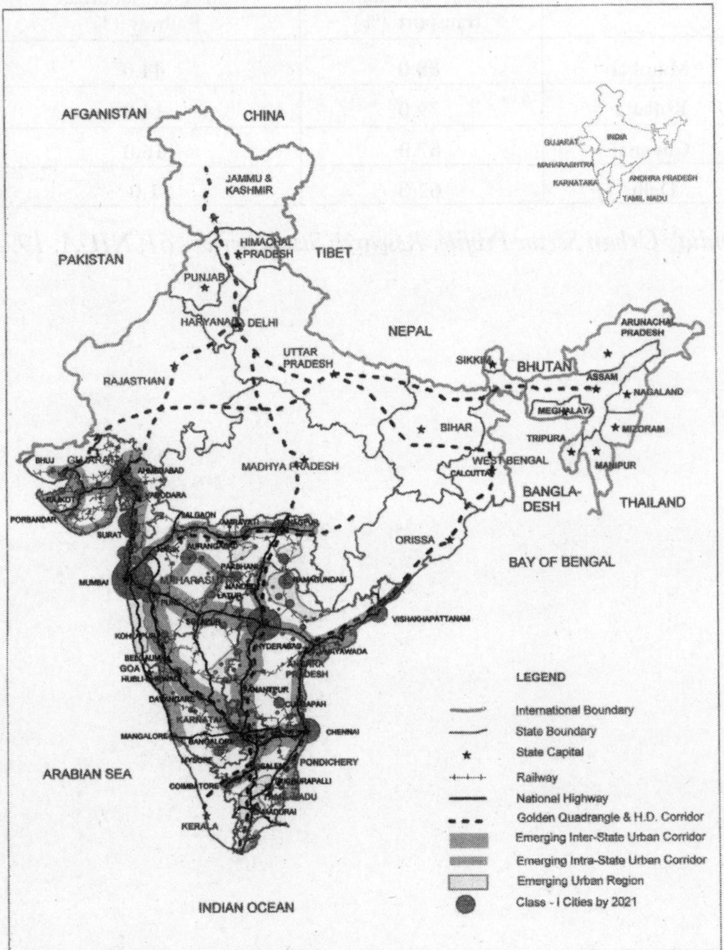


**EMERGING URBAN CORRIDORS IN SELECTED STATES**

GUJARAT, MAHARASHTRA , KARNATAKA, ANDHRA PRADESH & TAMIL NADU

## Annexure - 2

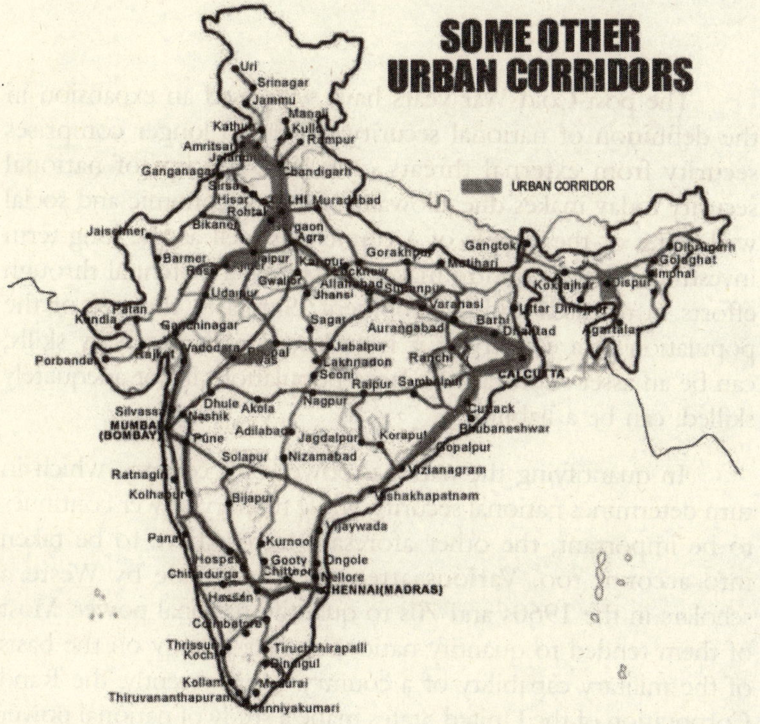
SOME OTHER
URBAN CORRIDORS
URBAN CORRIDOR
Uri
Srinagar
Jammu
Manali
Kullu
Rampur
Amritsar
Chandigarh
Ganganagar
Sirsa
Hisar
Rohtak
Muradabad
Bikaner
Agra
Jaisalmer
Barmer
Gangtok
Gorakhpur
Motihari
Gwalior
Jhansi
Udaipur
Varanasi
Patan
Kandia
Gandhinagar
Sagar
Aurangabad
Barhi
Vadodara
Jabalpur
Lakhnadon
Seoni
Ranchi
Porbandar
Rajkot
CALCUTTA
Raipur
Sambalpur
Silvassa
Dhule
Akola
Nagpur
Cuttack
Nashik
MUMBAI
(BOMBAY)
Bhubaneshwar
Pune
Adilabad
Jagdalpur
Koraput
Gopalpur
Solapur
Nizamabad
Vizianagram
Ratnagiri
Kolhapur
Bijapur
Vishakhapatnam
Vijaywada
Panaji
Kurnool
Hospet
Gooty
Ongole
Chitradurga
Nellore
CHENNAI(MADRAS)
Hassan
Coimbatore
Thrissur
Tiruchchirapalli
Kochi
Dindigul
Kollam
Madurai
Thiruvananthapuram
Kanniyakumari
Dibrugarh
Golaghat
Imphal
Kokrajhar
Dispur
Agartala

# National Security Index

*Satish Kumar*

The post-Cold War years have witnessed an expansion in the definition of national security which no longer comprises security from external threats only. The concept of national security today makes due allowance for the economic and social well-being of the people of a country as well as the long-term investment that a country makes in its power potential through efforts in research and development. Similarly, the size of the population of a country, if it is endowed with necessary skills, can be an asset. Contrarily, a large population, if not adequately skilled, can be a liability.

In quantifying the national power of a country, which in turn determines national security, while military power continues to be important, the other aforesaid factors have to be taken into account too. Various attempts were made by Western scholars in the 1960s and 70s to quantify national power. Most of them tended to quantify national power mainly on the basis of the military capability of a country. More recently, the Rand Corporation of the United States made a study of national power and came to the conclusion that national power should be measured on the basis of: i) National Resources (technology, enterprise, human resources, financial/capital resources, physical resources); ii) National Performance (infrastructure capacity, ideational resources); and iii) Military Capability (strategic resources, conversion capability, and combat proficiency).* It is obvious that all these factors are not quantifiable.

From the mid-1980s onwards, the Chinese scholars in consultation with the Chinese political leadership attempted to

---

* See Ashley J. Tellis, et.al., *Measuring National Power in the Postindustrial Age*, Rand-Arroyo Centre n.d., pp. 179-182.

determine the components of what they called comprehensive national power (CNP). According to the study conducted by Wang Songfen of the Chinese Academy of Social Sciences under the title: Comparative Studies of the Comprehensive National Power of the World's Major Nations, there should be eight major components of CNP, namely, Natural Resources, Domestic Economics, Foreign Economics, Science and Technology, Military Affairs, Government Capability, Foreign Affairs Capability, and Social Development.* Many of these factors again are not quantifiable.

Taking into account all these considerations, India's National Security Annual Review 2002 published a National Security Index (NSI) prepared by the National Security Council Secretariat of India. This was based on five variables, namely, defence capability, gross domestic product, human development levels, research and development levels, and the quantity and quality of population of different countries. This year's National Security Index prepared by INSAR is based on the same five variables except that the list of countries has been enlarged from 30 to 50, selected on the basis of highest defence expenditure in the descending order. Besides, the Defence Index (DI) this year is based not only on defence expenditure but also takes into account the number of personnel in armed forces with equal weightage given to both the factors. Further, the GDP Index (GDPI), although based on the same two factors, i.e. GDP and GDP growth rate, gives greater weightage to GDP growth rate than last year. This year's GDP Index gives 60 per cent weightage to GDP and 40 per cent to GDP growth rate as an important indicator of the potential economic strength of a country. The Human Development Index (HDI) has been taken as it is from the UNDP's Human Development Report 2002. This Index in itself is based on a number of sub-indices. The Research and

---

* See Michael Pillsbury, *China Debates the Future Security Environment,* Washington DC, National Defence University Press, January 2000, Chapter 5 titled "Geo-Political Power Calculations".

Development Index (RDI) takes into account three factors, i.e. the research and development expenditure incurred by a country as percentage of its GNP, the number of patents held by a country per million of its population, and the number of scientists and engineers of a country per million of its population. The weightage given to R&D expenditure is 60 per cent, whereas to patents and to the number of scientists and engineers it is 20 per cent each. The Population Index (PI) takes into account the size of population of a country, which is moderated by multiplying it with the Human Development Index (HDI) thereby arriving at a figure which is fairly representative of the quantity and quality both.

In the following tables, Table 1 gives the composite National Security Index and Table 2 gives the constituent five indices on which the National Security Index is based. Annexures 1 to 5 give details of each index for the 50 countries and the rank of each country in that Index. The sources from which data is taken are mentioned at the bottom of each Annexure.

Table 1: National Security Index

| Country | National Security Index | Rank |
|---|---|---|
| US | 0.687 | 1 |
| China | 0.551 | 2 |
| Japan | 0.481 | 3 |
| ROK | 0.404 | 4 |
| Sweden | 0.400 | 5 |
| Russia | 0.386 | 6 |
| Germany | 0.384 | 7 |
| India | 0.384 | 8 |
| France | 0.376 | 9 |
| UK | 0.358 | 10 |
| Israel | 0.352 | 11 |
| Switzerland | 0.344 | 12 |
| Australia | 0.334 | 13 |
| Netherlands | 0.324 | 14 |
| Norway | 0.321 | 15 |
| Canada | 0.320 | 16 |
| Denmark | 0.314 | 17 |
| Italy | 0.307 | 18 |
| Ukraine | 0.306 | 19 |
| Belgium | 0.304 | 20 |
| Austria | 0.297 | 21 |
| Spain | 0.291 | 22 |
| Egypt | 0.272 | 23 |
| Brazil | 0.267 | 24 |
| Greece | 0.266 | 26 |

| Poland | 0.258 | 25 |
|---|---|---|
| Iran | 0.257 | 27 |
| Singapore | 0.255 | 28 |
| Belarus | 0.255 | 29 |
| Portugal | 0.253 | 30 |
| Chile | 0.242 | 31 |
| Mexico | 0.238 | 32 |
| Finland | 0.233 | 33 |
| Vietnam | 0.230 | 34 |
| UAE | 0.225 | 35 |
| Uzbekistan | 0.223 | 36 |
| Thailand | 0.222 | 37 |
| South Africa | 0.221 | 38 |
| Venezuela | 0.220 | 39 |
| Oman | 0.219 | 40 |
| Argentina | 0.217 | 41 |
| Saudi Arabia | 0.216 | 42 |
| Malaysia | 0.214 | 43 |
| Kuwait | 0.213 | 44 |
| Columbia | 0.203 | 45 |
| Turkey | 0.202 | 46 |
| Algeria | 0.200 | 47 |
| Morocco | 0.198 | 48 |
| Pakistan | 0.193 | 49 |
| Angola | 0.136 | 50 |

Table 2: Constituent Indices of NSI

| Country | DI | GDPI | HDI | RDI | PI |
|---|---|---|---|---|---|
| Algeria | 0.026 | 0.256 | 0.697 | 0.000 | 0.022 |
| Angola | 0.025 | 0.246 | 0.403 | 0.000 | 0.005 |
| Argentina | 0.017 | 0.081 | 0.844 | 0.109 | 0.033 |
| Australia | 0.016 | 0.281 | 0.939 | 0.417 | 0.019 |
| Austria | 0.004 | 0.199 | 0.926 | 0.351 | 0.007 |
| Belarus | 0.016 | 0.274 | 0.788 | 0.197 | 0.000 |
| Belgium | 0.008 | 0.204 | 0.939 | 0.360 | 0.010 |
| Brazil | 0.074 | 0.230 | 0.757 | 0.133 | 0.141 |
| Canada | 0.019 | 0.242 | 0.940 | 0.396 | 0.002 |
| Chile | 0.018 | 0.239 | 0.831 | 0.110 | 0.013 |
| China | 0.570 | 0.423 | 0.726 | 0.034 | 1.000 |
| Columbia | 0.033 | 0.206 | 0.772 | 0.000 | 0.003 |
| Denmark | 0.003 | 0.195 | 0.926 | 0.441 | 0.005 |
| Egypt | 0.098 | 0.253 | 0.642 | 0.320 | 0.045 |
| Finland | 0.004 | 0.187 | 0.930 | 0.038 | 0.004 |
| France | 0.105 | 0.290 | 0.928 | 0.497 | 0.059 |
| Germany | 0.104 | 0.283 | 0.925 | 0.526 | 0.082 |
| Greece | 0.038 | 0.275 | 0.885 | 0.121 | 0.009 |
| India | 0.292 | 0.303 | 0.577 | 0.101 | 0.645 |
| Iran | 0.114 | 0.300 | 0.721 | 0.103 | 0.050 |
| Israel | 0.046 | 0.152 | 0.896 | 0.662 | 0.005 |
| Italy | 0.077 | 0.273 | 0.913 | 0.214 | 0.056 |
| Japan | 0.108 | 0.392 | 0.933 | 0.842 | 0.128 |
| Kuwait | 0.006 | 0.235 | 0.813 | 0.009 | 0.001 |

| Malaysia | 0.022 | 0.177 | 0.782 | 0.069 | 0.019 |
|---|---|---|---|---|---|
| Mexico | 0.046 | 0.190 | 0.796 | 0.072 | 0.085 |
| Morocco | 0.040 | 0.328 | 0.602 | 0.001 | 0.018 |
| Netherlands | 0.015 | 0.213 | 0.935 | 0.454 | 0.001 |
| Norway | 0.005 | 0.200 | 0.942 | 0.454 | 0.004 |
| Oman | 0.008 | 0.333 | 0.751 | 0.000 | 0.001 |
| Pakistan | 0.133 | 0.254 | 0.499 | 0.003 | 0.076 |
| Poland | 0.045 | 0.201 | 0.833 | 0.175 | 0.034 |
| Portugal | 0.008 | 0.210 | 0.880 | 0.160 | 0.009 |
| ROK | 0.161 | 0.265 | 0.882 | 0.669 | 0.045 |
| Russia | 0.307 | 0.382 | 0.781 | 0.337 | 0.122 |
| Saudi Arabia | 0.076 | 0.229 | 0.759 | 0.000 | 0.017 |
| Singapore | 0.014 | 0.112 | 0.885 | 0.263 | 0.003 |
| South Africa | 0.017 | 0.226 | 0.695 | 0.135 | 0.032 |
| Spain | 0.037 | 0.269 | 0.913 | 0.198 | 0.038 |
| Sweden | 0.008 | 0.205 | 0.941 | 0.836 | 0.008 |
| Switzerland | 0.005 | 0.210 | 0.928 | 0.571 | 0.006 |
| Thailand | 0.064 | 0.215 | 0.762 | 0.020 | 0.050 |
| Turkey | 0.118 | 0.008 | 0.742 | 0.091 | 0.052 |
| UAE | 0.014 | 0.296 | 0.812 | 0.000 | 0.001 |
| UK | 0.095 | 0.302 | 0.928 | 0.409 | 0.059 |
| Ukraine | 0.068 | 0.413 | 0.748 | 0.260 | 0.039 |
| US | 0.795 | 0.793 | 0.939 | 0.618 | 0.288 |
| Uzbekistan | 0.009 | 0.283 | 0.727 | 0.076 | 0.019 |
| Venezuela | 0.015 | 0.240 | 0.770 | 0.055 | 0.020 |
| Vietnam | 0.104 | 0.286 | 0.688 | 0.011 | 0.058 |

**Defence Index: Annexure 1**

| Countries | Defence Expenditure (US$ m) 2001 | DE Index | Number in Armed Forces (000) | Armed Forces Index | Composite Index |
|---|---|---|---|---|---|
| Algeria | 3149 | 0.006 | 124 | 0.047 | 0.026 |
| Angola | 1470 | 0.000 | 130.5 | 0.050 | 0.025 |
| Argentina | 4408 | 0.010 | 70.1 | 0.024 | 0.017 |
| Australia | 6752 | 0.017 | 50.7 | 0.015 | 0.016 |
| Austria | 1471 | 0.000 | 34.6 | 0.008 | 0.004 |
| Belarus | 1960 | 0.002 | 82.9 | 0.029 | 0.016 |
| Belgium | 3017 | 0.005 | 39.4 | 0.010 | 0.008 |
| Brazil | 10511 | 0.029 | 287.6 | 0.119 | 0.074 |
| Canada | 7745 | 0.020 | 56.8 | 0.018 | 0.019 |
| Chile | 2841 | 0.005 | 87.5 | 0.031 | 0.018 |
| China | 46049 | 0.139 | 2310 | 1.000 | 0.570 |
| Columbia | 2861 | 0.005 | 158 | 0.062 | 0.033 |
| Denmark | 2409 | 0.003 | 21.4 | 0.003 | 0.003 |
| Egypt | 4318 | 0.009 | 443 | 0.186 | 0.098 |
| Finland | 1432 | 0.000 | 32.3 | 0.007 | 0.004 |
| France | 32909 | 0.098 | 273.7 | 0.113 | 0.105 |
| Germany | 26902 | 0.080 | 308.4 | 0.128 | 0.104 |
| Greece | 5517 | 0.013 | 159.2 | 0.063 | 0.038 |
| India | 14167 | 0.040 | 1263 | 0.544 | 0.292 |
| Iran | 4698 | 0.011 | 513 | 0.217 | 0.114 |
| Israel | 10375 | 0.028 | 163.5 | 0.065 | 0.046 |
| Italy | 20966 | 0.061 | 230.4 | 0.094 | 0.077 |

| Japan | 39513 | 0.119 | 239.8 | 0.098 | 0.108 |
|---|---|---|---|---|---|
| Kuwait | 5029 | 0.012 | 15.5 | 0.000 | 0.006 |
| Malaysia | 3249 | 0.006 | 100.5 | 0.037 | 0.022 |
| Mexico | 5733 | 0.014 | 192.8 | 0.077 | 0.046 |
| Morocco | 1315 | 0.000 | 198.5 | 0.080 | 0.040 |
| Netherlands | 6257 | 0.015 | 50.4 | 0.015 | 0.015 |
| Norway | 2967 | 0.005 | 26.7 | 0.005 | 0.005 |
| Oman | 2831 | 0.005 | 43.4 | 0.012 | 0.008 |
| Pakistan | 2395 | 0.003 | 620 | 0.263 | 0.133 |
| Poland | 3408 | 0.007 | 206 | 0.083 | 0.045 |
| Portugal | 2226 | 0.003 | 43.6 | 0.012 | 0.008 |
| ROK | 11165 | 0.031 | 683 | 0.291 | 0.161 |
| Russia | 63684 | 0.194 | 977.1 | 0.419 | 0.307 |
| Saudi Arabia | 24266 | 0.071 | 201.2 | 0.081 | 0.076 |
| Singapore | 4280 | 0.009 | 60.5 | 0.020 | 0.014 |
| South Africa | 1829 | 0.002 | 89.2 | 0.032 | 0.017 |
| Spain | 6938 | 0.018 | 143.5 | 0.056 | 0.037 |
| Sweden | 3898 | 0.008 | 33.9 | 0.008 | 0.008 |
| Switzerland | 2840 | 0.005 | 26.8 | 0.005 | 0.005 |
| Thailand | 1831 | 0.002 | 306 | 0.127 | 0.064 |
| Turkey | 7219 | 0.018 | 515.1 | 0.218 | 0.118 |
| UAE | 3070 | 0.005 | 65 | 0.022 | 0.014 |
| UK | 34714 | 0.104 | 211.4 | 0.085 | 0.095 |
| Ukraine | 4899 | 0.011 | 303.8 | 0.126 | 0.068 |
| US | 322365 | 1.000 | 1367.7 | 0.589 | 0.795 |
| Uzbekistan | 1764 | 0.001 | 52 | 0.016 | 0.009 |
| Venezuela | 1896 | 0.002 | 82.3 | 0.029 | 0.015 |
| Vietnam | 2351 | 0.003 | 484 | 0.204 | 0.104 |

Source: *Military Balance 2002-2003,* London, Oxford University Press, 2002

**Defence: Annexure 1a**

| Country | Composite Defence Index | Rank |
|---|---|---|
| US | 0.795 | 1 |
| China | 1.000 | 1 |
| Russia | 0.307 | 3 |
| India | 0.292 | 4 |
| ROK | 0.161 | 5 |
| Pakistan | 0.133 | 6 |
| Turkey | 0.118 | 7 |
| Iran | 0.114 | 8 |
| Japan | 0.108 | 9 |
| France | 0.105 | 10 |
| Vietnam | 0.104 | 11 |
| Germany | 0.104 | 12 |
| Egypt | 0.098 | 13 |
| UK | 0.095 | 14 |
| Italy | 0.077 | 15 |
| Saudi Arabia | 0.076 | 16 |
| Brazil | 0.074 | 17 |
| Ukraine | 0.068 | 18 |
| Thailand | 0.064 | 19 |
| Israel | 0.046 | 20 |
| Mexico | 0.046 | 21 |
| Poland | 0.038 | 22 |
| Morocco | 0.037 | 23 |
| Greece | 0.038 | 24 |
| Columbia | 0.033 | 25 |

| | | |
|---|---|---|
| Algeria | 0.026 | 27 |
| Angola | 0.025 | 28 |
| Malaysia | 0.022 | 29 |
| Canada | 0.019 | 30 |
| Chile | 0.018 | 31 |
| South Africa | 0.017 | 32 |
| Argentina | 0.017 | 33 |
| Australia | 0.016 | 34 |
| Belarus | 0.016 | 35 |
| Venezuela | 0.015 | 36 |
| Netherlands | 0.015 | 37 |
| Singapore | 0.014 | 38 |
| UAE | 0.014 | 39 |
| Uzbekistan | 0.009 | 40 |
| Oman | 0.008 | 41 |
| Sweden | 0.008 | 42 |
| Belgium | 0.008 | 43 |
| Portugal | 0.008 | 44 |
| Kuwait | 0.006 | 45 |
| Norway | 0.005 | 46 |
| Switzerland | 0.005 | 47 |
| Austria | 0.004 | 48 |
| Finland | 0.004 | 49 |
| Denmark | 0.003 | 50 |

## Defence: Annexure 1b

| Country | Defence Expenditure Index | Rank | Country | Armed Forces Index | Rank |
|---|---|---|---|---|---|
| US | 1.000 | 1 | China | 1.000 | 1 |
| Russia | 0.194 | 2 | US | 0.589 | 2 |
| China | 0.139 | 3 | **India** | **0.544** | **3** |
| Japan | 0.119 | 4 | Russia | 0.419 | 4 |
| UK | 0.104 | 5 | ROK | 0.291 | 5 |
| France | 0.098 | 6 | Pakistan | 0.263 | 6 |
| Germany | 0.080 | 7 | Turkey | 0.218 | 7 |
| Saudi Arabia | 0.071 | 8 | Iran | 0.217 | 8 |
| Italy | 0.061 | 9 | Vietnam | 0.204 | 9 |
| **India** | **0.040** | **10** | Egypt | 0.186 | 10 |
| ROK | 0.031 | 11 | Germany | 0.128 | 11 |
| Brazil | 0.029 | 12 | Thailand | 0.127 | 12 |
| Israel | 0.028 | 13 | Ukraine | 0.126 | 13 |
| Canada | 0.020 | 14 | Brazil | 0.119 | 14 |
| Turkey | 0.018 | 15 | France | 0.113 | 15 |
| Spain | 0.018 | 16 | Japan | 0.098 | 16 |
| Australia | 0.017 | 17 | Italy | 0.094 | 17 |
| Netherlands | 0.015 | 18 | UK | 0.085 | 18 |
| Mexico | 0.014 | 19 | Poland | 0.083 | 19 |
| Greece | 0.013 | 20 | Saudi Arabia | 0.081 | 20 |
| Kuwait | 0.012 | 21 | Morocco | 0.080 | 21 |
| Ukraine | 0.011 | 22 | Mexico | 0.077 | 22 |
| Iran | 0.011 | 23 | Israel | 0.065 | 23 |

| | | | | | |
|---|---|---|---|---|---|
| Argentina | 0.010 | 24 | Greece | 0.063 | 24 |
| Egypt | 0.009 | 26 | Columbia | 0.062 | 26 |
| Singapore | 0.009 | 25 | Spain | 0.056 | 25 |
| Sweden | 0.008 | 27 | Angola | 0.050 | 27 |
| Poland | 0.007 | 28 | Algeria | 0.047 | 28 |
| Malaysia | 0.006 | 29 | Malaysia | 0.037 | 29 |
| Algeria | 0.006 | 30 | South Africa | 0.032 | 30 |
| UAE | 0.005 | 31 | Chile | 0.031 | 31 |
| Belgium | 0.005 | 32 | Belarus | 0.029 | 32 |
| Norway | 0.005 | 33 | Venezuela | 0.029 | 33 |
| Columbia | 0.005 | 34 | Argentina | 0.024 | 34 |
| Chile | 0.005 | 35 | UAE | 0.022 | 35 |
| Switzerland | 0.005 | 36 | Singapore | 0.020 | 36 |
| Oman | 0.005 | 37 | Canada | 0.018 | 37 |
| Denmark | 0.003 | 38 | Uzbekistan | 0.016 | 38 |
| Pakistan | 0.003 | 39 | Australia | 0.015 | 39 |
| Vietnam | 0.003 | 40 | Netherlands | 0.015 | 40 |
| Portugal | 0.003 | 41 | Portugal | 0.012 | 41 |
| Belarus | 0.002 | 42 | Oman | 0.012 | 42 |
| Venezuela | 0.002 | 43 | Belgium | 0.010 | 43 |
| Thailand | 0.002 | 44 | Austria | 0.008 | 44 |
| South Africa | 0.002 | 45 | Sweden | 0.008 | 45 |
| Uzbekistan | 0.001 | 46 | Finland | 0.007 | 46 |
| Austria | 0.000 | 47 | Switzerland | 0.005 | 47 |
| Angola | 0.000 | 48 | Norway | 0.005 | 48 |
| Finland | 0.000 | 49 | Denmark | 0.003 | 49 |
| Morocco | 0.000 | 50 | Kuwait | 0.000 | 50 |

## GDP Index: Annexure 2

| Countries | GDP, 2001 (in $ bn) | GDP Index | GDP in % 2000-01 | GDP growth Index | Composite GDP Index |
|---|---|---|---|---|---|
| Algeria | 50.7 | 0.004 | 3.50 | 0.634 | 0.256 |
| Angola | 9.0 | 0.000 | 3.20 | 0.614 | 0.246 |
| Argentina | 269.0 | 0.026 | -3.70 | 0.163 | 0.081 |
| Australia | 380.0 | 0.036 | 3.70 | 0.647 | 0.281 |
| Austria | 189.0 | 0.018 | 1.00 | 0.471 | 0.199 |
| Belarus | 90.0 | 0.008 | 4.10 | 0.673 | 0.274 |
| Belgium | 227.0 | 0.021 | 1.10 | 0.477 | 0.204 |
| Brazil | 504.0 | 0.049 | 1.50 | 0.503 | 0.230 |
| Canada | 700.0 | 0.068 | 1.50 | 0.503 | 0.242 |
| Chile | 66.4 | 0.006 | 2.80 | 0.588 | 0.239 |
| China | 1200.0 | 0.117 | 7.30 | 0.882 | 0.423 |
| Columbia | 83.0 | 0.007 | 1.50 | 0.503 | 0.206 |
| Denmark | 161.0 | 0.015 | 0.90 | 0.464 | 0.195 |
| Egypt | 93.8 | 0.008 | 3.30 | 0.621 | 0.253 |
| Finland | 124.0 | 0.011 | 0.70 | 0.451 | 0.187 |
| France | 1300.0 | 0.127 | 2.00 | 0.536 | 0.290 |
| Germany | 1800.0 | 0.176 | 0.60 | 0.444 | 0.283 |
| Greece | 114.0 | 0.010 | 4.10 | 0.673 | 0.275 |
| India | 490.0 | 0.047 | 4.30 | 0.686 | 0.303 |
| Iran | 82.0 | 0.007 | 5.10 | 0.739 | 0.300 |
| Israel | 110.0 | 0.010 | -0.60 | 0.366 | 0.152 |
| Italy | 1100.0 | 0.107 | 1.80 | 0.523 | 0.273 |
| Japan | 4100.0 | 0.401 | -0.40 | 0.379 | 0.392 |
| Kuwait | 42.3 | 0.003 | 2.70 | 0.582 | 0.235 |

| | | | | | |
|---|---|---|---|---|---|
| Malaysia | 87.0 | 0.008 | 0.40 | 0.431 | 0.177 |
| Mexico | 617.0 | 0.060 | -0.30 | 0.386 | 0.190 |
| Morocco | 32.0 | 0.002 | 6.30 | 0.817 | 0.328 |
| Netherlands | 384.0 | 0.037 | 1.10 | 0.477 | 0.213 |
| Norway | 164.0 | 0.015 | 1.10 | 0.477 | 0.200 |
| Oman | 20.0 | 0.001 | 6.50 | 0.830 | 0.333 |
| Pakistan | 55.8 | 0.005 | 3.40 | 0.627 | 0.254 |
| Poland | 176.0 | 0.016 | 1.10 | 0.477 | 0.201 |
| Portugal | 111.0 | 0.010 | 1.60 | 0.510 | 0.210 |
| ROK | 422.0 | 0.041 | 3.00 | 0.601 | 0.265 |
| Russia | 1522.0 | 0.148 | 5.00 | 0.732 | 0.382 |
| Saudi Arabia | 176.0 | 0.016 | 2.20 | 0.549 | 0.229 |
| Singapore | 85.0 | 0.007 | -2.10 | 0.268 | 0.112 |
| South Africa | 112.0 | 0.010 | 2.20 | 0.549 | 0.226 |
| Spain | 588.0 | 0.057 | 2.80 | 0.588 | 0.269 |
| Sweden | 209.0 | 0.020 | 1.20 | 0.484 | 0.205 |
| Switzerland | 247.0 | 0.023 | 1.30 | 0.490 | 0.210 |
| Thailand | 112.0 | 0.010 | 1.80 | 0.523 | 0.215 |
| Turkey | 148.0 | 0.014 | -6.20 | 0.000 | 0.008 |
| UAE | 67.0 | 0.006 | 5.00 | 0.732 | 0.296 |
| UK | 1400.0 | 0.136 | 2.20 | 0.549 | 0.302 |
| Ukraine | 226.0 | 0.021 | 9.10 | 1.000 | 0.413 |
| US | 10200.0 | 1.000 | 1.20 | 0.484 | 0.793 |
| Uzbekistan | 70.0 | 0.006 | 4.50 | 0.699 | 0.283 |
| Venezuela | 130.0 | 0.012 | 2.70 | 0.582 | 0.240 |
| Vietnam | 33.0 | 0.002 | 4.70 | 0.712 | 0.286 |

Source: *Military Balance 2002-2003,* London, Oxford University Press, 2002

**GDP: Annexure 2a**

| Country | Composite GDP Index | Rank |
|---|---|---|
| US | 0.793 | 1 |
| China | 0.423 | 2 |
| Ukraine | 0.413 | 3 |
| Japan | 0.392 | 4 |
| Russia | 0.382 | 5 |
| Oman | 0.333 | 6 |
| Morocco | 0.328 | 7 |
| **India** | **0.303** | **8** |
| UK | 0.302 | 9 |
| Iran | 0.300 | 10 |
| UAE | 0.296 | 11 |
| France | 0.290 | 12 |
| Vietnam | 0.286 | 13 |
| Uzbekistan | 0.283 | 14 |
| Germany | 0.283 | 15 |
| Australia | 0.281 | 16 |
| Greece | 0.275 | 17 |
| Belarus | 0.274 | 18 |
| Italy | 0.273 | 19 |
| Spain | 0.269 | 20 |
| ROK | 0.265 | 21 |
| Algeria | 0.256 | 22 |
| Pakistan | 0.254 | 23 |
| Egypt | 0.253 | 24 |

| | | |
|---|---|---|
| Angola | 0.246 | 26 |
| Canada | 0.242 | 25 |
| Venezuela | 0.240 | 27 |
| Chile | 0.239 | 28 |
| Kuwait | 0.235 | 29 |
| Brazil | 0.230 | 30 |
| Saudi Arabia | 0.229 | 31 |
| South Africa | 0.226 | 32 |
| Thailand | 0.215 | 33 |
| Netherlands | 0.213 | 34 |
| Switzerland | 0.210 | 35 |
| Portugal | 0.210 | 36 |
| Columbia | 0.206 | 37 |
| Sweden | 0.205 | 38 |
| Belgium | 0.204 | 39 |
| Poland | 0.201 | 40 |
| Norway | 0.200 | 41 |
| Austria | 0.199 | 42 |
| Denmark | 0.195 | 43 |
| Mexico | 0.190 | 44 |
| Finland | 0.187 | 45 |
| Malaysia | 0.177 | 46 |
| Israel | 0.152 | 47 |
| Singapore | 0.112 | 48 |
| Argentina | 0.081 | 49 |
| Turkey | 0.008 | 50 |

## GDP : Annexure 2b

| Country | GDP Index | Rank | Country | GDP growth Index | Rank |
|---|---|---|---|---|---|
| US | 1.000 | 1 | Ukraine | 1.000 | 1 |
| Japan | 0.401 | 2 | China | 0.882 | 2 |
| Germany | 0.176 | 3 | Oman | 0.830 | 3 |
| Russia | 0.148 | 4 | Morocco | 0.817 | 4 |
| UK | 0.136 | 5 | Iran | 0.739 | 5 |
| France | 0.127 | 6 | Russia | 0.732 | 6 |
| China | 0.117 | 7 | UAE | 0.732 | 7 |
| Italy | 0.107 | 8 | Vietnam | 0.712 | 8 |
| Canada | 0.068 | 9 | Uzbekistan | 0.699 | 9 |
| Mexico | 0.060 | 10 | India | 0.686 | 10 |
| Spain | 0.057 | 11 | Belarus | 0.673 | 11 |
| Brazil | 0.049 | 12 | Greece | 0.673 | 12 |
| India | 0.047 | 13 | Australia | 0.647 | 13 |
| ROK | 0.041 | 14 | Algeria | 0.634 | 14 |
| Netherlands | 0.037 | 15 | Pakistan | 0.627 | 15 |
| Australia | 0.036 | 16 | Egypt | 0.621 | 16 |
| Argentina | 0.026 | 17 | Angola | 0.614 | 17 |
| Switzerland | 0.023 | 18 | ROK | 0.601 | 18 |
| Belgium | 0.021 | 19 | Chile | 0.588 | 19 |
| Ukraine | 0.021 | 20 | Spain | 0.588 | 20 |
| Sweden | 0.020 | 21 | Kuwait | 0.582 | 21 |
| Austria | 0.018 | 22 | Venezuela | 0.582 | 22 |
| Poland | 0.016 | 23 | SaudiArabia | 0.549 | 23 |
| Saudi Arabia | 0.016 | 24 | South Africa | 0.549 | 24 |

| Norway | 0.015 | 26 | UK | 0.549 | 26 |
|---|---|---|---|---|---|
| Denmark | 0.015 | 25 | France | 0.536 | 25 |
| Turkey | 0.014 | 27 | Italy | 0.523 | 27 |
| Venezuela | 0.012 | 28 | Thailand | 0.523 | 28 |
| Finland | 0.011 | 29 | Portugal | 0.510 | 29 |
| Greece | 0.010 | 30 | Brazil | 0.503 | 30 |
| South Africa | 0.010 | 31 | Canada | 0.503 | 31 |
| Thailand | 0.010 | 32 | Columbia | 0.503 | 32 |
| Portugal | 0.010 | 33 | Switzerland | 0.490 | 33 |
| Israel | 0.010 | 34 | Sweden | 0.484 | 34 |
| Egypt | 0.008 | 35 | US | 0.484 | 35 |
| Belarus | 0.008 | 36 | Belgium | 0.477 | 36 |
| Malaysia | 0.008 | 37 | Netherlands | 0.477 | 37 |
| Singapore | 0.007 | 38 | Norway | 0.477 | 38 |
| Columbia | 0.007 | 39 | Poland | 0.477 | 39 |
| Iran | 0.007 | 40 | Austria | 0.471 | 40 |
| Uzbekistan | 0.006 | 41 | Denmark | 0.464 | 41 |
| UAE | 0.006 | 42 | Finland | 0.451 | 42 |
| Chile | 0.006 | 43 | Germany | 0.444 | 43 |
| Pakistan | 0.005 | 44 | Malaysia | 0.431 | 44 |
| Algeria | 0.004 | 45 | Mexico | 0.386 | 45 |
| Kuwait | 0.003 | 46 | Japan | 0.379 | 46 |
| Vietnam | 0.002 | 47 | Israel | 0.366 | 47 |
| Morocco | 0.002 | 48 | Singapore | 0.268 | 48 |
| Oman | 0.001 | 49 | Argentina | 0.163 | 49 |
| Angola | 0.000 | 50 | Turkey | 0.000 | 50 |

**Human Development Index: Annexure 3**

| Country | HDI |
|---|---|
| Algeria | 0.697 |
| Angola | 0.403 |
| Argentina | 0.844 |
| Australia | 0.939 |
| Austria | 0.926 |
| Belarus | 0.788 |
| Belgium | 0.939 |
| Brazil | 0.757 |
| Canada | 0.94 |
| Chile | 0.831 |
| China | 0.726 |
| Columbia | 0.772 |
| Denmark | 0.926 |
| Egypt | 0.642 |
| Finland | 0.93 |
| France | 0.928 |
| Germany | 0.925 |
| Greece | 0.885 |
| India | 0.577 |
| Iran | 0.721 |
| Israel | 0.896 |
| Italy | 0.913 |
| Japan | 0.933 |
| Kuwait | 0.813 |
| Malaysia | 0.782 |

| Country | HDI Index | Rank |
|---|---|---|
| Norway | 0.942 | 1 |
| Sweden | 0.941 | 2 |
| Canada | 0.94 | 3 |
| Australia | 0.939 | 4 |
| Belgium | 0.939 | 5 |
| US | 0.939 | 6 |
| Netherlands | 0.935 | 7 |
| Japan | 0.933 | 8 |
| Finland | 0.93 | 9 |
| France | 0.928 | 10 |
| Switzerland | 0.928 | 11 |
| UK | 0.928 | 12 |
| Austria | 0.926 | 13 |
| Denmark | 0.926 | 14 |
| Germany | 0.925 | 15 |
| Italy | 0.913 | 16 |
| Spain | 0.913 | 17 |
| Israel | 0.896 | 18 |
| Greece | 0.885 | 19 |
| Singapore | 0.885 | 20 |
| ROK | 0.882 | 21 |
| Portugal | 0.88 | 22 |
| Argentina | 0.844 | 23 |
| Poland | 0.833 | 24 |
| Chile | 0.831 | 26 |

| | |
|---|---|
| Mexico | 0.796 |
| Morocco | 0.602 |
| Netherlands | 0.935 |
| Norway | 0.942 |
| Oman | 0.751 |
| Pakistan | 0.499 |
| Poland | 0.833 |
| Portugal | 0.88 |
| ROK | 0.882 |
| Russia | 0.781 |
| Saudi Arabia | 0.759 |
| Singapore | 0.885 |
| South Africa | 0.695 |
| Spain | 0.913 |
| Sweden | 0.941 |
| Switzerland | 0.928 |
| Thailand | 0.762 |
| Turkey | 0.742 |
| UAE | 0.812 |
| UK | 0.928 |
| Ukraine | 0.748 |
| US | 0.939 |
| Uzbekistan | 0.727 |
| Venezuela | 0.77 |
| Vietnam | 0.688 |

| | | |
|---|---|---|
| Kuwait | 0.813 | 25 |
| UAE | 0.812 | 27 |
| Mexico | 0.796 | 28 |
| Belarus | 0.788 | 29 |
| Malaysia | 0.782 | 30 |
| Russia | 0.781 | 31 |
| Columbia | 0.772 | 32 |
| Venezuela | 0.77 | 33 |
| Thailand | 0.762 | 34 |
| Saudi Arabia | 0.759 | 35 |
| Brazil | 0.757 | 36 |
| Oman | 0.751 | 37 |
| Ukraine | 0.748 | 38 |
| Turkey | 0.742 | 39 |
| Uzbekistan | 0.727 | 40 |
| China | 0.726 | 41 |
| Iran | 0.721 | 42 |
| Algeria | 0.697 | 43 |
| South Africa | 0.695 | 44 |
| Vietnam | 0.688 | 45 |
| Egypt | 0.642 | 46 |
| Morocco | 0.602 | 47 |
| India | 0.577 | 48 |
| Pakistan | 0.499 | 49 |
| Angola | 0.403 | 50 |

Source: UNDP, *Human Development Report 2002,* New Delhi, Oxford University Press, 2002

## Research and Development Index: Annexure 4

| Country | Research Development Ex.p (as % of GNP) 1990-2000 | R&D Exp. Index | Patent to residents per million, 1998 | Patents Index | Scientists & Engineers in R&D per million, 1990-2000 | Scientists and Engineers Index | R&D Index |
|---|---|---|---|---|---|---|---|
| Algeria | 0 | 0.000 | 0 | 0.000 | 0 | 0.000 | 0.000 |
| Angola | 0 | 0.000 | 0 | 0.000 | 0 | 0.000 | 0.000 |
| Argentina | 0.5 | 0.132 | 8 | 0.008 | 711 | 0.143 | 0.109 |
| Australia | 1.7 | 0.447 | 75 | 0.075 | 3320 | 0.669 | 0.417 |
| Austria | 1.6 | 0.421 | 165 | 0.166 | 1605 | 0.324 | 0.351 |
| Belarus | 0.6 | 0.158 | 50 | 0.050 | 2296 | 0.463 | 0.197 |
| Belgium | 1.6 | 0.421 | 72 | 0.072 | 2307 | 0.465 | 0.360 |
| Brazil | 0.8 | 0.211 | 2 | 0.002 | 168 | 0.034 | 0.133 |
| Canada | 1.7 | 0.447 | 31 | 0.031 | 3009 | 0.607 | 0.396 |
| Chile | 0.6 | 0.158 | 0 | 0.000 | 370 | 0.075 | 0.110 |
| China | 0.1 | 0.026 | 1 | 0.001 | 459 | 0.093 | 0.034 |
| Columbia | 0 | 0.000 | 1 | 0.001 | 0 | 0.000 | 0.000 |

| | | | | | | | |
|---|---|---|---|---|---|---|---|
| Denmark | 1.9 | 0.500 | 52 | 0.052 | 3240 | 0.653 | 0.441 |
| Egypt | 1.9 | 0.500 | 0 | 0.000 | 493 | 0.099 | 0.320 |
| Finland | 0 | 0.000 | 187 | 0.188 | 0 | 0.000 | 0.038 |
| France | 2.2 | 0.579 | 205 | 0.206 | 2686 | 0.542 | 0.497 |
| Germany | 2.3 | 0.605 | 235 | 0.236 | 2873 | 0.579 | 0.526 |
| Greece | 0.5 | 0.132 | 0 | 0.000 | 1045 | 0.211 | 0.121 |
| India | 0.6 | 0.158 | 1 | 0.001 | 158 | 0.032 | 0.101 |
| Iran | 0.5 | 0.132 | 1 | 0.001 | 590 | 0.119 | 0.103 |
| Israel | 3.7 | 0.974 | 74 | 0.074 | 1570 | 0.317 | 0.662 |
| Italy | 1 | 0.263 | 13 | 0.013 | 1322 | 0.267 | 0.214 |
| Japan | 2.8 | 0.737 | 994 | 1.000 | 4960 | 1.000 | 0.842 |
| Kuwait | 0 | 0.000 | 0 | 0.000 | 214 | 0.043 | 0.009 |
| Malaysia | 0.4 | 0.105 | 0 | 0.000 | 154 | 0.031 | 0.069 |
| Mexico | 0.4 | 0.105 | 1 | 0.001 | 213 | 0.043 | 0.072 |
| Morocco | 0 | 0.000 | 3 | 0.003 | 0 | 0.000 | 0.001 |

| | | | | | | | |
|---|---|---|---|---|---|---|---|
| Netherlands | 2 | 0.526 | 189 | 0.190 | 2490 | 0.502 | 0.454 |
| Norway | 1.7 | 0.447 | 103 | 0.104 | 4095 | 0.826 | 0.454 |
| Oman | 0 | 0.000 | 0 | 0.000 | 0 | 0.000 | 0.000 |
| Pakistan | 0 | 0.000 | 0 | 0.000 | 78 | 0.016 | 0.003 |
| Poland | 0.7 | 0.184 | 30 | 0.030 | 1460 | 0.294 | 0.175 |
| Portugal | 0.6 | 0.158 | 6 | 0.006 | 1583 | 0.319 | 0.160 |
| ROK | 2.7 | 0.711 | 779 | 0.784 | 2139 | 0.431 | 0.669 |
| Russia | 1.1 | 0.289 | 131 | 0.132 | 3397 | 0.685 | 0.337 |
| Saudi Arabia | 0 | 0.000 | 0 | 0.000 | 0 | 0.000 | 0.000 |
| Singapore | 1.1 | 0.289 | 8 | 0.008 | 2182 | 0.440 | 0.263 |
| South Africa | 0.6 | 0.158 | 0 | 0.000 | 992 | 0.200 | 0.135 |
| Spain | 0.8 | 0.211 | 42 | 0.042 | 1562 | 0.315 | 0.198 |
| Sweden | 3.8 | 1.000 | 271 | 0.273 | 4507 | 0.909 | 0.836 |
| Switzerland | 2.6 | 0.684 | 183 | 0.184 | 3058 | 0.617 | 0.571 |
| Thailand | 0.1 | 0.026 | 1 | 0.001 | 102 | 0.021 | 0.020 |
| Turkey | 0.5 | 0.132 | 0 | 0.000 | 303 | 0.061 | 0.091 |

| UAE | 0 | 0.000 | 0 | 0.000 | 0 | 0.000 | 0.000 |
|---|---|---|---|---|---|---|---|
| UK | 1.8 | 0.474 | 82 | 0.082 | 2678 | 0.540 | 0.409 |
| Ukraine | 1 | 0.263 | 84 | 0.085 | 2121 | 0.428 | 0.260 |
| US | 2.5 | 0.658 | 289 | 0.291 | 4103 | 0.827 | 0.618 |
| Uzbekistan | 0 | 0.000 | 25 | 0.025 | 1754 | 0.354 | 0.076 |
| Venezuela | 0.3 | 0.079 | 0 | 0.000 | 194 | 0.039 | 0.055 |
| Vietnam | 0 | 0.000 | 0 | 0.000 | 274 | 0.055 | 0.011 |

Source: UNDP, Human Development Report 2002, New Delhi, Oxford University Press, 2002

### Research and Development: Annexure 4a

| Country | R & D Index | Rank |
|---|---|---|
| Japan | 0.842 | 1 |
| Sweden | 0.836 | 2 |
| ROK | 0.669 | 3 |
| Israel | 0.662 | 4 |
| US | 0.618 | 5 |
| Switzerland | 0.571 | 6 |
| Germany | 0.526 | 7 |
| France | 0.497 | 8 |
| Norway | 0.454 | 9 |
| Netherlands | 0.454 | 10 |
| Denmark | 0.441 | 11 |
| Australia | 0.417 | 12 |
| UK | 0.409 | 13 |
| Canada | 0.396 | 14 |
| Belgium | 0.360 | 15 |
| Austria | 0.351 | 16 |
| Russia | 0.337 | 17 |
| Egypt | 0.320 | 18 |
| Singapore | 0.263 | 19 |
| Ukraine | 0.260 | 20 |
| Italy | 0.214 | 21 |
| Spain | 0.198 | 22 |
| Belarus | 0.197 | 23 |
| Poland | 0.175 | 24 |
| Portugal | 0.160 | 26 |

| | | |
|---|---|---|
| South Africa | 0.135 | 25 |
| Brazil | 0.133 | 27 |
| Greece | 0.121 | 28 |
| Chile | 0.110 | 29 |
| Argentina | 0.109 | 30 |
| Iran | 0.103 | 31 |
| India | 0.101 | 32 |
| Turkey | 0.091 | 33 |
| Uzbekistan | 0.076 | 34 |
| Mexico | 0.072 | 35 |
| Malaysia | 0.069 | 36 |
| Venezuela | 0.055 | 37 |
| Finland | 0.038 | 38 |
| China | 0.034 | 39 |
| Thailand | 0.020 | 40 |
| Vietnam | 0.011 | 41 |
| Kuwait | 0.009 | 42 |
| Pakistan | 0.003 | 43 |
| Morocco | 0.001 | 44 |
| Columbia | 0.000 | 45 |
| Algeria | 0.000 | 46 |
| Angola | 0.000 | 47 |
| Oman | 0.000 | 48 |
| Saudi Arabia | 0.000 | 49 |
| UAE | 0.000 | 50 |

## Research and Development: Annexure 4b

| Country | R & D Expenditure Index | Rank |
|---|---|---|
| Sweden | 1.000 | 1 |
| Israel | 0.974 | 2 |
| Japan | 0.737 | 3 |
| ROK | 0.711 | 4 |
| Switzerland | 0.684 | 5 |
| US | 0.658 | 6 |
| Germany | 0.605 | 7 |
| France | 0.579 | 8 |
| Netherlands | 0.526 | 9 |
| Denmark | 0.500 | 10 |
| Egypt | 0.500 | 11 |
| UK | 0.474 | 12 |
| Australia | 0.447 | 13 |
| Canada | 0.447 | 14 |
| Norway | 0.447 | 15 |
| Austria | 0.421 | 16 |
| Belgium | 0.421 | 17 |
| Russia | 0.289 | 18 |
| Singapore | 0.289 | 19 |
| Italy | 0.263 | 20 |
| Ukraine | 0.263 | 21 |
| Brazil | 0.211 | 22 |
| Spain | 0.211 | 23 |
| Poland | 0.184 | 24 |

| Belarus | 0.158 | 26 |
|---|---|---|
| Chile | 0.158 | 25 |
| India | 0.158 | 27 |
| Portugal | 0.158 | 28 |
| South Africa | 0.158 | 29 |
| Argentina | 0.132 | 30 |
| Greece | 0.132 | 31 |
| Iran | 0.132 | 32 |
| Turkey | 0.132 | 33 |
| Malaysia | 0.105 | 34 |
| Mexico | 0.105 | 35 |
| Venezuela | 0.079 | 36 |
| China | 0.026 | 37 |
| Thailand | 0.026 | 38 |
| Algeria | 0.000 | 39 |
| Angola | 0.000 | 40 |
| Columbia | 0.000 | 41 |
| Finland | 0.000 | 42 |
| Kuwait | 0.000 | 43 |
| Morocco | 0.000 | 44 |
| Oman | 0.000 | 45 |
| Pakistan | 0.000 | 46 |
| Saudi Arabia | 0.000 | 47 |
| UAE | 0.000 | 48 |
| Uzbekistan | 0.000 | 49 |
| Vietnam | 0.000 | 50 |

| Country | Patent Index | Rank | Country | Scient-ists Engineers Index | Rank |
|---|---|---|---|---|---|
| Japan | 1.000 | 1 | Japan | 1.000 | 1 |
| ROK | 0.784 | 2 | Sweden | 0.909 | 2 |
| US | 0.291 | 3 | US | 0.827 | 3 |
| Sweden | 0.273 | 4 | Norway | 0.826 | 4 |
| Germany | 0.236 | 5 | Russia | 0.685 | 5 |
| France | 0.206 | 6 | Australia | 0.669 | 6 |
| Netherlands | 0.190 | 7 | Denmark | 0.653 | 7 |
| Finland | 0.188 | 8 | Switzerland | 0.617 | 8 |
| Switzerland | 0.184 | 9 | Canada | 0.607 | 9 |
| Austria | 0.166 | 10 | Germany | 0.579 | 10 |
| Russia | 0.132 | 11 | France | 0.542 | 11 |
| Norway | 0.104 | 12 | UK | 0.540 | 12 |
| Ukraine | 0.085 | 13 | Netherlands | 0.502 | 13 |
| UK | 0.082 | 14 | Belgium | 0.465 | 14 |
| Australia | 0.075 | 15 | Belarus | 0.463 | 15 |
| Israel | 0.074 | 16 | Singapore | 0.440 | 16 |
| Belgium | 0.072 | 17 | ROK | 0.431 | 17 |
| Denmark | 0.052 | 18 | Ukraine | 0.428 | 18 |
| Belarus | 0.050 | 19 | Uzbekistan | 0.354 | 19 |
| Spain | 0.042 | 20 | Austria | 0.324 | 20 |
| Canada | 0.031 | 21 | Portugal | 0.319 | 21 |
| Poland | 0.030 | 22 | Israel | 0.317 | 22 |
| Uzbekistan | 0.025 | 23 | Spain | 0.315 | 23 |
| Italy | 0.013 | 24 | Poland | 0.294 | 4 |

| | | | | | |
|---|---|---|---|---|---|
| Argentina | 0.008 | 26 | Italy | 0.267 | 26 |
| Singapore | 0.008 | 25 | Greece | 0.211 | 25 |
| Portugal | 0.006 | 27 | South Africa | 0.200 | 27 |
| Morocco | 0.003 | 28 | Argentina | 0.143 | 28 |
| Brazil | 0.002 | 29 | Iran | 0.119 | 29 |
| China | 0.001 | 30 | Egypt | 0.099 | 30 |
| Columbia | 0.001 | 31 | China | 0.093 | 31 |
| **India** | **0.001** | **32** | Chile | 0.075 | 32 |
| Iran | 0.001 | 33 | Turkey | 0.061 | 33 |
| Mexico | 0.001 | 34 | Vietnam | 0.055 | 34 |
| Thailand | 0.001 | 35 | Kuwait | 0.043 | 35 |
| Algeria | 0.000 | 36 | Mexico | 0.043 | 36 |
| Angola | 0.000 | 37 | Venezuela | 0.039 | 37 |
| Chile | 0.000 | 38 | Brazil | 0.034 | 38 |
| Egypt | 0.000 | 39 | India | 0.032 | 39 |
| Greece | 0.000 | 40 | Malaysia | 0.031 | 40 |
| Kuwait | 0.000 | 41 | Thailand | 0.021 | 41 |
| Malaysia | 0.000 | 42 | Pakistan | 0.016 | 42 |
| Oman | 0.000 | 43 | Algeria | 0.000 | 43 |
| Pakistan | 0.000 | 44 | Angola | 0.000 | 44 |
| Saudi Arabia | 0.000 | 45 | Columbia | 0.000 | 45 |
| South Africa | 0.000 | 46 | Finland | 0.000 | 46 |
| Turkey | 0.000 | 47 | Morocco | 0.000 | 47 |
| UAE | 0.000 | 48 | Oman | 0.000 | 48 |
| Venezuela | 0.000 | 49 | Saudi Arabia | 0.000 | 49 |
| Vietnam | 0.000 | 50 | UAE | 0.000 | 50 |

## Population Index: Annexure 5

| Countries | Population, 2001 in'000 | HDI | Population x HDI | Population Index |
|---|---|---|---|---|
| Algeria | 30900 | 0.697 | 21537.3 | 0.022 |
| Angola | 13500 | 0.403 | 5440.5 | 0.005 |
| Argentina | 37500 | 0.844 | 31650 | 0.033 |
| Australia | 19400 | 0.939 | 18216.6 | 0.019 |
| Austria | 8100 | 0.926 | 7500.6 | 0.007 |
| Belarus | 1000 | 0.788 | 788 | 0.000 |
| Belgium | 10300 | 0.939 | 9671.7 | 0.010 |
| Brazil | 172600 | 0.757 | 130658.2 | 0.141 |
| Canada | 3100 | 0.94 | 2914 | 0.002 |
| Chile | 15400 | 0.831 | 12797.4 | 0.013 |
| China | 1271900 | 0.726 | 923399.4 | 1.000 |
| Columbia | 4300 | 0.772 | 3319.6 | 0.003 |
| Denmark | 5400 | 0.926 | 5000.4 | 0.005 |

| Country | Population Index | Rank |
|---|---|---|
| China | 1.000 | 1 |
| India | 0.645 | 2 |
| US | 0.288 | 3 |
| Brazil | 0.141 | 4 |
| Japan | 0.128 | 5 |
| Russia | 0.122 | 6 |
| Mexico | 0.085 | 7 |
| Germany | 0.082 | 8 |
| Pakistan | 0.076 | 9 |
| UK | 0.059 | 10 |
| France | 0.059 | 11 |
| Vietnam | 0.058 | 12 |
| Italy | 0.056 | 13 |

| | | | | |
|---|---|---|---|---|
| Egypt | 65200 | 0.642 | 41858.4 | 0.045 |
| Finland | 5200 | 0.93 | 4836 | 0.004 |
| France | 59200 | 0.928 | 54937.6 | 0.059 |
| Germany | 82200 | 0.925 | 76035 | 0.082 |
| Greece | 10600 | 0.885 | 9381 | 0.009 |
| India | 1033400 | 0.577 | 596271.8 | 0.645 |
| Iran | 64700 | 0.721 | 46648.7 | 0.050 |
| Israel | 6400 | 0.896 | 5734.4 | 0.005 |
| Italy | 57700 | 0.913 | 52680.1 | 0.056 |
| Japan | 127100 | 0.933 | 118584.3 | 0.128 |
| Kuwait | 2000 | 0.813 | 1626 | 0.001 |
| Malaysia | 23800 | 0.782 | 18611.6 | 0.019 |
| Mexico | 99400 | 0.796 | 79122.4 | 0.085 |
| Morocco | 29200 | 0.602 | 17578.4 | 0.018 |
| Netherlands | 1600 | 0.935 | 1496 | 0.001 |
| Norway | 4500 | 0.942 | 4239 | 0.004 |

| | | |
|---|---|---|
| Turkey | 0.052 | 14 |
| Iran | 0.050 | 15 |
| Thailand | 0.050 | 16 |
| ROK | 0.045 | 17 |
| Egypt | 0.045 | 18 |
| Ukraine | 0.039 | 19 |
| Spain | 0.038 | 20 |
| Poland | 0.034 | 21 |
| Argentina | 0.033 | 22 |
| South Africa | 0.032 | 23 |
| Algeria | 0.022 | 24 |
| Venezuela | 0.020 | 26 |
| Malaysia | 0.019 | 25 |
| Uzbekistan | 0.019 | 27 |
| Australia | 0.019 | 28 |
| Morocco | 0.018 | 29 |

| Oman | 2500 | 0.751 | 1877.5 | 0.001 |
|---|---|---|---|---|
| Pakistan | 141500 | 0.499 | 70608.5 | 0.076 |
| Poland | 38700 | 0.833 | 32237.1 | 0.034 |
| Portugal | 10200 | 0.88 | 8976 | 0.009 |
| ROK | 47600 | 0.882 | 41983.2 | 0.045 |
| Russia | 144800 | 0.781 | 113088.8 | 0.122 |
| Saudi Arabia | 21400 | 0.759 | 16242.6 | 0.017 |
| Singapore | 4100 | 0.885 | 3628.5 | 0.003 |
| South Africa | 43200 | 0.695 | 30024 | 0.032 |
| Spain | 39500 | 0.913 | 36063.5 | 0.038 |
| Sweden | 8900 | 0.941 | 8374.9 | 0.008 |
| Switzerland | 7200 | 0.928 | 6681.6 | 0.006 |
| Thailand | 61200 | 0.762 | 46634.4 | 0.050 |
| Turkey | 66200 | 0.742 | 49120.4 | 0.052 |
| UAE | 2600 | 0.812 | 2111.2 | 0.001 |
| UK | 59900 | 0.928 | 55587.2 | 0.059 |

| Saudi Arabia | 0.017 | 30 |
|---|---|---|
| Chile | 0.013 | 31 |
| Belgium | 0.010 | 32 |
| Greece | 0.009 | 33 |
| Portugal | 0.009 | 34 |
| Sweden | 0.008 | 35 |
| Austria | 0.007 | 36 |
| Switzerland | 0.006 | 37 |
| Israel | 0.005 | 38 |
| Angola | 0.005 | 39 |
| Denmark | 0.005 | 40 |
| Finland | 0.004 | 41 |
| Norway | 0.004 | 42 |
| Singapore | 0.003 | 43 |
| Columbia | 0.003 | 44 |
| Canada | 0.002 | 45 |

| | | | | |
|---|---|---|---|---|
| Ukraine | 49100 | 0.748 | 36726.8 | 0.039 |
| US | 284000 | 0.939 | 266676 | 0.288 |
| Uzbekistan | 25100 | 0.727 | 18247.7 | 0.019 |
| Venezuela | 24600 | 0.77 | 18942 | 0.020 |
| Vietnam | 79500 | 0.688 | 54696 | 0.058 |

| | | |
|---|---|---|
| UAE | 0.001 | 46 |
| Oman | 0.001 | 47 |
| Kuwait | 0.001 | 48 |
| Netherlands | 0.001 | 49 |
| Belarus | 0.000 | 50 |

Source: Population figures from *World Bank, World Development Report 2003*, Washington DC, 2003 and HDI from the UNDP *Human Development Report 2002*, New Delhi, Oxford University Press, 2002. Population figures for Oman and UAE are of 2000 and have been taken from the UNDP *Human Development Report, 2002.*

## Composite National Security Index (Without Population Index): Annexure 6

| Country | DI | GDPI | HDI | RDI |
|---|---|---|---|---|
| Algeria | 0.026 | 0.256 | 0.697 | 0.000 |
| Angola | 0.025 | 0.246 | 0.403 | 0.000 |
| Argentina | 0.017 | 0.081 | 0.844 | 0.109 |
| Australia | 0.016 | 0.281 | 0.939 | 0.417 |
| Austria | 0.004 | 0.199 | 0.926 | 0.351 |
| Belarus | 0.016 | 0.274 | 0.788 | 0.197 |
| Belgium | 0.008 | 0.204 | 0.939 | 0.360 |
| Brazil | 0.074 | 0.230 | 0.757 | 0.133 |
| Canada | 0.019 | 0.242 | 0.940 | 0.396 |
| Chile | 0.018 | 0.239 | 0.831 | 0.110 |
| China | 0.570 | 0.423 | 0.726 | 0.034 |
| Columbia | 0.033 | 0.206 | 0.772 | 0.000 |

National Security Index

| Country | National Security Index | Rank |
|---|---|---|
| US | 0.786 | 1 |
| Japan | 0.569 | 2 |
| Sweden | 0.498 | 3 |
| ROK | 0.494 | 4 |
| Germany | 0.460 | 5 |
| France | 0.455 | 6 |
| Russia | 0.452 | 7 |
| Israel | 0.439 | 8 |
| China | 0.438 | 9 |
| UK | 0.433 | 10 |
| Switzerland | 0.428 | 11 |
| Australia | 0.413 | 12 |

| | | | | |
|---|---|---|---|---|
| Denmark | 0.003 | 0.195 | 0.926 | 0.441 |
| Egypt | 0.098 | 0.253 | 0.642 | 0.320 |
| Finland | 0.004 | 0.187 | 0.930 | 0.038 |
| France | 0.105 | 0.290 | 0.928 | 0.497 |
| Germany | 0.104 | 0.283 | 0.925 | 0.526 |
| Greece | 0.038 | 0.275 | 0.885 | 0.121 |
| India | 0.292 | 0.303 | 0.577 | 0.101 |
| Iran | 0.114 | 0.300 | 0.721 | 0.103 |
| Israel | 0.046 | 0.152 | 0.896 | 0.662 |
| Italy | 0.077 | 0.273 | 0.913 | 0.214 |
| Japan | 0.108 | 0.392 | 0.933 | 0.842 |
| Kuwait | 0.006 | 0.235 | 0.813 | 0.009 |
| Malaysia | 0.022 | 0.177 | 0.782 | 0.069 |
| Mexico | 0.046 | 0.190 | 0.796 | 0.072 |
| Morocco | 0.040 | 0.328 | 0.602 | 0.001 |
| Netherlands | 0.015 | 0.213 | 0.935 | 0.454 |

| | | |
|---|---|---|
| Netherlands | 0.404 | 13 |
| Norway | 0.400 | 14 |
| Canada | 0.399 | 15 |
| Denmark | 0.391 | 16 |
| Belgium | 0.378 | 17 |
| Ukraine | 0.372 | 18 |
| Austria | 0.370 | 19 |
| Italy | 0.369 | 20 |
| Spain | 0.354 | 21 |
| Greece | 0.330 | 22 |
| Egypt | 0.328 | 23 |
| Belarus | 0.319 | 24 |
| Singapore | 0.319 | 25 |
| India | 0.318 | 26 |
| Portugal | 0.314 | 27 |
| Poland | 0.313 | 28 |

| | | | | |
|---|---|---|---|---|
| Norway | 0.005 | 0.200 | 0.942 | 0.454 |
| Oman | 0.008 | 0.333 | 0.751 | 0.000 |
| Pakistan | 0.133 | 0.254 | 0.499 | 0.003 |
| Poland | 0.045 | 0.201 | 0.833 | 0.175 |
| Portugal | 0.008 | 0.210 | 0.880 | 0.160 |
| ROK | 0.161 | 0.265 | 0.882 | 0.669 |
| Russia | 0.307 | 0.382 | 0.781 | 0.337 |
| Saudi Arabia | 0.076 | 0.229 | 0.759 | 0.000 |
| Singapore | 0.014 | 0.112 | 0.885 | 0.263 |
| South Africa | 0.017 | 0.226 | 0.695 | 0.135 |
| Spain | 0.037 | 0.269 | 0.913 | 0.198 |
| Sweden | 0.008 | 0.205 | 0.941 | 0.836 |
| Switzerland | 0.005 | 0.210 | 0.928 | 0.571 |
| Thailand | 0.064 | 0.215 | 0.762 | 0.020 |
| Turkey | 0.118 | 0.008 | 0.742 | 0.091 |
| UAE | 0.014 | 0.296 | 0.812 | 0.000 |

| | | |
|---|---|---|
| Iran | 0.309 | 29 |
| Chile | 0.299 | 30 |
| Brazil | 0.299 | 31 |
| Finland | 0.290 | 32 |
| UAE | 0.280 | 33 |
| Mexico | 0.276 | 34 |
| Uzbekistan | 0.274 | 35 |
| Oman | 0.273 | 36 |
| Vietnam | 0.272 | 37 |
| Venezuela | 0.270 | 38 |
| South Africa | 0.268 | 39 |
| Saudi Arabia | 0.266 | 40 |
| Kuwait | 0.266 | 41 |
| Thailand | 0.265 | 42 |
| Argentina | 0.263 | 43 |
| Malaysia | 0.263 | 44 |

| | | | | |
|---|---|---|---|---|
| UK | 0.095 | 0.302 | 0.928 | 0.409 |
| Ukraine | 0.068 | 0.413 | 0.748 | 0.260 |
| US | 0.795 | 0.793 | 0.939 | 0.618 |
| Uzbekistan | 0.009 | 0.283 | 0.727 | 0.076 |
| Venezuela | 0.015 | 0.240 | 0.770 | 0.055 |
| Vietnam | 0.104 | 0.286 | 0.688 | 0.011 |

| | | |
|---|---|---|
| Columbia | 0.253 | 45 |
| Algeria | 0.245 | 46 |
| Morocco | 0.243 | 47 |
| Turkey | 0.240 | 48 |
| Pakistan | 0.222 | 49 |
| Angola | 0.169 | 50 |

# Acquisition of Arms and Military Technology by India and Its Neighbours*

*INSAR Research Staff*

## India

India's defence cooperation with Russia has been comprehensive including all aspects of defence equipment, aircrafts, missiles, ships and defence technology. There were a host of bilateral agreements between the two countries' defence industries. The contracts also include provisions for the joint research and development of next generation fighters along with other, as yet unspecified, weapons projects. The Indo-Russian Inter-Governmental Commission (IRIGC) for Military-Technical Cooperation created in 2002 is seen as a major landmark, which covers all major issues of procurement. The IRIGC protocol includes cooperation in developing fifth-generation fighters and the production of the jointly developed Brahmos anti-ship cruise missile. The Protocol agreement also envisaged a package of defence sales to India worth $3 billion. This included nuclear propelled submarines, strategic bombers and the setting up of joint ventures on the pattern of the supersonic Brahmos cruise missile. An agreement with Russia to jointly develop fifth-generation fighters as one of 12 Cooperative Projects has also been covered by the Protocol for Further Development of Military-Industrial Cooperation between Russia and India. The protocol agreed to establish service centers in India for logistics and product support for its military equipment. During the Third Meeting of the IRIGC on 8 January 2003 the two countries cleared several long-awaited contracts, including the acquisition of the aircraft carrier Admiral Gorshkov and the 'related' lease-purchase of two Akula (Bars) - Class Type 971 nuclear powered

* The information given in this chapter is derived from published sources (Editor).

submarines (SSNs) and four Tu-22M strategic bomber/maritime strike aircraft by the end of the fiscal year 2002-2003 in March. In another development, an agreement between the two reached on 3-5 December decided to set up a joint centre for the transfer of technology developed by the two countries to industries and other third countries.

On 21 June, the first batch of two-advanced SU-30MKI was delivered to India for induction into the Indian Air Force and in September another four was received. *The Hindu*, on 2 December, announced that India obtained "in-dept license" for the manufacture of Russia's most sophisticated SU-30MKI fighter plane including the advanced AL-31FP engine. Earlier in February, Russia also guaranteed with immediate effect, long term, uninterrupted spares supply as well as the creation of production facilities for critical items. Hindustan Aeronautics Limited, a Bangalore-based company signed an agreement, at Aero-India 2003, with Russia's Irkutsk Aviation Production Association to supply canards, tail fins, undercarriages and bay doors for the SU-30 MKI.

*Jane's Defence Weekly*, on 16 January, announced that the Indian Air Force fleet of 125 Mig-21 (BIS) is being upgraded under the Mig-21-93 standard programme, which is being carried out by Hindustan Aeronautics Limited (HAL) in cooperation with Sokol Nizhegorodsky Aviastroitelnyi Zavod Ao under a $340 million contract agreed in 1996. The first indigenously upgraded Mig-29-93 had successfully been test flown earlier. Presently, stealth modifications to the aircraft are reportedly being carried out. The principal features are a modernised avionics suite that includes the Phazotron Kopyo multi-mode radar and the ability to utilise advanced air-to-air and air-to-ground ordinance.

In February 2002, India and Russia reportedly signed a $700 million deal for 310 Main Battle Tanks, 124 of which are to be delivered in complete form while the rest are to be built at the Heavy Vehicles Factory in Avadi. Russian Deputy Prime

Minister, Ilya Klebanov, on 8 February, in New Delhi, announced that Russia would speed up supplies of 80 advanced T-90 tanks to India. Further, in a related development, a $73 million, T-72M1 MBT upgrade deal was also signed on 1 March with the Polish SKO-IT Drawa-T, for the Thermal Imaging Fire Control System (TIFCS).

Nuclear energy cooperation between the countries was also strengthened with the two countries signing an agreement on 7 November, to assist India in building two power reactors at Koodankulam in Tamil Nadu. Work, reportedly, had already begun at the Koodankulam station with the pouring of concrete on 31 March.

Defence cooperation between India and the United States has improved with the US lifting sanctions against India. One of the first indications of this development has been the US government's clearance, in February 2002, of the sale of Israel's Phalcon airborne early-warning system (AWACS) to India.

*Jane's Defence Weekly* reported in February that the Bush Administration cleared the sale of 20 US military items to India. A US military team that visited India on 20 February, an outcome of the renewed defence links between the two countries, cleared the sale of 40 General Electric F404-GE-F2J3 engines and advanced avionics for India's Light Combat Aircraft (LCA). During the period, negotiations for the sale of Raytheon AN/TPQ-37 Firefinder/weapon locating radar was also carried out. Further, the sale of submarine rescue facilities, and ground sensors and electronic fencing for use in Jammu and Kashmir state was negotiated. The US has also reportedly released in early February, 2003, an initial shipment of spare parts for the Indian Navy's 25-strong fleet of Sea King MK 42 anti-submarine warfare and utility helicopters.

*The Hindu*, on 8 December, reported that India's Mazagon Docks signed an agreement worth 1.8 billion Euro, in June, with the French Defence Electronics Group, Thales, for transfer of technology so that submarines can be built in India. On completion of the formalities, the deal will be the biggest ever deal by the Indian Navy for its shipyards at Mazagon Docks in Mumbai. Other deals with France include jointly developing and manufacturing a further development of the TM 333B Helicopter engine to power the locally designed, twin-engine Advanced Light Helicopter (ALH).

A report by *The Hindu*, on 8 October, announced that India, satisfied with the current batch of Israeli radars, has decided to purchase over 1000 more such mobile sensors at the cost of Rs. 350 crores. These systems to be used in conjunction with other hi-tech systems are expected to detect intrusions. The sensors are being purchased along with 8 Searcher-II unmanned aerial vehicles (UAVs) some of which could be used for detecting militants massed in low-altitude areas. Besides, Israeli technology will also be used for the armoured corps assets such as the T-72 tanks and armoured personnel carriers.

Further, on 8 January 2003, *Jane's Defence Weekly*, reported that Israel Military Industries will supply India with an unspecified quantity of Tavor 21 5.56mm assault rifles and Galil 7.62mm sniper rifles in an estimated $20 million deal signed earlier during the visit of the officials of the Indian Ministry of Defence Committee to Tel Aviv. The contract includes the provision of ammunition, night vision sights, laser range finders and other targeting equipment. The Tavor will replace the 5.56 M16 series of assault rifles currently in the service of the Indian Defence Forces.

India's recent development of indigenous armoured carrier includes the new Main Battle Tank (MBT) by amalgamating the turret from the locally designed Arjun MBT with the chassis of the Russian T-72 MIMBT, *Jane's Defence Weekly* reported on 6 March. Codenamed Tank EX, the Indian Defence Research and Development Organisation (DRDO) announced that the design had "successfully" undergone six months of trial in the Rajasthan desert region.

India is also reported to have carried out a series of test firings of the Russian Splav 300mm BM9A52 (12 round) Smerch Multiple Rocket System (MRS) in July 2002. With a range of more than 90 kms and enhanced warheads of high explosive and fuel-air explosive, the system is expected to considerably boost the firepower of the Indian army.

Bangalore-based Hindustan Aeronautics Limited (HAL), in April, is reported to have delivered 7 Advanced Light Helicopters (ALH), Dhruv two to the Air Force, three to the Army and one each to the Coast Guard and the Navy. Defence News reported on 9 September that the company will also begin undertaking mid-life upgrades for 100 Indian Air Force AN-32 transport aircrafts, including engine and avionics modifications in what is expected to cost around $200 million. The avionics modernisation includes installation of terrain-collision avoidance system and global positioning system navigation equipment. The modernisation will extend the service of the aircraft AI-20D engines and also increase the aircraft's range from 2200-3200 kms through the integration of two additional 3000-litre fuel tanks.

The second technology demonstrator (TD2) for India's long-delayed Light Combat Aircraft (LCA) has been flown at Bangalore, *Aviation Weekly & Space Technology* reported on 26 August. Once full production begins, the LCA is expected to replace India's aging fleet of some 450 Mig-21s.

The Indian air force will receive six refuelling aircraft currently being assembled in Ukraine, the Air Chief, S. Krishnaswamy, was reported to have revealed in October, the first batch of which would arrive in January 2003. Similar to the IAF Workhorse, the IL-76, the tanker has a more powerful engine and can also be used for ferrying troops and cargo. At the same time, the fuel acceptance capability of Jaguars, SU-30MKI and Mirage 2000 was being activated. Ten new Mirage 2000 fighters fitted with air-to-air refuelling capabilities are expected to arrive in India during September 2003.

India, on 12 November, inducted the first Fast Patrolling Vessel (FPV) CGH Sarojini Naidu into the Coast Guard to patrol the western region. This induction will specially check illegal activities in the region. Meanwhile, the India Navy is leasing four Russian aircraft for maritime patrol in the Indian Ocean.

It was reported in March 2002, that India made a breakthrough with regard to development of the indigenous cryogenic engine to replace the upper stage of the three-stage Geo-Synchronous Satellite Launch Vehicle (GSLV) with a 12 minute test firing of its 16, 875lb - 7u5 KN thrust CUSP liquid hydrogen-liquid oxygen engine. The Indian Space Research Organisation (ISRO) said that the engine would fly on the third GSLV. India, in October, also successfully launched the Technical Experiment Satellite (TES), which will give it independent access to high-resolution images from space. Security concerns in the wake of the Kargil conflict is supposed to have pushed India in this regard. In the missiles field, India successfully test-fired the 800 km medium-range Agni missile on 9 January 2003. India reportedly is in the advanced stages of further development of Agni II.

With regard to nuclear energy, India, on 18 September, started construction of two new 220 mw pressurised heavy water reactors at the Rajasthan Atomic Power Station (RAPS). With this, the total capacity of the six RAPS series of reactors is expected to reach 1180 mw.

**China**

China has developed a strong military cooperation with Russia. Instructive of this has been the host of defence agreements between the two. In a report by *Aviation Week & Space Technology*, on 3 June, China was reportedly developing a new active radar-guided beyond-visual-range air-to-air missile with technical support from Russia. The programme is codenamed Project 129 or R129. This will significantly improve the Chinese air force air-combat capability. In October, *Jane's Defence Weekly* reported that China will begin taking delivery from Russia of 4 Beriev A-50/A-50m/V (Mainstay) Airborne Early Warning and Control (AEW&C aircraft in a deal signed "a few months ago". In a related development, in February 2003, *Flight International* reported that China concluded a major $1 billion deal with Russia for additional acquisition of Su-30MKs. The latest batch of Su-30s will be equipped with the Zvezda KH-31A anti-ship missile and probably the new Raduga KH-59MK long-range anti-ship weapon.

In February, it was reported that China would buy two Russian-built Sovremenny Class destroyers. The new ships will be fitted with improved automated combat systems to counter surface vessels and will feature anti-ship, anti-submarine and air-defence capabilities. Each of the destroyers will carry a KA-27 helicopter. Further, Russia would also supply 8 kilo-class diesel electric submarines to China in a deal worth $1.6 billion signed on 3 May.

Complying with a new American demand, Israel suspended all contracts on the export of arms and security equipment to China. However, in January 2002, a Hong Kong-based company purchased two Israeli-built communications satellites in January, indicating renewed military contacts between Israel and China.

China has been focusing on indigenous production of defence equipment including aircrafts and ships. *Jane's Defence Weekly* reported on 27 February that China has begun indigenous construction, in Shanghai, of two major warships, although their type is not yet known. In March, China announced that it had completed the development of the JH-7A fighter for the Air Force, an improved version of the fighter/bomber JH-7, carrying the C-801K and Zvezda KH-31A anti-ship missiles. *Jane's Defence Weekly*, in December, reported that the Chengdu No. 611 Institute has reportedly completed conceptual design work on two advanced variants of its J-10 fighter aircrafts by enhancing its manoeuvrability through use of canards and engines with thrust-vectoring controls. During the same period, China also unveiled the Y-8 airlifter that it is developing with assistance from Ukraine's Antonov.

In January 2002, China reportedly released the China Cat a missile armed fast attack craft. Iran is believed to be its first customer. China Cat is 23m long and powered by two diesel engines with a maximum speed of about 50 kt. It has a lightweight surveillance radar at the top of the mast and an electro-optical director mounted on the platform. Four surface-to-surface missiles are mounted on the stern.

With regard to space technology, the successful launches of the Shenzhou series of spacecrafts has reportedly made it possible for China to launch humans into space. The Shenzhou IV spacecraft was successfully launched on 30 December 2002, and landed on the snow-covered Northern grasslands of Inner Mongolia, laying the solid foundation for the coming manned space mission. China's first manned spacecraft, Shenzhou V, has reportedly entered the overall assemblage testing phase. The Shenzhou is based on Russia's Soyuz spacecraft, but with a cockpit-equipped descent module that is 13 per cent larger.

In the nuclear power field, China's first CANDU Reactor, Qinshan-4, achieved criticality on 20 September, three weeks ahead of the project schedule. The Qinshan Phase III Project, located 80 miles from Shanghai includes two 728-Mwe CANDU 6 Units supplied by the Atomic Energy of Canada Limited. The first of the CANDU-6 pressurised heavy water reactors produced its first power to the grid on 20 November. According to Vendor Atomic Energy of Canada Ltd. (AECL), it is expected that the first unit will reach full power before the end of the year.

According to *Jane's Defence Weekly*, dated 4 September, China is to enhance its surveillance of the Taiwan Strait with the introduction of an aerostat-borne maritime patrol radar capability on the coast of its South Eastern Fujian Province. The new system comprises one Puma tethered aerostat to be supplied by Moscow's RosAero Systems Company and Sea Dragon Maritime Patrol Radar acquired from Leninets Holding Company of St. Petersburg.

**Pakistan**

As part of the continuing arms embargo, in the wake of Pakistan undertaking nuclear tests in May 1998, the Bush Administration announced that it will not transfer F-16 fighter jets bought years ago to Pakistan. However, in a report on 30 July, US surveillance equipment, including 3 fixed-wing planes and 5-armed helicopters worth $ 75 million was being shipped to Pakistan. *The Hindu* reported on 18 December that the US also handed over radio and communications equipment worth $4.5 million to Pakistan to enhance its security in what the US called an "appreciation" for being a "reliable ally" in the war against terrorism.

In February 2002, it was reported that Pakistan was expected to take delivery of the new generation F-7 series fighter aircraft from China in December. Totalling around 40 aircraft, the new F-7PG fighters were a further development of the Mig-21 with improved avionics and amore powerful engine than the Pakistan Air Force's current inventory of F-7MP Skybolt fighters. In a related development, *Jane's Defence Weekly* announced in January 2003 that Pakistan and China launched the production of the FC-1 lightweight fighter in an indication of increased defence cooperation between the two. The prototype FC-1 will be powered by a Russian supplied RD-93 turbofan engine and carry an Israeli-sourced EL/M-2032 airborne fire-control radar.

In a report in *The Hindu* on 11 June, Pakistan concluded a $100 million deal with Ukraine for 285 sets of engines and gearboxes for Pakistan's Al Khalid Main Battle Tanks (MBT). The 1200 hp engine reaches a maximum speed of 65 km/hr and can work reliably at air temperatures of upto 55 degrees centigrade.

The Pakistan Navy, in February, accepted its first Mesma air-independent propulsion system from Paris-based DCN International to power its three Agosta 903 submarines currently under construction. Pakistan had earlier bought one Agosta 90B submarine PNS Khalid from France in 1999 along with transfer of technology for two more such vessels along with AIP Systems. The submarine has four bow torpedo tubes, missiles and a combat electronics system.

In recent times, Pakistan has accorded considerable emphasis to the development of missiles. For the first time Pakistan tested a solid fuelled missile Ghaznavi (Haft-III), a 300 km medium range intermediate range missile capable of carrying a nuclear warhead in October 2001. It also test-fired the Hatf-IV medium range surface-to-surface missile for the second time in 5 days and said it was in continuation of the one conducted in October to "validate" certain additional parameters. It has been claimed that the ballistic missile could hit targets within a range of 750 kms. *The Hindu*, on 26 May 2002, reported that Pakistan successfully test fired the Hatf-V (Ghauri) Intermediate Range Ballistic Missile with a range of 1500-2000 kms and capable of carrying a nuclear warhead. Pakistan announced that the missile was indigenously built.

It has been reported that, Pakistan and Iran have decided to enhance defence cooperation covering the manufacture of small arms, ammunitions, artillery, tank ammunition, propellant and various kinds of explosives.

**Iran**

Iran's 25-year force modernisation programme has been oriented largely towards the purchase of Russian-made arms and military equipment. In February, the Russian RosoboronExport Armament Agency reportedly signed a $150 million contract with Iran for the delivery of 30 MI-171 military transport helicopters. Between 1-4 October, Iran signed an agreement with Russia for the upgradation of its armaments and the delivery of modern systems and equipment including air defence missile systems, anti-tank guided weapons and battlefield missile system (Tochka-V and Iskander-E). A $100 million contract for the delivery of 550 BMP-3 infantry combat vehicles was also being prepared during the period.

According to a *Jane's Defence Weekly* report of 4 September, Iran revealed a new surface-to-air missile (SAM) developed by the Air Defence Industries Group of the Aerospace Industries Organisation. Dubbed Shahab Thageb, the SAM is believed to have been in service with the air force for a number of years. The missile is guided by radio command to line-of-sight. The solid propellant single-stage rocket motor gives the missile a maximum speed of M2.2. The high explosive fragmentation warhead weighs 13.5 kg and is fitted with an infrared proximity fuse. The missile can engage targets to a maximum range of 12 kms, up to an altitude of 5.5 kms. *Jane's Defence Weekly*, on 4 December, reported that Iran's Aerospace Industries Organization (AIO) is working to develop and produce anti-ship missile systems in collaboration with China Aerospace Science and Industry Corporation, which includes both short-range C-701 and long-range C-802 missiles.

*Aviation Week & Space Technology* on 7 October reported that Iran developed and successfully tested a helicopter-launched anti-ship missile as part of its ongoing aim of creating an indigenous guided weapons industry. The missile called the Fajr-e Darya appears to be based on the obsolescent Italian Sea killer anti-ship missile. *Jane's Defence Weekly*, on 20 November, reported that advanced design work has already been completed for an all-new advanced trainer and attack aircraft, known as the Shafagh. The team working on the aircraft has already conducted wind-tunnel tests of the design using a 1/7-scale model and has also built a full-scale mock-up of the aircraft in Teheran.

Iran, on 26 May, carried out a fifth successful test flight and is reported to have begun serial production of its indigenously built Shahab 3 Medium Range Ballistic Missile (MRBM) with a range of 1300 kms. The engine reportedly relies on No Dong engines received from North Korea in 1999.

Iran's Aircraft Manufacturing Industries (HESA), in a *Jane's Defence Weekly* report of 18 December, is working with foreign partners, including Russia's Antonov, to develop two specialist military versions of the AN-140 commercial airliners the IR.AN 140 MP Maritime patrol and the IR.AN140 T C tactical transport.

In the nuclear field, Nucleonics Week, reported on 16 January that Iran has reportedly obtained design information to develop and construct gas centrifuges for uranium enrichment from Pakistan's nuclear programme, according to western intelligence sources.

**Afghanistan**

*Jane's Defence Weekly* reported on 10 April, that donors Bangladesh, China, Germany, India, Iran, Italy, Pakistan, Turkey, the United States and the United Kingdom pledged to create a 68,000-strong Afghan army in the post-Taliban period. Kabul had earmarked $235 million for military and security funding for 2002. The United States would provide an additional $278 million for this purpose.

Russia, on 6 September, during a visit by its Defence Minister, Sergei Ivanov, said that it would supply military transport aircraft, vehicles, communication equipment, spare parts as well as fuel and lubricants to Afghanistan. In addition, it also agreed to train Afghan junior officers in a Russian base in Tajikistan. Russia decided to provide all military aid gratis at first, but a paying arrangement was agreed to be worked out later, when the Afghan economy took off.

**Bangladesh**

Bangladesh, in July 2002, decided to dispose of 8 multi-role Mig-29 fighters because it could not afford the $1 billion a year needed for spare parts and maintenance. The Prime Minister, Khaleda Zia, announced on 16 July that "the country is losing money to keep them." *Daily Ittefaq* reported that the Prime Minister had already instructed the Air Force Chief to start the proceedings for the sale of the fighters.

Bangladesh's defence deals with China, signed in Beijing, in December, would not contain anything that would hurt the ties with India, the Foreign Minister, M. Morshed Khan announced in December to press persons.

**Myanmar**

Myanmar is expanding its naval facilities on Great Coco Islands, involving the construction of a jetty measuring 85m by 70m at a budgeted cost of 70 million Kyat ($11 million) with Chinese support. The project was launched with a foundation stone-laying ceremony, held on 4 November 2002.

In April 2002, it was reported that Myanmar was seeking to obtain the R-27 (NATO reporting name: A-10 Alamo) medium-to-long range, infrared and radar guided air-air-missile for 10 Mig-29 interceptor/ground attack fighters ordered in 2001.

*Nucleonics Week* reported on 25 October that Myanmar's attempt to develop atomic energy was cold-shouldered by the international community, when the International Atomic Energy Agency (IAEA) ignored a formal request to its Director General, Mohammad El Baradei, by Myanmar, for assistance in obtaining a research reactor. The IAEA said that they had no confidence that Myanmar either needs a reactor or has the infrastructure and funding required to support such a project.

## Nepal

In a report by *Flight International*, 24-30 September, PZL-Mielec delivered an M 28 Skytruck to Nepal. The Pratt & Whitney Canada PT6A-powered aircraft can carry 21 equipped soldiers and will be operated by the 11th Parachute Brigade, possibly replacing one of Nepal's two Shorts Skyvans. Nepal, the first Asian customer for the Skytruck, joins Poland and Venezuela as operators of the aircraft.

❖❖❖❖❖

# Indices of Violence in J&K

*Contributed by NSCS*

## Infiltration Index (Jan 2000 = 100)

| Months | 2000 | 2001 | 2002 | 2003 |
|---|---|---|---|---|
| January | 100 | 124 | 28 | 88 |
| February | 48 | 87 | 48 | 46 |
| March | 53 | 94 | 110 | 76 |
| April | 108 | 101 | 94 | 130 |
| May | 343 | 149 | 138 | 163 |
| June | 250 | 261 | 81 | 141 |
| July | 328 | 193 | 72 | 157 |
| August | 158 | 233 | 92 | 180 |
| September | 157 | 218 | 195 | 196 |
| October | 203 | 188 | 124 | - |
| November | 153 | 152 | 106 | - |
| December | 88 | 215 | 80 | - |

**Index of People Killed (Jan 2000 = 100)**

| Months | 2000 | 2001 | 2002 | 2003 |
|---|---|---|---|---|
| January | 100 | 104 | 142 | 96 |
| February | 100 | 119 | 95 | 67 |
| March | 127 | 121 | 150 | 124 |
| April | 125 | 140 | 158 | 125 |
| May | 149 | 161 | 163 | 144 |
| June | 175 | 155 | 120 | 127 |
| July | 132 | 205 | 138 | 125 |
| August | 210 | 199 | 167 | 138 |
| September | 187 | 203 | 186 | 182 |
| October | 168 | 209 | 167 | - |
| November | 168 | 213 | 139 | - |
| December | 106 | 153 | 106 | - |

**Index of Incidents (Jan 2000 = 100)**

| Months | 2000 | 2001 | 2002 | 2003 |
|---|---|---|---|---|
| January | 100 | 139 | 116 | 97 |
| February | 78 | 101 | 82 | 58 |
| March | 101 | 117 | 127 | 82 |
| April | 104 | 135 | 125 | 106 |
| May | 121 | 152 | 139 | 115 |
| June | 117 | 143 | 113 | 104 |
| July | 105 | 169 | 123 | 121 |
| August | 131 | 168 | 142 | 132 |
| September | 131 | 173 | 192 | 135 |
| October | 134 | 154 | 139 | - |
| November | 113 | 129 | 106 | - |
| December | 119 | 117 | 105 | - |

*NB: Calculated by NSCS on the basis of official figures.*

# II

# Chronology of Major Events

# Chronology of Major Events 2002

## United States

*Strategic Profile*

**16 January:** The US Secretary of State, Colin Powell, characterised President Musharraf's speech on 12 January as a historic one and hinted that he expected India to roll back some of the diplomatic sanctions on Pakistan, at a joint press conference with Pakistan's Foreign Minister, Abdul Sattar, in Islamabad.

**29 January:** President George W. Bush delivering his first State of the Union address to a joint session of the two houses of Congress stated that the USA would act against an 'axis of evil' formed by Iran, Iraq and North Korea. Bush accused the three countries of developing weapons of mass destruction and, in the case of Iraq and Iran, of harbouring and directing international terrorists.

**1 February:** Continuing the tough words on terrorism in his State of the Union Address on 29 January, the US President, George W. Bush, once again threatened countries that if they were deemed as backing terrorism, they would have to face justice.

**14 February:** In one of the clearest signals that the US's next target could be Iraq, the US President, George Bush, asked the State Department, Pentagon and CIA to draw up plans to remove the Iraqi President, Saddam Hussein.

**14 February:** The United States and Pakistan agreed to re-establish the Defence Consultation Group for reviving their close military relationship, the US Defence Secretary, Donald Rumsfeld, announced at the Pentagon after a meeting with the visiting Pakistan President, Pervez Musharraf, on 13 February.

**9 March:** Citing a classified Pentagon report, *The Los Angeles*

*Times* reported that the Bush administration had told the Defence Department to prepare, on a contingency basis, plans to use nuclear weapons against at least seven countries. The military was also directed to build smaller nuclear weapons for use in certain battlefield situations, the newspaper reported.

**10 March:** In an apparent damage control exercise, the US while confirming reports of preparing for possible nuclear attacks against seven countries including Russia, said the new guidance gives greater emphasis to potential use against China, North Korea and several "threatening" Middle Eastern states than against Moscow.

**13 March:** In a landmark move, the United Nations Security Council backed the idea of a Palestinian State after the United States surprised the Council by introducing a resolution to that effect.

**14 March:** The President, George W. Bush, declared that the Iraqi President, Saddam Hussein is a menace "and we're going to deal with him," and said Osama bin Laden — a man he once wanted dead or alive — has been reduced to a marginal figure in the war on terrorism.

**2 May:** The US Secretary of Defence, Donald Rumsfeld, and the Chinese Vice-President, Hu Jintao, on a visit to Washington, agreed to resume US-China military exercises, in cold storage since the downing of the US spy plane over South China Sea and the administration's later approval of a substantial arms package for Taiwan, which Mr. Jintao said would serve neither peace and stability nor the US-China relationship and the commitments of the two countries.

**28 May:** A new NATO-Russia Council came into being in Rome with Russia formally joining NATO in the presence of US President George Bush and Russian President Vladimir Putin.

**17 June:** *The Washington Times* reported that the US

President, George Bush has asked the CIA to use all necessary means to remove Mr. Saddam Hussein from power.

**1 July:** At the United Nations Security Council, the US exercised its veto to reject a six-month extension of the peacekeeping mission in Bosnia on the ground that American peacekeepers did not have immunity from the new Criminal Court.

**13 July:** A Pentagon report, submitted to Congress after it was signed by US Deputy Defence Secretary Paul Wolfowitz, has noted that China's short-range ballistic missiles and Russian-made submarines could threaten Taiwan. Secretary of State, Colin Powell, has affirmed that the report need not cause any concern.

**1 August:** At the ASEAN Regional Forum (ARF) at Bander Seri Begawan (Brunei), the US and ASEAN signed a joint declaration for cooperation to combat international terrorism. The US Secretary of State, Colin Powell, added that his country was "not looking for new bases or places at this time."

**10 August:** The Bush administration, making use of the provisions of the new anti-terrorism law, has warned that the countries which become members of the newly-constituted International Criminal Court without pledging to protect Americans serving in their countries could lose all American military assistance.

**6 September:** In a bid to build global coalition for his plans on Iraq, US President George Bush called up the Presidents, Jacques Chirac of France, Jiang Zemin of China, and Vladimir Putin of Russia. All three had voiced deep doubts about military action against Iraq.

**8 September:** The US President George Bush and the British Prime Minister Tony Blair, meeting at Camp David, Maryland, argued that the world must act against Mr. Saddam

Hussein, for he has flouted all UN resolutions over the past 11 years.

**12 September:** Addressing the UN General Assembly, US President George Bush challenged the UN to confront the threat from Iraq "decisively." Meanwhile, the UN Secretary General, Kofi Annan, addressing the General Assembly, argued that only the world body could authorise the use of force that goes beyond straightforward self-defence.

**12 September:** The US announced that it intended to rejoin the UN Educational, Scientific and Cultural Organisation (UNESCO) which it left in 1984, followed by the UK and Singapore in 1985, in protest against the organisation's then allegedly anti-US and anti-Western policies. The UK rejoined in 1997.

**20 September:** The US National Security Adviser, Condoleeza Rice, told reporters in Washington that the US intends to keep its military superiority in the world and will not allow another Soviet Union to rise to challenge that power.

**21 September:** The US President George Bush outlined a new security strategy that formally discards the strategy of deterrence. In his 35-page Annual Report to the Congress, America reserves the right to strike pre-emptively against emerging threats. The report further states that the US will not hesitate to act alone if necessary.

**27 September:** The US Secretary of State, Colin Powell, told the Senate Foreign Relations Committee in Washington that it would be irresponsible for the US not to consider the option of pre-emption and that perhaps pre-emption should be considered "more readily than we might (have) in the past."

**1 October:** The US Assistant Secretary of State for South Asia, Christina Rocca, made an unscheduled visit to Islamabad and met the Pakistan President, General Pervez Musharraf and the Minister of State for Foreign Affairs, Inamul Haq. They exchanged views on bilateral issues and the prevailing situation in the region. She called for a resumption of dialogue between India and Pakistan to defuse tensions in the region.

**2 October:** The White House spokesperson, Ari Fleischer, while talking about the various forms for the ouster of the Iraqi President, Saddam Hussein, remarked, "the cost of one bullet is cheaper and quicker than any military action." The White House clarified that there is no intent on the part of the Bush administration to relax the ban on assassinations in place through executive orders since 1976.

**4 October:** The US Under Secretary of State, John Bolton, and the Assistant Secretary of State for East Asia and Pacific Affairs, James Kelley, after talks in Beijing and Seoul, have stated that the US and its allies will bring the maximum pressure on North Korea to abandon its nuclear weapons programme.

**5 October:** The US State Department spokesperson, Richard Boucher, has observed that the Bush administration was disappointed with the testing of the Shaheen-I short-range ballistic missile by Pakistan and said that such tests further threaten regional and international security.

**8 October:** The US President, George Bush, in a television address from Cincinnati, Ohio, called the Iraqi leader Saddam Hussein, a "murderous tyrant", who may be planning to attack the US with chemical and biological weapons and warned that any delay in acting would spell disaster.

**11 October:** The US Congress has approved the use of military force against Iraq with a resounding majority of 77-23, in what was seen as a major foreign and national security policy victory for President Bush.

**16 October:** The White House spokesman, Ari Fleischer, has said that doctrines and policies have a 'local context' and that in the case of Iraq, it has to do with an "irrational" leader who has a history of using military force, who can acquire nuclear weapons and blackmail the world. He was responding to a question whether it would be lawful in the realm of international law for India and China to adopt the US policy on preventive attacks vis-à-vis Pakistan and Taiwan.

**16 October:** The US President has signed into law the Iraq resolution, which authorises the use of force, in a ceremony in the East room of the White House.

**28 October:** After meeting the Chinese President, Jiang Zemin, at his ranch in Texas on 25 October, US President George Bush declared that the US would enter into "a new dialogue on security issues" while staying engaged with China "through contacts at many levels." Mr. Jiang said that Sino-American relations should be seen from a "strategic height and with a long-term perspective."

**9 November:** The US President George Bush has said that the new UN Security Council Resolution 1441 which enjoins Iraq to hand over its weapons of mass destruction before 15 November was the final test for Mr. Saddam Hussein and urged all nations to pressure the Iraqi leader to comply with the resolution.

**12 November:** The US President George Bush has approved a tentative plan of the Defence Department that calls for a land, sea, and air force of up to 2,00,000 troops, ready to invade Iraq, ahead of the 15 November deadline for Iraq to disarm its weapons of mass destruction.

**20 November:** The US Senate has passed the Homeland Security Department Legislation by a margin of 90 to 9. This paves the way for the reorganisation of the Department of Defence, to form the Homeland Security Department by merging 22 federal agencies with a combined budget of $ 40 billion and a workforce of about 1,70,000.

**7 December:** As Iraq handed over a declaration containing details of its arms programme to the United Nations, the commander of US Central Command, Gen. Tommy Franks, arrived in Qatar to test a new mobile headquarters on the outskirts of Doha that could serve as the nerve-centre for a possible war against Iraq. Military exercises to test the capability of allied forces to launch a high-powered military campaign in the Arabian Desert would commence from this mobile headquarters from 9 December.

**11 December:** The Bush administration in a six-page White House document being sent to the Congress, titled the "National Strategy to Combat Weapons of Mass Destruction", has stated that the US will respond with "overwhelming force" in response to any attack with weapons of mass destruction on it, its troops or allies.

**14 December:** The US State Department spokesman, Richard Boucher, has affirmed that Iran was pursuing nuclear weapons development at the Natanz plant in central Iran. He urged Iran to cooperate fully with the IAEA and comply with its rules requiring complete disclosure of plan design information no later than 180 days before construction starts.

**18 December:** The US President has provided written legal authority to the CIA to hunt down and kill terrorists without seeking further approval each time the Agency is about to stage an operation, especially against terrorist leaders whose capture is impractical.

**20 December:** The US Secretary of State, Colin Powell, declared that Iraq had flagrantly violated the UN disarmament resolution 1441. Speaking to newspersons in Washington, he observed that the recently furnished Iraqi declaration was a "catalogue of recycled information and flagrant omissions."

**28 December:** The US ordered a major military force, comprising thousands of troops, two aircraft-carrier battle groups and scores of combat aircraft to the Persian Gulf in preparation for a possible war with Iraq.

***Relations with India***

**11 January:** The US intelligence apparatus, including the Central Intelligence Agency (CIA) and the National Security Agency, stepped up surveillance along the India-Pakistan border looking for deployment of nuclear arsenal by both countries, according to a report in *The New York Times*. However, an unnamed official was quoted as saying, "So far there is no evidence of that."

**13 January:** The United States President, George W. Bush, hailed the speech of the Pakistan President, Pervez Musharraf, delivered on 12 January and hoped that it would set the framework for a diplomatic solution to reducing tensions in the subcontinent.

**16 January:** The US Secretary of State, Colin Powell, on his South Asia trip, said India and Pakistan must focus on Kashmir by renewing a direct dialogue. These talks were more important than reducing tensions along the border by way of troop withdrawal, he told reporters travelling with him.

**22 January:** The US Secretary of State, Colin Powell, on a visit to India talked to the External Affairs Minister, Jaswant Singh and offered his sincere condolences to the families of those killed in the attack on the American Centre in Kolkata.

**23 January:** The United States President, Mr. George W. Bush, expressed concern about the violence in Kolkata where motorcycle-borne terrorists killed five policemen.

**25 January:** The US Secretary of State, Colin Powell, today lamented India's test of a short-range nuclear missile but added he did not believe it would further inflame tensions between India and Pakistan.

**20 March:** The US Central Intelligence Agency Director, George Tenet, said the chances of a war between India and Pakistan were the highest since 1971 and maintained that a conventional war between the two nations could escalate into a nuclear confrontation.

**28 March:** Even as the Prevention of Terrorism Act has come under severe criticism in India by the Opposition parties, the Bush administration has given its stamp of "approval" to the measure saying that India "seems" to have gone about the whole thing in a "constitutional way".

**2 April:** The Cabinet Committee on Security (CCS) has cleared a proposal envisaging joint patrolling by India and the United States of the strategic Malacca Straits. The Malacca Straits, which encompasses the Indonesian island of Sumatra on the one side and Malaysia, on the other, forms a vital channel through which an estimated $ 500 billion worth of trade is conducted annually.

**9 April:** The visiting US Assistant Secretary of State (South Asia), Christina Rocca, and the Joint Secretary (North) in the Ministry of External Affairs, Meera Shankar, held discussions on the Maoist insurgency in Nepal and the reconstruction of war-torn Afghanistan.

**23 April:** New Delhi has clarified that there is no joint patrolling of the Straits of Malacca by Indian and American navies but that an Indian ship, INS SHARDA, was just 'escorting' American vessels carrying 'high-value' cargo for the ongoing military operation in the Arabian Sea/ Persian Gulf.

**30 April:** The US International Trade Commission has imposed anti-dumping duties on the import of silico-manganese from India, Kazakhstan and Venezuela, arguing that the US was for free trade but only so long as its industry was not hurt.

**5 May:** In an exclusive interview to *The Hindu*, the US

Deputy Secretary of State, Richard Armitage, has said that infiltration from across the Line of Control (LoC) in Kashmir has declined recently.

**7 May:** The United States Commission on International Religious Freedom, in its annual report for 2002, has focused on the violence against minorities in India and urged the US government to pressure India to exercise its power to halt the atrocities and bring the perpetrators to justice. Ambassador Shirin Tahir-Kheli, one of the members of the Commission, averred that India is one of the two nations, the other being China, where the Commission has been barred from entering.

**21 May:** The State Department's *Report on Patterns of Global Terrorism for 2001* stated that though Pakistani support for organisations designated as 'Foreign Terrorist Organisations' has waned after 11 September, questions remained over whether President Musharraf's policy would be fully implemented and sustained.

**27 May:** According to *The New York Times*, Pentagon has estimated that a nuclear exchange between India and Pakistan would result in the "immediate death" of up to 12 million people.

**30 May:** US President George Bush told reporters in Washington that President Musharraf must stop incursions across the Line of Control and announced that he was sending his Secretary of Defence, Donald Rumsfeld, to the subcontinent early next week to reduce tensions.

**3 June:** Speaking at the "Asian Security Conference", organised by the International Institute of Strategic Studies (IISS) in Singapore, the US Deputy Defence Secretary, Paul Wolfowitz, maintained that the US sees India as a useful counterfoil to China and as an emerging strategic player in East Asia, and is encouraging New Delhi to increase its profile in the region.

**7 June:** The visiting US Deputy Secretary of State, Richard Armitage, told the Indian leadership that the American pressure on the Pakistan President to end cross-border terrorism had begun to yield results. At the same time, he stressed the American expectations of early reciprocal actions from India, which could lead to a step-by-step process of de-escalating the current India-Pakistan confrontation.

**12 June:** India conveyed to the visiting US Defence Secretary, Donald Rumsfeld, that it was willing to take more steps towards reduction of military tensions with Pakistan if Islamabad moved towards a comprehensive effort to end cross-border terrorism. Mr. Rumsfeld told reporters that there were 'indications' of Al-Qaeda terrorists operating near the LoC in Jammu and Kashmir and offered to provide ground sensors to monitor the militant incursion across the LoC.

**14 June:** According to a press report, India, the US and Britain are exploring ways to intensify intelligence gathering to evaluate accurately the Pakistan President's promise to end infiltration across the LoC. Foreign Minister Jaswant Singh told reporters in Delhi after a meeting of the Cabinet Committee on Security (CCS) that the US offer of providing sensors to India was being studied.

**24 June:** Annoyed by the Pakistan President, Pervez Musharraf's remark to *Newsweek* that he had not given any commitment to permanently stop cross-border terrorism, the US Secretary of State, Colin Powell, called up General Musharraf, who conveyed to him that he would stick to his promise.

**13 July:** At the two-day meeting of the Joint Working Group (JWG) on Counter-Terrorism in Washington, India and the US agreed to intensify cooperation and intelligence sharing not only to prevent terrorist acts but also to neutralise terrorist outfits.

**15 July:** The US Secretary of State, Colin Powell, has called the 13 July massacre of civilians in Jammu a "vicious killing committed by terrorist thugs" which was carried out to undermine efforts to ease tensions in South Asia.

**19 July:** The US Assistant Secretary of State for South Asia, Christina Rocca, at a hearing in the House International Relations Sub-Committee, brushed aside calls for a plebiscite in Jammu and Kashmir and said that it was for India and Pakistan to settle the issue bilaterally within the framework of the Shimla Agreement.

**22 July:** The US further eased its restrictions on American citizens travelling to India, thus acknowledging the easing of military tensions in the subcontinent.

**23 July:** A report in *The Washington Times* says that the US is not taking too kindly to the sale of the Israeli Arrow missile defence system to India and that the Secretary of State, Colin Powell, would carry the US's objection when he visits New Delhi on the 27 July.

**25 July:** Two senior Congressmen, Benjamin Gilman, and Gary Ackerman, Chairman and Ranking Member respectively of the House International Relations Sub-Committee on the Middle East and South Asia, have urged the Secretary of State, Colin Powell that he reiterate the message to General Musharraf that the halt to terrorist infiltration must be "permanent and visible."

**27 July:** The visiting US Secretary of State, Colin Powell, was told by India's Foreign Minister, Yashwant Sinha, that India had "legitimate concerns about Pakistan and its role in fomenting terrorism." The spokesperson of the Ministry of External Affairs, Nirupama Rao, told reporters that General Powell emphasised that the US does not see its relationship with India within the framework of India-Pakistan relations.

**31 July:** At the margins of the annual plenary of the ASEAN Regional Forum (ARF) at Bander Seri Begawan (Brunei), the

US Secretary of State, Colin Powell, in his talks with Foreign Minister, Yashwant Sinha, is understood to have indicated that the resolution of the Kashmir issue would be a matter for India and Pakistan to address and solve it bilaterally.

**6 August:** The US has condemned the attacks on the Amarnath pilgrims in Jammu and Kashmir, where nine pilgrims were killed and noted that such attacks were aimed at escalating tensions in the region.

**23 August:** The US Deputy Secretary of State, Richard Armitage, informed reporters in New Delhi that the US will continue to use its good offices to reduce tensions between India and Pakistan. He added that Washington wanted the elections in Jammu and Kashmir to be free, fair and open. India also expressed its desire to improve bilateral relations between the two countries and the possibility of working out a "strategic framework" with the United States.

**4 September:** A news report talks of the proposed Indo-US military exercises, 'Geronimo Thrust', to be held in Alaska involving Special Forces. About 100 Indian armed forces personnel along with the IAF's transport workhorse, 1L-76, will practise inter-operability with their American counterparts near the Elmendorf Air Force base at Fort Richardson in Anchorage, Alaska.

**19 September:** The US Ambassador to India, Robert Blackwill, has termed as "remarkable" the 48 per cent turnout in Jammu and Kashmir during the first phase of elections and hoped the trend would also continue in the next phase.

**24 September:** India and the US announced that they would continue discussions on all "outstanding non-proliferation differences" after talks between the visiting US Assistant Secretary of State for Non-Proliferation, John Wolf, and Joint Secretary (Disarmament), S. K. Sharma. Separately, a meeting exclusively devoted to Afghanistan was held between the US Assistant

Secretary of State for South Asia, Christina Rocca, and the US Special Coordinator for Afghanistan, David Johnson, with Arun Singh and Jayant Prasad, Joint Secretaries in the External Affairs Ministry.

**25 September:** The White House spokesman, Ari Fleischer, has condemned the terrorist attack on the Swaminarayan temple in Gujarat, calling it "horrific" and a "terrorist" attack.

**26 September:** The Prime Minister, Atal Behari Vajpayee, told reporters in New Delhi that US pressure on Pakistan was not working and added that India will have to fight terrorism on its own strength.

**30 September:** The Finance Minister, Jaswant Singh, in Washington to attend the annual meeting of the World Bank and the International Monetary Fund, observed that every country has the right to pre-emption and that this doctrine is not the prerogative of any one nation.

**1 October:** The United States Commission on International Religious Freedom (USCIRF) has recommended that the US Secretary of State, Colin Powell, designate India, along with other countries like China, North Korea, Iran, Iraq, Sudan, among other countries, as "Countries of Particular Concern" under the International Religious Freedom Act of 1998.

**3 October:** India and the US began their joint military exercises codenamed 'Geronimo Thrust 02' at Fort Richardson and Elmendorf Air Force Base, sponsored by the Pacific Command. The exercise is the first of its kind involving India's troops and airmen on American soil.

**7 October:** The State Department's 2002 Report on International Religious Freedom quotes "credible observers" to say that the "Gujarat fighting was aggravated by official inaction and in some cases, involvement." The report notes that the "growing assertiveness of Hindu extremists also seems to be the major contributing factor to societal discrimination."

**10 October:** The US State Department spokesman, Richard Boucher, has said in Washington that the US was pleased with the elections in Jammu and Kashmir but noted that the elections alone cannot solve the problems between India and Pakistan.

**17 October:** The first contingent of US Air Force personnel arrived in Agra to take part in the first-ever joint exercises to be held with their Indian counterparts, between 26-30 October. The exercises are funded, scheduled and sponsored by the US Pacific Air Forces.

**18 October:** The US Ambassador to India, Robert Blackwill, has called the troop pullback by India and Pakistan "a very major step in the right direction." He hoped that in the context of the de-escalation, the Jammu and Kashmir elections and the naming of a new Pakistani Prime Minister soon, a dialogue would begin between India and Pakistan.

**29 October:** Addressing a FICCI meeting on US-India Economic Relations in New Delhi, the US Ambassador, Robert Blackwill, asserted that India was a victim of terrorism, which was entirely "externally-driven." He added that India-US relations were rooted in "common interests, shared beliefs, and personal feelings."

**29 October:** The Director (Policy Planning Staff) in the US State Department, Richard Haass, talking to reporters in New Delhi, said that it is "undesirable" for the India-Pakistan relationship to be as 'thin' as it is and favoured a "bottom-up approach" to strengthen the ties. He added that the US looked forward to working with a government in Pakistan whatever be its complexion and composition.

**30 October:** India and the US have begun their first-ever

"Global Crises Forum", an occasion to discuss a range of issues on the social plane. The first round of talks held between Foreign Secretary, Kanwal Sibal, and the visiting US Under Secretary for Global Affairs, Paula Dobrinsky, discussed the issue of AIDS in the presence of Additional Secretary in the Union Health Ministry, Meenakshi Datta-Ghosh, who also heads the National AIDS Control Organisation (NACO). The two sides also discussed the issues of human rights in a multilateral context and the promotion of democracy.

**30 October:** The US President's Special Envoy on Afghanistan, Zalmay Khalilzad, told reporters in New Delhi that Washington will be "vigilant" in watching Pakistan's cooperation in the war against terrorism as a new government takes power in Islamabad.

**7 November:** The visiting US Under Secretary of State for Economics and Business affairs, Alan Larson, told the media in New Delhi that intra-regional trade in South Asia was very low and called for increased trade and economic interaction between India and Pakistan. He said this would also be good for rebuilding the war-ravaged country of Afghanistan.

**12 November:** The Defence Production and Supplies Secretary, N. S. Sisodia, after a meeting of the India-US Inter-governmental meeting on defence purchases, has questioned the reliability of the US as a long-term partner for defence equipment and warned the US of alternate supply sources if it continued to waffle on long-term product support.

**13 November:** At the end of a two-day visit by a US delegation led by US Under-Secretary of Commerce, Kenneth Juster, India and the US have decided to create an India-US High Technology Cooperation Group that will tackle contentious issues of increasing trade in "dual use" goods and technologies. The Foreign Secretary, Kanwal Sibal, led the Indian delegation.

**12 November:** The visiting US Treasury Secretary, Paul O'

Neill, has described India as one of the most restrictive countries in the world. He insisted that India could attain China's level of foreign direct investment by making changes in policies and procedures. He urged India to build up trade with its neighbours, just as Canada and Mexico are the US's largest trading partners.

**26 November:** The US has condemned the attack on the Raghunath temple in Jammu as a case of "senseless violence" and has noted that terrorism will not achieve the political goals of any group.

**10 December:** Speaking on Indo-US Relations in Kolkata on 27 November, the US Ambassador to India, Robert Blackwill, has said that India and the US share three 'big' overlapping vital national interests. These include promotion of peace and freedom in Asia, combating international terrorism, and slowing the spread of weapons of mass destruction. He added that close cooperation would endure over the long term because of convergence in democratic values and national interests.

**11 December:** India's National Security Adviser, Brajesh Mishra, after meeting top officials in Washington, maintained that there could be no dialogue with Pakistan unless cross-border terrorism stopped. He also pointed out that the US could not make Pakistan give up terrorism.

**18 December:** The US Ambassador to India, Robert Blackwill, speaking after gifting 20 vehicles to the Narcotics Control Bureau (NCB) in New Delhi, identified drug enforcement as a key area of cooperation between India and the US.

**26 December:** India and the US signed an agreement whereby neither country will surrender persons of the other country to any international tribunal without the other country's express consent. The Foreign Secretary, Kanwal Sibal, and the US Ambassador to India, Robert Blackwill, signed the agreement.

# EUROPE

## EUROPEAN UNION

*Strategic Profile*

**1 January:** Europeans rang in the New Year with a new currency, the Euro, which became legal tender for 300 million people.

**29 January:** The chasm of divide between the European Union and the United States over the fate of the Palestinian leader, Yasser Arafat, widened in recent weeks. The US President, George Bush, strongly criticised the Palestinian leader for his failure to stop acts of terror against Israel. But the EU renewed its political support for Mr. Arafat.

**14 February:** EU Foreign Ministers and their counterparts from the OIC met in Istanbul on 12-13 February, in a meeting called by Turkey aimed at fostering inter-cultural dialogue between the West and the Islamic world. The meeting brought together representatives from 71 countries.

**14 February:** Six EU countries – France, Belgium, Spain, Luxembourg, Portugal, and UK announced plans to introduce a new Europe arrest warrant, one year ahead of schedule, in early 2003. The arrest warrant was agreed to at the Laeken Summit in December 2001 to replace cumbersome extradition procedures between member states in cases of serious crimes.

**18 February:** EU Foreign Ministers voted in Brussels to take over full control of the 500-strong International Police Task Force (IPTF) in Bosnia from the UN at the end of 2002. It was the first time that the EU had agreed to run and fund such an operation in full by itself.

**28 February:** The EU launched the constitutional conventions agreed to in the Laeken Declaration in December

2001. Chaired by the former President of France, Valery Giscard d'Estaing, the 105-member convention, made up of representatives from the 15-member states, would draw up proposals on the future shape of the Union's institutions.

**17 March:** A summit conference of EU heads of government was held in Barcelona, Spain, on 15-16 March. The summit decided on a host of measures including the liberalisation of the common energy market, an increase in the amount of development aid for the world's poorest nations, and in spite of opposition from the US, approved the Galileo Satellite Navigation System, which would be a counter to the US Global Positioning System (GPS).

**29 May:** The European Commission (EC) President Romano Prodi announced in Brussels that Europe would recognise Russia as a market economy, a key step towards Russia's desire to join the World Trade Organisation (WTO).

**1 June:** All the 15 countries of the EU have ratified the Kyoto Protocol and urged the US to end its opposition to the Treaty. The Kyoto Protocol must be ratified by 55 countries, but the ratification must also include industrialised nations responsible for at least 55 per cent of the 1990 levels of the greenhouse gases blamed for heating the atmosphere. The EU action boosted the number of ratifications to about 70. The US backed out of the Protocol in 2001, saying it would cost the US economy $ 400 billion and 4.9 million jobs.

**21 June:** Leaders of the 15 EU countries began a two-day summit in Seville, Spain, over an agenda that includes tightening Western Europe's borders and enlisting poor countries in the fight to curb illegal immigration.

**24 July:** The EU Commissioner for Development and Humanitarian Aid, Poul Nielson, told reporters in Brussels that the EU will give an extra 32 million Euro to the UN Population Fund to make up for the US decision to withhold funds earmarked for UN family planning programmes. The US has charged that the funds go to Chinese agencies, which carry out "coercive programmes" involving abortion.

**13 December:** Ten new nations joined the European Union in Copenhagen. The countries include Latvia, Lithuania, Estonia, Poland, Hungary, the Czech Republic, Slovakia, Slovenia, Malta and Cyprus. Bulgaria and Romania will also become full members in 2007. The extended EU of "Solidarity and Unity" is structured on a common economic and political heritage, based on the key principles of multi-party democracy, rule of law, free-market economy, and border tariff-free trade.

*Relations with India*

**13 January:** Welcoming Pakistan President, Pervez Musharraf's 12 January address to the nation, the 15-nation European Union (EU) urged New Delhi and Islamabad to promptly renew dialogue to resolve the current tension.

**5 April:** The Ambassador of the European Commission in India, Michal Caillouet, ruled out any kind of mediation between India and Pakistan and affirmed that the best way to resolve the conflict was through bilateral negotiations.

**25 April:** The President of the EU, Spain, said that it was concerned about the escalation of violence in Gujarat, which could create tensions in the region. The Foreign Ministry spokesman, Louis Arias, was reacting to statements made by India's MEA spokesperson Nirupama Rao, asking foreign countries to refrain from interfering in the internal affairs of India.

**1 May:** A press report says that Indian participation in the European Union Seafood Exposition in Brussels has aroused wide expectations. India exports seafood worth $ 225 million to Europe, the second largest exporter of seafood after China and constituting 2 per cent of total European Union seafood imports from non-European sources.

**2 May:** A meeting of senior officials of the EU and India reviewed developments in India-EU relations preparatory to the India-EU summit to be held in Copenhagen in October, when Denmark would take over the EU presidency. The EU is India's largest trading partner.

**3 May:** The European Union moved to freeze the assets of 11 non-European terrorist organisations in attempts to combat post-11 September terrorism. Three groups operating in India, including the Pakistan-based Lashkar-e-Taiba, are on the list.

**7 May:** The Federal Minister of Finance of Austria, Karl Heinz Grasser, while addressing the Confederation of Indian Industry (CII) conference on "EU at the beginning of the 21st century" in New Delhi, has said that Austria has the potential to become the gateway for Indian investments to the EU. He added that Austria offered a stable economic environment, a tradition of strong fiscal discipline, well –trained work force, liberalised energy, and telecom services, well-developed transport network among other things.

**15 June:** The European Parliament in Brussels supported Indian's stance on cross-border terrorism and called upon Pakistan President Pervez Musharraf to "eradicate terrorist activities carried out from Pakistan, especially infiltration of terrorists." It also called for "the resumption of bilateral talks on the Kashmir question." All anti-India amendments, including one which called for mediation, were rejected.

**26 July:** The EU's High Representative for a Common Foreign and Security Policy, Javier Solana, told reporters in New Delhi after meeting Foreign Minister Yashwant Sinha that progress in reducing tensions between India and Pakistan had to be "sequential", i.e. if Pakistan did more to curb cross-border terrorism, then the Indian response would be positive.

**1 October:** A five-member European parliamentary delegation met the Prime Minister, Mr. Vajpayee, and the Defence

Minister, George Fernandes, and voiced concern over the killings of minorities in India, which they said detracted from India's future, given its secular character.

**2 October:** The European Commission, executive body of the EU, in its country analysis of India, titled "the EC-India Country Strategy Paper 2002-06", argued that the Kashmir issue remained the "major threat" to stability in South Asia. It said that India's growth was still "far below" the 10 per cent required to substantially reduce mass poverty within the decade.

**10 October:** At the third India-EU summit at Copenhagen, India and the EU differed publicly on issues of Kashmir, dialogue in South Asia and cross-border terrorism. The Danish Prime Minister and EU President, Anders Fogh Rasmussen, urged India to de-escalate the tense relations with Pakistan. Mr. Vajpayee insisted that de-escalation required a peaceful, congenial atmosphere.

**11 October:** The Danish Prime Minister, Anders Rasmussen, told reporters after his talks with the Indian Prime Minister, Mr. Vajpayee, that an end to cross-border infiltration was of vital importance to create a "positive climate for a fruitful dialogue" with Pakistan.

**13 October:** The EU, in a declaration issued in Copenhagen by the Danish presidency, welcomed the "strenuous efforts of the Indian Election Commission in promoting free and fair elections" and hoped that the future developments will lead to improvements in the governance and human rights situation in Kashmir. In sharp contrast, the EU Observers Mission in Pakistan said that the "Pakistani authorities engaged in actions which resulted in serious flaws in the electoral process."

# BRITAIN

*Strategic Profile*

**5 February:** UK and Spanish officials ended a protracted series of talks in Gibraltar aimed at finding a constitutional settlement for the dispute over the UK dependency of Gibraltar. Gibraltar's Chief Minister, Peter Carvana, boycotted the meeting. He claimed that the UK government had agreed in principle to give away "half the sovereignty" of Gibraltar.

**11 April:** The British Prime Minister, Tony Blair, backed the Saudi Arabian peace plan for the Middle East, called for deployment of British and European monitors to ensure compliance by both sides and an economic package to rebuild the Palestine infrastructure destroyed in Israel's military action.

**26 April:** The British Prime Minister, Tony Blair, has defended the close relationship between Britain and America, calling critics who call him an 'American poodle', a "destructive influence." Mr. Blair said in an interview with *The Guardian* that "a renewed sense of urgency" after September accounted for the conviction behind the close relationship.

**10 May:** In a bid to defuse a threatened revolt in his party and government, the British Prime Minister, Tony Blair, has assured his MPs that he would not back US military action against Baghdad without the backing of the UN Security Council.

**6 September:** The British Prime Minister, Tony Blair, told the BBC that Britain was willing to pay "the blood price" for its special relationship with America by supporting a US-led attack on Iraq.

**8 December:** The British Foreign Secretary, Jack Straw, rejected as a "pack of lies" Iraqi claims that it does not have any weapons of mass destruction. Mr. Straw's remarks came amid reports that Britain was willing to offer asylum to Iraqi scientists who might be in a position to disclose information about Baghdad's weapons of mass destruction.

*Relations with India*

**1 January:** The British Foreign Secretary, Mr. Jack Straw, urged Pakistan to have talks with India to defuse the tension in the region, and avoid a conflict.

**3 January:** After a massive media build-up, the Government sought to lower the expectations from the British Prime Minister, Tony Blair's visit to India and Pakistan saying he was not carrying a "peace plan" or intending to intervene in the dispute over Kashmir.

**8 January:** The British Prime Minister, Tony Blair, returned after a high- profile visit to the subcontinent, including a secret midnight stopover in Afghanistan, amid claims that he had succeeded in paving the way for a dialogue between New Delhi and Islamabad by getting the Pakistan President, Pervez Musharraf, to declare that his country "rejected terrorism in all its forms."

**22 January:** Britain made a renewed bid to push its long-pending one billion pound worth deal for 'Hawk' advanced jet trainer with India. The issue was raised by the British Defence Secretary, Geoff Hoon, at a luncheon he hosted in honour of the Defence Minister, George Fernandes, in London.

**4 February:** The National Security Adviser, Brajesh Mishra, held talks with the British Foreign Secretary, Jack Straw, in London mainly focusing on the "tension" on the border between India and Pakistan.

**16 April:** Officials of the Ministry of External Affairs met the British High Commission officials over a report in a section of the media that suggested that the British High Commission viewed the post-Godhra violence in Gujarat as pre-planned.

**23 April:** Opposition MPs in Britain have expressed concern that the sale of military hardware like Jaguar fighter jets and Hawk trainer-fighters would be in conflict with the British government's arms export guidelines on non-proliferation. Since India is not a signatory to the Nuclear Non-Proliferation Treaty (NPT), the MPs have demanded that India did not get the nuclear capable Jaguars.

**27 April:** British officials, after visiting Gujarat, have reported that the violence in Gujarat had "all the hallmarks of ethnic cleansing." According to the BBC, the report talks of the impossibility of reconciliation between Muslims and Hindus as long as the Chief Minister Narendra Modi stays in power.

**14 May:** The British Foreign Secretary, Jack Straw, has strongly condemned the terrorist attacks on the Army camp at Kaluchak and without naming Pakistan, has urged "all countries in the region to denounce it."

**23 May:** The British Foreign Secretary, Mr. Jack Straw told the BBC that Kashmir was an "unfinished business", and stressed that the question as to "who should run Kashmir was never fully addressed."

**28 May:** Amidst speculation over the future of arms supplies to India and Pakistan, the British Foreign Office Minister, Ben Bradshaw, insisted that there was no arms embargo and that no decision had been taken to freeze the £ 1 billion Hawk deal with India.

**29 May:** The British Foreign Secretary, Jack Straw, after meeting Prime Minister Vajpayee and Foreign Minister Jaswant Singh in New Delhi, told reporters that the international community looks to President Musharraf to implement the promises made by him. He added that terrorism could not be disguised as "freedom-fighting".

**7 June:** The British Defence Secretary, Geoff Hoon, has said that Britain is willing to send troops to act as neutral observers to monitor the LoC. Mr. Hoon's remarks came at the meeting of the Defence Ministers of NATO in Brussels, amid reports of a joint US-British plan for a helicopter-borne monitoring force to check cross-border infiltration.

**9 June:** *The Sunday Telegraph* has reported that Pakistan-based Kashmir terrorist groups are being financed to the tune of about £ 5 million a year by British Muslims. The report talks of the proof of this activity being presented to the visiting British Foreign Secretary, Jack Straw, by the Indian Foreign Minister, Jaswant Singh, when he was in New Delhi.

**20 June:** The British Prime Minister, Tony Blair has defended continuing arms supplies to India and Pakistan following widespread criticism that it is in breach of EU criteria, which prohibits exports of arms to a region where there is a risk of war.

**1 July:** For the first time in India, Britain has introduced a multiple entry visa, priced at Rs.11, 250, with a validity of ten years.

**3 July:** The British Defence Secretary, Geoff Hoon, after meeting the Defence Minister, George Fernandes, told reporters in New Delhi that Britain had asked Pakistan to effect significant reduction in cross-border infiltration into Jammu and Kashmir, while urging India to exercise restraint.

**19 July:** The British Foreign Secretary, Jack Straw, after talks with Foreign Minister, Yashwant Sinha, in New Delhi stressed the centrality of the Kashmir issue between India and Pakistan and added that "further steps" need to be taken before an active dialogue can take place.

**22 August:** The Deputy Prime Minister, L. K. Advani, was greeted by angry demonstrators protesting the recent events in Gujarat, when he visited the India House to unveil the bust of Sardar Vallabhai Patel in London.

**12 October:** During a meeting with the British Prime Minister, Tony Blair, in London, Prime Minister A. B. Vajpayee expressed concern at the success of fundamentalist parties in the just-concluded elections in Pakistan. Briefing the media, External Affairs Minister Yashwant Sinha stated that Britain had "endorsed" India's position that no dialogue was possible without an end to cross-border terrorism.

**17 October:** Britain welcomed India's decision to withdraw its troops from the border and Pakistan's offer to do the same, calling them "positive moves." The visiting British Foreign Office Minister, Mike O'Brien, expressed the hope that the move would lead to a process that can "resolve the issues which have caused the confrontation" between the two countries.

**21 October:** *The Guardian* has criticised the British Prime Minister, Tony Blair, for "lobbying" his Indian counterpart, A. B. Vajpayee, over the sale of Hawk Jets to India, when the two leaders met recently. The British Foreign Office spokesperson, reacting to the report, said that he can "make no apologies for lobbying in support of British defence industry".

**31 October:** The British Foreign Secretary, Jack Straw, after talks with the visiting Indian External Affairs Minister, Yashwant Sinha, who is in London for a meeting of the Commonwealth Ministerial Group, told reporters that London believed that "India should join the UN Security Council, along with Germany and Japan".

**15 November:** In an interview to the *New Statesman*, the British Foreign Secretary, Jack Straw, observed that Britain made "serious mistakes" over Kashmir and called the dispute between India and Pakistan a consequence of his country's colonial past.

## CYPRUS

*Relations with India*

**8 October:** Cyprus today pledged full support to India's quest for a permanent seat on the UN Security Council while India reciprocated with support for Cyprus' inclusion in the European Union. The statements in this regard were read out by Prime Minister A. B. Vajpayee and Cyprus President Clerides after talks between the two leaders in Nicosia on the second day of Vajpayee's visit to Cyprus.

## FRANCE

*Strategic Profile*

**13 September:** France increased its defence expenditure to 2.5 per cent of its GDP for the next year, compared with 1.8 per cent, in 2002. The stated aim was to reduce the gap between French and British military capability and to enable France to make a greater contribution to European defence and security cooperation. The plan included construction of a second aircraft carrier by 2015.

**26 September:** In an interview to an Indian daily, the French Foreign Minister, Dominique de Villepin, rejected the idea of unilateral action against Iraq and called for keeping the United Nations in the picture.

**8 October:** On the occasion of the Air Force Day, the Chief of Air Staff, S. Krishnaswamy, said that India and France would conduct joint air exercises at Gwalior early next year, the home base for the French-built Mirage-2000 aircraft. This will be the first occasion when a foreign air force will bring in contemporary combat aircraft to India and hold such exercises.

**17 December:** Indian Foreign Secretary, Kanwal Sibal, speaking at the French International Relations Institute in Paris, described India as a "country wounded by terrorism" and pilloried Western governments for adopting double standards in dealing with Pakistan. He insisted that President Musharraf had not delivered on the promises he made to halt cross-border terrorism.

*Relations with India*

**28 June:** A report in the daily *La Tribune* says that France's naval construction company DCN is to sign a contract in September or October to supply India six Scorpene-type submarines. The submarines are to be built at the Mazagaon Dock at Mumbai.

**2 August:** During the visit of the French Foreign Minister, Dominique de Villepin, to New Delhi, India sensitised France on the need for peace during the Jammu and Kashmir elections. The French minister called for respecting the Shimla and Lahore agreements.

**31 August:** The French Foreign Minister, Dominique de Villepin, while addressing a meeting in Paris for the Annual Review of the country's foreign policy said that the non-resolution of the Kashmir dispute between two nuclear powers harboured incalculable risks for the entire planet. He was of the opinion that India should initiate a dialogue while combating terrorism.

## GERMANY

*Strategic Profile*

**27 April:** The Bundestag (the lower house of the federal legislature) on 26 April approved a tightening of the anti-terrorism law adopted in December 2001, under which membership of or support for a foreign terrorist organisation would become a criminal offence.

**8 November:** German Defence Minister, Peter Struck, held talks in Washington DC with US Defence Secretary, Donald

Rumsfeld, who later said that US-German relations were now "un-poisoned", a reference to his assertion in September that they had been "poisoned" by the German government policy on Iraq.

**5 December:** German Defence Minister, Peter Struck, announced major cuts in military procurement intended to save about Euro 6 billion over five years and thus to contribute to government efforts to curb the budget deficit. Germany would reduce its order of 73 Airbus A400 military aircraft to 60 and also cut its order for 180 Euro-fighter combat aircraft.

*Relations with India*

**2 February:** India's National Security Adviser Brajesh Mishra, said in Munich that the disappearance of the Taliban and Al Qaeda leaders and activists after the US military campaign in Afghanistan was "a matter of immediate security concern" and made it clear that New Delhi would de-escalate only after seeing "concrete evidence" of decreasing terrorism from across its borders.

## ITALY

*Relations with India*

**21 September:** The Defence Minister, George Fernandes, addressing a seminar on "The Security Scenario" in Rome, called for greater international cooperation, especially among "threatened democracies" to combat terrorism on a war-footing. At a meeting between Mr. Fernandes and his Italian counterpart, Antonio Martino, the two sides decided to hold joint defence exercises and identified many areas of defence collaboration, including joint ventures.

## PORTUGAL

### *Relations with India*

**20 September:** Underworld don Abu Salem, one of the India's most wanted criminals, has been arrested by Interpol authorities in the Portuguese capital Lisbon, along with his companion, Bollywood starlet Monica Bedi, said a report. The Indian government expressed confidence, 22 September, that it would be able to get gangster Abu Salem back in the country despite agency reports from Lisbon that a Portuguese court had rejected his deportation to India.

## UKRAINE

### *Relations with India*

**3 October:** India and Ukraine signed an extradition treaty, a shipping agreement, and a treaty on mutual legal assistance in criminal matters, in the presence of the visiting Ukrainian President, Leonid Kuchma, and the Prime Minister, A. B. Vajpayee.

## RUSSIA

### *Strategic Profile*

**31 March:** The Russian Deputy Minister for Atomic Energy, E. A. Reshetnikov, maintained that the Russian government had no plans to help complete a nuclear power plant in North Korea. He was speaking at Koodankulam in Tamil Nadu during the commencement of construction of the main plant of the complex.

**5 April:** Russia reasserted its resolve to expand economic and military ties with Iran despite US objections. The Russian President, Vladimir Putin, conveyed this to the visiting Iranian Foreign Minister, Kamal Kharazzi. The US had earlier branded Iran as part of the 'axis' of 'evil'.

**18 April:** In his annual State of the Nation address to both Houses of Parliament, the Russian President Vladimir Putin observed that the Commonwealth of Independent States (CIS) is Russia's topmost foreign policy priority and emphasised relations with Europe as the number two priority, followed by ensuring global strategic stability.

**19 April:** The Russian President, Vladimir Putin, called for the establishment of an 'arc of stability', stretching from Europe to China. The 'arc' would rest on two pillars: a closer relationship between Russia and NATO and the Shanghai Cooperation Organisation (SCO), which unites Russia, China, and the four Central Asian Republics.

**25 April:** The first ever summit of the five nations bordering the Caspian Sea – Russia, Azerbaijan, Turkmenistan, Kazakhstan and Iran – ended without agreement on how to divide its oil and gas resources. Russia, Kazakhstan, and Azerbaijan want the seabed to be split along a median line into national sectors, corresponding roughly to the length of each country's shoreline. Iran, which would get a 14 per cent share under this dispensation, insists on all the five littoral states to get a 20 per cent share.

**26 April:** According to a report in the *Vremya Novostei* newspaper, Russia and China are forging a Defence pact under the umbrella of the Shanghai Cooperation Organisation (SCO), a regional security organisation that also unites Kazakhstan, Krygyzstan, Tajikistan, and Uzbekistan. The newspaper noted that the growing US presence in Central Asia has made Russia more amenable to Chinese participation in the regional security arrangements.

**29 April:** The US Defence Secretary, Donald Rumsfeld, and the Russian Defence Minister, Sergei Ivanov, discussed ways to further reduce each other's nuclear arsenal at Moscow. While President Bush was willing to reduce the US nuclear arsenal to

1700-2200 warheads, as against about 6000 each country is allowed under START-I, President Putin said that Russia would reduce its warheads to 1500.

**8 May:** Russia has criticised the US refusal to join the international war crimes tribunal and reiterated Moscow's support for the body. Russia signed the Rome statute in September 2000 but is yet to ratify it. American officials in Washington have said that the International Criminal Court (ICC) would threaten American sovereignty and that Washington would regard as "illegitimate" any moves by the court to assert jurisdiction over US citizens.

**15 May:** At a Summit in Reykjavik, Iceland, NATO Foreign and Defence Ministers approved an agreement in which Russia was accepted as a member. The new NATO-Russia Council would cooperate on issues related to terrorism, arms control, international crisis management, peacekeeping, and civil-emergency issues. As an 'Associate Member', Russia will not participate in any decision-making related to NATO's military initiatives.

**24 May:** The US President, George Bush, and the Russian President Vladimir Putin, have signed a landmark nuclear disarmament treaty in Moscow, which obliges both sides to reduce their nuclear arsenals to about 1200 to 2200 warheads over the next decade. The Treaty is the first strategic arms reduction treaty in nearly ten years.

**3 June:** The Russian Defence Minister, Sergei Ivanov, told reporters in Moscow after his trip to Beijing that increased relations with US and NATO should not damage its relations with China, which according to him viewed stronger cooperation between Moscow and the West as a positive development. He noted that Russia's state emblem, the double-headed eagle, symbolizes its policy of forging close ties with both the East and the West.

**12 June:** Russia would supply 8 kilo-class diesel-electric submarines to China in a deal worth $ 1 billion, according to *Novaya Gazeta*. This was the second deal Russia has signed with China this year. In January, it sealed a contract for the construction of two Sovremenny-class destroyers for China, in addition to two supplied in 2000.

**13 June:** The 1972 Anti-Ballistic Missile Treaty expired today with Russia voicing, "regret." Defence Minister Sergei Ivanov said that his country's task was to minimise the possible fallout from the US withdrawal from the ABM treaty.

**14 June:** After the death of the ABM treaty, Russia pulled out of START-II. The US ratified the treaty in 1996 while Russia did so in 2000 but linked its implementation to the Russian-American Memorandum on preserving the ABM pact. The decision would give Russia the freedom to continue to have land-based strategic missiles with multiple warheads.

**19 June:** Prospects for a unified state of Belarus and Russia further diminished as efforts of reunification broke out into a public row after the Belarussian President, Alexander Lukashenko, put forth a proposal for creating a federation with Russia in which Belarus was an equal partner. The Russian President dismissed the suggestion saying Belarus could not be equal with Russia as the size of its economy was only 3 per cent of that of Russia. Mr. Lukashenko said that his country was not willing to be the "north-western or north-eastern edge of any country."

**20 June:** Russia has sold MI-171 transport helicopters to Pakistan in what is believed to be the first transaction between the two countries involving that dual-purpose equipment. The MI-171 is an advanced version of the MI-17 helicopter, which India has in large numbers and that were very effective during the Kargil war. Russia sold the copters after receiving a written obligation from Pakistan not to use the copters for military purposes.

**28 June:** Russian Defence Minister told reporters after visiting Russia's only nuclear testing ground at the Novaya Zemlya Island beyond the Arctic Circle that Russia has no plans to resume nuclear weapons testing. He added that Russia would abide by the Comprehensive Test Ban Treaty (CTBT) as the State Duma (Russian Parliament's Lower House) has ratified it. Russia had unilaterally suspended nuclear testing in 1990 but has kept the test range in operational readiness.

**27 July:** Ignoring US opposition, Russia unveiled plans to expand trade and economic ties with Iran. Russia will also build ten nuclear power reactors, help Iran manufacture aircraft engines, build two steel plants and several petrochemical projects, as well as develop oil, gas and coal fields.

**1 August:** Media reports from Moscow talk of Russia selling 30-40 SU-30 MK2 jet fighters to China. This is a naval version of the multi-role SU-30 MKK fighters Russia sold China earlier. Armed with X-31 A anti-ship missiles and an operational range of over 3000 kms, the fighters will boost China's ability to challenge the US military might off Taiwan.

**10 August:** Russian Defence Minister, Sergei Ivanov, has accused Georgia of harbouring a "nest of international terrorism" on its territory. Russia had earlier accused Georgia of harbouring Chechen rebels in the Pankisi Gorge near its border with Chechnya.

**18 August:** The Russian Defence Minister, Sergei Ivanov, has said that Russia has abandoned plans to reduce its land-based nuclear missile forces. He added that Russia would continue to retain the deadly "Satan" (SS-18/ RS-20) missiles and the train-mounted mobile (RT-23 "Scalpel") missiles, armed with ten nuclear warheads each.

**19 August:** In a deal that will be a potential setback to the US efforts to isolate Iraq, Russia has announced a $ 40 billion trade agreement with Saddam Hussein. The agreement, which would have to be approved by the UN, contains dozens of separate deals involving oil, electrical energy, chemical products, irrigation, railroad construction, and transport, over the next five years.

**22 August:** The Prime Minister of China, Zhu Rongji, and Russian Prime Minister, Mikhail Khasyanov, after meeting in Shanghai have drafted a security resolution calling for mutual trust, equality and cooperation among the states as an alternative to the US framework of international security.

**2 September:** The Russian Foreign Minister, Igov Ivanov, after meeting the visiting Iraqi Foreign Minister, Naji Sabri, reiterated Russian opposition to a US attack on Iraq, while calling for resumption of UN inspections to pave the way for lifting the economic sanctions against Baghdad.

**22 October:** Russia rejected the revised draft of the UN Security Council Resolution on Iraq, brought by the United States, as disappointing and unacceptable. Russia has consistently opposed any unilateral US military action against Iraq.

**23 October:** Armed men and women, numbering around 50, reportedly from Chechnya, entered a crowded Moscow theatre and took the audience of over 700 people, hostage.

**26 October:** Russian Special Forces stormed the Moscow theatre where Chechen rebels held more than 700 people hostage, killing the 50 terrorists, including their leader, Movsar Barayev. The decision to storm the theatre was taken after the captors started executing hostages.

**9 November:** The Russian Foreign Ministry insisted that the new UN Security Council Resolution 1441 on Iraq gave the US no license for military action against Baghdad, should it obstruct international weapons inspections, citing the clause which calls for the Security Council to meet again to assess any serious violation before further action is taken.

**12 November:** At the EU-Russia Summit at Brussels, the Russian President Vladimir Putin, said that Western civilization faced a mortal threat from Muslim terrorists. A EU-Russian action plan to fight terrorism was agreed to at the mini-summit. The Danish Prime Minister, Anders Fogh RasMussen, occupying the Presidency of the EU, called on Moscow to abide by human rights agreements, prosecute war criminals in Chechnya, admit international observers to the conflict zone and seek a political settlement.

**1 December:** A report in *The Hindu* talks of the deployment of Russian military aircraft in Kyrgyzstan, Central Asia, including SU-25 ground attack fighters, IL-76 transport planes and SU-27 fighter jets. The report states that this could be an effort to balance American military presence in the region.

**2 December:** At the end of a visit to Beijing by the Russian President, Vladimir Putin, President Ziang Zemin stated that Russia and China will be "good neighbours, friends, and partners forever." The two sides stressed the need for the normalization of ties between North Korea and the United States. The two leaders also called for the creation of a nuclear weapons-free Korean peninsula.

**17 December:** The Russian President, Vladimir Putin, after talks with the visiting President of Yemen, Ali Abdullah Saleh, in a joint declaration called for the settlement of the Iraqi problem through "peaceful, political and diplomatic instruments, without resort to military force and on the basis of relevant UN resolutions."

**20 December:** A report in *The Hindu* says that Russia has reversed plans to scrap its nuclear tipped SS-18 'Satan' missiles in response to US President George Bush's decision to speed up the deployment of a missile shield. Russia's Commander of Strategic Missile Forces, Colonel General Nikolai Solovstsov, said in Moscow that Russia would keep its missiles on duty till 2010-2020.

*Relations with India*

**10 April:** The Russian Defence Minister, Sergei Ivanov, conveyed to his Indian counterpart, George Fernandes, that Russia has shipped the second batch of 40 T-90 tanks and also finalised the schedule for the delivery of the first lot of the upgraded SU-30 MKI fighter planes.

**11 April:** The Russian Defence Minister, Sergei Ivanov, said that India and Russia have decided to jointly design and produce weapons. While giving full support to India's stand on terrorism, he told Defence Minister George Fernandes that both countries have similar stands on issues of regional and global security.

**12 April:** The Russian-built kilo-class diesel submarine, INS SINDURATNA, was launched at a northern Russian shipyard after in-depth upgradation and repairs. It has been provided with a new acoustic system, information system, and navigation system. India has 10 kilo-class submarines.

**13 April:** Russian Prime Minister, Mikhail Khasyanov, meeting the Defence Minister, George Fernandes, invited India to join the six-member Shanghai Security Organisation (SSO), comprising Russia, China, and four Central Asian states.

**19 May:** After a meeting of the Cabinet Committee on Security (CCS) in New Delhi, India's Ambassador in Moscow, K. Raghunath, called on the Russian Deputy Foreign Minister, Alexander Losynkov, and passed on information about Pakistan's direct involvement in the Kaluchak massacre. This was in tune with the Indo-Russian bilateral pacts signed by President Yeltsin in January 1993 (The Friendship Treaty) and the Strategic Partnership Declaration of 2000, which provide for urgent consultations between the countries in case of a threat to the security of one of the contracting parties and close cooperation in jointly removing the threat.

**3 June:** The Russian Defence Minister, Sergei Ivanov, has accused Pakistan of whipping up tensions by allowing terrorists to cross over into India and by conducting missile tests. He endorsed the Western estimates that about 12 million could die instant deaths and 7 million would die a slow death in the event of a nuclear war in South Asia.

**4 June:** The Russian President, Vladimir Putin, told Prime Minister Atal Behari Vajpayee at Almaty, Kazakhstan, on the sidelines of the 16-nation "Conference on Interaction and Confidence-building Measures in Asia", that President Musharraf had given "serious and positive signals" to end the current military stand-off with India. Later, Mr. Putin compared the Indo-Pak stand-off to the Cuban missile crisis between the Soviet Union and the US in 1962.

**5 June:** India's National Security Adviser, Brajesh Mishra, after talks with the Russian Defence Minister, Sergei Ivanov, in Moscow has said that India is grateful to Russia for its support in the current stand-off with Pakistan. Mr. Ivanov maintained that Russia was greatly concerned about the crisis as "Kashmir lies in the middle of the 'arc of stability' Russia wants to build from Vancouver to Vladivostok."

**22 June:** The Russian Ambassador to India, Alexander M. Kadakin, told reporters in Bangalore that the centrality of the problem between India and Pakistan was not the issue of Kashmir, but trans-border infiltration and international terrorism.

**22 June:** A Russian scientist, Yuri Malenkov of the St. Petersburg State University, writing in the daily *Izvestia* has claimed that nearly half-a-billion people could die in the event of an Indo-Pak nuclear exchange owing to the industrial calamities they will trigger.

**24 June:** Russia has begun the delivery of the multi-role SU-30 MKI fighters to India. The IAPO, which builds the Sukhoi-series aircraft, is expected to supply a total of 10 SU-30

MKI fighters to India in the next couple of months, and another 22 planes next year. Alexander Varkin of the Indo-Russia Security Forum told *The Hindu* that the plane is a fourth generation plane and has the potential for modernisation to the level of a fifth generation aircraft.

**27 June:** A press report says that Russia will ship the third and last batch of 44 T-90 Main Battle Tanks (MBTs) to India in a month. Among the 310 T-90 MBT's that India has purchased, 124 will be delivered in fully assembled forms. The rest will be produced at Avadi Heavy Vehicles factory in Tamil Nadu from semi-knocked down kits and fully knocked down assembly kits.

**17 July:** At the India-Russia Joint Working Group on Afghanistan in New Delhi, the two countries agreed that there could not be any double standards in the fight against terrorism and that the world cannot distinguish between good and bad terrorists.

**7 September:** The Russian Foreign Minister, Igor Ivanov, told the visiting Indian Foreign Secretary, Kanwal Sibal, that the implementation by Islamabad of its commitment to end anti-India activity by terrorists holed-up on Pakistan-controlled territory is an indispensable condition for the de-escalation of tensions in the region.

**14 September:** India's Foreign Minister, Yahwant Sinha, met his Chinese counterpart, Tang Jiaxuan, and the Russian Foreign Minister, Igor Ivanov, on the sidelines of the 57th session of the UN General Assembly to discuss issues relating to counter-terrorism and greater economic cooperation.

**15 October:** Russia hailed the Jammu and Kashmir elections as "free and fair" and noted that "they had opened the way for an early normalisation in the region" and hoped that the formation of a coalition government would create fresh opportunities for speedy normalisation of the situation in Jammu and Kashmir.

**24 October:** India condemned the hostage crisis in a Moscow Theatre as a "cowardly act of terrorism directed against a friendly state." A statement of the Foreign Office in New Delhi remarked that the primary reason for the continued acts of terrorism around the world was the support and assistance such acts receive from outside forces.

**6 November:** India will participate in the Baku-Tblisi-Ceyhan (BTC) pipeline project that will bring crude oil from Azerbaijan in the Caspian zone to Ceyhan on the Turkish-Mediterranean coast. Punj Lloyd, a New Delhi based company, in partnership with a Turkish firm, has bagged the order for constructing 232 kms of pipeline, out of a total length of 1750 kms.

**26 November:** Russia strongly condemned the Raghunath temple attacks and demanded that Pakistan crackdown on terrorists operating from its territory.

**30 November:** The Russian President, in an interview to *The Hindu* and NDTV, on the eve of his visit to India from 3-5 December, expressed the fear that Pakistan's weapons of mass destruction could fall into the hands of "bandits and terrorists." While stressing that Moscow would fulfil its obligations under the Nuclear Non-Proliferation Treaty (NPT), he reiterated that there was a future for developing the Russia, China, India strategic triangle.

**4 December:** The visiting Russian President, Vladimir Putin, and the Prime Minister, A. B. Vajpayee, signed the 'Delhi Declaration' to enhance strategic cooperation. Both sides also set up a joint working group on combating terrorism and issued a joint declaration on strengthening economic, scientific and cultural cooperation. The Declaration stressed the need for Pakistan to end infiltration and called for a resolution of the Kashmir issue within the framework of the 1972 Simla Agreement and the Lahore Declaration of 1999.

**11 December:** The Prime Minister, A. B. Vajpayee, told the Rajya Sabha that no concrete steps had been taken to further trilateral cooperation among India, Russia and China. Earlier, he said that Mr. Putin's visit had underlined Moscow's and New Delhi's "mutual commitment" to constantly strengthen their strategic partnership.

## JAPAN

*Strategic Profile*

**5-9 January:** The Japanese Prime Minister, Junichiro Koizumi, toured five South East Asian Countries (Indonesia, Malaysia, Philippines, Singapore and Thailand) apparently to assert Japan's role at the centre of economic and security affairs within South East Asia and also to wrest some of the regional diplomatic initiative from China. A free trade agreement was signed with Singapore on 13 January. Koizumi also reiterated that Japan was committed to expanding the role of Japan's Self-Defence Force to tackle regional security issues.

**14 January:** Japanese Prime Minister, Junichiro Koizumi, while delivering the Singapore Lecture indicated that Japan was ready for a bigger role in South East and East Asia in tune with its international obligations. He said that ASEAN and Japan must tackle the issues of terrorism, piracy and energy security together. He also called for the creation of a larger East Asian community which would include Australia and New Zealand.

7 **February:** Japan was accused by North Korea of using the trial of a satellite-launching rocket as part of a military build up. The North Korean Foreign Ministry spokesman said Japan's test of a satellite-launching rocket was a covert attempt to bolster its arms programme. The spokesman also stated that Japan's launching of an H-2A rocket sought to revive militarism. Japan clarified that the H-2A was intended for launching commercial satellites.

**18 February:** During the US President George Bush's visit to Japan, he voiced concern that Japan's recession threatened to delay the recovery of the US economy. He implored the Japanese Prime Minister, Junchiro Koizumi, to speed efforts to restructure the world's second largest economy, while simultaneously expressing praise for Koizumi's commitment to reform. Koizumi reciprocated Bush's expressions of support by endorsing Washington's condemnation of Iran, Iraq and North Korea as an "axis of evil", and lauding the US administration's dealings with those countries as very calm and cautions.

**20 February:** President Bush, while addressing the Japanese Parliament said he foresaw a "pacific century" with the US playing a major role in defending the region against terrorism. Explicating his denunciation of an "axis of evil" formed by North Korea, Iraq and Iran, Bush assured the Diet in Tokyo that he was committed to fight if necessary to protect US allies. He promised that the US would "continue to show American power and purpose" in defence of the Philippines, Australia, Thailand, and South Korea and was committed to a forward presence in the region.

**8 April:** Ichiro Ozawa, leader of the Japanese Opposition Liberal Democratic Party, said that Japan was capable of producing thousands of nuclear warheads overnight to counter China's rapid military build up. He told an audience in Fukuoka that he had mentioned the nuclear option for Japan during a recent meeting with a Chinese official.

**31 May:** The Chief Cabinet Secretary of Japan, Yasuo Fakuda, affirmed that Japan might reconsider the long-standing policy of "not producing, not possessing, and not allowing nuclear weapons into the country." He said that if needed the constitution of Japan could be amended in this respect. Later, Prime Minister Junichiro Koizumi and Foreign Minister Yoriko Kawaguchi tried to quell fears among the neighbours of Japan arising from Fakuda's statement.

**11 July:** Japan's Defence White Paper for 2002 placed a new emphasis on terrorism and security cooperation with the US. Three major changes for Self-Defence Force (SDF) were introduced: they are, a greater emphasis on international activities under the aegis of the United Nations, improved preparedness to deal with aggression, and further enhancement of Japan-US Security Cooperation. The need to introduce legislation to clearly define the SDF's role in the eventuality of a foreign attack was also stressed. Unusually, it also addressed Japan's economic downturn. Apparently, it could undermine regional stability and security.

**13 July:** Japan and South Korea agreed on Saturday to seek dialogue with North Korea despite a deadly sea skirmish that chilled relations on the divided Korean peninsula and prompted Washington to withdraw a proposal for security talks with the communist North. The Japanese Foreign Minister, Yoriko Kawaguchi, who arrived in Seoul on 12 July met the South Korean Foreign Affairs and Trade Minister, Choi Sung-Hong and then visited the President, Kim Dae-Jung, for talks that focused on the 29 June gun battle between North and South Korean Patrol boats.

**17 September:** Meeting for the first time, in Pyonyang, Japanese Prime Minister, Junichiro Koizumi and North Korean leader Kim Jong II exchanged apologies for historical wrongs and agreed to pursue normalised diplomatic relations. Kim made some of his biggest overtures yet to the West, agreeing to extend a moratorium on missile tests beyond 2003 and to allow inspections by the International Atomic Energy Agency.

**19 November:** Japan expanded he mandate of its Self-Defence Force to allow military cooperation with a broader range of countries. The Japanese Cabinet meeting revised the SDF's basic operational plan under the Special Law to deal with Terrorism, enacted in October 2001. The revision calls for the maritime SDF to supplement its current operations in the Indian

Ocean, involving destroyers and combat support ships with the deployment of a transport ship to conduct sealift operations of foreign engineers and heavy construction equipment. The equipment will also be used to maintain an undisclosed airfield in Afghanistan.

**5 December:** The Japanese Prime Minister, Junichiro Koizmi ordered the dispatch of an Aegis equipped destroyer of the Maritime Self-Defence Force to the Indian Ocean to provide logistic support for the US and British warships engaged in anti-terrorism operations.

*Relations with India*

**11 January:** Japan's leader of the Opposition, Hatoyama Yukio, strongly condemned terrorism "in any form" and stated categorically that his country expected the Pakistan President, Pervez Musharraf, to take concrete action against terrorists and put an end to terrorism. Mr. Hatoyama, leader of Japan's Democratic Party, was in New Delhi at the invitation of the Bharatiya Janata Party.

**25 April:** India and Japan have agreed on the need for a permanent membership of the UN Security Council, said Japanese Ambassador to India Hiroshi Hirabayashi. In an interview to *The Times of India* on the occasion of the forthcoming 50th anniversary of diplomatic relations, Hirabayashi hinted that Japan was willing to modify its earlier fast track method for a joint approach that would ensure the entry of India and Japan, both of whom have been competing contenders in the past, along with some countries from Africa and Latin America.

**13 September:** India and Japan have agreed to broaden their areas of cooperation in economic and other fields and resolved to fight global terrorism. Sentiments to this effect were exchanged at the meeting between the Prime Minister, Atal Behari Vajpayee, and his Japanese counterpart, Junichiro Koizumi in New York.

**12 October:** Japan has called for the resumption of talks between India and Pakistan in the emerging ambience of what Tokyo sees as a positive development. While placing a premium on the fact that elections were held on schedule in Jammu and Kashmir in the face of terrorist attempts to disrupt them, Japan has also noted that a general election took place in Pakistan around the same time. According to a Foreign Ministry official in Tokyo, "Japan values that despite a number of terrorist disturbances, the local Assembly elections in Kashmir were conducted as scheduled."

## CHINA

***Strategic Profile***

**26 January:** China announced a significant softening of its policy towards Taiwan, released a political prisoner with American ties and pledged about $ 150 million towards the effort to rebuild Afghanistan. Analysts claimed that these moves were aimed at underscoring its desire for good relations with Washington before George Bush's visit to China in February.

**3 February:** A commentary which appeared in the official Xinhua news agency strongly criticized US President George Bush's comments calling North Korea, Iran and Iraq an "axis of evil." It suggested that the US was preparing the ground for widening this war on terrorism, while clarifying that no such axis existed between the three nations.

**5 February:** A senior Chinese official in a briefing to reporters said that China was exploring possibilities of opening direct shipping, trade and mail links with Taiwan and was ready to do so without involving the government on either side. This was an important development as it implied that China was willing to drop its precondition that Taiwan first recognize the "one China principle" before opening links with Taiwan.

**21 February:** The US President George Bush visited China

and held talks with President Jiang Zemin. Both countries downplayed their differences on the Taiwan issue. Bush asked China to stop the proliferation of missiles and other deadly technologies. The talks between China and the US were the second in four months. Jiang made a four-point proposition for the two countries to safeguard and develop the positive momentum in their bilateral relationship. Bush, while agreeing, said the US expects to expand and strengthen cooperation with China in various fields which will not only benefit the two countries but also be of significance to safeguarding world peace and promoting cooperation.

**22 February:** The US President, George Bush, and his Chinese counterpart, Jiang Zemin, at a press conference observed that they would work together to open negotiations between the US and North Korea. Jiang Zemin did not specify what China's role would be in the negotiations but said that he was firmly behind Bush's position. The two leaders reaffirmed the importance of the US-Chinese relationship and pushed aside the most contentious issues in the interests of their own agendas. The two countries also reaffirmed each of their country's position on Taiwan. Jiang Zemin averred that China should be reunified with Taiwan while Bush said that the US believed in a peaceful resolution of the issue. Bush, however, reiterated that the US would continue to support the Taiwan Relations Act guaranteeing Taiwan's security, a reminder that the US is bound by its own law to provide weapons to the island for its defence.

**5 March:** China rejected the US human rights report as fabricated and urged Washington to stop interfering in the internal affairs of other nations on the pretext of human rights.

**6 March:** China announced 17.6 per cent rise in the defence spending to $ 20.07 billion citing changes in the international situation and the need to modernise the 2.5 million strong People's Liberation Army.

**11 March:** China released its own version of human rights records in the US for 2001, in which it attacked American foreign policy, racism, domestic inequality, the position of women and children. The State Council of China prepared the report.

**16 March:** Chinese State owned television reported that China had strongly accused Washington of nuclear blackmail. Apparently the Vice-Foreign Minister Li Zhaoxing called the US ambassador Clark T. Randt Jr. to present him with solemn representations after a Pentagon nuclear policy review, which described contingency plans to aim nuclear weapons at China among several other countries, was released.

**19 March:** China's ambassador to the United Nations, Zhang Yan, specified his country's position on the fight against nuclear terrorism within the framework of the International Atomic Energy Agency (IAEA). He stressed the crucial importance of international cooperation, the indispensable role of government in the safety of nuclear material, and the role of the IAEA.

**25 March:** Indonesia and China moved to bolster bilateral diplomatic ties during Indonesian President, Megawati Soekarnoputri's five-day visit to China. The visit was aimed at boosting trade relations between the two countries. A number of MoU's were signed including one on the establishment of a Joint Energy Forum and on a US $ 6 million grant to Indonesia.

**26 March:** Chinese Premier, Zhu Rongji, at a meeting with visiting US Senators Daniel Inouye and Ted Stevens hoped sincerely that a peaceful reunification of the motherland would materialise and opposed US actions to obstruct China's efforts. He expressed appreciation for the two Senators' enduring efforts towards the progress of Sino-US relations and said that bilateral friendly cooperation was in the interests of both countries and is mutually supported by their people.

**26 April:** The Russian Newspaper, *Vremya Novostei,* reported that Russia and China are forging a defence pact under the umbrella of the Shanghai Cooperation Organisation (SCO). The other countries involved are Kazakhstan, Kyrgyzstan, Tajikistan, and Uzbekistan. The newspaper reported that the foreign ministers of the six countries met in Moscow to approved a charter which will be signed in June.

**2 May:** Hu Jintao, the Chinese Vice President, for the first time visited the US. He met President Bush, Secretary of State Colin Powell and other high-ranking officials. They discussed Taiwan, trade issues and US complaints about China's human rights record. Bush apparently told the Chinese leader that US-China relations were satisfactory, while urging China to respect religious freedom.

**2 July:** US sources reported that China test-fired a new air-to-air missile in a move that could, according to Washington prompt America to give Taiwan access to similar weapons. China apparently refused to confirm the reports.

**27 August:** China reportedly signed a contract with Russia to purchase 38 Sukhoi-30 MK fighter-bombers to increase the size of its combined fleet of SU-30s to nearly 200 jets by 2004.

**25 October:** Chinese President Jiang Zemin paid an official visit to the US in order to attend a summit meeting with his American counterpart George Bush in Crawford, Texas. At a press conference after the meeting both affirmed they would work closely together to rid North Korea of nuclear weapons and agreed to cooperate in fighting against terrorism and preventing the proliferation of weapons of massive destruction.

**15 November:** The Central Committee of the governing Communist Party of China (CPC) elected Hu Jintao as its new General Secretary. Jiang Zemin gave up the post on 14 November to facilitate a change of leadership based on consensus within the party. He will, however, retain the Presidency of China until his term is completed. Hu Jintao, currently Vice-President will succeed him.

**2 December:** The Russian President, Vladimir Putin, visited Beijing for a summit with his Chinese counterpart, Jiang Zemin. The theme of the summit was the evolution of a special strategic equation between the two countries. North Korea's declaration about its right to possess an arsenal of nuclear weapons was also discussed.

**9 December:** China's first defence policy paper in more than two years featured its preoccupation with Taiwan. The document also revealed China's concerns about non-traditional threats like terrorism and global crime. Although the US was not directly mentioned, the document extended support to the global war on terrorism.

**19 December:** The Chinese Foreign Ministry spokesman expressed concern over the move by the US President, George Bush, to hasten the deployment of an early version of a missile defence system by 2004. China emphasised that the Bush plan should not affect global strategic stability nor harm international and regional security.

**24 December:** China signed a "Good-Neighbourly Treaty of Friendship and Cooperation" with Kazakhstan. The treaty was signed by the Chinese President, Jiang Zemin and the visiting leader of Kazakhstan, Nursultan Nazarbayev, in Beijing. The treaty enables China to establish bilateral strategic ties with Kazakhstan. The treaty will optimise two-way trade, strengthen cooperation in the energy sector besides extending preferential treatment to investors from both sides on a reciprocal basis, and promote cultural exchanges.

### *Relations with India*

**13 January:** The Chinese Prime Minister, Zhu Rongji, arrived on a visit to India to explore the possibilities of expanding political cooperation with India. On his arrival, he made it clear that China had no intention of brokering peace between India and Pakistan.

**15 January:** China and India during Zhu Rongji's visit to New Delhi decided to build close economic ties and established a forum that would help in combating terrorism. A regular dialogue would also be held to expand cooperation in combating terrorism.

**17 January:** The Chinese Prime Minister, Zhu Rongji, visiting Bangalore, noted that China and India could work together to help each other to complement their respective strengths in information technology.

**29 March:** India's External Affairs Minister Jaswant Singh visited China and held extensive consultations with the Chinese leadership. In a major step towards an eventual resolution of the vexed boundary dispute, India and China agreed to complete the delineation of the Line of Actual Control on their contested borders within a reasonable time frame.

**30 March:** Jaswant Singh concluded consultations with the Chinese leadership. The significant decisions arrived at during this visit were accelerating the process of demarcating the LAC, initiation of the first ever bilateral dialogue on combating terrorism, and a political determination to intensify economic cooperation.

**17 June:** India and China began talks on the clarification of the Line of Actual Control on the Western sector of their long and contested boundary in Beijing. The Indian press reported that Indian and Chinese officials had apparently initiated the process of exchanging maps of the Western sector in Beijing.

**22 November:** The fourteenth meeting of the Joint Working Group (JWG) on the boundary question between India and China was held in New Delhi to resolve differences relating to the exchange of maps in the Western sector of the Line of Actual Control (LAC). While details were unavailable, the Indian Foreign Office spokesman said the talks were "good and forward looking".

# PAKISTAN

***Strategic Profile***

**4 January:** Gen. Musharraf in a transit stop at Beijing on his way to Kathmandu, discussed the tense situation in South Asia and the ongoing war on terrorism at a meeting with the Chinese Premier Zhu Rongji. He assured China that Pakistan was taking necessary measures to curb terrorism in Pakistan. In turn, Zhu Rongji expressed appreciation for Pakistan's adherence to seeking a dialogue amid the tense situation.

**6 January:** Pakistan President, Pervez Musharraf, in Kathmandu called upon the SAARC to take up bilateral contentious issues at its forum.

**10 January:** It was revealed by defence officials in Pakistan that China had supplied the first batch of 40 Chinese made fighter aircraft under a defence deal. The first batch of 10F-7 pg aircraft was delivered in December 2001, while the rest would be supplied later.

**17 February:** The US restored the International Military Education and Training (IMET) programme to the Pakistani army.

**19 February:** Ukraine, it was revealed, signed two major defence deals with Pakistan to help build its latest Main Battle Tanks (MBT) and to upgrade old ones. The deal amounted to about $100-120 million.

**20 February:** *The New York Times* reported that Pakistan had started winding up two major units of its Inter Services Intelligence (ISI) that had a close relationship with militants in Afghanistan and Kashmir.

**22 February:** Pakistan and Iran signed an agreement for a pre-feasibility study on laying the Indo-Iran gas pipeline project via Pakistan.

**14 March:** Pakistan President, Gen. Pervez Musharraf, while on a visit to Japan, met its Prime Minister Junichiro Koizumi. Both countries, among other issues, discussed Indo-Pak relations. Japan urged Pakistan to do more to ease tensions with India. Pakistan was not able to persuade Japan to resume economic assistance and investments in the region.

**2 July:** *The Dawn* reported that Pakistan had purchased border surveillance equipment including three fixed wing planes and five armed helicopters worth about $73 million, from the US.

**15 July:** An anti-terrorist court in Pakistan sentenced Omar Saeed Sheikh to death by hanging because of his involvement in the kidnapping and subsequent murder of the *Wall Street Journal* reporter, Daniel Pearl.

**20 July:** Pakistan deployed the five helicopters it received from the US for surveillance on the Afghanistan border to monitor infiltration by Al Qaeda and the Taliban.

**27 September:** Pakistan was elected as a non-permanent member of the United Nations Security Council for a two-year term that would start from January 2003. The Pakistani permanent envoy to the United Nations, Munir Akram, told the Pakistan-based news agency NNI in New York that the Kashmir issue would be raised at the appropriate time and that it was at the top of Pakistan's agenda.

**4 October:** Pakistan successfully test-fired a Medium Range Surface-to-Surface Ballistic Missile (MRSSBM), Hatf IV (Shaheen), which was capable of carrying a nuclear warhead and hit targets within a range of 700 kms.

**8 October:** Within a span of five days Pakistan for the second time tested Hatf IV MRSSBM ostensibly to validate certain additional parameters.

**8 October:** Japan in a statement requested Pakistan to desist from carrying out ballistic missile tests as planned saying that it could further ignite the ongoing missile race in South Asia.

**11 October:** In the general elections held on 10 October no single party emerged with a majority. The Mutthida Majlis-e-Amal (MMA), an alliance of right wing religious parties, forged ahead with 40 seats in the 272-member National Assembly.

**12 October:** The MMA in Pakistan asserted that it would not allow US troops to use Pakistani soil.

**12 October:** Releasing the preliminary findings of the European Union (EU) Election Observation Mission to Pakistan, its chief, John Cusnahan, suggested that pre-poll manipulation such as rules to bar top political leaders from contesting the elections had adversely impacted the outcome and he also raised serious doubts about the credibility of the electoral process because it was replete with serious flaws.

**1 November:** The Commonwealth Secretary-General, Don McKinnon, announced in London after a decision was taken by the Commonwealth Ministerial Action Group that Pakistan would remain suspended from the Commonwealth until the latter is satisfied that democracy had been fully restored there, in the light of the Commonwealth Observers report on the elections in Pakistan.

**6 November:** The US Under Secretary of State for Economic, Business and Agriculture Affairs, Alan P. Larson, on a visit to Pakistan announced that the US was committed to write off Pakistan's $ 1 billion debt and was rapidly moving towards an agreement with Pakistan on that account.

**13 November:** The Pakistani English daily *Dawn* reported that Pakistan had signed a Memorandum of Understanding (MoU) with the Russian energy firm Gazprom for the construction of a $ 3.5 billion trans-Pakistan gas pipeline from Iran to India.

**15 November:** An official statement announced in Pakistan that the 1973 constitution, which was suspended in the wake of the military coup on 12 October 1999, stood restored with certain changes.

**16 November:** The Pakistan National Assembly met after more than three years. Gen. Pervez Musharraf was sworn in as President for another five years on the basis of a referendum held in April.

**22 December:** *The Washington Times* reported from Iraqi secret service documents that Pakistan had deflected and frustrated a UN probe into an offer made by Islamabad to Iraq of nuclear weapons know-how, allegedly made in the 1990s on behalf of Abdul Qadir Khan, father of Pakistan's atomic bomb.

**26 December:** At the conclusion of Iranian President, Syed Mohammad Khatami's visit to Islamabad, both Pakistan and Iran, in an obvious reference to the Bush doctrine expressed opposition to what has been termed as unilateral or pre-emptive military operation against Iraq and rejected the thesis of a regime change.

***Relations with India***

**2 January:** Pakistan said that it was prepared to consider the extradition requests for the "20 fugitives" accused of having committed crimes in India and had taken shelter in Pakistan, if New Delhi gave credible evidence and rooted it through the SAARC anti-terrorism convention.

**3 January:** Foreign Minister Jaswant Singh in Kathmandu released a comprehensive document listing evidence provided to Islamabad during the past decade about the involvement of 20 criminals in terrorist acts whose extradition had been demanded by India.

**3 January:** Prime Minister Atal Behari Vajpayee at a press conference in Kathmandu made a veiled attack on Pakistan for abetting cross-border terrorism and asked the global coalition on terrorism to pressurize states sponsoring and sheltering terrorist organizations to abandon the policy.

**5 January:** At the opening session of the SAARC summit, Pakistan President, Pervez Musharraf, sought a renewed engagement with India, but Indian Prime Minister, Atal Behari Vajpyaee, insisted that Pakistan first end support to cross-border terrorism. While welcoming Gen. Musharraf's offer of friendship, Vajpayee demanded that Pakistan follow it up by gestures to stop any activity in Pakistan and its occupied part of Kashmir, which enabled terrorists to perpetrate mindless violence in India.

**9 January:** Pakistan President, Gen. Pervez Musharraf, constituted a "National Kashmir Committee" to be headed by the former Prime Minister and President of Pakistan-occupied Kashmir (PoK), Muhammad Abdul Qayyum Khan.

**12 January:** Pervez Musharraf, in a TV address, banned the Lashkar-e-Taiba and Jaish-e-Mohammad along with three other sectarian and religious extremist outfits and urged the Indian leadership to sit across the table for a resolution of the Kashmir dispute in accordance with the wishes of the people of the state. He ruled out handing over the 20 fugitives as demanded by India and pledged to continue moral, political and diplomatic support to the Kashmir cause. He assured that he would not allow terrorism to thrive in Pakistan, and that all madrasas in the country would be registered.

**13 January:** India welcomed Pakistan's decision to snap its support for terrorism in Kashmir and expressed its readiness for direct talks provided "deeds matched words."

**15 January:** At the inaugural address of the new National Kashmir Committee, in Pakistan, Gen. Pervez Musharraf asserted that Pakistan would never compromise on Kashmir and favoured a just solution that addressed the concerns and interests of the people of the state.

**20 January:** Pakistan refused to extend transit facility for the Indian wheat that was supplied to Afghanistan under the World Food Programme (WFP), on the grounds that it was infected.

**22 January:** In front of the American Centre in Kolkata, gunmen killed 4 policemen and wounded 20 people. Without elaborating, India's Home Minister, L. K. Advani, said that a group connected with the ISI of Pakistan was responsible for the attack.

**23 January:** The United Nations Secretary-General, Kofi Annan, on a visit to Islamabad affirmed that there was need for India and Pakistan to build on steps taken by Musharraf to defuse tensions between the two countries.

**24 January:** Kofi Annan urged India to withdraw its troops from the frontline positions to de-escalate tensions in South Asia.

**30 January:** India would "wait and watch" Pakistan's steps to end cross-border terrorism and abandon it as a matter of state policy before deciding on resumption of the Indo-Pak dialogue, the External Affairs Minister Jaswant Singh said in London.

**3 February:** Indian Prime Minister, Atal Behari Vajpayee, at a press conference noted that the issue of the return of Pakistan-occupied Kashmir (PoK) would top the agenda of any talks with Islamabad, but that it would not be a precondition for talks.

**5 February:** Addressing a joint session of the PoK Assembly and Council on the occasion of the Kashmir Solidarity Day, Musharraf observed that Kashmir was central to Indo-Pakistan relations and appealed to the international community for an early resolution of the dispute on the ground that bilaterism had proved to be a farce.

**6 February:** Indian Prime Minister, Atal Behari Vajpayee, asserted that the deployment of troops along the border would continue as long as Pakistan continued sponsoring terrorism.

He said India favoured a dialogue to resolve the Kashmir issue peacefully and that it was the responsibility of Pakistan to build mutual trust and a congenial atmosphere for talks.

**7 February:** The Director of the American Central Intelligence Agency (CIA), George Tenet, appearing before an open session of the Senate Intelligence Committee for the first time since the 11 September attacks said that once a conventional war breaks out between India and Pakistan it could escalate into a nuclear confrontation.

**11 February:** After the deportation of Aftab Ansari (a suspect in the Kolkata shoot out case) from UAE, India reiterated that Pakistan should take action on the list of 20 fugitives and issued a fresh verbal demarche to Pakistan Deputy High Commissioner, Jaleel Abbas Jilani.

**13 February:** Musharraf, during a visit to the US said that to have peace in South Asia, it was critical for the Kashmir issue to be resolved and that, it could not be resolved without third party mediation.

**14 February:** India reiterated its objection to third party intervention in Indo-Pakistan affairs and said that the differences between the two sides could only be resolved by direct talks.

**16 February:** Gen. Musharraf ruled out handing over the 20 fugitives wanted by India and said that Pakistan would not give any face saving device to enable India to withdraw its troops from the frontline.

**27 February:** Pakistan reacted sharply to observations made by the Indian President, K.R. Narayanan, in his address to the joint session of Indian Parliament on 25 February on cross-border terrorism supported by Pakistan. Pakistan rejected the charges and said that contrary to the allegations, Pakistan had taken steps to defuse tensions and pave the way for resumption of talks.

**7 March:** Indian Information and Broadcasting Minister,

Sushma Swaraj, visited Pakistan for the second SAARC Information Ministers' Conference. Pakistan President, Gen. Pervez Musharraf, announced that Pakistan would lift the ban on air links between the two countries if India reciprocated the gesture.

**1 July:** India's new Foreign Secretary, Kanwal Sibal, ruled out the resumption of a dialogue with Pakistan until the Pakistan President, Pervez Musharraf, demonstrated concretely that cross-border terrorism had ended in Jammu and Kashmir.

**4 July:** India's new External Affairs Minister, Yashwant Sinha, immediately after taking over warned that India be cautious in dealing with Musharraf as he had back tracked on assurances concerning cross-border terrorism in Jammu and Kashmir.

**8 July:** Indian Defence Minister, George Fernandes, alleged that cross-border terrorism continued in Jammu and Kashmir and that India stood by its proposal for joint patrolling with Pakistan of the Line of Control to stop infiltration.

**10 July:** Pakistan's newly appointed Minister of State for Foreign Affairs, Inam-ul Haq, appealed to the international community to engage itself in finding a just and durable solution to the Kashmir problem and said that the Pakistani forces would not be able to ensure that infiltration was absent.

**13 July:** A random terrorist attack on a slum in Jammu killed 27 persons.

**14 July:** The US State Department maintained that though there had been a significant decline in infiltration along the Line of Control in Kashmir, there was a perceived need to make the commitments made by Pakistan President permanent.

**15 July:** Pakistan initiated a series of 10-day war games involving senior military officers of Pakistan's nuclear command and control organisation, called "Sabut Kadam-II."

**19 July:** The Bush administration brushed aside calls for a plebiscite in Jammu and Kashmir saying that it was a bilateral issue.

**26 July:** The European Union's High Representative for a Common Foreign and Security Policy, Javier Solana, said in New Delhi that progress in reducing tensions between India and Pakistan would have to be sequential and that if Pakistan did more to curb cross-border terrorism then the Indian response would be positive.

**28 July:** Colin Powell while in New Delhi suggested that India allow outsiders to monitor the October polls in Jammu and Kashmir to add credibility to the process. He also indicated that India should take further de-escalatory steps as Pakistan stops supporting infiltration. In Pakistan later in his tour he said in an ambiguous note that both India and Pakistan should initiate a bilateral process towards a productive and sustainable dialogue.

**29 July:** Pakistan asserted that the ball was in India's court to defuse the tensions at the LoC as it had nothing more to offer and that it had done all it could to stop cross-border infiltration.

**31 July:** During a conversation on the sidelines of the ARF meeting in Brunei between Indian External Affairs Minister Yashwant Sinha and the US Secretary of State, Colin Powell, the latter was said to have assured India that the emergence of the Kashmir issue as a matter of international concern does not imply that the US would like the global community and more particularly Washington itself to play a role in the resolution of the dispute.

**31 July:** India's Deputy Prime Minister, L. K. Advani, while speaking in the Rajya Sabha said that infiltration along the Line of Control (LoC) had declined but not stopped.

**14 August:** General Musharraf in a speech on Pakistan's 55th Independence Day described the scheduled elections (in

October) in Jammu and Kashmir as farcical and said that there could never be peace in South Asia without the resolution of the Kashmir issue.

**21 August:** At the sidelines of the SAARC Council of Ministers Conference in Nepal, the Indian External Affairs Minister, Yashwant Sinha, noted that India and Pakistan could work towards de-escalation if Pakistan conceded that infiltration across the LoC was not in its control and came clean on the issue.

**22 August:** Pakistan's Minister of State for Foreign Affairs, Inam-ul-Haq, while addressing media-persons in Nepal said that Islamabad was not averse to considering the Indian proposal of joint patrolling of the LoC if tensions came down and confidence was built between the two countries.

**24 August:** US Deputy Secretary of State, Richard Armitage, on a visit to Islamabad said that some infiltration continued on the LoC and that Musharraf had reiterated his commitment to stop it. Talking to journalists, he said that no one believed that Pakistan could ensure the complete stoppage of infiltration across the LoC.

**12 September:** Prime Minister Vajpayee met the American President, George Bush, to discuss Pakistan's continued support to cross-border terrorism and its sustained attempts to disrupt elections in Jammu and Kashmir through violence.

**12 September:** Pakistan President, General Pervez Musharraf, in his address to the United Nations General Assembly (UNGA) targeted Hindu fanaticism in India and called on the international community to hold accountable those responsible for the murder of Muslims in Gujarat.

**13 September:** Prime Minister Vajpayee in his address to UNGA accused Pakistan of nuclear blackmail following India's efforts to stamp out cross-border terrorism and said that to succumb to such blatant nuclear terrorism would mean to forget the bitter lessons of 11 September. He also rebutted Pakistan's allegations and reaffirmed that cross-border terrorism would be suppressed by all means at India's command.

**14 September:** At a function in New York, General Musharraf asserted that he would be thrown out of office if he abandoned the Kashmir issue.

**19 September:** General Musharraf at a seminar on 'Peace and Security in South Asia', organised in Islamabad declared that there would be no more concessions from Pakistan for de-escalation of tensions with India and that New Delhi would have to take substantive reciprocal steps if it was serious about its declared intention of walking the high road to peace.

**26 September:** Indian Prime Minister, Atal Behari Vajpayee, said that US pressure on Pakistan was not working and that India would have to fight its own war against the menace, at an awards presentation ceremony.

**30 September:** Indian Finance Minister, Jaswant Singh, while in Washington to attend the annual meetings of the World Bank and the International Monetary Fund, at a news conference at the Indian embassy said that every country had the right to pre-emption and that this doctrine was not the prerogative of any one nation.

**11 October:** Indian Foreign Minister, Yashwant Sinha, in London speaking to the press observed that the strong performance by fundamentalists' parties in the elections in the Pakistani state of the North-West Frontier Province (NWFP) and Balochistan was an ominous signal.

**12 October:** Indian Prime Minister, Atal Behari Vajpayee, met his British counterpart, Tony Blair, in London. He apparently expressed concern at the success of the fundamentalist MMA in Pakistan's general elections. After the meeting, Yashwant Sinha briefing the press said that Tony Blair had endorsed India's position that no dialogue was possible without an end to cross-border terrorism.

**16 October:** India at a meeting of its Cabinet Committee on Security (CCS) decided to pull back its troops from the International Border (IB) with Pakistan.

**17 October:** Pakistan announced the withdrawal of its troops along the India-Pakistan border to peacetime locations.

**17 October:** The Chinese Foreign Ministry in a statement welcomed India's decision to withdraw its troops deployed on the IB with Pakistan saying that Beijing would welcome all efforts aimed at reducing the tensions that prevailed in South Asia.

**21 October:** Pakistan Foreign Office spokesperson, Aziz Ahmed Khan, maintained that a return to the negotiation table was the real measure of tensions subsiding in the region. Pakistan, he said, hoped that the withdrawal of troops would lead to the resumption of dialogue between India and Pakistan.

**11 November:** Pakistan Foreign Office spokesperson, Aziz Ahmad Khan, said that Pakistan would set a deadline for India and Bhutan to respond on the proposed SAARC summit in January.

**12 November:** The Indian External Affairs Minister, Yashwant Sinha, in Seoul to participate in the second Ministerial Conference of Democracies said that Pakistan could not set a deadline as SAARC works on consensus.

**12 November:** Indian Defence Minister, George Fernandes, stated that there had been a minor reduction in infiltration of terrorists from Pakistan into Jammu and Kashmir.

**23 November:** As Pakistan's new government led by Prime Minister Zafarullah Khan Jamali was sworn in, President Pervez Musharraf hoped that India would commence talks with the new civilian government.

**2 December:** Vajpayee endorsed the Russian President Vladimir Putin's fears on Pakistan's nuclear weapons falling into the hands of terrorists. He asked the international community to take note of the serious threat.

**4 December:** At the conclusion of the Russian President Vladimir Putin's visit to India, the Delhi Declaration included in its purview India's relations with Pakistan. Putin, without naming Pakistan appealed for the strengthening of the international non-proliferation regime to prevent weapons of mass destruction falling into the hands of terrorists. A joint statement also backed India's position on cross-border terrorism.

**14 December:** Pakistani authorities released Masood Azhar, chief of the banned militant outfit Jaish-e-Mohammad, after the Lahore High Court turned down the government's request to extend his remand for three months because the authorities failed to produce sufficient evidence to hold him for a longer period in custody without a charge.

**14 December:** The Indian Foreign Office spokesperson stated that the release of Masood Azhar made it clear that the charges against him had not been pursued with any seriousness by Islamabad.

**21 December:** The US White House spokesman, Ari Fleischer, said that Washington believed that tensions between India and Pakistan were no longer alarming as diplomatic efforts by Washington and the international community had brought them down to a markedly diminished point.

**29 December:** Indian Minister of State for Home, Vidyasagar Rao, announced that India planned to restrict the movement of Pakistani nationals to three Indian cities and begin a vigorous drive to round up those who had overstayed.

**30 December:** While addressing Air Force veterans in Karachi, Pakistani President, Gen. Pervez Musharraf, disclosed that he had conveyed several messages to the Indian Prime Minister, Atal Behari Vajpayee, during the stand off between India and Pakistan, that if Indian forces tried to cross the border the tension could escalate into a nuclear war. The spokesman of the Pakistani President, however, maintained that Gen. Musharraf did not mention a nuclear war and that his reference to unconventional war was in the context of support to the Pakistani government from the people of Pakistan and Kashmir.

**30 December:** The Pakistan Foreign Office spokesman asserted that Pakistan had no plans as of then to reciprocate measures contemplated by India to further tighten visa regulations on Pakistani nationals wanting to visit India.

## NEPAL

**19 January:** The US Secretary of State, Colin Powell, met with Nepal's top military officials to hear their needs for military aid in fighting an escalating Maoist insurgency.

**17 February:** In their deadliest strike, Maoist rebels killed 133 people, including 129 security personnel, in two separate assaults in Nepal, losing more than 100 of their cadres in counter-offensive.

**21 February:** At least 48 Maoist insurgents were killed and 15 others arrested by security forces in western Nepal, the Defence Ministry of Nepal said.

**22 February:** Barely hours after the Nepal Parliament extended the state of emergency, Maoist rebels unleashed a fresh wave of violence killing 44 people, including 34 policemen, while losing eight of its men to the security forces.

**20 March:** Prime Minister Sher Bahadur Deuba arrived for a weeklong visit to India. He intended to discuss ways to tackle the Maoist insurgency and steps to expand bilateral trade and economic cooperation, especially the development of water resources in his country.

**12 April:** The Maoist rebels have killed 102 people in the Dang district of south-western Nepal, including 84 policemen, in two attacks on police posts.

**12 April:** India will grant an assistance of Rs. 840 million to Nepal for setting up the 100 km East-West Highway Optical Fibre Cable (OFC) Network, which is expected to cover all the main cities and towns in the Himalayan kingdom.

**13 April:** Nearly 160 police and Maoist rebels were killed in the worst carnage in the six-year-old insurgency in Nepal.

**20 April:** Maoist rebels bombed the home of Nepal's Finance Minister, Ramsharan Mahat, even as security forces gunned down 10 terrorists across the country. The Minister was not at his village home when it was attacked.

**1 May:** At least 14 Maoists were killed in battles with Nepalese Security forces in the west of Himalayan kingdom. The fresh violence came ahead of a state visit to Washington on 1 May by Nepali Prime Minister, Sher Bahadur Deuba. The Bush administration has already asked the Congress for $ 20 million as military assistance to the kingdom.

**4 May:** The US has declared that it has no plans to set up a military base in Nepal to counter the Chinese influence.

**26 May:** After the Nepali Prime Minister Sher Bahadur Deuba asked King Gyanendra to dissolve the 205-member House of Parliament two years before the Parliament's term was to end in 2004, the ruling Nepali Congress (NC) expelled him for three years. Mr. Deuba recommended the dissolution after the party objected to a plan to extend the state of emergency to tackle the communist insurgency.

**21 June:** The spokesman of the Foreign Office in New Delhi emphasised that "constitutional monarchy and multiparty democracy are the twin pillars that will provide stability in Nepal" on the eve of the visit of King Gyanendra to Delhi, his first visit abroad after his ascension.

**21 June:** The Nepalese king held extensive talks with the President, K. R. Narayanan, the Prime Minister, Atal Behari Vajapayee, the Vice-President, Krishan Kant, and the External Affairs Minister, Jaswant Singh. President Narayanan expressed the hope that Nepal would overcome the 'grave challenges' facing it. The Defence Minister assured the King that New Delhi will continue to provide military assistance to help combat Maoist insurgency.

**19 August:** At the three-day India-Nepal Government Committee on Trade Transit and Cooperation to Control Unauthorised Trade, which concluded in New Delhi, India and Nepal agreed to tackle several irritants in bilateral trade, including a cut in customs-duty preference on Indian goods as well as continuing discrimination against export of cars from the country.

**31 August:** A group of 15-20 Maoists attacked the 'Taj and Karan', an Indian car dealership at Teku, damaging 22 vehicles, and causing a loss of Rs. 50 lakhs.

**14 September:** India and Nepal began a three-day consultative meeting to explore measures to strengthen trans-boundary cooperation on bio-diversity conservation, control illegal trade in timber, wild flora and fauna and their products.

**4 October:** Nepal's King Gyanendra dismissed the Prime Minister, Sher Bahadur Deuba, and his cabinet and declared himself the interim executive head of the Himalayan kingdom. This is the first time that the king has taken over the reins of the country after the restoration of multi-party democracy in the kingdom in 1990.

**6 October:** A press report says that India and Nepal have worked out a formula for deporting 'wanted' people from each other's territory during the visit of the Foreign Minister, Yashwant

Sinha, to Nepal in August, though the two countries do not have an extradition treaty.

**30 December:** Nepalese Prime Minister, Lokendra Bahadur Chand, while speaking at the 58th birth anniversary of the slain King Birendra, offered to make public the whereabouts of the rebels detained by the government. This was one of the conditions laid down by the Maoists to call off the strike that had crippled Nepal for the past two days.

## BANGLADESH

**4 January:** Dhaka expressed its readiness to support the peace process in post-Taliban Afghanistan as the British Prime Minister, Tony Blair, whose country heads the International Security Assistance Force (ISAF), ended his one-and-a-half-day brief "working visit" to Dhaka.

**9 January:** Several former Ministers of the Sheikh Hasina government were beaten up by the police during a country-wide hartal enforced by the Awami League in Bangladesh.

**10 January:** Though there was an angry denial from the Bangladesh Prime Minister, Begum Khaleda Zia, that there was any Taliban in her Government, Bangladesh's main Opposition seemed serious in claiming that the present Cabinet has "several Ministers" who have strong Taliban connections.

**7 February:** The Bangladesh Government denied the charge by some politicians and a section of the media in India that it has become the springboard for Pakistan's Inter-Services Intelligence (ISI) operations in India.

**11 February:** The Bangladesh Foreign Minister, Morshed Khan, denied the Tripura Chief Minister, Manik Sarkar's claim that there are over 30 camps of north-east "rebel groups" in Bangladesh.

**3 March:** The Bangladesh Government's Cabinet Committee on Law and Order decided to provide security to Hindu temples in Bangladesh to prevent any untoward incident. The ruling Bangladesh Nationalist Party (BNP) expressed its concern over the communal violence in India.

**10 March:** Prime Minister Khaleda Zia condemned the Gujarat killings, while lauding the Bangladesh police for preventing any backlash following the violence in Gujarat.

**1 April:** The Bangladesh Commerce Minister, Amir Khasrau Mahumud Choudhury, said that his country would review its trade relations with India. The Minister told Parliament that if India did not remove tariff and non-tariff barriers on Bangladesh products, he would have to announce remedial measures in his next budget.

**3 April:** The Bangladesh Government has lodged a strong protest with *The Far Eastern Economic Review* for publishing a cover story in its 4 April issue headlined "Beware of Bangladesh" which suggested an alarming rise of Islamic fundamentalism.

**6 April:** The Bangladesh Prime Minister has said that the Government intended to build friendly and cordial relations with India. She dismissed reports of 'persecution' of the minorities in her country and added that a large section of the Hindus had voted for her party and its alliance.

**10 April:** India and Bangladesh concluded their trade talks in Dhaka with New Delhi agreeing to give duty-free access to 16 categories of Bangladeshi products and Dhaka agreeing to discuss border trade and transhipment issues at the coming Joint Economic Commission (JEC) meeting.

**23 April:** Prime Minister, Khaleda Zia, met the tribal leaders of the Chittagong Hill Tracts (CHT) region and urged them to contribute to national development. The ruling Bangladesh Nationalist Party (BNP), while in opposition had opposed the CHT Peace Accord, which ended the decades-long tribal insurgency. She had called the accord an "Indian Machination".

**1 May:** Rejecting suggestions by the US Congressman Benjamin Gilman, the Chairman of the US Congressional South Asian Affairs Committee and Co-Chairman of the Bangladesh Caucus, for a new law to ensure the security of minority citizens, the Bangladesh Foreign Minister, Morshed Khan, has said that "there is no minority problem in Bangladesh."

**5 May:** The Bangladeshi Commerce Secretary, Sohel Ahmed, has said that India had not shown "any intention" to provide access to Bangladeshi products even a month after the last round of trade talks. In order to reduce the huge cumulative trade gap between the two countries, which was in India's favour to the tune of $ 1 billion in 2000-01, he said Bangladesh would continue to talk with India and demand preferential treatment as a least developed country.

**8 May:** The commander of the now-defunct tribal insurgent faction, Shanti Bahini, and current head of the Chittegong Hill Tracts Regional Council (CHTRC), J. B. Larma, has said that the Bangladesh National Party (BNP) led government needs to take "immediate steps" to implement the 1991 peace accord. He added that the non-implementation of the accord was at the heart of the deteriorating law and order situation.

**11 May:** The US has not dropped the idea of pushing forward the Status of Forces Agreement (SoFA) with Bangladesh, which Washington had proposed a few years ago but failed following stiff resistance from Dhaka. This was revealed by the US Ambassador, Mary Ann Peters, in Dhaka.

**29 May:** Amnesty International, the international human rights watchdog, in its annual report for 2001, has alleged widespread persecution and ill treatment of minority communities and women in Bangladesh, before and after last year's general election.

**17 June:** During talks between the visiting Bangladesh Foreign Minister, Morshed Khan, and the External Affairs Minister, Jaswant Singh, the two sides acknowledged that the two nations could not be "defeated by small difficulties", which included Dhaka's demand for duty free access to its products in the Indian market and New Delhi's quest for transit rights through Bangladesh territory to the Indian north-east.

**4 July:** The Bangladeshi Commerce Minister, Amir Khasru Mohammed Chowdhary, told newspersons in Dhaka that India was not keen on improving trade between the two countries. While commenting on duty-free access granted by India to 40 Bangladeshi products, he stated that most of their products were not produced in the country. At the ensuing Secretary-level talks with India, he said that it would be the priority of Bangladesh to get duty-free access to 160 Bangladeshi items.

**17 July:** The Bangladesh Prime Minister, Khaleda Zia, told reporters in Dhaka that her government had decided to sell the multi-role MIG-29 planes that the previous government of Sheikh Hasina had purchased two years ago as Bangladesh "cannot afford the $ 1 billion a year needed for spare parts and maintenance."

**1 August:** The Bangladesh High Commissioner, Tufail Haider, told a meeting organised by the Confederation of Indian Industry (CII) that Bangladesh regretted that India had not been able to resolve the issue of reducing tariff barriers on 25 product lines, as requested by his country. He added that Bangladesh may export a 'moderate' quantity of natural gas to India.

**24 August:** At talks between the visiting Foreign Minister, Yashwant Sinha, and his Bangladeshi counterpart, Morshed Khan, both the countries reached an agreement to combat terrorism and poverty. India also confirmed duty free access to 40 Bangladeshi products under 16 categories that was agreed to earlier.

**21 September:** The 'Bangladesh Puja Ujjapan Parishad', the central Hindu body to oversee celebration of religious functions of the community, said that it would protest the atrocities against the community by the country's ruling alliance during the coming festival of Durga Puja.

**22 September:** The Bangladesh Prime Minister, Khaleda Zia, told the 24-member Asia-Pacific Regional Consultative Workshop on Water and Poverty, that withdrawal of water by upper riparian states was degrading its vast areas of land and increasing the poverty.

**6 October:** The Bangladesh Acting Foreign Secretary, Anwarul Alam Shahid, called the Indian High Commissioner, M. L. Tripathi, and handed a protest note against media reports suggesting that an unidentified aircraft from its territory had intruded into airspace over West Bengal. Mr. Shahid said that such media reports in "no way contribute to the existing friendly ties between the two neighbouring countries."

**10 October:** The Bangladesh Prime Minister, Khaleda Zia, on the occasion of her completing the first year in power, told a meeting of foreign diplomats that tough measures had been taken to ensure "peaceful and joyous celebrations" of the Durga Puja.

**13 October:** Quoting sources in the Indian Intelligence and Bangladesh's largest Al Qaeda-allied terrorist group, the Harkat-ul-Jihad-al-Islami (HUJI), *Time* magazine has revealed that Bangladesh has become a hotbed of terrorists waging a war against India. The magazine said that agents of Bangladesh's military intelligence services (DGFI) maintain contact with their counterparts in Pakistan's ISI and have a long history of supporting rebels fighting Indian rule across the border.

**17 October:** The Bangladesh Foreign Secretary, Shamsher Chowdhary, has termed the report carried by *Time* magazine under the title "Deadly Cargo" as "fictitious and imaginative", and described it as part of "an anti-Bangladesh campaign".

**18 October:** The Bangladesh army carried out a massive countrywide crackdown on terrorists across the country. The opposition charged that by calling out the army, the Government had acknowledged failure of the civil administration in tackling the deteriorating law and order situation.

**19 October:** At the seminar-cum-mini trade summit on "Promotion of Trade and Investment between Bangladesh and North-Eastern States of India", organised by the Chittagong Chamber of Commerce and Industry (CCCI) and the Indian High Commission in Chittagong, the Bangladesh Commerce Minister, Amir Khasru Mahumud Chowdhury, underscored the need for a pro-active and friendly attitude from the members of SAARC, particularly India, to increase the volume of trade and investment in the region.

**1 November:** India and Bangladesh decided to set up a joint coordination committee to take care of border problems, during a meeting with the chief of India's BSF, Ajai Raj Sharma and head of Bangladesh Rifles (BDR), Maj. Gen. Rezaqul Haider. The BSF Chief raised the issue of insurgents of the north-eastern India finding shelter in Bangladesh.

**7 November:** The Deputy Prime Minister, L. K. Advani, after inaugurating the 51st All-India Police games at Bhiwani, Haryana, voiced serious concern over the growing activities of the Inter-Services Intelligence of Pakistan and the Al Qaeda in Bangladesh and asked the international community to treat Al Qaeda on a par with terrorist outfits like the Taliban.

**8 November:** Reacting to the charges made by the Deputy Prime Minister, L. K. Advani, the Bangladesh Foreign Office spokesman said that they were "totally baseless, motivated and irresponsible."

**27 November:** The External Affairs Minister, Yashwant Sinha, while replying to a question in the Lok Sabha, said that the

Pakistan mission in Dhaka had become the "nerve-centre" of ISI activities encouraging terrorism in India.

**28 November:** Bangladesh rejected India's charge that its territory was being used by Pakistan's ISI and the Al Qaeda for anti-India activities, but asked New Delhi to provide "credible evidence", saying it would investigate the allegations.

**29 November:** The Defence Minister, George Fernandes, said that India had intelligence information and "human evidence" to support its claim that Pakistan's ISI and the Al Qaeda were using Bangladesh territory for anti-India activities.

**11 December:** Bangladesh's Finance and Planning Minister, Saifur Rahman, addressing a seminar on "Bilateral Trade with India and Economic Security of Bangladesh" held at the Bangladesh Institute of International and Strategic Studies rejected any transit or transhipment facility for India, saying the country's entire road system would collapse if such facilities were given.

**24 December:** Bangladesh Prime Minister, Khalida Zia's visit to China unveiled a significant "umbrella defence agreement" between Dhaka and Beijing. The Bangladeshi daily *The Daily Star* reported the agreement, which would ostensibly rationalize the existing piecemeal agreements to enhance cooperation in training, maintenance and in some areas of production of defence equipment.

**29 December:** Bangladesh's Foreign Minister, M. Morshed Khan, while addressing presspersons after the visit of Prime Minister Khaleda Zia to Beijing, said that the just-concluded defence deal with China does not contain anything "destructive" and will not hurt ties with India.

## SRI LANKA

**5 January:** The LTTE has reiterated to Norway, the facilitator chosen by both sides, that a complete lifting of economic restrictions on areas under its control along with removal of restrictions on fishing in the north-east coast and on the movement and travel of Tamils, were essential prerequisites for the commencement of talks.

**10 January:** A team from Oslo arrived in Colombo for discussions with the Government on the peace process, as Sri Lanka publicly distanced itself from an LTTE proposal to hold peace talks in India, dismissing newspaper reports on the issue as "speculative" and saying it was too early in the process to start thinking of a venue.

**13 January:** Undeterred by strong opposition in India, the LTTE representative in London, Anton Balasingham, continues to hold that South India is the best venue for peace talks with the Sri Lankan Government, ruling out speculation that Kathmandu was being considered instead.

**20 January:** The LTTE extended its ceasefire, which was due to end at midnight on 24 January, by another month and asked the government to reciprocate.

**21 January:** Sri Lanka's Navy pulled back from a confrontation with a flotilla of Sea Tiger boats in the island's northern waters in the early hours, as the Government followed the LTTE in announcing an extension of the current truce till 24 February.

**27 January:** The Sri Lankan Prime Minister, Ranil Wickremesinghe, began canvassing support for lifting the ban on the Liberation Tigers of Tamil Eelam.

**12 February:** In yet another measure to normalise life in the North-East and assist the evolving peace process with the

LTTE, the Sri Lankan Government ended an era of control over travel to the Jaffna peninsula and areas controlled by the Tigers in the North-East.

**14 February:** The Sri Lankan President, Chandrika Kumaratunga, was "cautiously optimistic" about the peace process but wanted built into any agreement with the Liberation Tigers of Tamil Eelam safeguards on human rights of Tamil people in the north-east.

**21 February:** The director of the Central Bureau of Investigation, P.C. Sharma, said in Colombo that the LTTE leader, Velupillai Prabhakaran, remains a wanted man in India and the request for his extradition is pending with the Sri Lankan Government.

**22 February:** The Sri Lankan Government and the Liberation Tigers of Tamil Eelam (LTTE) were set to begin an indefinite and mutually agreed ceasefire from 23 February midnight for the first time since 1994, with both sides signing letters accepting the terms of the Norway-brokered truce.

**23 February:** The Prime Minister, Ranil Wickremesinghe, described the mutual truce between the Sri Lankan Government and the LTTE, which took effect from 23 February, as a "first step" that would render negotiations for a settlement "more likely to succeed."

**27 February:** The Sri Lankan President, Chandrika Kumaratunga, said she had no intention of hindering the negotiation process to end the nation's ethnic conflict, but maintained that some of the clauses in the Government's ceasefire agreement with the LTTE were of great concern to her.

**14 March:** Prime Minister Ranil Wickremansinghe began a two-day visit to Jaffna with a promise of equality to the Tamil people and an appeal to soldiers to uphold the ceasefire with the LTTE.

**31 March:** The Sri Lankan government is willing to discuss handing over power to the LTTE in the north-east as a precursor to the final solution to the ethnic conflict. The talks, to be held in Thailand in May, after India ignored the LTTE proposal for the talks to be held in one of the southern states, would discuss among other things, the setting up of an interim administration in the trouble-torn area.

**3 April:** The High Commissioner of India, Gopal Krishna Gandhi, visited an oil-storage facility in the eastern district of Trincomalee. The Indo-Sri Lanka Accord of 1987 gave India first preference in the running of the oil-storage facility in the district. The visit comes in the backdrop of a ceasefire between the Sri Lankan government and the LTTE, and amid moves to privatize the country's petroleum sector.

**11 April:** The LTTE leader, V. Prabhakaran, stated at a news conference at Killinochi that he wanted a political solution with the Sri Lankan government. He reiterated his commitment to an independent Tamil State, while expressing his desire to rebuild ties with India.

**14 April:** The leader of the Sri Lankan Muslim Congress (SLMC), Rauff Hakeem, has announced that the LTTE would stop the harassment of Muslims. In an agreement he signed with the LTTE leader V. Prabhakaran, the SLMC accepted the de facto authority of the LTTE in the north-east, widely expected to be legitimised by the Sri Lankan government through an interim administration.

**15 April:** The leader of the Ceylon Workers Congress (CWC) and senior cabinet minister Armugam Thondaman, met the LTTE leader, V. Prabhakaran and came to an understanding to work together for the resolution of the Tamil national question. This represented an effort by the LTTE to bring the Tamils of Central Sri Lanka, who had not so far identified with its cause or violent methods, under its wing.

**16 April:** Sri Lanka has extended its 'visa-on-arrival' facility to India to give a boost to tourism. So far, tourists from India, Iran, and Afghanistan visiting the island had to obtain visas in advance.

**17 April:** The Sri Lankan President, Chandrika Kumaratunga, wants the proposed interim administration in the north-east to reflect the pluralism of the region and has stressed that its setting up should be linked to a time-frame for talks with the LTTE for a permanent solution. This was revealed by the Presidential spokesman, Harris Peiris, in Colombo.

**19 April:** The US Deputy Secretary of State, Richard Armitage, told the visiting Sri Lankan Constitutional Affairs Minister, G. L. Peiris, in Washington that the US would not take the LTTE off its designated list of terrorist organisations even if the Sri Lankan government legalised the outfit ahead of the proposed talks.

**25 April:** Rocket launchers, machine guns, and grenades were among the arms and ammunition found in three LTTE boats apprehended by the Sri Lankan Navy off the eastern coast of Trincomalee. This was in violation of the ceasefire agreement signed by the LTTE and the Government in February. The government has filed a complaint against the LTTE with the Norwegian-led Sri Lanka Monitoring Mission (SLMM).

**30 April:** The Sri Lankan Prime Minister, Ranil Wickremansinghe, visited Buddhist chief priests in the town of Kandy and assured them that he would not concede parts of Sri Lanka as Tamil homeland, as demanded by the LTTE. This follows protests by monks, the Nationalist-Socialist Janatha Vimukti Peramuna (JVP) and the Sri Lanka Freedom Party, against moves by the Government to legalise the LTTE.

**7 May:** The Constitutional Affairs Minister, G. L. Peiris, has said that the Indian External Affairs Minister, Jaswant Singh, has offered constitutional and technical expertise to the Sri Lankan government in the ongoing peace process, particularly on aspects of the 13th Amendment to the Constitution, a result of the 1987 Indo-Sri Lanka Accord.

**13 May:** After hundreds of Buddhist monks protested in Colombo against the proposed interim administration on the grounds that it would lead to division of the country, the Sri Lankan Prime Minister, Ranil Wickremasinghe, assured them in a speech at the southern town of Motara that he would not enter a deal with the LTTE by himself and that it would first have to go through Parliament and be ratified by the people. He stressed that it was crucial to keep the LTTE within the framework of a peace process.

**17 May:** The Sri Lankan Foreign Minister, Tyronne Feranando, observed that the two-year extension of the ban on the LTTE by the Indian government would not affect the course of the peace process. The LTTE political wing chief, S.P. Thamilchelvan, has said that the move by the Government of India was a "wrong move".

**22 May:** Bernald Goonetilleka, the senior most government official in charge of the peace process, met the LTTE political wing chief S. P. Thamvilchelvan, over the slowing down of the peace process. The two sides reiterated their commitment and support to the peace process at the meeting, their first direct meeting in seven years.

**23 May:** Complying with one of the key provisions in the ceasefire agreement between the government and the LTTE, the Sri Lankan armed forces have withdrawn from almost all places of worship they were occupying in the north-east.

**25 May:** The Sri Lankan Cabinet has approved a proposal to give a strategically located oil storage facility in the eastern port city of Trincomalee on a long lease to the Indian Oil Corporation (IOC). The move could be opposed by the LTTE. Pro-LTTE website *Eelamnation.com* has said only the 'Tamil Ealam' had the right to take a decision on the leasing of the oil farm.

**25 May:** According to a press report, Sri Lanka and the US are to soon sign a defence fact for enhancing military cooperation between the two countries. The treaty would allow the US military the use of Sri Lanka's sea and air bases, particularly for refuelling, in return for training, assistance and supply of spare parts and repairs.

**28 May:** The Sri Lankan President, Chandrika Kumaratunga, told the Norwegian Deputy Foreign Minister, Vidar Helgesen, when he called on her that an interim administration for the north-east was not advisable till a final political solution to the ethnic conflict had been worked out.

**5 June:** The LTTE's political adviser, Anton Balasingham, told the *Tamil Guardians* weekly that Colombo was not implementing some of the provisions of the ceasefire agreement as quickly as the LTTE would like it and added that it was acting under the 'hawkish' influence of the Sri Lankan President, Chandrika Kumaratunga.

**6 June:** The Sri Lanka Development Forum, comprising 37 donor countries and multilateral agencies, agreed to a suggestion by the Sri Lankan Finance Minister, K. N. Choksy, and released $ 150 million of aid for the development of the north-eastern part of the country. Mr. Choksy had argued that the government's hand in the peace process would be strengthened if the people could reap the peace dividend straightaway.

**7 June:** India and Sri Lanka agreed to set up a working group for including trade in services in the bilateral Free Trade Agreement (FTA). The issue was taken up at the first Joint Ministerial Committee (JMC) meeting under the Indo-Sri Lanka FTA. Both sides agreed that there was a need to utilise the core competencies of both the countries in areas of trans-shipment, tourism, and professional services to mutual advantage.

**8 June:** The visiting Sri Lankan Prime Minister, Ranil Wickremasinghe, said that the tension between India and Pakistan was of concern to the region, but stressed that it had to be solved bilaterally.

**10 June:** The Indian Finance Minister, Yashwant Sinha, and the Commerce Minister, Murasoli Maran, met Mr. Wickremasinghe and offered to supply 3 lakh tonnes of wheat to Sri Lanka and simultaneously extended a $ 100 million credit line for export of products from India.

**10 June:** A report in *The Hindu* talks of a request by the Sri Lankan government to India on providing training to its armed forces. The Sri Lankan military is said to be interested in setting up a unit along the lines of India's highly trained National Security Guard (NSG).

**3 July:** Indian High Commissioner, Gopal Krishna Gandhi, and the Sri Lankan Finance Secretary, Charitha Ratwatte, signed two credit agreements in Colombo, under which India extended credit worth $ 51 million at concessionary interest rates. The first agreement provides $ 31 million for the purchase of 3,00,000 tonnes of wheat over a period of 20 months, while the second agreement provides $ 20 million in support of Sri Lanka's Economic Stabilization Programme, negotiated with the IMF.

**11 July:** India's Foreign Minister, Yashwant Sinha visiting Colombo, was briefed by the Sri Lankan Prime Minister, Ranil Wickremansinghe, on the ongoing peace process. In turn, Mr. Wickremasinghe was briefed on the Indo-Pak situation.

**12 July:** After talks with the Sri Lankan President, Mr. Sinha, said that there was no "contradiction" in India's demand for extradition of LTTE chief V. Prabhakaran and its support for the Sri Lankan peace process.

**31 July:** The Sri Lankan President, Chandrika

Kumaratunga, lauded the visiting Pakistan President Pervez Musharraf's role in the global coalition against terror and expressed her 'optimism' over the recent peace efforts launched in her country to end the decades long ethnic strife.

**8 August:** The Sri Lankan Foreign Minister, Tyronne Fernando, after meeting Foreign Minister, Yashwant Sinha, in New Delhi, told reporters that his country of 20 million people was concerned at the possession of nuclear weapons by India and Pakistan.

**14 August:** After talks between the Sri Lankan Minister for Economic Affairs, Milinda Moragoda, and the LTTE's Chief Negotiator, Anton Balasingham, at Oslo, Norway has announced that formal talks between the two sides would begin between 12-17 September at Thailand.

**18 August:** The Sri Lankan Prime Minister, Ranil Wickremasinghe, has advocated a "step-by-step" approach for the talks between his government and the LTTE and urged Sri Lankans to be "patient about the peace process".

**27 August:** The Sri Lankan Minister for Economic Affairs, Milinda Moragoda, during his meeting with the Deputy Chairman of the Planning Commission, K. C. Pant, proposed the setting up of a joint working group to coordinate economic relations, even as he sought India's assistance in the reconstruction and rehabilitation of the strife-torn country.

**2 September:** Hundreds of Buddhist monks took out a procession and passed a resolution against de-proscribing the LTTE before meeting the President, Chandrika Kumaratunga, who assured them that she was "strongly opposed" to the move and that there were "legal avenues" to check any such attempt.

**4 September:** The Sri Lankan Defence Minister, Mr. Milinda Morapane, told the Cabinet that he had decided to de-proscribe the separatist LTTE, thus meeting an crucial condition set by the rebels ahead of direct talks to start on 16 September.

**16 September:** Talks between Sri Lanka and the LTTE began at the Thai naval base in Sattahip. While the Sri Lankan Minister for Constitutional Affairs, G. L. Peiris, insisted a solution would have to be found within the, "unity and territorial integrity" of Sri Lanka, the LTTE's Anton Balasingham reiterated the Tamils "right to self-determination".

**18 September:** The LTTE's Chief Negotiator at the Thai peace talks, Anton Balasingham, has said that the Tigers would fight for political independence and statehood only when their demand for special autonomy and self-governance is rejected and if conditions of oppression continue. Sri Lankan Minister, G. L. Peiris, maintained that there has been a softening of position on both sides.

**31 October:** The second round of direct talks between Colombo and the LTTE, which started at Nakorn Pathom (Thailand), focused on issues relating to the disturbing security situation in Eastern Sri Lanka, especially the safety of Muslims residing there.

**1 November:** The Sri Lankan government and the LTTE arrived at a broad agreement on establishing a joint task force to address issues relating to the reconstruction of the North-East. The head of the Sri Lankan delegation, G. L. Peiris, said that the agreement would meet three important objectives of winning international confidence to invest in rebuilding the North-East, be acceptable to both the government and the Tigers and conform to the laws and procedures of Sri Lanka. The agreement provides for an eight-member sub-committee, comprising four representatives each from the government and the Tigers.

**9 November:** The visiting Norwegian Foreign Minister, Jan Petersen, after talks with Home Minister, L. K. Advani, and the External Affairs Minister, Yashwant Sinha, noted that the Sri Lankan government and the LTTE are ready for "painful compromises" in the pursuit of peace and commended regional approaches to conflict management.

**12 November:** The Sri Lankan President, Chandrika Kumaratunga, proposed the setting up of a National Commission for Ethnic Reconciliation and Sustainable Peace, with the participation of the LTTE to resolve the decade-long ethnic conflict.

**25 November:** The Oslo donor conference committed $70 million as "immediate financial assistance" and asked the Sri Lankan government and the LTTE to reach a political settlement "without recourse to violence".

**27 November:** In his annual Heroes Day speech, the LTTE leader, Mr. Prabhakaran, spelt out "regional self-rule" as the alternative to Tamil Eelam, but made it clear that he had not abandoned the option of secession. He added that "internal self-determination" entitles a people to regional self-rule.

**5 December:** The Sri Lankan government and the LTTE, meeting in Oslo, agreed to develop a government that would give the rebels regional autonomy. Both sides consented to pursue a peace based on the principle of "internal self-determination" in the Tamil-dominated areas of the North and the East.

## BHUTAN

**5 August:** India's Foreign Minister, Yashwant Sinha, in his meeting with the King of Bhutan in Thimpu, discussed the issue of camps belonging to India-based militant groups operating in Bhutan.

## MALDIVES

**10 July:** India's Foreign Minister, Yashwant Sinha, during a visit to the Indira Gandhi Memorial Hospital in Male, assured Maldives of India's support to improve its health sector. The hospital is the nation's largest with a 220-bed capacity. About 80 per cent of the doctors are Indians, employed by the Maldives government.

**22 September:** Prime Minister Atal Behari Vajpayee arrived on a four-day official visit to Male, as part of India's continuing efforts to "deepen and strengthen" bilateral ties with its neighbour.

**23 September:** In their bilateral talks, India and Maldives discussed terrorism, security, and South Asian regional cooperation. While interacting with Maldivian journalists, Mr. Vajpayee called for updating the SAARC Charter on terrorism. He also revealed that India is to undertake digital mapping and hydro-graphic survey of the Maldivian land mass and coastlines, besides assisting the island to set up an Information Technology Village.

## MAJOR GLOBAL DEVELOPMENTS

**5 February:** The World Economic Forum held its annual meeting of prominent leaders, financiers, and academics on 31 January - 4 February for the first time in New York City, USA, officially as a gesture of solidarity with the city after the attacks of 11 September 2001. The meeting's overall theme was "Leadership in Tough Times: A Vision for a Shared Future." The speeches were focused mostly on weaknesses of the economic and political system and the need to reduce poverty in developing countries in order to decrease the threat of terror.

**2 March:** Commonwealth leaders, at the CHOGM Summit in Coolum, Australia, adopted an action plan to combat terrorism.

**23 March:** The UN's International Conference on Financing for Development was held in Monterey, Mexico, on 18-22 March. Some 171 countries, international financial institutions such as the World Bank and the IMF attended it. The conference monitored the progress towards the Millennium

Development Goals adopted by the UNGA in 2000 and debated the relationship between poverty and political violence.

**3 April:** The OIC Foreign Minister have called on the international community to agree on a definition of terrorism that differentiates between legitimate national liberation struggles and acts of terrorism. It condemned Israel for its escalating military campaign against the Palestinian people and rejected any attempt to link terrorism to the struggle of the Palestinian people in the exercise of their inalienable right to establish their independent state with Al-Quds Al-Sharif (Jerusalem) as its capital.

**15 April:** The inaugural Boao Asia Forum, described as an Asian alternative to the World Economic Forum (WEF), was held on 12-14 April on the island of Hainan, Southern China. The Chinese government planned to host the conference annually.

**30 April:** The United Nations Trade and Development Report 2002 expects India and China to weather the reversal in the global economy in the Asian region. The report says that India and China, on account of their large size and relatively closed economies, were by and large immune from the downward pressure of world markets.

**3 May:** The South Asia workshop on "Adaptation to Climate Change for Agricultural Productivity", jointly organised in New Delhi by the Indian Ministry of Agriculture and the United Nations Environment Programme, has called for international funding support for developing countries to go in for adaptation strategies to mitigate the effects of global warning.

**6 May:** Governments have not lived up to promises made in 1990 to improve the lives of children around the world, according to the United Nations Childrens Emergency Fund (UNICEF), which is organising the second three-day summit on children in New York from 8 May. Out of the 27 goals set at the World Summit for Children in 1990, only 6 are considered notable successes. The New York summit is expected to work out a declaration and plan of action called "A World Fit for Children", to push for the fulfilment of these goals and set new targets for the coming decade.

**6 May:** At the Religious Affairs Ministers meeting of the Organization of Islamic Conference (OIC) at Kuala Lumpur, differences persisted over the suicide bombings in Israel, with the Saudi Minister calling them as 'martyrs', while the Malaysian Deputy Prime Minister, Abdullah Admed Badawi, saying that holy wars cannot be won with violence and suicide bombers.

**7 May:** The Bush administration has announced that the US is pulling out of the International Criminal Court on war crimes. While the conservatives in the US praised the move, human rights groups and US allies in Europe and Canada criticised the move.

**17 May:** Nearly 50 European and Latin American leaders in Madrid agreed to boost cooperation in fighting terrorism and drugs. The EU leaders urged Latin America to stick with democratic and economic reforms.

**18 May:** The Vienna-based United Nations Industrial Development Organisation (UNIDO) concluded its $25^{th}$ Industrial Development Board session at Vienna, with message to re-induct countries which had left the organisation, like the US, Australia, and Canada. UNIDO, the organisation giving industrial advice to developing countries (DCs) was in dire need of more funds to bolster its technical programmes. Japan, UNIDO's main donor, formulated a new strategy to address future developmental needs of the DCs.

**27 June:** At the G-8 Summit in Alberta, Canada, the leaders agreed to grant an extra $ 1 billion in debt relief to the world's 42 poorest countries. Under an initiative called the New Partnership for Africa's Development (NEPAD), the G-8 countries would pump in billions in annual investments in exchange for good political and economic governance. The leaders also clinched a $ 20 billion deal to finance a programme designed to keep Russia's vulnerable excess plutonium deposits out of the hands of terrorists.

**1 July:** The International Criminal Court opened in makeshift offices at The Hague. The budget and staff of the Court will be sanctioned in autumn by the 74 constituting states, which will then elect the Court's 18 judges and the Chief Prosecutor.

**4 July:** The African Union (AU) will be established at the 8-10 July Summit of African Heads of State, in place of the Organisation of African Unity (OAU), which existed for 39 years. The new AU will to a large extent oversee NEPAD, the New Programme for Africa's Development.

**26 August:** The UN World Summit on Sustainable Development (the Earth Summit) opened in Johannesburg with delegates set to grapple with issues on how to alleviate poverty worldwide while protecting the environment. The South African President, Thabo Mbeki, urged delegates to unite to overcome "global apartheid" in the path towards sustainable development.

**28 August:** Amidst fears that the Bush administration is planning to withdraw from the CTBT to test smart new nukes, the Preparatory Commission (Prepcom) of the Comprehensive Test Ban Treaty Organisation (CTBTO) concluded its 18th session at Vienna last week and resolved to go ahead with completing its International Monitoring System (IMS) worldwide to ensure absolute verification of the treaty.

**11 September:** After remaining neutral for 51 years, Switzerland became the 190th member of the UN with the General Assembly approving its admission with acclamation at its opening session.

**27 September:** East Timor (Timor-Leste) became the 191st member of the UN when its application, sponsored by Australia and Indonesia, was approved unanimously by the UNGA. In his address to the assembly, President Jose Xanana Gusmao proposed that the UN should declare a world peace week on 21-22 September each year.

**12 October:** The seventh session of the Conference of the States Parties to the 1993 Chemical Weapons Convention (CWC) was held on 7-11 October in The Hague, the Netherlands. The CWC entered into force in 1993 and had been ratified by 145 states, 109 of which attended the session. The conference granted an extension in principle to Russia of the deadlines for destruction of 11 per cent and 20 per cent of its category I chemical weapons stockpiles. Both India and the US had fulfilled their obligations in the destruction of 20% of their chemical weapons stockpiles.

**21 October:** The ninth Francophone summit meeting of 55-French speaking states was held on 18-20 October in Beirut, Lebanon. French President Jacques Chirac pledged his commitment to fight against terrorism, but said that it must not be fought at the expense of human rights and the principles of the UN.

**23 October:** The eighth Conference of Parties to the UN Framework Convention on Climate Change began in New Delhi with the developing countries, led by India, emphasising the need to bring the Kyoto Protocol into force without any further delay and for greater efforts to protect the poor who were the most vulnerable to the adverse impact of climate change.

**29 October:** A report presented by the UN Environment Programme (UNEP) to the eighth Conference of Parties (CoP-8) to the UN Framework Convention on Climate Change (UNFCCC) in New Delhi says that the loss due to natural disasters this year could be over $ 20 billion. According to UNEP Executive Director, Klaus Toepfer, the report highlights the real risks and economic perils the global financial community is facing as a result of human-influenced climate change.

**1 November:** The 'Delhi Declaration' was adopted at the

end of the UN Conference on Climate Change, in New Delhi. The document reiterates the principle of common but differentiated responsibilities of the countries in meeting the challenges of climate change, taking into account their priorities, objectives and socio-economic circumstances. The declaration emphasizes the need for the US, Russia and other developed countries, which are yet to ratify the Kyoto Protocol on Reduction of Green House Gases (GHG) emission, to do so at the earliest.

**2 November:** The Commonwealth Ministers Action Group (CMAG), meeting in London on 1 November, decided to maintain the suspension of Pakistan from the 54-member group, arguing that there was still no fully civilian government in place and that Musharraf's constitutional amendments had limited the restoration of democracy. CMAG's membership included Australia, Bahamas, Bangladesh, Botswana, India, Malta, Nigeria, and Samoa.

**3 November:** A global mountain summit was held on 29 October — 2 November at Bishkek, Kyrgyzstan, sponsored by the government of Kyrgyzstan and the UNEP. The summit, which was the culmination of the UN's International Year of The Mountains, adopted the Bishkek Mountain Platform, which organizers believe would be of practical use in protecting the mountains themselves and their inhabitants.

**8 November:** The UN Security Council unanimously voted on a tough new Iraq Resolution (1441) that warns the Iraqi leader, Saddam Hussain, that he must disarm before 15 November or face "serious consequences." All the 15 members of the Council voted for the resolution, which was agreed to after eight weeks of intense negotiations.

**16 November:** India said that it will not be a party to the International Code of Conduct against Ballistic Missile Proliferation (ICOC) to be signed by consenting countries at a conference in The Hague, Netherlands, on 25-26 November. Foreign Office spokesman said in New Delhi that India found it difficult to accept missile proliferation and space launch vehicles as an amalgam and the implied questioning of the right to peaceful uses of space technology.

**16 November:** The fifth review conference of 140 States Parties to the 1992 Convention on the Prohibition of the Development, Production, and Stockpiling of Bacteriological and Toxic Weapons and their Destruction (BTWC), also referred to as the Biological Weapons Convention (BWC), completed its deliberations in Geneva on 11-15 November. The session decided that BTWC acceding states would meet annually in the run-up to the sixth review conference in 2006, focusing on implementation measures short of the kind of enforcement, such as on-site inspectors, opposed by the US.

**21 November:** At the historic NATO Summit in Prague, NATO invited seven ex-communist countries under its security umbrella. These include Latvia, Estonia, Lithuania, Bulgaria, Romania, Slovakia, and Slovenia. The alliance agreed to set up a 20,000 strong rapid response force able to deploy within days against terrorists or rogue states as part of military reforms designed to ensure that the alliance will be relevant in the post-11 September era.

**7 December:** The Iraqi government delivered to the UN a declaration of more than 12,000 pages of technical details describing its chemical, nuclear and biological weapons. Iraq was required to do so under the UN Security Council Resolution 1441. The declaration, titled "Currently Accurate, Full and Complete Declarations", will be delivered to the UN Headquarters in New York and the International Atomic Energy Agency (IAEA) in Vienna.

# MAJOR REGIONAL DEVELOPMENTS

## EAST ASIA

**2 April:** The Indian External Affairs Minister, Jaswant Singh, arrived in Seoul to renew political contact with South Korea and intensify cooperation and engagement with one of India's important economic partners. His three-day visit to the country was seen by analysts as part of a conscious strategy to raise the Indian profile in the East Asian region.

**3 April:** Jaswant Singh conferred with the South Korean leadership: its President Kim Dae Jung and Foreign Minster Choi Sung-hong extensively. Building on growing convergence of their interests in Asia, both countries agreed to intensify contacts in the defence sector, initiate consultations on combating international terrorism, and expand political cooperation in multilateral forums.

**7 August:** Work on the Light Water Reactors at Kumho on the eastern coast of the Democratic Peoples Republic of Korea has started. The reactor was the centrepiece of the Agreed Framework that the US and North Korea worked out in 1994 in a bid to prevent North Korea's nuclear weapons development.

**17 October:** North Korea has admitted that it has a secret nuclear weapons programme and said that it no longer wishes to abide by an agreement signed with the Clinton administration in 1994.

**25 October:** North Korea has demanded that the US enter into a bilateral "Non-Aggression Treaty" so that the security concerns of both sides could be addressed in a manner that could bring about peace and stability to the Korean peninsula. The North Korean Foreign Ministry has said that the massive stockpiling of nuclear weapons in South Korea and its vicinity had complicated an already complex situation between the two countries.

**27 October:** On the fringes of the Asia-Pacific Economic Cooperation Forum in Las Cabos, Mexico, the US President, George Bush, South Korean President, Kim Dae-Jung and the Japanese Prime Minister, Junichiro Koizumi, reaffirmed a commitment for a peaceful Korean peninsula free of nuclear weapons. The leaders called upon North Korea to disassemble its nuclear weapons programme in a prompt and verifiable manner.

**12 December:** Raising fears of a nuclear crisis in the Korean peninsula, North Korea said that it would immediately reactivate a nuclear power plant that US officials suspect was being used to develop weapons. The Koreans suspended their nuclear programme under the 1994 Agreed Framework with the US.

**22 December:** North Korea has announced that it was now beginning to dismantle the monitors or surveillance devices at its nuclear power facilities. The move would enable Pyongyang to rid itself of constraints on its 'sovereign' rights to produce nuclear energy and put the spent fuel to other uses.

**South-East Asia**

**12 January:** The Burmese Foreign Minister Win Aung confirmed in an interview with the BBC that Burma intended to build a nuclear reactor for medical research near the town of Magive in 2002-03, with Russian assistance. *The Far Eastern Economic Review* of 3 January had earlier reported that Russia had already trained some 300 Burmese nuclear technicians.

**3 April:** The Indonesian President, Megawati Sukharnoputri, arrived in New Delhi for a bilateral visit. Sharing common perceptions both countries sought to define a durable partnership in the field of countering terrorism and energy security. India said that its relationship with Indonesia was the key to larger engagement with ASEAN.

**8 April:** The Indian Prime Minister, Atal Behari Vajpayee, on a visit to Singapore had extensive consultations with Singapore's Prime Minister, Goh Chok Tong. Both countries agreed to set up a Joint Study Group (JSG) to consider a comprehensive economic agreement. Two Memorandum of Understanding (MoUs) were also signed, one on greater cooperation in the telecom sector and another in the field of culture and heritage. The challenge posed by terrorism was also discussed.

**9 April:** The Indian Prime Minister, Atal Behari Vajapyee, arrived in Cambodia. This was the first visit by an Indian Prime Minister since 1954. He held consultations with the Cambodian Prime Minister Hun Sen. Three agreements which included one on the conservation and restoration of Ta Prohm temple, an air services pact, and the third on visa exemption for diplomatic and official passport holders were signed. India also offered a judge for the Khmer Rouge trial.

**21 April:** Officials of the ASEAN Regional Forum (ARF) met for three days in Bangkok and discussed among other things, plans to counter terrorism related to maritime and aviation security as well as more effective border control.

**7 May:** Malaysia, Indonesia, and the Philippines have signed an agreement to combat terrorism in South-East Asia. All the three countries have been plagued with the problems of Islamist militancy.

**20 May:** In a ceremony at Dili, East Timor became an independent state and the flag of the UN was lowered and replaced by the new black, red and gold flag of the country. The ceremony was attended by UN Secretary-General Kofi Annan and representatives of 92 countries, including 13 heads of State, amongst them Indonesian President Megawati Sukarnoputri and President Jorge Sampaio of Portugal, the former colonial power.

**18 June:** The Union Finance Minister, Yashwant Sinha told *The Hindu* in Cha-am, Thailand, that India, while supportive of the idea of Asian dialogue, believes that the whole concept of the Thai-backed Asian Cooperation Dialogue (ACD) will have to be "clearly defined." The ACD formally came into being on 19 June when 17 Asian Ministers signed it into existence. The next ACD ministerial meeting would be held in Chiang Rai, Thailand, in June 2003.

**31 July:** The ASEAN Regional Forum (ARF) meeting at Bander Seri Begawan underlined the need to "maintain the existing moratorium on nuclear-testing", and called upon all states to "work towards the objective of total elimination of nuclear weapons."

**1 August:** Foreign Ministers of the 10-member ASEAN held their 35th annual meetings at Bandar Seri Begawan, Brunei, from 29-30 July, followed by the 23-member ASEAN Regional Forum (ARF). A joint declaration was signed by the US Secretary of State, Colin Powell and the ASEAN Foreign Ministers for cooperation to combat international terrorism. The agreement provides a formal framework for the involvement of the USA in regional efforts to combat terrorism, including financial and technical assistance, exchange information and "capacity-building".

**15 September:** Addressing the ASEAN Economic Ministers (AEM)-India Consultation in Brunei Darussalam, the Commerce and Industry Minister, Murasoli Maran, said that India would like to have a Bilateral Regional Trade and Investment Agreements (RTA) or a Free Trade Agreement (FTA) with the ASEAN in the long run.

**5 November:** The first ASEAN-India summit was held at Phnom Penh, Cambodia, where leaders pledged to comprehensively combat "non-traditional security threats", inclusive of terrorism. The next summit will be held in Bali, Indonesia. Singapore's Prime Minister Goh Chok Tong described the event as the acquisition of full-fledged capabilities by the jumbo-aircraft called ASEAN, the other wing being made up of the ASEAN-plus caucus, where the organization is engaged with China, Japan, and South Korea.

**5 November:** Leaders of the 10-member ASEAN held a summit meeting on 3-5 November in Phnom Penh, Cambodia. Chinese Prime Minster Zhu Rongji and Indian Prime Minister A. B. Vajpayee also attended it. India and ASEAN announced the establishment of a task force to draft a framework for a free-trade agreement for consideration in 2003. India's trade with ASEAN area was worth US $ 10 billion, compared with China's US $ 40 billion, but analysts said that some ASEAN members saw India as a potential counterbalance to China's power.

**6 November:** India's Prime Minister Atal Behari Vajpayee on a visit to Laos and Cambodia held talks with Bounhang Varochit and Hun Sen in Vietnam and Phnom Penh respectively. In a clear commitment to help lesser-developed ASEAN countries, India announced a $ 10 million line of credit each for Laos and Cambodia on exceptionally preferential terms and signed a host of other agreements to boost trade and defence cooperation after the talks.

**7 November:** After discussions between Prime Minister Vajpayee and his Laotian counterpart Bounnhang Varochit, Laos agreed to cooperate closely with India in the fight against terrorism while stressing that all countries within the United Nations must implement the obligations of its resolution on terrorism passed after 9/11.

**9 December:** The Indonesian government and representatives of the separatist Free Aceh Movement (GAM) signed a peace agreement in Geneva, Switzerland, to end a rebellion in the north Sumatran province of Aceh that had begun in 1976 and cost 12,000 lives.

## Central Asia

**13 April:** The fourth meeting of signatories to the Commonwealth of Independent States (CIS) Collective Security Treaty, held in Almaty, Kazakhstan, concluded with an agreement to coordinate their activities against terrorism, drug smuggling and illegal immigration, and possibly to formalise international cooperation by converting the Collective Security Treaty into an international collective security organisation corresponding to the UN charter.

**14 May:** At a summit in Moscow, Russia, Krygystan, Tajikistan, Armenia, and Belarus decided to set up a full-fledged military alliance. The 10-year-old Treaty of Collective Security would now be called "Organisation of the Treaty of Collective Security." The new alliance will establish a joint military planning body, adopt common military-technical standards and training programmes, and set up a joint regional force for Central Asia. The Russian President Mr. Putin has said that the new organization can be an element in the new global structure, along with NATO and the Shanghai Cooperation Organisation (SCO).

**4 June:** The Conference for Interaction and Confidence Building Measures in Asia (CICA) held at Almaty and attended by 16 countries signed a declaration which was strongly advocated by New Delhi. They also adopted the Almaty Act, which recognized that terrorism was a trans-national threat and had to be eradicated from the continent through united efforts. The Declaration on Eliminating Terrorism and Promoting Dialogue Among Civilisations said that the signatories would be vigilant that the global fight against terrorism does not become a war targeting a particular culture, religion, or nation. The signatories to the Declaration and the Almaty Act were Russia, China, India, Pakistan, Afghanistan, Azerbaijan, Egypt, Iran, Israel, Kazakhstan, Kyrgystan, Mongolia, Palestine, Tajikistan, Turkey, and Uzbekistan.

**7 June:** At a summit in St. Petersburg, leaders of the six states of Kazakhstan, Uzbekistan, Kyrgyzstan, Tajikistan, China and Russia formally signed the charter of the Shanghai Cooperation Organisation (SCO), making it a full-fledged international body. The political declaration, which was also signed, lists out three priority tasks for the new grouping-regional security, economic cooperation and the fight against terrorism and separatism.

**18 September:** The construction of the 1760-km Baku-Ceyhan oil pipeline from Azerbaijan through Georgia and Turkey has started. The pipeline will carry Caspian energy resources, the world's third largest, to a Turkish port en route to Western markets.

**8 October:** A summit meeting of leaders of the Commonwealth of Independent States (CIS) was held in the Moldavian capital Chisinau, on 6-7 October. The Presidents of the members of the CIS Collective Security Treaty (Armenia, Belarus, Kyrgyzstan, Kazakhstan, Russia, and Tajikistan) signed a charter upgrading the Treaty's statutes to that of an international organisation.

**6 November:** Focused on becoming a player in the global energy market, India in partnership with Turkey acquired a foothold in a $ 4.2 billion pipeline project that would bring oil from the Caspian Sea to the Mediterranean Coast. The Baku-Tblisi-Ceyhan project, as it is called, would transport crude oil from Azerbaijan in the Caspian zone to Ceyhan on the Turkish Mediterranean Coast.

## West Asia

**27 March:** The 22 Members of the Arab League held their organisation's 14th ordinary summit in Beirut on 27-28 March. Two interdependent issues, the Arab-Israeli conflict and Iraq's relations with Kuwait dominated the summit. The center piece of the summit was the delivery on 27 March of a "land-for-peace" proposal to end the Arab-Israeli conflict by Saudi Arabian crown prince Abdullah Ibn-Abdul Aziz. He offered Israel security and normal relations from the entire Arab world in return for a full Israeli withdrawal from all occupied Arab territories.

## South-West Asia

**21 May:** The Iranian Foreign Minister, Kamal Kharrazi, on a visit to India, in an interview to *The Hindu* called for an early dialogue between India and Pakistan to defuse military tension in the subcontinent and also to find a political solution to the bilateral problem.

**21 October:** The Foreign Office spokesman in New Delhi has said that India does not believe that its relationship with Iran will have a bearing on its deepening ties with the United States. He was speaking in the context of the visit of the Foreign Secretary, Kanwal Sibal, to Iran on 19-20 October for consultations with his counterpart, the Deputy Foreign Minister, Aminzadeh and his talks with the Foreign Minister, Kamal Kharazzi, and the Secretary of Iran's National Security Council, Hasan Rahawi.

**22 December:** In recognition of India's status as a major player in Afghanistan, it was present as an observer when Pakistan, Tajikistan, Turkmenistan, Iran, Uzbekistan, and China issued a declaration on good neighbourly relations vis-à-vis Afghanistan. India shared the observer status with the G8 and OIC.

**22 December:** At a conference in Kabul, President Hamid Karzai signed a non-aggression pact with six neighbouring countries, committing all signatories to the principles of territorial integrity, mutual respect, and non-interference in each other's internal affairs. Karzai and Foreign Ministers from China, Iran, Pakistan, Tajikistan, Turkmenistan, and Uzbekistan signed the Kabul Declaration on Good Neighbourly Relations.

## SAARC

**2 January:** Prime Minister, Atal Behari Vajpayee visiting Kathmandu for the SAARC summit, called upon the South Asian countries to desist from aiding or abetting terrorism in any form, and declared that countering the menace would define the SAARC agenda in the next decade.

**6 January:** In a solid endorsement of India's position on cross-border terrorism, the SAARC summit in Kathmandu vowed to fight terrorism in all its forms and manifestations and pledged to prevent support and financing of organised terrorist activities in the member countries.

**9 April:** While addressing the South Asian Association for Regional Cooperation (SAARC) Finance-Planning Ministers conference on 'Poverty Alleviation' in Islamabad, the Deputy Chairman of the Indian Planning Commission, K. C. Pant, urged the countries of the region to fully tap their trade potential, where the inter-SAARC trade accounted for less than 5 per cent of the total volume.

**10 April:** The SAARC Finance-Planning Ministers meet on 'Poverty Alleviation' has endorsed an action plan for full operationalisation of SAPTA (South Asia Preferential Trade Agreement) and move faster towards SAFTA (South Asia Free Trade Agreement). Four rounds of negotiations had already been completed on SAFTA.

**20 August:** The Foreign Secretaries of the SAARC countries meeting in Kathmandu have agreed to update the 1987 SAARC Regional Convention on Suppression of Terrorism by drafting an additional protocol in the light of the UN Security Council Resolution 1373 on combating terrorism and the International Convention on Suppression of Financing of Terrorism.

**21 August:** Inaugurating the 23rd Session of the SAARC Council of Ministers at Kathmandu, the Nepalese Prime Minister,

Sher Bahadur Deuba, said that eradication of poverty, promotion of a free-trade zone and social upliftment had been identified as "core areas" for regional cooperation within the SAARC framework.

**21 September:** The ninth conference of the South Asian Association for Regional Cooperation in Law (SAARCLAW) began in Jaipur, with a call to bring a degree of uniformity in laws in SAARC and to promote interaction, facilitate entrepreneurship and protect the norms and social rights of their citizens.

**23 October:** India has made attendance at the scheduled SAARC summit in Islamabad next year conditional on solid progress being made on economic cooperation agreements within the regional grouping. India has pointed out in recent times to other member countries that Pakistan was holding up progress on greater economic cooperation.

**26 October:** Prime Minister A. B. Vajpayee while addressing the combined commanders' conference in New Delhi has suggested that a substantial agenda for action should first be finalised before agreeing on firm dates for the SAARC summit meet.

**2 November:** The Foreign Office spokesman in New Delhi has accused Pakistan of "tokenism" and "double standards" for the failure of the 30 October - 1 November fourth round of meeting under SAPTA in Kathmandu. He reiterated that India was prepared to have more engagement with Pakistan on economic issues.

**18 December:** The External Affairs Minister Yashwant Sinha told the Lok Sabha that India was "ready and willing to participate" in a SAARC summit whenever new dates are fixed and criticised Pakistan for postponing the summit for "specious" reasons.

# III

# Select Documents

# 1. US CIA Director's Unclassified Report to Congress on the Acquisition of Technology Relating to Weapons of Mass Destruction and Advanced Conventional Munitions 1 January through 30 June 2002

[Editor's Note: This Report was submitted to the US Congress in early 2003, and reported in the press on 21 April 2003]

## Acquisition by Country

### *Iran*

***Nuclear.*** Despite Iran's status in the Treaty on the Nonproliferation of Nuclear Weapons (NPT), the United States remains convinced Tehran is pursuing a nuclear weapons programme. To bolster its efforts to establish domestic nuclear fuel-cycle capabilities, Iran has technology that can also support fissile material production for Tehran's overall nuclear weapons programme.

Iran has continued to attempt using its civilian nuclear energy programme to justify its efforts to establish domestically or otherwise acquire assorted nuclear fuel-cycle capabilities. Such capabilities, however, are well suited to support fissile material production for a weapons programme, and we believe it is this objective that drives Iran's efforts to acquire relevant facilities. We suspect that Tehran is interested in acquiring foreign fissile material and technology for weapons development as part of its overall nuclear weapons programme.

Despite Bushehr being put under IAEA safeguards, Russia's provision of expertise and manufacturing assistance has helped Iran to develop its own nuclear technology infrastructure. In addition, facing economic pressures, some Russian entities have shown a willingness to provide assistance to other nuclear projects within Iran. For example, an institute subordinate to the Russian Ministry of Atomic Energy (MINATOM) had agreed to deliver in late 2000 equipment that was clearly intended for atomic vapour laser isotope separation, a technology capable of producing weapons-grade uranium. As a result of US protests, the Russian Government has halted the delivery of some of this equipment to Iran.

Chinese entities are continuing work on a zirconium production facility at Esfahan that will enable Iran to produce cladding for reactor fuel. As an adherent to the NPT, Iran is required to accept IAEA safeguards on its nuclear material. The IAEA's Additional Protocol requires states to declare production of zirconium fuel cladding and gives the IAEA the right of access to resolve questions or inconsistencies related to the declarations, but Iran has made no moves to bring the Additional Protocol into force. Moreover, Iran remains the only NPT adherent with a full-scope safeguards agreement that has not adopted a subsidiary agreement obligating early declaration of nuclear facilities. Zirconium production, other than production of fuel cladding, is not subject to declaration or inspection.

***Missile***. Ballistic missile-related cooperation from entities in the former Soviet Union, North Korea, and China over the years has helped Iran move towards its goal of becoming self-sufficient in the production of ballistic missiles. Such assistance during the reporting period continued to include equipment, technology, and expertise. Iran, already producing Scud short-range ballistic missiles (SRBMs), is in the late stages of developing the Shahab-3 medium-range ballistic missile (MRBM). In addition, Iran publicly has acknowledged the development of follow-on versions of the Shahab-3. It originally said that another version, the Shahab-4, is a more capable ballistic missile than its predecessor but later characterised it as solely a space launch vehicle with no military applications. Iran's Defence Minister has also publicly mentioned a "Shahab-5." Such statements strongly suggest that Tehran intends to develop a longer-range ballistic missile capability.

***Chemical***. Iran is a party to the Chemical Weapons Convention (CWC). Nevertheless, during the reporting period it continued to seek chemicals, production technology, training, and expertise from Chinese entities that could further Tehran's efforts at achieving an indigenous capability to produce nerve agents. Iran already has stockpiled blister, blood, and choking agents—and the bombs and artillery shells to deliver them—which it previously has manufactured. It probably also has made some nerve agents.

***Biological***. Even though Iran is part of the Biological Weapons Convention (BWC), Tehran probably maintains an offensive BW programme. Foreign dual-use biotechnical materials, equipment, and expertise—primarily, but not exclusively, from Eastern Europe—continued to feature prominently in Iran's procurement efforts. While such materials do have legitimate uses, Iran's biological warfare (BW) programme could also benefit from them. It is likely that Iran has capabilities to produce small quantities of BW agents, but has a limited ability to weaponise them.

***Advanced Conventional Weapons***. Iran continued to seek and acquire conventional weapons and production technologies, primarily from Russia, China, and North Korea. Since Russia announced in November 2000 that it was abrogating the Gore-Chernomyrdin Agreement, the Russian and Iranian Governments and firms have engaged in high-level discussions on a wide variety of military services and equipment — including air defence, naval, air and ground weapons, and technologies. In October 2001, Tehran and Moscow signed a new military-technical cooperation agreement, which laid the groundwork for negotiations and created a commission for future arms sales, but did not itself include sales contracts.

Contract negotiations, which may take years to complete, continued in the following months and at least one sale—apparently for helicopters—was concluded. Various Russian officials and academicians have suggested that sales under this new agreement could, in the next few years, make Iran Russia's third-largest arms customer, after China and India. Until that agreement is concluded, Russia will continue to deliver on existing contracts. Estimates of conventional arms sales to Iran of $300 million per year would put Iran's share of Russian sales worldwide at roughly 10 per cent, compared to more than 50 per cent going to China and India.

To facilitate new arms agreements, Russian oil enterprises entered an agreement with the Russian state arms trading firm Rosoboronexport to promote arms exports. Russian and Iranian arms dealers are to include such firms as Lukoil to coordinate "commercial conditions" and participate in projects proposed by the customer.

Outside the Russian market, Iran's search for conventional weapons is global. In particular, Iran capitalised on the specialised weapons services and lower prices that China and North Korea offered. Elsewhere, Iran sought out products, particularly weapons components and dual-use items, that are superior in quality to those available from Russia or that have proven difficult to acquire through normal government channels.

### *Iraq*

During the reporting period, Baghdad continued to deny UN inspectors entry into Iraq as required by Security Council Resolution 687 and subsequent Council resolutions, and no UN inspections took place during the first half of 2002. Moreover, the automated video monitoring systems installed by the UN at known and suspect WMD facilities in Iraq were not operating during this period. Furthermore, Iraq has engaged in extensive concealment efforts and has used the period since it refused inspections to attempt to reconstitute prohibited programmes.

***Nuclear***. More than ten years of sanctions and the loss of much of Iraq's physical nuclear infrastructure under IAEA oversight have not diminished Saddam's interest in acquiring or developing nuclear weapons. Iraq's efforts to procure tens of thousands of proscribed high-strength aluminum tubes are of significant concern. All intelligence experts agree that Iraq is seeking nuclear weapons and that these tubes could be used in a centrifuge enrichment programme. Most intelligence specialists assess this to be the intended use, but some believe that these tubes are probably intended for conventional weapons programmes.

Iraq had an advanced nuclear weapons development programme before the Gulf war that focused on building an implosion-type weapon using highly enriched uranium. Baghdad was attempting a variety of uranium enrichment techniques, the most successful of which were the electromagnetic isotope separation (EMIS) and gas centrifuge programmes. After its invasion of Kuwait, Iraq initiated a crash programme to divert IAEA-safeguarded, highly enriched uranium from its Soviet- and French-supplied reactors, but the onset of hostilities ended this effort. Iraqi declarations and the UNSCOM/IAEA inspection process revealed much of Iraq's nuclear weapons efforts.

Baghdad, however, has still not provided complete information on all aspects of its nuclear weapons programme. Iraq has withheld significant details relevant to its nuclear programme, including procurement logs, technical documents, experimental data, accounting of materials, and foreign assistance. Baghdad also continues to withhold other data about enrichment techniques, foreign procurement, weapons design, and the role of Iraqi security services in concealing its nuclear facilities and activities. In recent years, Baghdad has diverted goods contracted under the Oil-for-Food Programme for military purposes and has increased solicitations and dual-use procurements—outside the Oil-for-Food process—some of which almost certainly are going to prohibited WMD and other weapons programmes. Baghdad probably uses some of the money it gains through its illicit oil sales to support its WMD efforts.

Before its departure from Iraq, the IAEA made significant strides toward dismantling Iraq's nuclear weapons programme and unearthing the nature and scope of Iraq's past nuclear activities. In the absence of inspections, however, most analysts assess that Iraq is working to reconstitute its nuclear programme—unravelling the IAEA's hard-earned accomplishments.

Iraq retained its cadre of nuclear scientists and technicians, its programme documentation, and sufficient dual-use manufacturing capabilities to support a reconstituted nuclear weapons programme. Iraqi media have reported numerous meetings between Saddam and nuclear scientists over the past two years, signalling Baghdad's continuing interest in reviving a nuclear programme.

Iraq's expanding international trade provided growing access to nuclear-related technology and materials and potential access to foreign nuclear expertise. An increase in dual-use procurement activity in recent years may be supporting a reconstituted nuclear weapons programme. The acquisition of sufficient fissile material is Iraq's principal hurdle in developing a nuclear weapon. Iraq is unlikely to produce indigenously enough weapons-grade material for a deliverable nuclear device until the last half of this decade. Baghdad could produce a nuclear weapon within a year if it were able to procure weapons-grade fissile material abroad.

*Missile*. Iraq has developed a ballistic missile capability that exceeds the 150-kilometre range limitation established under UNSCR 687. During the 1980s, Iraq purchased 819 Scud B missiles from the USSR. Hundreds of these 300 km range missiles were used to attack Iranian cities during the Iran-Iraq War. Beginning in 1987, Iraq converted many of these Soviet Scuds into extended-range variants, some of which were fired at Tehran; some were launched during the Gulf War, and others remained in Iraq's inventory at war's end. Iraq admitted filling at least 75 of its Scud warheads with chemical or biological agents and deployed these weapons for use against Coalition forces and regional opponents, including Israel in 1991.

Most of the approximately 90 Scud-type missiles Saddam fired at Israel, Saudi Arabia, and Bahrain during the Gulf War were al-Husayn variants that the Iraqis modified by lengthening the airframe and increasing fuel capacity, extending the range to 650 kms.

Baghdad was developing other longer-range missiles based on Scud technology, including the 900km al-Abbas. Iraq was designing follow-on multi-stage and clustered medium range ballistic missile (MRBM) concepts with intended ranges up to 3,000 kms. Iraq also had a programme to develop a two-stage missile, called the Badr-2000, using solid-propellants with an estimated range of 750 to 1,000 kms. Iraq never fully accounted for its existing missile programmes. Discrepancies in Baghdad's declarations suggest that Iraq retains a small force of extended-range Scud-type missiles and an undetermined number of launchers and warheads. Further, Iraq never explained the disposition of advanced missile components, such as guidance and control systems, that it could not produce on its own and that would be critical to developmental programmes.

Iraq has continued to work on UN-authorised short-range ballistic missiles (SRBMs)—those with a range no greater than

150 kms—that help develop the expertise and infrastructure needed to produce longer-range missile systems. The al-Samoud-II liquid propellant SRBM and the al-Fat'h (Ababil-100) solid propellant SRBM, however, have both flown beyond the allowed 150-km range. Both missiles have been tested aggressively and are in early deployment. Other evidence strongly suggests that Iraq is modifying missile testing and production facilities to produce even longer-range missiles.

The Al-Rafah-North Liquid Propellant Engine Research, Development, Testing, and Evaluation (RDT&E) Facility is Iraq's principal site for the static testing of liquid propellant missile engines. Baghdad has been building a new test stand there that is larger than the test stand associated with al-Samoud engine testing and the defunct Scud engine test stand. The only plausible explanation for this test facility is that Iraq intends to test engines for longer-range missiles prohibited under UNSCR 687.

The Al-Mutasim Solid Rocket Motor and Test Facility, previously associated with Iraq's Badr-2000 solid-propellant missile programme, has been rebuilt and expanded in recent years. The Al-Mutasim site supports solid-propellant motor assembly, rework, and testing for the UN-authorised Ababil-100, but the size of certain facilities there, particularly those newly constructed between the assembly rework and static test areas, suggests that Baghdad is preparing to develop systems that are prohibited by the UN.

At the Al-Mamoun Solid Rocket Motor Production Plant and RDT&E Facility, the Iraqis, since the December 1998 departure of inspectors, have rebuilt structures damaged during the Gulf War and dismantled by UNSCOM that originally were built to manufacture solid-propellant motors for the Badr-2000 programme. They have also built a new building and are reconstructing other buildings originally designed to fill large Badr-2000 casings with solid propellant. Also at Al-Mamoun, the Iraqis have rebuilt two structures used to "mix" solid propellant for the Badr-2000 missile. The new buildings—about as large as the original ones—are ideally suited to house large, UN-prohibited mixers. In fact, the only logical explanation for the size and configuration of these buildings is that Iraq intends to develop longer-range, prohibited missiles.

Iraq has managed to rebuild and expand its missile development infrastructure under sanctions. Iraqi intermediaries have sought production technology, machine tools, and raw materials in violation of the arms embargo. The Iraqis have completed a new ammonium perchlorate production plant at Al-Mamoun that supports Iraq's solid propellant missile programme. Ammonium perchlorate is a common oxidiser used in solid-propellant missile motors. Baghdad would not have been able to complete this facility without help from abroad. In August 1995, Iraq was caught trying to acquire sensitive ballistic missile guidance components, including gyroscopes originally used in Russian strategic nuclear submarine-launched ballistic missiles, demonstrating that Baghdad has been pursuing proscribed, advanced, long-range missile technology for some time. Iraqi officials admitted that, despite international prohibitions, they had received a similar shipment earlier that year.

***Chemical***. We believe that, since December 1998, Iraq has increased its capability to pursue chemical warfare (CW) programmes. After both the Gulf War and Operation Desert Fox in December 1998, Iraq rebuilt key portions of its chemical production infrastructure for industrial and commercial use, as well as former dual-use CW production facilities and missile production facilities. Iraq has attempted to purchase numerous dual-use items for, or under the guise of, legitimate civilian use. Since the suspension of UN inspections in December 1998, the risk of diversion of such equipment has increased. In addition, Iraq appears to be installing or repairing dual-use equipment at CW-related facilities. Some of these facilities could be converted fairly quickly for production of CW agents.

UNSCOM reported to the Security Council in December 1998 that Iraq also continued to withhold information related to its CW programme. For example, Baghdad seized from UNSCOM inspectors an Iraqi Air Force document discovered by UNSCOM that indicated that Iraq had not consumed as many CW munitions during the Iran-Iraq War in the 1980s as had been declared by Baghdad. This discrepancy indicates that Iraq may have hidden an additional 6,000 CW munitions.

***Biological*** During this reporting period, Baghdad continued to pursue a BW programme. Iraq in 1995 admitted to having an offensive BW programme, but UNSCOM was unable to verify the full scope and nature of Iraq's efforts. UNSCOM assessed that Iraq was maintaining a knowledge base and industrial infrastructure that could be used to produce quickly a large amount of BW agents at any time. In addition, Iraq has continued dual-use research that could improve BW agent R&D capabilities. In light of Iraq's growing industrial self-sufficiency and the availability of mobile or possible covert facilities, we are concerned that Iraq is again producing BW agents.

***Advanced Conventional Weapons***. Iraq continued to pursue an unmanned aerial vehicle (UAV) programme that converted L-29 jet trainer aircraft originally acquired from Eastern Europe. In the past, Iraq conducted flights of the L-29, possibly to test system improvements or to train new pilots. We suspect that these refurbished trainer aircraft have been modified for delivery of chemical or, more likely, biological warfare agents. Iraq is also developing and testing smaller UAVs, some of which are well suited for dispensing chemical and biological agents.

Iraq aggressively continues to seek advanced conventional warfare (ACW) equipment and technology. A thriving grey arms market and porous borders have allowed Baghdad to acquire smaller arms and components for larger arms, such as spare parts for aircraft, air defence systems, and armoured vehicles. Iraq also acquires some dual-use and production items that have applications in the ACW arena through the Oil For Food programme.

### *North Korea*

***Nuclear*.** The United States has remained suspicious that North Korea has been working on uranium enrichment for several years. However, we did not obtain clear evidence indicating that North Korea had begun constructing a centrifuge facility until recently.

In 2001, North Korea began seeking centrifuge-related materials in large quantities. It also obtained equipment suitable for use in uranium feed and withdrawal systems. North Korea's goal appears to be a plant that could produce enough weapons-grade uranium for two or more nuclear weapons per year when fully operational. We continue to monitor and assess North Korea's nuclear weapons efforts which, given the North's closed society and the obvious covert nature of the programme, remains a difficult intelligence collection target.

***Missile*.** North Korea has also continued procurement of raw materials and components for its extensive ballistic missile programmes from various foreign sources. In the second half of 2002, North Korea continued to abide by its voluntary moratorium on flight tests, while announcing it may reconsider its September offer to extend the moratorium beyond 2003. The multiple-stage Taepo Dong-2—capable of reaching parts of the United States with a nuclear weapon-sized payload—may be ready for flight-testing. The North is probably also working on improvements to its current design. North Korea is nearly self-sufficient in developing and producing ballistic missiles and has demonstrated a willingness to sell complete systems and components that have enabled other states to acquire longer range capabilities earlier than would otherwise have been possible and to acquire the basis for domestic development efforts.

***Chemical.*** North Korea is not a party to the Chemical Weapons Convention (CWC). P'yongyang has acquired dual-use chemicals that could potentially be used to support P'yongyang's long-standing chemical warfare programme. North Korea's chemical warfare capabilities include the ability to produce bulk quantities of nerve, blister, choking and blood agent, using its sizeable, although aging, chemical industry. During the last half of 2002, we believed that North Korea possessed a sizeable stockpile of these agents and weapons, which it could have employed in a variety of delivery means.

***Biological.*** North Korea has acceded to the Biological and Toxin Weapons Convention, but nonetheless has pursued biological warfare (BW) capabilities since the 1960s. P'yongyang has acquired dual-use biotechnical equipment, supplies, and reagents that could be used to support North Korea's BW efforts. As of the last half of 2002, North Korea is believed to have possessed a munitions production infrastructure that would have allowed allow it to weaponise BW agents and may have such weapons available for use.

***Libya***

***Nuclear***. An NPT party with full-scope IAEA safeguards, Libya continued to develop its nuclear infrastructure. The suspension of UN sanctions provided Libya the means to enhance its nuclear infrastructure through foreign cooperation and procurement efforts. Tripoli and Moscow continued talks on cooperation at the Tajura Nuclear Research Centre and a potential power reactor deal. Such civil-sector work could present Libya with opportunities to pursue technologies that would also be suitable for military purposes. In addition, Libya participated in various technical exchanges through which it could try to obtain dual-use equipment and technology that could enhance its overall technical capabilities in the nuclear area. In 2001, Libya and other countries reportedly used their secret services to try to obtain technical information on the development of WMD, including nuclear weapons. Although Libya made political overtures to the West in an attempt to strengthen relations, Libya's continued interest in nuclear weapons and nuclear infrastructure upgrades raises concerns.

***Missile***. The suspension of UN sanctions in 1999 allowed Libya to expand its efforts to obtain ballistic missile–related equipment, materials, technology, and expertise from foreign sources. Outside assistance—particularly from Serbian, Indian, Iranian, North Korean, and Chinese entities—has remained critical to its ballistic missile development programmes. Libya's capability is improving and with continued foreign assistance it will probably achieve an MRBM capability—a long-desired goal—or extended-range Scud capability.

***Chemical and Biological***. Libya also remained heavily dependent on foreign suppliers for CW precursor chemicals and other key-related equipment. Following the suspension of UN sanctions, Tripoli reestablished contacts with sources of expertise, parts, and precursor chemicals abroad, primarily in Western Europe. Tripoli still appeared to be working towards an offensive CW capability and eventual indigenous production. Evidence suggested that Libya is also seeking to acquire the capability to develop and produce BW agents.

***Advanced Conventional Weapons***. Following the suspension of UN sanctions, Libyan and Russian firms have completed contracts for conventional weapons, munitions, and upgrades and refurbishment for Libya's existing inventory of Soviet-era weapons.

***Syria***

***Nuclear and Missile***. Syria—an NPT signatory with full-scope IAEA safeguards—has a nuclear research centre at Dayr Al Hajar. Russia and Syria have approved a draft cooperative programme on cooperation on civil nuclear power. In principal, broader access to Russian expertise provides opportunities for Syria to expand its indigenous capabilities, should it decide to pursue nuclear weapons. During the second half of 2001, Damascus continued to receive help from abroad on establishing a solid-propellant rocket motor development and production capability. Syria's liquid-propellant missile programme has and will continue to depend on essential foreign equipment and assistance—primarily from North Korean entities and Russian firms. Damascus also continued its efforts to assemble—probably with North Korean assistance—liquid-fuelled Scud C missiles.

*Chemical and Biological*. Syria sought CW-related precursors and expertise from foreign sources during the reporting period. Damascus already held a stockpile of the nerve agent sarin, but apparently is trying to develop more toxic and persistent nerve agents. Syria remained dependent on foreign sources for key elements of its CW programme, including precursor chemicals and key production equipment. It is highly probable that Syria also is continuing to develop an offensive BW capability.

*Advanced Conventional Weapons*. Syria continued to acquire relatively small quantities of ACW—mainly from Russia and other former Soviet-bloc suppliers. But Damascus' outstanding debt to Russia and inability to fund large purchases hampered negotiations for the large quantity of equipment Syria needs to revitalise its aging defence forces. Damascus wanted to acquire Russian SA-10 and SA-11 air defence systems, MiG-29 and Su-27 fighters, and T-80 or T-90 main battle tanks, as well as upgrades for the aircraft, armoured weapons, and air defence systems already in its inventory. No breakthroughs in the sales or debt issue have been noted since Syria's Defence Minister met with high-level Russian officials in Moscow in May 2001, although high-level delegations continued to discuss weapons trade.

### *Sudan*

***Chemical and Biological*.** Sudan, a party to the CWC, has been seeking the capability to produce chemical weapons for many years. It historically has obtained help from foreign entities, principally in Iraq. Sudan may be interested in a BW programme as well.

***Advanced Conventional Weapons*.** During the reporting period, Sudan sought to acquire a variety of military equipment from various sources. In the long-running civil war, Khartoum is seeking older, less expensive ACW and conventional weapons that nonetheless offer more advanced capabilities than the weapons of its opponents and their supporters in neighbouring countries. We remain concerned that Sudan may seek a ballistic missile capability in the future.

### *India*

***Nuclear*.** The underground nuclear tests in May 1998 were a significant milestone in India's continuing nuclear weapons development programme. Since the 1998 tests, New Delhi has continued efforts intended to lead to the development of more sophisticated nuclear weapons. During this reporting period, India continued to obtain foreign assistance for its civilian nuclear power programme, primarily from Russia.

***Missile*.** India still lacks engineering or production expertise in some key missile technologies. Entities in Russia and Western Europe remained the primary conduits of missile-related and dual-use technology transfers during 2001. During the reporting period, India flight-tested the Agni I ballistic missile and continued work with the Russians on the Brahmos cruise missile.

***Advanced Conventional Weapons*.** ACW acquisitions, primarily from Russia, continued to play an important role in India's across-the-board modernisation of its armed forces. Many key programmes have been plagued by delays, but New Delhi has received the first of a licensed upgrade of 125 MiG-21-93 fighter aircraft, working with Hindustan Aeronautics, Limited. In 2001, New Delhi concluded an $800 million contract with Russia for 310 T-90S main battle tanks and a smaller contract for KA-31 helicopters. India was also negotiating with Russia for nuclear submarines and an aircraft carrier. India also continued to explore options for leasing or purchasing several airborne early warning systems. In addition to purchasing the Green Pine radar from Israel, New Delhi also signed a $270 million contract with Tel Aviv for the ship-borne Barak-1 surface-to-air missile defence system. The Indian Air Force reopened the competition for jet trainer aircraft and is considering bids primarily from the Czech Republic and the United Kingdom.

Israel also sought to expand its defence cooperation with India. In recent months, India and Israel engaged in negotiations for the sale of the Arrow-2 anti-tactical-ballistic missile. Negotiations were also underway regarding the proposed sale of three PHALCON airborne early warning (AEW) aircraft for approximately $1 billion. India has already taken delivery of the Israeli Greenpine radar for installation at a ground site for use as an early warning platform—in conjunction with the PHALCON AEW aircraft. Israel has also reportedly sold the Harpy unmanned aerial vehicle (UAV) to India.

***Pakistan***

***Nuclear***. Pakistan's nuclear weapons tests in late May 1998 demonstrated its well-developed nuclear weapons programme. During the reporting period, it continued to acquire nuclear-related equipment, some of it dual-use, and materials from various sources—principally in Western Europe. If Pakistan chooses to develop more advanced nuclear weapons, seeking such goods will remain important. China provided extensive support in the past to Islamabad's nuclear weapons and ballistic missile programmes, but in May 1996 it pledged not to provide assistance to unsafeguarded nuclear facilities in any state, including Pakistan. We cannot rule out, however, the possibility of continued contacts between Chinese and Pakistani entities on Pakistani nuclear weapons development.

***Missile***. Pakistan's ballistic missile programme continued to benefit from significant Chinese entity assistance during the reporting period. With Chinese entity assistance, Pakistan continues to move towards serial production of solid-propellant SRBMs, such as the Shaheen-I, Abdali, and Ghaznavi. During the reporting period, Pakistan flight-tested three ballistic missiles: the Ghauri MRBM, the Hatf III (Ghaznavi) SRBM, and the Hatf II (Abdali) SRBM, and prepared to test the Shaheen I SRBM. Successful development of the two-stage Shaheen-II MRBM will require continued assistance from Chinese entities or other potential sources.

***Advanced Conventional Weapons***. Pakistan continues to rely on China and France for its ACW requirements. Islamabad received delivery of 40 upgraded Mirage IIIs and Vs from France, and received 40 additional F-7PG fighters from China.

**Chemical, Biological, Radiological, and Nuclear Terrorism**

The threat of terrorists using chemical, biological, radiological, and nuclear (CBRN) materials continued to rise—particularly in the aftermath of the attacks on 11 September 2001. Several of the 30 designated foreign terrorist organisations and other nonstate actors worldwide have expressed interest in CBRN—although terrorists probably will continue to favour long-proven conventional tactics such as bombings and shootings.

Increased publicity surrounding the anthrax incidents since the 11 September attacks has highlighted the vulnerability of civilian and government targets to CBRN attacks.

One of our highest concerns is Al-Qaeda's stated readiness to attempt unconventional attacks against us. As early as 1998, Osama bin Ladin publicly declared that acquiring unconventional weapons was "a religious duty."

Terrorist groups worldwide have ready access to information on chemical and biological, and to some extent, even nuclear weapons, via the Internet, publicly available scientific literature, and scientific conferences, and we know that Al-Qaeda was working to acquire some of the most dangerous chemical agents and toxins. A senior bin Ladin associate on trial in Egypt in 1999 claimed his group had chemical and biological weapons. Documents and equipment recovered from Al-Qaeda facilities in Afghanistan show that bin Ladin has a more sophisticated unconventional weapons research programme than was previously known.

We also know that Al-Qaeda has ambitions to acquire or develop nuclear weapons and has been receptive to any outside nuclear assistance that might become available. In February 2001, during the trial on the Al Qaeda bombings of the American Embassies in Tanzania and Kenya, a government witness—Jamal Ahmad Fadl—testified that Al-Qaeda pursued the sale of a quantity of purported enriched uranium (which in fact was probably scam material) in Sudan in the early 1990s.

We assess that terrorist groups are capable of conducting attacks using radiological dispersal devices. In addition, we must be alert to the possibility that Al-Qaeda or other terrorist groups might also try to launch conventional attacks against the chemical or nuclear industrial infrastructure of the United States to cause panic and economic disruption.

## Key Suppliers

### *Russia*

Russia's cash-strapped defence, biotechnology, chemical, aerospace, and nuclear industries continue to be eager to raise funds via exports and transfers. In addition, some Russian universities and scientific institutes have shown a willingness to earn much-needed funds by providing WMD or missile-related teaching and training for foreign students. Given the large potential proliferation impact of such exports, transfers, and training, monitoring the activities of specific entities as well as the overall effectiveness of the Russian Government's nonproliferation regime remains a high priority.

***Nuclear***. Russia has played a key role in supporting civilian nuclear programmes in Iran, primarily the Bushehr Nuclear Power Plant project. Even though the ostensible purpose of Russian assistance to Iran's nuclear infrastructure is for civilian applications, we assess that such support enhances Tehran's ability to support a nuclear weapons development effort.

President Putin in May 2000 amended the presidential decree on nuclear exports to allow Russia in exceptional cases to export nuclear materials, technology, and equipment to countries that do not have full-scope IAEA safeguards. For example, Russia supplied India with material for its civilian nuclear programme in 2001.

***Missile***. Russian entities during the reporting period continued to supply a variety of ballistic missile-related goods and technical know-how to countries such as Iran, India, and China. Iran's earlier success in gaining technology and materials from Russian entities has helped to accelerate Iranian development of the Shahab-3 MRBM, and continuing Russian entity assistance most likely supports Iranian efforts to develop new missiles and increase Tehran's self-sufficiency in missile production.

*Chemical and Biological*. During the first half of 2002, Russian entities remained a key source of dual-use biotechnology, chemicals, production technology, and equipment for Iran. Russia's biological and chemical expertise makes it an attractive target for Iranians seeking technical information and training on BW and CW agent production processes.

*Advanced Conventional Weapons*. Russia continues to be a major supplier of conventional arms. Following Moscow's abrogation of the Gore-Chernomyrdin agreement in November 2000, Russian officials stated that they see Iran as a significant source of potential revenue from arms sales and believe that Tehran can become Russia's third-largest conventional arms customer after China and India. In 2001, Russia was the primary source of ACW for China, Iran, Libya, and Sudan, and one of the largest sources for India. Russia actively markets its thermobaric weapons at international arms shows.

Russia continues to be the main supplier of technology and equipment to India's and China's naval nuclear propulsion programmes. In addition, Russia has discussed leasing nuclear-powered attack submarines to India.

*Export Controls.* The Duma enacted new export control legislation in 1999, and Putin in 2000 reorganised the export control bureaucracy. In 2001, Putin signed into effect several of the new law's implementing decrees, which updated export control lists for biological pathogens, chemicals, missiles, and related dual-use technologies and equipment. In May 2002, Russia amended its criminal code to allow for stricter punishment for violations involving the illegal export of material, equipment, and scientific-technical information that may be used in creating WMD or military equipment.

Despite progress in creating a legal and bureaucratic framework for Russia's export controls, lax enforcement remains a serious concern. To reduce the outward flow of WMD and missile-related materials, technology, and expertise, top officials must make a sustained effort to convince exporting entities—as well as the bureaucracy whose job it is to oversee them—that nonproliferation is a top priority and that those who violate the law will be prosecuted.

### *North Korea*

***Missile.*** Throughout the first half of 2002, North Korea continued to export significant ballistic missile-related equipment, components, materials, and technical expertise to the Middle East, South Asia, and North Africa. P'yongyang attaches high priority to the development and sale of ballistic missiles, equipment, and related technology. Exports of ballistic missiles and related technology are one of the North's major sources of hard currency, which fuel continued missile development and production.

### *China*

Over the past several years, Beijing has improved its nonproliferation posture through commitments to multilateral arms control regimes, promulgation of export controls, and strengthened oversight mechanisms, but Chinese entities remain key suppliers of WMD and missile-related technologies to countries of concern.

***Nuclear.*** In October 1997, China agreed to end cooperation with Iran on supplying a uranium conversion facility (UCF) and to undertake no new nuclear cooperation with Iran after completion of two existing projects. China also made bilateral pledges to the United States that go beyond its 1992 NPT commitment not to assist any country in the acquisition or development of nuclear weapons. For example, in May 1996, Beijing pledged that it would not provide assistance to unsafeguarded nuclear facilities. We cannot rule out, however, some continued contacts subsequent to the pledge between

Chinese entities and entities associated with Pakistan's nuclear weapons programme, and we are concerned that some interactions between Chinese and Iranian entities may run counter to Beijing's expressed bilateral commitments to the United States.

***Missile***. Beijing on several occasions has pledged not to sell Missile Technology Control Regime (MTCR) Category I systems but has not recognised the regime's key technology annex. China is not a member of the MTCR.

In November 2000, China committed not to assist, in any way, any country in the development of ballistic missiles that could be used to deliver nuclear weapons, and to enact at an early date a comprehensive missile-related export control system. Chinese entities continued to provide Pakistan with missile-related technical and material assistance during the reporting period. Pakistan has been moving towards domestic serial production of solid-propellant SRBMs with the help of Chinese entities. Pakistan also needs continued Chinese entity assistance to support development of solid-propellant MRBMs. In addition, firms in China have provided dual-use missile-related items, raw materials, and/or assistance to several other countries of proliferation concern—such as Iran, Libya, and to a lesser extent, North Korea.

***Chemical***. Since 1997, the US has imposed numerous sanctions against Chinese entities for providing material support to the Iranian CW programme. Evidence during the current reporting period continues to show that Chinese firms still provide dual-use CW-related production equipment and technology to Iran.

***Advanced Conventional Weapons***. China remains a primary supplier of advanced conventional weapons to Pakistan and Iran, and other countries. Beijing and Islamabad have also negotiated the sale of an additional 40 F-7 fighters for delivery to Pakistan.

## Emerging State and Non-State Suppliers

As nuclear, biological, chemical, and ballistic missile-applicable technologies continue to be more broadly available around the world, new sources of supply are emerging that are making the challenge of stemming WMD proliferation even more complex and difficult. Nuclear fuel-cycle and weapons-related technologies have spread to the point that, from a technical view, additional states may be able to produce sufficient fissile material and to develop the capability to weaponise it. As developing countries expand their chemical industries into pesticide production, they are also advancing towards at least latent chemical warfare capability. Likewise, additional non-state actors are becoming more interested in the potential of using biological warfare as a relatively inexpensive way to inflict serious damage. The proliferation of increasingly capable ballistic missile designs and technology poses the threat of more countries of concern developing longer-range missiles and posing greater risks to regional stability.

In this context, there is a growing concern that additional states that have traditionally been recipients of WMD and missile-related technology may follow North Korea's practice of supplying specific WMD-related technology and expertise to other countries or non-state actors. Even in cases where states take action to stem such transfers, there are growing numbers of knowledgeable individuals or non-state purveyors of WMD-related materials and technology who are able to act outside the constraints of governments. Such non-state actors are increasingly capable of providing technology and equipment that previously could only be supplied directly by countries with established capabilities.

Although Western European countries maintain rigorous and effective export controls on WMD and missile-related goods and materials, proliferators and associated networks nonetheless continue to seek machine tools, spare parts for dual-use equipment, and widely available materials, scientific equipment, and specialty metals. Western countries are also an important source for the proliferation of WMD-related information and training. The relatively advanced research of Western institutes, the availability of relevant dual-use studies and information, the enthusiasm of scientists for sharing their research, and the availability of dual-use training programmes and education may have shortened development time for some WMD programmes, particularly those of terrorist organisations.

(Source: http://www.cia.gov/cia/reports/721_reports/jan_jun2002.html)

❖❖❖❖❖

# 2. Declaration of the Eleventh SAARC Summit, Kathmandu, 5-6 January 2002

The Prime Minister of the People's Republic of Bangladesh, Her Excellency Begum Khaleda Zia; the Prime Minister of the Royal Government of Bhutan, His Excellency Lyonpo Khandu Wangchuk; the Prime Minister of the Republic of India, His Excellency Mr. Atal Behari Vajpayee; the President of the Republic of Maldives, His Excellency Mr. Maumoon Abdul Gayoom; the Prime Minister of the Kingdom of Nepal, Right Honourable Mr. Sher Bahadur Deuba; the President of the Islamic Republic of Pakistan, His Excellency General Pervez Musharraf; and the President of the Democratic Socialist Republic of Sri Lanka, Her Excellency Mrs. Chandrika Bandaranaike Kumaratunga met at the Eleventh Summit meeting of the South Asian Association for Regional Cooperation (SAARC) in Kathmandu, Nepal from 4 to 6 January 2002.

**Regional Cooperation**

1. The Heads of State or Government reaffirmed their commitment to regional cooperation through SAARC and underscored the importance of annual Summit meetings in charting common strategies for the realisation of the objectives and principles set out in the Charter of the Association. Meeting for the first time at the dawn of the new millennium, they solemnly renewed their pledge to strengthen the Association and make it more cohesive, result-oriented, and forward looking, by adopting clearly defined programmes and effective implementation strategies in line with popular expectations. To give effect to the shared aspirations for a more prosperous South Asia, the Leaders agreed to the vision of a phased and planned process eventually leading to a South Asian Economic Union.

2. The Heads of State or Government stressed that equitable sharing of the benefits of regional cooperation is essential to achieve and maintain a minimum acceptable level of economic and social development in each Member State. To this end, they expressed their commitment to a speedier process of harmonising their policies and practices and imbibing regional goals and strategies in their national development programmes.

3. The Heads of State or Government expressed their firm determination to benefit fully from the wealth of traditional wisdom, creativity and enterprise in the region. They also pledged to enhance transparency and accountability in governance and to encourage effective participation of the peoples and civil societies in the formulation as well as implementation of the programmes of cooperation.

4. Reiterating their resolve to promote South Asian regional identity and to strengthen cooperation at the international level, the Heads of State or Government also reemphasised the need to evolve common positions on issues of shared interest at the international fora.

**Cooperation in the Economic Sector**

5. The Heads of State or Government agreed to accelerate cooperation in the core areas of trade, finance and investment to realise the goal of an integrated South Asian economy in a step-by-step manner. They expressed their determination to make full use of regional synergy to maximise the benefits of globalisation and liberalisation and to minimise their negative impacts on the region. While recognising that trade and economic expansion is closely inter-linked, the Leaders made a commitment to widen and deepen the scope of regional networks of activities in trade and financial matters.

6. The Heads of State or Government noted with satisfaction

the outcomes of the successive meetings of the SAARC Commerce Ministers aimed at enlarging the scope of cooperation in the core areas. They recognised the importance of achieving a free trade area and reaffirmed that the treaty regime for creating a free trade area must incorporate, inter alia, binding timeframes for freeing trade, measures to facilitate trade and provisions to ensure an equitable distribution of benefits of trade to all states, especially for small and least developed countries, including mechanisms for compensation of revenue loss.

7. Recognising the need to move quickly towards a South Asian Free Trade Area, the Heads of State or Government directed the Council of Ministers to finalise the text of the Draft Treaty Framework by the end of 2002. They also directed that in moving towards the goal of SAFTA, the Member States expedite action to remove tariff and non-tariff barriers and structural impediments to free trade. They also instructed to conclude the meeting of the Inter Governmental Group on Trade Liberalisation for the Fourth Round of Trade Negotiations under SAPTA as early as possible according to the decision of the Tenth SAARC Summit in Colombo.

8. The Heads of State or Government renewed their commitment to encourage the participation of the private sector and assured their full support for their socially responsible economic initiatives. While welcoming the practice of holding trade fairs in cooperation with the private sector at the regional level, they appreciated the efforts of the SAARC Chamber of Commerce and Industry to promote regional economic cooperation in the spirit of public and private sector partnership.

9. The Heads of State or Government also decided to instruct the Secretary-General to facilitate the early finalisation of a

regionally agreed investment framework to meet investment needs of the SAARC Member States.

10. The Heads of State or Government recognised the immense tourism potential of South Asia and underlined the need to take measures to promote South Asia as a common tourist destination through joint efforts in areas such as upgrading of infrastructure, air linkages, simplification and harmonisation of administrative procedures and training and joint marketing.

**Poverty Alleviation**

11. The Heads of State or Government acknowledged that investment in poverty alleviation programmes contributes to social stability, economic progress and overall prosperity. They were of the view that widespread and debilitating poverty continued to be the most formidable developmental challenge for the region. Conscious of the magnitude of poverty in the region, and recollecting the decision of the UN Millennium Summit 2000 to reduce world poverty in half by 2015, and also recalling the commitments made at the five-year review of the World Summit for Social Development to reduce poverty through enhanced social mobilisation, the Heads of State or Government made a review of the SAARC activities aimed at poverty alleviation and decided to reinvigorate them in the context of the regional and global commitments to poverty reduction.

12. The Heads of State or Government expressed their firm resolve to combat the problem of poverty with a new sense of urgency by actively promoting the synergetic partnership among national governments, international agencies, the private sector, and the civil society. They reaffirmed their pledge to undertake effective and sustained poverty alleviation programmes through pro-poor growth strategies

and social as well as other policy interventions with specific sectoral targets. The Leaders also agreed to take immediate steps for the effective implementation of the programmes for social mobilisation and decentralisation, and for strengthening institution building and support mechanisms to ensure participation of the poor, both as stakeholder and beneficiary, in governance and the development process.

13. The Heads of State or Government decided to undertake sustained measures to extend rural micro-credit programmes with focus on women and the disadvantaged sections of society. They also stressed the need for widening the opportunities for gainful employment. While highlighting the importance of promoting agriculture, indigenous skills and small-scale and cottage industries to address the incidence of rural poverty, they decided to enhance cooperation in agricultural research, extension and adoption. They specifically instructed that the Technical Committees should identify programmemes and activities that impact on poverty alleviation. They urged the need to create gainful employment and promote cooperation in vocational training.

14. The Heads of State or Government emphasised the need to promote sharing of the best practices and experiences among the Member States and to this end, instructed the Secretary-General to disseminate such information to the Member States on a regular basis. They directed the Council of Ministers to review, on a continuous basis, the regional poverty profile to be prepared by the Secretary-General with the assistance of the related UN agencies, nodal agencies and independent research institutions specialised in the field.

15. In order to ensure social stability and to protect the vulnerable sections of population from the adverse impacts

of globalisation and liberalisation, the Heads of State or Government stressed the need to enhance cooperation to create and maintain appropriate safety nets.

16. The Heads of State or Government agreed that a Special Session on poverty alleviation at the Ministerial level should undertake a comprehensive review and evaluation of the status of implementation of poverty eradication policies and programmes carried out so far, and to recommend further concrete measures to enhance effective cooperation at the regional level to the Twelfth SAARC Summit. They also directed the Council of Ministers to take necessary steps to fully activate the existing three-tier mechanism for poverty alleviation.

17. The Leaders directed the Council of Ministers to coordinate efforts to integrate poverty alleviation programmes into the development strategies of Member States. In this context, they agreed to reconstitute the Independent South Asian Commission on Poverty Alleviation, with Nepal as its Convenor and Bangladesh as Co-convenor, for reviewing the progress made in cooperation on poverty alleviation and for suggesting appropriate and effective measures. They instructed the Chairman of the Council of Ministers to seek two nominations from each Member State by the end of January 2002 to enable the convening of its first meeting before the proposed Ministerial Meeting on Poverty Alleviation in Pakistan in April 2002.

18. Expressing concern at the region's special vulnerability in the slowdown in world economy and its negative impact on the poor and the marginalised, the Heads of State or Government called for a supportive international environment and an enhanced level of assistance by the international community for poverty alleviation programmes in South Asia.

**Cooperation in the Social and Cultural Sector**

19. The Heads of State or Government reiterated the need for an early finalisation of the SAARC Social Charter and instructed the Inter Governmental Expert Group to expedite their work on the basis of the draft to be submitted by the Secretary-General, as a working paper for its consideration and to complete the draft framework of the Charter as early as possible for consideration at the next meeting of the Council of Ministers. In drawing up the Charter, they also directed the Council of Ministers to include the important areas of poverty eradication, population stabilisation, the empowerment of women, youth mobilisation, human resources development, the promotion of health and nutrition and the protection of children as decided at the Tenth Summit.

20. The Leaders recognised the debilitating and widespread impact of the HIV/ AIDS, TB and other deadly communicable diseases on the population of South Asia and stressed the need for evolving a regional strategy to combat these diseases. The strategy should include, inter alia, culturally appropriate preventive measures, an affordable treatment regime and should specially target the vulnerable groups. In this regard, they felt that SAARC should collabourate with the international organisations and civil society. They also emphasised that the SAARC Tuberculosis Centre in Kathmandu should play a coordinating role in the related areas.

21. In accordance with the Colombo Declaration, the Heads of State or Government decided to mandate the Meeting of Ministers of Cultural Affairs in Sri Lanka to finalise the details relating to the establishment of the SAARC Cultural Centre including its financing and to submit its report to the next session of the Council of Ministers.

**Women and Children**

22. The Heads of State or Government welcomed the signing of the SAARC Convention on Preventing and Combating the Trafficking in Women and Children for Prostitution and expressed their collective resolve to treat the trafficking in women and children for commercial sexual exploitation as a criminal offence of a serious nature. They also welcomed the signing of the SAARC Convention on Regional Arrangements for the Promotion of Child Welfare in South Asia and observed that the Convention reflected their commitment to place the child first in the national and regional programmes of the Member States. They instructed the Secretary-General, in consultation with Member States and other specialised agencies, to present a report on measures for the effective implementation of the Conventions to the next meeting of the Council of Ministers.

23. The Heads of State or Government agreed to establish, on the basis of recommendations of the Regional Task Force responsible for the implementation of the provisions of the SAARC Convention on Preventing and Combating Trafficking in Women and Children for Prostitution, a voluntary fund with contributions from Member States, individuals, and donor countries and agencies for the rehabilitation and reintegration of the victims of trafficking.

24. The Leaders recognised the need to form an autonomous advocacy group of prominent women personalities from the Member States with a view to making recommendations to the SAARC bodies on a broad spectrum of gender-related issues. They directed the Council of Ministers to take necessary steps to prepare and present, for consideration at their next meeting, the Terms of Reference for the purpose.

25. The Heads of State or Government recognised the need to actively pursue and promote social development through empowerment of women and to achieve their full participation in decision-making at all levels. They reaffirmed their commitment to uplift the social status of the people, women and children in particular, in the region and expressed their common resolve to accord the highest priority to promoting social development through specific and targeted programmes. The Leaders directed the Council of Ministers to take necessary measures to ensure the enjoyment by women and girl children of their inherent potential. They also directed the Council of Ministers to constitute a Task Force to review the status of implementation of past decisions related to the social sector and to suggest guidelines for their effective implementation in the future.

26. The Leaders directed the Council of Ministers to take concrete steps to give priority to investing in children as an effective means for poverty reduction in the long run. Reaffirming their commitment to the Colombo Plan of Action and the Rawalpindi Declaration and recalling the declaration of 2001 to 2010 as the SAARC Decade of the Rights of the Child, the Heads of State or Government noted with appreciation the South Asia High-level Meeting on Children held in Kathmandu in May 2001. They reaffirmed their conviction that the children in South Asia deserve urgent and focused attention to enhance the long-term and overall progress of the countries of the region.

27. The Heads of State or Government agreed to mobilise the necessary resources and intensify broad-based actions to achieve a set of priority goals related to improving the status of children, such as polio eradication by 2005, protection of children from mother-to-child transmission of HIV/ AIDS, and quality basic education to the children within a time-bound period.

## Education

28. The Heads of State or Government instructed the concerned Ministries of Governments to devise appropriate strategies for raising the quality of education through the exchange of information among the universities in the region. While emphasising the importance of mutual recognition of the educational institutions, they agreed to give the necessary impetus to realise the goal of a common regional educational standard through uniform methods of instruction and teaching aids. They were unanimous in recognising the benefit of introducing SAARC in the national curricula at appropriate levels of study in order to enhance the awareness about the Association's goals and objectives.

29. The Heads of State or Government recognised that access to quality education was an important element for the empowerment of all segments of society, and undertook to develop or strengthen national strategies and action plans to ensure that all children, particularly the girl child have access to quality primary education by 2015; and to improve levels of adult literacy by fifty per cent by eliminating gender disparities in access to education as envisaged in the Dakar Framework for Action on Education for All adopted by the World Education Forum held at Dakar in April 2000.

## International Political and Economic Environment

30. The Heads of State or Government reiterated their firm support for the principles and purposes of the United Nations in order to create a just, balanced and equitable world order. They reaffirmed their commitment to continue working with the NAM and other like-minded countries for the reform and democratisation of the United Nations System with a view to making it an effective and more

democratic institution for international peace, security, progress and cooperation.

31. The Heads of State or Government were of the view that stability, peace and security in South Asia should be promoted together with efforts to improve the global security environment. They underscored their commitment to general and complete disarmament including nuclear disarmament on a universal basis, under effective international control. They agreed that global non-proliferation goals could not be achieved in the absence of progress towards nuclear disarmament and in this context called upon all nuclear weapon states, whether party or non-party to the NPT, to engage constructively through a transparent and credible process of negotiations at the Conference on Disarmament. The Leaders also recognised the linkage between disarmament and development.

32. The Leaders emphasised the need to take appropriate measures to make international financial institutions and the global trading regime more responsive to the needs and concerns of the developing countries. They reiterated the call for genuine partnership among the developed and developing countries in international trade and finance and for the reform of the global financial architecture with an enhanced level of resources.

33. The Leaders also called upon the developed countries to facilitate and ensure an unimpeded and enhanced level of market access to products from the developing, the least developed and the land-locked countries.

34. Recognising the important role that trade can play in advancing the overall development of a country, thus contributing to an equitable and sustainable world order, the Heads of State or Government also called for an early realisation of a rule-based and non-discriminatory world

trade regime. In this context, they appreciated the positive elements of the Fourth WTO Ministerial Conference held in Doha and called upon the developed countries to fulfil their commitments to address the particular concerns and needs of the developing and the least developed countries. The Leaders also instructed the forthcoming meeting of the Committee on Economic Cooperation to devote at least half a day for discussions on the evaluation of the decisions of the recently concluded Doha Conference in order to evolve better coordinated positions among the Member States on all WTO issues. They further stressed the need to intensify coordination among the SAARC missions in Geneva and begin the necessary preparation to advance the common interest of the region in the Fifth WTO Ministerial Conference.

35. The Heads of State or Government noted with serious concern the adverse impact of the shrinking Official Development Assistance (ODA) and other concessional financial flows on developing countries in general, and the least developed among them in particular. They further noted with concern the current trend of the global economic slowdown and its adverse effects on these economies. Taking into account the interdependent nature of the global economy, the Leaders urged the developed countries to enhance the level of ODA flows to meet the internationally agreed targets.

36. Recalling the recommendations of the Third United Nations Conference on the Least Developed Countries held in Brussels in May 2001 and the decisions of the Zanzibar Declaration of July 2001, the Leaders urged the developed countries to adopt more liberal trade and aid policies responsive to the particular needs of the least developed countries. Referring to the forthcoming International Conference on Financing for Development to be held in Mexico in March 2002, the Leaders urged the international

community to strengthen cooperation for development by addressing international and systemic issues related to financing for development in the developing and the least developed countries in a holistic manner.

37. The Heads of State or Government welcomed the initiative of the donor countries to relieve the external debt burden of the Highly Indebted Poor Countries. They urged the international donor community and financial institutions to widen the scope and extent of debt relief initiatives to cover all those developing and the least developed countries, which are facing developmental difficulties particularly due to the current global recession. In the context of growing global interdependence, they underlined the importance of forging cooperative partnership between the developed and the developing countries to ensure equitable benefits to all.

38. The Heads of State or Government expressed concern over the continued violence and bloodshed in the Middle East, and the set backs suffered by the peace process. They reaffirmed their support for the achievement of a just, lasting and comprehensive peace based on Security Council Resolution 242 (1967) and Resolution 338 (1973) and the establishment of a sovereign Palestine State under the leadership of the PLO, which could coexist with its neighbours in peace, security and harmony.

**Security of Small States**

39. The Heads of State or Government recognised that due to their particular vulnerability, small states require special measures for support from the international community for the safeguarding of their sovereign independence and territorial integrity. They reiterated that the real protection of small states should be firmly rooted in the scrupulous adherence to the UN Charter, the rule of law and the strict

adherence to universally accepted principles and norms related to sovereign rights and territorial integrity of all states, irrespective of size. This, they stressed, should be ensured by all the countries, either severally or collectively through the pursuit of appropriate action.

**Terrorism**

40. The Heads of State or Government were convinced that terrorism, in all its forms and manifestations, is a challenge to all states and to all of humanity, and cannot be justified on ideological, political, religious or on any other ground. The Leaders agreed that terrorism violates the fundamental values of the United Nations and the SAARC Charter and constitutes one of the most serious threats to international peace and security in the 21st century.

41. The Heads of State or Government emphasised the need for the urgent conclusion of a Comprehensive Convention on Combating International Terrorism. They also emphasised that international cooperation to combat terrorism should be conducted in conformity with the UN Charter, international law and relevant international conventions.

42. The Heads of State or Government reiterated their support to the United Nations Security Council Resolution 1373 of 28 September 2001 and affirmed their determination to redouble efforts, collectively as well as individually, to prevent and suppress terrorism in all its forms and manifestations, including by increased cooperation and full implementation of the relevant international Conventions relating to terrorism to which they are parties. In this context, they called on all states to prevent and suppress the financing of terrorist acts by criminalising the collection of funds for such acts and refraining from organising, instigating, assisting or participating in terrorist acts in

states or acquiescing in organised activities within its territory directed towards the commission of such acts. The Leaders reaffirmed that the fight against terrorism in all its forms and manifestations has to be comprehensive and sustained.

43. The Heads of State or Government were unanimous in recognising the distinct ominous link between terrorism, drug-trafficking, money laundering and other transnational crimes and emphasised the need to coordinate efforts at the national and regional levels to strengthen the global response to this serious challenge and threat to international security. They called upon the international community to assist Member States of SAARC to deal effectively with the adverse economic effects of terrorism in general and to meet the rising insurance and security related costs in particular.

44. The Heads of State or Government reaffirmed their commitment to SAARC Regional Convention on Suppression of Terrorism, which, among others, recognises the seriousness of the problem of terrorism as it affects the security, stability, and development of the region. They also reiterated their firm resolve to accelerate the enactment of enabling legislation within a definite time-frame for the full implementation of the Convention, together with strengthening of SAARC Terrorist Offences Monitoring Desk and the SAARC Drug Offences Monitoring Desk in an effective manner.

**Report of the Group of Eminent Persons**

45. The Leaders noted with appreciation that the Report of the Group of Eminent Persons (GEP) was an important contribution in the ongoing process of introspection into the functioning of the Association as well as in setting out a perspective plan of action for that purpose. They endorsed

the report of the Council of Ministers on the implementation of the recommendations of the GEP Report, and directed the Council of Ministers to undertake a review of progress in this regard.

**Enhancing Political Cooperation**

46. The Heads of State or Government reaffirmed their commitment to the promotion of mutual trust and understanding and, recognising that the aims of promoting peace, stability and amity and accelerated socio-economic cooperation may best be achieved by fostering good neighbourly relations, relieving tensions and building confidence, agreed that a process of informal consultations would prove useful in this regard. The Leaders further recognised that this process would contribute to the appreciation of each other's problems and perceptions as well as for decisive action in agreed areas of regional cooperation. They underlined the importance of informal political consultations in promoting mutual understanding and reinforcing the confidence building process among the Member States.

**Sub-regional Cooperation**

47. The Heads of State or Government reaffirmed the validity of the idea of encouraging the development of specific projects relevant to the individual needs of three or more Member States under the provisions of Articles VII and X of the SAARC Charter.

**South Asian Development Fund (SADF)**

48. The Heads of State or Government underlined the urgent need to make the South Asian Development Fund operational by making utilisation of the existing funds. They also instructed the Secretary-General to submit a proposal for seeking possible assistance from regional and

international sources for the implementation of specific regional poverty alleviation priority projects.

**Environment**

49. The Heads of State or Government noted with satisfaction the growing public awareness on the need for protecting the environment within the framework of regional cooperation. They reiterated their call for the early and effective implementation of the SAARC Environment Plan of Action as endorsed by the SAARC Environment Ministers. They directed their Environment Ministers to take this into account and come up with an agreed position in their forthcoming meeting.

50. The Heads of State or Government also felt a strong need to devise a mechanism for cooperation in the field of the early warning on as well as preparedness and management of natural disasters, along with programmes to promote conservation of land and water resources.

51. The Heads of State or Government also stressed the need to develop a cooperative mechanism for the protection, enrichment and utilisation of bio-diversity as provided for in the UN Convention on Biological Diversity and to establish a regional bio-diversity database with a view to providing equitable benefits to all Member States. They also underscored the importance of protecting associated knowledge and other indigenous intellectual manifestations for the advancement of the region. They also directed the Council of Ministers to explore the possibility of establishing a SAARC Seed Security Reserve to strengthen cooperation in the field of agriculture and to protect IPRs of the seeds of the Reserve.

**People-to-People Contact**

52. The Heads of State or Government were unanimous in

recognising the need for further promoting a sense of regional identity amongst the peoples of the region. The Leaders lauded the roles played by intellectuals, professionals and eminent persons in promoting people-to-people contacts within the region and agreed to encourage such endeavours as a healthy sign of regional cohesion and fraternity. In this context, they took note of the activities of the SAARCLAW including other recognised bodies. They also took note of the First Meeting of the Chief Election Commissioners of SAARC Countries held in Kathmandu in February 1999 and appreciated the initiative on free and fair election. The Leaders instructed the Secretary-General to collect on a regular basis study reports and other relevant documents and information from the civil society on matters relating to regional cooperation for dissemination to Member States.

**Rationalisation and Institutional Issues**

53. The Heads of State or Government were in agreement that the Summit and all other meetings of SAARC needed to be made more business-like and result-oriented with focus on programmes and activities supported by informed regional inputs from the cross-sections of the society. They directed the Chairman of the Council of Ministers to undertake a review of the functioning and operation of the SAARC Secretariat, and to make recommendations to advance the process of rationalisation and to make SAARC more functional and business-like, to the next meeting of the Council of Ministers.

**SAARC Award**

54. The Heads of State or Government noted with appreciation the proposal made by Nepal to institute a SAARC Award to honour the outstanding work of individuals and organisations within the region in the fields of peace,

development, poverty alleviation and regional cooperation, and requested His Majesty's Government of Nepal to submit a concept paper for consideration by the next session of the Council of Ministers.

**Date and Venue of the Twelfth Summit**

55. The Heads of State or Government welcomed with appreciation the offer of the Government of the Islamic Republic of Pakistan to host the Twelfth Summit Meeting of the Heads of State or Government of the South Asian Association for the Regional Cooperation (SAARC) in Pakistan in early 2003.

56. The Heads of State or Government of Bangladesh, Bhutan, India, Maldives, Pakistan and Sri Lanka expressed their deep appreciation for the exemplary manner in which the Right Honourable Prime Minister of Nepal conducted the proceedings of the Eleventh SAARC Summit in his capacity as Chairperson. They also expressed their deep gratitude for the generous hospitality extended to them by His Majesty's Government and people of Nepal, and for the excellent arrangements made for the Summit.

(Source: http://www.saarc-sec.org/ summits/3ss-decl.htm)

# 3. President General Pervez Musharraf's Address to the Nation 12 January 2002

I begin in the name of God, the most Beneficent, the most Merciful.

Pakistani Brothers and Sisters!

As you would remember, ever since I assumed office, I launched a campaign to rid the society of extremism, violence and terrorism and strived to project Islam in its true perspective. In my first speech on 17 October 17 1999, I had said and I quote; "Islam teaches tolerance, not hatred; universal brotherhood, not enmity; peace, and not violence. I have a great respect for the Ulema and expect them to come forward and present Islam in its true light. I urge them to curb elements which are exploiting religion for vested interests and bringing a bad name to our faith." After this, I initiated a number of steps in this regard. First, in the year 2000, I started interacting with the Taliban and counselled them to inculcate tolerance and bring moderation in their ways. I also told them that those terrorists who were involved in terrorist acts in Pakistan and seeking refuge in Afghanistan should be returned to us. Unfortunately, we did not succeed.

In the year 2001, I think it was January, we sealed the Pak-Afghan borders and I gave directions that no students of any Madarissah (religious seminaries) should be allowed to cross into Afghanistan without relevant documents. After this, I despatched a number of delegations to meet Mullah Omar.I continued to advise them tolerance and balance. Later, on 15 February 2001, we promulgated the Anti-Weaponisation Ordinance. Through this law, we launched a de-weaponisation campaign in Pakistan.

On 5 June, on the occasion of the Seerat Conference, I addressed Ulema belonging to all Schools of thought and spoke firmly to them against religious extremism. On 14 August 2001, we finally took a very important decision to ban Lashkar-e-Jhangvi and Sipah-e-Muhammad and placed Sipah-e-Sahaba and TJP (Tehrik-e-Jafria Pakistan) under observation. In addition, on a number of occasions, I called Ulema and Mashaikh and held extensive consultations with them. The objective was to take them on board in our campaign against terrorism and extremism. These measures have been continuing since our government assumed office in 1999. I am explaining all this to you in great detail only because of the fact that the campaign against extremism undertaken by us from the very beginning is in our own national interest. We are not doing this under advice or pressure from anyone. Rather, we are conscious that it is in our national interest. We are conscious that we need to rid society of extremism and this is being done right from the beginning.

This domestic reforms process was underway when a terrorist attack took place against the United States on 11 September. This terrorist act led to momentous changes all over the world. We decided to join the international coalition against terrorism and in this regard I have already spoken to you on a number of occasions. We took this decision on principles and in our national interest.

By the grace of God Almighty our decision was absolutely correct. Our intentions were noble and God Almighty helped us. I am happy to say that the vast majority of Pakistanis stood by this decision and supported our decision. I am proud of the realistic decision of our nation. What really pains me is that some religious extremist parties and groups opposed this decision. What hurts more was that their opposition was not based on principles. At a critical juncture in our history, they preferred their personal and party interests over national interests. They tried their utmost to mislead the nation, took out processions and resorted to agitation. But their entire efforts failed. The people of Pakistan frustrated their designs. As I have said, I am proud of the people of Pakistan who support correct decisions and do not pay heed to those who try to mislead them.

I have interacted with the religious scholars on a number of occasions and exchanged views with them. I am happy to say that our discussions have been very fruitful. A majority of them are blessed with wisdom and vision and they do not mix religion with politics. Some extremists, who were engaged in protests, are people who try to monopolise and attempt to propagate their own brand of religion.

They think as if others are not Muslims. These are the people who considered the Taliban to be a symbol of Islam and that the Taliban were bringing Islamic renaissance or were practising the purest form of Islam.

They behaved as if the Northern Alliance, against whom the Taliban were fighting, were non-Muslims! Whereas, in fact, both were Muslims and believers. These extremists were those people who do not talk of "Haqooqul Ibad" (obligations towards fellow human beings). They do not talk of these obligations because practising them demands self-sacrifice. How will they justify their Pajeros and expensive vehicles? I want to ask these extremists as to who was responsible for misleading thousands of Pakistanis to their massacre in Afghanistan? These misled people were let down by the very people in whose support they had gone. All of us should learn a lesson from this. We must remember that we are Pakistanis. Pakistan is our identity, our motherland. We will be aliens outside Pakistan and be treated as aliens.

Pakistan is our land. It is our soil. If we forsake it, we will face difficulties. This lesson we must learn.

Sectarian terrorism has been going on for years. Everyone of us is fed up of it. It is becoming unbearable. Our peace-loving people are keen to get rid of the Klashinkov and weapon culture. Every one is sick of it. It was because of this that we banned

Lashkar-e-Jhangvi and Sipah-e-Muhammad. Yet little improvement occurred. The day of reckoning has come. Do we want Pakistan to become a theocratic state? Do we believe that religious education alone is enough for governance or do we want Pakistan to emerge as a progressive and dynamic Islamic welfare state? The verdict of the masses is in favour of a progressive Islamic state. This decision, based on the teaching of the Holy Prophet (Peace Be Upon Him) and in line with the teachings of Quaid-e-Azam and Allama Iqbal will put Pakistan on the path of progress and prosperity. Let us honestly analyse what the few religious extremists have attempted to do with Pakistan and Islam. First, with regard to Afghanistan, they indulged in agitational activities.

Look at the damage it has caused! Pakistan's international image was tarnished and we were projected by the international media as ignorant and backward. Our economy suffered. A number of export orders already placed with Pakistani industry were cancelled and no new orders materialised. This led to closure of some factories and unemployment. The poor daily wage earners lost their livelihood. Extremists also formed a Pakistan-Afghanistan Defence Council! Apart from damaging Pakistan, they had negative thinking and had no idea of anything good for Afghanistan. Did they ever think of bringing about peace to Afghanistan through reconciliation among the Taliban and Northern Alliance? Did they counsel tolerance to them? Did they ever think of collecting funds for the welfare, rehabilitation and reconstruction of the war-ravaged Afghanistan, or to mitigate sufferings of the poor Afghan people? Did they think of a solution to the hunger, poverty and destruction in Afghanistan? To my knowledge, only Maulana Abdul Sattar Edhi, God bless him, and some foreign NGOs and the UN organisations were providing the Afghans with food and medicines. These extremists did nothing except contributing to bloodshed in Afghanistan. I ask of them, whether they know any thing other then disruption and sowing seeds of hatred? Does Islam preach this?

Now, let us see their activity outside Afghanistan. They initiated sectarian feuds.

Sects and different schools of thought in Islam have existed for some time.

There is nothing wrong with intellectual differences flowing from freedom of thought as long as such differences remain confined to intellectual debates.

Look at what this extremist minority is doing? They are indulging in fratricidal killings. There is no tolerance among them. Quaid-e-Azam declared that Pakistan belonged to followers of all religions; that everyone would be treated equally. However, not to mention other religions, Muslims have started killing each other.

I think, these people have declared more Muslims as Kafirs (infidels) than motivating the non-Muslims to embrace Islam. Look at the damage they have caused? They have murdered a number of our highly qualified doctors, engineers, civil servants and teachers who were pillars of our society. Who has suffered? The families of the dead, no doubt. But a greater loss was inflicted on Pakistan because, as I said, we lost the pillars of our society. These extremists did not stop here. They started killing other innocent people in mosques and places of worship.

Today, people are scared of entering these sacred places of worship. It is a matter of shame that police have to be posted outside for their protection. We claim Islam as Deen or a complete way of life.

Is this the way of life that Islam teaches us? That we fight amongst ourselves and feel scared of fellow Muslims, scared of visiting our places of worship where police have to be deputed outside for protection? Mosques are being misused for propagating and inciting hatred against each other's sect and beliefs and against the government, too.

I would like to inform you that a number of terrorist rings have been apprehended. In Karachi, the Inspector General of Police, while briefing me, informed me that the leader of one of these groups is the Pesh Imam (Prayer Leader) of a mosque in Malir. The Imam has confessed to murdering many people himself. This is the state of affairs. To what purpose are we using our mosques for? These people have made a state within a state and have challenged the writ of the government.

Now, I would like to dwell upon the subject of Madaris or Religious Schools in some detail. These schools are excellent welfare set-ups where the poor get free board and lodge. In my opinion, no NGO can match their welfare aspects. Many of the madaris are imparting excellent education. In addition to religious teachings, other subjects such as science education and computer training are also being imparted there.

I am thankful to them for undertaking excellent welfare measures without State funding. I would also like to say that I have projected madaris internationally and with various heads of states time and again. I think no one else in Pakistan has done so much for their cause. However,there are some negative aspects of some madrasas. These few impart only religious education and such education which produces semi-literate religious scholars. This is a weakness. Very few madaris, I repeat very few of them, are under the influence of politico-religious parties or have been established by them. I know that some of these promote negative thinking and propagate hatred and violence instead of inculcating tolerance, patience and fraternity. We must remember that historically, the madrasa was a prestigious seat of learning. They were citadels of knowledge and beacons of light for the world.

When Islam was at its zenith, every discipline of learning, e.g. mathematics, science, medicine, astronomy and jurisprudence were taught at these institutions. Great Muslim luminaries such as Al-Beruni, Ibn-e-Sina (Avesina) and Ibn Khuldoon, were the products of these same madaris. And if we study history, we see that from the 7th to 15th century AD, transfer of technology took place from the Muslims to the rest of the world.

Look at Muslims' condition today. Islam teaches us to seek knowledge, even if it involved travel to China. I am sure you are aware that the Prophet (Peace Be Upon Him) had told prisoners of war in the Battle of Badar that they would be set free if each of them imparted education to ten Muslims.

Quite obviously, this education could not have been religious education as the prisoners were non-Muslims. So the Prophet (Peace Be Upon Him) was actually referring to worldly education. If we do not believe in education, are we following the teachings of Islam or violating them? We must ask what direction are we being led into by these extremists? The writ of the government is being challenged. Pakistan has been made a soft state where the supremacy of law is questioned. This situation can not be tolerated any more. The question is what is the correct path? First of all, we must rid the society of sectarian hatred and terrorism, promote mutual harmony. Remember that mindsets can not be changed through force and coercion. No idea can ever be forcibly thrust upon anyone. Perhaps the person changes outwardly but minds and hearts can never be converted by force. Real change can be brought about through personal example, exemplary character and superior intellect. It can be brought about by Haqooq-ul-ibad (Obligation towards fellow beings).

Have we forgotten the example of the Holy Prophet (Peace Be Upon Him) where Islam was spread by virtue of his personal conduct, true leadership and that is how changes in the world took place at that time? We have forgotten the teaching of revered personalities of Islam like Hazrat Data Ganj Bakhsh, Hazrat Lal Shahbaz Qalandar, Fareed Ganj Shakar, Baha-uddin Zakria, etc.

Was Islam spread by them through force and coercion? No. They preached Islam by personal example. I give these examples because it hurts me to see where we have relegated ourselves now. We must restore the status of madaris to what they originally were. We have to change the state of affairs and take them on the path of improvement.

The second thing I want to talk about is the concept of Jehad in its totality. I want to dilate upon it because it is a contentious issue, requiring complete comprehension and understanding. In Islam, Jehad is not confined to armed struggles only. Have we ever thought of waging Jehad against illiteracy, poverty, backwardness and hunger? This is the larger Jehad. Pakistan, in my opinion, needs to wage Jehad against these evils.

After the battle of Khyber, the Prophet (Peace Be Upon Him) stated that Jehad-e-Asghar (Smaller Jehad) is over but Jehad-e-Akbar (Greater Jehad) has begun. This meant that armed Jehad, i.e. the smaller Jehad was now over and the greater Jehad against backwardness and illiteracy had started.

**Pakistan needs Jehad-e-Akbar at this juncture.**

By the way, we must remember that only the government of the day and not every individual can proclaim armed Jehad. The extremist minority must realise that Pakistan is not responsible of waging armed Jehad in the world.

I feel that in addition to Haqooq Allah (Obligations to God), we should also focus on Haqooq-Al-ebad (obligations towards fellow human beings). At schools, colleges and madaris, obligations towards fellow beings should be preached. We know that we have totally ignored the importance of correct dealings with fellow humans beings. There is no room for feuds in Islamic teachings. It is imperative that we teach true Islam, i.e. tolerance, forgiveness, compassion, justice, fair play, amity and harmony, which is the true spirit of Islam. We must adopt this. We must shun negative thinking.

We have formulated a new strategy for madaris and there is

need to implement it so as to galvanise their good aspects and remove their drawbacks. We have developed a new syllabi for them providing for teaching of Pakistan studies, Mathematics, Science and English along with religious subjects. Even if we want these Madaris to produce religious leaders they should be educated along these lines. Such people will command more respect in society because they will be better qualified. To me, students of religious schools should be brought into the mainstream of society. If any one of them opts to join college or university, he would have the option of being equipped with modern education. If a child studying at a madrasa does not wish to be a prayer leader and he wants to be a bank official or seek employment elsewhere, he should be facilitated.

It would mean that the students of madaris should be brought into the mainstream through a better system of education. This is the crux of the madrasa strategy.

This by no means is an attempt to bring religious educational institutions under government control nor do we want to spoil the excellent attributes of these institutions. My only aim is to help these institutions in overcoming their weaknesses and providing them with better facilities and more avenues to the poor children at these institutions.

We must check abuse of mosques and madaris and they must not be used to spread political and sectarian prejudices. We want to ensure that mosques enjoy freedom and we are here to maintain it. At the same time we expect a display of responsibility along with freedom. If the Imam of mosques fail to display responsibility, curbs would have to be placed on them. After this analysis, now, I come to some conclusions and decisions: - First, we have to establish the writ of the government. All organisations in Pakistan will function in a regulated manner. No individual, organisation or Party will be allowed to break the law of the land. The internal environment has to be improved.

Maturity and equilibrium have to be established in the

society. We have to promote an environment of tolerance, maturity, responsibility, patience and understanding. We have to check extremism, militancy, violence and fundamentalism. We will have to forsake the atmosphere of hatred and anger.

We have to stop exploitation of simple poor people of the country and not to incite them to fueds and violence. We must concern ourselves with our own country. Pakistan comes first. We do not need to interfere and concern ourselves with others. There is no need to interfere in other countries.

Now I turn to other important issues. In my view there are three problems causing conflict and agitation in our minds. They include; first the Kashmir cause, secondly all political disputes at the international level concerning Muslims and thirdly internal sectarian disputes and differences.

These are the three problems which create confusion in our minds. I want to lay down rules of behaviour concerning all three.

Let us take the Kashmir cause first. Kashmir runs in our blood. No Pakistani can afford to sever links with Kashmir. The entire Pakistan and the world knows this. We will continue to extend our moral, political and diplomatic support to Kashmiris. We will never move an inch from our principle stand on Kashmir. The Kashmir problem needs to be resolved by dialogue and peaceful means in accordance with the wishes of the Kashmiri people and the United Nations resolutions. We have to find a solution to this dispute. No organisation will be allowed to indulge in terrorism in the name of Kashmir. We condemn the terrorist acts of 11 September, 1 October and 13 December. Anyone found involved in any terrorist act would be dealt with sternly.

Strict action will be taken against any Pakistani individual, group or organisation found involved in terrorism within or outside the country. Our behaviour must always be in accordance with international norms.

On this occasion, as President of Pakistan, I want to convey a message to Prime Minister Vajpaee: If we want to normalise relations between Pakistan and India and bring harmony to the region, the Kashmir dispute will have to be resolved peacefully through a dialogue on the basis of the aspirations of the Kashmiri people. Solving the Kashmir Issue is the joint responsibility of our two countries. Let me repeat some of the observations made by you, Mr. Vajpayee, some time ago, and I quote: "Mind-sets will have to be altered and historical baggage will have to be jettisoned. I take you up on this offer. Let us start talking in this very spirit.

Now as Commander of the Armed Forces of Pakistan, I wish to convey another message. The Armed Forces of Pakistan are fully prepared and deployed to meet any challenge. They will spill the last drop of their blood in the defence of their country. Let there be no attempt of crossing the border in any sector as it will be met with full force. Do not entertain any illusions on this count.

I would also like to address the international community, particularly the United States on this occasion. As I mentioned earlier on a number of occasions, Pakistan rejects and condemns terrorism in all its forms and manifestations.

Pakistan will not allow its territory to be used for any terrorist activity anywhere in the world. Now you must play an active role in solving the Kashmir dispute for the sake of lasting peace and harmony in the region. We should be under no illusion that the legitimate demand of the people of Kashmir can ever be suppressed without their just resolution. Kashmiris also expect that you ask India to bring an end to state terrorism and human rights violations. Let human rights organisations, Amnesty International, the international media and UN peacekeepers be allowed to monitor activities of the Indian occupation forces.

Now we come to the second problem, which causes confusion in our minds and is of our particular concern. It relates to conflicts involving Muslims. Our religious leaders involve themselves in such conflicts without giving serious thought to them. I don't want to talk at length on this.

It is for the government to take a position on international issues. Individuals, organisations and political parties should restrict their activities to expression of their views. I request them to express their views on international issues in an intellectual spirit and in a civilised manner through force of argument.

Views expressed with maturity and moderation have greater convincing power.

Expressing views in a threatening manner does not create any positive effect and anyone who indulges in hollow threats is taken as an unbalanced person by the world at large.

I would request that we should stop interfering in the affairs of others.

First, we should attain the strength and the importance where our views carry weight when we express them.

**Now we come to internal decisions.**

The third issue causing conflict in our minds relates to sectarian differences. As I have already pointed out that writ of the government will be established. No individual, organisation or party will be allowed to break the law of the land. All functioning will be in a regulated manner and within rules.

Now I come to the extremist organisations. Terrorism, and sectarianism must come to an end. I had announced a ban on Lashkar-e-Jhangvi and Sipah-e-Mohammad on 14 August last year. On that occasion, I had pointed out that Sipah-e-Sahaba and TJP would be kept under observation.

I am sorry to say that there is not much improvement in the situation. Sectarian violence continues unabated. We have busted several gangs involved in sectarian killings. You would be astonished to know that in the year 2001 about 400 innocent people fell victim to sectarian and other killings.

Many of the gangs apprehended include people mostly belonging to Sipah-e-Sahaba and some to TJP. This situation cannot be tolerated any more.

I, therefore, announce banning of both Sipah-e-Sahaba and TJP. In addition to these, TNSM (Tehrik-e-Nifaz-e-Shariat Mohammadi) being responsible for misleading thousands of simple poor people into Afghanistan also stands banned.

This organisation is responsible for their massacre in Afghanistan.

The government has also decided to put the Sunni Tehreek under observation. No organisation is allowed to form Lashkar, Sipah or Jaish. The government has banned Jaish-e-Mohammad and Lashkar-e-Taiba. Any organisation or individual would face strict punitive measures if found inciting the people to violence in internal or external contexts.

Our mosques are sacred places where we seek the blessings of God Almighty. Let them remain sacred. We will not allow the misuse of mosques. All mosques will be registered and no new mosques will be built without permission. The use of loudspeakers will be limited only to call for prayers, and Friday Sermon and Vaaz. However, I would like to emphasise that special permission is being given for "Vaaz" (Sermon). If this is misused the permission will be cancelled.

If there is any political activity, inciting of sectarian hatred or propagation of extremism in any mosque, the management would be held responsible and proceeded against according to law.

I appeal to all Pesh Imams to project the qualities of Islam in the mosques and invite the people to piety. Talk of obligations towards fellow beings, exhort them to abstain from negative thoughts and promote positive thinking. I hope that all Nazims, Distt. Police officers and Auqaf Department officials will take quick action against violators of these measures.

On madaris, a detailed policy will be issued through a new Madrasa Ordinance. The Ordinance will be issued in a few days. I am glad that the Madrasa policy has been finalised in consultation with religious scholars and Mashaikh. I have touched on the merits and shortcomings prevailing in the madaris. Merits have to be reinforced while shortcomings have to be rooted out. Under the Madrasa policy, their functioning will be regulated.

These madaris will be governed by the same rules and regulations applicable to other schools, colleges and universities. All madaris will be registered by 23 March 2002 and no new madrasa will be opened without permission of the government.

If any madrasa (religious school) is found indulging in extremism, subversion, militant activity or possessing any types of weapons, it will be closed. All madaris will have to adopt the new syllabi by the end of this year. Those madaris which are already following such syllabi are welcome to continue. The government has decided to provide financial assistance to such madaris. The government will also help the madaris in the training of their teachers. The Ministry of Education has been instructed to review courses of Islamic education in all schools and colleges also with a view to improving them. So far as foreign students attending madaris are concerned, we have set rules for them. Foreign students who do not have proper documents would be required to comply with the formalities by 23 March 2002, otherwise they can face deportation.

Any foreigner wanting to attend madaris in Pakistan will

have to obtain the required documents from his/her native country and NOC from the government.

Only then, will he or she get admission. The same rules will apply to foreign teachers.

Certain ulema were of the view that some poor people who come to Pakistan for religious education should not be deported to the countries of their origin.

I agree that this is a genuine demand but such people should regularise their stay in Pakistan through their respective embassies. As I have said, all such activity has to be regulated and the writ of the government must be established.

With a view to ending conflict, I have explained to you at great length the three areas causing confusion in our minds. Making rules, regulations and issuing ordinances is easy but their implementation is difficult. However, I feel all the measures I have announced are of utmost importance. We have to implement them. In this regard, the law enforcement agencies including police must perform their duty.

We are introducing reforms in the police with a view to improving their efficiency. A great responsibility lies on their shoulders.

I have directed the police to ensure implementation of the steps announced by the government and I have no doubt they will be motivated to perform their duty. After reforms we expect they will be better trained and equipped to discharge their duty. Rangers and civil armed forces will be in their support.

We are also taking steps in consultation with the judiciary for speedy trial of cases relating to terrorism and extremism. Anti terrorist courts are being strengthened and necessary orders will be issued in a few days.

Apart from these issues, I would also like to inform you,

my brothers and sisters, that we have been sent a list of 20 people by India.

I want to clear our position on this. There is no question of handing over any Pakistani. This will never be done. If we are given evidence against those people, we will take action against them in Pakistan under our own laws. As far as non-Pakistanis are concerned, we have not given asylum to anyone. Anyone falling under this category will be proceeded against whenever one is found.

**My brothers and sisters,**

Pakistan is an Islamic Republic. There are 98 per cent Muslims living in this country. We should live like brothers and set an example for the rest of the Islamic countries. We should strive to emerge as a responsible and progressive member of the comity of nations.

We have to make Pakistan into a powerful and strong country. We have resources and potential. We are capable of meeting external danger. We have to safeguard ourselves against internal dangers. I have always been saying that internal strife is devouring us like termites. Don't forget that Pakistan is the citadel of Islam and if we want to serve Islam well we will first have to make Pakistan strong and powerful. There is a race for progress among all nations.

We cannot achieve progress through a policy of confrontation and feuds. We can achieve progress through human resource development, mental enlightenment, high moral character and technological development. I appeal to all my compatriots to rise to the occasion. We should get rid of intolerance and hatred and instead promote tolerance and harmony.

May God guide us to act upon the true teachings of Islam. May He help us to follow the Quaid-e-Azam's motto: "Unity,

Faith and Discipline." This should always be remembered. We will be a non-entity without unity.

And I would again like to recite a couplet from Allama Iqbal.

Fard Qaim Rabte Millat Say Hai Tanha Kuch Naheen.

Mauj Hai Darya Main Aur Baroon-e-Darya Kuch Naheen.

English:

Amongst the community do individuals survive; not alone;

Like waves that exist in rivers and out of water are not known.

Pakistan Paindabad.

(Source: http://www.forisb.org/president/pres2002-01-12.htm)

# 4. State of the Union Address by President George W. Bush to a Joint Session of US Congress, Washington, DC, 29 January 2002

[Excerpts]

Thank you very much. Mr. Speaker, Vice President Cheney, members of Congress, distinguished guests, fellow citizens: As we gather tonight, our nation is at war, our economy is in recession, and the civilised world faces unprecedented dangers. Yet the state of our Union has never been stronger. (Applause.)

We last met in an hour of shock and suffering. In four short months, our nation has comforted the victims, begun to rebuild New York and the Pentagon, rallied a great coalition, captured, arrested, and rid the world of thousands of terrorists, destroyed Afghanistan's terrorist training camps, saved a people from starvation, and freed a country from brutal oppression. (Applause.)

The American flag flies again over our embassy in Kabul. Terrorists who once occupied Afghanistan now occupy cells at Guantanamo Bay. (Applause.) And terrorist leaders who urged followers to sacrifice their lives are running for their own. (Applause.)

America and Afghanistan are now allies against terror. We'll be partners in rebuilding that country. And this evening we welcome the distinguished interim leader of a liberated Afghanistan: Chairman Hamid Karzai. (Applause.)

The last time we met in this chamber, the mothers and daughters of Afghanistan were captives in their own homes, forbidden from working or going to school. Today women are free, and are part of Afghanistan's new government. And we welcome the new Minister of Women's Affairs, Doctor Sima Samar. (Applause.)

Our progress is a tribute to the spirit of the Afghan people, to the resolve of our coalition, and to the might of the United States military. (Applause.) When I called our troops into action, I did so with complete confidence in their courage and skill. And tonight, thanks to them, we are winning the war on terror. (Applause.) The men and women of our Armed Forces have delivered a message now clear to every enemy of the United States: Even 7,000 miles away, across oceans and continents, on mountaintops and in caves — you will not escape the justice of this nation. (Applause.)

For many Americans, these four months have brought sorrow, and pain that will never completely go away. Every day a retired firefighter returns to Ground Zero, to feel closer to his two sons who died there. At a memorial in New York, a little boy left his football with a note for his lost father: Dear Daddy, please take this to heaven. I don't want to play football until I can play with you again some day.

..........................

Our cause is just, and it continues. Our discoveries in Afghanistan confirmed our worst fears, and showed us the true scope of the task ahead. We have seen the depth of our enemies' hatred in videos, where they laugh about the loss of innocent life. And the depth of their hatred is equalled by the madness of the destruction they design. We have found diagrams of American nuclear power plants and public water facilities, detailed instructions for making chemical weapons, surveillance maps of American cities, and thorough descriptions of landmarks in America and throughout the world.

What we have found in Afghanistan confirms that, far from ending there, our war against terror is only beginning. Most of the 19 men who hijacked planes on 11 September were trained in Afghanistan's camps, and so were tens of thousands of others. Thousands of dangerous killers, schooled in the methods of murder, often supported by outlaw regimes, are now spread throughout the world like ticking time bombs, set to go off without warning.

Thanks to the work of our law enforcement officials and coalition partners, hundreds of terrorists have been arrested. Yet, tens of thousands of trained terrorists are still at large. These enemies view the entire world as a battlefield, and we must pursue them wherever they are. (Applause.) So long as training camps operate, so long as nations harbour terrorists, freedom is at risk. And America and our allies must not, and will not, allow it. (Applause.)

Our nation will continue to be steadfast and patient and persistent in the pursuit of two great objectives. First, we will shut down terrorist camps, disrupt terrorist plans, and bring terrorists to justice. And, second, we must prevent the terrorists and regimes who seek chemical, biological or nuclear weapons from threatening the United States and the world. (Applause.)

Our military has put the terror training camps of Afghanistan out of business, yet camps still exist in at least a dozen countries. A terrorist underworld — including groups like Hamas, Hezbollah, Islamic Jihad, Jaish-i-Mohammed — operates in remote jungles and deserts, and hides in the centres of large cities.

While the most visible military action is in Afghanistan, America is acting elsewhere. We now have troops in the Philippines, helping to train that country's armed forces to go after terrorist cells that have executed an American, and still hold hostages. Our soldiers, working with the Bosnian government, seized terrorists who were plotting to bomb our embassy. Our Navy is patrolling the coast of Africa to block the shipment of weapons and the establishment of terrorist camps in Somalia.

My hope is that all nations will heed our call, and eliminate the terrorist parasites who threaten their countries and our own. Many nations are acting forcefully. Pakistan is now cracking down on terror, and I admire the strong leadership of President Musharraf. (Applause.)

But some governments will be timid in the face of terror. And make no mistake about it: If they do not act, America will. (Applause.)

Our second goal is to prevent regimes that sponsor terror from threatening America or our friends and allies with weapons of mass destruction. Some of these regimes have been pretty quiet since 11 September. But we know their true nature. North Korea is a regime arming with missiles and weapons of mass destruction, while starving its citizens.

Iran aggressively pursues these weapons and exports terror, while an unelected few repress the Iranian people's hope for freedom.

Iraq continues to flaunt its hostility towards America and to support terror. The Iraqi regime has plotted to develop anthrax, and nerve gas, and nuclear weapons for over a decade. This is a regime that has already used poison gas to murder thousands of its own citizens — leaving the bodies of mothers huddled over their dead children. This is a regime that agreed to international inspections — then kicked out the inspectors. This is a regime that has something to hide from the civilised world.

States like these, and their terrorist allies, constitute an axis of evil, arming to threaten the peace of the world. By seeking weapons of mass destruction, these regimes pose a grave and growing danger. They could provide these arms to terrorists, giving them the means to match their hatred. They could attack our allies or attempt to blackmail the United States. In any of these cases, the price of indifference would be catastrophic.

We will work closely with our coalition to deny terrorists and their state sponsors the materials, technology, and expertise to make and deliver weapons of mass destruction. We will develop and deploy effective missile defences to protect America and our allies from sudden attack. (Applause.) And all nations should know: America will do what is necessary to ensure our nation's security.

We'll be deliberate, yet time is not on our side. I will not wait on events, while dangers gather. I will not stand by, as peril draws closer and closer. The United States of America will not permit the world's most dangerous regimes to threaten us with the world's most destructive weapons. (Applause.)

Our war on terror is well begun, but it is only begun. This campaign may not be finished on our watch — yet it must be and it will be waged on our watch.

We can't stop short. If we stop now — leaving terror camps intact and terror states unchecked — our sense of security would be false and temporary. History has called America and our allies to action, and it is both our responsibility and our privilege to fight freedom's fight. (Applause.)

Our first priority must always be the security of our nation, and that will be reflected in the budget I send to Congress. My budget supports three great goals for America: We will win this war; we'll protect our homeland; and we will revive our economy.

September the 11th brought out the best in America, and the best in this Congress. And I join the American people in applauding your unity and resolve. (Applause.) Now Americans deserve to have this same spirit directed towards addressing problems here at home. I'm a proud member of my party — yet as we act to win the war, protect our people, and create jobs in America, we must act, first and foremost, not as Republicans, not as Democrats, but as Americans. (Applause.)

It costs a lot to fight this war. We have spent more than a billion dollars a month — over $30 million a day — and we must be prepared for future operations. Afghanistan proved that expensive precision weapons defeat the enemy and spare innocent lives, and we need more of them. We need to replace aging aircraft and make our military more agile, to put our troops anywhere in the world quickly and safely. Our men and women in uniform deserve the best weapons, the best equipment, the best training — and they also deserve another pay raise. (Applause.)

My budget includes the largest increase in defence spending in two decades — because while the price of freedom and security is high, it is never too high. Whatever it costs to defend our country, we will pay. (Applause.)

............................

In this moment of opportunity, a common danger is erasing old rivalries. America is working with Russia and China and India, in ways we have never before, to achieve peace and prosperity. In every region, free markets and free trade and free societies are proving their power to lift lives. Together with friends and allies from Europe to Asia, and Africa to Latin America, we will demonstrate that the forces of terror cannot stop the momentum of freedom. (Applause.)

............................

Thank you all. May God bless. (Applause.)

(Source: http://www.whitehouse.gov/news/releases/ 2002/01/ 20020129-11.html)

# 5. Joint Declaration of India and Kazakhstan New Delhi, 12 February 2002

The people of India and Kazakhstan have an ancient tradition of close and friendly relations which resulted in the development especially of cultural and economic cooperation. The relations will strengthen further due to our common heritage and commitment to the ideals of tolerance, democracy, secularism and the desire for peace. The Prime Minister of India expressed his happiness at the visit of the President of the Republic of Kazakhstan on the tenth anniversary of the establishment of diplomatic relations between the two countries. The two leaders expressed their common resolve that Kazakhstan and India should further enhance their cooperation and mutual consultations on bilateral, regional and international issues so as continue to contribute towards stability and prosperity of their common neighbourhood in Asia and the world;

Afghanistan: We have noted with satisfaction the developments in Afghanistan, the establishment of the Interim Administration, the elimination of the oppressive Taliban regime and support the resolve of the international community not to allow Afghanistan to be used as a safe haven for terrorism. We agree that further efforts need to be made by the international community for the long-term establishment of a broad based multi-ethnic government in an independent Afghanistan.

Terrorism: Recalling the strong and forthright condemnation by Kazakhstan of the terrorist attack on the Indian Parliament on 13 December 2001, we affirm that terrorism cannot be justified in any form, for any cause or for any reason used as an excuse. We also reiterate our strong belief that the fight against terrorism has to be global, comprehensive and sustained for the objective of total elimination of terrorism everywhere. In this context we recall our commitment to UN Security Council Resolution 1373, and also declare our intent to set up a bilateral forum on counter terrorism. We reiterate that the global fight against terrorism must also address those who instigate, assist or acquiesce as much as those who perpetuate terrorism.

Regional Initiatives: We acknowledge the importance of frequent consultations to promote peace, stability and prosperity in the region. We have noted with satisfaction the progress of the Conference on Interaction and Confidence Building Measures in Asia (CICA), which represented a unique initiative and agree that the forthcoming summit will be a significant step forward. We have also noted the progress being made by the Shanghai Cooperation Organisation (SCO) as a regional organisation. Kazakhstan expressed the belief that considering India's geographical proximity in the neighbourhood and its active participation on regional and global matters of cooperation, India's membership of SCO would add to the strength of that organisation. We have also agreed on the need to give impetus to regional economic cooperation for the common benefit of the people of the two countries and the region. In this context, Kazakhstan with its substantial hydro carbon resources could become an important source of energy to India, which is expected to become one of the largest energy consumers in the world. Similarly, India's prowess in Information Technology would be of great benefit to the needs of Kazakhstan's economy. We have agreed that concrete projects in these sectors will be worked out with a view to early implementation.

Bilateral: We have noted with satisfaction the results of the Fourth Session of Kazakhstan-India Joint Commission on Trade-Economic, Scientific and Technical Cooperation which was held in New Delhi on 11 February 2002. During the session of the Commission, which was held in the spirit of mutual understanding and constructiveness, new areas of mutually beneficial cooperation were identified. We agreed that effective measures should be taken to implement the agreements reached thereby, which would serve to further strengthen the cooperation in various spheres. We have also agreed that early action should be taken for finalising agreements in educational, tourism, military and technical cooperation sectors as well as for the extradition treaty. The Prime Minister of India noted with satisfaction that the official visit of H.E. Mr. N.A. Nazarbayev, the President of the Republic of Kazakhstan to India made a substantial contribution to the strengthening of relations in political, trade and economic, military-technical, cultural and humanitarian spheres, and expressed confidence that it would promote further activisation of the entire range of bilateral cooperation and search for new ways of collabouration. We have agreed upon the expediency of expanding the Security Council of the United Nations Organisation to make it more representative and efficient. The President of the Republic of Kazakhstan, noting the role being played by India in the world affairs, supports India as an appropriate candidate as a permanent member of a restructured UN Security Council. The President of Kazakhstan invited the Prime Minister of India to visit Kazakhstan at an early date. The invitation was accepted with pleasure.

A.B. Vajpayee, Prime Minister of India

N.A. Nazarbayev, Republic of President of the Republic of Kazakhstan

(Source: http://www.meadev.nic.in/ foreign/almaty-decl.htm)

# 6. CICA Declaration on Eliminating Terrorism and Promoting Dialogue among Civilisations Almaty, 5 June 2002

[Editor's Note: The signatories to this Declaration were: Afghanistan, Azerbaijan, China, Egypt, India, Iran, Israel, Kazakhstan, Kyrgyzstan, Mongolia, Pakistan, Palestine, Russia, Tajikistan, Turkey, and Uzbekistan]

We, Heads of State or Government of the Member States of the Conference on Interaction and Confidence Building Measures in Asia (CICA), gathered in Almaty for the First CICA Summit, do hereby declare the following:

We are deeply concerned by the increase in all acts of terrorism worldwide, including in CICA Member States.

We are fully committed to fighting terrorism and strengthening bilateral, regional and international cooperation, in accordance with the UN Charter, required to meet this challenge.

We emphasise the central role of the United Nations, its General Assembly and Security Council, in developing the framework for this.

We express our deepest sorrow over the loss of innocent lives in all acts, methods or practices of terrorism and convey our sympathies and condolences to the families of the victims.

We condemn all forms and manifestations of terrorism, committed no matter when, where or by whom, as barbaric offences and criminal acts indiscriminately directed at the life and well-being of innocent individuals and peoples as well as threatening the peaceful coexistence among nations. No considerations whatsoever can be invoked to justify terrorism.

We are convinced that terrorism constitutes a direct violation of human rights and, in particular, the right to life, freedom, security and development.

We emphasise that eliminating terrorism is the common goal of all cultures and civilisations.

We believe that all religions of the world reject violence and terrorism and advocate the protection of human rights. We underline that terrorism cannot be attributed to religion, nationality, or civilisation.

We believe that it is essential not to allow terrorists to lure us into a conflict of religions, cultures or civilisations. We also pledge to be particularly vigilant, in order to ensure that the global fight against terrorism does not become a war targeting particular cultures, regions or nations. We all stand united in this fight.

We reaffirm our strong commitment to all norms and principles of international law, the purposes and principles of the UN Charter, including the right to self-determination, and the CICA Almaty Act concerning the maintenance of international peace and security and the promotion of good-neighbourly and friendly relations and cooperation among countries.

We actively support efforts undertaken by the international community, in accordance with the UN Charter, to combat terrorism. The fight against terrorism should be global, comprehensive and sustained, and not selective or discriminatory and should avoid applying double standards. We are also against using the fight against terrorism as a pretext for interference in the internal affairs of sovereign States. We reject the use of force not in compliance with the UN Charter against sovereign States.

We reaffirm the key significance of, and pledge to fully support implementation of UN Security Council Resolution No. 1373 and other relevant UN resolutions on combating terrorism which provide the basic framework for national, regional and international obligations and efforts to combat this universal evil. We underscore the need to respect human rights and rule of law in combating terrorism.

We encourage States Parties to the various UN anti-terrorism Conventions to consult and cooperate, in accordance with the provisions of these Conventions, to ensure their effective implementation.

We will contribute to the early elabouration and adoption by the UN of the other appropriate instruments, such as the Comprehensive Convention on International Terrorism and the International Convention for the Suppression of Acts of Nuclear Terrorism.

We are open for cooperation in combating terrorism with all other states, regional and international organisations and forums. Taking into account the tans-national character of terrorism, as well as its close links with other challenges and threats to security such as organised crime, narcotics and human trafficking as well as illicit arms trafficking, we will seek to foster cooperation between our relevant authorities and to maintain regular exchange of information in order to enhance international capacity to stop financing of terrorism and eliminate it.

We consider as one of the primary tasks of the international community to strengthen efforts to eliminate poverty, unemployment, illiteracy, extremism, intolerance, entrenched hatred and all forms of discrimination. We believe that it is necessary to ensure sustainable development of all regions of the world and to pay more attention to the socio-economic impact of globalisation. It will also be of high importance for our cause to encourage the peaceful settlement of regional and international crises and conflicts. We support international efforts for the rehabilitation and reconstruction of Afghanistan in order to help revive this country as a stable and prosperous member of the international community.

The CICA Member States intend to strengthen cooperation and dialogue among them in order to promote common values, mutual understanding and confidence for the benefit of the joint fight against terrorism. We consider CICA as a unique Asian forum, which comprises states of different cultures and traditions making it one of the most important mechanisms to promote dialogue among civilisations and cultures. In this context we reconfirm our full support for the UN General Assembly resolution no. A/RES/56/6 on Dialogue among Civilisations and are convinced that implementation of its Programme of Action positively contributes to international efforts to attain universal peace, welfare and stability. The CICA Member States intend to comprehensively and actively promote such a dialogue taking into account that Eurasia has not only been a cradle of some of the world's largest civilisations but has also served as a bridge between them.

(Source: http://www.meadev.nic.in/speeches/4decdelhi-decorationrussia.htm)

# 7. Annual Report on the Military Power of the People's Republic of China, July 2002

[Editor's Note: This Report was submitted to the US Congress by the Secretary of Defence in July 2002 pursuant to the requirement of National Defence Authorisation Act, FY2000. Reproduced below are Sections II and III of the report dealing with Goals and Trends in Chinese Strategy and PRC Military Modernisation, respectively.]

## II. Goals and Trends in Chinese Strategy

### A. Grand Strategy

***Goals of Grand Strategy***

China has not publicly articulated an authoritative, official statement of its "grand strategy." Chinese military strategists define grand strategy as the "overall strategy of a nation or an alliance of nations in which they use overall national strength" to achieve national political goals, especially those related to national security and development.

China's grand strategy attempts to balance two often competing objectives: one is developing what it calls the nation's "comprehensive national power" (CNP). The other is exploiting

---

1. There is no Western equivalent to the concept of "shi." Chinese linguists explain it as "the alignment of forces," the "propensity of things," or the "potential born of disposition," that only a skilled strategist can exploit to ensure victory over a superior force. Similarly, only a sophisticated assessment by an adversary can recognise the potential exploitation of "*shi*."

2. This definition of Comprehensive National Power is used primarily by the PLA Academy of Military Science (AMS). However, the China Academy of Social Sciences (CASS) uses a slightly different set of measures: politics, economics, science and technology, and foreign affairs. See Chapter 5 of *China Debates the Future Security Environment* (National Defence University Press, 2000).

to maximum advantage the existing "strategic configuration of power" or "shi," to preserve national independence and enable China to build "momentum" in its effort to increase national power. The relative priority that the national leadership places on these two objectives is subject to adjustment and change, depending on how China assesses the opportunities and challenges in the "strategic configuration of power."

"Comprehensive national power" (CNP) is the concept by which China's strategic planners evaluate and measure national standing in relation to other nations. The concept of CNP first appeared in conjunction with former paramount leader Deng Xiaoping's national development strategy in the early 1980s. It represents an adaptation of Western methodologies for monitoring and assessing national power, fused with traditional Chinese concepts of statecraft and strategy, which placed a heavy emphasis on calculations and estimates of relative power among nations. The current approach applies quantitative and qualitative evaluations of politics, economics, military, science and technology, and foreign affairs to determine relative CNP.

While China's national leadership is focused primarily on national development, it is constantly assessing the broader "strategic configuration of power" for potential challenges or threats that might prompt it to adjust or change its grand strategy, as well as for opportunities to advance national interests. In particular, China's leaders believe that three essential "conditions" — national unity, stability, and sovereignty — must exist if China is to survive and develop as a nation. Among these conditions, Beijing judges that national unity is the most important. Beijing's preoccupation with maintaining unity is driven by China's internal and external security environment and national condition, historical experience, national goals, and, perhaps most importantly, challenges to the Chinese Communist Party's (CCP's) legitimacy.

Ensuring domestic stability and a secure international

environment is crucial to Beijing's national development strategy. Senior leaders currently are focused on the short-term task of ensuring regime stability by maintaining domestic order and leadership control while dealing with several sources of internal unrest and instability. Chinese leaders also believe they must maintain conditions of state sovereignty and territorial integrity. This is reflected in China's response to a range of international issues, including human rights and democracy, and territorial and resource disputes with its neighbours.

Should China become involved in a major war, the relative priority it places on its national goals is likely to change. Deng Xiaoping and current CCP General Secretary and State President Jiang Zemin have indicated publicly that the goal of reestablishing a favourable "strategic configuration of power" would override the goal of developing national power if China faced a fundamental threat to its national unity, internal stability, or sovereignty. Such circumstances were defined as situations in which China faced the credible prospect of a military invasion of the mainland, or the nation was involved in a large-scale war, such as a major war between China and Taiwan that included direct US military intervention. While Deng and Jiang indicated that ensuring a favourable strategic "configuration of power" would be the primary national goal in such situations, they also clearly emphasised that one of China's war aims would be to end the war on favourable terms as soon as possible so that Beijing could refocus on the goal of developing national power.

### *Sources of Grand Strategy*

China's grand strategy has been influenced primarily by a combination of the ancient tenets of Chinese statecraft as well as more modern national development theory. While ancient Chinese statecraft and national development theories are dominant, other factors also shape China's grand strategy. China has had a long-standing geopolitical challenge in maintaining control over the heartland of China and major elements of "Inner

Asia," and in securing a vast periphery of coastal and land boundaries as well as maritime territory in a region populated by traditional rivals and enemies. These challenges shape how China approaches grand strategy, especially its emphasis on maintaining a favourable domestic and international "strategic configuration of power." Moreover, Maoist and Marxist ideology, as well as lessons from the Sino-Japanese war and the civil war, are prevalent in China's approach to grand strategy. Finally, the Chinese study how other nations approach international security affairs, to include grand strategy, in an effort to enhance their own approach to the issues of strategy, security, and development.

Beijing has sought to describe its long-term political goals of developing CNP and ensuring a favourable strategic configuration of power in positive, passive, cooperative, benign, and peaceful themes. These themes include China's emphasis on "peace and development," the non-use of force in settling international disputes, non-intervention in the internal affairs of other countries, the defensive nature of China's military strategy, its "no-first-use of nuclear weapons" declaration, its support for nuclear-free weapons zones, and claims that China would never deploy its military forces on foreign soil.

These principled themes should not, however, obscure the ambitious nature of China's national development programme and the nature of China's approach to the use of force, which is contingent, rather than inherently passive or defensive, as Chinese commentators often vigorously assert. In particular, Beijing probably calculates that ambiguity in international discourse helps to buy China time in developing its national power.

One of Deng Xiaoping's key directives to China's security and development establishment was the so-called "24 character strategy": "keep cool-headed to observe, be composed to make reactions, stand firmly, hide our capabilities and bide our time, never try to take the lead, and be able to accomplish something" (emphasis added). This often-quoted maxim not only suggests a desire to downplay China's ambitions; it also affirms a long-term strategy to build up China's CNP with a view to maximising China's options in the future.

From Beijing's perspective, strategic ambiguity, including strategic denial and deception, is a mechanism to influence the policies of foreign governments and the opinions of the general public and elites in other countries. China's leaders believe that ambiguity and stressing the "just nature" of PRC actions have the effect of "drawing out" those who oppose and those who support China's interests abroad. Once China's leaders make the distinction between friends and adversaries, they can develop and tailor themes to counter opposition and advance their overall agenda. Moreover, such distinctions position China to reward "friends" abroad, or alternatively, punish "enemies" to enhance its own position in the balance of power.

## B. Security Strategy

### *Security Assessment*

As with its "grand strategy," China has not publicly articulated a "national security strategy" in a format similar to that used by the United States. China's efforts to accomplish its security goals involve an integrative strategy that applies diplomatic, informational, military, and economic instruments of national power. China's national security leadership structure is based on a traditional Leninist model in which the party apparatus mirrors the state system and plays the dominant role in strategy and policy formulation and oversight. The party function is facilitated by "cross leadership" — the practice of "dual hatting" party cadres with government positions. For example, Communist Party General Secretary Jiang Zemin also serves as the State President.

While seeing opportunity and benefit in interactions with the United States — primarily in terms of trade and technology — Beijing apparently believes that the United States poses a significant long-term challenge. China's leaders have asserted that the United States seeks to maintain a dominant geostrategic position by containing the growth of Chinese power, ultimately "dividing" and "Westernising" China, and preventing a resurgence of Russian power. Beijing has interpreted the strengthened US-Japan security alliance, increased US presence in the Asia-Pacific region, and efforts to expand NATO as manifestations of Washington's strategy. Most importantly, China has adopted an ambivalent if not sceptical attitude towards the US presence in the Asia-Pacific region. As China's 2000 Defence White Paper states:

> There are new negative developments in the security of the Asia-Pacific region. The United States is further strengthening its military presence and bilateral alliances in this region advocating the development of the TMD system and planning to deploy it in East Asia. Japan has passed a bill relating to measures in the event of a situation in the areas surrounding Japan. All this goes against the tide of the times. Joint military exercises have increased in the region to the detriment of trust between countries...Encroachments on China's sovereignty and interest in the South China Sea are not infrequent, and some extra-regional countries are attempting to interfere in this issue...

Beijing apparently calculates that US efforts to develop missile defences will challenge the credibility of China's nuclear deterrent and eventually be extended to protect Taiwan, degrading the coercive value of its growing conventional theatre ballistic missile capability opposite the island.

Chinese analyses indicate a concern that Beijing would have difficulty in managing potential US military intervention in crises in the Taiwan Strait or the South China Sea. There are even indications of a concern that the United States might intervene in China's internal disputes with ethnic Tibetan or Muslim minorities. Chinese concerns about US intervention likely have been reinforced by their perceptions of the US response to the 1995-1996 Taiwan Strait crises, Operation Allied Force in Kosovo, and more recent US-led military operations to combat international terrorism. Over the longer term, China often expresses concern over the prospects for the expansion of Japanese military power in the region.

Beyond these more traditional security concerns, China's strategic planners are beginning to recognise global and transnational threats such as HIV/AIDS, international crime and narcotics trafficking, terrorism, and the proliferation of weapons of mass destruction. In addition, in part stemming from over two decades of "reform and opening up," China's leaders increasingly perceive threats to "economic security," "information security," and the erosion of national independence as a consequence of globalisation. These concerns will only grow in future years with China's entry into the World Trade Organisation (WTO).

While assuming the primacy of economic power, China's leaders view the military as necessary to ensure that China's economic power will rise; to protect important national interests; and, to support China's eventual emergence as a great power and the preeminent power in Asia. Nevertheless, Chinese leaders since Deng have placed military modernisation behind other priorities such as development in agriculture, industry, and science and technology. This placement is based on a calculation that broad-based modernisation will raise overall levels of industry, technology, and human resources to sustain long-term military modernisation.

Debate over the proper ordering of China's national priorities has surfaced periodically — particularly in the face of external challenges to China's security interests. For example, following Operation Allied Force in 1999, Beijing seriously considered upgrading the priority attached to military modernisation. While the senior leadership has since reaffirmed its stress on economic growth and development, it nevertheless agreed to provide significant additional resources and funding to support accelerated military modernisation.

A key variable in assessing long-term trends in the PRC's security strategy is Taiwan. One of Beijing's priority security interests is to prevent further steps by Taiwan towards permanent separation from the mainland and to secure the eventual resolution of the Taiwan issue on the PRC's terms. Taiwan's integration under mainland authority is considered to be an essential step towards completion of "national reunification." China's leaders will remain determined to secure unification on Beijing's terms.

Beijing assesses that the permanent separation of Taiwan from the mainland could serve as a strategic foothold for the United States. At the same time, securing control over Taiwan would allow the PRC to move its defensive perimeter further seaward. The PRC's Taiwan strategy will continue to emphasise a coercive approach towards Taipei, and Beijing's decision-makers have affirmed that they will resort to force if Taiwan's present de facto separation becomes official, either through a declaration or international recognition as such. Moreover, China's leaders have threatened force if they fail to make progress towards "reunification" objectives.

In addition to preventing Taipei's moves toward de jure independence, Beijing seeks to counter what it perceives to be Japan's growing military cooperation with the United States and to prevent a rebirth of Japanese militarism. At the same time, it will continue to value the economic benefits it derives from access to Japanese technology, trade, and foreign investment. Beijing's other important security goals in East Asia include preventing the development and implementation of a regional theatre missile defence system, particularly one involving Taiwan; coping with challenges to its claims in the East and South China Seas; and supporting its economic interests through bilateral and multilateral mechanisms, such as the Association of Southeast Asian Nations (ASEAN), the Asia-Pacific Economic Cooperation (APEC) process, and the ASEAN Regional Forum (ARF).

The United States will remain central to these regional priorities. Consequently, China's actions in the region will be shaped by its assessment of US policies, particularly our regional alliance and defence relationships. While seeking a stable relationship with Washington, Beijing will continue to seek opportunities to diminish US regional influence.

### *Key Trends in Security Strategy*

Three key factors likely will remain fundamental in shaping Chinese security policy over the long term, regardless of the outcome of a Taiwan conflict or the change in the nature of the Chinese regime.

First, China's leaders will be unlikely to maintain a monolithic state. Future leaders probably will continue to pursue economic growth and technology, which, combined with the information revolution and bureaucratic professionalisation, will reinforce this trend. Second, globalisation and China's linkage to the outside world will continue and expand. Third, there will be pressure for political change. China will continue to face economic and internal challenges; the demands on the regime from both internal and external sources will persist. Consequently, China will continue to perceive challenges from the West. Beijing will continue to seek technology, wealth, and power associated with the Western system, but will maintain that Western political concepts and culture are antithetical to its interests.

## *C. Military Strategy*

China's leaders believe that the control and use of the armed forces and other coercive instruments of power are essential components of their security strategy. China does not have a document directly equivalent to the US "National Military Strategy." The closest approximation is a document referred to as the "National Military Strategic Guidelines for the New Period."

PLA strategists are beginning to discuss in professional journals issues such as the efficiency accrued through limited applications of force to accomplish political goals. Moreover, advances in military technologies will provide China's leaders over the long term with an expanded set of options. These enhanced capabilities have given rise to and will sustain a trend in which China's warfighting strategies increasingly favour coercive over annihilative approaches.

### *Trends in Military Strategy*

The principal area where China appears to be making advances in coercive military capabilities involves airpower, to include missiles and information operations. Military coercion can also be effected through the use of blockades or quarantines. Further, the use of ground forces may provide the "shock value" necessary to weaken the adversary's will. Finally, China's leaders may also employ economic coercion through the manipulation of stock and currency exchanges and banking, as well as political and psychological intimidation.

## III. PRC Military Modernisation

Preparing for a potential conflict in the Taiwan Strait is the primary driver for China's military modernisation. Beijing is pursuing the ability to force Taiwan to negotiate on Beijing's terms regarding unification with the mainland. It also seeks to deter, deny, or complicate the ability of foreign forces to intervene on Taiwan's behalf. Beijing has been influenced by the emerging revolution in military affairs and is seeking the means to counter advances the United States could make in this area. PRC doctrine stresses surprise, deception, and preemption as a means to offset weaknesses in equipment and other areas. Currently, China's conventional short-range ballistic missile force is its most credible **and immediate threat to Taiwan.**

## A. PRC Operational Doctrine

### *Evolution of PRC Operational Doctrine*

The evolution of PLA operational doctrine has mirrored changes that have taken place in PRC security and military strategy since the mid-1980s.

Impact of the Revolution in Military Affairs. China's more forward-looking strategists note the Persian Gulf War's role in bringing the emerging revolution in military affairs (RMA) into sharp focus for the PLA. In particular, PLA observers witnessed how quickly the force, equipped with high-tech weapons systems, defeated the Iraqi force that resembled the PLA in many ways. The force and capability displayed by the coalition during that conflict prompted PLA theorists to alter their perceptions of the character of future wars, highlighting the role of air and air defence operations, electronic and information warfare, and long-range precision strikes.

At the same time, the PLA observers judged that the technological advances surrounding the RMA also increased the demands on military forces in other areas, to include greater emphasis on command, control, communications, computers, intelligence, surveillance, and reconnaissance (C4ISR), joint service and combined arms operations, the need for professional, technically qualified personnel to operate and maintain advanced equipment, and the need, especially, for a professional corps of non-commissioned officers.

US observations of the RMA have also migrated into PLA thinking on the impact of the RMA on future warfare. As an example, Zhou Fangyin, of the China Institute of Contemporary International Relations, appeared to pull from US academic writing when he indicated that "war in the information age will be manifested not as 'platform-centred warfare,' but rather as 'network-centred warfare.'" The internalisation of RMA concepts, over time, is manifest in actual changes in doctrine, strategy, tactics, and equipment.

China's military planners are working to incorporate the concepts of modern warfare attributed to the "revolution in military affairs" and have placed a priority on developing the technologies and tactics necessary to conduct rapid tempo, high-technology warfare in Asia.

On balance, PLA authors assess that the current RMA holds the potential for producing radical new forms of warfare, enhanced information warfare, networks of systems, and "digitised" combat forces. At the same time, however, based on observations and lessons learned from the Gulf War and, later, Operation Allied Force, Beijing perceives certain weaknesses in the US over-reliance on the advances offered by the RMA. Consequently, revised PLA doctrine, rather than seeking to capture and pursue RMA advances, emphasises measures to target and exploit its weaknesses.

Evolution Since the Persian Gulf War. Operation Allied Force in 1999 appears to have had at least as much impact on PLA thinking as the Persian Gulf War, although more as a validation of earlier assessments of the trends of modern warfare than as a catalyst for change. PLA commentary on NATO's Kosovo air operation concluded that a superior enemy's situational awareness and precision-strike systems could be stymied through effective, and often low-tech, counter-reconnaissance measures such as camouflage and concealment, simple decoys, dispersion, and frequent movement of forces. NATO air operations reinforced the PLA's focus on the use of underground facilities, landline communications, and well-concealed supply depots.

The Serbs' survival in a modern battlefield against a superior force reportedly impressed PLA observers. These observers, however, also noted that the Serbs suffered from inferior equipment, inadequate defence of civilian installations, and poor logistics.

The PLA implemented lessons from Operation Allied Force in the restructured "Three Attacks, Three Defences" air defence training regime. "Three Attacks, Three Defences" concentrates on attacking stealth aircraft, cruise missiles, and helicopters, while defending against precision strikes, electronic warfare, and enemy reconnaissance. Many PLA training events also now incorporate this new training regime.

### *Current PLA Operational Doctrine*

Doctrinal literature is developed by the PLA Academy of Military Science (AMS) under the authority of the CMC and in close coordination, probably, with the PLA General Staff Department (GSD). The AMS is responsible for the development of theoretical and applied military strategy, operational theory and methodology, and combat tactics for China's armed forces. Service-specific tactics, techniques, and procedures are developed variously by the PLA Navy, Air Force, and Second Artillery; however, each service must adhere to the greater context and guidance for military strategy and operations at the theatre level of war and above promulgated by the AMS. Officers from the AMS Campaign and Tactics Department had a major role in developing the new operational regulations. This department is also responsible for drafting and writing documents and manuals that are the functional equivalents of US Joint Publications and Field Manuals. Very little is known about the actual substance of the new operational directives that emerged in 1999.

### *The Role of Surprise and Pre-Emption in Local Conflicts*

PLA operational theory reflects the transition undertaken during the 1990s to shift from predominately annihilative to coercive war-fighting strategies. Shock and surprise are considered by PLA strategists as crucial to successful coercion. Accordingly, PLA operational theory emphasises achieving surprise and accruing "shock power" during the opening phase of a campaign. The pre-eminent role that surprise and pre-emption have in potential conflicts is best illustrated in the fundamental principles of "Actively Taking the Initiative" and "Catching the Enemy Unprepared" in PLA operational doctrine.

"Actively Taking the Initiative" stresses the necessity of attack at the optimal point and time to catch the enemy unprepared.

"Catching the Enemy Unprepared" emphasises the role of concealment of intentions and capabilities through camouflage, deception, feints, and the use of stratagem to allow a relatively small amount of force to dominate the enemy through surprise.

Throughout the 1990s, PLA writers have highlighted pre-emptive strikes as a means to offset advantages that a technologically superior power brings to the fight. Lessons from Kosovo added impetus to developing a capacity for offensive operations against targets at the operational and strategic levels of warfare. PLA writers have asserted that offensive strike assets, which are more cost effective than defensive assets, must focus on an opponent's ability to carry out strikes and/or conduct counterattack operations. The measure of effectiveness, in this context, is not the capture of territory but the effects the strikes have on an enemy's ability to resist. The defender is thrown into a state of passivity owing to his inability to conduct operations.

The PLA believes that surprise is crucial for the success of any future campaign, and it is likely that it would not be willing to initiate any military action unless assured of a significant degree of strategic surprise. With no apparent political prohibitions against pre-emption, the PLA requires shock as a force multiplier, to catch Taiwan or another potential adversary such as the United States, unprepared. Observers such as PLAAF Chief of Staff LTG

Zheng Shenxia have noted that without adopting a pre-emptive doctrine, the chances of a PLA victory are limited.

PLA writings indicate a number of methodologies that could enhance the success of surprise, including strategic and operational deception, electronic warfare, and wearing down or desensitising an opponent's political and military leadership. At least one objective would be to reduce indications and warning of military action.

### *Operational Considerations Against Technologically Superior Adversaries*

The relative technological inferiority of the PLA and the overarching primacy of economic development have led to the exploration of asymmetric methods enabling "the inferior to defeat the superior."

PLA writings suggest that China's armed forces remain relatively confident of their ability to defeat a regional military force of comparable technological development with traditional battles of annihilation, or operations that rely on mass and attrition to attack the enemy forces, formations, and troops directly. The PLA is also convinced that this traditional approach to campaigns will not suffice against an enemy with advanced technologies. Consequently, there is an emphasis on conducting operations that will paralyse the high-tech enemy's ability to conduct its campaign, including operations to disrupt and delay the enemy campaign at its inception, and operations that are highly focused on identifying the types and locations of enemy high-tech weapons that pose the greatest threat. After identifying those weapons, the PLA must then attempt to neutralise them, either through hard-kill methods (e.g. firepower, special operations, etc.) or soft-kill methods also termed technological interdictions. Degrading a high-tech adversary's ability to process or gather information is viewed as an absolutely essential task if weak forces are to defeat the strong, especially if that high-tech adversary is perceived to be overly dependent upon information systems to enable its own operations.

Captain Shen Zhongchang from the Chinese Navy Research Institute, for example, envisages a weaker military defeating a superior one by attacking its spaced-based communications and surveillance systems. "The mastery of outer space will be a requisite for military victory, with outer space becoming the new commanding heights for combat." He also noted that "lightning attacks and powerful first strikes will be more widely used in the future." In future wars, Shen highlights radar, radio stations, communications facilities, and command ships as priority targets vulnerable to smart weapons, electronic attack, and electromagnetic pulse (EMP) weapons.

Ultimately, the PLA seeks to level the technological playing field at the outset of a campaign in order to enhance its chances of operational success. Consequently, PLA operational theory calls for operations aimed at:

- Destroying the enemy command system;
- Crippling the enemy information systems;
- Destroying the enemy's most advanced weapons systems;
- Crippling the enemy support (logistic) systems; and
- Disrupting the critical links in the enemy's campaign systems (i.e. denying the enemy the synergies that accrue from its technological superiority).

## B. PRC Conventional Military Modernisation and Training

China retains the world's largest military, yet it lacks the technology and logistical support to project and sustain conventional forces much beyond its borders. Military Modernisation is directed towards training and equipping the services to be capable of fighting short-duration, high-intensity conflicts. Recognising that comprehensive Modernisation will take many years, the PLA is pursuing force multipliers.

**Air**. Although the PLA has approximately 3,400 aircraft, only about 100 are considered modern, fourth-generation fighters. Development and acquisition efforts have been aimed primarily at defeating the regional air forces, defending against aircraft at long ranges from China's coast, defeating high-value air assets, denying US naval operations, and striking other targets such as airbases and air defence sites. A force-wide modernisation focused on the acquisition of advanced systems, improved training realism, new tactics to complement modern technology, and technically proficient personnel is intended to improve combat capability over the next decade and help to extend operations further beyond land and sea borders. By the end of the decade, China is expected to have a more robust fleet of fourth-generation fighters augmented by modern missiles, electronic countermeasures, and several AWACS-type aircraft. Although PRC pilot capabilities will remain poor by Western standards, improvements across the board will increase their potential.

**Navy**. The PLA Navy (PLAN) is making efforts to improve its regional force projection options by improving the capability to deploy submarines on extended patrols, and outfitting surface ships with more capable air defence assets and more lethal anti-ship cruise missiles. In addition, the Navy is attempting to address weaknesses in anti-submarine warfare. Despite incremental gains, the PLAN still lacks fleet air defence, over-the-horizon targeting, and sufficient sea/air lift for major amphibious operations. The PLA is addressing these deficiencies, but does not appear likely to make significant gains in those areas until at least 2005. Regardless, the PLAN will remain a large force that could pose a threat to regional navies.

**Ground**. Force reductions and selective new equipment acquisitions are creating a more mobile, combat-ready core within the larger ground force. Since the mid-1990s, the army has shrunk from about 100 divisions to approximately 50, with many of the units downsizing to brigades. The PLA also has three Airborne divisions and two Marine brigades. However, the army's ability to project force much beyond China's land borders remains limited owing to a shortage of amphibious ships, heavy cargo carrying aircraft, long-range transports, and other logistical shortcomings. Although the PLA has improved its amphibious attack capabilities in recent years, there are no signs that Beijing is serious about increasing its heavy lift capacity or conducting sustained ground operations.

**Conventional Missile Forces.** Modernisation and training developments in recent years highlight China's continuing effort quantitatively and qualitatively to improve the capabilities of its conventionally-armed SRBM force. There are approximately 350 SRBMs already in the deployed inventory; this number is increasing at about 50 missiles per year. The accuracy and lethality of this force is expected to increase through the use of satellite-aided guidance systems.

### *Air Forces Modernisation*

The PLA Air Force (PLAAF) and PLA Naval Air Force (PLANAF) are equipped with approximately 3,400 fighters of mostly obsolete Soviet design. Modernisation efforts through the 1990s were highlighted by the purchase of Su-27 and Su-30 FLANKER fighters from Russia and a license agreement to produce additional Su-27s in China. Beijing also has continued to pursue domestic aircraft programmes, including the FB-7, and upgrades to the F-7 and F-8 fighters.

**Combat Aircraft.** The PLA has used some of its increased modernisation funding to purchase modern arms from Russia, to include Su-27 air defence fighters and Su-30 multi-mission fighters. Domestic production of the Su-27 is proceeding, albeit very slowly. China also continues to upgrade fighters already in the inventory. The primary focus is on improving sensors, weapons, electronic warfare capabilities, and information connectivity on aircraft in order to increase the lethality of the otherwise outdated airframes. To bolster strike capabilities, China reportedly is developing an improved version of the FB-7. The twin-engine FB-7 is an all-weather, supersonic, medium-range fighter-bomber with an anti-ship mission. Improvements to the FB-7 likely will include a better radar, night attack avionics, and weapons. Over the next 20 years, production efforts for the air forces are expected to focus on an indigenous fourth-generation-type aircraft, the improved FB-7 fighter-bomber, and possible upgrades to the Su-27/Su-30.

**Special Mission Aircraft.** Since the Gulf War, China has sought to improve the capabilities of its special-mission aircraft, with a focus on electronic warfare aircraft, C4ISR platforms and tankers. China reportedly has developed jamming versions of several of its larger aircraft, and may have several programmes underway to deploy new standoff and escort jammers using bombers, transports, tactical aircraft, and UAV platforms.

*The PLA Air Force is building up its multi-role fighter force. The most powerful strike-fighter deployed in the Taiwan theatre is the PLAAF's Russian-built Sukhoi Su-30MKK, which can deliver precision-guided missiles in all weather conditions.*

China has been actively pursuing an advanced airborne surveillance and control aircraft since the early 1990s. In 1999, it introduced an airborne early warning (AEW) aircraft, the Y-8AEW. The cancellation last year of the more capable PHALCON programme forced Beijing to pursue other alternatives, to include the possible acquisition of A-50 MAINSTAY AWACS aircraft from Russia.

**Air-to-Air Refuelling.** China began developing its air-to-air refuelling capability in the mid-1980s using a converted B-6/BADGER bomber as an aerial tanker. PLANAF fighters and tanker aircraft successfully transferred fuel during aerial operations over the South China Sea in April 2000, suggesting that the

PLANAF has achieved a very limited, clear weather, daytime aerial refuelling capability. Training, however, remains rudimentary and it will be several years before either the PLAAF or the PLANAF incorporate aerial refuelling into routine operations.

**Unmanned Aerial Vehicles (UAVs).** China is investing considerably in the development of UAVs. China already has a number of short-range and longer-range UAVs in its inventory for reconnaissance, surveillance, and electronic warfare (EW) roles. Research efforts are also underway across a range of UAV technologies with several developmental UAV programmes underway related to reconnaissance, surveillance, communications, and EW.

**Munitions.** China's approach to the development of conventional munitions for its air forces has been altered irrevocably since the Gulf War, where precision-guided munitions (PGMs) were introduced on a large and effective scale. Ensuing

campaigns such as Operations Allied Force and Enduring Freedom have demonstrated an increasing use of PGMs that has reinforced Beijing's desire to develop its own cruise missiles. The PLANAF has operated the B-6/BADGER as a weapons platform for the C-601/KRAKEN anti-ship cruise missile for over ten years. Another variant of the B-6/BADGER is being developed to carry land-attack cruise missiles (LACMs) in the future. PLAAF and PLANAF tactical forces also are developing and acquiring PGMs. The Su-30 is equipped to use anti-radiation missiles (ARMs), and eventually could carry laser, TV, and radar-guided missiles and munitions. Future aircraft also are expected to employ a variety of both indigenously produced and Russian-made LACM, ASCM, and ARM PGMs.

**Evolving Capabilities.** Since China received its first fourth-generation fighter, the Su-27, in 1992, training, tactics and operational concepts progressed slowly as China integrated the new technologies and capabilities into the force structure. This protracted learning phase has allowed China to prepare for the introduction of larger numbers of fourth-generation aircraft into its inventories. Over the past two years, new Su-27s and Su-30s have been more rapidly integrated into operational units. Meanwhile, air combat tactics continue to evolve and training is becoming more advanced. By 2010, the PLA will have all the elements of a modern air force and should have developed the operational concepts and the training needed to fight as an integrated force. Although not all the PLAAF and PLANAF will be equipped with modern weapons by that time, a core of units will be in place to allow the PLA to execute the type of regional combat operations envisaged by its current military doctrine.

### *Maritime Forces Modernisation*

The PLA Navy (PLAN) numbers 290,000 personnel, with approximately 60 destroyers and frigates, about 50 diesel and six nuclear submarines, and some 40 amphibious landing ships. Approximately 350 auxiliary and smaller patrol vessels, as well as a naval air arm of over 500 fixed-wing aircraft and 50 helicopters, complement this force. Over the last decade, the Navy has streamlined and modernised its forces by eliminating large numbers of older ships and replacing them with fewer, more modern units. The number of submarines has declined by about one-half. The Navy's entire inventory of US-built, Second World War - vintage landing ships has been replaced by newer ships produced in China. In addition, there is a large fleet of about 600 landing craft, both military and civilian, that could be used for ship-to-shore operations, as well as a handful of air cushion vehicles. The PLAN also has hundreds of smaller landing craft, barges, and troop transports, all of which could be used together with fishing boats, trawlers, and civilian merchant ships to augment the naval amphibious fleet. The size of the major surface combatant fleet has been relatively stable, with older ships slowly being replaced by newer Chinese-built destroyers and frigates.

The PLAN seeks to push its maritime defence perimeter further seaward. This change in operations will require newer, more modern warships and submarines capable of operating out to the Ryukyu Islands and into the South China Sea. At these extended ranges, the platforms will have to be better armed to enable defence from all methods of attack. The Navy has been conducting research and acquiring foreign technology in an effort to improve the broad range of naval warfare capabilities; it also is acquiring new classes of ships that will be better suited for operations out to the limits of the East and South China Seas.

*A PLA Navy Russian-built Sovremennyy-class destroyer leads a line of warships during exercises last year. China's navy now has two Russian Sovremennyy-class destroyers that fire a supersonic anti-ship missile that cannot be shot down by any Asian navy.*

**Major Surface Combatants.** The acquisition of two Russian-built SOVREMENNYY Class destroyers has improved China's surface fleet capabilities. These ships are equipped with SS-N- 22/SUNBURN ASCMs and the SA-N-7 SAM system. The SOVREMENNYYs also are fitted with the AK-630M 30-mm Gatling gun and 130-mm dual-purpose gun. China's best domestically constructed surface combatant, the 6,000-ton LUHAI Class destroyer, is equipped with C-802 ASCMs. It is also equipped with a naval variant of the HQ-7 SAM system.

China has signed a contract for two additional SOVREMENNYY destroyers and could acquire additional Russian-made major surface combatants. Not only would these foreign acquisitions provide China with immediate improvement to its warfighting capabilities; they would also provide the PLAN with the opportunity to reverse-engineer more modern weapons and associated systems.

By 2010, another new destroyer class probably will begin to enter the fleet, as could a new frigate. By 2020, China is expected to have its new destroyer classes in full production, with several in service or on the way. The new frigate is likely to experience a similar rate of production. As they go into service, these platforms will replace the older JIANGHU I/II Class frigates. By 2020, China will probably have phased out most of the LUDA Class DD.

**Aircraft Carrier.** While continuing to research and discuss possibilities, China appears to have set aside indefinitely plans to acquire an aircraft carrier.

**Air Defence.** The PLAN continues to have long-standing concerns about its capability to engage enemy aircraft, cruise missiles and precision-guided munitions. This problem is becoming more significant as the Navy strives to operate away from the protection of land-based air defences. PLAN surface combatants have a limited, and primarily self-defence, anti-air warfare (AAW) capability. Only about twelve of its destroyers and frigates are outfitted with SAM systems; the others are armed only with AAA and possibly man-portable air defence systems. In addition, PLAN warships lack the modern air surveillance systems and data links required for area air defence missions. The combination of short-range weapons and lack of modern surveillance systems limits the PLAN to self-defence and point-defence anti-air warfare only. Consequently, except in unusual circumstances, no PLAN ship is capable of conducting air defence of another ship. Additionally, the PLAN could not reliably defend against either current or projected anti-ship cruise missiles (ASCM). China has recognised the importance of countering low-observable aircraft and cruise missiles. Engineering efforts to develop air defence systems capable of detecting and eventually engaging these systems are underway.

Air defence improvements include the development of SAMs to provide area defence. This effort has led to continuing exchanges with Russia on air defence-related radars and missiles. The SA-N-7 provides the most capable system in the near term. Technology from the SA-N-7 could probably assist with the development of an indigenous naval SAM system. Over the next ten years, the PLAN could develop a naval missile roughly equivalent to the shore-based SA-10s purchased from Russia. While indigenous SAM development is preferred, it is uncertain if China will be able to build its own equivalent within an acceptable period of time, and purchase of additional, more advanced Russian weapons may be required.

The land-based version of the long-range HQ-9 is in development and will probably incorporate technology from the Russian SA-10. Based on precedents, China will probably produce a naval variant of the HQ-9. HQ-9 is designed to be a long-range SAM to counter high-performance aircraft, cruise missiles, air-to-surface missiles (ASMs), and tactical ballistic missiles (TBMs). Technology from advanced Western systems may also be incorporated into the HQ-9.

**Submarines.** The PLA Navy intends to maintain a large submarine force. China is producing more modern submarines and is acquiring Russian technology to improve future units, with likely upgrades to the current fleet accomplished during overhauls. Although the force is oriented principally towards interdicting surface ships using torpedoes and mines, development of the YJ-82 ASCM for the SONG submarines will eventually give the Navy a submerged-launch cruise missile. A second major improvement will entail the use of advanced mobile mines to augment the Navy's large inventory of submarine-laid mines. While the primary mission of China's submarine force remains anti-surface warfare, China's ASW capabilities will also continue to improve in light of the acquisition of Russian-built KILO Class submarines.

*A new advanced version of the SONG-class conventional submarine is expected to incorporate advanced air-independent propulsion. SONG-class submarines, equipped with submerged launched cruise missiles, could play a significant role in countering US aircraft craft battle groups operating in the Western Pacific Ocean.*

**Diesel Electric Submarines.** In addition to the roughly 30 obsolete Soviet-designed ROMEO Class submarines remaining in the force, China has produced two domestically designed diesel-electric attack submarine classes: the MING and the SONG Class SS. China has launched 21 MINGs and three SONGs. The MING essentially is an improved version of the ROMEO. The SONG, on the other hand, is China's first new-design, conventionally powered submarine.

The SONG is a blend of Chinese and Western technology and has several key features that point to a major shift in diesel submarine design philosophy. It is the first Chinese submarine to have a skewed propeller. The SONG is also the first Chinese submarine designed to carry the developmental YJ-82, China's first encapsulated ASCM capable of launching from a submerged submarine. SONGs are probably fitted with flank-array sonars of French design. Chinese diesel submarines are fitted with German MTU diesel engines.

The PLAN has taken delivery of four Russian-built KILO Class SS. Two are standard export version Project 877 EKM KILO SS and two are Project 636 KILO SS (the improved KILO design). In purchasing the KILO SS, the PLAN has acquired one of the quietest diesel-electric submarines in the world. Armed with such weapons as the wire-guided Test-71ME heavyweight torpedo and the 53-65KE wake-homing torpedo, the KILO provides Beijing with access to previously unavailable

quieting and weapons technology. China most likely will try to incorporate aspects of this submarine into its domestic programmes, although it will take several years before these technologies could be used effectively.

By 2010, China will have withdrawn the ROMEO Class submarines from service. By 2020, China's non-nuclear submarine inventory probably will include MING, SONG, and KILO SS. China will continue using Russian technology to improve quieting, propulsion, and submarine design; it is also incorporating foreign technology into its existing submarines. China will also benefit from the maturation of its domestic submarine research and development (R&D) infrastructure to achieve a capability to design and manufacture modern submarines domestically.

*Wake homing torpedoes are a "fire-and-forget" weapon that can sense and follow a vessel's wake. Even crews with minimal proficiency can deploy this weapon effectively. China's acquisition of wake homing torpedoes makes its submarines potent anti-ship platforms.*

**Nuclear-Powered Submarines.** The PLAN has five HAN nuclear attack submarines (SSNs) in its inventory, all launched between 1970 and 1990. China's sole nuclear-powered ballistic missile submarine (SSBN) - the XIA Class - was overhauled in 1995-1998 and most likely will be extended through at least 2011. Next-generation nuclear submarine programmes will reflect Russian influence and technology. China will acquire a new nuclear-powered attack submarine class, the Type 093 Class SSN, which will have technology similar in quality to the Russian VICTOR III SSN. The Type 093 Class will carry wire-guided and wake-homing torpedoes and cruise missiles. The first Type 093 Class SSN will probably be operational soon after 2005. It will eventually replace the HAN Class SSNs, all of which China will withdraw from service by 2020. The Type 094 SSBN is expected to carry an advanced submarine-launched ballistic missile (SLBM).

**Mines.** China has enough mine warfare assets to lay a good defensive and a modest offensive minefield using a wide range of launch platforms. China is believed to have a variety of mine types available including bottom and moored influence, mobile mines, remotely controlled mines, and propelled-warhead mines. China recently has begun advertising some advanced mines, indicating that it may have even more sophisticated mines in its inventory.

**Torpedoes.** China's modernisation efforts are likely to be focused on developing torpedoes with state-of-the-art homing

and propulsion systems capable of operating in acoustically challenging shallow-water environments. China may also seek advanced torpedo countermeasures like mobile decoys and hard-kill anti-torpedo torpedoes to increase the survivability of its surface ships and submarines.

**Submarine Sonars.** Most PLAN submarines are believed to have obsolete sonar systems based on older analog designs. A limited number of Chinese submarines have more modern digital sonar systems based probably on 1980s Western technology. The Chinese have an extensive research and development infrastructure in shallow-water acoustics and have experience using modern commercial off-the-shelf (COTS) computer processing technology. It is likely that current Chinese sonar designs are similar to commercially available Western submarine sonar systems and feature modern COTS processors and displays.

**Submarine Quieting.** PLAN submarines are assessed to incorporate a wide range of quieting technologies, most of which are imported. China nonetheless desires to develop the capability to produce indigenously quiet submarines. The main submarine quieting technologies are machinery mounts, hull coatings, and propellers. Future PLA Navy submarine designs are expected to incorporate lower propeller rotational rates and more advanced propeller designs, machinery mounts, and hull coatings. China's apparent goal is to design and construct quiet submarines independently of other countries. This effort is evident in China's large investment in research, development and manufacturing.

### *Ground Forces Modernisation*

China's ground forces are divided among approximately 20 group armies, more than 40 manoeuvre divisions, and some 40 manoeuvre brigades. More than a dozen of these divisions and several of these brigades are designated "rapid reaction" units. China completed a 500,000-man force reduction in 2000 in an effort to streamline the force further and free up funding for modernisation. This reduction was achieved primarily through the deactivation of several group army headquarters; the transfer of personnel to the People's Armed Police; and the downsizing of approximately 30 combat divisions to brigades. Recent improvements have also focused on increasing the capability of reserve and militia units. The size of the PLA ground forces suggests that continued modernisation would remain slow, deliberate, and limited through at least 2010. By 2020, infantry, airborne, armour and army aviation units will comprise a much larger percentage of the force.

**Armour Modernisation.** The PLA has begun a programme to upgrade the main gun on its mainstay Type 59 main battle tanks, as well as maintain over 1,000 tanks already equipped with the 105-mm gun. In addition, several new or updated armour assets are gradually making their way into the PLA ground force inventory, to include a light tank, an amphibious tank, and an amphibious APC. Production of the Type 96 tank continues, with 1,800 expected to be deployed by 2005, according to open sources.

**Fire Support Modernisation.** Artillery research, development and production have continued to emphasise qualitative improvements to the PLA's artillery forces over quantitative production. Progress on an advanced multiple rocket launcher and a self-propelled amphibious howitzer continues.

**Special Operations Forces.** In addition to conventional warfare modernisation, the PLA has devoted considerable resources to the development of Special Operations Forces (SOF). SOF units are an integral element of ground force modernisation. They are expected to play an important role in achieving objectives in which limited goals, scale of force and time would be crucial to victory. SOF missions are likely to include conducting surveillance and battle damage assessment; locating or destroying C4I assets, transport nodes, and logistics depots; capturing or destroying airfields and ports; supporting invasion forces; destroying air defence assets; and, conducting denial and deception and information operations.

**Army Aviation.** China's Army Aviation forces can provide only minimal support to ground or amphibious operations despite a slowly growing inventory of helicopters, which currently numbers about 300 aircraft. Army Aviation has been acquiring small numbers of attack and medium lift helicopters over the last several years, but still lacks a dedicated attack helicopter.

While PLA ground forces continue to make advances in several areas, they remain faced with several key challenges, including:

> Downsizing and Restructuring. China's leadership still considers its ground forces as too "infantry-heavy." Beijing probably believes that further troop reductions accompanied by additional restructuring are required in order to make the force a more appropriately balanced combined arms force with increased mobility, lethality, and survivability.

The Pace of Modernisation. Recent fielding of new equipment has thus far been in limited numbers and, therefore, has not improved appreciably the capabilities of most of the PLA's ground forces. Even with the consolidation of ground force assets into progressively fewer units, the army remains so large as to impede rapid equipment modernisation throughout its force structure. However, new equipment, while not being deployed throughout the whole of China, is being deployed to the PLA's strategically important areas, especially the southeast.

### *Conventional Second Artillery Missile Modernisation*

Beijing's growing conventionally armed missile force provides China with a military capability that avoids the political and practical constraints associated with the use of nuclear-armed missiles. The CSS-6 and CSS-7 SRBMs provide China with a survivable and effective conventional strike force, as will future conventionally armed CSS-5s and LACMs.

*China maintains various types of conventional ballistic missiles.*

### *Ground-Based Air and Missile Defence Modernisation*

China currently lacks a coherent, national, strategic-level integrated air defence system (IADS). It has a variety of major defensive weapon systems; however, the bulk of China's air defence system is based on obsolete weapon systems, which, when combined with an antiquated and inefficient C3 system, allow for routine operations, such as providing point air defence for major cities and other high-value assets, but does not allow for an in-depth or flexible air defence throughout the country.

China's air defences consist of strategic assets operated by the PLAAF and tactical assets operated by the PLA's ground forces. Historically, Beijing relied upon its large inventory of interceptors along with PLA anti-aircraft artillery units to defend the country. However, the acquisition of modern SAMs may be precipitating a change to the historical strategy in which SAMs had not been the primary choice of engagement. Modern SAMs are primary weapons against cruise missiles, SRBMs and tactical aircraft at close range. PLAAF aircraft would be primary weapons for engaging tactical aircraft at a greater distance. Until additional SAM units become operational, China will only be able to defend effectively against isolated intrusions and small-scale attacks.

Much of China's more recent air defence modernisation efforts extend from Beijing's observation of Western military campaigns beginning with the Gulf War in early 1991 and Operation Allied Force in mid-1999. During the Gulf War, the employment of precision-guided munitions, stealth aircraft, and airborne C4I apparently awakened Beijing to the limitations of its air defence capabilities. The design of the HQ-9 SAM was reportedly influenced by these observations, and plans were made to upgrade China's C4I system. Late model Russian SAMs such

as the SA-10 and the SA-15 were purchased to provide a stop-gap measure against a perceived cruise missile threat, and external assistance was sought to develop a robust air defence system.

**Anti-Radiation Missile Development.** Reports of a Chinese anti-radiation SAM, the FT-2000, first surfaced in sales brochures at the September 1998 Farnborough Air Show. The FT-2000 is a mobile system based on the HQ-9/SA-10 with a maximum advertised range in excess of 100 kms. It has been described as an "AWACS killer." There are also indications that China is promoting the development of another anti-radiation SAM, the FT-2000A, which is an update of the antiquated CSA-1; it is a fixed-based SAM system with a range of under 100 kms. The intended targets for anti-radiation SAM systems would be AWACS aircraft or any airborne asset emitting radio signals. There is no information indicating that any country, including China, has expressed an interest in acquiring either system or that either system has progressed beyond the conceptual phase.

*Training and Exercises*

PLA combined-arms training in 2001 reportedly emphasised amphibious warfare with limited multi-service participation. Several major exercises were conducted, some of which focused on aspects of amphibious warfare. The PLAN, Air Force, and Second Artillery all conducted service-specific training.

**Ground Forces Training and Exercises.** PLA ground forces training and exercises since the mid-1990s have focused on various themes, although without a predictable pattern or sequence from year to year. Training activity in 2001 reportedly emphasised maritime and amphibious training, and integration of conventional ground units with Marines, Airborne, and SOF. It built on previous years and included more combat units, which incrementally improved the PLA's abilities to deploy and sustain the force, and to conduct amphibious operations in a multi-service environment.

**PLA Navy Training and Exercises.** PLAN training and exercise activity in 2001 was limited, with the Navy reportedly participating in only a handful of exercises. Moreover, the normal end-of-year multifleet exercise apparently was cancelled.

**PLA Air Training and Exercises.** The PLAAF and

PLANAF fighter pilot tactical training continues, albeit slowly. During 2001, some of the PLAAF's more advanced aircraft reportedly conducted advanced tactical training involving fighters of dissimilar types. Advanced tactics training is part of the PLA's push to modernise combat tactics against regional air forces. The tactics being practised are a significant departure from traditional PLA training. PLAAF/PLANAF exercise activity during 2001 reportedly concentrated on mobility, air defence, and support to amphibious assault forces. Air defence exercises, apparently smaller in number than last year, were said to be highly scripted and the scenarios lacked realism, limiting the benefit PLA pilots could have gained from the exercises.

**C. Strategic Force Modernisation**

China is in the midst of a ballistic missile modernisation programme that is improving its force, both qualitatively and quantitatively, in all classes of missiles. This modernisation programme will improve both China's nuclear deterrence by increasing the number of warheads that can target the United States as well as improving its operational capabilities for contingencies in East Asia.

***Intercontinental Ballistic Missiles (ICBM)***

China is replacing CSS-4 Mod 1 ICBMs with longer range CSS-4 Mod 2s. The replacement of all the approximately 20 CSS-4 Mod 1s will be completed by mid-decade. In addition, China is developing three solid propellant ICBMs. Development of the DF-31 is progressing and deployment should begin before mid-decade. China is also developing two follow-on extended range versions of the DF-31: a solid-propellant, mobile ICBM and a solid-propellant submarine launched ballistic missile (SLBM). Deployment of these two DF-31 follow-ons should begin by mid-to-late-decade. China will also retain the dozen CSS-3 ICBMs through the end of the decade.

Intermediate and Medium Range Ballistic Missiles (IRBM and MRBM)

The Second Artillery is continuing the replacement of the liquid propellant CSS-2 IRBM with the solid-propellant, mobile CSS-5 MRBM.

*Submarine-launched Ballistic Missiles (SLBM)*

China is expected to deploy a medium-range SLBM aboard the XIA SSBN before the end of the year. The DF-31 follow-on SLBM will be deployed on a new, more capable submarine by the end of the decade.

*Missile Deployment Trends*

China currently has around 20 ICBMs capable of targeting the United States. This number will increase to around 30 by 2005 and may reach 60 by 2010.

*Likely Countermeasures to US Missile Defence Deployments*

China's ballistic missile modernisation began before it assessed that the United States would deploy a missile defence, but China will take measures to improve its ability to defeat the defence system in order to preserve its strategic deterrent. The measures likely will include improved penetration packages for its ICBMs, an increase in the number of deployed ICBMs, and perhaps development of a multiple warhead system for an ICBM, most probably for the CSS-4.

*China is developing a longer range version of the DF-31 that can reach much of the US*

## D. Intelligence, Surveillance, and Reconnaissance (ISR)

China is enhancing its battlespace awareness for a Taiwan Strait conflict. The acquisition of modern intelligence, surveillance, and reconnaissance (ISR) systems remains a critical aspect of Beijing's military modernisation. China is developing its ISR capabilities based upon indigenous developments, supplemented by foreign technology acquisition, and procurement of complete foreign systems. Its procurement of new space systems, airborne early warning aircraft, long-range unmanned aerial vehicles, and over-the-horizon radar will enhance its ability to detect, monitor, and target naval activity in the Western Pacific Ocean.

### *Space-based ISR Development*

Exploitation of space and acquisition of related technologies remain high priorities in Beijing. China is placing major emphasis on improving space-based reconnaissance and surveillance, including electro-optical, synthetic aperture radar, and other satellite reconnaissance systems. These systems, when fully deployed, are expected to provide regional and potentially a hemispheric, continuous surveillance capability. China has begun to embrace new satellite architecture emphasising common satellite buses. This approach to satellite construction is based on the use of a standard, versatile satellite bus module, with minor modifications to accommodate various payloads. In addition to indigenous development, China will probably continue to use commercial satellite imagery and may seek to join an international consortium-owned constellation. China is cooperating with a number of countries, including Russia,

Ukraine, Brazil, Great Britain, France, Germany, and Italy, in order to advance its objectives in space.

*Airborne ISR Development*

Unmanned Aerial Vehicles. China's armed forces have operated the Chang Hong (CH-1) long-range, air-launched autonomous reconnaissance drone since the 1980s. China developed the CH-1 by reverse-engineering US Firebee reconnaissance drones recovered during the Vietnam War. An upgraded version of the system was displayed at the 2000 Zhuhai air show and is being offered for export. A PRC aviation periodical reported the CH-1 can carry either a daylight still, TV or infrared camera. It is not equipped with a data-link, which would allow remote control operation, nor is it capable of providing real-time payload feedback to the remote operator. China's armed forces also operate other UAVs, primarily for battlefield reconnaissance or electronic warfare.

**Manned Aircraft.** In addition to the Y-8 AEW and efforts to procure and produce an AWACS capability, China has several other aircraft that can perform ISR missions such as the Tu-154 multi-role special mission aircraft equipped for ELINT collection missions and possibly electronic warfare. The PLAAF reportedly has several aircraft - both fighters and bombers - capable of performing an imagery reconnaissance function.

*Ground-based ISR Development*

**Over-the-Horizon Radar (OTHR).** China may have as many as three OTH sky-wave radar systems that China aspires to use to target aircraft carriers. These systems could be used in an early warning capacity. China may also have deployed at least one surface-wave OTHR.

*Sea-Based ISR Development*

China may have developed passive acoustic sensors for use in coastal waters. China may also have at least one underwater acoustic range. This range could be used to track torpedoes during training exercises. Because of China's interest in ASW, development and deployment of additional underwater sensors is probable in the next 5-10 years and will expand through 2020. Some of these future systems may be installed as far offshore as the edge of the continental shelf. Passive sensors would provide only a few miles of coverage against quiet submarines, but could detect merchant shipping and noisy combatants at greater distances.

## E. Battle Management/Command, Control and Communications

### *Theatre-level Weapons Management*

Currently, the PLA conducts joint battle and weapon management functions manually at the theatre level. The theatre-level commander determines which weapons will accomplish the task and communicates these decisions to subordinate weapon controllers. The weapon controllers provide feedback, enabling the theatre-level commanders to determine the next course of action. China is developing a battle management system that will be used by the entire PLA for strategic, campaign, and tactical planning and operations.

China's ongoing development of a common, joint C4ISR system recognises the importance of accurate sensors. China also aims to improve the characteristics of its sensors in terms of all-weather capability, miniaturisation, artificial intelligence, survivability, and integration with other sensors.

Over the next ten years, China is projected to have several functioning AWACS-type platforms. The technical ability could exist for these aircraft to display a coordinated air picture, with the capability to command and control airborne assets. With the enhancement of an air refuelling capability, this air capability could extend into the South China Sea and beyond. In the interim, China has reportedly leased several A-50 aircraft from Russia, with first delivery expected this year. China may be negotiating with the Belarusian firm Agat to produce C4I software and equipment capable of performing joint battle management. Analysis of brochures for Agat's PANORAMA C2 system suggests it is capable of performing joint battle management. Although a purchase has yet to be confirmed, acquisition of the PANORAMA C2 system would be one way China could make progress in developing a joint C4ISR architecture.

### *Communications Networks*

China has an extensive network of hardened, underground shelters and command and control facilities for both its military and civilian leadership. Fear of a possible war with the former Soviet Union in the 1960s and 1970s prompted Beijing to expend considerable resources constructing national-level command posts, civil defence facilities and associated communications. These facilities are intended to ensure survival of China's leadership and provide a refuge from which it can maintain control over the country's military forces.

China's national command and control (C2) facilities are supported by both civilian and military communications networks. The military communications network is separate from the civilian telecommunications network. It supports all levels of the military and civilian leadership. The military communications network provides the backbone support to China's national military command and data network. PLA national level C3 is carried over multiple transmission systems to include coaxial and fibre optic cable, satellite communications, microwave radio relay, and long-range high frequency (HF) radio. China's communications networks, both civil and military, would be capable of supporting a wide range of military operations.

### *Information Operations*

China views information operations/information warfare (IO/IW) as a strategic weapon for use outside traditional operational boundaries. China is particularly sensitive to the potential asymmetric applications IO/IW can have in any future conflict with a technologically superior adversary.

Both the Academy of Military Science and the National Defence University have published several books devoted, in part or completely, to this subject. These writings indicate a growing sophistication in the PLA's understanding of all aspects of IO. In addition to developing wartime applications for its robust information control and perception management capability, China is pursuing IO/IW development as part of its overall military modernisation. Combining information warfare such as computer hacking with irregular special and guerilla operations, would allow China to mount destructive attacks within the enemy's own operations systems, while avoiding a major head-on confrontation.

The PLA has increased the amount and complexity of IO/IW components in several recent exercises. Efforts have focused on increasing the PLA's proficiency in defensive measures, most notably against the threat of computer viruses. This concern apparently is driving anti-viral and network security research and development within the PLA and military-supported academia. The research is facilitated by the dual-use nature of Information Technology (IT) and the growth in China's technology base. Increases in network defence likely will enhance China's understanding of virus propagation and behaviour, creating a solid knowledge base not only for computer network defence (CND), but potentially also for computer network attack (CNA) through malicious software development.

In an effort to improve its skill base in the IT field, the PLA has been recruiting specialists via its reserve officer selection programme. The programme involves sponsoring students, particularly those in high technology fields, through college or offering to repay loans after graduation in return for a military service commitment. This programme is intended to help provide

China with a more technically skilled officer corps that would improve, among other things, the PLA's ability to design, comprehend, and execute a full-spectrum IO/IW campaign.

China has the capability to penetrate poorly protected US computer systems and could potentially use CNA to attack specific US civilian and military infrastructures. This anti-access strategy is centred on targeting operational centres of gravity, including C41 centres, airbases, and aircraft carrier battle groups located around the periphery of China.

### *Role of Nationalistic Hacking*

In the near term, nationalistic hacking is likely to occur during periods of tension or crises. Chinese hacking activities would involve extensive web page defacements with themes sympathetic to China. Although the extent of Chinese government involvement would be difficult to ascertain, official statements concerning the leveraging of China's growing presence on the Internet, and the application of the principles of "Peoples War" in "net warfare," suggest the government will have a stronger role in future nationalistic hacking.

## G. Electronic Warfare

China's electronic warfare (EW) efforts are focused on technology and design development, accomplished mainly through cooperation with Western companies, through reverse engineering efforts, and through the procurement of foreign systems. The inventory of Chinese EW equipment includes a combination of 1950s-1980s technologies, with only a few select military units receiving the most modern components. China's newer designs, offered for sale at air and trade shows, show significant improvements over older systems. China is procuring state-of-the-art technology to improve its intercept, direction finding, and jamming capabilities. In addition to providing extended imagery reconnaissance and surveillance and electronic intelligence (ELINT) collection, Beijing's unmanned aerial vehicle programmes will probably yield platforms for improved radio and radar jammers. Additionally, existing earth stations can be modified to interfere with satellite communications. The PLA is also developing an electronic countermeasures (ECM) doctrine and has performed structured training in an ECM environment.

## H. Counterspace Development

Publicly, China opposes the militarisation of space, and seeks to prevent or slow the development of anti-satellite (ASAT) systems and space-based missile defences. Privately, however, China's leaders probably view ASATs and offensive counterspace systems, in general as well as space-based missile defences as inevitabilities. In addition to passive counterspace measures such as denial and deception China is said to be acquiring a variety of foreign technologies, which could be used to develop an active ASAT capability.

China probably has a thorough knowledge of US and foreign space operations, based, in part, on access to open-source information on US space systems and space operations. Beijing may already have acquired technical assistance that could be applied to the development of laser radars used to track and image satellites and may be seeking an advanced radar system with the capability to track satellites in low earth orbit. It may also be developing jammers that could be used against Global Positioning System (GPS) receivers. In addition, China may already possess the capability to damage, under specific conditions, optical sensors on satellites that are very vulnerable to damage by lasers. Beijing may also have acquired high-energy laser equipment and technical assistance, which could probably be used in the development of ground-based ASAT weapons. Given China's current level of interest in laser technology, Beijing could probably develop a weapon that could destroy satellites in the future. Although specific Chinese programmes for laser

ASAT have not been identified, press articles indicate an interest in developing this capability and Beijing may be working on appropriate technologies. For example, a Hong Kong newspaper article in January 2001 reported that China had developed and tested an ASAT system described as a "parasitic microsatellite." This claim is being evaluated. Nonetheless, a number of countries, including China, are developing and proliferating microsatellite (10- to 100-kg mass) and nanosatellite (1- to 10-kg mass) technologies.

## I. Space Launch Capabilities

Since 1998, China and the United States have signed three intergovernmental agreements on launching services. Several US satellite-manufacturing companies have signed contacts on commercial satellite launching services, involving a total of some 30 satellites.

Beijing is developing a new modular family/class of heavy-lift space launch vehicles (SLVs), which will reportedly use ecologically clean propellants. China's objective is a capability to launch 25 tons to low earth orbit and 14 tons to geosynchronous orbit by 2007. Beijing has also begun to develop a new small, solid propellant SLV.

China continues to make progress with its manned space programme. The first unmanned test launch occurred in November 1999. A second unmanned test flight occurred in January 2001. There is some concern that at least the recovery portion of the second mission experienced some difficulty, since Beijing has not released any photography of the recovery capsule (it did release pictures of the capsule used in the November 1999 mission shortly after recovery). While one of the strongest immediate motivations for this programme appears to be political prestige, China's manned space efforts almost certainly will contribute to improved military space systems in the 2010-2020 time frame.

China may launch its first manned space mission by 2003 or 2004. It also has long-term plans to launch its own space station, and possibly a reusable space plane as well.

## J. "New Concept" Weapon Systems

China is pursuing research and development programmes to introduce so-called "new concept" weapon systems into the PLA inventory. Key weapon systems in this category include laser and radio frequency weapons.

### *Laser Weapons*

China is pursuing a robust research and development programme for laser weapons. The Chinese have openly stated that their scientists have "laid a firm technical foundation" in laser technology and are capable of developing laser weapons. China is reportedly focusing its laser weapon development on anti-personnel, counter-precision guided munitions air defence, and ASAT roles.

China's research into laser weapon technologies has already resulted in the development and fielding of several systems. In 1995, China North Industries Corporation (NORINCO), a military trading company, introduced the ZM-87 laser weapon at defence exhibitions in Manila and Abu Dhabi. Since that time, Chinese writings indicate a continuing effort to develop additional laser systems. A second system was unveiled at the 50th Anniversary Military parade in 1999, when the Chinese displayed a probable laser-based ATGM countermeasure on its Type 90-II tanks. Additional Chinese ground combat systems include laser pointers, laser range finders, and laser target designators. These devices are routinely marketed at defence exhibitions. In the future, China can be expected to continue to develop and field military weapon and non-weapon laser systems. Using a combination of indigenous capabilities and foreign assistance, China could emerge as a leading producer and exporter of military lasers by 2020.

### *Radiofrequency Weapons*

China has reportedly placed a priority on the development of radio frequency (RF) weapons. PRC officials have indicated publicly that the PLA will need RF weapons that would defeat enemy electronics in the 21st century. Although the PLA most likely does not have an RF weapon at this time, it is believed to have a programme to develop the high-power RF technologies that could form the basis for some types of RF weapons. In addition to indigenous research, China is working closely with foreign scientists and is seeking foreign technology associated with high-power RF generation. Chinese scientists have published on efforts to develop explosively driven RF weapons technology that could potentially be used in missile warheads or aircraft bombs, and are studying the effects of RF pulses on electronics and the propagation of RF energy through the atmosphere.

Within the next decade, China may be able to develop and field air defence RF weapons intended to defeat missiles or aircraft by targeting the electronics in guidance, altimeter, fire-control, communications, navigation or other critical subsystems. While the PRC has discussed the use of high-power RF technology for air defence, there is little evidence that a programme to produce an RF weapon for this mission has been initiated. Nevertheless, China may consider working with Russia to support research and development on a high-powered microwave system (HPM), referred to as Ranets-E, which would target the electronics onboard precision-guided weapons. If the Russians succeed in developing the system - and China purchases it - the PLA could have a number of these systems available before 2020.

China is known to be conducting research on explosively driven RF weapons; however, there are questions regarding the technological feasibility and military utility of RF warheads. Even if China could produce significant amounts of RF energy by means of an explosive driver, it is still not clear whether it is possible to build an RF warhead that will negate electronics at a significantly greater range than a conventional warhead of the same size would cause blast/fragmentation damage. China is unlikely to possess effective RF warheads until after the year 2010 even if such weapons do prove to be feasible.

Finally, China may consider RF weapons with an ASAT capability. An ASAT mission is undoubtedly one of the most stressing RF weapon applications. For a ground-based system beaming RF energy into space, HPM sources operating at very high power levels as well as large transmitting antennas having high gain would be required. For an RF weapon delivered via a direct-ascent missile or deployed as an orbital system, there are severe constraints on system size and mass and the question of competitiveness with other ASAT systems that must also approach the target. Even if the Chinese commit resources to a major ASAT RF development programme, they will be unable to deploy such a weapon for at least fifteen years.

#### *Low Observable Technologies*

China reportedly embarked on an extensive national effort to understand and develop low observable (LO) technology in the 1980s. Indigenous efforts have grown in maturity and understanding so as to allow analysis of foreign capabilities and attempt to duplicate past research. Chinese scientists are said to have an excellent theoretical understanding of LO technology, but apparently lack practical experience that comes with decades of applied research. China appears to have begun multiple programmes to apply basic signature reduction technologies to its fighter aircraft programmes and is reportedly developing new fighter aircraft that will incorporate LO technology.

### K. Technology Acquisition

The PRC's efforts to develop, acquire and gain access to

advanced technologies that would enhance military capabilities are multi-faceted and include the use of traditional military actors, commercial entities and individuals involved in basic scientific research. The production of advanced weapon systems requires not only the transfer or development of the technology, but also the transfer or development of associated knowledge, including training, education, technical skills and manufacturing know-how.

In 1979, China began modernising its weapons facilities through a policy emphasising production of both military and civilian goods throughout its defence industrial base. This policy shift reflects China's aspiration to attain long-term self-sufficiency through the acquisition of key foreign dual-use technologies and knowledge. Once such technology is obtained, defence-affiliated institutes and factories may apply them to the design and production of commercial and/or military end-items. Moreover, design and production of commercial goods by the defence industrial base can generate revenue and foreign exchange to finance the acquisition of advanced technology. Since 1979, thousands of PRC business entities have been established in the United States. The bulk of the business conducted by these entities is probably legitimate, but an undetermined number may target dual-use commodities and controlled technologies restricted from sale to the PRC.

Recently, two authoritative PRC journals recommended an increase in the use of overseas ethnic-Chinese scientists to transfer foreign technology. The journals endorsed building databases of such overseas scientists, entrusting them with research of interest to Beijing, and maintaining secrecy through the use of intermediaries and third countries. Recruitment through intermediaries was recommended to avoid complications due to policies and sensitivities of the targeted nation. One journal suggested private sector intermediary organisations and international talent exchange associations be used for recruiting. The journals also suggested setting up an "Overseas Chinese

Experts Data Centre" operated by the Ministry of Science, fed by multiple sources, and organised by region, country, and profession. This data would be collected through privately owned service organisations supported by the State, over Internet websites hosted in China and the target country, by the private sector's foreign offices, and by science attaches in PRC embassies and consulates abroad.

Using academic exchange as a medium to train scientists and to develop ties between scientists, China appears to be building an informal S&T network around the world that could not only contribute to basic research but also to the development of commercial and military technologies. The close relationships between the personnel and organisations involved often makes it difficult to separate the research, funding and cooperation triangle among Chinese universities, government institutes and businesses.

### *Collection of Technical Information*

In 1991, the China Defence Science and Technology Information Centre (CDSTIC) - then the information arm for the Commission on Science, Technology and Industry for National Defence published a science and technology (S&T) collection manual titled "Sources and Techniques of Obtaining National Defence Science and Technology Intelligence." The manual suggested that 80 per cent of China's defence S&T needs are met through open and grey source (purchase/subscription) materials. This manual provided detailed information on foreign open sources on defence technology and noted that there are roughly 4,000 individual intelligence organisations operating in China (as of 1991). Many of these organisations are associated with state-owned enterprises, research institutes and academies affiliated with China's defence industrial base.

The collection of technical information probably continues to be orchestrated by CDSTIC - now under the PLA General

Equipment Department (GED). The GED reportedly oversees a complex web of factories, institutes, and academies that are subordinate to China's nuclear, aeronautics, electronics, ordnance, shipbuilding, and astronautics industries. Each of these institutions has an import/export corporation to facilitate the import of technology and knowledge.

***China's Defence Industrial Base***

National Defence Science, Technology and Industry. China's defence industrial base - also known as National Defence Science, Technology and Industry (NDST&I) - is a well-organised and redundant structure, consisting of the factories, institutes, and academies subordinate to the organisations that represent the nuclear, aeronautics, electronics, ordnance, shipbuilding, and astronautics industries.

Before the reforms of 1998, five corporations and one ministry represented China's defence industrial base:

- Ministry of Electronics Industry
- China National Nuclear Corporation (CNNC)
- Aviation Industries of China (AVIC)
- China North Industries Corporation (CNIC)
- China State Shipbuilding Corporation (CSSC)
- China Aerospace Corporation (CASC)

In 1998, each of the five corporations split into two competing corporations in the shipbuilding, aviation, nuclear, ordnance and missile/aerospace arenas. The Ministry of Electronics Industry merged with the Ministry of Posts and Telecommunications to become the Ministry of Information Technology and Telecom Industry. The current organisation of China's defence industrial base is:

- Ministry of Information Technology and Telecom Industry (MTTI)

- China State Shipbuilding Corporation (CSSC)
- China State Shipbuilding Industry Corporation (CSIC)
- China Aviation Industry Corporation I (AVIC I)
- China Aviation Industry Corporation II (AVIC II)
- China National Nuclear Corporation (CNNC)
- China National Engineering Construction Corporation (CNEC)
- China North Industries Group Corporation (CNIGC)
- China South Industries Group Corporation (CSIGC)
- China Aerospace Science and Industry Corporation (CASIC)
- China Aerospace Science and Technology Corporation (CASC)

Each of these corporations and MTTI have subordinate import/export corporations. These sub-corporations facilitate the import of technology and the export of commercial and military goods for profit. All of these import/export corporations have at least one branch office operating in the United States. The import/export corporations are:

- China Nuclear Energy Industry Corporation
- China Aero-Technology Import/Export Corporation
- China North Industries Corporation
- China National Electronics Import/Export Corporation
- China Shipbuilding Trading Corporation
- China Great Wall Industries Corporation
- China Precision Machinery Import/Export Corporation

Chinese Academy of Sciences. The Chinese Academy of Sciences (CAS), directly subordinate to the State Council, is China's highest academic institution for comprehensive research in the natural and applied sciences. Research is conducted in the basic sciences, such as mathematics, physics, chemistry, astronomy, and geology, as well as in newer scientific fields, such as systems engineering, remote sensing, computers, automation, robotics, semiconductors and lasers. CAS has branches with subordinate institutes in Shanghai, Nanjing, Hefei, Guangzhou, Wuhan, Changchun, Shenyang, Chengdu, Kunming, Xian, Lanzhou, and Xinjian - cities also strongly associated with China's defence industrial base. As a consequence, these organisations often work closely with the military in applied research, with products funded or developed for use by the military.

## L. Military Budget Trends

In March 2002, Chinese finance minister Xiang Huaicheng announced that China is increasing military spending in 2002 by 17.6 per cent, or $3 billion, bringing the publicly reported total to $20 billion. The publicly disclosed figures do not include major spending for weapons research and for the purchase of foreign weapons like two Russian-built destroyers China bought last year. Actual military spending, including the large but difficult-to-assess off-budget financing portion, could total $65 billion, making China the second largest defence spender in the world after the United States and the largest defence spender in Asia.

Additional double-digit defence budget growth is likely, at least through the Tenth Five-Year Plan (2001-05). These increases will be used to offset losses from divested PLA commercial enterprises, underwrite escalating personnel costs, and fund PLA modernisation. Beijing's 2000 White Paper on National Defence and its predecessor editions detail the official PLA budget, but only by poorly defined resource categories and not by service or mission. The release of the white papers may be an attempt by China to appear to be increasing its military transparency to the West while in reality keeping much secret.

Although Xiang cited modernisation as one reason for the budget increase, most defence modernisation spending occurs outside the PLA budget. Imported weapon systems are financed by separate hard-currency allocations from the State Council and are not charged against the PLA budget. The PLA pays for domestically produced Chinese equipment, which makes up about half of the modernisation effort, but it pays only the incremental cost of manufacturing one system and none of the substantial R&D or startup costs. Such costs appear in the budget of the state-owned industry that produces the equipment, including substantial hard-currency costs for foreign technology and assistance.

The PLA receives funding from numerous, extra-budgetary sources. These sources include special allocations for procurement, at least partially derived from arms sales profits; sales of military unit services (e.g. construction) and products (e.g. farm produce) and other traditional PLA self-sufficiency activities; earnings from PLA enterprises remaining after divestment, which still produce civilian services and products; and, defence-related allocations in other ministries (e.g. state science and technology budgets and agencies at the provincial and local levels). In addition, China's proliferation of weapons of mass destruction (WMD)-associated technology and conventional munitions may help subsidise certain force modernisation programmes. Tracking these sources complicates the process of identifying and assessing defence budgetary trends.

Projecting Chinese defence spending over a long period of time is problematic, especially given that even total defence spending is not adequately defined or reported. However, anticipated economic growth would define somewhat the boundaries of future defence expenditures. Using this method, annual defence spending could increase in real terms over threefold to fourfold between now and 2020.

(Source:http://www.defencelink.mil/news/Jul2002/d20020712china.pdf)

# 8. Speech of US President George W. Bush at the United Nations General Assembly

## New York, 12 September 2002

The President: Mr. Secretary General, Mr. President, distinguished delegates, and ladies and gentlemen: We meet one year and one day after a terrorist attack brought grief to my country, and brought grief to many citizens of our world. Yesterday, we remembered the innocent lives taken that terrible morning. Today, we turn to the urgent duty of protecting other lives, without illusion and without fear.

We've accomplished much in the last year — in Afghanistan and beyond. We have much yet to do — in Afghanistan and beyond. Many nations represented here have joined in the fight against global terror, and the people of the United States are grateful.

The United Nations was born in the hope that survived a world war — the hope of a world moving towards justice, escaping old patterns of conflict and fear. The founding members resolved that the peace of the world must never again be destroyed by the will and wickedness of any man. We created the United Nations Security Council, so that, unlike the League of Nations, our deliberations would be more than talk, our resolutions would be more than wishes. After generations of deceitful dictators and broken treaties and squandered lives, we dedicated ourselves to standards of human dignity shared by all, and to a system of security defended by all.

Today, these standards, and this security, are challenged. Our commitment to human dignity is challenged by persistent poverty and raging disease. The suffering is great, and our responsibilities are clear. The United States is joining with the world to supply aid where it reaches people and uplifts lives, to extend trade and the prosperity it brings, and to bring medical care where it is desperately needed.

As a symbol of our commitment to human dignity, the United States will return to UNESCO. (Applause.) This organisation has been reformed and America will participate fully in its mission to advance human rights, tolerance and learning.

Our common security is challenged by regional conflicts — ethnic and religious strife that is ancient, but not inevitable. In the Middle East, there can be no peace for either side without freedom for both sides. America stands committed to an independent and democratic Palestine, living side by side with Israel in peace and security. Like all other people, Palestinians deserve a government that serves their interests and listens to their voices. My nation will continue to encourage all parties to be aware of their responsibilities as we seek a just and comprehensive settlement to the conflict.

Above all, our principles and our security are challenged today by outlaw groups and regimes that accept no law of morality and have no limit to their violent ambitions. In the attacks on America a year ago, we saw the destructive intentions of our enemies. This threat hides within many nations, including my own. In cells and camps, terrorists are plotting further destruction, and building new bases for their war against civilisation. And our greatest fear is that terrorists will find a short cut to their mad ambitions when an outlaw regime supplies them with the technologies to kill on a massive scale.

In one place — in one regime — we find all these dangers, in their most lethal and aggressive forms, exactly the kind of aggressive threat the United Nations was born to confront.

Twelve years ago, Iraq invaded Kuwait without provocation. And the regime's forces were poised to continue their march to seize other countries and their resources. Had Saddam Hussein been appeased instead of stopped, he would have endangered the peace and stability of the world. Yet this aggression was stopped — by the might of coalition forces and the will of the United Nations.

To suspend hostilities, to spare himself, Iraq's dictator accepted a series of commitments. The terms were clear, to him and to all. And he agreed to prove he is complying with every one of those obligations.

He has proven instead only his contempt for the United Nations, and for all his pledges. By breaking every pledge — by his deceptions, and by his cruelties — Saddam Hussein has made the case against himself.

In 1991, Security Council Resolution 688 demanded that the Iraqi regime cease at once the repression of its own people, including the systematic repression of minorities — which the Council said, threatened international peace and security in the region. This demand goes ignored.

In 2001, the UN Commission on Human Rights found that Iraq continues to commit extremely grave violations of human rights, and that the regime's repression is all pervasive. Tens of thousands of political opponents and ordinary citizens have been subjected to arbitrary arrest and imprisonment, summary execution, and torture by beating and burning, electric shock, starvation, mutilation, and rape. Wives are tortured in front of their husbands, children in the presence of their parents ¾ and all these horrors concealed from the world by the apparatus of a totalitarian state.

In 1991, the UN Security Council, through Resolutions 686 and 687, demanded that Iraq return all prisoners from Kuwait and other lands. Iraq's regime agreed. It broke its promise. In 2001 the Secretary General's high-level coordinator for this issue reported that Kuwait, Saudi, Indian, Syrian, Lebanese,

Iranian, Egyptian, Bahraini, and Omani nationals remain unaccounted for — more than 600 people. One American pilot is among them.

In 1991, the UN Security Council, through Resolution 687, demanded that Iraq renounce all involvement with terrorism, and permit no terrorist organisations to operate in Iraq. Iraq's regime agreed. It broke this promise. In violation of Security Council Resolution 1373, Iraq continues to shelter and support terrorist organisations that direct violence against Iran, Israel, and Western governments. Iraqi dissidents abroad are targeted for murder. In 1993, Iraq attempted to assassinate the Emir of Kuwait and a former American President. Iraq's government openly praised the attacks of 11 September. And Al-Qaeda terrorists escaped from Afghanistan and are known to be in Iraq.

In 1991, the Iraqi regime agreed to destroy and stop developing all weapons of mass destruction and long-range missiles, and to prove to the world it has done so by complying with rigorous inspections. Iraq has broken every aspect of this fundamental pledge.

From 1991 to 1995, the Iraqi regime said it had no biological weapons. After a senior official in its weapons programme defected and exposed this lie, the regime admitted to producing tens of thousands of litres of anthrax and other deadly biological agents for use with Scud warheads, aerial bombs, and aircraft spray tanks. UN inspectors believe Iraq has produced two to four times the amount of biological agents it declared, and has failed to account for more than three metric tons of material that could be used to produce biological weapons. Right now, Iraq is expanding and improving facilities that were used for the production of biological weapons.

United Nations' inspections also revealed that Iraq maintains stockpiles of VX, mustard and other chemical agents, and that the regime is rebuilding and expanding facilities capable of producing chemical weapons.

And in 1995, after four years of deception, Iraq finally admitted it had a crash nuclear weapons programme before the Gulf War. We know now, were it not for that war, the regime in Iraq would likely have possessed a nuclear weapon no later than 1993.

Today, Iraq continues to withhold important information about its nuclear programme — weapons design, procurement logs, experiment data, an accounting of nuclear materials and documentation of foreign assistance. Iraq employs capable nuclear scientists and technicians. It retains physical infrastructure needed to build a nuclear weapon. Iraq has made several attempts to buy high-strength aluminium tubes used to enrich uranium for a nuclear weapon. Should Iraq acquire fissile material, it would be able to build a nuclear weapon within a year. And Iraq's state-controlled media has reported numerous meetings between Saddam Hussein and his nuclear scientists, leaving little doubt about his continued appetite for these weapons.

Iraq also possesses a force of Scud-type missiles with ranges beyond the 150 kilometres permitted by the UN Work at testing and production facilities shows that Iraq is building more long-range missiles that it can inflict mass death throughout the region.

In 1990, after Iraq's invasion of Kuwait, the world imposed economic sanctions on Iraq. Those sanctions were maintained after the war to compel the regime's compliance with Security Council resolutions. In time, Iraq was allowed to use oil revenues to buy food. Saddam Hussein has subverted this programme, working around the sanctions to buy missile technology and military materials. He blames the suffering of Iraq's people on the United Nations, even as he uses his oil wealth to build lavish palaces for himself, and to buy arms for his country. By refusing to comply with his own agreements, he bears full guilt for the hunger and misery of innocent Iraqi citizens.

In 1991, Iraq promised UN inspectors immediate and unrestricted access to verify Iraq's commitment to rid itself of weapons of mass destruction and long-range missiles. Iraq broke this promise, spending seven years deceiving, evading, and harassing UN inspectors before ceasing cooperation entirely. Just months after the 1991 cease-fire, the Security Council twice renewed its demand that the Iraqi regime cooperate fully with inspectors, condemning Iraq's serious violations of its obligations. The Security Council again renewed that demand in 1994, and twice more in 1996, deploring Iraq's clear violations of its obligations. The Security Council renewed its demand three more times in 1997, citing flagrant violations; and three more times in 1998, calling Iraq's behaviour totally unacceptable. And in 1999, the demand was renewed yet again.

As we meet today, it's been almost four years since the last UN inspectors set foot in Iraq, four years for the Iraqi regime to plan, and to build, and to test behind the cloak of secrecy.

We know that Saddam Hussein pursued weapons of mass murder even when inspectors were in his country. Are we to assume that he stopped when they left? The history, the logic, and the facts lead to one conclusion: Saddam Hussein's regime is a grave and gathering danger. To suggest otherwise is to hope against the evidence. To assume this regime's good faith is to bet the lives of millions and the peace of the world in a reckless gamble. And this is a risk we must not take.

Delegates to the General Assembly, we have been more than patient. We've tried sanctions. We've tried the carrot of oil for food, and the stick of coalition military strikes. But Saddam Hussein has defied all these efforts and continues to develop weapons of mass destruction. The first time we may be completely certain he has nuclear weapons is when, God forbids, he uses one. We owe it to all our citizens to do everything in our power to prevent that day from coming.

The conduct of the Iraqi regime is a threat to the authority of the United Nations, and a threat to peace. Iraq has answered a decade of UN demands with a decade of defiance. All the world now faces a test, and the United Nations a difficult and defining moment. Are Security Council resolutions to be honoured and enforced, or cast aside without consequence? Will the United Nations serve the purpose of its founding, or will it be irrelevant?

The United States helped found the United Nations. We want the United Nations to be effective, and respectful, and successful. We want the resolutions of the world's most important multilateral body to be enforced. And right now those resolutions are being unilaterally subverted by the Iraqi regime. Our partnership of nations can meet the test before us, by making clear what we now expect of the Iraqi regime.

If the Iraqi regime wishes peace, it will immediately and unconditionally forswear, disclose, and remove or destroy all weapons of mass destruction, long-range missiles, and all related material.

If the Iraqi regime wishes peace, it will immediately end all support for terrorism and act to suppress it, as all states are required to do by UN Security Council resolutions.

If the Iraqi regime wishes peace, it will cease persecution of its civilian population, including Shi'a, Sunnis, Kurds, Turkomans, and others, again as required by Security Council resolutions.

If the Iraqi regime wishes peace, it will release or account for all Gulf War personnel whose fate is still unknown. It will return the remains of any who are deceased, return stolen property, accept liability for losses resulting from the invasion of Kuwait, and fully cooperate with international efforts to resolve these issues, as required by Security Council resolutions.

If the Iraqi regime wishes peace, it will immediately end all illicit trade outside the oil-for-food programme. It will accept UN administration of funds from that programme, to ensure that the money is used fairly and promptly for the benefit of the Iraqi people.

If all these steps are taken, it will signal a new openness and accountability in Iraq. And it could open the prospect of the United Nations helping to build a government that represents all Iraqis — a government based on respect for human rights, economic liberty, and internationally supervised elections.

The United States has no quarrel with the Iraqi people; they've suffered too long in silent captivity. Liberty for the Iraqi people is a great moral cause, and a great strategic goal. The people of Iraq deserve it; the security of all nations requires it. Free societies do not intimidate through cruelty and conquest, and open societies do not threaten the world with mass murder. The United States supports political and economic liberty in a unified Iraq.

We can harbour no illusions — and that's important today to remember. Saddam Hussein attacked Iran in 1980 and Kuwait in 1990. He's fired ballistic missiles at Iran and Saudi Arabia, Bahrain, and Israel. His regime once ordered the killing of every person between the ages of 15 and 70 in certain Kurdish villages in northern Iraq. He has gassed many Iranians, and 40 Iraqi villages.

My nation will work with the UN Security Council to meet our common challenge. If Iraq's regime defies us again, the world must move deliberately, decisively to hold Iraq to account. We will work with the UN Security Council for the necessary resolutions. But the purposes of the United States should not be doubted. The Security Council resolutions will be enforced — the just demands of peace and security will be met — or action will be unavoidable. And a regime that has lost its legitimacy will also lose its power.

Events can turn in one of two ways: If we fail to act in the face of danger, the people of Iraq will continue to live in brutal submission. The regime will have new power to bully and dominate and conquer its neighbours, condemning the Middle East to more years of bloodshed and fear. The regime will remain unstable — the region will remain unstable, with little hope of freedom, and isolated from the progress of our times. With every step the Iraqi regime takes towards gaining and deploying the most terrible weapons, our own options to confront that regime will narrow. And if an emboldened regime were to supply these weapons to terrorist allies, then the attacks of 11 September would be a prelude to far greater horrors.

If we meet our responsibilities, if we overcome this danger, we can arrive at a very different future. The people of Iraq can shake off their captivity. They can one day join a democratic Afghanistan and a democratic Palestine, inspiring reforms throughout the Muslim world. These nations can show by their example that honest government, and respect for women, and the great Islamic tradition of learning can triumph in the Middle East and beyond. And we will show that the promise of the United Nations can be fulfilled in our time.

Neither of these outcomes is certain. Both have been set before us. We must choose between a world of fear and a world of progress. We cannot stand by and do nothing while dangers gather. We must stand up for our security, and for the permanent rights and the hopes of mankind. By heritage and by choice, the United States of America will make that stand. And, delegates to the United Nations, you have the power to make that stand, as well.

Thank you very much. (Applause.)

(Source: http://www.un.org/ webcast/ga/57/statements/ 020912usaE.htm)

# 9. Prime Minister Atal Bihari Vajpayee's Address at the $57^{th}$ Session of the United Nations General Assembly

## New York, 13 September 2002

*Mr. President,*

I congratulate you on your election as President of the 57th General Assembly. We wish you success and pledge our whole-hearted support.

I also extend my best wishes to Secretary General Kofi Annan in this first year of his second term in office.

*Mr. President,*

Two days ago, we commemorated the first anniversary of a terrible event, which focused the collective global consciousness on international terrorism. Terrorism did not start on 11 September. It was on that day that it brazenly announced itself on the global stage, flaunting its immunity from distance and power.

As a country exposed to the depredations of terrorism for decades, India empathised with the pain of the American people, admired their resilience in coming to terms with the consequences, and supported the bold decision to counterattack terrorism at its very source.

The international community has taken some collective decisions in the global effort to combat terrorism and to choke off its lifelines. The UN Security Council Resolution 1373 contains the essence of these decisions. Its Counter-Terrorism Committee should now move beyond information compilation and legal assistance to enforcing compliance by states known to be sponsoring, sheltering, funding, arming and training terrorists.

In our South Asian region, nuclear blackmail has emerged over the last few months as a new arrow in the quiver of State-sponsored terrorism. Dark threats were held out that actions by India to stamp out cross-border terrorism could provoke a nuclear war. To succumb to such blatant nuclear terrorism would mean forgetting the bitter lessons of the 11 September tragedy.

As far as India is concerned, we have repeatedly clarified that no one in our country wants a war — conventional or otherwise. Nor are we seeking any territory.

But absolutely everyone in India wants an end to the cross-border terrorism which has claimed thousands of innocent lives and denied entire generations their right to a peaceful existence with normal economic and social activity. We are determined to end it with all the means at our command. Let there be no doubt about it in any quarter.

***Mr. President,***

Yesterday we heard the extraordinary claim in this Assembly that the brutal murder of innocent civilians in Jammu & Kashmir is actually a "freedom struggle." And that the forthcoming elections in that state are a "farce", since they cannot be a substitute for a plebiscite demanded over 50 years ago.

It requires an effort of logical acrobatics to believe that carnage of innocents is an instrument for freedom and elections are a symbol of deception and repression!

If the elections are a mere fraud, why are terrorists being trained and infiltrated into India at the command of the Inter-Services Intelligence Agency of Pakistan to kill election candidates and to intimidate voters?

If Pakistan claims to be a crucial partner in the international coalition against terrorism, how can it continue to use terrorism as an instrument of state policy against India?

How can the international coalition condone Pakistan-directed killings of thousands of innocent civilians — women and children included — to promote a bizarre version of "self-determination"?

Those who speak of "underlying" or "root" causes of terrorism, offer alibis to the terrorists and absolve them of responsibility for their heinous actions — such as the 11 September attacks on the United States or the 13 December attack on our Parliament.

General Musharraf has himself admitted that rigging was responsible for his winning the referendum by a dubious margin of 90 per cent in April this year. As for the "true" democracy he intends to establish in Pakistan, he has rendered it impotent even before the elections are held next month.

Those who had to "adjust" voting and counting procedures to win a referendum — and achieved constitutional authority by the simple expedient of writing their own constitution — are ill-placed to lecture others on freedom and democracy.

***Mr. President,***

Yesterday we heard yet another patently false and self-serving claim that in India, Muslims and other minorities are the target of "Hindu extremists." With 150 million, India has the second largest Muslim population in the world, more than in Pakistan. We are proud of the multi-religious character of our society. Equal respect for all faiths, and non-discrimination on the basis of religion, is not just our Constitutional obligation. As the whole world knows, it is the signature tune of India's civilisation and culture.

***Mr. President,***

We have to recognise that the developmental divide

between the North and the South is becoming wider and deeper by the day. The challenges that face us are stark and there is no alternative to all the countries of the world joining hands to face them together.

Over the last decade, 10 million people have been joining the ranks of the poor each year. A quarter of the world's population lives in extreme poverty.

A million lives are lost to malaria each year. Tuberculosis claims twice as many lives annually. One-fifth of humanity does not have access to safe drinking water.

We have to find US$ 24 billion annually for investment in poor countries if we are to achieve the World Food Summit goal of halving hunger by 2015.

It was this bleak picture that we addressed in our Millennium Declaration in 2000 with a time-bound road map for poverty eradication, with goals and targets to be achieved by 2015. The Monterrey Conference on Financing for Development was an encouraging beginning in the effort to enhance international financing for development.

Continuation of widespread poverty, at a time when unimaginable wealth is concentrated in a small social layer, is totally unacceptable. The 21st century has all the means to end this sad legacy of the past centuries. What is lacking is the political will among the developed countries to sincerely and speedily address the legitimate developmental needs of the developing countries, especially the least developed ones.

The poor of the world, as also the more enlightened sections of the rich around the world, would like the United Nations to spearhead efforts to end the systemic indifference towards poverty. The agenda of action that would achieve this objective is clear:

- **One,** asymmetry in trading relations between developing and developed nations; the problem of declining prices for commodities from developing countries; and all unjustified barriers to their exports must be removed.

- **Two**, extreme volatility in global energy markets has been causing havoc with the trade and fiscal balances of developing countries. This must end.
- **Three,** unpredictability in global capital movements, which periodically devastate the economies of developing countries, must be controlled.
- **Four**, malfeasant corporate practices, which drain off the natural resources and traditional knowledge base of developing countries without fair compensation, must be dealt with sternly.

Casting an even longer shadow over this grim developmental canvas is global climate change from which the poor will suffer the most, though they contributed the least to it. The recent floods and forest fires in Europe are a forewarning that the countries of Asia and Africa are not the only victims of the fury of a degraded environment. The Earth's atmosphere and biosphere know no national boundaries. The choice before the global community is stark: Either we take urgent steps to protect the environment, or be prepared for far worse natural calamities.

Early this month, the Johannesburg Summit for Sustainable Development debated some of the linkages between poverty, trade, environment, national, international and corporate governance and global financial flows. We emerged from the Summit with some encouraging outcomes, but these fell well short of the demands of our time.

It has become a categorical imperative to understand, and address, man's developmental needs in their totality and not in isolated parts. It is disconcerting that the highways of development are jammed by the noisy and unruly traffic of materialism and its brash cousin, consumerism. Human values have become mute bystanders in most political, economic and social activities.

The result of this imbalance between our material and non-material needs can never be happy for mankind. On the contrary, by placing compassion, care, fellow feeling, cooperation and other human values in the driver's seat, we are bound to get the right solutions to every problem on our planet.

Humanity is crying out for a harmonious integration of the economic, social, political, environmental and spiritual dimensions of development. This task calls for the closest possible cooperation among nations and communities, with a readiness to accept the best from every cultural and spiritual tradition around the globe. The United Nations needs to take up newer and bigger initiatives in this direction.

In this Assembly, less than a year ago — and in the US Congress the year before — I had extended India's offer to coordinate a Comprehensive Global Development Dialogue. I reiterate that offer today. If we are to achieve the development goals we have promised ourselves by 2015, we need such a dialogue urgently.

***Mr. President,***

As we come together once again at the United Nations, at a time of new and varied challenges, we should reflect on our collective commitment to the UN Charter, its purposes and principles. There is a growing perception — particularly among the weaker and poorer countries — that responses to issues of far-reaching impact often seem arbitrary or contradictory.

A common destiny is at stake. The world needs collective multilateralism. It needs the United Nations — the coming together and working together of all its nations in the development of a common and collective perspective.

Conflicts arise when there is no spirit of democracy within

and among nations. A genuinely democratic framework enables us to respect alternative points of view, to value diversity, and to fashion solutions responsive to the aspirations of the people.

India's own experience as a hugely populated and diverse nation shows how complex problems can be addressed within a constitutional and democratic framework.

These values need to be assiduously nurtured in our societies, so that at least a future generation is rid of the scourge of poverty, intolerance, obscurantism and religious extremism.

Democratic societies are far less prone to ideologies based on violence or militarist yearnings, since they do not have their fingers permanently on the trigger of a gun. We have to be vigilant against threats to democracy worldwide arising from forces that are opposed to it, be they rooted in fundamentalist political dogmas or extremist religious ideologies.

***Mr. President,***

All of us are aware of the challenges. Most of us are agreed that a stable global order has to rest on the four strong pillars of peace, security, sustainable development and democracy. We have to ensure that each of these pillars is strong and resilient.

We are conscious of our collective responsibility. It is the leap from this theoretical understanding to its practical realisation, which we have often failed to execute. We should not fail again. Our future generations will not forgive us if we do.

Thank you.

(Source: http://meadev.nic.in/ speeches/pm-address-un.htm)

# 10. The National Security Strategy of the United States of America

# The White House, Washington, 20 September 2002

[Editor's Note: The National Security Strategy of the United States was presented by President George W. Bush in his Annual Report to the US Congress on 20 September 2002.]

[Excerpts]

## III. Strengthen Alliances to Defeat Global Terrorism and Work to Prevent Attacks Against us and our Friends

The United States of America is fighting a war against terrorists of global reach. The enemy is not a single political regime or person or religion or ideology. The enemy is terrorism – premeditated, politically motivated violence perpetrated against innocents.

In many regions, legitimate grievances prevent the emergence of a lasting peace. Such grievances deserve to be, and must be, addressed within a political process. But no cause justifies terror. The United States will make no concessions to terrorist demands and strike no deals with them. We make no distinction between terrorists and those who knowingly harbour or provide aid to them.

The struggle against global terrorism is different from any other war in our history. It will be fought on many fronts against a particularly elusive enemy over an extended period of time. Progress will come through the persistent accumulation of successes—some seen, some unseen.

Today our enemies have seen the results of what civilised nations can, and will, do against regimes that harbour, support, and use terrorism to achieve their political goals. Afghanistan has been liberated; coalition forces continue to hunt down the Taliban and Al-Qaeda. But it is not only this battlefield on which we will engage terrorists. Thousands of trained terrorists remain at large with cells in North America, South America, Europe, Africa, the Middle East, and across Asia.

Our priority will be first to disrupt and destroy terrorist organisations of global reach and attack their leadership; command, control, and communications; material support; and finances. This will have a disabling effect upon the terrorists' ability to plan and operate.

We will continue to encourage our regional partners to take up a coordinated effort that isolates the terrorists. Once the regional campaign localises the threat to a particular state, we will help ensure the state has the military, law enforcement, political, and financial tools necessary to finish the task.

The United States will continue to work with our allies to disrupt the financing of terrorism. We will identify and block the sources of funding for terrorism, freeze the assets of terrorists and those who support them, deny terrorists access to the international financial system, protect legitimate charities from being abused by terrorists, and prevent the movement of terrorists' assets through alternative financial networks.

However, this campaign need not be sequential to be effective, the cumulative effect across all regions will help achieve the results we seek.

We will disrupt and destroy terrorist organisations by:

- direct and continuous action using all the elements of national and international power. Our immediate focus will be those terrorist organisations of global reach and any terrorist or state sponsor of terrorism which attempts to gain or use weapons of mass destruction (WMD) or their precursors;

- defending the United States, the American people, and our interests at home and abroad by identifying and destroying the threat before it reaches our borders. While the United States will constantly strive to enlist the support of the international community, we will not hesitate to act alone, if necessary, to exercise our right of self-defence by acting preemptively against such terrorists, to prevent them from doing harm against our people and our country; and
- denying further sponsorship, support, and sanctuary to terrorists by convincing or compelling states to accept their sovereign responsibilities.

We will also wage a war of ideas to win the battle against international terrorism. This includes:

- using the full influence of the United States, and working closely with allies and friends, to make clear that all acts of terrorism are illegitimate so that terrorism will be viewed in the same light as slavery, piracy, or genocide: behaviour that no respectable government can condone or support and all must oppose;
- supporting moderate and modern government, especially in the Muslim world, to ensure that the conditions and ideologies that promote terrorism do not find fertile ground in any nation;
- diminishing the underlying conditions that spawn terrorism by enlisting the international community to focus its efforts and resources on areas most at risk; and
- using effective public diplomacy to promote the free flow of information and ideas to kindle the hopes and aspirations of freedom of those in societies ruled by the sponsors of global terrorism.

While we recognise that our best defence is a good offense, we are also strengthening America's homeland security to protect against and deter attack.

This Administration has proposed the largest government reorganisation since the Truman Administration created the National Security Council and the Department of Defence. Centred on a new Department of Homeland Security and including a new unified military command and a fundamental reordering of the FBI, our comprehensive plan to secure the homeland encompasses every level of government and the cooperation of the public and the private sector.

This strategy will turn adversity into opportunity. For example, emergency management systems will be better able to cope not just with terrorism but with all hazards. Our medical system will be strengthened to manage not just bioterror, but all infectious diseases and mass-casualty dangers. Our border controls will not just stop terrorists, but improve the efficient movement of legitimate traffic.

While our focus is protecting America, we know that to defeat terrorism in today's globalised world we need support from our allies and friends. Wherever possible, the United States will rely on regional organisations and state powers to meet their obligations to fight terrorism. Where governments find the fight against terrorism beyond their capacities, we will match their willpower and their resources with whatever help we and our allies can provide.

As we pursue the terrorists in Afghanistan, we will continue to work with international organisations such as the United Nations, as well as non-governmental organisations, and other countries to provide the humanitarian, political, economic, and security assistance necessary to rebuild Afghanistan so that it will never again abuse its people, threaten its neighbours, and provide a haven for terrorists.

In the war against global terrorism, we will never forget that we are ultimately fighting for our democratic values and way of life. Freedom and fear are at war, and there will be no quick or easy end to this conflict. In leading the campaign against terrorism, we are forging new, productive international relationships and redefining existing ones in ways that meet the challenges of the 21st entury.

### IV. Work with Others to Defuse Regional Conflicts

Concerned nations must remain actively engaged in critical regional disputes to avoid explosive escalation and minimise human suffering. In an increasingly interconnected world, regional crisis can strain our alliances, rekindle rivalries among the major powers, and create horrifying affronts to human dignity. When violence erupts and states falter, the United States will work with friends and partners to alleviate suffering and restore stability.

No doctrine can anticipate every circumstance in which US action—direct or indirect—is warranted. We have finite political, economic, and military resources to meet our global priorities. The United States will approach each case with these strategic principles in mind:

- The United States should invest time and resources into building international relationships and institutions that can help manage local crises when they emerge.
- The United States should be realistic about its ability to help those who are unwilling or unready to help themselves. Where and when people are ready to do their part, we will be willing to move decisively.

The Israeli-Palestinian conflict is critical because of the toll of human suffering, because of America's close relationship with the state of Israel and key Arab states, and because of that region's importance to other global priorities of the United States. There can be no peace for either side without freedom for both sides. America stands committed to an independent and democratic Palestine, living beside Israel in peace and security. Like all other people, Palestinians deserve a government that serves their interests and listens to their voices. The United States will continue to encourage all parties to be aware of their responsibilities as we seek a just and comprehensive settlement to the conflict.

The United States, the international donor community, and the World Bank stand ready to work with a reformed Palestinian government on economic development, increased humanitarian assistance, and a programme to establish, finance, and monitor a truly independent judiciary. If Palestinians embrace democracy, and the rule of law, confront corruption, and firmly reject terror, they can count on American support for the creation of a Palestinian state.

Israel also has a large stake in the success of a democratic Palestine. Permanent occupation threatens Israel's identity and democracy. So the United States continues to challenge Israeli leaders to take concrete steps to support the emergence of a viable, credible Palestinian state. As there is progress towards security, Israel forces need to withdraw fully to positions they held before 28 September 2000. And consistent with the recommendations of the Mitchell Committee, Israeli settlement activity in the occupied territories must stop. As violence subsides, freedom of movement should be restored, permitting innocent Palestinians to resume work and normal life. The United States can play a crucial role but, ultimately, lasting peace can only come when Israelis and Palestinians resolve the issues and end the conflict between them.

In South Asia, the United States has also emphasised the need for India and Pakistan to resolve their disputes. This Administration invested time and resources building strong bilateral relations with India and Pakistan. These strong relations then gave us leverage to play a constructive role when tensions in the region became acute. With Pakistan, our bilateral relations have been bolstered by Pakistan's choice to join the war against terror and move towards building a more open and tolerant society. The Administration sees India's potential to become one of the great democratic powers of the 21st century and has worked hard to transform our relationship accordingly. Our involvement in this regional dispute, building on earlier investments in bilateral relations, looks first to concrete steps by India and Pakistan that can help defuse military confrontation. Indonesia took courageous steps to create a working democracy and respect for the rule of law. By tolerating ethnic minorities, respecting the rule of law, and accepting open markets, Indonesia may be able to employ the engine of opportunity that has helped lift some of its neighbours out of poverty and desperation. It is the initiative by Indonesia that allows US assistance to make a difference.

In the Western Hemisphere we have formed flexible coalitions with countries that share our priorities, particularly Mexico, Brazil, Canada, Chile, and Colombia. Together we will promote a truly democratic hemisphere where our integration advances security, prosperity, opportunity, and hope. We will work with regional institutions, such as the Summit of the Americas process, the Organisation of American States (OAS), and the Defence Ministerial of the Americas for the benefit of the entire hemisphere.

Parts of Latin America confront regional conflict, especially arising from the violence of drug cartels and their accomplices. This conflict and unrestrained narcotics trafficking could imperil the health and security of the United States. Therefore we have developed an active strategy to help the Andean nations adjust their economies, enforce their laws, defeat terrorist organisations, and cut off the supply of drugs, while—as important—we work to reduce the demand for drugs in our own country.

In Colombia, we recognise the link between terrorist and

extremist groups that challenge the security of the state and drug trafficking activities that help finance the operations of such groups. We are working to help Colombia defend its democratic institutions and defeat illegal armed groups of both the left and right by extending effective sovereignty over the entire national territory and provide basic security to the Colombian people.

In Africa, promise and opportunity are juxtaposed with disease, war, and desperate poverty. This threatens both a core value of the United States preserving human dignity—and our strategic priority—combating global terror. American interests and American principles, therefore, lead in the same direction: we will work with others for an African continent that lives in liberty, peace, and growing prosperity. Together with our European allies, we must help strengthen Africa's fragile states, help build indigenous capability to secure porous borders, and help build up the law enforcement and intelligence infrastructure to deny havens for terrorists.

An ever more lethal environment exists in Africa as local civil wars spread beyond borders to create regional war zones. Forming coalitions of the willing and cooperative security arrangements are key to confronting these emerging transnational threats.

Africa's great size and diversity requires a security strategy that focuses on bilateral engagement and builds coalitions of the willing. This Administration will focus on three interlocking strategies for the region:

- Countries with a major impact on their neighbourhood such as South Africa, Nigeria, Kenya, and Ethiopia are anchors for regional engagement and require focused attention;
- Coordination with European allies and international institutions is essential for constructive conflict mediation and successful peace operations; and

- Africa's capable reforming states and sub-regional organisations must be strengthened as the primary means to address transnational threats on a sustained basis.

Ultimately the path of political and economic freedom presents the surest route to progress in sub-Saharan Africa, where most wars are conflicts over material resources and political access often tragically waged on the basis of ethnic and religious difference. The transition to the African Union with its stated commitment to good governance and a common responsibility for democratic political systems offers opportunities to strengthen democracy on the continent.

## V. Prevent Our Enemies from Threatening Us, Our Allies, and Our Friends with Weapons of Mass Destruction

The nature of the Cold War threat required the United States with our allies and friends to emphasise deterrence of the enemy's use of force, producing a grim strategy of mutual assured destruction. With the collapse of the Soviet Union and the end of the Cold War, our security environment has undergone profound transformation.

Having moved from confrontation to cooperation as the hallmark of our relationship with Russia, the dividends are evident: an end to the balance of terror that divided us; an historic reduction in the nuclear arsenals on both sides; and cooperation in areas such as counterterrorism and missile defence that until recently were inconceivable.

But new deadly challenges have emerged from rogue states and terrorists. None of these contemporary threats rival the sheer destructive power that was arrayed against us by the Soviet Union. However, the nature and motivations of these new adversaries, their determination to obtain destructive powers hitherto available only to the world's strongest states, and the greater likelihood that they will use weapons of mass destruction against us, make today's security environment more complex and dangerous.

In the 1990s we witnessed the emergence of a small number of rogue states that, while different in important ways, share a number of attributes. These states:

- brutalise their own people and squander their national resources for the personal gain of the rulers;
- display no regard for international law, threaten their neighbours, and callously violate international treaties to which they are party;
- are determined to acquire weapons of mass destruction, along with other advanced military technology, to be used as threats or offensively to achieve the aggressive designs of these regimes;
- sponsor terrorism around the globe; and
- reject basic human values and hate the United States and everything for which it stands.

At the time of the Gulf War, we acquired irrefutable proof that Iraq's designs were not limited to the chemical weapons it had used against Iran and its own people, but also extended to the acquisition of nuclear weapons and biological agents. In the past decade, North Korea has become the world's principal purveyor of ballistic missiles, and has tested increasingly capable missiles while developing its own WMD arsenal. Other rogue regimes seek nuclear, biological, and chemical weapons as well. These states' pursuit of, and global trade in, such weapons has become a looming threat to all nations.

We must be prepared to stop rogue states and their terrorist clients before they are able to threaten or use weapons of mass destruction against the United States and our allies and friends. Our response must take full advantage of strengthened alliances, the establishment of new partnerships with former adversaries, innovation in the use of military forces, modern technologies, including the development of an effective missile defence system, and increased emphasis on intelligence collection and analysis.

Our comprehensive strategy to combat WMD includes:

- *Proactive counterproliferation efforts.* We must deter and defend against the threat before it is unleashed. We must ensure that key capabilities—detection, active and passive defences, and counterforce capabilities—are integrated into our defence transformation and our homeland security systems. Counterproliferation must also be integrated into the doctrine, training, and equipping of our forces and those of our allies to ensure that we can prevail in any conflict with WMD-armed adversaries.
- *Strengthened nonproliferation efforts to prevent rogue states and terrorists from acquiring the materials, technologies, and expertise necessary for weapons of mass destruction.* We will enhance diplomacy, arms control, multilateral export controls, and threat reduction assistance that impede states and terrorists seeking WMD, and when necessary, interdict enabling technologies and materials. We will continue to build coalitions to support these efforts, encouraging their increased political and financial support for nonproliferation and threat reduction programmes. The recent G-8 agreement to commit up to $20 billion to a global partnership against proliferation marks a major step forward.
- *Effective consequence management to respond to the effects of WMD use, whether by terrorists or hostile states.* Minimising the effects of WMD use against our people will help deter those who possess such weapons and dissuade those who seek to acquire them by persuading enemies that they cannot attain their desired ends. The United States must also be prepared to respond to the effects of WMD use against our forces abroad, and to help friends and allies if they are attacked. *14 National Security Strategy*

It has taken almost a decade for us to comprehend the true nature of this new threat. Given the goals of rogue states and terrorists, the United States can no longer solely rely on a reactive posture as we have in the past. The inability to deter a potential attacker, the immediacy of today's threats, and the magnitude of potential harm that could be caused by our adversaries' choice of weapons, do not permit that option. We cannot let our enemies strike first.

- In the Cold War, especially following the Cuban missile crisis, we faced a generally status quo, risk-averse adversary. Deterrence was an effective defence. But deterrence based only upon the threat of retaliation is less likely to work against leaders of rogue states more willing to take risks, gambling with the lives of their people, and the wealth of their nations.

- In the Cold War, weapons of mass destruction were considered weapons of last resort whose use risked the destruction of those who used them. Today, our enemies see weapons of mass destruction as weapons of choice. For rogue states these weapons are tools of intimidation and military aggression against their neighbours. These weapons may also allow these states to attempt to blackmail the United States and our allies to prevent us from deterring or repelling the aggressive behaviour of rogue states. Such states also see these weapons as their best means of overcoming the conventional superiority of the United States.

- Traditional concepts of deterrence will not work against a terrorist enemy whose avowed tactics are wanton destruction and the targeting of innocents; whose so-called soldiers seek martyrdom in death and whose most potent protection is statelessness. The overlap between states that sponsor terror and those that pursue WMD compels us to action.

For centuries, international law recognised that nations need not suffer an attack before they can lawfully take action to defend themselves against forces that present an imminent danger of attack. Legal scholars and international jurists often conditioned the legitimacy of preemption on the existence of an imminent threat—most often a visible mobilisation of armies, navies, and air forces preparing to attack.

We must adapt the concept of imminent threat to the capabilities and objectives of today's adversaries. Rogue states and terrorists do not seek to attack us using conventional means. They know such attacks would fail. Instead, they rely on acts of terror and, potentially, the use of weapons of mass destruction—weapons that can be easily concealed, delivered covertly, and used without warning.

The targets of these attacks are our military forces and our civilian population, in direct violation of one of the principal norms of the law of warfare. As was demonstrated by the losses on 11 September 2001, mass civilian casualties is the specific objective of terrorists and these losses would be exponentially more severe if terrorists acquired and used weapons of mass destruction.

The United States has long maintained the option of preemptive actions to counter a sufficient threat to our national security. The greater the threat, the greater is the risk of inaction—and the more compelling the case for taking anticipatory action to defend ourselves, even if uncertainty remains as to the time and place of the enemy's attack. To forestall or prevent such hostile acts by our adversaries, the United States will, if necessary, act preemptively.

The United States will not use force in all cases to preempt emerging threats, nor should nations use preemption as a pretext for aggression. Yet in an age where the enemies of civilisation openly and actively seek the world's most destructive technologies, the United States cannot remain idle while dangers gather.

We will always proceed deliberately, weighing the consequences of our actions. To support preemptive options, we will:

- build better, more integrated intelligence capabilities to provide timely, accurate information on threats, wherever they may emerge;
- coordinate closely with allies to form a common assessment of the most dangerous threats; and
- continue to transform our military forces to ensure our ability to conduct rapid and precise operations to achieve decisive results.

The purpose of our actions will always be to eliminate a specific threat to the United States or our allies and friends. The reasons for our actions will be clear, the force measured, and the cause just.

## VI. Ignite a New Era of Global Economic Growth through Free Markets and Free Trade

A strong world economy enhances our national security by advancing prosperity and freedom in the rest of the world. Economic growth supported by free trade and free markets creates new jobs and higher incomes. It allows people to lift their lives out of poverty, spurs economic and legal reform, and the fight against corruption, and it reinforces the habits of liberty.

We will promote economic growth and economic freedom beyond America's shores. All governments are responsible for creating their own economic policies and responding to their own economic challenges. We will use our economic engagement with other countries to underscore the benefits of policies that generate higher productivity and sustained economic growth, including:

- pro-growth legal and regulatory policies to encourage business investment, innovation, and entrepreneurial activity;
- tax policies—particularly lower marginal tax rates—that improve incentives for work and investment;
- rule of law and intolerance of corruption so that people are confident that they will be able to enjoy the fruits of their economic endeavours;
- strong financial systems that allow capital to be put to its most efficient use;
- sound fiscal policies to support business activity;
- investments in health and education that improve the well-being and skills of the labour force and population as a whole; and
- free trade that provides new avenues for growth and fosters the diffusion of technologies and ideas that increase productivity and opportunity.

The lessons of history are clear: market economies, not command-and-control economies with the heavy hand of government, are the best way to promote prosperity and reduce poverty. Policies that further strengthen market incentives and market institutions are relevant for all economies — industrialised countries, emerging markets, and the developing world.

A return to strong economic growth in Europe and Japan is vital to US national security interests. We want our allies to have strong economies for their own sake, for the sake of the global economy, and for the sake of global security. European efforts to remove structural barriers in their economies are particularly important in this regard, as are Japan's efforts to end deflation and address the problems of non-performing loans in the Japanese banking system. We will continue to use our regular consultations with Japan and our European partners—including through the Group of Seven (G-7)—to discuss policies they are adopting to promote growth in their economies and support higher global economic growth.

Improving stability in emerging markets is also key to global economic growth. International flows of investment capital are needed to expand the productive potential of these economies. These flows allow emerging markets and developing countries to make the investments that raise living standards and reduce poverty. Our long-term objective should be a world in which all countries have investment-grade credit ratings that allow them access to international capital markets and to invest in their future.

We are committed to policies that will help emerging markets achieve access to larger capital flows at lower cost. To this end, we will continue to pursue reforms aimed at reducing uncertainty in financial markets. We will work actively with other countries, the International Monetary Fund (IMF), and the private sector to implement the G-7 Action Plan negotiated earlier this year for preventing financial crises and more effectively resolving them when they occur.

The best way to deal with financial crises is to prevent them from occurring, and we have encouraged the IMF to improve its efforts doing so. We will continue to work with the IMF to streamline the policy conditions for its lending and to focus its lending strategy on achieving economic growth through sound fiscal and monetary policy, exchange rate policy, and financial sector policy.

The concept of "free trade" arose as a moral principle even before it became a pillar of economics. If you can make something that others value, you should be able to sell it to them. If others make something that you value, you should be able to buy it.

This is real freedom, the freedom for a person—or a nation—to make a living. To promote free trade, the Unites States has developed a comprehensive strategy:

- *Seize the global initiative.* The new global trade negotiations we helped launch at Doha in November 2001 will have an ambitious agenda, especially in agriculture, manufacturing, and services, targeted for completion in 2005. The United States has led the way in completing the accession of China and a democratic Taiwan to the World Trade Organisation. We will assist Russia's preparations to join the WTO.
- *Press regional initiatives.* The United States and other democracies in the Western Hemisphere have agreed to create the Free Trade Area of the Americas, targeted for completion in 2005. This year the United States will advocate market-access negotiations with its partners, targeted on agriculture, industrial goods, services, investment, and government procurement. We will also offer more opportunity to the poorest continent, Africa, starting with full use of the preferences allowed in the African Growth and Opportunity Act, and leading to free trade.
- *Move ahead with bilateral free trade agreements.* Building on the free trade agreement with Jordan enacted in 2001, the Administration will work this year to complete free trade agreements with Chile and Singapore. Our aim is to achieve free trade agreements with a mix of developed and developing countries in all regions of the world. Initially, Central America, Southern Africa, Morocco, and Australia will be our principal focal points.
- *Renew the executive-congressional partnership.* Every administration's trade strategy depends on a productive partnership with Congress. After a gap of eight years, the Administration reestablished majority support in the

Congress for trade liberalisation by passing Trade Promotion Authority and the other market opening measures for developing countries in the Trade Act of 2002. This Administration will work with Congress to enact new bilateral, regional, and global trade agreements that will be concluded under the recently passed Trade Promotion Authority.

- *Promote the connection between trade and development.* Trade policies can help developing countries strengthen property rights, competition, the rule of law, investment, the spread of knowledge, open societies, the efficient allocation of resources, and regional integration—all leading to growth, opportunity, and confidence in developing countries. The United States is implementing the Africa Growth and Opportunity Act to provide market-access for nearly all goods produced in the 35 countries of sub-Saharan Africa. We will make more use of this act and its equivalent for the Caribbean Basin and continue to work with multilateral and regional institutions to help poorer countries take advantage of these opportunities. Beyond market access, the most important area where trade intersects with poverty is in public health. We will ensure that the WTO intellectual property rules are flexible enough to allow developing nations to gain access to critical medicines for extraordinary dangers like HIV/AIDS, tuberculosis, and malaria.
- *Enforce trade agreements and laws against unfair practices.* Commerce depends on the rule of law; international trade depends on enforceable agreements. Our top priorities are to resolve ongoing disputes with the European Union, Canada, and Mexico and to make a global effort to address new technology, science, and health regulations that needlessly impede farm exports and improved agriculture. Laws against unfair trade practices are often abused, but the international community must be able to address genuine concerns about government subsidies and

dumping. International industrial espionage which undermines fair competition must be detected and deterred.

- *Help domestic industries and workers adjust.* There is a sound statutory framework for these transitional safeguards which we have used in the agricultural sector and which we are using this year to help the American steel industry. The benefits of free trade depend upon the enforcement of fair trading practices. These safeguards help ensure that the benefits of free trade do not come at the expense of American workers. Trade adjustment assistance will help workers adapt to the change and dynamism of open markets.
- *Protect the environment and workers.* The United States must foster economic growth in ways that will provide a better life along with widening prosperity. We will incorporate labour and environmental concerns into US trade negotiations, creating a healthy "network" between multilateral environmental agreements with the WTO, and use the International Labour Organisation, trade preference programmes, and trade talks to improve working conditions in conjunction with freer trade.
- *Enhance energy security.* We will strengthen our own energy security and the shared prosperity of the global economy by working with our allies, trading partners, and energy producers to expand the sources and types of global energy supplied, especially in the Western Hemisphere, Africa, Central Asia, and the Caspian region. We will also continue to work with our partners to develop cleaner and more energy efficient technologies.

Economic growth should be accompanied by global efforts to stabilise greenhouse gas concentrations associated with this growth, containing them at a level that prevents dangerous human interference with the global climate. Our overall objective is to reduce America's greenhouse gas emissions relative to the size of our economy, cutting such emissions per unit of economic activity by 18 per cent over the next ten years, by the year 2012. Our strategies for attaining this goal will be to:

- remain committed to the basic UN Framework Convention for international cooperation;
- obtain agreements with key industries to cut emissions of some of the most potent greenhouse gases and give transferable credits to companies that can show real cuts;
- develop improved standards for measuring and registering emission reductions;
- promote renewable energy production and clean coal technology, as well as nuclear power—which produces no greenhouse gas emissions, while also improving fuel economy for US cars and trucks;
- increase spending on research and new conservation technologies, to a total of $ 4.5 billion—the largest sum being spent on climate change by any country in the world and a $700 million increase over last year's budget; and
- assist developing countries, especially the major greenhouse gas emitters such as China and India, so that they will have the tools and resources to join this effort and be able to grow along a cleaner and better path.

..........................

## VIII. Develop Agendas for Cooperative Action with the Other Main Centres of Global Power

America will implement its strategies by organising coalitions—as broad as practicable — of states able and willing to promote a balance of power that favours freedom. Effective coalition leadership requires clear priorities, an appreciation of others' interests, and consistent consultations among partners with a spirit of humility.

There is little of lasting consequence that the United States can accomplish in the world without the sustained cooperation of its allies and friends in Canada and Europe. Europe is also the seat of two of the strongest and most able international institutions in the world: the North Atlantic Treaty Organisation (NATO), which has, since its inception, been the fulcrum of transatlantic and inter-European security, and the European Union (EU), our partner in opening world trade.

The attacks of 11 September were also an attack on NATO, as NATO itself recognised when it invoked its Article V self-defence clause for the first time. NATO's core mission—collective defence of the transatlantic alliance of democracies— remains, but NATO must develop new structures and capabilities to carry out that mission under new circumstances. NATO must build a capability to field, at short notice, highly mobile, specially trained forces whenever they are needed to respond to a threat against any member of the alliance.

The alliance must be able to act wherever our interests are threatened, creating coalitions under NATO's own mandate, as well as contributing to mission-based coalitions. To achieve this, we must:

- expand NATO's membership to those democratic nations willing and able to share the burden of defending and advancing our common interests;
- ensure that the military forces of NATO nations have appropriate combat contributions to make in coalition warfare;
- develop planning processes to enable those contributions to become effective multinational fighting forces;
- take advantage of the technological opportunities and economies of scale in our defence spending to transform NATO military forces so that they dominate potential aggressors and diminish our vulnerabilities;

- streamline and increase the flexibility of command structures to meet new operational demands and the associated requirements of training, integrating, and experimenting with new force configurations; and
- maintain the ability to work and fight together as allies even as we take the necessary steps to transform and modernise our forces.

If NATO succeeds in enacting these changes, the rewards will be a partnership as central to the security and interests of its member states as was the case during the Cold War. We will sustain a common perspective on the threats to our societies and improve our ability to take common action in defence of our nations and their interests. At the same time, we welcome our European allies' efforts to forge a greater foreign policy and defence identity with the EU, and commit ourselves to close consultations to ensure that these developments work with NATO. We cannot afford to lose this opportunity to better prepare the family of transatlantic democracies for the challenges to come.

The attacks of 11 September energised America's Asian alliances. Australia invoked the ANZUS Treaty to declare that 11 September was an attack on Australia itself, following that historic decision with the dispatch of some of the world's finest combat forces for Operation Enduring Freedom. Japan and the Republic of Korea provided unprecedented levels of military logistical support within weeks of the terrorist attack. We have deepened cooperation on counter-terrorism with our alliance partners in Thailand and the Philippines and received invaluable assistance from close friends like Singapore and New Zealand.

The war against terrorism has proven that America's alliances in Asia not only underpin regional peace and stability, but are flexible and ready to deal with new challenges. To enhance our Asian alliances and friendships, we will:

- look to Japan to continue forging a leading role in regional and global affairs based on our common interests, our common values, and our close defence and diplomatic cooperation;
- work with South Korea to maintain vigilance towards the North while preparing our alliance to make contributions to the broader stability of the region over the longer term;
- build on 50 years of US-Australian alliance cooperation as we continue working together to resolve regional and global problems—as we have so many times from the Battle of the Coral Sea to Tora Bora;
- maintain forces in the region that reflect our commitments to our allies, our requirements, our technological advances, and the strategic environment; and
- build on stability provided by these alliances, as well as with institutions such as ASEAN and the Asia-Pacific Economic Cooperation forum, to develop a mix of regional and bilateral strategies to manage change in this dynamic region.

We are attentive to the possible renewal of old patterns of great power competition. Several potential great powers are now in the midst of internal transition—most importantly Russia, India, and China. In all three cases, recent developments have encouraged our hope that a truly global consensus about basic principles is slowly taking shape.

With Russia, we are already building a new strategic relationship based on a central reality of the 21st century: the United States and Russia are no longer strategic adversaries. The Moscow Treaty on Strategic Reductions is emblematic of this new reality and reflects a critical change in Russian thinking that promises to lead to productive, long-term relations with the Euro-Atlantic community and the United States. Russia's top leaders have a realistic assessment of their country's current weakness and the policies—internal and external—needed to reverse those weaknesses. They understand, increasingly, that Cold War approaches do not serve their national interests and that Russian and American strategic interests overlap in many areas.

United States policy seeks to use this turn in Russian thinking to refocus our relationship on emerging and potential common interests and challenges. We are broadening our already extensive cooperation in the global war on terrorism. We are facilitating Russia's entry into the World Trade Organisation, without lowering standards for accession, to promote beneficial bilateral trade and investment relations. We have created the NATO-Russia Council with the goal of deepening security cooperation among Russia, our European allies, and ourselves. We will continue to bolster the independence and stability of the states of the former Soviet Union in the belief that a prosperous and stable neighbourhood will reinforce Russia's growing commitment to integration into the Euro-Atlantic community.

At the same time, we are realistic about the differences that still divide us from Russia and about the time and effort it will take to build an enduring strategic partnership. Lingering distrust of our motives and policies by key Russian elites slows improvement in our relations. Russia's uneven commitment to the basic values of free-market democracy and dubious record in combating the proliferation of weapons of mass destruction remain matters of great concern. Russia's very weakness limits the opportunities for cooperation. Nevertheless, those opportunities are vastly greater now than in recent years—or even decades.

The United States has undertaken a transformation in its bilateral relationship with India based on a conviction that US interests require a strong relationship with India. We are the two largest democracies, committed to political freedom protected by representative government. India is moving towards greater economic freedom as well. We have a common interest in the free flow of commerce, including through the vital sea lanes of the Indian Ocean. Finally, we share an interest in fighting terrorism and in creating a strategically stable Asia.

Differences remain, including over the development of India's nuclear and missile programmes, and the pace of India's economic reforms. But while in the past these concerns may have dominated our thinking about India, today we start with a view of India as a growing world power with which we have common strategic interests. Through a strong partnership with India, we can best address any differences and shape a dynamic future.

The United States relationship with China is an important part of our strategy to promote a stable, peaceful, and prosperous Asia-Pacific region. We welcome the emergence of a strong, peaceful, and prosperous China. The democratic development of China is crucial to that future. Yet, a quarter century after beginning the process of shedding the worst features of the Communist legacy, China's leaders have not yet made the next series of fundamental choices about the character of their state. In pursuing advanced military capabilities that can threaten its neighbours in the Asia-Pacific region, China is following an outdated path that, in the end, will obstruct its own pursuit of national greatness. In time, China will find that social and political freedom is the only source of that greatness.

The United States seeks a constructive relationship with a changing China. We already cooperate well where our interests overlap, including the current war on terrorism and in promoting stability on the Korean peninsula. Likewise, we have coordinated on the future of Afghanistan and have initiated a comprehensive dialogue on counter terrorism and similar transitional concerns. Shared health and environmental threats, such as the spread of HIV/AIDS, challenge us to promote jointly the welfare of our citizens.

Addressing these transnational threats will challenge China to become more open with information, promote the development of civil society, and enhance individual human rights. China has begun to take the road to political openness, permitting many personal freedoms and conducting village-level elections, yet remains strongly committed to national one-party rule by the Communist Party. To make that nation truly accountable to its citizen's needs and aspirations, however, much work remains to be done. Only by allowing the Chinese people to think, assemble, and worship freely can China reach its full potential.

Our important trade relationship will benefit from China's entry into the World Trade Organisation, which will create more export opportunities and ultimately more jobs for American farmers, workers, and companies. China is our fourth largest trading partner, with over $100 billion in annual two-way trade. The power of market principles and the WTO's requirements for transparency and accountability will advance openness and the rule of law in China to help establish basic protections for commerce and for citizens. There are, however, other areas in which we have profound disagreements. Our commitment to the self-defence of Taiwan under the Taiwan Relations Act is one. Human rights is another. We expect China to adhere to its nonproliferation commitments. We will work to narrow differences where they exist, but not allow them to preclude cooperation where we agree.

The events of 11 September 2001, fundamentally changed the context for relations between the United States and other main centres of global power, and opened vast, new opportunities. With our long-standing allies in Europe and Asia, and with leaders in Russia, India, and China, we must develop active agendas of cooperation lest these relationships become routine and unproductive. Every agency of the United States Government shares the challenge. We can build fruitful habits of consultation, quiet argument, sober analysis, and common action.

In the long-term, these are the practices that will sustain the supremacy of our common principles and keep open the path of progress.

(Source: http://www.whitehouse.gov/nsc/nss.pdf)

# 11. The Indo-US Military Relationship: Expectations and Perceptions October 2002

[Editor's Note: Reproduced below is the Executive Summary of the Report prepared for the Director, Net Assessment, Office of the Secretary of Defence, Government of the United States, in October 2002]

### Executive Summary

**Study Objectives**

Through in-depth interviews, this study explores the thinking of decision-makers in the United States and India who are responsible for building a closer Indo-US military relationship. It examines their understandings of the strategic rationale for the relationship; what the relationship should achieve and what it should avoid; expectations, reservations, and prejudices of each side towards the other; and how each side believes the relationship might best be organised and towards what ends. The Director, Net Assessment, Office of the Secretary of Defence sponsored this study to reveal opportunities for and impediments to military-to-military cooperation that might not be obvious to everyone, expose areas of agreement and misunderstandings that can affect decision-making, and enrich the dialogue between the two sides

**Different Views of the Strategic Environment**

The interview revealed stark differences how the Indians and Americans view Asia generally, and the Indian Ocean region specifically.

For Indian military personnel, strategists and policy-makers alike, India's key strategic interests extend from the Persian Gulf to the Strait of Malacca and from Central Asia to Antarctica: the

"Indian Ocean Basin." They argue that Indian sits in the centre of this region, and that the strategic challenges are interrelated, interactive, and not easily disaggregated into discrete national security problems. Moreover, India aspires to play a larger role in all of the regions that compose the Indian Ocean Basin. Specifically, India seeks to be regarded as "an economic and political role model" and to act as a regional stabiliser. This role will require new and expanded applications of military power. India will endeavour to ensure that no element inimical to India's interests emerges in this region. In particular, this means preventing the Indian Ocean Basin from becoming a battleground for super-power competitions.

The dynamic Indian Ocean Basin is plagued with fragile governments, porous borders, ethnic and religious diversity, economic underdevelopment, and an assertive regional power – China. The threats most frequently cited by the Indians include:

- **China:** China was repeatedly identified as a long-term strategic threat that is "encircling" India and as an economic competitor. For the Indians, the threats posed by China and multidimensional — strategic, military, economic, environmental and social.
- **Pakistan:** Indians view Pakistan as an increasingly destabilising threat for India and the region because of its three-pronged strategy against India: terrorism (sub-conventional warfare), proxy war, and finally, nuclear blackmail, which permits Pakistan to prosecute its sub-conventional strategy; and because of Pakistan's ability to leverage outside linkages to pursue each component of this strategy.
- **Energy Security/ Maritime Security:** Piracy and terrorist threats to energy and merchant traffic threaten the sea-lanes crisscrossing the Indian Ocean. For Indians, ensuring the safe passage of energy and other merchant ships through the Indian Ocean Basin promotes stability across Asia.

- **Demography:** The illegal influx of immigrants from Bangladesh and Nepal foments social tension, particularly between Muslims and Hindus.
- **Transnational Threats:** Narco-trafficking, terrorism, and Islamic fundamentalism are used by states or non-state actors either separately or in combination to threaten India or destabilise the region generally.

Indians would like the United States to play three roles as a strategic partner in their region, as described by an Indian brigadier: Indians expect the United States to be: 1) a stabilising force in the region, 2) a protecting force when shared values and interests may be threatened, and 3) an enabling force that assists India in protecting its own national security interests.

For Americans, the Indian Ocean Basin as defined by the Indians does not exist as one discrete region. US military and policy-making organisations divide Asia into different theatres or regions (e.g. the Middle East, Southeast Asia, Central Asia, Near East, South Asia, Asia-Pacific) and apply multiple and overlapping analytical policy filters that include India in different contexts. Some Americans described the Indian Ocean Basin as lying on the periphery of other important regions that demand American attention (e.g. Middle East, Southeast Asia, Central Asia). Others called it a "strategic crossroads" at which other discrete regions – the Middle East, Southeast Asia, South Asia, and East Africa – converge. From a military perspective, the Indian Ocean is divided down the centre and assigned to two Unified Commands — US Pacific Command (PACOM) and US Central Command (CENTCOM). One American colonel underscored the different strategic views of Asia and the Indian Ocean Basin with this observation:

When you see a map of Asia on the wall at the Indian Ministry of Defence, India sits at the centre of Asia. The Indians see themselves located at the centre of the world. For Americans, India has never been thought of as the centre of Asia, but it lies on the periphery of regions where the United States has national security interests.

Americans consistently defines US concerns in a larger Asian context:

- "Tinderboxes" in Asia – China-Taiwan, the Korean Peninsula, and India-Pakistan.
- Renewed and emboldened insurgent groups in Southeast Asia that will destabilise the region.
- Weak global economy – Globalisation ensures that a weak economy in the United States could destabilise Asian states that are closely tied to the US economy.
- Destabilising transborder threats – migration, narco-trafficking, cross-border terrorism, and piracy.
- Failing states – Lack of good governance in key critical countries (e.g. Indonesia and Pakistan) could have cascading destabilising effects.

For Americans, a strategic and military relationship with India is a hedge against an uncertain and possibly threatening future security environment in Asia. If India is a partner, interviewees argued, the future environment may be less threatening and more easily managed.

**Areas of Strategic Convergence and Divergence**

Interviews revealed that strategic interests converge on many issues, but that the American and Indian interpretation of these issues and their understanding of the role the United States or India should play often differed significantly.

**Sea Lane Protection – "the Most Promising Area of Cooperation."** Protection of the sea lanes of communication (SLOCs) from the Persian Gulf to the Strait of Malacca represents the strongest area of strategic convergence. India and American military officers believe that sea lane protection should include anti-piracy, counter-drug, counter-arms, anti-pollution and environmental remediation, and search and rescue operations. Indian policy-makers cautioned that naval cooperation should go beyond the eastern SLOCs in the Bay of Bengal and Strait of Malacca to include the Strait of Hormuz and the Arabian Sea.

**China.** Indian and American views of China were strikingly similar:

- China is an emerging power regionally and globally whose strategic ambitions and military capabilities cannot be clearly defined.
- A viable, long-term Indo-US relationship cannot be based on "containing" China, although China will loom large in the relationship.
- China must be kept out of the Indian Ocean region.

Indians noted that post-9/11, the Chinese feel "encircled by the Americans", and they worry that China will respond by putting indirect pressure on areas that pose direct challenges to India's security, for example, in Myanmar, Nepal, Pakistan, and in the Persian Gulf.

Virtually all Indians wondered how India factors into US thinking about China. Lurking beneath the surface of most interviews with Indians was a fear that the United States is a fickle and uncertain strategic partner, that it has not made a solid strategic choice to partner with India, and that it might change partners in Asia to India's detriment, as political administrations change.

**Central Asia.** For Indians, Central Asia touches most of their strategic hot buttons: terrorism, encirclement by China, energy exploration and transport, relations with Russia and Iran, proliferation of weapons of mass destruction (WMD), and drug smuggling. It is a region that they know well, where Indians believe many of their strategic interests intersect and converge with US interests, and where cooperation between the United States and India would have a stabilising effect on the region. In contrast, only a few American interviewees cited Central Asia (and Afghanistan) as an important area of Indo-US military cooperation.

**Persian Gulf.** All Indians pointed to the Persian Gulf as a region for potential cooperation and strategic dialogue because five key security interests hinge on or include the Persian Gulf in important ways: energy security, regional stability, future of the Islamic world, WMD proliferation, and counter-terrorism. Most Indian interviewees see many unexplored opportunities for wide-reaching discussions about mutual concerns in the Persian Gulf (or West Asia) and believe that India is uniquely placed for three reasons: 1) India sits in the centre of the Islamic world that spans from Northern Africa to Southeast Asia. 2) India has a close relationship with nearly all Islamic states in the Persian Gulf and Southeast Asia that could be leveraged for mutual benefit. 3) As the second largest Muslim country in the world, India can help the United States understand the "Muslim psyche."

In contrast, fewer than a quarter of the American interviewees – all but two of them were located in Washington – mentioned the Persian Gulf as an area of India's strategic concern and even fewer identified the Persian Gulf as an area where US and Indian interests might converge.

**Non-Proliferation.** Americans and Indians share a commitment to basic non-proliferation principles (e.g. impeding proliferation of WMD to other states and non-state actors, and security all nuclear material and facilities). Moreover, both militaries believe that cooperation on non-proliferation issues would be a "win-win situation." At the same time, both militaries are concerned that non-proliferation policies will continue to plague the military-to-military relationship because a relatively small but determined non-proliferation constituency in the United States refuses to accept India's nuclear capability and treats

India as a proliferator.

Indians assert that non-proliferation will continue to be an obstacle to greater cooperation until the United States accepts India as a nuclear power and treats it as a nuclear "friend." Indians complained about what they see as different policies coming from the US Department of State – which tends to treat India as a dangerous "proliferator" – and the US Department of Defence (DOD) – which accepts India's nuclear capability and wants to embrace India as a strategic partner.

**War on Terrorism.** The war on terrorism created a new context and impetus for the Indo-US relationship. Despite the success of existing counter-terrorism initiatives under the Joint Working Group on Terrorism, American and Indians cited three reasons for doubting sustained convergence on counter-terrorism: American and Indians define the terrorist threat differently (e.g. regional versus international view of the threat); divergent views on the roots and sources of terrorism (e.g. Pakistan is the root of the problem, not part of the solution); and Indian concerns about spill over during the next phase of the US war on terrorism, particularly if the next phase of the campaign destabilises the Persian Gulf.

**Common Democratic Values.** Both Indians and Americans claim that democracy is an important rationale for a military relationship and both extol the virtue of spreading democratic values but the rhetoric about democratic values also engenders cynicism among the Indians, who bridle at US tolerance of undemocratic Pakistan. Moreover, Indians believe that the appropriate "democratic" model is better attuned to the challenges faced by developing countries; and second, Indians have more confidence in democracy's resilience and strength to organise and stabilise societies.

**Economic Cooperation.** Indians and Americans agree that a strong economic relationship will bolster military cooperation and will be the "glue" of an enduring relationship. Moreover, Indians believe that increased US economic stakes in India will mitigate the unpredictability of congressional policies aimed at India and could reduce the risk of future sanctions.

Americans believe if a robust economic relationship is to develop, the responsibility for building this foundation lies solely with the Indians – India must create the environment that will attract US business. In contrast, many Indians believe that a stronger Indo-US economic relationship will naturally flow from a strategic relationship, as was the case when the United States "opened China" in the early 1970s. An underlying theme emerges from all the Indian interviews: India is opening to the world, and it is an opportunity for the United States either to seize or to lose.

**Pakistan.** American and Indian perceptions diverge fundamentally on the nature or extent of US involvement in the Indo-Pakistan conflict. Americans tend to believe that the United States should play a role in resolving this historic conflict; that without US intervention of some kind a conflict might escalate out of control; and that solving the Kashmir conflict will fundamentally change the region, freeing the United States of having to choose sides each time a crisis erupts. For Americans, the United States is trying to balance short-term, crisis management priorities in the war on terrorism with Pakistan, with a long-term objective of building a strategic relationship with India.

In contrast, most Indians rejected any role for the United States as a peace-maker/mediator between India and Pakistan in the Kashmir dispute and doubt that the problems between India and Pakistan will be resolved with an agreement over Kashmir. The route of the problem with Pakistan lies not with Kashmir but with the Pakistani's anti-India ideology. Therefore, Indians stressed that the US role in the Indo-Pakistan conflict should be confined to putting strong pressure on Pakistan to change the character of the Pakistani state – e.g. to make it democratic, economically viable, and terrorist free. For Indians, Pakistan has successfully kept India tied down and prevented India from being able to extend itself beyond South Asia. One Indian strategic thinker described Pakistan as a "ball and chain around India's neck."

Americans' characterisations of US relations with India and Pakistan ranged from "the United States is sitting on the hyphen between Pakistan and India, trying to jawbone both sides" to "the United States will not balance its policy between the two states but treat each state based on its own merits." Indians argued that former characterisation of US policy best reflects US actions, and warn against any attempt to balance US relations with two states that are not equal – India is superior in all areas and has more to offer the United States.

**India's Relationship with Russia.** For Indians, Russia represents India's "most dependable strategic partner" – which includes being a reliable weapons supplier – and its most valuable "strategic option." Indians continue to harbour deeply held fears that the American tendency "to view the world as black and white" might force India to choose between the United States and Russia or limit its relationship with Russia. Indians asserted that any relationship with the United States must be "mutually exclusive." But many Indians (mostly retired military officers also argued that if they had to choose tomorrow between the United States and Russia they would opt for Russia – the suppliers of 70 per cent of its military equipment and joint-development agreements – due to the current uncertainty about access to advanced US technologies and the possible unreliability of the United States as a supplier. Nevertheless, over the medium and long-term, the Indian military seeks to reduce its dependence on Russia by diversifying defence suppliers, particularly since Russia no longer offers the special ruble-rupee deals that India enjoyed during the Soviet era.

In contrast, Americans were not worried about India's strategic relationship with Russia, though many conceded that residual American suspicion of the Indo-Russia relationship will influence technology transfer decisions.

### Military Cooperation: Objectives, Priorities, Approaches

The interviews suggest that Indians and Americans have different ideas about the ultimate objectives for a military-to-military relationship and how to achieve them.

**The American View.** The US military wants a capable partner in Asia that can take on more responsibility for low-end operations in Asia; that provides new training opportunities; and that will ultimately provide basing and access for US power projection. For many, India is the most attractive partner in the region because of its strategic location and size and relative sophistication of its military. Eventual US military access to Indian military infrastructure would represent a critical "strategic hedge" against dramatic or evolutionary changes in traditional US relationships in Asia (e.g. Japan, South Korea and Saudi Arabia). To achieve these objectives, American military officers seek to build trust, communication, and understanding of each other's systems through service-to-service initiatives (e.g. joint training exercises, multilateral exercises, IMET exchanges), focusing on areas where both militaries benefit, such as high-altitude training, joint exercises with special forces, and search and rescue exercises. Over time, they believe that the military relationship should result in shared technology and capabilities; and ultimately they would like to be able to respond jointly to regional crises.

**The Indian View.** The Indian priorities for building a military relationship are the reverse. Although they recognise that the relationship will develop slowly, they demand tangible and immediate results that demonstrate the United States' commitment.

- *Technology Transfer: India's Touchstone Issue*. Most Indians explicitly linked technology cooperation (or technology transfer) to success at other levels of military cooperation (e.g. service-to-service cooperation and strategic dialogue). Indians' concerns about husbanding and applying technology arise from India's historical experience of repeatedly being defeated by invaders with superior historical experience of repeatedly being defeated by invaders with superior technology. The message from the Indians at all levels was nearly uniform: Technology transfer must be the engine of the relationship and the "acid test" of US commitment. For Indians, technology transfer carries both practical and symbolic importance. Regarding the latter, technology transfer demonstrates US confidence and trust in the relationship, confirms American understanding of India's strategic importance, and signals that the United States will treat India as a friend.

- *Increased US Investment in the Indian Defence Sector.* For most Indians, the centrepiece of any military relationship will be economic. Linking the two defence industrial bases (DIBs) will create many opportunities for collabouration (e.g. space cooperation, co-development, cooperative research and development), and will insulate the relationship from political changes (in either country) and policy disagreements.

- *A Partnership of Equals*. All Indian interviewees warned that only a military-to-military relationship based on equality would be acceptable to Indian leadership. They expect "an adult-to-adult" relationship, not a "patron-client" or a "parent-child" relationship. For Indians, equality means how they are treated more than what should be expected of them.

- *Reciprocity*. Indians believe that equal treatment is embodied, above all else, in reciprocity. For example, the Indians complained of an "asymmetry of access" in which the

Americans are receiving greater access to Indian officials in Delhi than Indians are receiving to Americans in Washington, and warned that if this persisted, it could slowly strangle the relationship because it gives the Indians the appearance of a "patron-client" arrangement.

- *Normalcy*. Indian policy-makers want a normal relationship in which India is treated the same way the United States would treat its other friends and allies.
- *Symbiosis*. Indians believe that they will benefit from the military relationship if they are connected to infrastructure on the continental United States (CONUS).
- *Sensitivity*. Indians want American policy-makers to be more sensitive to India's concerns and interests in its "extended security horizon." This includes increased consultation in developing security policy in regions of shared concern that have a direct or indirect impact on India's security interests.

In an obvious contradiction, Indians expect the US military, as the "senior partner," to take the lead in building the military-to-military relationship. For the Indian military, all actions required to push the relationships forward (e.g. treating India an equal partner giving India assess to technology, building a robust economic relationship) rest on American shoulders, no the Indians.

**Impediments to Building an Enduring Strategic Relationships**

The interviews revealed that both the US and Indian systems are poorly organised to build a robust military relationship that maximises the strategic benefits for both sides.

Both sides complained about the bureaucratic hurdles in each other's system. Indians complained that the US bureaucracy can be as impenetrable and non-responsive as the Indian bureaucracy, particularly the US licensing process. Many Americans accuse their Indian counterparts of being "non-responsive" because Indian communication with their American counterparts are inevitably late, incomplete, or non-existent, and they describe the Indian bureaucracy as rigid and centralised, and unwilling to support individual decision-making. Americans and Indians agreed that as the Indo-US military relationship begins to evolve beyond high-level talks, it will and in some cases, already has confronted structural constraints and institutional obstacles on both sides.

**On the US side:**

**The PACOM-CENTCOM Divide.** India sits along the PACOM and CENTCOM seam, thereby confusing both the strategic rationale for engaging India and the organisational means to do so. Both Americans and Indians understand that India is lost in a kind of "strategic ether" between two powerful unified commands. The Indians asked repeatedly why the US military divides South Asia down the middle, when it makes perfect sense to them to join strategic issues that stretch through India from the Persian Gulf to Southeast Asia. This divide frustrates the Indians for three reasons:

- PACOM covers only half of India's strategic interests and concerns. Indians argue that many of India's most pressing strategic concerns and the areas, in their minds, most conducive to Indo-US military cooperation lie outside the PACOM's area of responsibility (AOR): countering cross-border terrorism and Islamic fundamentalism; promoting stability in Central Asia, Afghanistan, and the Persian Gulf; and protecting energy flows from the Persian Gulf.
- This CENTCOM-PACOM divide creates serious breakdowns in communications between Washington and Delhi on these important issues, as was the case immediately after the terrorist attacks of 9/11. The message conveyed by the Indians was nearly uniform: they believe PACOM has neither the authority nor the means to engage the US military across India's full range of strategic interests.

- Indians note that they frequently seek to bypass PACOM by going straight to Washington to talk about issues that extend beyond the PACOM AOR or fall outside PACOM's authority (e.g. technology transfer).

In contrast, most Americans touted the benefits of dividing India and Pakistan into separate AORs, arguing that including both states in the same AOR would compromise the credibility of each commander and make it impossible for them to build trust and forge a satisfactory relationship with either state. Americans believe that Indians fundamentally misunderstand the unified commands' central role in designing and executing the military's security cooperation programmes, which includes wielding power and authority and allocating the bulk of resources. (Indians counter that they understand the US structure perfectly. They are not adverse to dealing with PACOM, but PACOM fails to serve all their interests both geographically and functionally).

**Lack of Common US Engagement Objectives, Guidelines, and Practices.** No shared view of India's importance to US national security interests emerged from the interviews. Moreover, the interviews reveal that no common vision or programmatic guidelines inform the way different US military organisations identify priorities or build engagement plans with India, leading to confusion, inconsistency, and, occasionally, contradictions among those DOD elements entrusted with building a military-to-military relationship. Different offices responsible for policy planning for the Office of the Secretary of Defence (OSD), the services and the Joint Staff all place India in different strategic or operational contexts. India's strategic location in Asia is defined in at least five distinct ways – Asia-Pacific; Middle East, Africa, and South Asia; South and Southeast Asia; Southeast and Central Asia; and Near East/South Asia. Both Americans and Indians observed that the US engagement process lacks coordination and that few linkages appear to exist between the different components of a military-to-military relationship (e.g. foreign military sales and counter visits on one side, and security cooperation initiatives on the other). The organisations responsible for these different components of the relationship appear to base their decision on different priorities and requirements, and each develops and implements its programme with little understanding of how its decision and activities might affect the activities of other US national security entities.

These different approaches confuse the Indians, who sense a dichotomy on the American side between security cooperation strategy that flows from PACOM, on the one hand, and, on the other, the means to achieve it – i.e. high level exchanges, technology transfer, and foreign military sales (FMS) – that flow exclusively from the service headquarters. They argue that their natural inclination is to bypass PACOM to deal directly with service headquarters in Washington.

**"Owning" India: Long on Rhetoric and Short on Leadership and Resources.** Many Americans believe the Indo-US relationship requires that senior military leaders assume "ownership" of this rapidly evolving relationship. They worry that US commitment to the new relationship is not deep enough to build trust with the Indians because real commitment will require that US policy in other areas – such as space, non-proliferation, nuclear policy, and arms exports – change. The consensus view among American military interviewees [as of February 2002] is that no senior leadership has assumed "ownership" of security cooperation with India.

**On the Indian side:**

**India Lacks the Bureaucratic Capacity to Support the Relationship.** Many Americans believe that India's organisational structure and its bureaucracy lack the capacity to support broad-based military cooperation and that these structural factors could dampen enthusiasm for engaging India in the future because its persistent unresponsiveness shapes the perceptions of future military leaders, who then might be less willing to work with the Indians. Americans identify three potential problems that stem from India's bureaucratic structure.

- *Asymmetry in Institutional Capacity.* India lacks the institutional capability to support a broad-based relationship. Americans who interface with the MOD and military services have the impression that their Indian counterparts can handle only one initiative at a time.
- *Chokepoints in Bureaucratic Channels Impede Programmes.* The Indian military's insulation from foreigners, except with approval of the Directorate General for Military Intelligence (DGMI), impedes programme initiatives and the development of personal relationships.
- *Centralised Decision-making Contributes to Non-responsiveness and Indecisiveness.* India's highly centralised decision-making process in the MOD contrasts greatly from the US system in which decision-making is decentralised and responsibility is delegated downward. Americans believe that India's structure slows the decision-making process significantly because lower level staff have little authority to make decisions, and more opportunities exist for issues to die before they reach decision-makers.

**Civilian Control of the Military.** Many active and retired Indian military officers convey a uniform message: The Indian military must act within the highly restrictive boundaries created by their political leadership. For this reason, the Indian military prefers a top-down approach to building a relationship. They note that unprecedented agreement within the Indian establishment to build a military-to-military relationship with the United States has lowered many internal obstacles that obstructed direct military contact in the past, and the success of the reinvigorated Defence Policy Group (DPG) has provided Indian military officers with the political "cover" to discuss and plan security cooperation initiatives in more detail at an operational level at the service ESGs.

**Department of State: A Major Impediment.** Americans and Indians believe the US Department of State represents a serious obstacle to developing the military-to-military relationship because it does not share DOD's longer term strategic view, and it possesses the power to stall the licensing process for technology transfer.

## Indian and American Perceptions of Each Other

The interviews revealed strongly held and often contradictory perceptions by the Indians and Americans of each other. Several themes emerged clearly from the interviews:

**Mutual Admiration.** All Indian military officers emphasised that their perceptions of the US military are shaped by great respect and admiration for the US military and the United States as a country. American views of the Indians range from being a professional and well-trained potential partner in Asia to a capable military constrained by poor quality equipment and infrastructure. American and Indian military offices argued that if the two militaries were left alone, they could naturally build a strong military relationship, observing that in the past, political obstacles repeatedly blocked progress.

**Persistent Distrust.** The Indians and Americans approach the prospects of a military-to-military relationship with persistent, and in some cases, deep-seated distrust that stems from different sources:

**From the Indian side:**

- *United States' Decades-long Support for Pakistan.* Indians worry that the US military's past experience and comfort level with the Pakistani military might undermine cooperation because it generates a "default US response to depend on Pakistan" to address problems in the region.

The US immediate response to the terrorist attacks on 9/11 reinforced this perception.

- *Unreliable Partner and Supplier.* All Indians questioned the willingness of the United States to enter into long-term strategic relationships. The America that Indians see is quick to entice and then dismiss strategic partners when US interests change, and the Indians pointed repeatedly to America's on-again-off-again relationships with Pakistan and China as evidence. In particular, Indians distrust the United States as a potential supplier of arms and equipment because of the US Congress' history of curtailing the transfer of supplies and technology to India from the United States and from third parties.

- *Uncertainty about America's Larger Strategic Vision.* Indians repeatedly asked: what does the United States want in India's part of the world, and where does India fit in this vision? Why is the United States so interested in India now/ they worry about US intentions in the region because they do not fully understand them? This uncertainty engenders anxiety about what the Indian military might have to give in any relationship with the United States.

- *US Superpower Status Could Limit India's Options.* Indians are resigned to the world being unipolar for many decades, recognising that the United States will have the ability to act alone for the foreseeable future. For this reason, Indian military officers, in particular, believe that India must engage the US military. But this realisation also raises fears of India losing its freedom of action and strategic options, even when US and Indian interests coincide, and of the second and third order consequences of US actions that might have a direct impact on Indian security concerns.

- *American Ignorance of India's Political Culture.* Indians characterise most Americans as being ignorant of India's history and the complexities of India's internal political culture, which Indians insist influence and often constrain their policy choices and strategies.

**From the American side:**

- *Indo-Soviet/ Russia Relationship.* American views are shaped by India's past close relationship with the Soviet Union and its ongoing supplier/co-production relationship with Russia. One American colonel commented that the US Government continues to be uncomfortable about sharing technology with India if "Russian scientists are running around the country."
- *Negative Experiences Working with the Indians in the Past.* Some Americans do not trust the Indians and believe the Indian assertions about China and Pakistan are designed to manipulate US policy to achieve India's security objectives.
- *Inadequate Export Laws and Procedures.* Americans worry about the potential leakage of technology owing to India's lack of export laws and procedures to guarantee the safeguarding of technologies.
- *Indian Sensitivity about Sovereignty.* Americans described Indians as hypersensitive about their "sovereignty", which, Americans believe, stems from India's history of foreign occupation. Consequently, Indians tend to view every unwanted/ unanticipated American action with great suspicion and concern that it might adversely affect India's security or undermine its freedom of action.
- *Indians' Protocol Consciousness.* In American eyes, Indians are too protocol conscious, which leads to small missteps posing disproportionate difficulties to the relationship. A common theme from Americans is that, for Indians, the act is much more important than the substance; the theory is more important than the execution; and the tactic is

more important than the strategy.

**Most Promising Opportunity for Cooperation**

Americans and Indians broadly agree that naval cooperation represents one of the most promising areas of service-to-service cooperation for a number of reasons:

- Naval cooperation supports the strongest area of strategic convergence – sea lane protection.
- Naval cooperation in the Strait of Malacca represents the first concrete example of Indo-US military cooperation.
- The Indian Navy is best equipped to lead military cooperation with the US military because its mission dovetails naturally with the larger cooperation agenda.
- Naval cooperation can occur without causing political anxieties in India – the US Navy leaves no "footprint" in India.
- India's Joint Eastern Command on the Nicobar Island represents the only joint structure in the Indian military.

(Source: The Indo-US Military Relationship: Expectations and Perceptions, October 2002. Prepared for the Director, Net Assessment, Office of the Secretary of Defence, US Government, pp. iii-xv.)

# 12. Speech by Russian Ambassador, Mr. Alexander M. Kadakin, at a Seminar on "Indo-Russian Strategic Partnership" held under the auspices of Indian Defence Review, New Delhi, 29 November 2002

Relations between Russia and India have a long and rich history. At all times. These were not merely contacts between two powers but profound, sincere and highly inspired civilisation interaction of two friends that know and understand each other well. On the threshold of the new age, when Russia, in the words of the 19th century Chancellor Prince Alexander Gorchakov, was "concentrating", having abandoned a number of olden illusions was building a new model of development in a radically changed international environment. We have cherished our adherence to the basic interests, with one constant – friendly and durable relations with India immune to considerations of expediency.

Two years ago the President of Russia, Vladimir Putin, and the Prime Minster of India, A. B. Vajpayee, signed the Declaration on Strategic Partnership. This innovative document not only heralded the recognition of the proximity of national interests and geopolitical priorities, but also signified mutual readiness to act together in the international arena and continue advancing our relations on the basis of trust, taking into account each other's interests and concerns for decades to come.

Our strategic partnership has become a weighty contribution of our countries to today's diplomacy, having completed the transition from the bipolar configuration of confrontation towards equal and mutually beneficial cooperation. Our ties have not lost their historical mileage and have not shrunk to *realpolitik* pragmatism. Together we advocate the ideals of equality and non-violence, supremacy of international law amidst the central role of the United Nations; we jointly fight on the anti-terror front and react to world crises, searching for ways of responding to new challenges and threats, and closely cooperate in the United Nations and other international organisations.

Our partnership in foreign policy has evolved into a major factor of international life and has acquired a global dimension. Among our achievements one can name earnest participation in the disarmament process, active protection of non-proliferation principles, mutual support in preventing the militarisation of space and subject-wise cooperation in addressing the problems of the Afghan settlement.

Bilateral cooperation in our fight against international terrorism has become a tangible embodiment of strategic partnership. In this field, Moscow and New Delhi stand as old and time-tested allies. It is worth recalling our joint activities in Afghanistan long before and during the anti-terrorist campaign. We cooperate not only in the framework of the global antiterrorist coalition but also bilaterally, as we stated in the Moscow Declaration on International Terrorism signed in November 2001 during Prime Minister A. B. Vajpayee's visit to Russia. There exists an institutionalised departmental interaction on anti-terrorism within the framework of joint working groups of the Security Councils and Foreign Offices. We work together at promoting in the United Nations the Indian Draft Comprehensive Convention on Combating International Terrorism and the Russian Draft Convention for the Suppression of Acts of Nuclear Terrorism.

Our countries share a common vision of a peaceful and stable South Asia. The near-crisis tensions of the summer of 2002 have shown that terrorism can damage the system of interstate relations and global stability, if there is a temptation to garb international bandits as "freedom fighters" or use them for accomplishing some foreign policy agenda.

It is exactly this threat that emanates from extremist groups that found shelter in Pakistan-controlled territories. We pay tribute to Indian leadership's wisdom, restraint and political acumen for having taken steps to reduce tensions and, hopefully, eventually having taken the option of a diplomatic settlement of bilateral issues. We hope that Pakistan will fully and unconditionally deliver on its promises to put an end to cross-border terrorism and eliminate the terror infrastructure on its territory, thus opening up avenues for a resumed long-overdue peaceful dialogue between India and Pakistan on the whole gamut of bilateral issues.

The lesson learnt from the recent India-Pakistan crisis is that the countries, claiming the right to possess nuclear capacities should be enrolled in a system of internationally recognised safeguards and obligations which would create for them common space for security and responsibility.

Russia's viewpoint on the Kashmir problem remains unchanged – i.e. peaceful bilateral negotiations on the basis of the Simla Agreement of 1972 and the Lahore Accords, without internationalisation, and any outside interference or mediation. Another thing also becomes clear: regardless of one's mindset on the Kashmir problem, terrorism only aggravates, rather than solves it. One should proceed not from the assumption that the Kashmir issue hampers the normalisation of relations but that the cessation of cross-border acts of terror and overall normalisation of relations will remove barriers to resolving the problems.

The Russian diplomacy in its South Asian vector is open and balanced, drawing from age-old trust of the regional countries. One of the recent examples is the President of Russia Vladimir Putin's personal involvement when in June 2001 he met the leaders of India and Pakistan in Alma-Aty. It was those meetings that signalled the gradual de-escalation of tensions in the India-Pakistan confrontation, which by then had almost reached a boiling point. We do not want and will not don the mantle of a mediator but world rather be ready to catalyse the two countries' advancement towards mutual understanding. At the same time, in no way are we going to shut the door for a constructive dialogue with Pakistan if it genuinely eliminates all elements of its terror infrastructure.

Bilateral and multilateral interaction on the pan-Asian problems and regional issues in Central Asia, South-East Asia and Asia-Pacific is one of the priorities of the Russian-Indian strategic partnership. Russia, as a Eurasian power, is naturally interested in seeing Asia as a peaceful, sustainable, economically growing and integrated continent, free from geopolitical rivalry or claims for dominance, whatever their source.

We think that our Indian partners' interest in the activities of the Shanghai Organisation of Cooperation (SOC) is justified. The process of the SOC's coming of age and developing into a well-established system is nearing completion. This is an open organisation with a broad all-Asia agenda.

The approaches of Russia and India to reforming the UN are close. For the Security Council to be more sustainable and balanced, it has to include at a certain juncture most influential developing countries, with India a frontrunner among the candidates.

The fact that the positions of Moscow and New Delhi on most international issues coincide is not a reflection of any kind of compromise. At its basis lie the historically syntonised commonality of vital national interests. But, nuances or differences in approaches on certain matters exist which is quite logical and natural. We are not inclined to dramatise them.

For instance, India is one of our key partners in international cooperation on the whole gamut of issues relating to strategic stability, nuclear and missile non-proliferation and disarmament. This happens despite India's unwillingness to join the CTBT and its criticism of the NPT. We believe it was correct when in 1998, after the nuclear explosions notwithstanding the fact that we did not like it at all; we did not impose any sanctions against India. Our cooperation in the peaceful use of nuclear energy is progressing successfully.

The two years of Russian-Indian strategic partnership have been marked with unprecedented intensity of the bilateral agenda. Close and regular confidential contacts with President Putin and Prime Minister Vajpayee have become an annual affair and serve as a beacon for bilateral relations at all levels. These include meetings between the Foreign Ministers and Foreign Offices, interdepartmental consultations, parliamentary and cultural exchanges and, finally, grassroots contacts and mutual affection between common people that have become a well-established and deep-rooted popular tradition.

A solid legal basis for economic and investment cooperation has been created. It covers a wide range of interstate and interdepartmental agreements in a number of specific spheres including such projects as the international "North-South" transport corridor and the joint production of the IL-214 airliner. Russia participates in the construction of hydel-power stations and highways on the Indian soil, in erection and reconstruction of metallurgical plants, prospecting for oil and natural gas in the Bay of Bengal. Investment cooperation has received a powerful boost after ONGC had invested $ 1.7 billion into the promising "Sakhalin-I" project. This year the construction of the $ 2 billion "Kudankulam" nuclear power plant in India's South with Russia's participation has started.

The amplitude of our interaction is really impressive – from the ocean depths high into the sky. But even the sky is not the limit for us. The recent launch of an Indian Satellite with Russian technologies is a vivid illustration of our long-standing cooperation in peaceful exploration of the outer space. Joint production of hi-tech, razor-edge equipment remains a priority in our economic ties.

Our military and technical cooperation is progressing successfully. Its feature nowadays is a smooth transition from the "pay and bye" relations to joint long-term programmes of scientific and production cooperation between the military-industrial complexes of two countries, transfer of licenses and technologies of the most up-to-date military hardware. A mighty, stable and prospering India meets the national interests of the Russian Federation.

Strategic partnership is the optimal model of bilateral and foreign policy interaction between Russia and India today, aimed at a long-term prospect. It has convincingly proved its vitality and efficiency and is acquiring global importance. We look into the future with confidence. Relations with India are amongst the highest priorities of Russia's foreign policy. It is no wonder that they are the subjects of close and permanent attention personally by the President of Russia. The forthcoming visit to India of President Putin will no doubt expand considerably. Our partnership's agenda will open up news vistas of cooperation in all fields and will help further strengthen the tradition of affection and amity for each other.

The outstanding Russian artist and philosopher, Nicholas K. Roerich, who made India his second home, very aptly described the feelings of our nations towards each other:

"India's heart is reaching for the infinite Russia. The great Indian magnet is attracting Russian hearts. How joyful it is to see vitality in Indian-Russian ties... There exists beauty in the Indian-Russian magnet."

*No doubt, these prophetic words of the "Indian Maharishi", as Nicholas Roerich was named by Prime Minister A. B. Vajpayee remain true today. This powerful and mysterious magnet will forever attract the two great nations towards each other.*

(Source: Text of the Speech as distributed at the Seminar)

# 13. Delhi Declaration on Further Consolidation of Strategic Partnership between the Republic of India and the Russian Federation

## New Delhi, 4 December 2002

[Editor's Note: This Declaration was signed by President Vladimir Putin of Russia and Prime Minister Atal Behari Vajpayee of India during the former's visit to New Delhi.]

The Republic of India and the Russian Federation, - relying on long-standing traditions of friendship' and good-neighbourliness; - recalling the Treaty of Friendship and Cooperation between the Republic of India and the Russian Federation of 28 January 1993 and the Declaration on Strategic Partnership between the Republic of India and the Russian Federation of 5 October 2000; - proceeding from the fact that the strategic partnership between India and Russia is founded on the complementarity of national interests and geopolitical priorities of the two countries; - determined to elevate their strategic partnership to an even higher and qualitatively new level in both bilateral and international arenas; - recognising respect for national sovereignty, territorial integrity, plurality, diversity and tolerance as the cornerstone of a stable and enduring multi-polar world; - recognising also their unique role and responsibility as multi-ethnic and pluralistic States in contributing to a stable world order, as envisaged in the United Nations Millennium Declaration of 8 September 2000 and the Moscow Declaration by the Republic of India and the Russian Federation of 30 June 1994 on the Protection of Interests of Pluralistic States, and in contributing to peace, stability and prosperity in Asia and all over the world; - determined to counter new challenges and threats to security - primarily international terrorism - through mechanisms of bilateral and multilateral cooperation; hereby declare:

Our strategic partnership provides a solid framework for long-term and all-round development of relations. Mutual security, development and prosperity of our peoples are core objectives of this partnership. It also contributes to countering global challenges and threats and promoting strategic stability at the international level. The established practice of holding annual meetings at summit level as well as at Ministerial and working levels, and exchanges between Parliamentary, judicial and other constitutional bodies would be further intensified. There would be particular emphasis on deepening the economic content of bilateral relations. People-to-people contacts would be strengthened through an expanding network of ties between the two societies. Internationally accepted standards of democracy and the rule of law, as enshrined in our respective Constitutions, are basic components of our political systems. They are reliable guarantees for a pluralistic political, social and economic framework and for the promotion and protection of the aspirations of our peoples for human rights, life with dignity, and freedom from want and fear. These are standards which shall also guide our relations with other countries. As large multi-ethnic and pluralistic states, we are convinced of our special responsibility to combat and bring to an end challenges posed to our unique attributes, including our territorial integrity, by forces of terrorism, extremism and separatism. We reiterate our support for each other's territorial integrity and respect for each other's sovereignty, enshrined in our respective Constitutions. Neither side shall take any actions which might threaten or impair the security of the other. Both sides shall be guided by this principle in determining their security and defence policies as well as in military technical cooperation with third countries.

Bilateral cooperation as well as cooperation with other countries would be further enhanced to meet the various challenges of globalisation, in particular the mitigation of its negative manifestations. Globalisation and national identity represent complementary components of world order. Recognition of and respect for diversity is a necessary precondition for human progress, and an essential component of the Dialogue between Civilisations. Enduring ties of friendship, trust and confidence and commonality of interests confer on India and Russia a unique capability to contribute to the evolution of a new world order, which would be stable, secure, equitable and sustainable and will be based on the respect for the principles of the UN Charter and international law. To fulfil this vision, both sides would endeavour to strengthen relevant international institutions and mechanisms. Both countries reaffirm that now more than ever before there is a need for the international community to commit itself to the UN and multilateralism. Both countries favour strengthening of the UN's central role in promoting international security in a multipolar world. They stand for enhancing the efficiency of the UN and its Security Council and making them more reflective of the contemporary geo-political and economic realities and rendering them more representative of the interests of the vast majority of the UN members by completing the process of rationally reforming the Organisation based on the broadest consensus of its member-states. In this context, Russia reaffirms its support to India as a strong and appropriate candidate for permanent membership in an expanded United Nations Security Council. We take note of the outcome of the World Summit on Sustainable Development at Johannesburg and in this context, welcome the reaffirmation of the Rio principles. Taking note of the importance attached to the issue of climate change by both the countries, we welcome the results of the Eighth Conference of Parties to the United Nations Framework Convention on Climate Change hosted by India in October-November 2002 and the initiative of the President of the Russian Federation to convene in Moscow in Autumn 2003 the World Conference on Climate Change.

Both the countries reiterate their commitment to work

towards a new cooperative security order that recognises the legitimate security interests of all countries and promotes global peace and stability at lower levels of armaments, and strengthens non-proliferation and disarmament goals. India and Russia are convinced that the promotion of the disarmament process, including reduction and eventual elimination of nuclear weapons, is one of the most important components of security both in Asia and in the world at large. We call for early start of multilateral talks aimed at preparing a comprehensive arrangement on non-deployment of weapons in outer space, non-use or threat of use of force in respect of space-based objects and preserving the use of space for a full-range of cooperative, peaceful and developmental activities. Situation in our common neighbourhood – Afghanistan and Central Asia – is of vital security interest to both the countries. We feel that there is a need to continuously assess the evolving Afghan situation and intend to continue and expand the close cooperation on Afghanistan. We welcome the successful implementation of the Bonn Agreement and extend full support to the Transitional Administration, aimed at promoting national reconciliation, reconstruction of the Afghan economy and rebuilding the Afghan institutions, including indigenous security structures, which are important for countering and defeating internal and external threats to Afghanistan's security. India and Russia agree to cooperate closely in the reconstruction efforts in Afghanistan and agreed that these should be driven by Afghan priorities. We underline the need for the United Nations and the international community to remain engaged for ensuring the revival of Afghanistan as a sovereign and independent state, free from terrorism, drugs and external interference. Both sides have a vital interest in maintaining security, stability and a secular order in the Central Asian region. We call for containment of the spiral of violence in the Middle East and resumption, in good faith, of the negotiations towards establishment of a just and durable peace on the basis of UN Security Council Resolutions 242 (1967), 338 (1973) and 1397(2002).

Both the countries support the continuation of political and diplomatic efforts to fully implement all the United Nations Security Council Resolutions on Iraq. India and Russia have been victims of terrorism and, as democratic and open societies, have been vulnerable to the threats posed by globalisation of terror, including new manifestations of linkage between terrorism and weapons of mass destruction. Terrorism constitutes a gross violation of human rights, particularly the most fundamental right — the right to life — and is a crime against humanity. India and Russia firmly condemn all acts of terrorism wherever they may occur and whatever may be their motivation. Terrorism cannot be justified on any grounds and must be condemned unambiguously wherever it exists. Both the countries strongly condemn those who support terrorism or finance, train, harbour or support terrorists. States that aid, abet or shelter terrorists are as guilty of the acts of terrorism as their perpetrators. We are fully determined to strengthen our cooperation in the fight against terrorism, separatism and extremism, and the support these phenomena receive from organised crime and illicit arms and drugs trafficking. Both the countries regard these as global threats, which can be effectively countered only through collective, comprehensive, determined and sustained efforts of the international community. The fight against terrorism must not admit of any double standards and should also target the financial and other sources of support to terrorism. Both the countries reaffirm the relevance of the Moscow Declaration by the Republic of India and the Russian Federation on International Terrorism of 6 November 2001. In this regard, they also stress the paramount importance of strict implementation of UN Security Council Resolutions on the fight against terrorism, in particular Resolution 1373, and universal anti-terrorist conventions, which create the basic framework for national, regional and international obligations and cooperation of the international community in combating terrorism, in accordance with the UN Charter. India and Russia remain fully committed to implement this Resolution and call for an early agreement on, and entry into force of, the

Comprehensive Convention on International Terrorism and the Convention for the Suppression of Acts of Nuclear Terrorism. As victims of terrorism having its roots in our common neighbourhood, we have a particular interest in putting an end to this common threat through preventive and deterrent measures nationally and bilaterally. The two countries agree to enhance bilateral cooperation in order to combat terrorism, including in the context of the cooperation under the aegis of the Joint Working Group on Afghanistan and the Group on terrorism set up by the National Security Council of India and the Security Council of the Russian Federation. The agreement to set up an Indio-Russian Joint Working Group on Counter-terrorism will further strengthen our cooperation in this sphere. Both sides recognise that factors influencing global energy production and supplies constituted an element of vital national interest and would be the subject of regular bilateral discussions through relevant mechanisms. India and Russia would strengthen cooperation in all areas of the energy sector taking into account the needs of sustainable development and environmental protection. The Republic of India and the Russian Federation are convinced that this Declaration will widen and strengthen the framework of the existing cooperation in different areas and will contribute to consolidation of our strategic partnership.

(Sd/-)
Prime Minister of the Republic of India
President of the Russian Federation
4 December 2002

(Source: http://www.meadev.nic.in/speeches/4decdelhi-decorationrussia.htm)

# 14. China's Defence Policy Paper for 2002
# 9 December 2002

**[Excerpts]**

[Editor's Note: Only Section 4: National Defence Building; Section 5: Armed Forces Building; and Section 7: Arms Control and Disarmament, of this Report have been reproduced below.]

..........................

## 4. National Defence Building

China's national defence building is an important part of the country's modernisation drive. To meet the needs of safeguarding its national security, China insists on modernising its national defence according to its own conditions.

### Legal System

During the past two years, the legal system relating to China's national defence has made great headway. In March 2000, the National People's Congress (NPC) enacted the Legislation *Law of the PRC,* which for the first time expressly defined the legislative power of the CMC and all general headquarters/ departments, all services and arms, and all military area commands. The CMC may formulate military statutes in accordance with the Constitution and laws. The general headquarters/departments, services and arms, and military area commands may, within their respective authorities, formulate military regulations in accordance with the law and the military statutes, decisions and orders of the CMC. The military statutes and regulations are implemented within the armed forces. Procedures for formulation, amendment and nullification of military statutes and regulations shall be stipulated by the CMC in accordance with the principles specified in the provisions of the said law. The above stipulations have provided for the important position of the military legislative system within the overall legislative system of the state.

Since 2000, China has issued 3 decisions, 56 statutes and 420 regulations in respect of laws and law-related issues concerning national defence and armed forces building. *The National Defence Education Law of the PRC* enacted by the Standing Committee of the NPC has provided a legal basis for national defence education. The newly revised *Law of the PRC on Officers in Active Service* has further perfected the military service system pertaining to PLA officers. The State Council and the CMC have jointly formulated the *Implementation Measures for the Law of the PRC on Protecting Military Facilities*, which expressly provides for the organisational leading system regarding the protection of military facilities, as well as specific protection and penalty measures. The newly revised *Routine Service Regulations of the PLA and Discipline Regulations of the PLA* provide a powerful legal guarantee for enhancing the effort of running the armed forces according to law under the new conditions.

To safeguard the interests of national defence and the legitimate rights and interests of military personnel in an age of reform and opening-up, China has reformed its military judicial system. Authorised by the Supreme People's Court of the PRC, military courts have begun to adjudicate civil cases within the armed forces, including cases on contract, marriage and family, real estate, intellectual property rights, damage claims in medical accidents, and applications for adjudication of the missing or death of servicemen, thus exercising the function of civil adjudication inside the armed forces. Relevant organs of local governments at various levels and the armed forces are trying to create a favourable legal environment for national defence and armed forces building by establishing and improving the mechanism of protecting the legitimate rights and interests of the service personnel and their families.

Under unified arrangement by the state, the Chinese armed forces launched in 2001 the Fourth Five-Year Programme on Education to Popularise Knowledge of Laws. The main contents include studying the Constitution, basic laws of the state and laws and regulations in relation to national defence and armed forces building, performance of the armed forces' functions, development of the socialist market economy, and the vital interests of the officers and men. The contents of the military law, the law of war and armed conflicts, etc have been included in the legal courses at military colleges and schools, and the training programmes of the armed forces. The PLA has set up courses for field-grade officers of the Army, Navy and Air Force on the armed conflict law once every two years, and organised lectures on the armed conflict law for officers of the division level and above, who are enrolled at the National Defence University every year.

**Mobilisation**

At each level of the people's government from the county up to the state, there is a national defence mobilisation commission, which has under it, offices and coordinating bodies responsible for the mobilisation of the people's armed forces, national economy and transportation, civil air defence, and national defence education. The premier of the State Council takes the position of chairman of the State National Defence Mobilisation Commission, and vice-premiers of the State Council and vice-chairmen of the CMC are vice-chairmen. Other members include heads of relevant ministries and commissions under the State Council, leaders of the general headquarters/departments of the PLA and heads of their subordinate offices. The chairman of the local national defence mobilisation commission is the principal leader of the local government at the same level. The vice-chairmen are the deputy leaders at the local government of the same level and principal leaders of the military organ at the same level.

The state conducts mobilisation preparations in peacetime by integrating mobilisation of the armed forces, the national economy and transportation, civil air defence, and defence education into the state's overall development plan and relevant programmes. Mobilisation of the armed forces refers to the mobilisation of the active and reserve forces of the PLA, the Armed Police Force, the militia and the reserve personnel, as well as the mobilisation of appropriate weapons, equipment and logistical materials. Its main task is to prepare in peacetime for manpower mobilisation and, in case of need, call up the reservists and other citizens of service age, ensure a quick expansion and reorganisation of the PLA, and expansion of the other forces, and organise the masses to support and join in the operations of the armed forces. Mobilisation of the national economy includes mobilisation of industry, agriculture, science and technology, material supplies, commerce and trade, and finance. Its main task is, in peacetime, to integrate the preparation for mobilisation with economic development in an organised and planned way, and in time of war, reallocate economic resources, and exercise centralised control and use of national financial and material resources so as to increase the production of weapons, equipment and other military supplies, and meet the needs of war. Mobilisation for civil air defence includes mobilisation of civilians and people with special civil air defence skills, material and technical support for civil air defence projects, and civil air defence early-warning systems. Its main task is to mobilise social forces in construction of air defence projects, establish and train specialised air defence service, conduct civil air defence publicity and education, organise evacuations and sheltering, assist in air defence operations, and deal with the aftermath of air raids. Mobilisation of transportation includes mobilisation of transportation, communications and postal services. Its main task is to organise in peacetime the formation of professional transportation and communications support force, defence infrastructure construction, equipment build-up, war material storage and mobilisation preparations of civil transportation means and in time of war, organise the rush repair and construction of transportation and communications facilities, and transportation support for troop movement and material supply.

In recent years, some army units and local governments have, pursuant to relevant laws and regulations, jointly organised defence mobilisation drills for transportation and air defence. China is further improving its defence mobilisation laws and regulations, perfecting its defence mobilisation system, and actively promoting modernisation in this area.

**Education**

China emphasises popularising and strengthening national defence education with patriotism at its core, strives to enhance the national defence awareness of the whole people, and helps citizens perform defence duties conscientiously.

The nationwide defence education is under the leadership of the State Council, with the assistance of the CMC. The State Defence Education Office is responsible for the planning, organisation, direction and coordination of the nation's defence education. Local people's governments at all levels exercise leadership over defence education in their respective administrative areas. All relevant departments perform their respective duties, cooperate with one another, and, combined with their own work, ensure that defence education activities are carried out smoothly. The *National Defence Education Law of the PRC* was formally promulgated and came into force on 28 April 2001, putting China's national defence education on the legal track.

China implements a military training system in institutions of higher learning, senior middle schools and schools corresponding to senior middle schools. Since 1985, more than 200,000 officers and men have helped these institutions and schools organise military training for students, and more than 30 million students have been trained. In the past several years, the percentage of university and college freshmen receiving military training has reached about 60 per cent. Commencing in 2002, students of all regular institutions of higher learning and senior middle schools are obliged to take military training in accordance with relevant regulations and plans.

On 31 August 2001, the NPC Standing Committee set the third Saturday of September every year as the National Defence Education Day. This has provided a vehicle for the participation of the entire population in national defence educational activities, which helps ensure enhanced and continued implementation of the educational programmes in this area.

**Defence Expenditure**

The Chinese government has always been strict in its control, management and supervision of defence spending, and has established a complete system of relevant laws and regulations for that purpose. Pursuant to the *National Defence Law of the PRC,* the entire defence expenditure comes from the state financial budget. In order to meet the defence needs, the Chinese government exercises a system of financial appropriation of defence funds, and implements administration in accordance with the *Budget Law of the PRC.* China's defence budget and final accounts are reviewed and approved by the NPC. The state and armed forces' auditing organs exercise strict auditing and supervision of the execution process of the budget.

In recent years, in line with financing and budgeting reforms in the government, the administration of defence expenditure has undergone a whole array of reforms, including reform in the defence expenditure budgeting method, centralised payment for weapon and equipment procurement, and a tendering and bidding system for the procurement of defence materials, projects and services. Defence funds are therefore managed in a more just, fair and transparent way.

Based on the continuous economic growth, China's defence expenditure has increased somewhat. The proportion of annual defence spending in the GDP was 1.09 per cent in 1995, and 1.50 per cent in 2001 (see Chart 1). However, China's defence expenditure has been kept at a fairly low level, and the increased part is basically of a compensatory nature. From 1979 to 2001, the proportion of defence expenditure in the state financial spending is on a declining curve (see Chart 2) from 17.37 per cent in 1979 to 7.65 per cent in 2001 — a drop of nearly 10 percentage points.

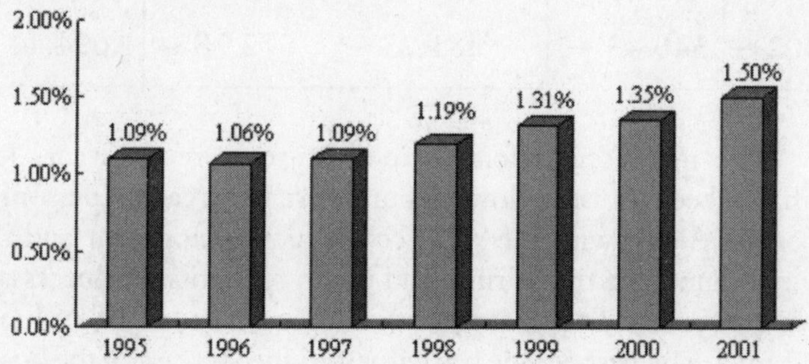


Chart 1 : Percentage of China's Annual Defence Expenditure in GDP(1995-2001)

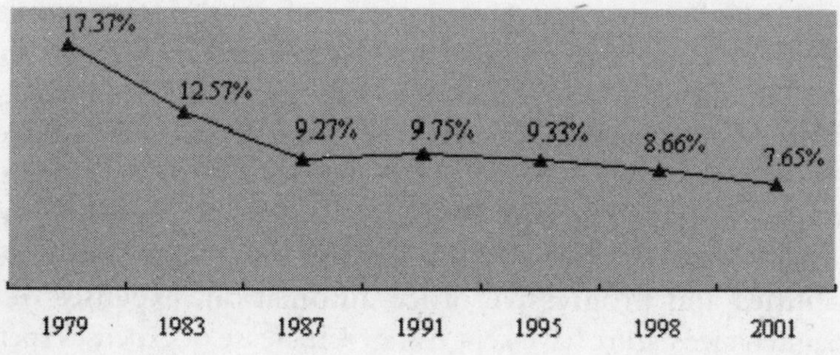

China's defence spending was RMB 120.754 billion yuan in 2000, and 144.204 billion yuan in 2001. The budget for defence expenditure in 2002 is 169.444 billion yuan (see table on p. 26), accounting for 7.60 per cent, 7.65 per cent and 8.03 per cent of the state financial expenditure in the same year, respectively.

| Item / Years | Personnel | Maintenance & Operations | Equipment | Total |
|---|---|---|---|---|
| 2000↵ | 405.50 ↵ | 412.74↵ | 389.30↵ | 1,207.54↵ |
| 2001↵ | 461.63 ↵ | 485.81↵ | 494.60↵ | 1,442.04↵ |
| 2002↵ | 540.43 ↵ | 581.23↵ | 572.78↵ | 1,694.44↵ |

The increased defence expenditure in recent years has primarily been for the following purposes: 1.Increase of personnel expenses. Along with the socio-economic development and the per-capita income rise of rural and urban residents, it is necessary to improve the living standards and conditions of military personnel. The past decade has witnessed the increase of the board expenses in the armed forces on five occasions, and an 84 per cent salary raise for officers and 92 per cent allowance raise for soldiers. 2.Establishment and gradual improvement of a social security system for servicemen. In accordance with the requirements of the market economy, China has, since 1998, established such systems as injury and death insurance for servicemen, medical insurance for demobilised servicemen and housing subsidies for servicemen, and adjusted and enhanced living expense standards for PLA retirees. 3.Increase of expenses of a maintenance nature. Since the armed forces stopped commercial activities in 1998, the budget for training has increased year by year. With the gradual improvement of living facilities and progressive office automation, expenses of a maintenance nature have kept rising. 4.Increase of expenses spent on cooperation with the international community in anti-terrorism activities. 5.Appropriate increase of expenses for the improvement of military equipment to enhance defence capabilities under the conditions of modern technologies, particularly high technologies.

On the whole, China's defence expenditure has remained at a fairly low level in the world in 2002 (see Chart 3). Compared with the USA, Russia, UK and France, the percentage of China's defence expenditure in its GDP and the state financial expenditure is also fairly low (see Chart 4).

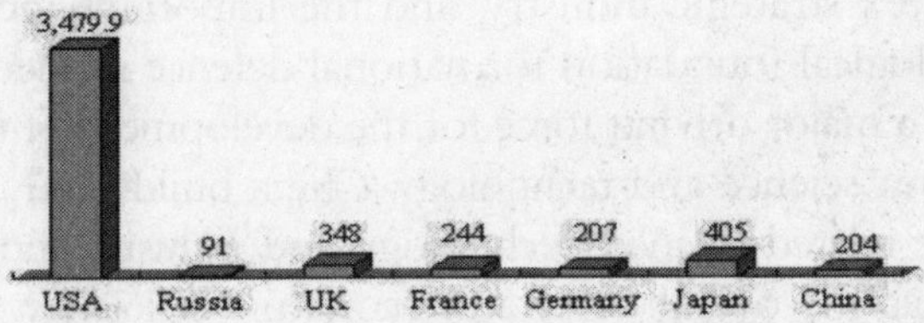


Chart 3 : Comparison of Defence Expenditures of Some Countries in 2002 (unit : 100 million US dollars)

Note 1: The exchange rate used here is based on that announced by China's State Administration of Exchange Control in 2002, which is US$ 1.0˜RMB 8.28 yuan.
Note 2: Statistics in the chart are sourced from the national defence reports, financial reports and other government reports published by the said countries.

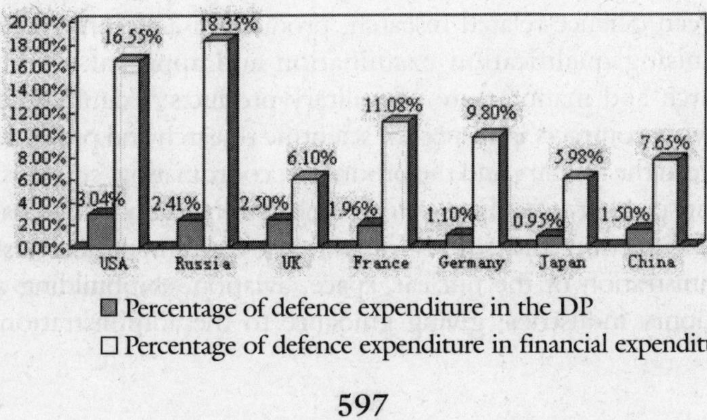


■ Percentage of defence expenditure in the DP
□ Percentage of defence expenditure in financial expenditure

Chart 4: Comparison of the Percentages of Defence Expenditure in the GDP and Financial Expenditure of China and Some Other Countries in 2001

Note: Statistics in the chart are sourced from the national defence reports, financial reports and other government reports published by the said countries.

**Science, Technology and Industry for National Defence**

China's defence-related science, technology and industry is the state's strategic industry, and the important industrial and technological foundation for national defence modernisation, as well as a major driving force for the development of the national economy, science and technology. China builds and develops its defence-related science, technology and industry independently, enhances the overall level and economic efficiency of defence-related science, technology and industry, and promotes the coordinated development of national defence and economy.

The Commission of Science, Technology and Industry for National Defence of the PRC is an organ under the State Council in charge of work in this regard. It is responsible for researching and formulating principles and policies, as well as laws, rules and regulations in respect of the development of defence-related science, technology and industry; deliberating the development plan for defence-related science, technology and industry, and overseeing the overall planning of and proper connections between defence-related research, production and construction; organising qualification examination and approval work for research and manufacture of military products; examining and verifying contracts in respect of scientific research and production between the military and the producers; coordinating, supervising and inspecting execution of ordering contracts so as to ensure the production and supply of military equipment; exercising administration of the nuclear, space, aviation, shipbuilding and weaponry industries; giving guidance to the administration of the military-related electronics sector; organising, studying and implementing reform of the system of defence-related science, technology and industry; organising adjustment of the capability, structure and layout of the defence-related science, technology and industry; drawing up plans for investment in fixed as-sets in respect of defence-related science, technology and industry, and for technical transformation and development of defence conversion technologies, and organising the implementation of such plans; and conducting foreign exchanges and international cooperation in the field of defence-related science, technology and industry.

After decades of development, China has formed a defence-related science, technology and industry system, which is by and large complete in disciplines and coordinated with regard to means of research and production; trained and fostered a contingent of professionals with a good mastery of advanced technology and a sound work style; and laid an important material and technological foundation for independent research and manufacture of military equipment in China. Currently, China has 11 military industrial group corporations, namely, China National Nuclear Corporation, China Nuclear Engineering and Construction Corporation, China Aerospace Science and Technology Corporation, China Aerospace Science and Industry Corporation, China Aviation Industry Corporation I, China Aviation Industry Corporation II, China State Shipbuilding Corporation, China Shipbuilding Industry Corporation, China North Industries Group Corporation, China South Industries Group Corporation, and China Electronic Science and Technology Corporation. Each is responsible for the organisation and administration of its R&D and manufacture, and exercising the rights of an investor authorised by the state over state-owned assets in its subordinate enterprises.

China's defence-related science, technology and industry gives priority to the development of new- and high-tech weaponry and equipment, and strives to raise their modernisation level. It is imperative to speed up the adjustment of capability, structure and layout, enhance capability in research and production of new- and high-tech weaponry, streamline the work force of military industry, optimise the industrial layout, and gradually establish a new system of defence-related science, technology and industry. It is imperative to further strengthen the development of defence-related science and technology, promote the progress of science and technology, concentrate resources to make breakthroughs in a number of key technologies, enhance the capability of self-reliance and innovation and sustained development capability in defence-related science, technology and industry, and strive to achieve leapfrog technological progress. It is imperative to bring up talented people and create a well-structured contingent of high-calibre people in a whole array of disciplines needed for the development of defence-related science, technology and industry. At present, in China's defence-related science, technology and industry, 141 academicians of the Chinese Academy of Sciences and the Chinese Academy of Engineering are active, of which 52 are academicians of the Chinese Academy of Sciences, 95 are academicians of the Chinese Academy of Engineering, and 6 belong to both academies.

The Chinese government has always stressed the peaceful use of military industrial technology, and encouraged and supported defence-related science, technology and industry to bring its techno-logical and human resource advantages into full play, and develop dual-purpose technologies and new and high-tech industries, and thus promoted the development of the national economy. Nuclear power for civil use should be industrialised. Civil aerospace technologies have made remarkable achievements in the applied satellite, carrier rocket, and manned spaceship. The "Long March" series of carrier rockets have successfully launched 27 foreign-made satellites, entitling China to a position in the international commercial satellite launching service market. In 1999, 2001 and 2002, China successfully launched in succession three experimental unmanned spaceships, marking a breakthrough for China in mastering basic manned spaceship technology. This has provided a solid foundation for China to send a manned spaceship into space. The aviation industry for civil use, while strengthening technological research, expanding sub-contracting scope for production, and improving existing plane models, has made important headway in manufacturing general purpose aircraft and the "Xinzhou 60" aircraft, and has begun the R&D of new feeder liners. The shipbuilding industry for civil use has already become a highly competitive pillar export industry among China's electro-mechanical industries. In recent years, China's shipbuilding output has continuously increased, ranking third in the world for seven consecutive years. The accomplished shipbuilding output in 2001 accounted for 6 per cent of the world's total.

China's defence-related science, technology and industry endeavors to establish and perfect an organisational system and an operational mechanism tailored to the needs of national defence building and the socialist market economy. It encourages a specialised division of labour, gradually forms a new multi-tiered cooperative system of principal weaponry contractors, sub-contractors and suppliers of parts and components. It also presses forward with the strategic reorganisation of military industrial enterprises and institutions, optimises the allocation of resources, develops core industries, and gradually forms a batch of internationally competitive conglomerates. It makes efforts to deepen the reform of military industrial enterprises, establish a modern enterprise system, and push forward the diversification of investors of the enterprises and transformation of operational mechanisms so as to enable these enterprises to turn into market competitors operating independently and responsible for their own profits or losses. The defence-related science, technology and industry stresses the reform of its sci-tech system, strengthens the organic integration of production, education and research, and transforms the defence-related science and technology into actual productivity. In addition, the defence-related science, technology and industry adheres to opening-up, and actively participates in international exchanges and cooperation in line with the principles of the complementarity of each other's strengths, reciprocity, mutual benefit and common development.

**Land and Sea Border Defence**

China pursues a policy of good neighbourliness and friendship. It defends and administers its land borders and seas under its jurisdiction, safeguards the country's territorial sovereignty and maritime rights and interests, and secures both its land and sea borders strictly in accordance with treaties and agreements it has signed with neighbouring countries, and the United Nations Convention on Law of the Sea.

China advocates settling unresolved border and maritime demarcation issues through negotiation, and demarcating maritime boundaries with neighbouring countries or countries contiguous to opposite coasts based on the principle of equity, and opposes the use of force or provocative acts. China has solved or basically solved boundary issues left over by history with most of its adjacent countries. In December 2000, China and Viet Nam entered into the Beibu Gulf Demarcation Agreement. In May 2002, China and Tajikistan signed the Supplementary Agreement on the Boundary Between the People's Republic of China and the Republic of Tajikistan.

China attaches importance to having frontier defence exchanges and cooperation with neighbouring countries, and jointly maintaining order along the borders. China has signed treaties, agreements and understandings with Mongolia, Russia, Myanmar, Viet Nam, Laos and India on border control and handling border affairs, setting up confidence-building measures, and preventing dangerous military activities. Since 1995, the Chinese Ministry of National Defence has signed frontier cooperation agreements with the General Administration of

Frontier Defence of the Russian Federation and the Administration of Frontier Guards of Mongolia. In January 2002, Chinese Ministry of National Defence and the National Security Commission of Kazakhstan signed the Frontier Defence Cooperation Agreement Between China and Kazakhstan. In April 2002, China sent a delegation to attend the meeting of leaders of frontier defence authorities of the member states of the Shanghai Cooperation Organisation (SCO) held in Alma-Ata. At the meeting, the leaders of the frontier defence authorities of China, Russia, Kazakhstan, Kyrgyzstan and Tajikistan agreed that the frontier defence authorities of the five states will, within the framework of the relevant documents of the SCO and in accordance with the circumstances of the areas of common borders of the member states, strengthen exchanges of information in respect of frontier defence; further deepen corresponding bilateral and multilateral cooperation; take effective measures for the joint fight against terrorism, separatism and extremism, and for preventing cross-border criminal activities of all forms; safeguard order along the common borders of member states; and provide powerful guarantee for the development of good neighbourliness and friendship and economic, trade and cultural relations between the member states. China's frontier authorities and frontier troops faithfully implement relevant treaties, agreements and understandings, actively establish or improve the systems for consultation, frontier defence talks and meetings with counterparts of neighbouring countries, carry out frontier defence contacts and cooperation at various levels, and deal appropriately with border affairs. Therefore, mutual understanding, trust and friendship between China and neighbouring countries have been increased, and a peaceful and friendly atmosphere along borders has been created.

The Chinese government attaches importance to border area development and endeavours to promote transportation, communications, culture, education, public health, radio and television services in border areas. Since 1996, the State Frontier

Defence Commission has organised the construction of frontier defence infrastructure on a large scale in nine overland frontier provinces and autonomous regions, which has effectively improved the administrative conditions of border areas, and given impetus to economic and social development there. While earnestly performing their duties and unremittingly improving themselves, the land and sea border defence forces have actively participated in and supported local economic development and the building of spiritual civilisation. This has helped to strengthen the relations between the armed forces and the local governments, and between the military and civilians, and to safeguard political and social stability, and the unity of ethnic groups in frontier regions.

**Civil Air Defence**

China's civil air defence sector implements the concept of people's war. In view of wartime requirements, and based on the economic capability of the country, it relies on the broad masses, gives play to the initiatives of the central and local governments, ensures its readiness to provide effective protection. The basic tasks of civil air defence include: spreading knowledge of air defence among the people; building all types of protection projects; setting up a civil air defence communications and warning system; making plans for personnel and material evacuation; organising and training specialised air defence contingents; guarding and protecting important facilities of the national economy; and in wartime, organising and directing people to protect themselves against air-raids. In accordance with the needs for preparation against war, China has identified cities and regions for the conduct of civil air defence, and urban civil air defence is taken as the focal point of civil air defence.

The civil air defence sector adopts a system of joint leadership by the people's governments and military organs. The State Council and the CMC exercise leadership over civil air defence nationwide. Authorised by the State Council and the

CMC, the military area commands exercise leadership over civil air defence in their respective regions. Local people's governments at the county level and above and the corresponding military organs exercise leadership over civil air defence in their respective administrative areas. The administrative organ in charge of nationwide civil air defence is in the General Staff Head-quarters, and those in charge of the military area civil air defence are in the headquarters of the military area commands. The administrative organs in charge of civil air defence at the county level and above are in the people's governments at the same level. The relevant departments in charge of planning, programming and construction in the people's governments at the county level and above are responsible for relevant civil air defence within their respective scopes of duties.

The civil air defence sector adheres to the policy of long-term readiness, construction of key projects, and combination of peacetime footing with wartime footing, and implements the principle of developing in coordination with economic construction and in combination with urban construction. In peacetime, the state carries out civil air defence construction, divides cities into different categories for protection, incorporates civil air defence construction into the national socio-economic development programme, integrates the civil air defence construction plan into the overall urban development plan, and ensures the smooth operation of the civil air defence communications and warning system. The state protects civil air defence facilities from being damaged, adopts a preferential policy toward construction of air defence facilities, and encourages and supports enterprises, institutions, social organisations and individuals to invest in civil air defence construction projects. In peacetime, the state encourages submission of civil air defence projects to the service of economic development and people's daily needs; the use of civil air defence communications and warning facilities for emergency rescue and disaster relief, and assumption by civil air defence organs and specialised contingents of rescue and relief missions assigned by people's governments. To meet the needs of the changing situations, civil air defence will gradually be integrated with disaster prevention, and capabilities in rapid-reaction, damage-resistance, emergency rescue and self-improvement will be enhanced so as to cope with modern warfare and serious disasters and accidents, and effectively protect citizens' lives and property.

China has promulgated and implemented the Civil Air Defence Law of the PRC, and formulated a number of auxiliary civil air defence regulations. China sets store by cooperation and exchanges in respect of civil air defence with countries worldwide, and joined the International Civil Defence Organisation in 1992.

### Participating and Supporting the Development of the Western Region

The development of China's western region is important to the country's economy, politics and national defence. In accordance with the strategic decision for the large-scale development of the western region made by the state, the CMC has established a special leading group and a dedicated office, and made unified arrangements. The PLA and the Armed Police Force have contributed more than 1.5 million troops and 450,000 motor vehicles and machines to actively participate in and support the western region development efforts.

**Concentrating strength on supporting the construction of key infrastructure projects.** The Chinese armed forces regard the participation in the construction of transportation, energy, water conservancy and communications projects as the focal points in supporting the development of the western region. They have engaged in the expansion or reconstruction of 8 airports, 3 national highways and 4 expressways; the construction of 9 energy facilities such as pipelines, natural gas fields and oil-and-gas fields; the construction of 7 hydropower stations and 19 trunk diversion channels; and the laying of 8 optic telecommunications cables totalling more than 20,000 km.

**Taking part in the protection and construction of the ecological environment.** The armed forces stationed in the western region have, in order to improve the ecological environment, taken an active part in activities such as forestation, sand prevention and control, closing mountains to facilitate forestation, and restoring the reclaimed land to forests and grasslands. They have planted trees in an area of more than 3 million mu (one mu equals one fifteenth of a hectare), sown grass on more than 1.8 million mu of land, and restored more than 1.5 million mu of reclaimed land to forests and grasslands. Technical troops specialising in mapping, meteorology, water supply and aviation have provided such services as geographic survey, weather forecast, water source exploration, aerial sowing and artificial precipitation in the western region.

**Providing talented personnel, and intellectual and technical support.** Chinese armed forces have selected and transferred professionals from military colleges and schools, hospitals and scientific research institutes to support the development of the western region; arranged, in a planned way, demobilised officers to work in the western region; encouraged or persuaded demobilised soldiers from densely populated areas to settle in the west; and assigned increased numbers of soldiers from the western region to units stationed in developed areas, so as to help the cultivation of talents and the renewal of thinking for the development of the western region. Some colleges and schools, hospitals and scientific research institutes have actively provided services to the western region by way of jointly running schools, sponsoring short-term training courses, offering diseases prevention and treatment assistance, and transferring achievements of scientific and technological research.

**Opening and developing military facilities.** On the premise of ensuring military security, the armed forces have opened 5 military airports, more than 200 military rail lines, 30 oil pipelines,

70 communication lines and more than 100 rear area warehouses for civilian use. Some of the military farms, real estate, support enterprises and army horse-breeding farms have been handed over to local authorities. The armed forces have improved such facilities for preparation against war as air traffic control and frontier defence roads, in order to support the development of the civil transportation.

**Carrying out activities to help the poor and needy.** The armed forces stationed in the western region have sent officers and men to help repair roads, install electricity lines, sink wells, teach useful skills and develop a diversified economy. These efforts have enabled more than 200,000 local people to eliminate poverty. The armed forces have also helped build or enlarge more than 300 middle and primary schools, and helped more than 50,000 school dropouts return to class. In addition, 100 PLA hospitals have made arrangements with 105 local county hospitals in the poor areas of the western region to provide assistance.

## 5. Armed Forces Building

In compliance with the general requirements of being qualified politically and competent militarily and having a fine style of work, strict discipline and adequate logistical support, and focusing on the two historic tasks of being capable of winning and never degenerating, the PLA strives to strengthen its overall development and form a revolutionary, modernised and regularised people's army.

### Military Training

The PLA strives to adapt itself to the characteristics of modern warfare, takes enhancement of the capability of defensive operations under high-tech conditions as the main objective, and continuously strengthens and improves military training.

Over the past two years, the PLA has accelerated its steps

in transforming the training - from the conventional training to one featuring new technology. It has made full use of modern science and technology to organise and implement military training. In October 2000, the General Staff Headquarters organised a large-scale high-tech military exercise in the vicinity of Beijing and used such new and high technologies as computer networking, reconnaissance sensing, ECM and simulation to drill and test the new operational concepts, weaponry and training methods. The latest achievements gained in military training featuring new technologies were exchanged among the troops.

In line with the new generation of operational doctrines, the PLA focuses on the studies and training of joint operations. The annual regular exercises organised by the military area commands and ser-vices and arms all concentrate on joint operations. In the spring and summer of 2001, both Nanjing and Guangzhou military area commands organised field exercises with joint landing operations as the backdrop, focusing on the coordination of joint and combined arms landing operation, and drew useful lessons on how to organise, support and manage joint training, ground force amphibious landing training, and training of rapid reserve mobilisation. In addition, the general headquarters/departments organised successive studies and exercises of communications and command at the joint operational level, training of landing and mountain operations, and research on methods of joint penetration operations, and explored the features and patterns of integrated network and electronic warfare.

The PLA has enforced new military training regulations and strengthened regularised training. On the basis of extensively absorbing the achievements of the armed forces' training reform and the experience gained in troop training featuring new technologies, the General Staff Headquarters revised and adjusted the system of content of the PLA's military training, promulgated the Outline of Military Training and Evaluation in July 2001, and organised a training course of the Outline in a combined corps in northern China in September 2001. In September 2002, the CMC promulgated the new Regulations on Military Training of the PLA comprehensively and systematically standardising the organisation, leadership and administration of military training.

The PLA has continued to deepen the reform of institutional education. In line with the general concept of "running schools in large-scale, modernising teaching, regularising administration and outsourcing logistic support," the PLA has further improved its new system of institutional education and established a teaching system consonant with military, sci-tech and educational developments. In recent years, on the basis of fulfilling the major construction tasks of 18 colleges and schools, 60 disciplines and 31 laboratories, the PLA has launched the Key Construction Project of Military Colleges and Schools, whereby efforts are being focused on 67 domains of disciplines and specialties, and 178 research centres. So far 58 have been qualified as state-level key disciplines and specialties. The general headquarters/departments have promulgated the first catalogue of disciplines and specialties of the PLA's colleges and schools, thus setting up a new system of disciplines and specialties. Deepening teaching reform with teaching content as the focal point, colleges and schools of the PLA have formulated a new teaching programme, implemented a key teaching material development project, and perfected the teaching appraisal system. At the same time, informationisation and networking of teaching have been promoted, and an information network platform for the armed forces' teaching and scientific research has been initially put in place, giving shape to a training information network linking PLA's colleges and schools and having nearly 100,000 websites and centres.

**Political Work**

The political work of the PLA is the ideological and organisational work of the CPC in the armed forces. It is the fundamental guarantee for the absolute leadership of the Party over the armed forces, and the assurance on maintaining and improving combat effectiveness of the troops. It is the lifeline of the PLA.

The PLA's political work implements the aim of serving the people wholeheartedly; guarantees the Party's absolute leadership over the armed forces; adheres to the principle of seeking unity between officers and men and between the military and the people, and demoralising and disintegrating the enemy, with ideological-political education as the central link; operates a system featuring political democracy, economic democracy and military democracy; and enforces the Three Main Rules of Discipline and the Eight Points for Attention. The PLA's political work implements the Party committee (Party branch) system, political leader system and political organ system. The Party committee (Party branch) system stipulates that a Party committee shall be set up in a unit at or above the regiment level, a grass-roots Party committee in a unit at the battalion or corresponding level, and a Party branch in a unit at the company or corresponding level. Party committees (Party branches) at various levels are the core of the centralised leadership and unity of the unit concerned. The sys-tem of leading cadres assuming separate responsibilities under the unified collective leadership of the Party committee (Party branch) is the fundamental system for Party leadership over the armed forces. The political leader system stipulates that a political commissar shall be appointed to a unit at or above the regiment level, a political director to a battalion, and a political instructor to a company. The political commissar, political director and political instructor, together with the chief military officers at the same level, are the chief leaders of their units, assuming joint responsibility for all work in their units under the leadership of the Party committees (Party branches) at the same level. The political commissar, political director and political instructor are organisers of the day-to-day work of the Party committees (Party branches) and leaders of political work. The political organ system stipulates that a political department (section) shall be set up in a unit at or above the regiment level, and a general political department for the PLA; and that the political organs are the leading body of the political work in a unit, responsible for administering Party work and organising the implementation of the political work.

The political work of the PLA persists in advancing with the times, breaking new ground and making innovations, keeping pace with profound changes in the international situation and the military field, adapting itself to the rapid development of the socialist market economy, striving to provide strong spiritual motivation for winning future high-tech wars, and furnishing a reliable political guarantee for maintaining the nature, character and work style of the people's army. In recent years, the CPC Central Committee has promulgated the new Regulations on the Political Work of the PLA, the CMC has promulgated the Outline for Armed Forces Construction at the Grass-Roots Level, and the General Political Department has released Decisions on Some Issues Concerning the PLA Ideological-Political Work Under the Conditions of the Reform and Opening-up and the Development of a Socialist Market Economy and Opinions on Strengthening and Improving Ideological-Political Education of the Army in the New Situation. The PLA has actively studied and implemented the important thought of the "Three Represents," organised the rank and file to study the Constitution and other state laws, the Party's basic theories, and scientific and cultural knowledge, and conducted education in patriotism, collectivism and revolutionary heroism by establishing military history museums in units at and above the regiment level, and honor exhibition in companies. The PLA has issued an ethical code for servicemen, organised the composition of moral songs, set up a PLA-wide publicity, cultural and information network, improved cultural facilities in barracks, set up cultural clubs in companies, and established cultural centres in units at and above the regiment level. The PLA has carried out psychological education and legal consultation, and has established psychological education and legal consultation mechanisms that rely mainly on brigade or regiment political organs and grass-roots political officers and integrate the political work system with the related specialty system.

**Logistical Support**

The PLA strives actively to reform its logistical structure and system, construct a modern logistical support system and constantly enhance its logistical support capabilities.

The introduction of the joint logistics system is a major reform of the logistical support system of the PLA. The joint logistics system is based on military area commands. It combines regional support with organic system support and general supply support with special supply support. Unified general-purpose material supply and service support are provided by military area commands, and special material supply and service support are provided by the services and arms through their organic channels. The General Logistics Department is in charge of the PLA's joint logistics work. The military area command's joint logistics department is in charge of the joint logistics work within a theatre of war. And the joint logistics sub-department is mainly responsible for organising and implementing the general-purpose support of the services and arms within its support area. After more than two years' practice of reform, the joint logistics system has been standardised gradually with notably improved efficiency. The system will be further developed into one that integrates the three armed services, unites the army with the people, and combines peacetime and wartime footing.

In order to streamline the logistical support organisations and improve the cost-effectiveness of defence expenditures, the PLA has carried out a reform featuring the socialisation of logistical support in non-combat units at and above the corps level, and in military colleges and schools and hospitals in large and medium-sized cities. After nearly three years of effort, substantial progress has been achieved in this regard, including reform in food and commercial services, barracks, and the administration of civilian employees. Reform has also been carried out, on a trial basis, in non-military transportation, fuel supply and the monetised supply of clothing. So far, the PLA has already had more than 1,500 messes run by civilian services, more than 1,000 post exchanges integrated into civilian service systems, more than 1,800 barracks managed by real estate companies, approximately 300 support enterprises and farms transferred to central and local authorities, reducing a total number of more than 300,000 institutional and business employees. In order to promote the reform of socialisation of military logistical support and to ensure the development of the reform, in September 2002, the State Council and the CMC issued an Announcement Concerning the Issues of Advancing the Reform of Military Logistical Support, and in October, the CMC approved and transmitted the General Logistics Department's Opinions on Some Is-sues Concerning the Socialisation of Military Logistical Support.

In March 2001, the PLA began to reform the budgetary planning system. Drawing on the internationally adopted budgeting method, the PLA reformed its budgeting form, method and content extensively, with emphasis placed on implementation of the zero-base budget method, so as to give full play to the budget's macro-control role and gradually establish a new budgeting pattern featuring the concentration of financial power and resources, scientific distribution of military expenditures, concrete and transparent itemisation, and tight supervision and control.

In January 2002, the PLA carried out an across-the-board reform of the procurement system, focusing mainly on concentrated procurement and procurement through public bidding, and set up a mechanism for sectional management, which features cooperation with proper division of labour and mutual restriction. High-value, large-quantity, general-purpose materials are procured in a concentrated way by relying mainly on the material procurement departments. Bulk materials with one-time procurement value exceeding RMB 500,000 Yuan, and projects newly built, expanded, or revamped each involving an investment of over RMB 2 million Yuan are undertaken through public bidding.

Currently, the method of combining military support with social support, government house with self-owned house, and supply in kind with supply in money is adopted for PLA officers' housing system. Officers of all ranks and all military branches are provided with appropriate housing support. Active-service officers live mainly in government houses. Retired officers are entitled mainly to purchase the houses they are living in or other affordable houses. Demobilised officers and noncommissioned officers transferred to civilian posts should be ensured of housing benefits mainly by subsidies and incorporation into the social security system.

The PLA constantly strengthens the development of its logistical equipment and upgrades its logistical support means. In 2001, it carried out coordinative experiments in the overall support capability of logistical equipment organically and systematically; developed logistical equipment in seven aspects - rapid maritime rescue and treatment of the wounded, shore party support, air field support, mobility support for missile units, air-dropped material support, individual support and field logistics command; and completed the demonstration, R&D and testing of 86 kinds of new equipment. In order to obtain and process information on the resources, requirements and conditions of logistical support real-time and in a precise and transparent way, the PLA is doing research on a video logistics system. In July 2002, the CMC promulgated the Regulations on the Logistical Equipment of the PLA to promote the regularised development of logistical equipment.

**Weaponry and Equipment**

In line with the needs of high-tech military developments and defence operations, the PLA conscientiously implements the principle of building a strong military through science and technology and giving first place to quality, so as to upgrade and accelerate the development of military equipment.

The weaponry and equipment management system and mechanism have further improved. Following the founding of the General Armaments Department in April 1998, the services and arms, military area commands and combat units at the corps, division and regiment levels have all set up their armaments departments (sections), and further strengthened unified leadership over weaponry and equipment development, and the across-the-board and life-cycle management of military equipment, thus effectively improving the overall efficiency. In December 2000, the CMC promulgated the first Regulations on Armaments of the PLA, which standardises the organisation and leadership, division of responsibilities and management procedures of the PLA's armament-related work. The CMC promulgated the Regulations on the Armament Maintenance Work of the PLA in June 2002, and the Outline of Operational Equipment Support of the PLA in October 2002. These rules and regulations concerning armament-related work have promoted the development of the work along scientific, regularised and legal lines.

The modernisation level of weaponry and equipment has undergone constant improvement. The PLA persists in stressing self-reliance and independent innovation, and actively develops military equipment with advanced foreign technology. In compliance with the needs of future defence operations in high-tech conditions, the PLA mainly develops weaponry and equipment featuring new and high technology, while upgrading and modernising current weaponry and equipment selectively, so as to accomplish the historical tasks of mechanisation and IT-application of military equipment. A Chinese-style weaponry and equipment system, with a relatively complete variety and a good structure, has thus come into shape.

Weaponry and equipment management capability has been notably enhanced. The PLA manages and uses existing weaponry and equipment conscientiously and in a proper way, and constantly enhances its ability to manage new-type weapons. The forces at and below the corps level have universally established and improved rules and regulations for weaponry management, exercised standardised management of equipment-related finance, and carried out examination and appraisal relating to the scientific, institutional and regular management of weaponry and equipment. At the same time, they have organised training courses in the use and management of new-type equipment, trained personnel in equipment management and technological support, improved the management of support facilities, and succeeded in developing the combat and support capabilities of military equipment organically and systematically.

The weapon and equipment procurement system is being gradually reformed. The PLA seeks actively to meet the requirements of the socialist market economy and improvement of weapons and equipment, and vigorously promotes the reform. The armament departments perform the functions of the principal responsible party in weapon and equipment ordering, and institutes contractual management in the research, procurement and maintenance of weapons and equipment in accordance with state and PLA regulations. In recent years, the PLA has persisted in introducing the mechanism of competition into its procurement process, gradually instituted a public bidding and tendering system, introduced and improved mechanisms of competition, appraisal, supervision and motivation, further strengthened the fostering of factory-based military representatives, and perfected the quality certification system, thereby improving the efficiency of the weapon and equipment expenditures, and the cost-effectiveness of weaponry research and production.

**Cadre Training**

The PLA persists in taking the training of high-quality military personnel of a new type as a fundamental measure for promoting a leapfrog development of the armed forces' modernisation.

Cadres of the PLA include officers and non-ranking cadres. In recent years, the PLA has constantly raised the training level of officer candidates, adjusted the sources of officer candidates, and established a scientific and justified system for training such candidates, resulting in a marked improvement in the training level, quality and efficiency of military personnel. At present, more than 80 per cent of the PLA's cadres have received junior college or higher education. More than 30,000 have doctor's or master's degrees, and many of them hold leading posts at the division or regiment level. At the same time, in order to draw on the useful armed forces building experiences of other countries, particularly developed countries, the PLA has since 1996 sent nearly 1,000 servicemen to study in over 20 countries, a considerable number of them being commanding or technical officers at the division or regiment level.

Both the Law of the PRC on Officers in Active Service passed by the Standing Committee of the NPC in December 2000 and the Regulations on Non-Ranking Officers of the PLA issued by the CMC in June 1999 explicitly stipulate that commanding officers and non-ranking officers without technical specialty, as well as ranking officers with technical specialty and non-ranking officers with technical specialty should receive training at relevant colleges and schools or other training institutions before their promotion; and that cadres in leading organs should have undergone training at appropriate colleges or schools. Cadre's on-the-job training is gradually undergoing a change from academic credentials education to all-round continuing education. Except for a small number of cadres who have to take academic credentials education, the overwhelming majority of cadres would update their knowledge mainly through short-term training.

In May 2000, the State Council and the CMC promulgated the Decision on Establishing a System for Training Military Cadres by Reliance on Regular Institutions of Higher Learning, clearly stressing the role of regular higher education in the modernisation of national defence and the armed forces, so as to widen the channel for the selection and training of high-caliber personnel for the military. So far, more than 50 institutions of higher learning, including Peking University and Tsinghua University, have undertaken the task of training personnel for the armed forces, providing a large batch of outstanding personnel for the PLA each year.

To meet the requirement of building a strong military through science and technology, the PLA pays great attention to the training of high-level personnel. In the past two years, the PLA's mobile post-doctoral stations and doctor's or master's degree authorisation centres have increased by large margins, the academic degree authorisation system has been improved gradually, and the training scale has been enlarged substantially. In May 2002, the Academic Degree Commission under the State Council examined and approved the Plan of Setting Up Specialties for the Master Degree of Military Science, and decided on the setting up of specialties for the master degree of military science as an experiment, marking a new stage in the training of high-level professionals for the armed forces.

The PLA regards the exchange of cadres as an important channel for training and tempering them and raising their quality. The Law of the PRC on Officers in Active Service further clarifies and standardises the exchange of officers. The Regulations on the Appointment and Removal of the PLA Officers in Active

Service promulgated by the CMC in January 2002 lays down concrete stipulations on the condition, scope, organisation and implementation of officer exchange. In accordance with the Interim Provisions on the Rotation of Cadres of the PLA Garrison in Hong Kong promulgated in December 1998, a regular rotation system has been instituted for all cadres of the garrison force in Hong Kong, and three batches of cadres have so far been rotated. A rotation system of this kind has also been instituted for the PLA Garrison in Macao.

.........................

## 7. Arms Control and Disarmament

After the end of the Cold War, a series of achievements were made in the field of international arms control, disarmament and non-proliferation. However, this momentum has been hampered by a host of negative developments in recent years. In the current situation, it is vitally important to maintain the global strategic balance and stability and the legal system governing international arms control and disarmament. The existing legal system is an important component of the global collective security framework centred around the United Nations. The Chinese government is willing, together with the international community, to contribute to the maintenance of the legal system for international arms control and disarmament, and the advancement of the process of arms control, disarmament and non-proliferation.

### Nuclear Disarmament

China has consistently advocated the complete prohibition and thorough destruction of nuclear weapons. On the very first day it came into possession of nuclear weapons, China solemnly declared that at no time and under no circumstances would it be the first to use such weapons. Later, China undertook unconditionally not to use or threaten to use nuclear weapons against non-nuclear-weapon states or nuclear-weapon-free zones, and has consistently urged all nuclear-weapon states to enshrine these commitments in a legal form. China has always exercised utmost restraint on the development of nuclear weapons, and its nuclear arsenal is kept at the lowest level necessary for self-defence only. China holds that countries having the largest nuclear arsenals bear a special and primary responsibility towards nuclear disarmament, and that they should take the lead in drastically reducing their nuclear arsenals and destroy the reduced nuclear weapons. China welcomes the new treaty signed by the US and Russia on the reduction of their offensive strategic weapons, and hopes that these two countries will adopt effective measures to ensure the "verifiability" and "irreversibility" of nuclear disarmament, and continue to further the process of nuclear disarmament, so as to genuinely promote world peace and stability.

The Comprehensive Nuclear Test Ban Treaty (CTBT) is an important step taken in the process of nuclear disarmament. As one of the first countries to sign the Treaty, China has always actively participated in the work of the Preparatory Commission of the Treaty Organisation, and earnestly carried out the preparatory work for the implementation of the Treaty in China. The Chinese government has submitted the Treaty to the NPC Standing Committee for examination and approval. Together with the international community, China is ready to work for the early entry into force of the Treaty. China maintains that the conclusion of a Fissile Material Cut-off Treaty (FMCT) will help to accelerate the process of nuclear disarmament and nuclear non-proliferation, and supports an early start of the negotiations on such a Treaty on the basis of a comprehensive and balanced work plan of the Conference on Disarmament (CD).

**Chemical and Biological Disarmament**

China has consistently advocated the complete prohibition and thorough destruction of chemical weapons. As a State Party to the Chemical Weapons Convention (CWC), China actively supports its purposes and objectives and has conscientiously and strictly fulfilled all its obligations under the Convention. China has set up a national authority for the implementation of the Convention, and submitted its initial declaration and all sorts of annual declarations in time. So far, China has accepted 55 inspections by the Organisation for the Prohibition of Chemical Weapons (OPCW), and has co-sponsored, together with the OPCW, several training courses and symposiums for inspectors.

Today, large quantities of chemical weapons abandoned by the Japanese invaders still remain on Chinese soil. China urges Japan to earnestly implement the obligations under the CWC for the destruction of these weapons, and expedite the pace of the relevant work in accordance with the Memorandum on the Destruction of Japanese Abandoned Chemical Weapons in China between the governments of China and Japan, so as to commence as soon as possible the substantive part of the destruction process.

China has always stood for the complete prohibition and thorough destruction of biological weapons. China acceded to the Biological Weapons Convention (BWC) in 1984, and has fully and conscientiously fulfilled its obligations under the Convention. Since 1987, China has, on an annual basis, provided the UN with information on confidence-building measures, in accordance with the decisions of the Review Conferences of the Convention.

China supports the enhancement of the effectiveness of the BWC in a comprehensive manner, and has actively participated in the work of the ad hoc group of the states parties to the Convention set up for the negotiation of a BWC protocol. China regrets that the protocol has not been reached as scheduled and that the Fifth Review Conference of the Convention has had to adjourn. China holds that the conclusion of a protocol with balanced contents and effective measures through multi-lateral negotiations remains the best way to enhance the effectiveness of the BWC. China is willing, together with all other parties concerned, to continue to explore measures along this line on the basis of the universal participation of all countries and within a multilateral framework.

**Missile Defence and Prevention of an Arms Race in Outer Space**

China's stand on the issue of missile defence is consistent and clear-cut. China understands the relevant countries' concern over the proliferation of weapons of mass destruction (WMD) and their means of delivery. But, like many other countries, China holds that this issue should be resolved through political and diplomatic means, with the common efforts of the international community.

China regrets the abrogation of the Anti-Ballistic Missile Treaty (ABM). It is China's consistent view that maintaining the global strategic stability and the international system of arms control, disarmament and non-proliferation is vitally important and in conformity with the fundamental interests of all countries. China hopes that the relevant countries will heed the opinions of the international community, and act prudently on the issue of missile defence. At the same time, China is willing to conduct constructive dialogue with all the parties involved, and make joint efforts to safeguard international peace and security.

China is concerned about certain countries' joint research and development of theatre missile defence (TMD) systems with a view to their deployment in the Northeast Asian region. This will lead to the proliferation of advanced missile technology and be detrimental to peace and stability in the Asia-Pacific region. China resolutely opposes any country which provides Taiwan with TMD assistance or protection in any form.

Outer space belongs to all mankind, and the peaceful use of outer space is the common aspiration of all humanity. At present, outer space is faced with the danger of weaponisation, and protection of outer space from weaponisation and an arms race has become a very urgent and realistic issue. The international community should negotiate and conclude the necessary legal instrument as soon as possible to prohibit the deployment of weapons in outer space and the use or threat of use of force against objects in outer space, so as to ensure peace and tranquillity therein. China holds that the Conference on Disarmament in Geneva is the suitable place for negotiations on this matter. China has submitted several working papers to the Conference, putting forward its suggestions on the main points of a future international legal instrument. In June 2002, China, Russia and some other countries jointly submitted to the Conference a working paper titled "Possible Elements for a Future International Legal Agreement on the Prevention of the Deployment of Weapons in Outer Space, the Threat or Use of Force Against Outer Space Objects" (Draft), setting forth their concept on the general structure and concrete contents of such a document. The above-mentioned working paper has received favourable responses from many countries. China hopes that the Conference will carry out substantive work on this issue at an early date, and start negotiating an international legal instrument, thus making positive efforts for the prevention of the weaponisation of outer space and an arms race therein.

**Non-Proliferation of Weapons of Mass Destruction and their Means of Delivery**

China has always been opposed to the proliferation of WMD and their means of delivery. It supports the international community's active efforts of non-proliferation, and has made its own contributions in this area. China maintains that the efforts of non-proliferation should not be confined to non-proliferation itself and should also include the identification and resolution of its root causes. Establishing a fair and rational new international order and realising the universal improvement of international relations are the fundamental way to eliminate the threat of WMD. Preventing terrorist organisations and other non-state entities from obtaining WMD is a common task confronting the international community. China is willing, together with the international community, to make common efforts for the establishment of a fair, rational and effective multilateral non-proliferation regime based on the participation of all countries.

China is a State Party to the Treaty on the Non-Proliferation of Nuclear Weapons (NPT). It has always abided by its obligations under the Treaty, and pursues a policy of not advocating, not encouraging and not engaging in the proliferation of nuclear weapons, and not helping other countries to develop nuclear weapons. China has also formulated three principles governing its nuclear exports: guarantees for peaceful use only, acceptance of the safeguards of the International Atomic Energy Agency (IAEA), and no re-transfer to the third country without prior approval of China. In order to strengthen its nuclear ex-port control mechanism, China joined the Zangger Committee in 1997, and has established and improved on its relevant domestic legal system. China promulgated, respectively in September 1997 and June 1998, the Regulations on the Control of Nuclear Export and Regulations on the Control of Nuclear Dual-Use Items and Related Technologies Export, under which China exercises control over the export of materials and technologies included in the list of the Zangger Committee and the list of nuclear dual-use items and technologies currently in use internationally. These regulations stipulate that China's nuclear exports shall be done exclusively by specialised companies designated by the government, that a licensing system shall be instituted for nuclear export, and that China shall not provide any assistance to any nuclear facility which is not under the IAEA safeguards. In order to strengthen the effectiveness of the IAEA safeguard system and fulfill its own non-proliferation obligations, China formally notified the IAEA on 28 March 2002 that it had completed the domestic legal procedures necessary for the entry into force of the Protocol Additional to the Agreement Between China and IAEA for the Application of Safeguards in China, and that the Protocol became effective for China on the same day. China was the first of the nuclear-weapon states to complete the above-mentioned procedures.

China is in favour of IAEA making its contributions to the protection against potential nuclear terrorist activities in accordance with purposes and principles of its Statute, and will provide appropriate assistance to the anti-terrorism activities of the Agency. Strengthening the physical protection of nuclear facilities and material is conducive to nuclear non-proliferation and prevention of nuclear terrorism. China has actively participated in the revision of the Convention on the Physical Protection of Nuclear Material, and is ready to make every effort to facilitate this process.

China strictly adheres to its obligations under the CWC and BWC, and will not in any way help or encourage any country to obtain chemical or biological weapons. China has consistently adopted a prudent and responsible attitude towardsq the export of chemicals or biological agents, as well as related production equipment and technologies. To ensure that exports of such material from China are not used for manufacturing chemical or biological weapons, the Chinese government has promulgated and implemented the Regulations of the PRC on the Administration of the Controlled Chemicals, and the detailed rules for its implementation, thereby placing the export of related material under stringent control. The Amendments to the Criminal Law of the PRC promulgated in December 2001 designates as criminal offences such acts of endangering public security as using, illegally manufacturing, trafficking, transporting and stockpiling radioactive substances, toxic materials or infectious disease pathogens, and stipulates corresponding penalties for these acts. In order to further strengthen the export control of the chemicals and dual-use biological products and related technologies and equipment, the Chinese government promulgated in October 2002 the Measures on Export Control of Certain Chemicals and Related Equipment and Technologies (including its control list), the Regulations of the PRC on the

Export Control of Dual-Use Biological Agents and Related Equipment and Technologies (including its control list), and the newly revised Regulations of the PRC on the Administration of Arms Export.

In recent years, the question of missile proliferation has aroused extensive concern in the international community. China also attaches great importance to this issue. The international community should, on the basis of such principles as non-discrimination and undiminished security for all countries, seek a solution to this issue through dialogue and cooperation, including exploring the possibility of establishing a new multilateral mechanism. China supports the United Nations in its efforts to play an important role in this field, and has actively participated in the UN Group of Governmental Experts on Missiles. China adopts an open attitude towards the new proposals made by countries concerned, and has, with a constructive stance, participated in international discussions on the International Code of Conduct Against Ballistic Missile Proliferation and the Proposal on a Global System for Non-proliferation of Missile Technologies. With respect to the prevention of missile proliferation, the Chinese government has al-ways adopted a serious, conscientious and responsible attitude, has not helped any country to develop ballistic missiles that can be used to deliver nuclear weapons, and has exercised strict control over the export of missiles and related material and technologies. In August 2002, the Chinese government formally promulgated the Regulations on the Export Control of Missiles and Missile-Related Items and Technologies and its control list. This is a major measure taken by the Chinese government to implement its policy of missile non-proliferation, further tightening control over the export of missiles and related material and technologies, and strengthening the administration of exports on a legal basis. In the future, China will, based on its own export control practice, continue to improve its legal system of export control. It is also willing to enhance exchanges and cooperation with all countries in this respect, actively participate in the discussions concerning the international non-proliferation mechanisms, and work for the final establishment of a fair, rational and effective international non-proliferation regime.

**Small Arms and Anti-Personnel Landmines**

China has always treated seriously the issue of illicit trafficking and excessive accumulation of small arms, and consistently taken a responsible attitude towards the manufacture and transfer of such arms. China has also actively participated in the endeavors of the international community in this regard. With a constructive attitude, China attended the UN Conference on the Illicit Trade in Small Arms and Light Weapons in All Its Aspects in July 2001, and is taking actions to implement the Programme of Action adopted at the Conference. China has actively participated in the negotiations of the Firearms Protocol to the UN Convention Against Transnational Organised Crimes, making its contributions to the conclusion of the Protocol. China is positively considering signing the Protocol. Both the Law of the PRC on the Control of Firearms and the Regulations of the PRC on the Administration of Arms Export have contained detailed stipulations on the manufacture, transportation, sales, equipment, and entry and exit control of firearms and ammunition, put in place strict controls over the export of small arms and other military items, and laid out severe penalties for violations. In 2001, China launched a nationwide campaign to eliminate illegal firearms, in the course of which large quantities of illegal firearms were confiscated and destroyed.

Since its ratification of the Amended Protocol II to the Convention on Certain Conventional Weapons in 1998, China has continued to carry out its commitment not to export anti-personnel landmines (APL) that are not in conformity with the standards set out in the Protocol, and has made considerable progress in other aspects of the implementation of the Protocol. The PLA has held a number of training courses on the Protocol.

Relevant departments are now formulating a series of rules and standards in accordance with the provisions of the Protocol, including the state military standards related to the technical performance of APLs and marking of minefields.

China continues to promote domestic and international mine clearance efforts. China is now basically safe from landmine hazards on its own territory. In 2001, China donated large quantities of demining equipment to Cambodia, Ethiopia, Eritrea, Mozambique, Rwanda, Namibia and Angola. In 2002, it contributed more than US$ 3 million for international mine clearance cooperation, mainly in aid to the demining operations in Eritrea and Lebanon. Apart from providing the two countries with demining equipment, China has sent a group of mine clearance experts to Eritrea to give on-the-spot guidance.

..........................

(Source: http://www.china.org.cn/e-white/20021209/index.htm)

# 15. National Strategy to Combat Weapons of Mass Destruction Released by President George W. Bush of the United States,

# 11 December 2002

[Editor's Note: The National Strategy to Combat Weapons of Mass Destruction is based on the classified National Security Presidential Directive 17, which the President signed in September 2002. That directive is official US policy.]

**Text Begins:**

*"The gravest danger our nation faces lies at the crossroads of radicalism and technology. Our enemies have openly declared that they are seeking weapons of mass destruction, and evidence indicates that they are doing so with determination.*

*The United States will not allow these efforts to succeed. ...History will judge harshly those who saw this coming danger but failed to act. In the new world we have entered, the only path to peace and security is the path of action."*

President Bush in "The National Security Strategy of the United States of America, 17 September 2002."

**Introduction**

Weapons of mass destruction (WMD)-nuclear, biological, and chemical-in the possession of hostile states and terrorists represent one of the greatest security challenges facing the United States. We must pursue a comprehensive strategy to counter this threat in all its dimensions.

An effective strategy for countering WMD, including their use and further proliferation, is an integral component of the

National Security Strategy of the United States of America. As with the war on terrorism, our strategy for homeland security, and our new concept of deterrence, the US approach to combat WMD represents a fundamental change from the past. To succeed, we must take full advantage of today's opportunities, including the application of new technologies, increased emphasis on intelligence collection and analysis, the strengthening of alliance relationships, and the establishment of new partnerships with former adversaries.

Weapons of mass destruction could enable adversaries to inflict massive harm on the United States, our military forces at home and abroad, and our friends and allies. Some states, including several that have supported and continue to support terrorism, already possess WMD and are seeking even greater capabilities, as tools of coercion and intimidation. For them, these are not weapons of last resort, but militarily useful weapons of choice intended to overcome our nation's advantages in conventional forces and to deter us from responding to aggression against our friends and allies in regions of vital interest. In addition, terrorist groups are seeking to acquire WMD with the stated purpose of killing large numbers of our people and those of friends and allies-without compunction and without warning.

We will not permit the world's most dangerous regimes and terrorists to threaten us with the world's most destructive weapons. We must accord the highest priority to the protection of the United States, our forces, and our friends and allies from the existing and growing WMD threat.

**Pillars of Our National Strategy**

Our National Strategy to Combat Weapons of Mass Destruction has three principal pillars:

**Counterproliferation to Combat WMD Use.** The possession and increased likelihood of use of WMD by hostile states and terrorists are realities of the contemporary security environment. It is therefore critical that the US military and appropriate civilian agencies be prepared to deter and defend against the full range of possible WMD employment scenarios. We will ensure that all needed capabilities to combat WMD are fully integrated into the emerging defence transformation plan and into our homeland security posture. Counterproliferation will also be fully integrated into the basic doctrine, training, and equipping of all forces, in order to ensure that they can sustain operations to decisively defeat WMD-armed adversaries.

*Strengthened Nonproliferation to Combat WMD Proliferation.* The United States, our friends and allies, and the broader international community must undertake every effort to prevent states and terrorists from acquiring WMD and missiles. We must enhance traditional measures-diplomacy, arms control, multilateral agreements, threat reduction assistance, and export controls-that seek to dissuade or impede proliferant states and terrorist networks, as well as to slow and make more costly their access to sensitive technologies, material, and expertise. We must ensure compliance with relevant international agreements, including the Nuclear Nonproliferation Treaty (NPT), the Chemical Weapons Convention (CWC), and the Biological Weapons Convention (BWC). The United States will continue to work with other states to improve their capability to prevent unauthorised transfers of WMD and missile technology, expertise, and material. We will identify and pursue new methods of prevention, such as national criminalisation of proliferation activities and expanded safety and security measures.

*Consequence Management to Respond to WMD Use.* Finally, the United States must be prepared to respond to the use of WMD against our citizens, our military forces, and those of friends and allies. We will develop and maintain the capability to reduce to the extent possible the potentially horrific consequences of WMD attacks at home and abroad

The three pillars of the US national strategy to combat

WMD are seamless elements of a comprehensive approach. Serving to integrate the pillars are four cross-cutting enabling functions that need to be pursued on a priority basis: intelligence collection and analysis on WMD, delivery systems, and related technologies; research and development to improve our ability to respond to evolving threats; bilateral and multilateral cooperation; and targeted strategies against hostile states and terrorists.

## Counterproliferation

We know from experience that we cannot always be successful in preventing and containing the proliferation of WMD to hostile states and terrorists. Therefore, US military and appropriate civilian agencies must possess the full range of operational capabilities to counter the threat and use of WMD by states and terrorists against the United States, our military forces, and friends and allies.

### *Interdiction*

Effective interdiction is a critical part of the US strategy to combat WMD and their delivery means. We must enhance the capabilities of our military, intelligence, technical, and law enforcement communities to prevent the movement of WMD materials, technology, and expertise to hostile states and terrorist organisations.

### *Deterrence*

Today's threats are far more diverse and less predictable than those of the past. States hostile to the United States and to our friends and allies have demonstrated their willingness to take high risks to achieve their goals, and are aggressively pursuing WMD and their means of delivery as critical tools in this effort. As a consequence, we require new methods of deterrence. A strong declaratory policy and effective military forces are essential elements of our contemporary deterrent posture, along with the full range of political tools to persuade potential adversaries not to seek or use WMD. The United States will continue to make clear that it reserves the right to respond with overwhelming force—including through resort to all our options—to the use of WMD against the United States, our forces abroad, and friends and allies.

In addition to our conventional and nuclear response and defence capabilities, our overall deterrent posture against WMD threats is reinforced by effective intelligence, surveillance, interdiction, and domestic law enforcement capabilities. Such combined capabilities enhance deterrence both by devaluing an adversary's WMD and missiles, and by posing the prospect of an overwhelming response to any use of such weapons.

*Defence and Mitigation*

Because deterrence may not succeed, and because of the potentially devastating consequences of WMD use against our forces and civilian population, US military forces and appropriate civilian agencies must have the capability to defend against WMD-armed adversaries, including in appropriate cases through preemptive measures. This requires capabilities to detect and destroy an adversary's WMD assets before these weapons are used. In addition, robust active and passive defences and mitigation measures must be in place to enable US military forces and appropriate civilian agencies to accomplish their missions, and to assist friends and allies when WMD are used.

Active defences disrupt, disable, or destroy WMD en route to their targets. Active defences include vigorous air defence and effective missile defences against today's threats. Passive defences must be tailored to the unique characteristics of the various forms of WMD. The United States must also have the ability rapidly and effectively to mitigate the effects of a WMD attack against our deployed forces.

Our approach to defend against biological threats has long

been based on our approach to chemical threats, despite the fundamental differences between these weapons. The United States is developing a new approach to provide us and our friends and allies with an effective defence against biological weapons.

Finally, US military forces and domestic law enforcement agencies as appropriate must stand ready to respond against the source of any WMD attack. The primary objective of a response is to disrupt an imminent attack or an attack in progress, and eliminate the threat of future attacks. As with deterrence and prevention, an effective response requires rapid attribution and robust strike capability. We must accelerate efforts to field new capabilities to defeat WMD-related assets. The United States needs to be prepared to conduct post-conflict operations to destroy or dismantle any residual WMD capabilities of the hostile state or terrorist network. An effective US response will not only eliminate the source of a WMD attack but will also have a powerful deterrent effect upon other adversaries that possess or seek WMD or missiles.

**Nonproliferation**

***Active Nonproliferation Diplomacy***

The United States will actively employ diplomatic approaches in bilateral and multilateral settings in pursuit of our nonproliferation goals. We must dissuade supplier states from cooperating with proliferant states and induce proliferant states to end their WMD and missile programmes. We will hold countries responsible for complying with their commitments. In addition, we will continue to build coalitions to support our efforts, as well as to seek their increased support for nonproliferation and threat reduction cooperation programmes. However, should our wide-ranging nonproliferation efforts fail, we must have available the full range of operational capabilities necessary to defend against the possible employment of WMD.

### *Multilateral Regimes*

Existing nonproliferation and arms control regimes play an important role in our overall strategy. The United States will support those regimes that are currently in force, and work to improve the effectiveness of, and compliance with, those regimes. Consistent with other policy priorities, we will also promote new agreements and arrangements that serve our nonproliferation goals. Overall, we seek to cultivate an international environment that is more conducive to nonproliferation. Our efforts will include:

✧ Nuclear

- Strengthening of the Nuclear Nonproliferation Treaty and International Atomic Energy Agency (IAEA), including through ratification of an IAEA Additional Protocol by all NPT states parties, assurances that all states put in place full-scope IAEA safeguards agreements, and appropriate increases in funding for the Agency;
- Negotiating a Fissile Material Cut-Off Treaty that advances US security interests; and
- Strengthening the Nuclear Suppliers Group and Zangger Committee.

✧ Chemical and Biological

- Effective functioning of the Organisation for the Prohibition of Chemical Weapons;
- Identification and promotion of constructive and realistic measures to strengthen the BWC and thereby to help meet the biological weapons threat; and
- Strengthening of the Australia Group.

✧ Missile

- Strengthening the Missile Technology Control Regime (MTCR), including through support for universal adherence to the International Code of Conduct Against Ballistic Missile Proliferation.

*Nonproliferation and Threat Reduction Cooperation*

The United States pursues a wide range of programmes, including the Nunn-Lugar programme, designed to address the proliferation threat stemming from the large quantities of Soviet-legacy WMD and missile-related expertise and materials. Maintaining an extensive and efficient set of nonproliferation and threat reduction assistance programmes to Russia and other former Soviet states is a high priority. We will also continue to encourage friends and allies to increase their contributions to these programmes, particularly through the G-8 Global Partnership Against the Spread of Weapons and Materials of Mass Destruction. In addition, we will work with other states to improve the security of their WMD-related materials.

*Controls on Nuclear Materials*

In addition to programmes with former Soviet states to reduce fissile material and improve the security of that which remains, the United States will continue to discourage the worldwide accumulation of separated plutonium and to minimise the use of highly-enriched uranium. As outlined in the National Energy Policy, the United States will work in collaboration with international partners to develop, recycle and fuel treatment technologies that are cleaner, more efficient, less waste-intensive, and more proliferation-resistant.

*US Export Controls*

We must ensure that the implementation of US export controls furthers our nonproliferation and other national security goals, while recognising the realities that American businesses face in the increasingly globalised marketplace.

We will work to update and strengthen export controls using existing authorities. We also seek new legislation to improve the ability of our export control system to give full weight to both nonproliferation objectives and commercial interests. Our overall goal is to focus our resources on truly sensitive exports to hostile states or those that engage in onward proliferation, while removing unnecessary barriers in the global marketplace.

### *Nonproliferation Sanctions*

Sanctions can be a valuable component of our overall strategy against WMD proliferation. At times, however, sanctions have proven inflexible and ineffective. We will develop a comprehensive sanctions policy to better integrate sanctions into our overall strategy and work with Congress to consolidate and modify existing sanctions legislation.

## WMD Consequence Management

Defending the American homeland is the most basic responsibility of our government. As part of our defence, the United States must be fully prepared to respond to the consequences of WMD use on our soil, whether by hostile states or by terrorists. We must also be prepared to respond to the effects of WMD use against our forces deployed abroad, and to assist friends and allies. The National Strategy for Homeland Security discusses US Government programmes to deal with the consequences of the use of a chemical, biological, radiological, or nuclear weapon in the United States. A number of these programmes offer training, planning, and assistance to state and local governments. To maximise their effectiveness, these efforts need to be integrated and comprehensive. Our first responders must have the full range of protective, medical, and remediation tools to identify, assess, and respond rapidly to a WMD event on our territory.

The White House Office of Homeland Security will coordinate all federal efforts to prepare for and mitigate the consequences of terrorist attacks within the United States, including those involving WMD. The Office of Homeland Security will also work closely with state and local governments to ensure their planning, training, and equipment requirements are addressed. These issues, including the roles of the Department of Homeland Security, are addressed in detail in the National Strategy for Homeland Security.

The National Security Council's Office of Combating Terrorism coordinates and helps improve US efforts to respond to and manage the recovery from terrorist attacks outside the United States. In cooperation with the Office of Combating Terrorism, the Department of State coordinates interagency efforts to work with our friends and allies to develop their own emergency preparedness and consequence management capabilities.

**Integrating the Pillars**

Several critical enabling functions serve to integrate the three pillars—counterproliferation, nonproliferation, and consequence management—of the US National Strategy to Combat WMD.

***Improved Intelligence Collection and Analysis***

A more accurate and complete understanding of the full range of WMD threats is, and will remain, among the highest US intelligence priorities, to enable us to prevent proliferation, and to deter or defend against those who would use those capabilities against us. Improving our ability to obtain timely and accurate knowledge of adversaries' offensive and defensive capabilities, plans, and intentions is key to developing effective counter- and nonproliferation policies and capabilities. Particular emphasis must be accorded to improving: intelligence regarding WMD-related facilities and activities; interaction among US intelligence, law enforcement, and military agencies; and intelligence cooperation with friends and allies.

### *Research and Development*

The United States has a critical need for cutting-edge technology that can quickly and effectively detect, analyse, facilitate interdiction of, defend against, defeat, and mitigate the consequences of WMD. Numerous US Government departments and agencies are currently engaged in the essential research and development to support our overall strategy against WMD proliferation.

The new Counterproliferation Technology Coordination Committee, consisting of senior representatives from all concerned agencies, will act to improve interagency coordination of US Government counterproliferation research and development efforts. The Committee will assist in identifying priorities, gaps, and overlaps in existing programmes and in examining options for future investment strategies.

### *Strengthened International Cooperation*

WMD represent a threat not just to the United States, but also to our friends and allies and the broader international community. For this reason, it is vital that we work closely with like-minded countries on all elements of our comprehensive proliferation strategy.

### *Targeted Strategies Against Proliferants*

All elements of the overall US strategy to combat WMD must be brought to bear in targeted strategies against supplier and recipient states of WMD proliferation concern, as well as against terrorist groups which seek to acquire WMD.

A few states are dedicated proliferators, whose leaders are determined to develop, maintain, and improve their WMD and delivery capabilities, which directly threaten the United States,

US forces overseas, and/or our friends and allies. Because each of these regimes is different, we will pursue country-specific strategies that best enable us and our friends and allies to prevent, deter, and defend against WMD and missile threats from each of them. These strategies must also take into account the growing cooperation among proliferant states-so-called secondary proliferation-which challenges us to think in new ways about specific country strategies.

One of the most difficult challenges we face is to prevent, deter, and defend against the acquisition and use of WMD by terrorist groups. The current and potential future linkages between terrorist groups and state sponsors of terrorism are particularly dangerous and require priority attention. The full range of counterproliferation, nonproliferation, and consequence management measures must be brought to bear against the WMD terrorist threat, just as they are against states of greatest proliferation concern.

**End Note**

Our National Strategy to Combat WMD requires much of all of us—the Executive Branch, the Congress, state and local governments, the American people, and our friends and allies. The requirements to prevent, deter, defend against, and respond to today's WMD threats are complex and challenging. But they are not daunting. We can and will succeed in the tasks laid out in this strategy; we have no other choice.

(Source: http://www.armscontrol.org/act/2003_01-02/document_janfeb03.asp)

# IV

# Basic Statistics

# BASIC STATISTICS

*Compiled by INSAR Research Staff*

## I. INDIA'S STATISTICAL PROFILE

### Table 1: India-Selected Socio-Economic Indicators

| | |
|---|---|
| Population | 1.027 billion (1 March 2001) |
| Birth Rate | 25.8 per 1,000 (2000) |
| Death Rate | 8.5 per 1,000 (2000) |
| Urban Population | 27.8% (2001) |
| Density of Population | 324 persons per sq. km (2001) |
| Sex Ratio | 933 Females per 1,000 Males (2001) |
| Poverty – Numbers | 260.3 Million (1999-00) |
| Poverty Ratio | 26.10% (1999-2000) |
| India's Ranking in UNDP Human Development Index (HDI) | 124/173 (2000) |
| HDI | 0.577 (2000) |
| Literacy Rate | 65% (2001) |
| GDP | 2094.0 (Rs thousand crores) |
| Average Annual Growth Rate 1997-2002 | 5.36% |
| Gross Domestic Capital Formation | 25.6 % of GDP (2001-02) |
| Gross Domestic Savings | 24.0% of GDP at Current Market Prices (2001-02) |
| Gross Domestic Investment | 23.7% of GDP at Current Market Prices (2001-02) |

| External Debt/GDP ratio | 20.9% (2002) |
|---|---|
| Debt Service to Current Receipts | 13.8% (2002) |
| Total Foreign Trade (Export + Import) | 454217 (Rs crores) (2001-02) |
| Exports | $43.827 billion (2001-02) |
| Imports | $51.413 billion (2001-02) |
| Average Rate of Inflation (WPI) | 3.6 (2001-2002) |
| Average Rate of Inflation (CPI) | 3.8 (2001) |
| Electricity Generated | 515.2 billion Kwh (2001-02) |
| Foodgrains Production | 183.2 Million Tonnes (2001-02) |

Source: *Economic Survey, 2002-2003,* Government of India, pp. S-1, 2, 7, 230, 213, 211, S-26, 79, 100, 125.

**Table 2: India's GDP: Total and Growth Rates**

(Rs. Thousand Crore)

| Year | GDP at Factor Cost (at 1993-94 prices) | Growth Rate |
|---|---|---|
| 1993-94 | 781.34 | 5.9 |
| 1994-95 | 838.03 | 7.3 |
| 1995-96 | 899.56 | 7.3 |
| 1996-97 | 970.08 | 7.8 |
| 1997-98 | 1016.59 | 4.8 |
| 1998-99 | 1082.74 | 6.5 |
| 1999-00 | 1148.44 | 6.1 |
| 2000-01 | 1198.68(Provisional) | 4.4(P) |
| 2001-02 | 1265.42(Quick estimate)) | 5.6(Q) |
| 2002-03 | 1320.7(Advance Estimate) | 4.4(A) |

Source: *Economic Survey, 2002-2003,* Government of India.pp.2, S-1

**Table 3: Foreign Exchange Reserves of India**

| Year | FE Reserves (including Gold, SDR and foreign currency assets) in US $ Billion |
|---|---|
| 1995-96 | 21.69 |
| 1996-97 | 26.42 |
| 1997-98 | 29.37 |
| 1998-99 | 32.49 |
| 1999-2000 | 38.04 |
| 2000-01 | 42.28 |
| 2001-02 | 54.10 |
| 2002-03 (Dec) | 70.44 (Provisional) |

Source: *Economic Survey, 2002-2003,* Government of India. p.2, S-69.

**Table 4: India's Share in World Economy**

| | |
|---|---|
| Rank in Global Exporters in World Merchandise Trade | 30 (2001) |
| Share | 0.7% |
| Rank in Global Importers in World Merchandise Trade | 27(2001) |
| Share | 0.8% |
| Rank in Global Exporters in World Trade in Commercial Services | 19(2001) |
| Share | 1.4% |
| Rank in Global Importers in World Trade in Commercial Services | 18(2001) |
| Share | 1.6% |
| Global Rank as Debtor | 9 |
| Country Total External Debt | $1,01,132mn (2001-Revised) |

Source: World Trade Organisation, *International Trade Statistics, 2002,* pp.25 and 27. *Economic Survey, 2002-2003,* Government of India, pp.125 and 127.

**Table 5: Foreign Investments in India**

| Year | Foreign Direct Investment Inflows in US $ Billion | Total Foreign Investment Inflows (Direct & Portfolio) in US $ Billion |
|---|---|---|
| 1990-91 | 0.10 | 0.10 |
| 1991-92 | 0.13 | 0.13 |
| 1992-93 | 0.32 | 0.56 |
| 1993-94 | 0.59 | 4.15 |
| 1994-95 | 1.31 | 5.14 |
| 1995-96 | 2.14 | 4.89 |
| 1996-97 | 2.82 | 6.13 |
| 1997-98 | 3.56 | 5.39 |
| 1998-99 | 2.46 | 2.40 |
| 1999-2000 | 2.16 | 5.18 |
| 2000-01 | 2.34 | 5.10 |
| 2001-02 | 3.90 | 5.92 |

Source: *Economic Survey, 2002-2003,* Government of India. p. 119.

**Table 6: India's External Dependence for Energy Sources (Crude Oil)**

| Year | Domestic Production in Million | Imports in Million Tonnes | Total in Million | Import Dependency |
|---|---|---|---|---|
| 1995-96 | 35.2 | 27.3 | 62.5 | 44% |
| 1996-97 | 32.9 | 33.9 | 66.8 | 51% |
| 1997-98 | 33.9 | 34.5 | 68.4 | 50% |

| 1998-99 | 32.7 | 39.8 | 72.5 | 55% |
|---|---|---|---|---|
| 1999-2000 | 31.9 | 45.0 | 76.9 | 59% |
| 2000-01 | 32.4 | 74.1 | 106.5 | 70% |
| 2001-02 | 32.0 | 78.7 | - | - |

Source: *Economic Survey, 2002-2003,* Government of India, p. S-30.

**Table 7: Trends in Growth Rates of Infrastructure Sectors (in percent)**

| Items | Unit | 1997 | 1998 | 1999 | 2000 | 2001 | 2001 | 2002 |
|---|---|---|---|---|---|---|---|---|
| **I. Energy** | | | | | | | **April to December** | |
| 1. Coal production | Mn. Tonnes | 3.6 | -2.1 | 3.1 | 3.5 | 4.2 | 4.1 | 5.1 |
| 2. Electricity generated | Bn. Kwh | 6.6 | 6.6 | 7.2 | 3.9 | 3.1 | 2.8 | 3.7 |
| A) Hydel | " | 8.5 | 11.1 | -2.5 | -7.6 | -0.7 | -3.7 | -9.6 |
| B) Thermal (incl. Nuclear) | " | 6.2 | 5.7 | 9.3 | 6.3 | 3.8 | 4.1 | 6.1 |
| 3. Petroleum | | | | | | | | |
| A) Crude oil production | Mn. Tonnes | 3 | -3.4 | -2.4 | 1.5 | -1.2 | -1.9 | 3.7 |
| B) Refinery throughout | " | 3.7 | 5.2 | 25.4 | 20.3 | 3.8 | 4.3 | 3.6 |
| II. Steel | " | 6.3 | 1.4 | 15 | 6.5 | 2.5 | 2.4 | 8.1 |
| III. Cement | " | 9.1 | 5.7 | 14.2 | -0.9 | 7.4 | 4.9 | 9.7 |
| *Average growth rate of I to iii* | | *5.7* | *2.8* | *9.1* | *5.1* | *3* | *2.5* | *5.4* |

Source: *Economic Survey, 2002-2003,* Government of India, p. 178.

**Table 8: Movement in Sectoral Shares in GDP at Current Prices in Some Select Asian Countries**

| | Agriculture | | | Industry | | | Services | | |
|---|---|---|---|---|---|---|---|---|---|
| Country | 1980 | 1990 | 2001 | 1980 | 1990 | 2001 | 1980 | 1990 | 2001 |
| China | 30.1 | 27 | 15.2 | 48.5 | 41.6 | 51.1 | 21.4 | 31.3 | 33.6 |
| India# | 38.1 | 31 | 24.7 | 25.9 | 29.3 | 26.4 | 36 | 39.7 | 48.8 |
| Indonesia | 24.8 | 19.4 | 16.4 | 43.4 | 39.1 | 46.5 | 31.8 | 41.5 | 37.1 |
| Korea | 14.9 | 8.5 | 4.4 | 41.3 | 43.1 | 41.4 | 43.7 | 48.4 | 54.1 |
| Malaysia | ... | 15.2 | 8.4 | ... | 42.2 | 49.6 | ... | 42.6 | 41.9 |
| Pakistan# | 29.6 | 26 | 25 | 25 | 25.2 | 23 | 45.5 | 48.8 | 52 |
| Philippines | 25.1 | 21.9 | 15.1 | 38.8 | 34.5 | 31.6 | 36.1 | 43.6 | 53.3 |
| Thailand | 23.2 | 12.5 | 8.6 | 28.7 | 37.2 | 42.1 | 48.1 | 50.3 | 49.3 |

# For India and Pakistan, data are based on GDP at current factor cost.
Source: *Economic Survey, 2002-2003,* Government of India, p.11.

**Table 9: FDI Inflows in Select Asian Economies**

| | 1996 | 1997 | 1998 | 1999 | 2000 | 2001 |
|---|---|---|---|---|---|---|
| **World** | 386140 | 478082 | 694457 | 1088263 | 1491934 | 7351146 |
| **Developed economies** | 219908 | 267947 | 484239 | 837761 | 1227476 | 503144 |
| **Developing economies** | 152685 | 191022 | 187611 | 225140 | 237894 | 204801 |
| Asia | 93331 | 105828 | 96109 | 102779 | 133707 | 102066 |
| South, East and South East Asia | 87843 | 96338 | 86252 | 99990 | 131123 | 94365 |
| A. China | 40180 | 44237 | 43751 | 40319 | 40772 | 46846 |
| B. India | 2525 | 3619 | 2633 | 2168 | 2319 | 3403 |
| C. Indonesia | 6194 | 4677 | -356 | -2745 | -4550 | -3277 |
| D. Korea | 2325 | 2844 | 5412 | 9333 | 9283 | 3198 |
| E. Malaysia | 7296 | 6324 | 2714 | 3895 | 3788 | 554 |
| F. Philippines | 1520 | 1249 | 1752 | 578 | 1241 | 1792 |
| G. Singapore | 8608 | 10746 | 6389 | 11803 | 5407 | 8609 |
| H. Thailand | 2271 | 3626 | 5143 | 3561 | 2813 | 3759 |

Source: *Economic Survey, 2002-2003,* Government of India, p.120.

**Table 10: External Environment**

*(Annual percent change unless otherwise noted)*

| | | *Projections* | | | |
|---|---|---|---|---|---|
| | | **2000** | **2001** | **2002** | **2003** |
| **World output** | | 4.7 | 2.2 | 2.8 | 3.7 |
| | **Advanced economies** | 3.8 | 0.8 | 1.7 | 2.5 |
| | United States | 3.8 | 0.3 | 2.2 | 2.6 |
| | European Union | 3.5 | 1.6 | 1.1 | 2.3 |
| | Japan | 2.4 | -0.3 | -0.5 | 1.1 |
| | Other advanced economies | 5.3 | 1.6 | 2.6 | 3.3 |
| | Newly industrialised Asian economies | 8.5 | 0.8 | 4.7 | 4.9 |
| | **Developing economies** | 5.7 | 3.9 | 4.2 | 5.2 |
| | Developing Asia | 6.7 | 5.6 | 6.1 | 6.3 |
| | China | 8 | 7.3 | 7.5 | 7.2 |
| | India | 5.4 | 4.1 | 5 | 5.7 |
| | ASEAN-4* | 5.1 | 2.6 | 3.6 | 4.2 |
| | **Countries in transition** | 6.6 | 5 | 3.9 | 4.5 |
| | Russia | 9 | 5 | 4.4 | 4.9 |

| | | | | | |
|---|---|---|---|---|---|
| **World trade volume** (Goods and services) | | 12.6 | -0.1 | 2.1 | 6.1 |
| | Manufactures | -5.2 | -2.3 | 2.6 | 4.2 |
| | Oil | 57 | -14 | 0.5 | -0.8 |
| **World trade prices (in US$ terms)** | Non-fuel primary commodities | 1.8 | -5.4 | 4.2 | 5.7 |
| Net private capital flows to emerging market economies | | 29.4 | 24.9 | 62.4 | 64.9 |

Source: *Economic Survey, 2002-2003,* Government of India, p.98.

* Includes Indonesia, Malaysia, Philippines and Thailand.

**Table 11a: Military Capabilities of India, Pakistan and China (Army)**

| | India | Pakistan | China |
|---|---|---|---|
| No. of Personnel | 1,298,000 | 620,000 | 2,270,000 |
| MBT | 3,898 | 2,357 | 7,010 |
| Towed Artillery | 4,175 | 1,467 | 14,000 |
| SSM | 3-5 Launchers (Prithvi) | 80 Hatf I, 50 Hatf III Shaheen I, 12Ghauri | 20+ ICBM (CSS-4, CSS-9), 130-150 IRBM (CSS-3, CSS-2, CSS-5), 12 SLBM (CSS-N-3) on *ixia* SSBN & 335+ SRBM (CSS- 6/M9, CSS- 7/M-11) |

Source: IISS, *Military Balance 2002-03 (2002),* pp. 129-131, 133-135 and 145-148

**Table 11b: Military Capabilities of India, Pakistan and China (Navy)**

| | India | Pakistan | China |
|---|---|---|---|
| No. of Personnel | 53,000 | 25,000 | 250,000 |
| Submarines | 16 | 10 | 69 |
| Principal Surface Combatants | 27 | 8 | 63 |
| Patrol and Coastal Combatants | 39 | 9 | 368 |
| Aircrafts | 35 | 6 | 472 |
| Helicopters | 50 | 9 | 45 |

Source: IISS, *Military Balance 2002-03 (2002)*, pp. 129-131, 133-135 and 145-148

**Table 11c: Military Capabilities of India, Pakistan and China (Air Force)**

| | India | Pakistan | China |
|---|---|---|---|
| No. of Personnel | 145,000 | 45,000 | 420,000 |
| Strike Aircraft | 510 | 110 | 838 |
| Fighter Aircraft | 155 | 202 | 948 |
| Attack Helicopters | 20 | 0 | 0 |
| Reconnaissance Aircraft | 22 | 11 | 290 |
| Transport Aircraft/Helicopters | 203/125 | 30 | 513/170 |

Source: IISS, *Military Balance, 2002-03 (2002)*, pp.129-131, 133-135 and 145-148

**Table 12: GDP and Defence Expenditures: India, Pakistan, and China**
(In US$ Billion)

| Year | India | | | Pakistan | | | China | | |
|---|---|---|---|---|---|---|---|---|---|
| | GDP | Defence Exp. | Defence Exp. as % of GDP | GDP | Defence Exp. | Defence Exp. as % of GDP | GDP | Defence Exp. | Defence Exp. as % of GDP |
| 1993-94 | L269.73 (92) | L 8.07 (91) | 2.99 | 44.06 (92) | 3.55 (92) | 8.05 | 434.08 (92) | L 21.76 (92) | 5.01 |
| 1994-95 | L 290.4 (93) | 7.0 (93) (93) | 2.41 | 50.8 (93) | 3.3 (93) | 6.49 | 507.5 (93) | 27.4 (93) | 5.39 |
| 1995-96 | 270.2 (94) | L7.43 (94) | 2.74 | 51.2 (94) | 3.3 (94) | 6.44 | 509 (94) | 28.5 (94) | 5.59 |
| 1996-97 | 330 (95) | 8.3 (95) (95) | 2.51 | 56 (95) | 3.6 (95) | 6.42 | 560 (95) | L 31.7 (95) | 5.66 |
| 1997-98 | 371 (96) | 10.4 (96) | 2.80 | 64 (96) | 3.7 (96) | 5.78 | 616 (96) | L 38 (96) | 6.16 |
| 1998-99 | 385 (97) | 12.2 (97) | 3.16 | 61 (97) | 3.4 (97) | 5.57 | 639 (97) | 36.6 (97) | 5.72 |

| | | | | | | | | | |
|---|---|---|---|---|---|---|---|---|---|
| 999-2000 | 469 (98) | 14.1 (98) | 3.00 | 61 (98) | 4.0 (98) | 6.55 | 703 (98) | L 37.5 (98) | 5.33 |
| **2000-01** | **440 (99)** | **14.2 (99)** | **3.22** | **61.6 (99)** | **3.5 (99)** | **5.68** | **732 (99)** | **L 39.5 (99)** | **5.39** |
| **2001-02** | **471 (2000)** | **14.7 (2000)** | **3.12** | **62.8 (2000)** | **3.65 (2000)** | **5.81** | **794 (2000)** | **L 42 (2000)** | **5.28** |
| 2002-03 | 490 (01) | 14.3 (01) | 2.91 | 55.8 (01) | 2.4 (01) | 4.30 | 1200 (01) | L 47 (01) | 3.91 |

Source: IISS, *Military Balance, 1993-94 to 2002-03*

Note: Figures in parenthesis indicate the year of the given data.

**Table 13: India's Power Profile**

| | |
|---|---|
| World Surface Area | 2.4% |
| World Population | 16.7% |
| Population | 1027015 (2001), (In ,000) |
| GDP | $490 bn |
| Growth Rate | 4.30% |
| Total Foreign Trade | $1,11,089 mn |
| Foreign Exchange | $20,835 millions |
| Total Military Personnel | 1,298,000 |
| MBT | 3,898 |
| Principal Naval Combatants | 43 |
| Total Combatant Aircraft | 701 |

Source: IISS, *Military Balance, 2002-03; EPW,* EPW Research Foundation, 17-23 May 2003, Vol. xxxviii, No. 20, p.1914, and Tables 1-12.

## II. WORLD POWER STRUCTURE

**Table 14: Share in World Military Expenditure (Year 2001)**

| Countries | Share in Percentage |
|---|---|
| USA | 38.59 |
| Russia | 7.62 |
| China | 5.51 |
| Japan | 4.73 |
| UK | 4.15 |
| France | 3.94 |
| Germany | 3.22 |
| Saudi Arabia | 2.90 |
| Italy | 2.51 |
| India | 1.69 |
| South Korea | 1.33 |
| Brazil | 1.25 |
| Israel | 1.24 |
| Canada | 0.92 |
| Turkey | 0.86 |
| Spain | 0.83 |
| Australia | 0.80 |
| Netherlands | 0.74 |
| Mexico | 0.68 |
| Greece | 0.66 |
| Kuwait | 0.60 |

Source: *IISS, Military Balance, 2002-03.*

**Table 15: Share in World Gross Domestic Product (Year 2001)**

| Countries | Share in Percentage |
|---|---|
| USA | 32.51 |
| Japan | 13.57 |
| Germany | 5.99 |
| UK | 4.50 |
| France | 4.16 |
| China | 3.70 |
| Italy | 3.49 |
| Canada | 2.16 |
| Mexico | 1.97 |
| Spain | 1.85 |
| Brazil | 1.61 |
| India | 1.53 |
| South Korea | 1.35 |
| Netherlands | 1.20 |
| Australia | 1.18 |
| Russia | 0.99 |
| Saudi Arabia | 0.55 |
| Turkey | 0.47 |
| Greece | 0.37 |
| Israel | 0.35 |
| Kuwait | 0.12 |

Source: The World Bank, *World Development Report, 2003*

**Table 16: Share in World Manufacturing Value Added (Year 2000)**

| Countries | Share in Percentage |
|---|---|
| USA | 26.51 |
| Japan | 17.42 |
| Germany | 6.82 |
| China | 6.31 |
| UK | 3.97 |
| France | 3.62 |
| Italy | 3.46 |
| South Korea | 2.44 |
| Mexico | 1.81 |
| Canada | 1.78 |
| Spain | 1.74 |
| Brazil | 1.35 |
| India | 1.11 |
| Netherlands | 1.03 |
| Australia | 0.77 |
| Turkey | 0.46 |
| Greece | 0.19 |
| Israel | .. |
| Kuwait | .. |
| Russia | .. |
| Saudi Arabia | .. |

Source: The World Bank, *World Development Report, 2003*

**Table 17: Share in World Commercial Energy Production (Year 2000)**

| Countries | Share in Percentage |
|---|---|
| USA | 16.74 |
| China | 11.07 |
| Russia | 9.66 |
| Saudi Arabia | 4.87 |
| India | 4.21 |
| Canada | 3.74 |
| UK | 2.72 |
| Australia | 2.32 |
| Mexico | 2.29 |
| Brazil | 1.42 |
| Germany | 1.34 |
| France | 1.31 |
| Kuwait | 1.11 |
| Japan | 1.05 |
| Netherlands | 0.57 |
| South Korea | 0.34 |
| Spain | 0.32 |
| Italy | 0.27 |
| Turkey | 0.26 |
| Greece | 0.06 |
| Israel | 0.01 |

Source: The World Bank, *World Development Indicators, 2003*

**Table 18: Share in World Trade (Year 2001)**

| Countries | Share in Percentage |
|---|---|
| USA | 15.27 |
| Germany | 8.49 |
| Japan | 6.03 |
| France | 5.13 |
| UK | 4.84 |
| China | 4.07 |
| Canada | 3.92 |
| Italy | 3.79 |
| Israel | 3.79 |
| Netherlands | 3.50 |
| Mexico | 2.67 |
| South Korea | 2.33 |
| Spain | 2.04 |
| Russia | 1.25 |
| Australia | 1.02 |
| Brazil | 0.93 |
| Saudi Arabia | 0.80 |
| India | 0.75 |
| Turkey | 0.57 |
| Greece | 0.29 |
| Kuwait | 0.19 |

Source: The World Bank, *World Development Indicators, 2003.*

**Table 19: Share in World Merchandise Exports (Year 2001)**

| Countries | Share in Percentage |
|---|---|
| USA | 11.86 |
| Germany | 9.24 |
| Japan | 6.57 |
| France | 5.18 |
| UK | 4.44 |
| China | 4.32 |
| Canada | 4.25 |
| Italy | 3.91 |
| Israel | 3.91 |
| Netherlands | 3.73 |
| Mexico | 2.57 |
| South Korea | 2.44 |
| Spain | 1.80 |
| Russia | 1.67 |
| Saudi Arabia | 1.11 |
| Australia | 1.03 |
| Brazil | 0.94 |
| India | 0.71 |
| Turkey | 0.51 |
| Kuwait | 0.26 |
| Greece | 0.14 |

Source: The World Bank, *World Development Indicators, 2003.*

**Table 20: Share in World High Tech Exports (Year 2001)**

| Countries | Share in Percentage |
|---|---|
| USA | 18.97 |
| Japan | 8.54 |
| Germany | 8.32 |
| UK | 6.88 |
| Netherlands | 5.97 |
| France | 5.96 |
| Israel | 4.89 |
| China | 4.32 |
| South Korea | 3.54 |
| Canada | 3.19 |
| Mexico | 2.83 |
| Italy | 1.96 |
| Brazil | 0.85 |
| Spain | 0.72 |
| Russia | 0.67 |
| Australia | 0.51 |
| India | 0.21 |
| Turkey | 0.13 |
| Greece | 0.06 |
| Kuwait | 0.01 |
| Saudi Arabia | 0.00 |

Source: The World Bank, *World Development Indicators, 2003.*

**Table 21: Share in World FDI Outflow (Year 2001)**

| Countries | Share in Percentage |
|---|---|
| USA | 18.36 |
| France | 13.34 |
| Netherlands | 7.09 |
| Germany | 6.97 |
| UK | 6.36 |
| Japan | 6.14 |
| Canada | 5.71 |
| Spain | 4.48 |
| Italy | 3.46 |
| Australia | 1.80 |
| Mexico | 0.60 |
| Russia | 0.42 |
| South Korea | 0.42 |
| China | 0.29 |
| Israel | 0.19 |
| India | 0.12 |
| Turkey | 0.08 |
| Kuwait | 0.05 |
| Brazil | 0.00 |
| Saudi Arabia | -0.05 |
| Greece | -0.10 |

Source: UNCTAD, *World Investment Report, 2003*

**Table 22: Share in World Scientific Journal Articles (Year 1999)**

| Countries | Share in Percentage |
|---|---|
| USA | 30.93 |
| Japan | 9.05 |
| UK | 7.51 |
| Germany | 7.06 |
| France | 5.18 |
| Canada | 3.72 |
| Italy | 3.24 |
| Russia | 2.96 |
| Australia | 2.37 |
| Spain | 2.32 |
| China | 2.21 |
| Netherlands | 1.98 |
| India | 1.74 |
| South Korea | 1.26 |
| Brazil | 0.97 |
| Israel | 0.95 |
| Turkey | 0.52 |
| Mexico | 0.43 |
| Greece | 0.42 |
| Saudi Arabia | 0.10 |
| Kuwait | 0.05 |

Source: The World Bank, *World Development Indicators, 2003.*

**Table 23: Share in World Patent Applications Filed (Year 2000)**

| Countries | Share in Percentage |
|---|---|
| Japan | 5.15 |
| USA | 3.51 |
| Germany | 2.78 |
| UK | 2.47 |
| Spain | 2.14 |
| South Korea | 1.82 |
| France | 1.70 |
| Netherlands | 1.53 |
| Italy | 1.50 |
| Greece | 1.49 |
| China | 1.30 |
| Russia | 0.95 |
| Canada | 0.91 |
| Australia | 0.86 |
| Israel | 0.72 |
| Turkey | 0.72 |
| Mexico | 0.71 |
| Brazil | 0.69 |
| India | 0.65 |
| Saudi Arabia | 0.01 |
| Kuwait | |

Source: The World Bank, *World Development Indicators, 2003.*

**Table 24: US Dominance in World Power Structure**

| Countries | A | B | C | D | E | F | G | H | I | J |
|---|---|---|---|---|---|---|---|---|---|---|
| Australia | 0.81 | 1.18 | 0.77 | 2.32 | 1.02 | 1.03 | 0.51 | 1.8 | 2.37 | 0.86 |
| Brazil | 1.26 | 1.61 | 1.35 | 1.42 | 0.93 | 0.94 | 0.85 | 0 | 0.97 | 0.69 |
| Canada | 0.93 | 2.16 | 1.78 | 3.74 | 3.92 | 4.25 | 3.19 | 5.71 | 3.72 | 0.91 |
| China | 5.51 | 3.7 | 6.31 | 11.07 | 4.07 | 4.32 | 4.32 | 0.29 | 2.21 | 1.3 |
| France | 3.94 | 4.16 | 3.62 | 1.31 | 5.13 | 5.18 | 5.96 | 13.3 | 5.18 | 1.7 |
| Germany | 3.22 | 5.99 | 6.82 | 1.34 | 8.49 | 9.24 | 8.32 | 6.97 | 7.06 | 2.78 |
| Greece | 0.66 | 0.37 | 0.19 | 0.06 | 0.29 | 0.14 | 0.06 | -0.1 | 0.42 | 1.49 |
| India | 1.7 | 1.53 | 1.11 | 4.21 | 0.75 | 0.71 | 0.21 | 0.12 | 1.74 | 0.65 |
| Israel | 1.24 | 0.35 | .. | 0.01 | 3.79 | 3.91 | 4.89 | 0.19 | 0.95 | 0.72 |
| Italy | 2.51 | 3.49 | 3.46 | 0.27 | 3.79 | 3.91 | 1.96 | 3.46 | 3.24 | 1.5 |
| Japan | 4.73 | 13.6 | 17.42 | 1.05 | 6.03 | 6.57 | 8.54 | 6.14 | 9.05 | 5.15 |
| Kuwait | 0.6 | 0.12 | .. | 1.11 | 0.19 | 0.26 | 0.01 | 0.05 | 0.05 | .. |
| Mexico | 0.69 | 1.97 | 1.81 | 2.29 | 2.67 | 2.57 | 2.83 | 0.6 | 0.43 | 0.71 |
| Netherlands | 0.75 | 1.2 | 1.03 | 0.57 | 3.5 | 3.73 | 5.97 | 7.09 | 1.98 | 1.53 |
| Russia | 7.62 | 0.99 | .. | 9.66 | 1.25 | 1.67 | 0.67 | 0.42 | 2.96 | 0.95 |

| | | | | | | | | | | |
|---|---|---|---|---|---|---|---|---|---|---|
| Saudi Arabia | 2.91 | 0.55 | .. | 4.87 | 0.8 | 1.11 | 0 | -0.1 | 0.1 | 0.01 |
| South Korea | 1.34 | 1.35 | 2.44 | 0.34 | 2.33 | 2.44 | 3.54 | 0.42 | 1.26 | 1.82 |
| Spain | 0.83 | 1.85 | 1.74 | 0.32 | 2.04 | 1.8 | 0.72 | 4.48 | 2.32 | 2.14 |
| Turkey | 0.86 | 0.47 | 0.46 | 0.26 | 0.57 | 0.51 | 0.13 | 0.08 | 0.52 | 0.72 |
| UK | 4.16 | 4.5 | 3.97 | 2.72 | 4.84 | 4.44 | 6.88 | 6.36 | 7.51 | 2.47 |
| USA | 38.6 | 32.5 | 26.51 | 16.74 | 15.27 | 11.9 | 18.97 | 18.4 | 30.9 | 3.51 |

A. Share in World Military Expenditure (Year 2001). Source: IISS, *Military Balance, 2002-03*.

B. Share in World Gross Domestic Product (Year 2001). Source: World Bank, *World Development Report, 2003*.

C. Share in World Manufacturing Value Added (Year 2000). Source: The World Bank, *World Development Report, 2003*.

D. Share in World Commercial Energy Production (Year 2000). Source: The World Bank, *World Development Indicators, 2003*.

E. Share In World Trade (Year 2001). Source: The World Bank, *World Development*.

F. Share in World Merchandise Exports (Year 2001). Source: The World Bank, *World Development Indicators, 2003*.

G. Share in World High Tech Exports (Year 2001). Source: The World Bank, *World Development Indicators, 2003*.

H. Share in World FDI Outflow (Year 2001). Source: UNCTAD, *World Investment Report, 2003*.

I. Share in World Scientific Journal Articles (Year 1999). Source: The World Bank, *World Development Indicators, 2003*.

J. Share in World Patent Applications Filed (Year 2000). Source: The World Bank, *World Development Indicators, 2003*.

* Includes Indonesia, Malaysia, Philippines and Thailand.

# Index

India Research Press is a collectively run book publisher with support of Authors and Editors. Since our founding in 1999, we have tried to meet the needs of readers who are exploring, or are committed to the politics of change.

Our goal is to publish books that encourage critical thinking and constructive action on the key political, cultural, social, economic and ecological issues shaping life in the Indian Sub-continent and in the world. In this way, we hope to give expression to a wide diversity of democratic and social movements.

India Research Press publishes Original works-as well as-works under Rights with various University and Academic publishers throughout the world.

Since our conception, we have added two new imprints to our existing line of Academic publishing.The Group now has three seperate divisions & editors for its publishing programme and many new titles, scheduled in the coming months. The India Research Press also has New Overseas Distributors for the sale of its titles in the USA and the European continent. The group is proud to introduce its three divisions of publishing.

India Research Press **Academic Publishing Division.**

TARA press **General Division – Mass Market including Fiction.**

Swankit **General Division – Health, Non Fiction and Educational titles.**

The group is headed by Anuj Bahri Malhotra, its CEO & Commissioning Manager. He is assisted by an efficient and professional staff of Editors, Administrator, Office Assistants and Accountant. Born to a bookseller's family, running the most sought after bookshop [ Bahri Sons ] in the country, Anuj has a long 23 years experience in the Indian Book Industry.